Frommer's

Barcelona

1st Edition

by Suzanne Wales

Here's what the critics say about Frommer's:

"Amazingly easy to use. Very portable, very complete."
—*Booklist*

"Detailed, accurate, and easy-to-read information for all price ranges."
—*Glamour Magazine*

"Hotel information is close to encyclopedic."
—*Des Moines Sunday Register*

"Frommer's Guides have a way of giving you a real feel for a place."
—*Knight Ridder Newspapers*

WILEY

Wiley Publishing, Inc.

About the Author

Australian **Suzanne Wales** moved to Barcelona with a barrage of other journalists in 1992, the city's Olympic year, and she has not been enticed to change her adopted country since. She has written on travel and architecture for *Wallpaper, Vogue Entertaining + Travel, Spain Magazine, Blueprint,* and *Elle Decór,* as well as documentary programs on Catalonia and Spain. She resides in the old fishing quarter of Barceloneta and, when not gazing at her view of the Mediterranean, is busy hunting for old-style bars and cafes before they disappear.

Published by:

Wiley Publishing, Inc.

111 River St.
Hoboken, NJ 07030-5774

ISBN-13: 978-0-7645-7792-5
ISBN-10: 0-7645-7792-1

Editor: Kathleen Warnock
Production Editor: Suzanna R. Thompson
Cartographers: Nick Trotter and Dorit Kreisler
Photo Editor: Richard Fox
Production by Wiley Indianapolis Composition Services

Front cover photo: Exterior of Gaudí's Batllo House (1904–06) at night.
Back cover photo: Sardana Monument with Barcelona skyline in distance.

For information on our other products and services or to obtain technical support, please contact our Customer Care Department within the U.S. at 800/762-2974, outside the U.S. at 317/572-3993 or fax 317/572-4002.

Wiley also publishes its books in a variety of electronic formats. Some content that appears in print may not be available in electronic formats.

Manufactured in the United States of America

5   4   3   2   1

Contents

10   Majorca   246

by Suzanne Wales & Tara Stevens

11   Bilbao   275

Appendix A: Barcelona Past & Present   305

Appendix B: The Catalan Culture   311

Appendix C: Useful Terms & Phrases   321

Index   324

List of Maps

An Invitation to the Reader

In researching this book, we discovered many wonderful places—hotels, restaurants, shops, and more. We're sure you'll find others. Please tell us about them, so we can share the information with your fellow travelers in upcoming editions. If you were disappointed with a recommendation, we'd love to know that, too. Please write to:

Frommer's Barcelona, 1st Edition
Wiley Publishing, Inc. • 111 River St. • Hoboken, NJ 07030-5774

An Additional Note

Please be advised that travel information is subject to change at any time—and this is especially true of prices. We therefore suggest that you write or call ahead for confirmation when making your travel plans. The authors, editors, and publisher cannot be held responsible for the experiences of readers while traveling. Your safety is important to us, however, so we encourage you to stay alert and be aware of your surroundings. Keep a close eye on cameras, purses, and wallets, all favorite targets of thieves and pickpockets.

Other Great Guides for Your Trip:

Frommer's Spain

Spain For Dummies

Frommer's Spain's Best Loved Driving Tours

Frommer's Seville, Granada & the Costa del Sol

Frommer's Madrid

Frommer's Gay & Lesbian Europe

Frommer's Europe

Frommer's Star Ratings, Icons & Abbreviations

Every hotel, restaurant, and attraction listing in this guide has been ranked for quality, value, service, amenities, and special features using a **star-rating system.** In country, state, and regional guides, we also rate towns and regions to help you narrow down your choices and budget your time accordingly. Hotels and restaurants are rated on a scale of zero (recommended) to three stars (exceptional). Attractions, shopping, nightlife, towns, and regions are rated according to the following scale: zero stars (recommended), one star (highly recommended), two stars (very highly recommended), and three stars (must-see).

In addition to the star-rating system, we also use **seven feature icons** that point you to the great deals, in-the-know advice, and unique experiences that separate travelers from tourists. Throughout the book, look for:

Finds	Special finds—those places only insiders know about
Fun Fact	Fun facts—details that make travelers more informed and their trips more fun
Kids	Best bets for kids and advice for the whole family
Moments	Special moments—those experiences that memories are made of
Overrated	Places or experiences not worth your time or money
Tips	Insider tips—great ways to save time and money
Value	Great values—where to get the best deals

The following **abbreviations** are used for credit cards:

AE	American Express	DISC	Discover	V	Visa
DC	Diners Club	MC	MasterCard		

Frommers.com

Now that you have the guidebook to a great trip, visit our website at **www.frommers.com** for travel information on more than 3,000 destinations. With features updated regularly, we give you instant access to the most current trip-planning information available. At Frommers.com, you'll also find the best prices on airfares, accommodations, and car rentals—and you can even book travel online through our travel booking partners. At Frommers.com, you'll also find the following:

- Online updates to our most popular guidebooks
- Vacation sweepstakes and contest giveaways
- Newsletter highlighting the hottest travel trends
- Online travel message boards with featured travel discussions

The Best of Barcelona

Unlike many monumental European cities, the Catalan capital's charm lies in a sum of many small parts. You could fall in love with the city over an encounter with the mélange of street performers along the famous boulevard Les Ramblas or at your first close encounter with a fanciful work of the master architect Antoni Gaudí. It could be the fact that fine city beaches, splendid Gothic palaces, elegant green parkland, cutting edge cafes, and sophisticated shopping are all within arm's length in this compact metropolis and its inherent easygoing nature means that as much time can be spent on chilling as cultural pursuits. It could be the fact that Barcelona (and Catalonia) are truly distinct from the rest of Spain and therefore many pre-conceptions of what it *will* be like give way to the discovery of a language, landscape, and people you may have known little about.

Over the centuries the Catalan people have clung fiercely to their culture, which General Francisco Franco systematically and often brutally tried to eradicate. Catalonia endured, becoming an autonomous region of Spain in which Catalan culture and language flourishes. Barcelona, the region's lodestar, has truly come into its own. In 2003 nearly four million visitors came to the city, many on charter flights from Northern Europe. The explosion of low-cost, Internet airlines, plus the good value at hotels and restaurants compared to other European cities, has made Barcelona the European weekender capital. Many come to party, some to soak up the unbeatable Mediterranean climate and most find the time to see a few of its outstanding cultural and architectural offerings.

The city's most powerful monuments open a window onto its history: the intricately carved edifices of the Barri Gòtic, the most intact Gothic Quarter in Europe; the florid, curvilinear *modernisme* (Catalan Art Nouveau), the seminal works of Picasso and Miró, plus daring new projects from national and international names of the ilk of Frank Gehry, Jean Nouvel, and Toyo Ito, Barcelona is a crucial incubator for 20th-century art and architecture. Gastronomy is another regional plus; led by Ferran Adrià, a chef whom *Time* listed as one of the 100 most influential people in the world today, "New Catalan Cuisine" has even been hailed by the French as the next great culinary wave. In 2004 six restaurants in the region received the coveted Michelin star.

Barcelona is on the doorstep of some of Europe's great playgrounds and vacation retreats. The Balearic Islands lie to the east, the Costa Brava to the north, the monastery at Montserrat to the west, and to the south, the Roman city of Tarragona, and the playground resort of Sitges.

A revitalized Barcelona welcomed thousands of visitors to the 1992 Summer Olympic Games, but the action didn't end when the last medal was handed out. With a culturally savvy local government, the city has become a model for intelligent development. On any weekend, as locals enjoy a new park or promenade, an outdoor concert or *fiesta,* it is clear that this proud population has an enduring love affair with their city. Of course the downside of all this progress is that the sound of the jackhammer is never far off. But the Barcelonese believe that while the past must be respected, the future is to be embraced.

1 Frommer's Favorite Barcelona Experiences

- **A Stroll along the Ramblas:** Barcelona's most famous promenade pulses with life. The array of living statues, street musicians, performers, hustlers, and eccentrics ensure there is never a dull moment by the time you reach the end of your kilometer-long stroll. See p. 56.

- **A Drink at Sunset on the Beach:** The closest thing to an Ibizan experience on the mainland, Barcelona's city beaches are dotted with *chiringuitos* (beach bars) and the Mediterranean provides a perfect backdrop for that end-of-day drink, often accompanied by the music of an in-house DJ. See p. 211.

- **Exploring the El Born Neighborhood:** This port-side pocket of Barcelona was once one of its seediest; now the "in" crowds converge on its narrow, tangle of streets by day to check out the latest in cutting edge fashion and design and by night for the plethora of bars and restaurants churning out the ultimate in New Catalan cuisine. See p. 58.

- **A Concert at the Palau de la Música Catalana:** This masterpiece of *modernista* (Art Nouveau) architecture must be one of the most lavish concert halls in the world. All strains of classical and jazz are played, but even the most finicky music lover will be moved by the Palau's onslaught of decorative detail. See p. 202.

- **Breakfast at the Boqueria:** There are about a dozen bars and restaurants in the city's main food market. Rub shoulders with Barcelona's top chefs and gourmands over a coffee and croissant and watch the day's deliveries coming in. See p. 192.

- **Barhopping in the Barri Gòtic:** Whether it's the iconic, smoke filled tapas bar, an Irish pub frequented by expats, or a cocktail lounge filled with minimalist furniture and minimally clad patrons, Barcelona's Old City is a wateringhole mecca, bar none. One of the best (at time of print, Barcelona's bar scene is famously fickle) is **Ginger,** a comfy, classy tapas and wine bar with the feel of a private club. See p. 207.

- **Sundays on Montjuïc:** The mountain of Montjuïc is the first sight that greets visitors arriving at the port. Behind its rocky seaside face are acres of pine-dotted parkland that cyclists, joggers, and strollers make a beeline for on the weekend; a tranquil contrast to the hustle of the city below and some welcome breathing room. See p. 161.

- **A Trip to Tibidabo on the Tramvía Blau:** The summit of the highest point on the city's hilly backdrop can be reached by a "blue tram," built as a people carrier to the amusement park on the mountain's peak. For most, the fun starts here, as the century-old tram rattles its way up the mountainside and reveals breathtaking views of the city below. See p. 63.

- **Dining at Els Quatre Gats:** The original was the preferred hang out of a young Picasso and his Bohemian contemporaries and acted as a fraternity house for late 18th-century dandies. While most of the art adorning the walls is now reproductions, this classic

Catalan restaurant still screams with history. The resident pianist and general formality only add to the atmosphere. See p. 110.

- **The First Glance of the Sagrada Família:** Nothing quite prepares you for the first glimpse of Gaudí's most famous work. Erupting from the center of a suburban city block like some retro-futurist grotto, the temple's four towers immediately draw your eyes skyward, before they drop down to the facade rich in religious symbolism. And that's before you step over the threshold to the (yet still unfinished) interior. See p. 156.

- **People-Watching at the MACBA:** The forecourt of the Museum of Contemporary Art is a snapshot of the new multicultural Barcelona; spend some time at one of its outside bars watching Pakistani cricket players, local kids playing soccer and Northern European skateboarders in a fascinating melting pot of recreational activity. See p. 153.

- **Staying Up until Dawn:** A long dinner, a few drinks at a bar, onto a club and then before you know it the sun is rising over the Mediterranean's party capital, throwing a warm glow over the city's palm-filled plazas and streets. Nothing beats a slow walk home at this magical hour (preferably through the Old City). If you manage to catch up on your sleep during the day, chances are you will repeat the experience that night.

2 The Best Hotel Bets

- **Best for a Romantic Getaway:** Lovebirds have good reasons not to leave the confines of **Gran Hotel La Florida,** Carretera de Tibidabo s/n (✆ **93-259-30-00**), a fabulous, newly opened historic hotel—and not all of those reasons are to be found in the bedrooms. The stainless-steel lap pool, spa, and gardens offering sweeping views of the city are enticement enough to keep you holed up for days. See p. 100.

- **Best for Art Lovers:** As well as being one of the city's most stylish five-stars, the **Hotel Claris,** Pau Claris 150 (✆ **93-487-62-62**), has rooms and foyers dotted with early Egyptian art and artifacts, 19th-century Turkish kilims, and even a couple of Roman mosaics, a fruit of the owner's passion for collecting. See p. 83.

- **Best for Business Travelers:** In the heart of business district, the **AC Diplomatic,** Pau Claris 122 (✆ **93-272-38-10**), exudes efficiency. The highly tasteful interior and amenities have just the right balance of detail and function, allowing those with a job to do to get on with it in comfort. See p. 86.

- **Best for Celebrity Spotting:** Preferred choice of top models and temperamental rock stars (P. Diddy reportedly partied up a storm when he came to Barcelona to host the 2002 MTV Awards) the **Hotel Arts,** Marina 19–21 (✆ **93-221-10-00**), has remained a jet-set playground and symbol of "cool Barcelona" for over a decade. See p. 96.

- **Best for Service:** As well as being a well above average four-star, the **Prestige,** Passeig de Gràcia 62 (✆ **93-272-41-80**), offers a unique service to its clients. The role of the concierge is replaced with "Ask Me," specially trained information officers on call to find the answers to the most challenging queries; from how to score soccer tickets to where to find halal restaurants. See p. 85.

- **Best Grande Dame:** Since it opened its doors in 1919, the city's **Hotel Ritz,** Gran Vía 668 (✆ **93-318-52-00**), has survived a civil war, a world war, an anarchist occupation and the fall of a dictatorship, all while retaining an impeccable level of service and tradition. During all this, distinguished guests such as the Duke of Windsor, Ava Gardner, and Salvador Dalí have chosen to stay in its gilt and marble surroundings and take refuge in the elegant tearoom and restaurant. See p. 84.

- **Best In-House Restaurant:** When celebrated chef Fermin Puig took over the food department the highly regarded **The Majestic,** Passeig de Gràcia 70 (✆ **93-488-17-17**), he not only revolutionized what clients receive on their breakfast tray but also created **Drolma,** one of the country's most celebrated haute cuisine restaurants. Officially recognized with a Michelin star, Puig's take on traditional Catalan and Southern French cooking has left most gourmands drooling at the mouth. See p. 121.

- **Best Historic Hotel:** The *modernista* masterpiece **Hotel Casa Fuster,** Passeig de Gràcia 132 (✆ **93-225-30-00**), was an emblematic building *before* it was recently converted into this luxury five star. The rooms have been restored to turn-of-the-20th-century opulence, but with all the mod-cons expected by today's high society. See p. 81.

- **Best Modern Design:** Combining the best of local talent, **Hotel Omm,** Rosselló 265 (✆ **93-445-40-00**), was almost conceived as homage to the city's vibrant design culture. Daring concepts prevail from the metal facade and the sleek open-plan suites and private terraces. On the ground floor, the Omm's restaurant, Moo, is fast becoming the place to see and be-seen among Barcelona's arts elite. See p. 84.

- **Best for Sheer Atmosphere:** If faded glory is your thing then look no further than the **Hotel España,** Sant Pau 11, 08001 Barcelona (✆ **93-318-17-58**). Designed by a contemporary of Gaudí's, the street-level dining room, filled with florid motif and brass fixtures, will whisk you back to the early nineteen hundreds, when it was filled with chattering patrons taking supper after a trip to the opera house next door. See p. 80.

- **Best Location:** In terms of location the **Hotel Colón,** Av. de la Catedral 7 (✆ **93-301-14-04**), is the envy of every hotel in the city. Placed directly in front of the cathedral's main entrance, across an expansive square that buzzes day and night, a front room with a balcony is the one to ask for when booking this highly recommended four-star. See p. 73.

- **Best for Architecture Buffs:** Hailing from the early '50s, the **Park Hotel,** Av. Marquès de L'Argenteria 11 (✆ **93-319-60-00**), was the first example of post-war *modernista* architecture in the city. The renovation carried out four decades later only enhances its singular style, and it sports one of the most striking staircases in existence. See p. 78.

- **Best Boutique Hotel:** The boutique concept took its time coming to Barcelona. Forefront of the movement was **Banys Orientals,** Argenteria 37 (✆ **93-268-84-60**), and it remains the best. It's perfectly located in the middle of El Born district, Barcelona's bastion of urban chic. See p. 79.

- **Best Small Hotel: Hostal D'Uxelles,** Gran Vía 688 and 667 (✆ **93-265-25-60**), looks like it has stepped straight off the pages of one of those rustic-interiors magazines. Located on the first floor of two adjacent buildings, each of the 14 rooms have a character all of their own, but all include canopied beds, antique furniture, and Andalusian-style ceramic bathrooms. See p. 90.

- **Best for Sea Views:** Imagine stepping off a luxury cruise liner and straight into a five-star hotel. That is pretty-much possible at **Hotel Grand Marina,** World Trade Centre, Moll de Barcelona (© **93-603-90-00**). Housed in the western-wing of the city's World Trade Centre, which in itself is built on a man-made island in the port, Mediterranean vistas greet you at every turn. See p. 96.

- **Best Inexpensive Hotel:** Serenity and character abound in **Hotel Peninsular,** Sant Pau 34–36 (© **93-302-31-38**), a nunnery-turned-hotel. Located on a colorful street just off Les Ramblas, the Art Nouveau lift, long hallways in tones of green and white and

inner-courtyard with its abundance of hanging plants is an oasis from the hustle and bustle outside. But book ahead. See p. 80.

- **Best for Families Who Don't Want to Break the Bank:** The family-run **Marina Folch,** Carrer del Mar 16, principal (© **93-310-37-09**), is the only one in the beachside neighborhood of Barceloneta, with plenty of open-air bars and open spaces for the kids to run wild. Ask for a room at the front for a balcony with a view of the port. See p. 98.

- **Best Hostal:** Forget faded curtains and floral wallpaper. **Gat Raval,** Joaquín Costa 44 (© **93-481-66-70**), is a streamlined hostal fitted out in acid green and black that has been conceived for the modern world traveler on a budget. On-demand Internet access and touches of abstract art add toits contemporary ambience and the foyer is always abuzz with travelers exchanging information. See p. 78.

3 The Best Restaurant Bets

- **Hottest Chef:** Carles Abellán has been hailed as the new wunderkind of nouvelle Catalan cuisine. His restaurant, **Comerç 24,** Comerç 24 (© **93-319-21-02**), was conceived as a playful take on all that's hot in the tapas world. Delights such as "kinder egg surprise" (a soft-boiled egg with truffle-infused yolk) and tuna sashimi pizza await the adventurous. See p. 109.

- **Best Newcomer:** Even rival chefs are talking about Jordi Villa's **Alkimia,** Indústria 79 (© **93-207-61-15**), for his vanguard versions of classic Catalan and French dishes. The unstinting minimalism of the interior is a fitting setting for what is an unforgettable gastronomic experience. See p. 123.

- **Best Place for a Business Lunch:** The sleek, urban decor and smoked-glass mirrors, black-clad waitstaff, and imaginative Spanish-Italian dishes have made **Noti,** Roger de Llúria 35 (© **93-342-66-73**)—in the heart of the power district—a hit with the city's media set and other assorted movers and shakers. See p. 125.

- **Best Spot for a Celebration:** You can make as much noise as you like at **Mesón David,** Carretes 63 (© **93-441-59-34**), an old-school eatery with an interminable menu of dishes from all regions of Spain. Chances are you will be sitting next to a raucous group celebrating a birthday or engagement with waiters often joining in the revelry themselves. See p. 114.

- **Best Wine List:** You will be spoiled for choice at **La Vinya del Senyor,** Plaça Santa María 5 (© **93-310-33-79**), a gorgeous wine bar opposite the towering Santa María del Mar church. Mull over the 300 varieties on offer while taking in its facade from the outside terrace, then order some of their delicious tapas to accompany your choice. See p. 138.
- **Best for Paella:** A paella-on-the-beach is one of the quintessential Barcelona experiences and there is no place better to do it than **Can Majó,** Almirall Aixada 23 (© **93-221-54-55**). Right on the seafront, this restaurant prides itself on its paellas and *fideuàs* (which replace noodles for rice) and is an established favorite among the city's most well heeled families. See p. 136.
- **Best Modern Catalan Cuisine:** With over 10 restaurants, the legendary Tragaluz group has revolutionized Barcelona's gastronomic panorama. its flagship eatery, **Tragaluz,** Passatge de la Concepció 5 (© **93-487-06-21**), defines not only the city's contemporary design aesthetic, but also its "market" cuisine: The freshest seasonal ingredients are executed to a very high standard. See p. 127.
- **Best Traditional Catalan Cuisine: Via Veneto,** Ganduxer 10 (© **93-200-72-44**), exudes old-fashioned class and serves up some of the finest Catalan cooking in the land. Some of the serving methods, such as the sterling silver duck press, seem to belong to another century (as do some of the clients). See p. 139.
- **Best for Kids:** Children are welcome almost everywhere in Spanish restaurants, but why not give them a real treat by heading for **La Paradeta,** Comercial 7 (© **93-268-19-39**)? As close as you can get to

the Catalan version of a fish and chippery, all kinds of seafood laid out on ice greet you as you walk in. You pick what you want and a few minutes later, *bingo!* Out it comes, hot and steaming, in a cardboard box. See p. 114.
- **Best Fusion Cuisine:** Born in Catalonia but raised in Canada, chef Jordi Artal instinctively knows how to fuse Old and New World cuisines. The five-course tasting menu in his upscale **Cinc Sentits,** Aribau 58 (© **93-323-94-90**), is a memorable way to sample his expertise; a range of tiny dishes using carefully sourced produce that surprise and delight. See p. 123.
- **Best for Tapas: Taller de Tapas,** Plaça Sant Josep Oriol 9 (© **93-301-80-20**) and Argenteria 51 (© **93-268-85-59**), was conceived to take the mystery out of tapas. Multilingual staff and menus ensure you don't get pig's cheeks when you order green leeks and the rest of the delectable dishes are a perfect initiation for the novice. See p. 118.
- **Best for People-Watching:** The food may not win any awards but that doesn't stop soccer stars, models and other assorted semi-celebs from flocking to **CDLC,** Passeig Marítim 32 (© **93-244-04-70**). Right on the waterfront in the Olympic Village and decked out in fashionable faux-Thai chic, the real fun starts with the post-dinner disco, and you're not sure whether the breeze is rolling in off the Mediterranean or the rush of air kisses. See p. 137.
- **Best Outdoor Dining Area:** As well as being one of the best-value restaurants in the city, the **Café de L'Academia,** Lledó 1 (© **93-315-00-26**), is blessed with one of the prettiest settings; a charming square in the Old Town flanked by Gothic

buildings and an ancient water fountain. At night the warm glow of the table candles bounces off the stone walls, ensuring you linger long on after the last liquor. See p. 108.

- **Best View:** Dine on top of the world, or at least 75m (246 ft.) up in **Torre d'Alta Mar,** Passeig Joan de Borbón 88 (© **93-221-00-07**), located in a cable-car tower. The view couldn't be more mesmerizing, allowing you to take an almost-360-degree view of the city's skyline and the surrounding sea in one swoop. See p. 134.

- **Best for Seafood:** Although good seafood is abundant in Barcelona, many swear that the best catches end up in **Cal Pep,** Plaça des les Olles 8 (© **93-310-79-61**), a tiny bar near the port. Mountains of the stuff are prepared in front of your eyes by lightning-quick staff and your dexterity is put to test as you try not to elbow your neighbor while peeling your prawns. See p. 109.

- **Best Wine Bar:** Bathed in Bordeaux red, with large arched windows looking out onto a tranquil square, **Vinissim,** Sant Doménech del Call 12 (© **93-301-45-75**), has a mind-boggling array of wines from all corners of the globe, plus a scrumptious array of tapas to soak them up. It offers a pleasing experience for all the senses. See p. 119.

- **Best for Sunday Lunch:** The queues say it all: **7 Portes,** Passeig Isabel II no. 14 (© **93-319-30-33**), one of the oldest restaurants in Barcelona, is a Sunday institution. Extended families can be seen dining on their excellent meat and fish dishes in turn of the century surrounds and the photographic memorabilia on the walls denotes its perennial popularity. See p. 134.

- **Best Vegetarian Restaurant:** True vegetarian dining is still quite rare in Barcelona. Thank heavens for **Organic,** Junta de Comerç 11 (© **93-301-09-02**), a barn-like place with communal wooden tables, an all-you-can-eat salad bar, and tempting rice, pasta, and tofu dishes. See p. 115.

- **Best for a Sweet Tooth:** Sweet but never sickly, **Espai Sucre,** Princesa 53 (© **93-268-16-30**), is perhaps the world's only restaurant that offers a menu made up entirely of desserts. Foodies rave about it and its reputation has spread far and wide as a once-in-a-lifetime gastronomic experience. Some savory dishes are available. See p. 110.

- **Best for Morning or Afternoon Tea:** The tiny street of Petritxol in the Old City is renowned for its *granjas,* cafes specializing in cakes, pastries, and hot chocolate. As well as all this **Xocoa,** Petritxol 11 (© **93-301-11-97**), makes its own mouth-watering chocolates and presents them up in funky wrappers; worthy of picking up to pop in your hand luggage. See p. 185.

- **Best for Consistency: Pla,** Carrer de Bellafila 5 (© **93-412-65-52**), strikes that right balance between hip and highly creative without scaring you off. The menu focuses on local market produce with a touch of Asian and Arabic and the staff are unusually friendly and helpful. See p. 112.

- **Best Snack on the Go:** Before you embark on a visit to the Museum of Contemporary Art, fuel-up at **Foodball,** Elisabets 9 (© **93-270-13-63**), a new concept in fast food. Wholegrain rice balls filled with tofu, wild mushrooms, chickpeas, and the like, plus fresh juices and smoothies are served in a quirky setting where you can also eat in. See p. 117.

- **Best Retro Interior:** For an authentic touch of the '70s, head up to **Flash-Flash Tortillería,**

Granada del Penedès 25 (© **93-237-09-90**). Bathed in dramatic red and white, the photo-murals of a model that adorn the walls were taken by Leopoldo Pomés, one of the founders and a top fashion photographer during the city's swinging decade. See p. 131.

4 The Best Bars & Pubs

• **Best Champagne Bar:** Sparkling wine in Spain is called *cava,* and often there is very little difference between the local version and what you get north of the border in France. **El Xampanyet,** Montcada 22 (© **93-319-70-73**), a tiny, ceramic-lined *cava* bar opposite the Picasso Museum, has been serving up its house variety for generations and is one of the more atmospheric places to down a bottle or two. See p. 217.

• **Best View:** The trek up to the peak of Tibidabo is worth it for **Mirablau,** Plaça Doctor Andreu s/n (© **93-418-58-79**), a chic bar that provides an unparalleled, panoramic view of the city from its floor-to-ceiling glass windows. See p. 216.

• **Best for Predinner Drinks:** Strategically located just off the top end of Les Ramblas, **Boadas,** Tallers 1 (© **93-318-88-26**), is another historic watering hole, this time with its roots in Havana, Cuba. Predictably *mojitos* and daiquiris are a specialty, and it's relaxed enough to wander in casually dressed. See p. 206.

• **Best Irish Pub:** While Barcelona abounds with good Celtic-style pubs, their wood-lined interiors and leather seating are not altogether congenial on a summer night. **The Fastnet,** Passeig Juan de Borbón 22 (© **93-295-30-05**), has an outdoor terrace that looks out onto the port, and is a favorite hangout of visiting yachties and beach-loving expats. See p. 212.

5 The Best for Kids

• **Sightseeing:** Anything by Antoni Gaudí, the city's most famous architect, immediately appeals to young eyes and imaginations. His whimsical **Parque Güell** (p. 169) with its imagery from the animal kingdom and hidden grottoes is a particular favorite. Speaking of animals, the city's world-class **Aquarium** (p. 167) with its walkthrough tunnels and superb collection of Mediterranean marine-life is also a good bet. The somewhat older and less-funded **Parque Zoológico** (p. 152) has a fantastic primate collection and is located in the **Parque Ciutadella** (p. 151) which also boasts a lake with row boats for hire, swings and other assorted kiddie attractions.

Museum-wise, a trip to the **Maritime Museum** (p. 167) could be combined with a jaunt on **Las Golondrinas** (p. 176); quaint, double-decker pleasure boats that take you from the port to the breakwater. The **Museu de la Cera** (**Wax Museum;** p. 146), may not be of the standard of its counterpart in London, but is interesting enough to make it worth a visit. Older children will also find the **Chocolate Museum** (p. 150) enticing and the newly opened **Science Museum** (p. 171) has excellent hands-on exhibits for all ages. Then, of course, there are the beaches—most with showers, toilets, bars, and hammocks for hire.

- **Trips:** An all-time favorite is the **Parc d'Atraccions Tibidabo** (p. 174); an amusement park on top of the city's highest peak, has death-defying attractions and a few gentler ones from bygone days. The **Parc del Laberint d' Horta** (p. 175) is neoclassical park complete with a maze in an outer suburb of the city. Further afield, **Montserrat** (p. 219); Catalonia's "spiritual heart" offers plenty of walking tracks on its rocky terrain, caves to visit, and a monastery.

2

Planning Your Trip to Barcelona

In this chapter, you'll find out the when, where and how of your trip—the advance planning required to get it together and take it on the road.

1 Visitor Information

VISITOR INFORMATION

TOURIST OFFICES The Tourist Office of Spain's official page is **www.okspain.org**.

In the U.S. 666 Fifth Ave., 35th Floor, New York, NY 10103 (© **212/265-8822;** fax 212/265-8864); 845 N. Michigan Ave., Suite 915E, Chicago, IL 60611 (© **312/642-1992;** fax 312/642-9817); 8383 Wilshire Blvd., Suite 956, Beverly Hills, CA 90211 (© **323/658-7188;** fax 323/658-1061); 1221 Brickell Ave., Suite 1850, Miami, FL 33131 (© **305/358-1992;** fax 305/358-8223).

In Canada 2 Bloor St. W., Suite 3402, Toronto, ON M5S 1M9 (© **416/961-3131;** fax 416/961-1992).

In the U.K. 22–23 Manchester Sq., London W1M 5AP (© **00891/66-99-20** or 020/7486-8077; fax 020/7486-8034).

WEBSITES For general info on the Net, check out **www.okspain.org**, the official page of the Tourist Office of Spain and www.spaininfo.com, which has loads of practical tips on driving, destinations, bringing in pets, and even learning Spanish. More Catalonia-specific information can be found on www.barcelonaturisme.com. The official site of city hall www.bcn.es is slow to load, but useful for things such as opening times and upcoming events (in English). The *Barcelona Metropolitan,* the local magazine in English (www.barcelona-metropolitan.com) is mainly aimed at expats, but will appeal to the visitor who wants more of an insider look at the city. For one-stop tour, hotel and activity booking try www.barcelona.com. If you want to pre-book train tickets www.renfe.es, the official site of Spain's rail network, lets you do it online (and effortlessly).

2 Entry Requirements & Customs

ENTRY REQUIREMENTS

Visas are not needed by U.S., Canadian, Australian, or New Zealand citizens for visits of less than 3 months but they must enter with a valid passport. British, Irish, and other E.U. citizens have no time limit on their visit and can enter with either a valid passport or ID (although I always recommend you carry a passport anyway).

Safeguard your passport in an inconspicuous, inaccessible place like a money belt. If you lose it, visit the nearest consulate of your native country as soon as possible for a replacement.

For information on how to get a passport, go to the Fast Facts section in the next chapter—the websites listed provide downloadable passport applications as well as the current fees

Destination Spain: Red Alert Checklist

- Most major venues have their own websites. Have you tried to book ahead for any concerts or events you want to attend?
- Remember most museums and galleries close at lunchtime on Sundays and all day Mondays. Have you included other weekdays in your itinerary?
- If you purchased traveler's checks, have you recorded the check numbers, and stored the documentation separately from the checks?
- Did you stop the newspaper and mail delivery, and leave a set of keys with someone reliable?
- Did you pack your camera and an extra set of camera batteries, and purchase enough film? If you packed film in your checked baggage, did you invest in protective pouches to shield film from airport X-rays?
- Do you have a safe, accessible place to store money?
- Did you bring your ID cards that could entitle you to discounts such as AAA and AARP cards, student IDs, and so on?
- Did you bring emergency drug prescriptions and extra glasses and/or contact lenses?
- Did you find out your daily ATM withdrawal limit?
- Do you have your credit card PINs? Is there a daily withdrawal limit on credit card cash advances?
- If you have an e-ticket, do you have documentation?
- Did you leave a copy of your itinerary with someone at home?
- Do you have the measurements for those people you plan to buy clothes for on your trip?
- Do you have the address and phone number of your country's embassy with you?

for processing passport applications. For an up-to-date country-by-country listing of passport requirements around the world, go to the "Foreign Entry Requirement" Web page of the U.S. State Department at **http://travel.state.gov/foreignentryreqs.html**.

CUSTOMS
WHAT YOU CAN BRING INTO SPAIN
According to E.U. conventions, you cannot take any animal-based food products (including any form of meat or dairy) into Spain. The exception is powdered baby milk, of which you can bring in up to one kilogram. You can bring into Spain personal effects (including jewelry, personal computers, and cameras) and items destined

for gifts, although if you are carrying large quantities, the application of duty (or not) will be left to the discretion of the customs officer. Travelers over 18 can carry in either 200 cigarettes, 100 small cigars, 50 cigars, or 250 grams of loose tobacco. As for alcohol, you are allowed to bring up to 1 liter of spirits (alcoholic content 22%), or 2 liters if the alcoholic content is less than 22%. Also note that fragrances are limited to 50 ml of perfume or 250 ml of eau de toilette. Cash amounts of over 6,010€ must be declared.

WHAT YOU CAN TAKE HOME FROM SPAIN
Returning **U.S. citizens** who have been away for at least 48 hours are

Spain

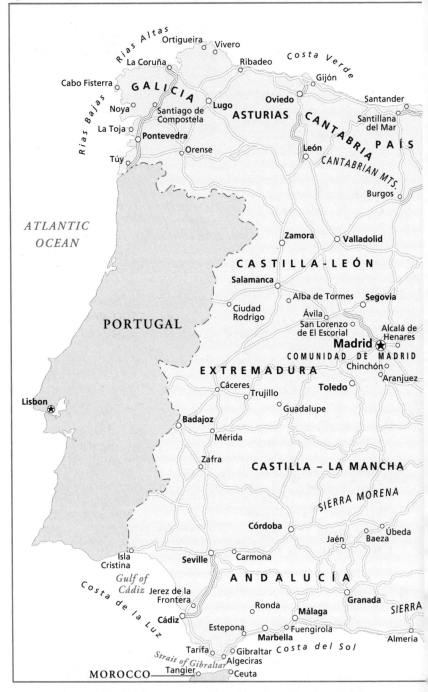

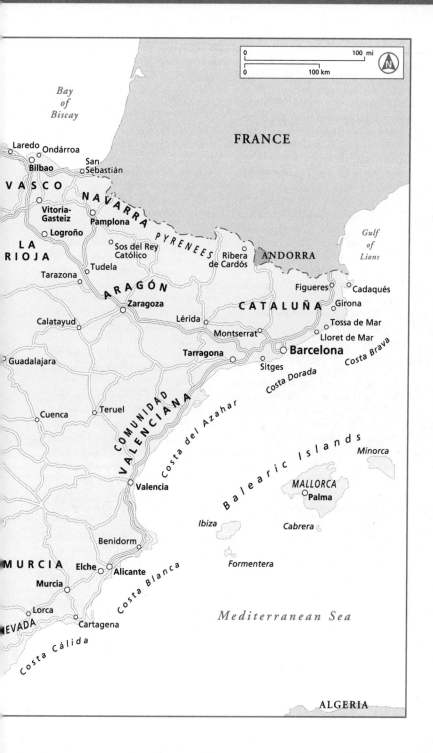

allowed to bring back, once every 30 days, $800 worth of merchandise duty-free. You'll be charged a flat rate of 4% duty on the next $1,000 worth of purchases. Be sure to have your receipts handy. On mailed gifts, the duty-free limit is $200. With some exceptions, you cannot bring fresh fruits and vegetables into the United States. For specifics on what you can bring back, download the invaluable free pamphlet *Know Before You Go* online at **www.customs.gov.** (Click on "Travel," then "Know Before You Go Online Brochure.") Or contact the **U.S. Customs Service,** 1300 Pennsylvania Ave. NW, Washington, DC 20229 (℡ **877/287-8667**), and request the pamphlet.

For a clear summary of **Canadian** rules, write for the booklet *I Declare,* issued by the **Canada Customs and Revenue Agency** (℡ **800/461-9999** in Canada, or 204/983-3500; www.ccra-adrc.gc.ca). Canada allows its citizens a C$750 exemption, and you're allowed to bring back duty-free one carton of cigarettes, 1 can of tobacco, 40 imperial ounces of liquor, and 50 cigars. In addition, you're allowed to mail gifts to Canada valued at less than C$60 a day, provided they're unsolicited and don't contain alcohol or tobacco (write on the package "Unsolicited gift, under $60 value"). All valuables should be declared on the Y-38 form before departure from Canada, including serial numbers of valuables you already own, such as expensive foreign cameras. ***Note:*** The $750 exemption can only be used once a year and only after an absence of 7 days.

Citizens of the U.K. who are **returning from a European Union (E.U.) country** will go through a separate Customs Exit (called the "Blue Exit") especially for E.U. travelers. In essence, there is no limit on what you can bring back from an E.U. country, as long as the items are for personal use (this includes gifts), and you have already paid the necessary duty and tax. However, customs law sets out guidance levels. If you bring in more than these levels, you may be asked to prove that the goods are for your own use. Guidance levels on goods bought in the E.U. for your own use are 3,200 cigarettes, 200 cigars, 400 cigarillos, 3 kilograms of smoking tobacco, 10 liters of spirits, 90 liters of wine, 20 liters of fortified wine (such as port or sherry), and 110 liters of beer.

The duty-free allowance in **Australia** is A$400 or, for those under 18, A$200. Citizens can bring in 250 cigarettes or 250 grams of loose tobacco, and 1,125 milliliters of alcohol. If you're returning with valuables you already own, such as foreign-made cameras, you should file form B263. A helpful brochure available from Australian consulates or Customs offices is *Know Before You Go.* For more information, call the **Australian Customs Service** at ℡ **1300/363-263,** or log on to www.customs.gov.au.

The duty-free allowance for **New Zealand** is NZ$700. Citizens over 17 can bring in 200 cigarettes, 50 cigars, or 250 grams of tobacco (or a mixture of all three if their combined weight doesn't exceed 250g); plus 4.5 liters of wine and beer, or 1,125 milliliters of liquor. New Zealand currency does not carry import or export restrictions. Fill out a certificate of export, listing the valuables you are taking out of the country; that way, you can bring them back without paying duty. Most questions are answered in a free pamphlet available at New Zealand consulates and Customs offices: *New Zealand Customs Guide for Travellers, Notice no. 4.* For more information, contact **New Zealand Customs,** The Customhouse, 17–21 Whitmore St., Box 2218, Wellington (℡ **04/473-6099,** or 0800/428-786 in New Zealand; www.customs.govt.nz).

3 Money

CURRENCY

The **euro** (€), the new single European currency, became the official currency of Spain and 11 other participating countries on January 1, 1999. However, the euro didn't go into general circulation until early in 2002. The old currency, the Spanish peseta, disappeared into history on March 1, 2002, replaced by the euro, whose official abbreviation is "EUR." Exchange rates of participating countries are locked into a common currency fluctuating against the dollar. For more details on the euro, check out **www.europa.eu.int/euro**.

Since the introduction of the euro and the country's economic coming-of-age, Spain is regrettably no longer a budget destination. However, compared to other major European cities, it does offer excellent value for money. Barcelona is often quoted as the most expensive city in Spain (in studies based on everything from the cost of renting an apartment to the price of a loaf of bread), but compared to London or Paris, it can be a bargain. Of course, once you move beyond Barcelona and into the rural areas you will find that the price of things (particularly hotels and restaurants) drops noticeably.

Much noise was made about the "rounding off" of prices upon the introduction of the Euro, not just in Spain, but throughout Europe. Basically this meant that, if the normal price of a coffee in pesetas came out at say 81 eurocents, after January 1st 2002 it was hiked up to an "even" euro. This practice was especially widespread in the hospitality sector and anyone who has visited the country in the days of the peseta will notice a considerable difference in prices in bars and restaurants. Unfortunately for U.S. visitors, in the last couple of years, the euro has gone from basically a one-to-one exchange rate with the dollar to a much stronger position. If you're from an expensive city in the U.S., you will probably find a lot of the prices comparable, but if you're not used to large-city prices, you could have a bit of sticker shock.

The old adage "You get what you pay for" is as true in Barcelona as any other European city, up to a point. Reflecting a modern, cosmopolitan city that has to cater all budgets, you can choose to go either up- or down-market in your choice of dining and accommodations. Often you will find that the most memorable experience is not wholly dependent on the price tag. Staying away from the tourist traps and seeking out family-run restaurants will generally make you more inclined to hand over your credit card with a smile when the check comes. In a climate of stiff competition (especially from the holiday apartment sector) hotels are usually clean and comfortable. Trains are very reasonably priced, fast and on time, and most service personnel treat you with respect.

Regarding the Euro

Since the euro's inception, the U.S. dollar and the euro have traded almost on par (i.e., $1 equals approximately 1€); therefore, all prices in this book are given in euros. But as this book went to press, 1€ was worth approximately $1.15 and gaining, so your dollars might not go as far as you'd expect. (I give euro/dollar conversions at this rate). For up-to-the minute exchange rates between the euro and the dollar, check the currency converter website www.xe.com/ucc.

Tips Small Change

When you change money, ask for some small bills or loose change. Petty cash will come in handy for tipping and public transportation. Consider keeping the change separate from your larger bills, so that it's readily accessible and you'll be less of a target for theft.

In Spain, many prices for children—generally defined as ages 6 to 17—are lower than for adults. Fees for children under 6 are generally waived.

It's a good idea to exchange at least some money—just enough to cover airport incidentals and transportation to your hotel—before you leave home, so you can avoid lines at airport ATMs (automated teller machines). You can exchange money at your local American Express or Thomas Cook office or your bank. If you're far away from a bank with currency-exchange services, American Express offers traveler's checks and foreign currency, though with a $15 order fee and additional shipping costs, at www.american express.com or **800/807-6233**.

ATMs

The easiest and best way to get cash away from home is from an ATM (automated teller machine). The **Cirrus** (✆ **800/424-7787;** www.mastercard. com) and **PLUS** (✆ **800/843-7587;** www.visa.com) networks span the globe (and are plentiful in Spain); look at the back of your bankcard to see which network you're on. ATMs are plentiful in Barcelona and even the tiniest village will have at least at least a few of them. Be sure you know your personal identification number (PIN) before you leave home and find out your daily withdrawal limit before you depart. Also keep in mind that most banks impose a fee every time a card is used at a different bank's ATM, and that fee can be higher for international transactions (up to $5 or more) than for domestic ones (where they're rarely more than $1.50).

On top of this, the bank from which you withdraw cash may charge its own fee (although this is often stated at the time of withdrawal). To compare banks' ATM fees within the U.S., use **www. bankrate.com**. For international withdrawal fees, ask your bank. Most ATMs in Barcelona are multilingual; displaying instructions in the language of your choice. Some are located on street level, while some are located inside a "chamber" (guarded by CCTV) that is accessed with your bankcard. Note that these type of ATMs in central Barcelona are often closed after 9pm, leaving only the street level ones at your disposal. If you feel nervous about using these at night, try to withdraw money during working hours when the bank is open and staff is on hand for any possible hitches. Also be warned that theft and scams at ATM points are on the rise (for more information, see p. 24).

You can also get cash advances on your credit card at an ATM. Keep in mind that credit card companies try to protect themselves from theft by limiting the funds someone can withdraw outside their home country, so call your credit card company before you leave home.

TRAVELER'S CHECKS

Traveler's checks are something of an anachronism from the days before the ATM made cash accessible at any time. Traveler's checks used to be the only sound alternative to traveling with dangerously large amounts of cash. They were as reliable as currency, but, unlike cash, could be replaced if lost or stolen.

These days, traveler's checks are less necessary because most cities (including Barcelona) have 24-hour ATMs that allow you to withdraw small amounts of cash as needed. A disadvantage to this convenience is that you will likely be charged an ATM withdrawal fee if the bank is not your own, so if you're withdrawing money every day, you might be better off with traveler's checks—provided that you don't mind showing ID every time you want to cash one.

You can get traveler's checks at almost any bank. **American Express** offers denominations of $20, $50, $100, $500, and (for cardholders only) $1,000. You'll pay a service charge ranging from 1% to 4%. You can also get American Express traveler's checks over the phone by calling © **800/221-7282;** Amex gold and platinum cardholders who use this number are exempt from the 1% fee.

Visa offers traveler's checks at Citibank locations nationwide, as well as at several other banks. The service charge ranges between 1.5% and 2%; checks come in denominations of $20, $50, $100, $500, and $1,000. Call © **800/732-1322** for information. AAA members can obtain checks without a fee at most AAA offices. **MasterCard** also offers traveler's checks. Call © **800/223-9920** for a location near you.

Foreign currency traveler's checks are useful if you're traveling to one country, or to the euro zone; they're accepted at locations such as bed & breakfasts where dollar checks may not be, and they minimize the amount of math you have to do at your destination. **American Express** offers checks in Australian dollars, Canadian dollars, British pounds, euros, and Japanese yen. **Visa** checks come in Australian, Canadian, British, and euro versions; **MasterCard** offers those four plus yen and South African rands.

If you choose to carry traveler's checks, be sure to keep a record of their serial numbers separate from your checks in the event that they are stolen or lost. You'll get a refund faster if you know the numbers.

CREDIT CARDS

Credit cards are a safe way to carry money, they provide a convenient record of all your expenses, and they generally offer good exchange rates. You can also withdraw cash advances from your credit cards at banks or ATMs, provided you know your PIN. If you've forgotten yours, or didn't even know you had one, call the number on the back of your credit card and ask the bank to send it to you. It usually takes 5 to 7 business days, though some banks will provide the number over the phone if you tell them your mother's maiden name or some other personal information. Your credit card company will likely charge a commission (1%–2%) on every foreign purchase you make, but don't sweat this small stuff; for most purchases, you'll still get the best deal with credit cards when you factor in things like ATM fees and higher traveler's check exchange rates.

In Spain, American Express, Diners Club, MasterCard, and Visa are commonly accepted, with the latter two cards predominating. For tips and telephone numbers to call if your wallet is stolen or lost, go to "Police" in the "Fast Facts" section in the next chapter. Also note that in Spain you are required to show some form of photo ID (driver's license, passport, and so on) when making a purchase with a credit card, although for some reason this is waived in restaurants.

For tips and telephone numbers to call if your wallet is stolen or lost, go to the "Lost & Found" in the "Fast Facts" section of chapter 3.

4 When to Go

Barcelona is blessed with a benign, Mediterranean climate. Spring and fall are ideal times to visit, especially May to June and September to October. Even in the winter, days are crisp to cold (due to its proximity to the mountains) but often sunny. Snow is rare and never lasts more than a day or two. Most of the rainfall occurs in April but some quite spectacular storms, as is typical of the Mediterranean, can occur all year round. July and August are hot and humid, even at night as the temperature often only drops minimally. The surrounding sea is warm enough to swim in from the end of June to early October. Inland the temperatures drop slightly, as does the humidity. North on the Costa Brava, a strong wind known as the *tramontana* often blows.

August is the major vacation month in Europe. The traffic from France, the Netherlands, and Germany to Spain becomes a veritable migration, and low-cost hotels along the coastal areas are virtually impossible to find unless booked well in advance. To compound the problem, many restaurants and shops also decide it's time for a vacation, thereby limiting the visitors' selections for both dining and shopping. That said, Barcelonese also head out of town for cooler climes, leaving tourists to enjoy the city for themselves. Barcelona is also a major international trade fair and conference destination. These happen throughout the year so if you plan to stay in a mid to high range hotel it should be booked well in advance. Barcelona is officially Spain's most popular destination, and tourism is now year-round. The only time you may not be rubbing shoulders with fellow travelers is Christmas!

Weather Chart for Barcelona

	Jan	Feb	Mar	Apr	May	June	July	Aug	Sept	Oct	Nov	Dec
Temp. (°F)	48	49	52	55	61	68	73	73	70	63	55	50
Temp. (°C)	9	9	11	13	16	20	23	23	21	17	13	10
Rainfall (in.)	1.70	1.40	1.90	2.00	2.20	1.50	.90	1.60	3.10	3.70	2.90	2.00

CATALAN & NATIONAL HOLIDAYS

Holidays observed are January 1 (New Year's Day), January 6 (Feast of the Epiphany), March/April (Good Friday and Easter Monday), May 1 (May Day), May/June (Whit Monday) June 24 (Feast of St. John), August 15 (Feast of the Assumption), September 11 (National Day of Catalonia), September 24 (Feast of Our Lady of Mercy), October 12 (Spain's National Day), November 1 (All Saints' Day), December 8 (Feast of the Immaculate Conception), and December 25 (Christmas) and December 26 (Feast of St. Stephen).

If a holiday falls on a Thursday or Tuesday, many people also take off the weekday in between creating an extra-long weekend. While this only really affects those doing business in the city, you should book hotels well ahead of time on these popular *puentes* (bridges).

BARCELONA CALENDAR OF EVENTS

Barcelona is *fiesta* city, bar none; whether it's a rip-roaring street carnival or a culture fest, the year's calendar is sprinkled with events to keep in mind when planning your trip. Note that on official holidays (see above) shops, banks, and some restaurants and museums close for the day.

The dates for festivals and events given below may not be precise. Sometimes the exact days are not announced until 6 weeks before the actual festival. Also days allotted to celebrate Easter Carnival and some other religious days change each year. Check with the Barcelona Tourist Office (see "Visitor Information," earlier in this chapter) if you're planning to attend a specific event.

January

Día de los Reyes (Three Kings Day). Parades are held around the country on the eve of the Festival of the Epiphany, which is traditionally when Christmas gift giving is done (the concept of "Santa Claus" has crept into the culture in the past years, meaning that people now also exchange gifts on Christmas). In Barcelona, the three "kings" arrive by boat at the port in the evening to dispense candy to all the incredibly excited children. January 5.

February

Carnival. Compared to other parts of Spain, particularly Cádiz in the south, Carnival in Barcelona is a low-key event. The most dressing up you are likely to see is done by groups of children or stall owners in the local markets who organize a competition between themselves for "best costume" (buying fresh fish off a woman dressed in full Louis VI regalia is one of those "only in Barcelona" experiences you will treasure) as well as the city's main Carnival parade. Just south of the city however in the seaside town of Sitges locals, especially the local gay community, go all out and many Barcelonese take the short train ride to celebrate along with them. Just before Lent (Feb 21–28 in 2006).

March/April

Semana Santa (Holy Week). Catalonia has some Easter traditions not found in the rest of the country. The Mona is a whimsical chocolate and pastry creation given in the same way we give Easter eggs. On Palm Sunday, palm leaves are blessed in Gaudí's Sagrada Família and the city's main cathedral has the curious L'ou com balla; a hollowed out egg shell that is placed on top of a fountain in the city's cathedral's cloister to bob around and "dance." Out of town, the ominously named Dansa de la Mort (Dance of Death) sees men dressed as skeletons performing a "death" dance in the village of Verges near Girona, and various Passion Plays are also performed, the most famous in the village of Esparraguera, 40km (25 miles) outside of Barcelona. 1 week before Easter.

La Diada de St. Jordi. Saint George (St. Jordi in Catalan) is the patron saint of Catalonia, and his name day coincides with the deaths of *Don Quixote* writer Miguel Cervantes and William Shakespeare. On this day men give a single red rose to the significant women in their lives (mother, girlfriend, sister, and so on), and women give a book in return (although, in the interest of gender equality, many men now give women a book). This is one of the most colorful days in Catalonia, as thousands of rose-sellers take to the streets and bookshops set up

---

Fun Fact St. George Conquers the World

In 1995, and taking a cue from Catalonia, UNESCO declared April 23 "World Book Day" to encourage people to buy books, to think about books, and simply read more. In the U.K., children receive a book token and online chat rooms are set up with well-known authors. The idea seems to be catching on with as many as 30 countries participating.

open-air stalls along the major thoroughfares. April 23.

May

May Day. Also known as Labor Day, this day sees a huge march by the city's trade union members. On this day, dozens of herbs, natural remedies, and wholesome goodies are sold along the Carrer de l'Hospital in the Fira de Sant Ponç. May 1.

Corpus Christi. During this festival, the streets of Sitges are carpeted in flowers. Can fall in May or June.

June

Verbena de Sant Juan. Catalonia celebrates the Twelfth Night with fiery activities that can keep even grannies up till dawn. Families stock up on fireworks a week in advance before setting them off in streets and squares and even off balconies. Bonfires are lit along the beachfront, and the sky is ablaze with smoke and light. Lots of champagne is consumed, and it is traditional to have the first dip in the sea of the year at dawn (officially the first day of summer). Madcap fun. June 23.

Sonar. This dance-music and multimedia festival has gained the reputation of being one of the best on the world circuit. Thousands from all over Europe descend on the city for the DJs, live concerts, and other related events. During the day events are held at the Museum of Contemporary Art; at night, they move to the enormous trade fair buildings. Purchase tickets to this wildly popular festival well in advance at www.sonar.es. Early to mid-June.

July

El Grec. International names in all genres music and theatre come to the city to perform in various open-air venues, including the mock-Greek theater, namesake of the city's main culturefest. Beginning of July.

August

Festa Major de Gràcia. This charming weeklong fiesta is held in the village-like neighborhood of Gràcia. All year long, the residents of Gràcia work on elaborate decorations with themes such as marine life, the solar system, or even local politics to hang in the streets. By day, long trestle tables are set up for communal lunches and board games; at night, thousands invade the tiny streets for outdoor concerts, balls, and general revelry. Early to mid-August.

September

La Diada de Catalunya. This is the most politically and historically significant holiday in Catalonia. Although it celebrates the region's autonomy, the date actually marks the day the city was besieged by Spanish and French troops in 1714 during the War of Succession. Demonstrations calling for greater independence are everywhere, wreath-laying ceremonies take place at tombs of past *políticos,* and the *senyera,* the flag of Catalonia, is hung from balconies. Not your typical tourist fare, but interesting for anyone who wishes to understand Catalan nationalism. September 11.

La Mercè. This celebration honors Our Lady of Mercy (La Mercè), the city's patron saint. Legend has it she rid Barcelona of a plague of locusts, and the Barcelonese give thanks in rip-roaring style. Free concerts, from traditional to contemporary music, are held in the plazas (particularly Plaça de Catalunya and Plaça Sant Jaume), and folkloric figures such as the *gigants* (giants) and *cap grosses* (fat heads) take to the streets. People come out to perform the *sardana* (the traditional Catalan dance) and to watch the nail-biting *castellers* (human towers). Firework displays light up the night, and the hair-raising *correfoc,* a parade of

The Pooping Catalan

When you go to the Fira d' Santa Lucia, be on the lookout for one unique personage amongst the Magi, farm animals, and other *pessebre* figurines. The *caganer* is a small fellow, usually dressed in the garb of a peasant farmer (but also seen in anything from formal attire to the Barcelona Football Club attire). He is squatting, has his pants down and a stream of excrement connects his bare buttocks to the earth. His origins are lost in folklore but it is generally believed that he sprang from the Catalan philosophy of "giving back to the earth what one takes from it." The artist Joan Miró placed him in *La Granja* (The Farm), one of his most famous works that is on display at Barcelona's Miró Foundation.

firework-brandishing "devils" and dragons is the grand finale. One of the best times to be in Barcelona, especially for children. September 24.

October

Dia de la Hispanitat. Spain's national day (which commemorates Columbus' "discovery" of the New World) is met with mixed receptions in Catalonia, due to the region's overriding sense of independence. The only street events you are likely to see are demonstrations calling for exactly that, or low-key celebrations from groups of people from other regions of Spain. October 12.

November

All Saints' Day. This public holiday is reverently celebrated, as relatives and friends lay flowers on the graves (or *nichos*—in Spain, people are buried one on top of another in tiny compartments) of the dead. The night before, some of the bars in the city hold Halloween parties, another imported custom that seems to be catching on. November 1.

December

Nadal (Christmas). In mid-December stallholders set up Fira d' Santa Lucia, a huge open air market held in the streets around the main cathedral. Thousands come to buy handicrafts, Christmas decorations, trees, and the figurines for their *pessebres* (nativity dioramas) that are hugely popular here. The Betlem Church on Les Ramblas holds an exhibition of them throughout the month and a life-size one is constructed outside the city hall in the Plaça Sant Jaume. December 25.

5 Travel Insurance

Check your existing insurance policies and credit-card coverage before you buy travel insurance. You may already be covered for lost luggage, canceled tickets, or medical expenses.

The cost of travel insurance varies widely, depending on the cost and length of your trip, your age and health, and the type of trip you're taking, but expect to pay between 5% and 8% of the vacation itself. Insurance that at least covers loss or theft of baggage and personal effects is particularly recommended when traveling to Spain.

TRIP-CANCELLATION INSURANCE Trip-cancellation insurance helps you get your money back if you have to back out of a trip, if you have to go home early, or if your travel supplier goes bankrupt. Allowed reasons for cancellation can range from sickness to natural disasters to the State

Department declaring your destination unsafe for travel. (Insurers usually won't cover vague fears, though, as many travelers discovered who tried to cancel their trips in Oct 2001 because they were wary of flying.) In this unstable world, trip-cancellation insurance is a good buy if you're getting tickets well in advance—who knows what the state of the world, or of your airline, will be in 9 months? Insurance policy details vary, so read the fine print—and especially make sure that your airline or cruise line is on the list of carriers covered in case of bankruptcy. For information, contact one of the following insurers: **Access America** (© 866/807-3982; www. accessamerica.com); **Travel Guard International** (© 800/826-4919; www.travelguard.com); **Travel Insured International** (© 800/243-3174; www.travelinsured.com); and **Travelex Insurance Services** (© 888/457-4602; www.travelex-insurance.com).

LOST-LUGGAGE INSURANCE
On international flights (including

U.S. portions of international trips), coverage on baggage is limited to approximately $9.05 per pound, up to approximately $635 per checked bag. If you plan to check items more valuable than the standard liability, see if your valuables are covered by your homeowner's policy, get baggage insurance as part of your comprehensive travel-insurance package, or buy Travel Guard's "BagTrak" product. Don't buy insurance at the airport, as it's usually overpriced. Be sure to take any valuables or irreplaceable items with you in your carry-on luggage, as many valuables (including books, money, and electronics) aren't covered by airline policies.

If your luggage is lost, immediately file a lost-luggage claim at the airport, detailing the luggage contents. For most airlines, you must report delayed, damaged, or lost baggage within 4 hours of arrival. The airlines are required to deliver luggage, once found, directly to your house or destination free of charge.

6 Health & Safety

STAYING HEALTHY
Visiting Spain and Catalonia does not pose any major health hazards. The rich cuisine may be too much for some people's digestion, and even though the water is generally safe, drink mineral water only. Fish and shellfish from the Mediterranean should only be eaten if cooked. Over-the-counter medicine is easy to get and most pharmacists will supply the Spanish equivalent of your prescription drugs without a written prescription if you run out. To be sure, ask your regular doctor for the chemical name of your medication before leaving home.

COMMON AILMENTS
DIETARY RED FLAGS The rich cuisine—garlic, olive oil, and wine—may give some travelers mild diarrhea, so take along some anti-diarrhea

medicine, and moderate your eating habits if necessary. Vegetarian restaurants and restaurants using organic products are becoming more common, although it should be noted that *carne,* the word for "meat" in Spanish, only refers to red meat. Vegetarians should double check that their orders do not contain fish or white meat in restaurants, as should those with allergies to nuts and other foodstuffs. In the hot weather, be wary of tapas containing mayonnaise or pastries with creamy fillings, as salmonella poisoning is a risk. To be on the safe side do not drink the water in mountain streams, regardless of how clear and pure it looks.

EXPOSURE In the hot weather, do as the locals do and avoid the sun between noon and 4pm. Use a sunscreen with a high protection factor and apply it liberally. Remember that children need more protection than adults do.

Urban beaches in Barcelona have lifeguards on duty and are marked by flags; green is safe, yellow means you should take caution and red means stay out. Where there are no guards on duty use your common sense and note that, particularly north of Barcelona along the Costa Brava, the seabed is rocky. Over the past years much has been done to improve the standard of Spain's beaches in terms of water pollution, leading to a consistently high rating in terms of cleanliness. At the onset of summer, jellyfish can be a problem. They are not poisonous but do have a nasty sting. If you do get bitten, seek assistance from the nearest *farmacia* (drugstore).

RESPIRATORY ILLNESSES Nonsmoking areas in restaurants and bars are virtually non-existent in Spain, so if smoke bothers you, try and secure a table on an outside *terraza*. Smoking has recently been banned in airports, post offices, banks, the Metro, and other public places but the general population has been slow to adhere to these new laws.

Lodged between the mountains and the sea, Barcelona can often trap smog from its nearby industrial belt. While the quality of the air is monitored, local media does not publish "high risk" days. Although the problem is nowhere near the level of say Tokyo, common sense is required for people with respiratory illnesses.

WHAT TO DO IF YOU GET SICK AWAY FROM HOME

Spanish medical facilities are among the best in the world. If a medical emergency arises, your hotel staff can usually put you in touch with a reliable doctor. If not, contact the American embassy or a consulate; each one maintains a list of English-speaking doctors or consult the local magazine for expatriates *The Barcelona Metropolitan* (www.barcelona-metropolitan. com). Medical and hospital services aren't free, so be sure that you have appropriate insurance coverage before you travel.

If you worry about getting sick away from home, consider purchasing **medical travel insurance** and carry your ID card in your purse or wallet. In most cases, your existing health plan will provide the coverage you need.

If you suffer from a chronic illness, consult your doctor before your departure. For conditions like epilepsy, diabetes, or heart problems, wear a **Medic Alert Identification Tag** (✆ 800/825-3785; www.medic alert.org), which will immediately alert doctors to your condition and give them access to your records through Medic Alert's 24-hour hot line.

Pack **prescription medications** in your carry-on luggage, and carry prescription medications in their original containers, with pharmacy labels—otherwise they won't make it through airport security. Also bring along copies of your prescriptions in case you lose your pills or run out. Don't forget an extra pair of contact lenses or prescription glasses. Carry the generic name of prescription medicines, in case a local pharmacist is unfamiliar with the brand name.

Contact the **International Association for Medical Assistance to Travelers (IAMAT;** ✆ 716/754-4883 or 416/652-0137; www.iamat.org) for tips on travel and health concerns in the countries you're visiting, and lists of local, English-speaking doctors. The United States **Centers for Disease Control and Prevention** (✆ 800/311-3435; www.cdc.gov) provides up-to-date information on necessary vaccines and health hazards by region or country. Any foreign consulate can provide a list of area doctors who speak English. If you get sick, consider asking your hotel concierge to recommend a local doctor—even his or her own. The emergency rooms at local hospitals have walk-in clinics for urgent cases that are not life threatening and, at least in Barcelona and resorts, are used to dealing with tourists. You may not get immediate attention, but you won't pay the high price of a private doctor.

In Barcelona, the **Centre d'Urgències Perecamps,** located near Les Ramblas at Av. de las Drassanes 13–15, is a good bet. *Farmacias* (pharmacies) are everywhere and their highly trained staff is normally extremely helpful and can often replace a trip to the doctor (most drugs are available over the counter). Pharmacies work on a shift basis; when one is closed they display a list of nearby 24-hour or extended-hour pharmacies on their front door.

Herbolistarias (herb shops) are also common, and many Spaniards use them for natural remedies for milder aliments such as colds and stomach upsets. As with *farmacias,* their staff is trained to diagnose and prescribe accordingly.

STAYING SAFE

The ETA terrorist organization remains active in Spain. Although ETA efforts have historically been directed against police, military, and other Spanish government targets, in March 2001, ETA issued a communiqué announcing its intention to target Spanish tourist areas. Americans have not been the specific targets of ETA activities. The Spanish government is vigorously engaged in combating terrorism at home and abroad and has been able to avert many terrorist activities. Over the years, ETA has conducted many successful attacks, many of which have resulted in deaths and injuries. In 2002 ETA attacks included a number of car bomb incidents, which occurred in areas frequented by tourists, including the Madrid and Málaga airports. While there were no tourist fatalities from any of these incidents, a number of bystanders suffered injuries. A smaller Marxist group, GRAPO, has also mounted several attacks since 1999 and killed three people.

U.S. tourists traveling to Spain should exercise caution and refer to the guidance offered in the Worldwide Caution Public Announcements issued in the wake of the September 11, 2001, terrorist attacks.

While most of Spain has a moderate rate of crime, and most of the estimated one million American tourists have trouble-free visits to Spain each year, the principal tourist areas have been experiencing an increase in petty crime. Madrid and Barcelona, in particular, have in the past reported growing incidents of muggings, pick-pocketing, and tourist-targeted scams, although in Barcelona at least the situation is slowly improving due to perpetrators now being fast-tracked through the courts. Criminals frequent tourist areas and major attractions such as museums, monuments, restaurants, hotels, beach resorts, trains, train stations, airports, subways, and ATMs. Travelers should exercise caution and common sense, carry limited cash and credit cards, and leave extra cash, credit cards, passports, and personal documents in a safe location. Crimes have occurred at all times of day and night.

Thieves often work in teams or pairs. In most cases, one person distracts a victim while the accomplice performs the robbery. For example, a stranger might wave a map in your face and ask for directions or "inadvertently" spill something on you. While your attention is diverted, an accomplice makes off with the valuables. A group of assailants may surround the victim, maybe in a crowded

Dealing with Discrimination

A fierce sense of national pride might lead many Spaniards to bristle at the suggestion that racism is a problem in their country, but certain events and a report by Amnesty International have brought to the fore concerns over racism and racial profiling in Spain. In January 2002, Rodney Mack, an African American and the principal trumpet player with the Barcelona Symphony Orchestra, was attacked and beaten in Madrid by four police officers who later said they mistook the musician for a car thief. The thief had been described as a black man of roughly Mr. Mack's height, and a police official later admitted that Mack was singled out because of "the color of his skin and his height." In April 2002, Amnesty International cited the Mack case in an exhaustive report accusing Spain of "frequent and widespread" mistreatment of foreigners and ethnic minorities. The report investigated more than 320 cases of abuse from 1995 to 2002, including deaths and rapes while in police custody, as well as beatings, verbal abuse, and the use of racial profiling by police. The report claims that an increase in racist attacks in Spain has coincided with a dramatic growth in the country's immigrant population over the last 20 years. Spanish officials, however, rejected the report, and Congressman Ignacio Gil-Lázaro of Spain's ruling Popular Party said, "The police and Civil Guard confront immigration in a deeply humanitarian way."

While Amnesty's report may rightfully dispel the notion that Spain is exempt from the problems of racism, it does not suggest that the country is Europe's only offender. Travelers of color may have a perfectly enjoyable trip in Spain, but visitors to the area should travel with the knowledge that racism and xenophobia may well be as serious a problem in Spain as anywhere in Europe or the United States. If you encounter discrimination or mistreatment while traveling in Spain, please report it to your embassy immediately, or contact **S.O.S. Racisme,** an independent anti-discrimination organization that has an office in Barcelona at Carrer Bou de Sant Pere, 3° izq. (✆ **93-301-05-97;** www.sosracisme.org).

—*John Vorwald*

popular tourist area or on public transportation, and only after the group has departed does the person discover he/she has been robbed.

Theft from parked cars is also common. Small items like luggage, cameras, or briefcases are often stolen from parked cars. Travelers are advised not to leave valuables in parked cars and to keep doors locked, windows rolled up, and valuables out of sight when driving. One of the more common methods is the lifting of bags from the passenger seat while the driver is waiting at a traffic light. "Good Samaritan" scams are unfortunately common, especially on the highways. A passing car will attempt to divert the driver's attention by indicating there is a mechanical problem. If the driver stops to check the vehicle, accomplices steal from the car while the driver is looking elsewhere. Drivers should be cautious about accepting help from anyone other than a uniformed

Spanish police officer or Civil Guard. In outside bars, never leave bags or other valuables hanging from the back of a chair, and walk away from women who approach you in the street selling carnations; they are expert in lifting bills from your wallet while you are fumbling around for change. Always use an ATM in pairs, ensuring your PIN cannot be seen by a third party.

The loss or theft abroad of a U.S. passport should be reported immediately to the local police and the nearest U.S. embassy or consulate. U.S. citizens may refer to the Department of State's pamphlet, *A Safe Trip Abroad,* for ways to promote a more trouble-free journey. The pamphlet is available by mail from the Superintendent of Documents, U.S. Government Printing Office, Washington, DC 20402, via the Internet at www.gpoaccess.gov/index.html, or via the Bureau of Consular Affairs home page at http://travel.state.gov.

7 Specialized Travel Resources

FOR TRAVELERS WITH DISABILITIES

Most disabilities shouldn't stop anyone from traveling. There are more options and resources out there than ever before.

Because of the endless flights of stairs in most buildings in Barcelona and narrow footpaths, visitors with disabilities may have difficulty getting around, but conditions are slowly improving. Newer hotels are more sensitive to the needs of those with disabilities, and the more expensive restaurants, in general, are wheelchair-accessible. Most museums in the city are also now equipped for the disabled as are most buses and some Metro stations. However, since many places have limited, if any, facilities for people with disabilities, you might consider taking an organized tour specifically designed to accommodate travelers with disabilities.

Organizations that offer assistance to travelers with disabilities include the **MossRehab Hospital** (www.mossresourcenet.org), which provides a library of accessible-travel resources online; the **Society for Accessible Travel and Hospitality** (© 212/447-7284; www.sath.org; annual membership fees: $45 adults, $30 seniors and students), which offers a wealth of travel resources for all types of disabilities and informed recommendations on destinations, access guides, travel agents, tour operators, vehicle rentals, and companion services; and the **American Foundation for the Blind** (© 800/232-5463; www.afb.org), which provides information on traveling with Seeing Eye dogs.

For more information specifically targeted to travelers with disabilities, the community website **iCan** (www.icanonline.net/channels/travel/index.cfm) has destination guides and several regular columns on accessible travel. Also check out the quarterly magazine **Emerging Horizons** ($15 per year, $20 outside the U.S.; www.emerginghorizons.com); **Twin Peaks Press** (© 360/694-2462), offering travel-related books for travelers with special needs; and *Open World Magazine,* published by the Society for Accessible Travel and Hospitality (see above; subscription: $18 per year, $35 outside the U.S.).

In Barcelona itself, TMB (the public transportation system, both bus and Metro) has a help line for disabled travelers (© 93-486-07-52) and ECOM is a federation of private disabled organizations (© 93-451-55-50).

FOR GAY & LESBIAN TRAVELERS

In 1978 Spain legalized homosexuality among consenting adults. In April

1995, the parliament of Spain banned discrimination based on sexual orientation and marriage between same-sex couples looks set to become legal in 2005. Catalonia has helped paved the way in rights for gay couples, pre-empting national laws by granting same-sex couples the same official status and conjugal rights as heterosexual ones and has given the green light for changes in the law that would facilitate same-sex couples adopting. Barcelona is one of the major centers of gay life in Spain, and two of the most popular resorts for gay travelers, Sitges (south of Barcelona) and the island of Ibiza, are within close proximity.

Before you go, consider picking up a copy of *Frommer's Gay & Lesbian Europe,* which contains chapters on Madrid, Barcelona, Sitges, and Ibiza.

The International Gay & Lesbian Travel Association (IGLTA; ℂ 800/448-8550 or 954/776-2626; www.iglta.org) is the trade association for the gay and lesbian travel industry, and offers an online directory of gay and lesbian-friendly travel businesses; go to their website and click on "Members."

Many agencies offer tours and travel itineraries specifically for gay and lesbian travelers. **Above and Beyond Tours** (ℂ 800/397-2681; www.abovebeyondtours.com) is the exclusive gay and lesbian tour operator for United Airlines. **Now, Voyager** (ℂ 800/255-6951; www.nowvoyager.com) is a well-known San Francisco–based gay-owned and -operated travel service. The following travel guides are available at most travel bookstores and gay and lesbian bookstores. *Out and About* (ℂ 800/929-2268 or 415-644-8044; www.outandabout.com), which offers guidebooks and a newsletter 10 times a year packed with solid information on the global gay and lesbian scene; *Spartacus International Gay Guide* and *Odysseus,* both good, annual English-language guidebooks focused on gay men; the *Damron* guides, with annual books for gay men and lesbians; and *Gay Travel A to Z: The World of Gay & Lesbian Travel Options at Your Fingertips,* by Marianne Ferrari (Ferrari Publications; Box 35575, Phoenix, AZ 85069), a good gay and lesbian guidebook series.

FOR SENIOR TRAVELERS

Mention the fact that you're a senior when you make your travel reservations. Although all of the major U.S. airlines except America West have canceled their senior discount and coupon book programs, many hotels, especially the state-run *paradors* (www.parador.es) still offer discounts for seniors. In Barcelona, people over the age of 60 qualify for reduced admission to theaters, museums, and other attractions.

Members of **AARP** (formerly known as the American Association of Retired Persons), 601 E St. NW, Washington, DC 20049 (ℂ **800/424-3410** or 202/434-2277; www.aarp.org), get discounts on hotels, airfares, and car rentals. AARP offers members a wide range of benefits, including *AARP The Magazine* and a monthly newsletter. Anyone over 50 can join.

Many reliable agencies and organizations target the 50-plus market. **Elderhostel** (ℂ 877/426-8056; www.elderhostel.org) arranges study programs for those 55 and over (and a spouse or companion of any age) in the U.S. and in more than 80 countries around the world. Most courses last 5 to 7 days in the U.S. (2–4 weeks abroad), and many include airfare, accommodations in university dormitories or modest inns, meals, and tuition. **ElderTreks** (ℂ **800/741-7956;** www.eldertreks.com) offers small-group tours to off-the-beaten-path or adventure-travel locations, restricted to travelers 50 and older.

Recommended publications offering travel resources and discounts for seniors include the quarterly magazine *Travel 50 & Beyond* (www.travel50 andbeyond.com); *Travel Unlimited: Uncommon Adventures for the Mature Traveler* (Avalon); *101 Tips for Mature Travelers,* available from Grand Circle Travel (℡ **800/221-2610** or 617/350-7500; www.gct. com); *The 50+ Traveler's Guidebook* (St. Martin's Press); and *Unbelievably Good Deals and Great Adventures That You Absolutely Can't Get Unless You're Over 50* (McGraw-Hill).

FOR BLACK TRAVELERS

Agencies and organizations that provide resources for black travelers include: **Rodgers Travel** (℡ **215/473-1775;** www.rodgerstravel.com), a Philadelphia-based travel agency with an extensive menu of tours in destinations worldwide, including heritage and private group tours.

The Internet offers a number of helpful travel sites for the black traveler. **Black Travel Online** (www.black travelonline.com) posts news on upcoming events and includes links to articles and travel-booking sites. **Soul of America** (www.soulofamerica.com) is a more comprehensive website, with travel tips, event and family reunion postings, and sections on historically black beach resorts and active vacations.

For more information, check out the following collections and guides: *Go Girl: The Black Woman's Guide to Travel & Adventure* (Eighth Mountain Press), a compilation of travel essays by writers including Jill Nelson and Audre Lorde, with some practical information and trip-planning advice; *Travel and Enjoy Magazine* (℡ **866/266-6211;** www.travelandenjoy.com; subscription: $24 per year), which focuses on discounts and destination reviews; and the more narrative *Pathfinders Magazine* (℡ **877/977-PATH;** www.pathfinderstravel.com; subscription: $15 per year), which includes articles on everything from Rio de Janeiro to Ghana.

8 Planning Your Trip Online

SURFING FOR AIRFARES

The "big three" online travel agencies, **Expedia.com, Travelocity.com,** and **Orbitz.com** sell most of the air tickets bought on the Internet. (Canadian travelers should try expedia.ca and Travelocity.ca; U.K. residents can go for expedia.co.uk and opodo.co.uk.) Each has different business deals with the airlines and may offer different fares on the same flights, so it's wise to shop around. Expedia and Travelocity will also send you **e-mail notification** when a cheap fare becomes available to your favorite destination. Of the smaller travel agency websites, **Side-Step** (www.sidestep.com) has gotten the best reviews from Frommer's authors. It's a browser add-on that purports to "search 140 sites at once," but in reality only beats competitors' fares as often as other sites do.

Also remember to check **airline websites,** especially those for low-fare carriers whose fares are often misreported or simply missing from travel agency websites. Even with major airlines, you can often shave a few bucks from a fare by booking directly through the airline and avoiding a travel agency's transaction fee. But you'll get these discounts only by **booking online:** Most airlines now offer online-only fares that even their phone agents know nothing about. For the websites of airlines that fly to and from your destination, go to "Getting There," later in this chapter.

Great **last-minute deals** are available through free weekly e-mail services provided directly by the airlines. Most of these are announced on Tuesday or Wednesday and must be purchased online. Most are only valid for travel that weekend, but some can be booked weeks or months in advance. Sign up for weekly e-mail alerts at airline websites or check megasites that compile comprehensive lists of last-minute specials, such as **Smarter Living** (smarterliving.com). For last-minute trips, **site59.com** in the U.S. and **lastminute.com** in Europe often have better deals than the major-label sites.

If you're willing to give up some control over your flight details, use an **opaque fare service** like **Priceline** (www.priceline.com; www.priceline.co.uk for Europeans) or **Hotwire** (www.hotwire.com). Both offer rock-bottom prices in exchange for travel on a "mystery airline" at a mysterious time of day, often with a mysterious change of planes en route. The mystery airlines are all major, well-known carriers. Priceline usually has better deals than Hotwire, but you have to play their "name our price" game. If you're new at this, the helpful folks at **BiddingForTravel** (www.biddingfortravel.com) do a good job of demystifying Priceline's prices. Priceline and Hotwire are great for flights within North America and between the U.S. and Europe.

Note: In 2004 Priceline added non-opaque service to its roster. You now have the option to pick exact flights, times, and airlines from a list of offers—or opt to bid on opaque fares as before.

For much more about airfares and savvy air-travel tips and advice, pick up a copy of *Frommer's Fly Safe, Fly Smart* (Wiley Publishing, Inc.).

For cheap airfares within Spain, check out the national airline Iberia (www.iberia.es). Their website offers lower fares than you would encounter through a travel agent. You book and pay on line, but must pick up the ticket at an Iberia office before you fly. The new Barcelona-based company **Vueling** (www.vueling.com) flies to Seville, Palma de Majorca and Ibiza and **Spanair** (www.spanair.com) often has good deals to major Spanish destinations. If you are flying to Barcelona from the U.K. there are plethora of Internet air carriers to choose from, the largest being **EasyJet** (www.easyjet.com).

SURFING FOR HOTELS

Shopping online for hotels is becoming easier the world over and that

---

Frommers.com: The Complete Travel Resource

For an excellent travel-planning resource, we highly recommend Frommers.com (www.frommers.com). We're a little biased, of course, but we guarantee that you'll find the travel tips, reviews, monthly vacation giveaways, and online-booking capabilities thoroughly indispensable. Among the special features are our popular **Message Boards,** where Frommer's readers post queries and share advice (sometimes even our authors show up to answer questions); **Frommers.com Newsletter,** for the latest travel bargains and insider travel secrets; and **Frommer's Destinations Section,** where you'll get expert travel tips, hotel and dining recommendations, and advice on the sights to see for more than 3,000 destinations around the globe. When your research is done, the **Online Reservations System** (www.frommers.com/book_a_trip) takes you to Frommer's preferred online partners for booking your vacation at affordable prices.

includes Spain. Of the "big three" sites, **Expedia** may be the best choice, thanks to its long list of special deals. **Travelocity** runs a close second. Hotel specialist sites **hotels.com** and **hotel discounts.com** are also reliable. An excellent free program, **TravelAxe** (www.travelaxe.net), can help you search multiple hotel sites, even ones you may never have heard of.

Priceline and Hotwire are even better for hotels than for airfares; with both, you're allowed to pick the neighborhood and quality level of your hotel before offering up your money. Priceline's hotel product even covers Europe and Asia, though it's much better at getting five-star lodging for three-star prices than at finding anything at the bottom of the scale. *Note:* Hotwire overrates its hotels by one star—what Hotwire calls a four-star is a three-star anywhere else.

Some Barcelona-based Internet hotel booking services include **Barcelona On Line** (www.barcelona-on-line.es) and **www.hotel-barcelona.com**. If you have a hotel in mind, search for their own website as discounts and special deals are often available for web bookers. Self-catering accommodations in Barcelona are done almost exclusively on the Net. Google "tourist apartment Barcelona" and you will be surprised how many hits come up.

SURFING FOR RENTAL CARS

For booking rental cars online, the best deals are usually found at rental-car company websites, although all the major online travel agencies also offer rental-car reservations services. Priceline and Hotwire work well for rental cars, too; the only "mystery" is which major rental company you get, and for most travelers the difference between Hertz, Avis, and Budget is negligible.

9 The 21st-Century Traveler

INTERNET ACCESS AWAY FROM HOME

Travelers have any number of ways to check their e-mail and access the Internet on the road. Of course, using your own laptop—or even a PDA (personal digital assistant) or electronic organizer with a modem—gives you the most flexibility. But even if you don't have a computer, you can still access your e-mail and even your office computer from cybercafes. These are plentiful in Barcelona, particularly in the Old Town.

WITHOUT YOUR OWN COMPUTER

It's hard nowadays to find a city that *doesn't* have a few cybercafes. Although there's no definitive directory for cyber-cafes—these are independent businesses, after all—three places to start looking are at **www.cybercaptive.com**, **www.netcafeguide.com**, and **www. cybercafe.com**.

Most major airports now have **Internet kiosks** scattered throughout their gates. These kiosks, which you'll also see in shopping malls, hotel lobbies, and tourist information offices around the world, give you basic Web access for a per-minute fee that's usually higher than cybercafe prices. The kiosks' clunkiness and high price means they should be avoided whenever possible.

To retrieve your e-mail, ask your **Internet service provider (ISP)** if it has a Web-based interface tied to your existing e-mail account. If your ISP doesn't have such an interface, you can use the free **mail2web** service (www. mail2web.com) to view (but not reply to) your home e-mail. For more flexibility, you may want to open a free, Web-based e-mail account with **Yahoo! Mail** (mail.yahoo.com). (Microsoft's Hotmail is another popular option, but Hotmail has severe spam problems.)

Your home ISP may be able to forward your e-mail to the Web-based account automatically.

If you need to access files on your office computer, look into a service called **GoToMyPC** (www.gotomypc. com). The service provides a Web-based interface for you to access and manipulate a distant PC from anywhere—even a cybercafe—provided your "target" PC is on and has an always-on connection to the Internet (such as with Road Runner cable). The service offers top-quality security, but if you're worried about hackers, use your own laptop rather than a cybercafe to access the GoTo-MyPC system.

WITH YOUR OWN COMPUTER

Major Internet service providers have **local access numbers** around the world, allowing you to go online by simply placing a local call. Check your ISP's website or call its toll-free number and ask how you can use your current account away from home, and how much it will cost.

If you're traveling outside the reach of your ISP, the **iPass** network has dial-up numbers in most of the world's countries. You'll have to sign up with an iPass provider, who will then tell you how to set up your computer for your destination(s). For a list of iPass providers, go to www.ipass.com and click on "Individuals." One solid provider is **i2roam** (✆ **866/811-6209** or 920/235-0475; www.i2roam.com).

Wherever you go, bring a **connection kit** of the right power and phone adapters, a spare phone cord, and a spare Ethernet network cable.

Most business-class hotels throughout the world offer dataports for laptop modems, and many hotels in Barcelona now offer high-speed Internet access using an Ethernet network cable. You'll have to bring your own cables either way, so **call your hotel in advance** to find out what the options are.

USING A CELLPHONE

The three letters that define much of the world's **wireless capabilities** are GSM (Global System for Mobiles), a big, seamless network that makes for easy cross-border cellphone use throughout Europe and dozens of other countries worldwide. In the U.S., T-Mobile, AT&T Wireless, and Cingular use this quasi-universal system; in Canada, Microcell and some Rogers customers are GSM, and all Europeans and most Australians use GSM.

If your cellphone is on a GSM system, and you have a world-capable multiband phone such as many Sony Ericsson, Motorola, or Samsung models, you can make and receive calls across civilized areas on much of the globe, from Andorra to Uganda. Just call your wireless operator and ask for "international roaming" to be activated on your account. Unfortunately, per-minute charges can be high—usually $1 to $1.50 in Western Europe and up to $5 in places like Russia and Indonesia.

That's why it's important to buy an "unlocked" world phone from the get-go. Many cellphone operators sell "locked" phones that restrict you from using any other removable computer memory phone chip (called a **SIM card**) card other than the ones they supply. Having an unlocked phone allows you to install a cheap, prepaid SIM card (found at a local retailer) in your destination country. (Show your phone to the salesperson; not all phones work on all networks.) You'll get a local phone number—and much, much lower calling rates. Getting an already locked phone unlocked can be a complicated process, but it can be done; just call your cellular operator and say you'll be going abroad for several months and want to use the phone with a local provider.

For many, **renting** a phone is a good idea. While you can rent a phone

Online Traveler's Toolbox

Veteran travelers usually carry some essential items to make their trips easier. Following is a selection of handy online tools to bookmark and use.

- **Airplane Seating and Food.** Find out which seats to reserve and which to avoid (and more) on all major domestic airlines at www.seatguru.com. And check out the type of meal (with photos) you'll likely be served on airlines around the world at www.airlinemeals.com.
- **Foreign Languages for Travelers** (www.travlang.com). Learn basic terms in more than 70 languages and click on any underlined phrase to hear what it sounds like.
- **Intellicast** (www.intellicast.com) and **Weather.com** (www.weather.com). Give weather forecasts for all 50 states and for cities around the world.
- **Mapquest** (www.mapquest.com). This best of the mapping sites lets you choose a specific address or destination, and in seconds, it will return a map and detailed directions.
- **Subway Navigator** (www.subwaynavigator.com). Download subway maps and get savvy advice on using subway systems in dozens of major cities around the world.
- **Time and Date** (www.timeanddate.com). See what time (and day) it is anywhere in the world.
- **Travel Warnings** (http://travel.state.gov, www.fco.gov.uk/travel, www.voyage.gc.ca, www.dfat.gov.au/consular/advice). These sites report on places where health concerns or unrest might threaten American, British, Canadian, and Australian travelers. Generally, U.S. warnings are the most paranoid; Australian warnings are the most relaxed.
- **Universal Currency Converter** (www.xe.com/ucc). See what your dollar or pound is worth in more than 100 other countries.
- **Visa ATM Locator** (www.visa.com), for locations of PLUS ATMs worldwide, or **MasterCard ATM Locator** (www.mastercard.com), for locations of Cirrus ATMs worldwide.
- The **Guia del Ocio** (www.guiadelocio.com) is a comprehensive "what's on" in Barcelona (Spanish only).
- **Tickets** for theatrical, musical and sporting events in Barcelona can be bought in advance from www.telentrada.com.

from any number of overseas sites, including kiosks at airports and at car-rental agencies, I suggest renting the phone before you leave home. That way you can give loved ones and business associates your new number, make sure the phone works, and take the phone wherever you go—especially helpful for overseas trips through several countries, where local phone-rental agencies often bill in local currency and may not let you take the phone to another country.

Phone rental isn't cheap. You'll usually pay $40 to $50 per week, plus airtime fees of at least a dollar a minute.

If you're traveling to Europe, though, local rental companies often offer free incoming calls within their home country, which can save you big bucks. The bottom line: Shop around.

In Barcelona, however, there is only one company that offers this service: you can rent a cell phone from **Rent A Phone,** Carrer Numància 212 (© **93-280-21-31;** www.rphone.es). Rent a Phone charge by *pasos,* which translates into units of a call. A call to another cell phone in Spain is likely to cost 80 cents per minute, rising to 1.50€ ($1.70) per minute for calls to the States. A deposit of 1.50€ ($1.70) is also required.

Two good wireless rental companies in the U.S. are **InTouch USA** (© **800/872-7626;** www.intouchglobal.com) and **RoadPost** (© **888/290-1606** or 905/272-5665; www.roadpost.com). Give them your itinerary, and they'll tell you what wireless products you need. InTouch will also, for free, advise you on whether your existing phone will work overseas; simply call © **703/222-7161** between 9am and 4pm ET, or go to http://intouchglobal.com/travel.htm.

For trips of more than a few weeks spent in one country, **buying a phone** becomes economically attractive, as many nations have cheap, no-questions-asked prepaid phone systems. Once you arrive at your destination, stop by a local cellphone shop and get the cheapest package; you'll probably pay less than $100 for a phone and a starter calling card. Local calls may be as low as 10¢ per minute, and in many countries incoming calls are free. Note that in Spain you must show your passport when you buy a phone and/or phone card.

10 Getting There

BY PLANE

FROM NORTH AMERICA   Flights from the U.S. east coast to Spain take 6 to 7 hours. The national carrier of Spain, **Iberia Airlines** (© **800/772-4642;** www.iberia.com), has more routes into and within Spain than any other airline. It offers almost daily services from most major U.S. cites (New York, Washington, Chicago, Atlanta) either direct to Barcelona or via Madrid. Also available are attractive rates on fly/drive packages within Iberia and Europe; they can substantially reduce the cost of both the air ticket and the car rental.

A good money-saver to consider is **Iberia**'s **SpainPass.** Available only to passengers who simultaneously arrange for transatlantic passage on Iberia, the SpainPass consists of coupons equivalent to a one-way/one-person ticket to destinations on mainland Spain and the Balearic Islands. Travelers must purchase a three-coupon minimum (228€/$275) and extra coupons can be bought at 60€ ($72) each. Their **EuroPass** services European destinations. Coupons (minimum of two) for destinations such as Rome, Geneva, Vienna, and Istanbul cost $139 each or $169 for Cairo or Tel Aviv. The EuroPass can only be purchased as a part of an Iberian Air itinerary from your home country.

Iberia's main Spain-based competitor is **Air Europa** (© **888/238-7672;** www.air-europa.com), which offers a daily service from Newark Airport using Continental Airlines to Madrid, with connecting flights to Barcelona. Fares are usually lower than Iberia's.

Delta (© **800/241-4141;** www.delta.com) runs daily nonstop service from Atlanta (its worldwide hub) and New York (JFK) to Barcelona. Delta's Dream Vacation department offers independent fly/drive packages, land packages, and escorted bus tours.

United Airlines (© **800/241-6522;** www.ual.com) does not fly into Spain directly. It does, however, offer airfares from the United States to Spain with United flying as far as Zurich, and then using another carrier to complete the journey. United also offers fly/drive packages and escorted motor coach tours.

FROM THE U.K. British Airways (© 0845/773-3377; www.british airways.com) **Iberia** (© 020/7830-0011 in London) and **EasyJet** (www. easyjet.com) are the three major carriers flying between England and Spain. More than a dozen daily flights, on either BA or Iberia, depart from London's Heathrow and Gatwick airports. About the same number of EasyJet flights depart daily from Stansted, Luton, and Gatwick airports. EasyJet also has direct flights from Liverpool and Newcastle and another Internet service **MyTravelite** (www.mytravelite. com) offers a daily service from Birmingham. **Ryanair** (www.ryanair.com) which uses Girona (Gerona) airport, located about an hour outside of Barcelona, flies in from Bournemouth, Dublin and the East Midlands, as well as London. (There is a connecting bus service from Girona Airport to central Barcelona). The best air deals on scheduled flights from England are those requiring a Saturday night stopover.

Budget airlines are giving the major carriers a run for their money and many have now had to slash their fares to compete. The efficiency of these services has been proven (both EasyJet and Ryanair have excellent "on time" records) and most travelers seem happy to forgo the frills and arrive in Barcelona with a few more euros in their pocket.

Charter flights to the regional Catalan airports of Reus and Girona leave from many British regional airports. Girona serves those heading to the Costa Brava north of Barcelona while Reus is mainly used by those holidaying on the resorts on the Costa Daurada in the south. **Trailfinders** (© 020/7937-5400 in London; www.trailfinder.com), operates charters to both destinations.

In London, there are many bucket shops around Victoria Station and Earls Court that offer cheap fares. Make sure the company you deal with is a member of the IATA, ABTA, or ATOL. These umbrella organizations will help you if anything goes wrong.

CEEFAX, the British television information service, runs details of package holidays and flights to Europe and beyond. Just switch to your CEEFAX channel and you'll find travel information.

FROM AUSTRALIA From Australia, there are a number of options to fly to Spain. The most popular is Qantas/British Airways (© 612/13-13-13), which flies daily via Asia and London. Other popular and cheaper options are Qantas/Lufthansa via Asia and Frankfurt, Qantas/Air France via Asia and Paris, and Alitalia via Bangkok and Rome. The most direct option is on Singapore Airlines, with just one stop in Singapore. Alternatively, there are flights on Thai Airways via Bangkok and Rome, but the connections are not always good.

GETTING INTO TOWN FROM THE AIRPORT

El Prat, Barcelona's airport is 13km (8 miles) from the city center and there are several options you can use to get into town.

The **Aerobús** leaves just outside all three terminals every 15 minutes from 6am to midnight. Its journey takes about 20 to 25 minutes (leave a few more minutes for the return journey, as the bus takes a slightly different route) and costs 3.60€ ($4.15). The bus stops at Plaça Espanya, Plaça Universitat, and Plaça Catalunya—all major hubs.

El Prat also has its own train station. While this is convenient for those traveling further afield by train (its journey finishes at Sants, the city's major terminal, which also has connections to

BARCELONA

B A R C E L O N A

Palau de la Música Catalana de Ll. Domènech i Montaner, any 1908.
Sala foyer a la planta baixa.

▶ TRIANGLE POSTALS / Foto Pere Vivas, Ricard Pla

3952

8 424455 339522

D.L. B. 14953-1997

the Metro) the station itself is a short walk from the airport terminal, which makes it inconvenient for those with lots of luggage. Trains leave every 30 minutes from 6:15am to 11:40pm and the 25-minute journey costs 2.50€ ($2.90).

There are taxi ranks outside all terminals. The 20-minute journey to the center should cost about 18€ ($21) including the 3€ ($3.45) airport surcharge. Luggage that goes in the trunk is .85€ ($1) per piece.

GETTING THROUGH THE AIRPORT

With the federalization of airport security, security procedures at U.S. airports are more stable and consistent than ever. Generally, you'll be fine if you arrive at the airport **2 hours** before an international flight; if you show up late, tell an airline employee and she'll probably whisk you to the front of the line.

Bring a **current, government-issued photo ID** such as a driver's license or passport. Keep your ID at the ready to show at check-in, the security checkpoint, and sometimes even the gate. (Children under 18 do not need government-issued photo IDs for domestic flights, but they do for international flights to most countries.)

In 2003 the TSA phased out **gate check-in** at all U.S. airports. And **e-tickets** have made paper tickets nearly obsolete. Passengers with e-tickets can beat the ticket-counter lines by using airport **electronic kiosks** or even **online check-in** from your home computer. Online check-in involves logging on to your airlines' website, accessing your reservation, and printing out your boarding pass—and the airline may even offer you bonus miles to do so! If you're using a kiosk at the airport, bring the credit card you used to book the ticket or your frequent-flier card. Print out your boarding pass from the kiosk and simply proceed to the security checkpoint with your pass and a photo

ID. If you're checking bags or looking to snag an exit-row seat, you will be able to do so using most airline kiosks. Even the smaller airlines are employing the kiosk system, but always call your airline to make sure these alternatives are available. **Curbside check-in** is also a good way to avoid lines, although a few airlines still ban curbside check-in; call before you go.

Security checkpoint lines are getting shorter than they were, but some doozies remain. If you have trouble standing for long periods of time, tell an airline employee; the airline will provide a wheelchair. Speed up security by **not wearing metal objects** such as big belt buckles. If you've got metallic body parts, a note from your doctor can prevent a long chat with the security screeners. Keep in mind that only **ticketed passengers** are allowed past security, except for folks escorting disabled passengers or children.

Federalization has stabilized **what you can carry on** and **what you can't.** The general rule is that sharp things are out, nail clippers are okay, and food and beverages must be passed through the X-ray machine—but that security screeners can't make you drink from your coffee cup. Bring food in your carry-on rather than checking it, as explosive-detection machines used on checked luggage have been known to mistake food (especially chocolate, for some reason) for bombs. Travelers in the U.S. are allowed one carry-on bag, plus a "personal item" such as a purse, briefcase, or laptop bag. Carry-on hoarders can stuff all sorts of things into a laptop bag; as long as it has a laptop in it, it's still considered a personal item. The Transportation Security Administration (TSA) has issued a list of restricted items; check its website (www.tsa.gov/public/index.jsp) for details.

Airport screeners may decide that your checked luggage needs to be

---

Tips Don't Stow It—Ship It

If ease of travel is your main concern and money is no object, you can ship your luggage and sports equipment with one of the growing number of luggage-service companies that pick up, track, and deliver your luggage (often through couriers such as FedEx) with minimum hassle for you. Traveling luggage-free may be ultraconvenient, but it's not cheap: One-way overnight shipping can cost from $100 to $200, depending on what you're sending. Still, for some people, especially the elderly or the infirm, it's a sensible solution to lugging heavy baggage. Specialists in door-to-door luggage delivery are **Virtual Bellhop** (www.virtualbellhop.com), **SkyCap International** (www. skycapinternational.com), **Luggage Express** (www.usxpluggageexpress. com), and **Sports Express** (www.sportsexpress.com).

---

searched by hand. You can now purchase luggage locks that allow screeners to open and re-lock a checked bag if hand-searching is necessary. Look for Travel Sentry certified locks at luggage or travel shops and Brookstone stores (you can buy them online at www.brookstone.com). These locks, approved by the TSA, can be opened by luggage inspectors with a special code or key. For more information on the locks, visit www.travelsentry.org. If you use something other than TSA-approved locks, your lock will be cut off your suitcase if a TSA agent needs to hand-search your luggage.

FLYING FOR LESS: TIPS FOR GETTING THE BEST AIRFARE

Passengers sharing the same airplane cabin rarely pay the same fare. Travelers who need to purchase tickets at the last minute, change their itinerary at a moment's notice, or fly one-way often get stuck paying the premium rate. Here are some ways to keep your airfare costs down.

- Passengers who can book their ticket **long in advance,** who can **stay over Saturday night,** or who **fly midweek** or **at less-trafficked hours** may pay a fraction of the full fare. If your schedule is flexible, say so, and ask if you can

secure a cheaper fare by changing your flight plans.

- You can also save on airfares by keeping an eye out in local newspapers for **promotional specials** or **fare wars,** when airlines lower prices on their most popular routes. You rarely see fare wars offered for peak travel times, but if you can travel in the off-months, you may snag a bargain.

- Search **the Internet, especially the Internet-only airlines** for cheap fares (see "Planning Your Trip Online," earlier in this chapter).

- Try to book a ticket **in its country of origin.** For instance, if you're planning a one-way flight from Johannesburg to Bombay, a South Africa–based travel agent will probably have the lowest fares. For multileg trips, book in the country of the first leg; for example, book New York–London–Amsterdam–Rome–New York in the U.S. Two of the biggest providers in Barcelona are **Halcon Viajes** (© **90-243-00-00;** www.halcon viajes.com) and **Viajes Iberia** (© **90-240-05-00;** www.viajes iberia.com).

- **Consolidators,** also known as bucket shops, are great sources for international tickets, although they usually can't beat the Internet on fares within North America. Start by looking in Sunday newspaper travel sections; U.S. travelers should focus on the *New York Times,* the *Los Angeles Times,* and the *Miami Herald.* For less-developed destinations, small travel agents who cater to immigrant communities in large cities often have the best deals. ***Beware:*** Bucket shop tickets are usually nonrefundable or rigged with stiff cancellation penalties, often as high as 50% to 75% of the ticket price, and some put you on charter airlines with questionable safety records. Several reliable consolidators are worldwide and available on the Net. **STA Travel** (**www.sta.com**) is now the world's leader in student travel, thanks to its purchase of Council Travel. It also offers good fares for travelers of all ages. **Flights.com** (✆ **800/ TRAV-800;** www.flights.com) started in Europe and has excellent fares worldwide, but particularly to that continent. It also has "local" websites in 12 countries. **FlyCheap** (✆ **800/FLY-CHEAP;** www.1800flycheap.com) is owned by package-holiday megalith MyTravel and so has especially good access to fares for sunny destinations. **Air Tickets Direct** (✆ **800/778-3447;** www.airtickets direct.com) is based in Montreal and leverages the currently weak Canadian dollar for low fares; it'll also book trips to places that U.S. travel agents won't touch, such as Cuba.

- Join **frequent-flier clubs.** Accrue enough miles, and you'll be rewarded with free flights and elite status. It's free and you'll get the best choice of seats, faster response to phone inquiries, and prompter service if your luggage is stolen, your flight is canceled or delayed,

or if you want to change your seat. You don't need to fly to build frequent-flier miles—**frequent-flier credit cards** can provide thousands of miles for doing your everyday shopping.

BY CAR

If you're touring the rest of Europe in a rented car, you might, for an added cost, be allowed to drop off your vehicle in a major city such as Barcelona.

Highway approaches to Spain are across France on expressways. The most popular border crossing is near Biarritz, but there are 17 other border stations between Spain and France. If you're going to Barcelona or Catalonia and along the Levante coast (Valencia), take the expressway in France to Toulouse, then the A-61 to Narbonne, and then the A-9 toward the border crossing at La Jonquera. You can also take the RN-20, with a border station at Puigcerdà.

If you're driving from Britain, make sure you have a cross-Channel reservation, as traffic tends to be very heavy, especially in summer.

You can take the Chunnel, the underwater Channel Tunnel linking Britain (Folkestone) and France (Calais) by road and rail. **Eurostar** tickets, for train service between London and Paris or Brussels, are available through Rail Europe (✆ **800/EUROSTAR;** www. eurostar.com for information). In London, make reservations for Eurostar at ✆ **0870/530-00-03;** in Paris at ✆ 01-44-51-06-02; and in the United States at ✆ 800/EUROSTAR. The tunnel also accommodates passenger cars, charter buses, taxis, and motorcycles, transporting them under the English Channel from Folkestone, England, to Calais, France. It operates 24 hours a day, 365 days a year, running every 15 minutes during peak travel times, and at least once an hour at night. Tickets may be purchased at the tollbooth at the tunnel's entrance. With "Le Shuttle," gone are the days of weather-related delays, seasickness, and advance reservations.

Once you land, you'll have about an 18-hour drive to Barcelona.

If you plan to transport a rental car between England and France, check in advance with the rental company about license and insurance requirements and additional drop-off charges. And be aware that many car-rental companies, for insurance reasons, forbid transport of one of their vehicles over the water between England and France.

BY TRAIN

If you're already in Europe, you might want to go to Barcelona by train, especially if you have a **EurailPass.** Even without a pass, you'll find that the cost of a train ticket is relatively moderate. Rail passengers who visit from Britain or France should make couchette and sleeper reservations as far in advance as possible, especially during the peak summer season.

Since Spain's rail tracks are of a wider gauge than those used for French trains (except for the TALGO and Trans-Europe-Express trains), you'll probably have to change trains at the border unless you're on an express train (see below). For long journeys on Spanish rails, seat and sleeper reservations are mandatory.

The most comfortable and the fastest trains in Spain are the TER, TALGO, and Electrotren. However, you pay a supplement to ride on these fast trains. Both first- and second-class fares are sold on Spanish trains. Tickets can be purchased in the United States or Canada at the nearest office of Rail Europe or from any reputable travel agent. Confirmation of your reservation takes about a week.

If you want your car carried aboard the train, you must travel Auto-Expreso in Spain. This type of auto transport can be booked only through travel agents or rail offices once you arrive in Europe.

To go from London to Barcelona by rail, you'll need to change not only the train but also the rail terminus in Paris. Trip time from London to Paris is about 6 hours (unless you take the Eurostar, in which case it's 2½ hr.) and from Paris to Barcelona 12 hours. Many different rail passes are available in the United Kingdom for travel in Europe.

BY BUS

Bus travel to Spain is possible but not popular—it's quite slow (service from London will take 24 hr. or more). But coach services do operate regularly from major capitals of Western Europe, and once in Spain, usually head for Barcelona. The major bus line running from London to Spain is **Eurolines Limited,** 52 Grosvenor Gardens, London SW1W 0AU, UK (© **0870/514-32-19** or 020/7730-8235).

11 Packages for the Independent Traveler

Before you start your search for the lowest airfare, you may want to consider booking your flight as part of a travel package. Package tours are not the same thing as escorted tours. Package tours are simply a way to buy the airfare, accommodations, and other elements of your trip (such as car rentals, airport transfers, and sometimes even activities) at the same time

and often at discounted prices—kind of like one-stop shopping. Packages are sold in bulk to tour operators—who resell them to the public at a cost that usually undercuts standard rates.

One good source of package deals is the airlines themselves. Most major airlines offer air/land packages, including **American Airlines Vacations** (© 800/321-2121; www.aavacations.

com), **Delta Vacations** (✆ 800/221-6666; www.deltavacations.com), **Continental Airlines Vacations** (✆ 800/301-3800; www.coolvacations.com), and **United Vacations** (✆ 888/854-3899; www.unitedvacations.com). Among the airline packagers, **Iberia Airlines** (✆ 800/772-4642, or 90-240-05-00 in Spain; www.iberia.com) leads the way.

Several big **online travel agencies**—Expedia, Travelocity, Orbitz, Site59, and Lastminute.com—also do a brisk business in packages. If you're unsure about the pedigree of a smaller packager, check with the Better Business Bureau in the city where the company is based, or go online at www.bbb.org.

If a packager won't tell you where it's based, don't fly with them.

Solar Tours (✆ 800/388-7652; www.solartours.com) is a wholesaler that offers a number of package tours to Barcelona, as well as to major beach resorts. **Spanish Heritage Tours** (✆ 800/456-5050; www.shtours.com) is known for searching for low-cost airfare deals to Spain. **Homeric Tours** (✆ 800/223-5570 or 212/753-1000; www.homerictours.com/contact.asp), the marketing arm of Iberia, is the most reliable tour operator and the agency used for air and land packages to some of the highlights of Spain.

12 Escorted General-Interest Tours

Escorted tours are structured group tours, with a group leader. The price usually includes everything from airfare to hotels, meals, tours, admission costs, and local transportation.

There are many escorted tour companies to choose from, each offering transportation to and within Catalonia, prearranged hotel space, and such extras as bilingual tour guides and lectures. Many of these tours to Catalonia include excursions to other parts of Spain.

Some of the most expensive and luxurious tours are run by **Abercrombie & Kent International** (✆ 800/323-7308 or 630/954-2944; www.abercrombiekent.com), including 10-day tours of the Iberian Peninsula on which kicks off in Barcelona. Guests stay in fine hotels, ranging from a late medieval palace to the exquisite Alfonso XIII in Seville.

American Express Travel (✆ 800/941-2639 in the U.S. and Canada; www.travelimpressions.com) is one of the biggest tour operators in the world. Its offerings are comprehensive, and unescorted customized package tours are available, too.

Alternative Travel Group Ltd. (✆ 01865/310-399; www.atg-oxford.co.uk) is a British firm that organizes walking and cycling vacations. The "Wilds of Catalonia" package takes you to forests, natural pools and waterfalls, abandoned monasteries and hermitages as well as the rugged mountain of Montserrat on foot, finishing at the luxury *parador* in Cardona. ✆ 01865/315-663.

Petrabax Tours (✆ 800/634-1188; www.petrabax.com) attracts those who prefer to see Spain by bus, although fly/drive packages are also offered. The 14-day "Splendors of Northern Spain" deal starts off in Barcelona, before heading to Basque Country and Bilbao.

The U.K.-based **Magic Travel Group** (✆ 800/980-3378; www.magictravelgroup.co.uk) has designed the ultimate culture vulture tour of Barcelona and Catalonia. Travelers are shown the architectural and artistic splendors of Barcelona before going on to explore the surrounding countryside and its influence on the regions great artists such as Picasso, Miró, and Dalí. Guides are qualified art experts and historians.

Archetours, Inc. (© 800/770-3051; www.archetours.com), offers a similar tour focusing on Barcelona's splendid contemporary architecture, together with a side trip to Bilbao and the Frank Gehry's Guggenheim.

Many people derive a certain ease and security from escorted trips. Escorted tours—whether by bus, motor coach, train, or boat—let travelers sit back and enjoy their trip without having to spend lots of time behind the wheel. All the little details are taken care of; you know your costs upfront; and there are few surprises. Escorted tours can take you to the maximum number of sights in the minimum amount of time with the least amount of hassle—you don't have to sweat over the plotting and planning of a vacation schedule. Escorted tours are particularly convenient for people with limited mobility.

On the downside, an escorted tour often requires a big deposit upfront, and lodging and dining choices are pre-determined. As part of a cloud of tourists, you'll get little opportunity for serendipitous interactions with locals. The tours can be jam-packed with activities, leaving little room for individual sightseeing, whim, or adventure—plus they also often focus only on the heavily touristed sites, so you miss out on the lesser-known gems.

Before you invest in an escorted tour, ask about the **cancellation policy:** Is a deposit required? Can they cancel the trip if they don't get enough people? Do you get a refund if they cancel? If *you* cancel? How late can you cancel if you are unable to go? When do you pay in full? *Note:* If you choose an escorted tour, think strongly about purchasing trip-cancellation insurance, especially if the tour operator asks you to pay upfront. See the section on "Travel Insurance," earlier in this chapter.

You'll also want to get a complete **schedule** of the trip to find out how much sightseeing is planned each day and whether enough time has been allotted for relaxing or wandering solo.

The **size** of the group is also important to know upfront. Generally, the smaller the group, the more flexible the itinerary, and the less time you'll spend waiting for people to get on and off the bus. Find out the **demographics** of the group as well. What is the age range? What is the gender breakdown? Is this mostly a trip for couples or singles?

Discuss what is included in the **price.** You may have to pay for transportation to and from the airport. A box lunch may be included in an excursion, but drinks might cost extra. Tips may not be included. Find out if you will be charged if you decide to opt out of certain activities or meals.

Before you invest in a package tour, get some answers. Ask about the **accommodations choices** and prices for each. Then look up the hotels' reviews in a Frommer's guide and check their rates for your specific dates of travel online. You'll also want to find out what **type of room** you get. If you need a certain type of room, ask for it; don't take whatever is thrown your way. Request a nonsmoking room, a quiet room, a room with a view, or whatever you fancy.

Finally, if you plan to travel alone, you'll need to know if a **single supplement** will be charged and if the company can match you up with a roommate.

13 Special-Interest Trips

Spain is one of the best destinations in Europe for enjoying the outdoors and Catalonia is no exception. Lounging on the beach leads the list of activities for most travelers, but there's a lot more to do. The Pyrénées mountains lure thousands of mountaineers and hikers as well as skiers and fishing and hunting are long-standing Iberian obsessions. Watersports ranging from sailing to windsurfing are prime summer attractions.

In addition to sports and adventures, I've also detailed some of the best educational and cultural programs below.

Note: The inclusion of an organization in this section is in no way to be interpreted as a guarantee. This information is presented only as a preview, to be followed by your own investigation.

BIKING, HIKING & WALKING

In England, the **Cyclists' Touring Club,** 69 Meadrow, Godalming, Surrey GU7 3HS, UK (© **0870/873-0060;** www.ctc.org.uk), charges £27 ($43) a year for membership; part of the fee provides for information and suggested cycling routes through Catalonia and Spain and dozens of other countries.

To venture into the more rugged countryside of Catalonia, contact **Ramblers Holidays,** P.O. Box 43, Welwyn Garden AL8 6PQ, UK (© **01707/331-133;** www.ramblers holidays.co.uk). Walking tours through the Pyrénées, are conducted by **Waymark Holidays,** 44 Windsor Rd., Slough SL1 2EJ, UK (© **01753/516-477;** www.waymarkholidays.co.uk).

An outfit known for its luxurious and pricey tours is **Abercrombie & Kent International,** 1520 Kensington Rd., Oak Brook, IL 60521 (© **800/323-7308** or 630/954-2944; www. abercrombiekent.com). They conduct a 9-day "Walking the Pyrénées" tour on the Spanish side of the mountainous border with France. Special emphasis is placed on the medieval churches that provided rest and hope to 10th-century pilgrims on their way to Santiago.

Another upmarket operator, the Canada-based **Butterfield and Robinson** (© **800/678-1147;** www. butterfield.com) offers 6-day, 5-night biking tours of the Pyrénées, Girona, and picturesque villages in between,

staying in top-class hotels and chalets. There is also a family option that combines biking, walking, and train trips. Naturally meals are taken in the region's best restaurants.

In addition to a walking tour of the Costa Brava, **Saranjan Tours,** P.O. Box 292, Kirkland, WA 98033 (© **800/858-9594** or 425/869-8636; www.saranjan.com), can show you Barcelona and Catalonia's wine country (walking a minimum of 2km/1¼ miles per day) while staying in quaint inns and rustic-style accommodations.

Un Cotxe Menys (One Less Car), Carrer de Esparteria 3 (© **93 268 21-05;** www.bicicletabarcelona.com), is a Barcelona company that organizes lively bike tours around the Old Town with a stop off in a bar or two along the way. Independent bike hire and trips further afield can also be arranged.

Another quirky local outfit is **Follow the Baldie** (© **61-703-99-56;** www.followthebaldie.com), which offers 1-day, low-impact night and day hikes around lesser-known pockets of Catalonia. Groups are small, the incredibly informed "baldie" speaks both English and Dutch, and most excursions include at least one visit to a local bar, a deserted castle, and lots and lots of local color.

GOLF

In recent decades, thousands of British retirees have settled in Spain, and their presence has sparked the development of dozens of new golf courses. Although the Costa Blanca in the south, with more than a third of the country's approximately 160 courses contained within its southern tier, has traditionally been the golfing mecca, Catalonia's Costa Brava is catching up. The International Association of Golf Tour Operators recently voted the Costa Brava the "Best Emerging Golf Destination," and with beautifully, landscaped courses, many with stunning mountain and fairways dotted with local flora its not hard to see why.

Generally regarded as the jewel in the crown is PGA course (© **972/472-2577,** www.pgacatalunya.com), but there are at least 10 others within easy reach of Barcelona.

As most visiting golfers still head down to Southern Spain, packages for Catalonia are limited. The U.K. School of Golf (© **1702/711-191;** www.ukschoolofgolf.com) has some very inviting options using courses on both the Costa Brava and Costa Daurada (near Tarragona) to suit all budgets and combining time on the green with city and cultural excursions, nights on the town and spa treatments and so on. To tailor your own trip, see www.barcelonagolf.com, an English-language website that has tons of information on courses, classes and accommodations for golfers.

HORSEBACK RIDING

Can Sort (© **97-256-03-35;** www.cansort.com) is a 15-room *masia* (Catalan country home) dating from 1789 with its own stable of horses. Located just inland from the northern-most point of the Costa Brava, the surrounding countryside is some of the most beautiful in the region. Accommodations are upscale rustic, and meals are taken communally with the other guests. Horse-hire is charged separately, meaning you can choose to either mount up or lay back by the open fire.

SAILING & WATERSPORTS

Llaüts i Velers (Boats and Yachts; © **97-260-09-57;** www.llautsivelers.com) located in the resort of Palamós on the Costa Brava, can sort you out with a motorboat or yacht, with or without skipper for periods of a day or a week. **Azul Sailing** (© **93-284-76-64;** fax 93-396-89-67; www.azulsailing.com) is a larger operation with a state-of-the-art fleet of sailing and motor yachts and catamarans that tour the Catalan Coast and the Balearic Islands. Airport pickup and special itineraries can be arranged.

Windsurfing facilities are located all along the Costa Brava. Barcelona's urban beaches are also an excellent spot for windsurfing and kayaking. Equipment can be hired at the **Base Nàutica de Mar Bella**, Avinguda del Litoral (© **93-221-04-32;** www.basenautica.org), providing you pass a test first to prove that you are competent. For those that aren't, courses are also available.

GASTRONOMY & COOKING

Thanks to chefs of the caliber of Ferran Adriá, the secret is out on Catalan cooking. The region's gastronomy is wildly different from the rest of the Peninsula (heavier, with unusual fusions of meat and fish, nuts, and fruits) and a new breed of Catalan cooks is busy re-inventing classic dishes through technology and imagination. Given the buzz on national grub, there are now more options than ever for the food tourist.

One is **Saboroso,** Comte d' Urgell 45, Barcelona (© **93-451-50-10;** www.saboroso.com). Run by a pair of food critics, the company provides all sorts of culinary activities; tapas tours of the Old Town, excursions to Catalunya's wine country (with wine tastings and lunch), and even cooking classes using local produce (in English). **Euroadventures,** Velázquez Moreno 9, fourth floor, 36201, Vigo (© **98-622-13-99;** www.euroadventures.net), is a specialist tour operator based in western Spain. Its 7-night "Mediterranean Morsel" holiday kicks off in Barcelona at the Boqueria Market before heading to the Costa Brava for some fine restaurants, wine tastings, and classes and the famous Ampurdan Cooking School.

LEARNING VACATIONS

See "Specialized Travel Resources," earlier in this chapter, for details on Interhostel and Elderhostel programs for seniors.

STUDYING Given the bilingual nature of the city where both Spanish and Catalan are spoken (and sometimes even mixed together) purists argue that Barcelona is not the ideal place to learn the language of Cervantes (that award generally goes to Salamanca and Madrid). That said, you will find enough situations and willing locals with which to practice your newly acquired linguistic skills. Keep in mind that Barcelona is a cosmopolitan city and you are just as likely to hear Arabic, French, and English spoken in the streets as Spanish and/or Catalan.

There is an abundance of private language academies in Barcelona, the two most reputable being **International House,** Trafalgar 14 08010 (© **93-268-45-11;** www.ihes.com/bcn/), and **Don Quijote,** Gran Vía 629, 08010 (© **92-326-88-74;** www.donquijote.org). Both have various courses to choose from (all levels, Spanish for specific purposes, and so on) and can arrange accommodations.

Another good source of information about courses in Catalonia and Spain is the **American Institute for Foreign Study (AIFS),** River Plaza, 9 W. Broad St., Stamford, CT 06902 (© **800/727-2437** or 203/399-5000; www.aifs.com). This organization can set up transportation and arrange for summer courses, with bed and board included.

The biggest organization dealing with higher education in Europe is the **Institute of International Education (IIE),** 809 United Nations Plaza, New York, NY 10017 (© **800/445-0443** or 212/883-8200; www.iie.org). A few of its booklets are free, but for $47, plus $6 for postage, you can purchase the more definitive *Vacation Study Abroad.* To order the book, call © **800/445-0443.** For both the above organizations, students should check whether the course they are interested in is conducted in Spanish or Catalan.

One recommended clearinghouse for academic programs throughout the world is the **National Registration Center for Study Abroad (NRCSA),** 823 N. 2nd St., Milwaukee, WI 53203 (© **414/278-0631;** fax 414/224-3466; www.nrcsa.com). The organization maintains language-study programs throughout Spain, including two in Barcelona, with lodgings in private homes with Spanish-speaking families included as part of the price and part of the experience. Tuition begins at around $893 for an intensive 2-week language course.

A clearinghouse for information on at least nine different Spain-based language schools is **Lingua Service Worldwide,** 75 Prospect St., Suite 4, Huntington, NY 11743 (© **800/394-LEARN** or 631/424-0777; fax 631/271-3441; www.linguaservice worldwide.com). Maintaining information about learning programs in 10 languages in 17 countries outside the United States, it represents organizations devoted to the teaching of Spanish and culture in 11 cities of Spain, with 3 in Barcelona including International House and Don Quijote, both mentioned above.

For more information about study abroad, contact the **Council on International Educational Exchange (CIEE),** 205 E. 42nd St., New York, NY 10017 (© **020/7478-2000** or 212/822-2700; www.ciee.org).

Based in Barcelona, **COINED,** Av. Mistral 36, Entresuelo 2ª, 08015 (© **93-425-49-01;** www.coined-spain.org), is a unique organization that sets up internships, teaching and volunteer positions for foreigners. Offers are as diverse as two months assisting instructors in the city's top tennis club, or as a PA in a marketing company. An intermediate level of Spanish is often required and get-togethers and excursions with other interns are part of the deal. **Best Programs,** Calle Solano 11,

3-C, 28223 Madrid (© **91-518-71-10;** www.bestprograms.org), operates in the same way, but places interns in not-for-profit organizations such as AIDS, animal welfare groups, or reforestation in Madrid, Barcelona, and Bilbao. All internships start with a two-week initiation course on language and Spanish customs.

14 Getting Around

BY CAR

A car offers the greatest flexibility while you're touring, even if you're just doing daytrips from Barcelona. Don't, however, plan to drive *in* Barcelona; it's too congested, street parking is a nightmare, and garage or lot parking expensive. Theoretically, rush hour is Monday through Saturday from 8 to 10am and 4 to 7:30 pm. In reality, it's always busy.

CAR RENTALS Many of North America's biggest car-rental companies, including Avis, Budget, and Hertz, have offices in Spain. Although several Spanish car-rental companies exist, I've gotten lots of letters from readers of previous editions telling me they've had a hard time resolving billing irregularities and insurance claims, so you might want to stick with the U.S.-based rental firms.

Note that tax on car rentals is a whopping 15%, so don't forget to factor that into your travel budget. Usually, prepaid rates do not include taxes, which will be collected at the rental kiosk itself. Be sure to ask explicitly what's included when you're quoted a rate.

Avis (© **800/331-1084;** www.avis.com) maintains about 100 branches throughout Spain, including eight in Barcelona. If you reserve and pay your rental by telephone at least 2 weeks before your departure from North America, you'll qualify for the company's best rate, with unlimited kilometers included. You can usually get competitive rates from **Hertz** (© **800/654-3001;** www.hertz.com) and **Budget** (© **800/472-3325;** www.budget.com); it always pays to comparison shop. Budget doesn't have a drop-off charge if you pick up in one Spanish city and return to another. All three companies require that drivers be at least 21 years of age and, in some cases, not older than 72. To be able to rent a car, you must have a passport and a valid driver's license; you must also have a valid credit card or a prepaid voucher. An international driver's license is not essential, but you might want to present it if you have one; it's available from any North American office of the American Automobile Association (AAA).

Two other agencies of note include **Kemwel Holiday Auto** (© **800/678-0678;** www.kemwel.com) and **Auto Europe** (© **800/223-5555;** www.autoeurope.com).

Many packages include airfare, accommodations, and a rental car with unlimited mileage. Compare these prices with the cost of booking airline tickets and renting a car separately to see if these offers are good deals. Internet resources can make comparison shopping easier. **Microsoft Expedia** (www.expedia.com) and **Travelocity** (www.travelocity.com) help you compare prices and locate car-rental bargains from various companies nationwide. They will even make your reservation for you once you've found the best deal. See "Planning Your Trip Online," earlier in this chapter, for tips.

DRIVING RULES Spaniards drive on the right side of the road. Drivers should pass on the left; local drivers sound their horns when passing another car and flash their lights at you if you're driving slowly (slowly for high-speed Spain) in the left lane.

Autos coming from the right have the right-of-way.

Spain's express highways are known as *autopistas,* which charge a toll, and *autovías,* which don't. Catalonia has an excellent *autopista* network, and these are always preferable to using the poorly maintained *autovías,* despite the cost. All road signs in Catalonia are bilingual. To exit, follow the *salida* or *sortida* (exit) sign. On most express highways, the speed limit is 120kmph (75 mph) or 80kmph (50 mph) for people with trailers. On other roads, speed limits range from 90kmph (56 mph) to 100kmph (62 mph). You will see many drivers far exceeding these limits.

Along the *autopistas,* gas stations and cafes/restrooms are plentiful. At the tollgates, you can choose to either pay with cash or credit card (there are separate booths for each so make sure you line up at the right one). Some routes with multiple exits give you a card and you pay for your journey when you hop off the motorway while with others you must pay upfront. Congestion at these gates, particularly on Sunday afternoons and the evenings before public holidays, is quite heavy.

If you must drive through Barcelona or any other sizable Catalan city such as Girona or Llerida, try to avoid morning and evening rush hours. In Barcelona, take advantage of the *litoral:* a ring road that has exits to the major motorways. Never park your car facing oncoming traffic, as that is against the law. If you are fined by the highway patrol *(Guardia Civil de Tráfico),* you must pay on the spot. Penalties for drinking and driving are very stiff and random Breathalyzer checks common.

MAPS   For one of the best overviews of the Iberian Peninsula (Spain and Portugal), get a copy of Michelin map no. 990 (for a folding version) or no. 460 for the same map in a spiral-bound version. For more detailed looks at Spain, Michelin has a series of six maps (nos. 441–446), showing specific regions, complete with many minor roads.

For extensive touring, purchase *Mapas de Carreteras-España y Portugal,* published by Almax Editores and available at most leading bookstores in Spain. This cartographic compendium of Spain provides an overview of the country and includes road and street maps of some of its major cities as well.

The **American Automobile Association** (© **800/222-4357;** fax 407/444-4300; www.aaa.com) publishes a regional map of Spain that's available free to members at most AAA offices in the United States. Also available free to members is a guide of approximately 60 pages, *Motoring in Europe,* that gives helpful information about road signs and speed limits, as well as insurance regulations and other relevant matters. Incidentally, the AAA is associated with the **Real Automóvil Club de España,** Diagonal 687, 08028 Barcelona (© **93-495-50-58;** www.racc.es). This organization can supply helpful information about road conditions in Spain, including tourist and travel data. It will also provide limited road service, in an emergency, if your car breaks down.

BREAKDOWNS   These can be a serious problem. If you're driving a Spanish-made vehicle, you'll probably be able to find spare parts, if needed. But if you have a foreign-made vehicle, you may be stranded. Have the car checked out before setting out on a long trek through Spain. On a major motorway you'll find strategically placed emergency phone boxes. On secondary roads, call for help by asking the operator to locate the nearest Guardia Civil, which will put you in touch with a garage that can tow you to a repair shop.

As noted above, the Spanish affiliate of AAA can provide limited assistance in the event of a breakdown.

BY TRAIN

Catalonia has a comprehensive network of rail lines. Hundreds of trains depart every day for points around the region or to more far-flung destinations such as Paris, Madrid, Southern Spain or even Milan.

If you plan to travel a great deal on the European railroads, it's worth buying a copy of the *Thomas Cook Timetable of European Passenger Railroads*. It's available exclusively in North America from **Forsyth Travel Library**, 44 S. Broadway, White Plains, NY 10601 (© **800/FORSYTH**; www. forsyth.com), at a cost of $28, plus $4.95 postage priority air mail in the United States plus $2 for shipments to Canada.

All trains in Catalonia are operated by **Spanish State Railways (RENFE)**. For day and overnight trips, the comfortable high-speed trains of the TALGO, TER, and Electrotren types are the ones you will be likely to catch. At present, the only AVE (high-speed train) connection is Barcelona–Valencia, although rails are presently being laid for Barcelona–Madrid and Barcelona to the French border connections. RENFE's easy-to-navigate website (www.renfe.es) has information in English on timetables and train types.

BY BUS

Areas not serviced by trains (such as the Pyrénées mountains) can be reached by bus. The biggest national bus company is **Alsa Enatcar** (© **90-242-22-42**, www.alsa.es). These buses, and most other companies leave from the Estació del Nord, Carrer d'Ali Bei 80, 08003, Barcelona. This terminal also has its own telephone and on-line booking service (© **90-226-06-06;** www.barcelonanord.com).

15 Tips on Accommodations

From castles converted into hotels to modern high-rise resorts overlooking the Mediterranean, Catalonia has some of the most varied hotel accommodations in the world—with equally varied price ranges. Accommodations are broadly classified as follows:

ONE- TO FIVE-STAR HOTELS

The Spanish government rates hotels by according them stars. At the top of the list are five-star **Grand-Luxe (GL)** hotels, which are truly deluxe, with deluxe prices. A one-star hotel is the most modest accommodations officially recognized as a hotel by the government. A four-star hotel offers first-class accommodations; a three-star hotel is moderately priced; and a one- or two-star hotel is inexpensively priced. The government grants stars based on such amenities as elevators, private bathrooms, and air-conditioning. If a hotel is classified as a *residencia,* it means that it serves breakfast (usually) but no other meals.

HOSTALS

Not to be confused with a hostel for students, an *hostal* is a modest hotel without services, where you can save money by carrying your own bags and the like. An *hostal* is identified by the letter H (or HR for *hostal-residencia*) on the blue plaque by the door. *Hostales* are ranked between one and three stars. An *hostal* with three stars is about the equivalent of a hotel with two stars.

PENSIONS

These boardinghouses are among the least expensive accommodations, but you're required to take either full board (three meals) or half-board, which is breakfast plus lunch or dinner. *Pensiones* are ranked with one or two stars.

CASAS HUESPEDES & FONDAS

These are the cheapest places in Spain and can be recognized by the light-blue plaques at the door displaying CH and F, respectively. They are invariably basic but respectable establishments and, at least in Catalonia, mainly found in rural areas.

Some chains of hotels are unknown outside Spain. **AC-Hoteles** (℡ **90-229-22-95;** www.ac-hoteles.com) is known for its stylish four-stars and is adding new destinations to its list all the time. NH (℡ **91-398-44-00;** www.nh-hoteles.com) aims to please the business traveler, with comfortable, streamlined rooms and excellent service. In the same vein, but slightly more geared to the tourist is **Catalonia** (℡ **90-030-10-78;** www.hoteles-catalonia.es).

PARADORS

The Spanish government runs a series of unique state-owned inns called paradors (*paradores* in Spanish), which now blanket the country. Deserted castles, monasteries, palaces, and other buildings have been taken over and converted into hotels. Today there are 86 paradors in all, and they're documented in a booklet called *Visiting the Paradors,* available at Spanish tourist offices (see "Visitor Information," earlier in this chapter).

At great expense, modern bathrooms, steam heat, and the like have been added to these buildings, yet classic Spanish architecture, where it existed, has been retained. Establishments are often furnished with antiques or at least good reproductions and decorative objects typical of the country.

Meals are also served in these government-owned inns. Usually, typical dishes of the region are featured. Paradors are likely to be overcrowded in the summer months, so advance reservations, arranged through any travel agent, are wise.

The government also operates a type of accommodations known as *albergues.* These are comparable to motels, standing along the roadside and usually built in hotel-scarce sections for the convenience of passing motorists. A client is not allowed to stay in an *albergue* for more than 48 hours, and the management doesn't accept reservations.

In addition, the government runs *refugios* **(refuges),** mostly in remote areas, attracting hunters, fishers, and mountain climbers. *Refugios* offer shared sleeping accommodations and you must take bedding with you. They operate on a "first-come, first-served" basis.

The central office of paradors is **Paradores de España,** Requeña 3, 28013 Madrid (℡ **91-516-66-66;** www.parador.es). The U.S. representative for the Paradores of Spain is **Marketing Ahead,** 381 Park Ave. S., New York, NY 10016 (℡ **800/223-1356** or 212/686/9213). Travel agents can also arrange reservations.

RENTING A HOUSE OR APARTMENT

If you rent a home or an apartment, you can save money on accommodations and dining and still take daily trips to see the surrounding area.

Apartments in Catalonia generally fall into two different categories: government-recognized *apartment-Hotels* (HA) and privately owned self-catering apartments. The *apartment-Hotels* have full facilities, with chamber service, equipped kitchenettes, and often restaurants and bars. The latter does not normally include daily room cleaning, and facilities vary, but due to their abundance and lower-cost, they are fast becoming the accommodations type of choice in Barcelona. Most of these are booked through the Net and stays are a minimum of three days.

One rental company that has a good selection of apartments in Barcelona and elsewhere is the U.K.-based **Selfcatering Hols** (℡ **1270-820-682;** www.selfcateringhols.com), who have an excellent selection, from one-bedroom old-town studios to more luxe apartments in key areas. There are dozens of local providers as well; a Google search will yield a mountain of results. Be sure to ask to see photos of your choice and check for amenities such as lifts and any extra costs such as cleaning. Most operators offer a "meet and greet" service.

Another agency is **ILC (International Lodging Corp.; © 800/ SPAIN-44** or 212/228-5900; www.ilc web.com), which rents privately owned apartments, houses, and villas, for a week or more. It also offers access to suites in well-known hotels for stays of a week or longer, sometimes at bargain rates. Rental units, regardless of their size, usually contain a kitchen. The company's listings cover accommodations in Madrid, Seville, Granada, and Majorca and Barcelona.

SAVING ON YOUR HOTEL ROOM

The **rack rate** is the maximum rate that a hotel charges for a room. Hardly anybody pays this price, however, except in high season or on holidays. To lower the cost of your room:

- **Ask about special rates or other discounts.** Always ask whether a room less expensive than the first one quoted is available, or whether any special rates apply to you. You may qualify for corporate, student, military, senior, or other discounts. Mention membership in AAA, AARP, frequent-flier programs, or trade unions, which may entitle you to special deals as well. Find out the hotel policy on children— do kids stay free in the room or is there a special rate?
- **Dial direct.** When booking a room in a chain hotel, you'll often get a better deal by calling the individual hotel's reservation desk rather than the chain's main number.
- **Book online.** Many hotels offer Internet-only discounts, or supply rooms to Priceline, Hotwire, or Expedia at rates much lower than the ones you can get through the hotel itself. Shop around. And if you have special needs—a quiet room, a room with a view—call the hotel directly and make your needs known after you've booked online.
- **Remember the law of supply and demand.** Resort hotels are most crowded and therefore most expensive on weekends, so discounts are usually available for midweek stays. Business hotels in downtown locations are busiest during the week, so you can expect big discounts over the weekend. Many hotels have high-season and low-season prices, and booking the day after "high season" ends can mean big discounts.
- **Look into group or long-stay discounts.** If you come as part of a large group, you should be able to negotiate a bargain rate, since the hotel can then guarantee occupancy in a number of rooms. Likewise, if you're planning a long stay (at least 5 days), you might qualify for a discount. As a general rule, expect 1 night free after a 7-night stay.
- **Avoid excess charges and hidden costs.** When you book a room, ask whether the hotel charges for parking. Use your own cellphone, pay phones, or prepaid phone cards instead of dialing direct from hotel phones, which usually have exorbitant rates. And don't be tempted by the room's minibar offerings: Most hotels charge through the nose for water, soda, and snacks. Finally, ask about local taxes and service charges, which can increase the cost of a room by 15% or more. If a hotel insists upon tacking on a surprise "energy surcharge" that wasn't mentioned at check-in or a "resort

---

Tips Dial E for Easy

For quick directions on how to call Spain, see the "Telephone" listing in the "Fast Facts" section at the end of chapter 3.

---

fee" for amenities you didn't use, you can often make a case for getting it removed.

- Consider the pros and cons of **all-inclusive** resorts and hotels. The term "all-inclusive" means different things at different hotels. Many all-inclusive hotels will include three meals daily, sports equipment, spa entry, and other amenities; others may include all or most drinks. In general, you'll save money going the "all-inclusive" way—as long as you use the facilities provided. The down side is that your choices are limited and you're stuck eating and playing in one place for the duration of your vacation.

- **Book an efficiency.** A room with a kitchenette allows you to shop for groceries and cook your own meals. This is a big money saver, especially for families on long stays.

LANDING THE BEST ROOM

Somebody has to get the best room in the house. It might as well be you. If you choose to stay at a chain hotel, you can start by joining the hotel's frequent-guest program, which may make you eligible for upgrades. A hotel-branded credit card usually gives its owner "silver" or "gold" status in frequent-guest programs for free. Always ask about a corner room. They're often larger and quieter, with more windows and light, and they often cost the same as standard rooms. When you make your reservation, ask if the hotel is renovating; if it is, request a room away from the construction. Ask about nonsmoking rooms, rooms with views, rooms with twin, queen- or king-size beds. If you're a light sleeper, request a quiet room away from vending machines, elevators, restaurants, bars, and discos. Ask for a room that has been most recently renovated or redecorated. If you aren't happy with your room when you arrive, ask for another one. Most lodgings will be willing to accommodate you.

In resort areas, particularly in warm climates, ask the following questions before you book a room:

- What's the view like? Cost-conscious travelers may be willing to pay less for a back room facing the parking lot, especially if they don't plan to spend much time in their room.

- Does the room have air-conditioning or ceiling fans? Do the windows open? If they do, and the nighttime entertainment takes place alfresco, you may want to find out when show time is over.

- What's included in the price? Your room may be moderately priced, but if you're charged for beach chairs, towels, sports equipment, and other amenities, you could end up spending more than you bargained for.

- How far is the room from the beach and other amenities? If it's far, is there transportation to and from the beach, and is it free?

16 Recommended Books

ECONOMIC, POLITICAL & SOCIAL HISTORY

For a first-hand account of the civil war and its devastating effects on Barcelona and Catalonia, George Orwell's *Homage to Catalonia* remains a classic. Irish writer Colm Tóibin takes a more light-hearted look at post-Orwell Barcelona, with plenty of anecdotes and colors through the eyes of a *güiri* (foreigner) in *Homage to Barcelona.* The city's most prolific writer, poet and essayist is the late Manuel Vázquez Montalbán. His *Barcelonas* is more of an insider guidebook, which combines lively accounts of Catalan history, character, and culture with scathing wit and insight.

Barça: A People's Passion, by Jimmy Burns (Bloomsbury, 2000), is a dramatic history of the city's soccer team, the richest and possibly most politically charged soccer club in the world.

THE ARTS

Antoni Gaudí is the Catalan architect who most excites visitors' curiosity. The latest study is *Gaudí: A Biography,* by Gijs van Hensbergen (Perennial, 2003). The author claims Gaudí was "drunk on form," and that the architect still has not lost his power to astonish with his idiosyncratic and innovative designs.

Spain's most famous artist was the Malaga-born Pablo Picasso. Picasso spent his formative years in Barcelona and the most controversial book about the late painter is *Picasso, Creator and Destroyer,* by Arianna Stassinopoulos Huffington (Simon & Schuster).

Catalonia's other headline-grabbing artist was Salvador Dalí. In *Salvador Dalí: A Biography* (Dutton), author Meryle Secrest asks: Was he a mad genius or a cunning manipulator?

Residents of Catalonia truthfully maintain that their unique language, culture, and history have been overshadowed (and squelched) by the richer and better-publicized accomplishments of Castile. Robert Hughes, a former art critic at *Time,* has written an elegant testament to the glories of the capital of this region: *Barcelona* (Knopf). This book offers a well-versed and witty articulation of the city's architectural and cultural legacy. According to the *New York Times,* the book is probably destined to become "a classic in the genre of urban history."

CUISINE

One of the best books out on the local gastronomy is written by an American. *Catalán Cuisine: Europe's Last Great Culinary Secret* (Grub Street, U.K.), by Colman Andrews, is a colorful exposé of food, wine and culinary customs of Catalonia. Andrews's conversations with chefs, his descriptions of wild mushroom-picking and village food markets and explanations of why the Catalans eat how they do makes terrific reading.

3

Getting to Know Barcelona

Blessed with rich and fertile soil, an excellent harbor, and a hardworking population, Barcelona has always prospered. When Madrid was still a dusty Castilian backwater, Barcelona was a powerful, diverse capital, influenced by the empires that had their eye on this Mediterranean jewel. Rome, North African Muslims, the Visigoths, Charlemagne-era France, and Castile all overran Barcelona, and each left a unique and indelible mark on the region's identity.

The Catalans themselves are also marked by a character that is distinct from other parts of Spain. In their own words, they are a mixture of *seny* (common sense) and *rauxa* (which can best be translated as being predisposed to moments of madness). These two poles are evident in almost every aspect of Barcelonese life; a group of suited businessmen singing along in a local bar, an elegant street that features a mad piece of sculpture, or the entire city stopping to watch their beloved soccer team, Barça, compete against their archrivals, Madrid. They equate to a modern and vibrant European metropolis with an enormous respect for tradition and culture.

Landmark Gothic buildings and world-class museums fill the historic city of Barcelona and the whimsical creations of the *modernisme* movement and cutting edge contemporary architecture the new. And an array of nightlife (Barcelona is a *big* party town) and shopping possibilities, plus nearby wineries, ensure that you'll be entertained round the clock. It makes for some serious sightseeing; you'll need plenty of time to take them all in and just as much to appreciate the city's unique, hidden charm.

1 Essentials

VISITOR INFORMATION

Barcelona has two types of tourist offices. The autonomous government (the Generalitat) office deals with **Catalonia** in general. Its office is in the grandiose **Palau Robert,** Passeig de Gràcia 107 (© **93-238-40-00**), where there are often exhibitions on aspects of Catalan culture. It's open daily from 10am to 7pm. The city council *(ajuntament)* runs **Turisme de Barcelona,** the source for information on the city of Barcelona. Its main office is located underground at the Plaça de Catalunya s/n (© **80-711-72-22** from inside Spain, or © **93-368-37-30** from outside; www.barcelonaturisme.com). It has loads of information on the city, a hotel booking service, a gift shop, and a branch of the bank Caixa de Catalunya where you can change money. The office is open daily from 9am to 9pm.

The same organization has an office at the **Estació Central de Barcelona-Sants (Sants Railway Station),** Plaça dels Països Catalans (no phone; Metro: Sants-Estació). In summer, it is open daily from 8am to 8pm; in the off season, it is open Monday through Friday from 8am to 8pm, Saturday and Sunday from 8am to 2pm. Another branch is located on the Plaça Sant Jaume (Carrer Ciutat 2). It's

Greater Barcelona

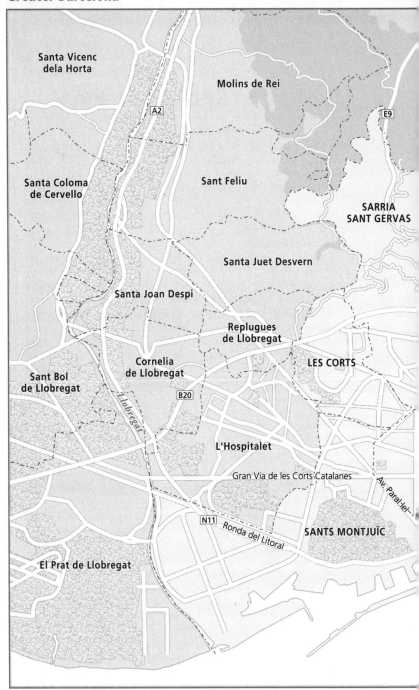

Santa Vicenc dela Horta

Molins de Rei

A2

E9

Santa Coloma de Cervello

Sant Feliu

SARRIA SANT GERVAS

Santa Juet Desvern

Santa Joan Despi

Replugues de Llobregat

Cornelia de Llobregat

LES CORTS

Sant Bol de Llobregat

Llobregat

B20

L'Hospitalet

Gran Via de les Corts Catalanes

Av. Paral·lel

N11

Ronda del Litoral

SANTS MONTJUÏC

El Prat de Llobregat

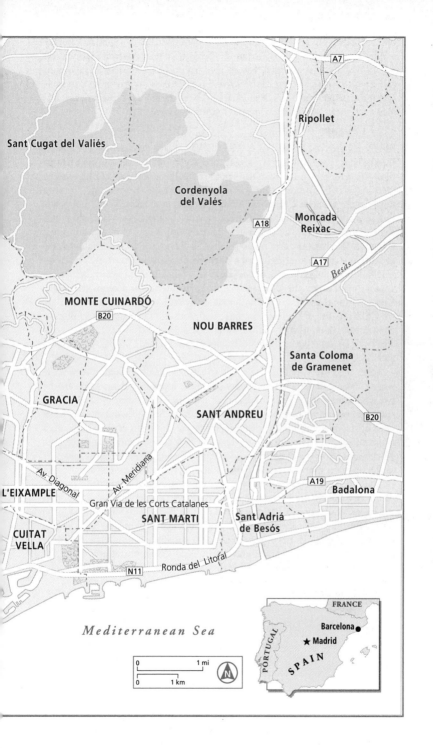

Sant Cugat del Valiés

Ripollet

A7

Cordenyola
del Valés

Moncada
Reixac

A18

A17

Besós

MONTE CUINARDÓ

B20

NOU BARRES

Santa Coloma
de Gramenet

GRACIA

SANT ANDREU

B20

Av. Diagonal

Av. Meridiana

A19

Badalona

L'EIXAMPLE

Gran Via de les Corts Catalanes

SANT MARTI

Sant Adriá
de Besós

CUITAT
VELLA

Ronda del Litoral

N11

Mediterranean Sea

FRANCE

PORTUGAL

Barcelona ●

★ Madrid

SPAIN

0   1 mi

0   1 km

N

open Monday through Friday 9am to 8pm, Saturday 10am to 8pm and Sunday and holidays 10am to 2pm. There are also branches at the Barcelona airport at terminals A and B that are open 9am to 9pm daily. These offices are the places to pick up discount sightseeing cards such as the *Barcelona Card* (see below). In summer the Casaques Vermelles (Red Jackets) take to the streets. These are multilingual hosts ready to answer any queries tourists may have.

CITY LAYOUT

MAIN SQUARES, STREETS & ARTERIES   Plaça de Catalunya (**Plaza de Cataluña** in Spanish) is the city's heart; the world-famous **Les Ramblas (Rambles)**, its main artery. Les Ramblas begins at the Plaça Portal de la Pau, with its 49m-high (161-ft.) monument to Columbus, opposite the port and stretches north to the Plaça de Catalunya. Along this wide promenade you'll find newsstands, stalls selling birds and flowers, portrait painters, and cafe tables and chairs, where you can sit and watch the passing parade. Moving northwards along Les Ramblas, the area on your left is **El Raval,** the largest neighborhood in Barcelona and to your right is the **Barri Gòtic (Gothic Quarter).** These two neighborhoods, plus the area of **La Ribera** which lies further to your right across another main artery the Vía Laietana, make up the sizable **Ciutat Vella (Old City).** Within these three neighborhoods are two sub-regions the infamous **Barrio Chino (Chinese Quarter)** on the lower, port side of El Raval and El Born—Barcelona's bastion of cool—in the lower, port side pocket of La Ribera. As this area is the largest, I have sub-divided all its attractions into El Raval, Barri Gòtic, and La Ribera.

Across the Plaça Catalunya Les Ramblas becomes **Rambla Catalunya** with the elegant **Passeig de Gràcia** running parallel to the immediate right. These are the two main arteries of the **L'Eixample,** or the *extension.* This is where most of the jewels of the *modernisme* period, including key works by Antoni Gaudí, dot the harsh grids of this graceful, middle class neighborhood. Both end at the **Diagonal,** a major cross town artery that also serves as the city's business and commercial hub. Northwards across the Diagonal is the suburb of **Gràcia.** Once a separate village, it makes up for in sheer atmosphere what it lacks on notable monuments.

The other areas of interest for the visitor are **Montjuïc,** the bluff to the east of the city and the maritime area of **Barceloneta** and the beaches. The first is the largest green zone in the city, contains some its top museums, and was the setting for the principal events of the 1992 Summer Olympic Games. The second is a peninsula that has long been the city's populist playground, with dozens of fish restaurants, some facing the beaches that sprawl northwards along the coast. The "other" mountain is **Tibidabo,** in the northwest, which boasts great views of the city and the Mediterranean. It also has an amusement park.

Tips   **Officer! Officer!**

There are four police forces in Catalonia: the Guardia Urbana (whose main responsibility is traffic), the Policía Nacional (National Police), the Guardia Civil (Civil Guard), and the Mossos d'Escuadra (Catalonia's autonomous police force). Tourists are more likely to deal with the latter at the Turisme-Atenció station, Les Ramblas 43 (© **93-344-13-00**). It's open 24 hours, and there are officers who speak various languages. This is where you can report petty theft for insurance purposes. For more on health and safety, see p. 22.

Value **The Barcelona Card**

An ideal way to appreciate Barcelona better and save money at the same time is with the Barcelona Card. It's definitely a bargain if you stay in the city for more than an afternoon and do any sightseeing at all. For adults, it costs 17€ ($20) for 1 day and 20€ ($23) for 2 days, 23€ ($26) for 3 days, 25€ ($29) for 4 days and 27€ ($31) for 5 days. For children, the card costs 3€ ($3.45) less on all options.

The 24-hour card covers unlimited travel on all public transport, and is valid for a free walking tour.

Culture vultures who hold the card can get discounts of 20% to 100% in all museums. Discounts on a host of theaters, shows, and attractions such as the Aquarium and the Goldrinas pleasure boats are also on the menu, as are discounts in bars, restaurants, and some shops. The cards specify where they can be used. They're for sale at the tourist offices at the airport, Sants train station, and in the Plaça de Catalunya (see "Visitor Information," above).

FINDING AN ADDRESS/MAPS Finding a Barcelona address doesn't generally pose too many problems. The L'Eixample district is built on a grid system, so by learning the cross street you can pretty much easily find the place you are looking for. Barcelona is hemmed in on one side by the sea *(mar)* and the mountain of Tibidabo *(montaña)* on the other, so often people just describe a place as being on the *mar* or *montaña* side of the street in L'Eixample. The Ciutat Vella or Old City is a little more confusing and you will need a good map (available in the news kiosks along Les Ramblas) to find specific places. However, the city abounds with long boulevards and spacious squares, making it easier to navigate. The designation S/N *(sin número)* means that the building has no number, however this is mainly limited to large buildings and monuments, so its pretty obvious once you get there where it is. In built up Barcelona, the symbol º designates the floor (for example, the first floor is 1º). Street names are in Catalan. Some people still refer to them in Spanish but there is very little difference between the two so it shouldn't cause any confusion. The word for "street" *(carrer* in Catalan and *calle* in Spanish) is nearly always dropped; that is, Carrer Ferran is simply referred to as Ferran. *Passeig* (or *paseo* in Spanish) and *avinguda* (or *avenida* in Spanish), meaning respectively "boulevard" and "avenue," are nearly always kept, as in Passeig de Gràcia and Avinguda de Tibidabo. *Rambla* means a long, pedestrianized avenue and *plaça* (or *plaza* in Spanish), a square.

THE NEIGHBORHOODS IN BRIEF

I've briefly described the location of the major neighborhoods in "City Layout," above; here I take a look at what makes each unique, its style, and its form.

Ciutat Vella (Old Town)

Barri Gòtic Next to the excesses of the 19th-century *modernista* period, Barcelona's golden age was between the 13th and 15th centuries, the Gothic period. The city expanded rapidly in medieval times, so much so that it could no longer be contained within the old Roman walls. So new ones were built. They originally ran from the port northwards along what was to become Les

Ramblas, down the Ronda Sant Pere to Calle Rec Comtal and back to the sea again. Except for a few remaining sections along the Vía Laietana, most of them have now been destroyed. But the ensemble of 13th- to 15th-century buildings (or parts of) that remain make up the most complete Barri Gòtic (Gothic Quarter) on the continent. These include government buildings, churches (including the main cathedral), and guild houses.

Guilds (*gremis*) were a forerunner to the trade unions and the backbone of Barcelona medieval life. Many of their shields can be seen on buildings dotted around the Barri Gòtic, which would have denoted the headquarters of each particular trade. Tiny workshops were also enclosed in the area and even now many street names bear the name of the activity that went on there for centuries—such as Escudellers (shield makers) and Brocaters (brocade makers), to name a few. El Call, the original Jewish ghetto, is also located within the Barri Gòtic. A tiny area around the Carrer del Call and L'Arc de Sant Ramon del Call was the scene of the sacking of the Jews by Christian mobs in the late 1400s.

Apart from the big attractions such as the **Cathedral de la Seu,** the **Plaça Sant Jaume** (which contains the two organs of Catalan politics, the Ajuntament and the Generalitat), and the medieval palace of the **Plaça del Rei,** where Columbus was received after returning from the New World, the Barri Gòtic's charm lies in its details. Smaller squares, such as the **Plaça Felip Neri** with its central fountain, the oasis-like courtyard of the **Frederic Marés Museum,** gargoyles peering down from ancient towers and small chapels set into the sides of medieval buildings; this

is what makes the area so fascinating. Most of them can only be discovered on foot, ideally at sunset when the fading Mediterranean light lends the stone buildings a warm hue and musicians, mainly of the classical nature, jostle for performance spaces around the Cathedral.

Some of the sites in the Barri Gòtic are not medieval at all (architecture and history purists argue that the name has remained simply for the sake of tourism) but are of no less merit. The most famous of these is the so-called "Bridge of Sighs" (nothing like the Venetian original) in Carrer del Bisbe, built during the city's Gothic Revival in the 1920s. But even modern additions do nothing to deter from the character of the Barri Gòtic. The abundance of specialist shops, from old fan and espadrille makers to more cutting edge designer ware is another attraction, as are the dozens of outdoor eateries where you can enjoy a coffee or two looking out onto an ancient edifice.

The sizable Barri Gòtic is hemmed in on one side by the ugly Vía Laietana and on the other by **Les Ramblas.**

The most famous promenade in Spain, ranking with Madrid's Paseo del Prado, it was once a sewer. These days, street entertainers, flower vendors, news vendors, cafe patrons, and strollers flow along its length. The gradual 1.5km (1-mile) descent toward the sea has often been called a metaphor for life because its bustling action combines cosmopolitanism and crude vitality.

Les Ramblas actually consists of five sections, each a particular *rambla*—Rambla de Canaletes, Rambla dels Estudis, Rambla de Sant Josep, Rambla dels Caputxins, and Rambla de Santa Mónica. The shaded pedestrian esplanade runs from the Plaça de Catalunya to the port—all the way to the Columbus Monument. Along the way you'll pass the **Gran Teatre del Liceu,** on Rambla dels Caputxins, one of the most magnificent opera houses in the world, restored to its former glory after a devastating fire in 1994. Watch out for the giant sidewalk mosaic by Miró halfway down at the Plaça de la Boqueria.

El Raval On the opposite side of Les Ramblas lies El Raval, Barcelona's largest inner-city neighborhood. This is where the ambitious plans for the post-Olympic "New Barcelona" are at their most evident as entire blocks of dank apartment buildings were bulldozed to make way for cutting edge new edifices, squares, and boulevards. El Raval has recently been cited as the neighborhood with the most multicultural mix in Europe and a quick stroll around its maze of streets, where Pakistani fabric merchants and South American spice sellers sit side by side along traditional establishments selling dried cod and local wine seems to confirm the fact. The *Adhan* (the Muslim call to prayer) wafts from mosques located in ground-floor locales located next to neo-hippie bars, yoga schools, and contemporary art galleries. The largest of these is the **MACBA (Museum of Contemporary Art),** a luminous white behemoth designed by the American architect Richard Meir; the MACBA resides on a huge concrete square that has, since its opening in 1995, become the neighborhood's most popular playground. At any time of the day, the space will be inundated by kids playing cricket and soccer, skateboarders cruising the ramps of the museum's forecourt and housewives on their way to the nearby **Boqueria** market. Another favorite stomping ground is the newer Rambla del Raval; a wide, airy pedestrianized avenue lined with cafes. A new five-star hotel and the city's **Filmoteca (Cinema Foundation)** are currently being built on its northern side, a sign that the neighborhood's reputation as a seedy inner-city slum is now firmly in the past. Signs of gentrification are everywhere in El Raval. While this still attracts its fair share of criticism, no one can deny the life enhancing benefits of the projects mentioned above for a neighborhood historically devoid of light and breathing space.

Change is slower to come to the so-called **Barrio Chino,** the lower half of El Raval near the port. Despite the name ("Chinese Quarter"), this isn't Chinatown—in fact most attribute its nickname to an American journalist visiting the area in the '20s; it apparently reminded him of a gangland back home. A decade later the French writer Jean Genet wrote *A Thief's Journal* during a stint in one if its peseta-a-night whorehouses. In some pockets of the Chino, you would be forgiven for thinking that little has changed; while drug dealing has been largely shipped out to the outer suburbs, prostitution still openly exists as does the general seediness of many of the streets. But, as with all of the Old City, the times are a changin' and you may find yourself wandering down here at night to attend the opening of a new bar or club. Petty thieves, prostitutes, drug dealers, and purse-snatchers are just some of the neighborhood "characters," so exercise caution.

La Ribera Another neighborhood that stagnated for years but is now well into a renaissance, is La Ribera. Across the noisy artery Vía Laietana and southwards of Calle Princesa, this small neighborhood is bordered in by the **Port Vell (Old Port)** and the **Parc de la Ciutadella.** Like the

Barrio Chino (see above) **El Born** is La Ribera's "neighborhood within a neighborhood." But far from being a rough diamond, El Born is a polished pastiche of the Old Town where designer clothing and housewares showcases occupy medieval buildings and workshops. The centerpiece is the imposing **Santa María del Mar,** a stunningly complete Gothic basilica that was built with funds from the cashed-up merchants that once inhabited the area. Many of them lived in the mansions and palaces along the Carrer de Montcada, today home to a trio of top museums including the Museu Picasso. Most of the mansions in this area were built during one of Barcelona's major maritime expansions, principally in the 1200s and 1300s. During this time, El Born was the city's principal trade area. The recently refurbished **La Llotja,** the city's first stock exchange, lies on its outer edge on the Plaça Palau; although the facade dates from 1802, the interior is pure Catalan Gothic. The central **Passeig del Born** got its name from the medieval jousts that used to occur here. At the northern end, the wrought iron Mercat del Born was the city's principal wholesale market until the mid-1970s. Recent excavation work has revealed entire streets and homes dating back to the 18th century, sealing the edifice's fate as a new museum where these ruins can be viewed via glass flooring and walkways. Behind the Mercat del Born the Parc de la Ciutadella is a tranquil oasis replete with a man-made lake, wide, leafy walkways, and yet more museums.

More Central Barcelona

Barceloneta, the Beaches & the Harbor Although Barcelona has a long seagoing tradition, its waterfront stood in decay for years. Today, the waterfront promenade,

Passeig del Moll de la Fusta, bursts with activity. The best way to get a bird's-eye view of the area is to take an elevator to the top of the Columbus Monument in Plaça Portal de la Pau at the port end of Les Ramblas.

Near the monument are the **Reials Drassanes,** or royal shipyards, a booming place during the Middle Ages. Years before Columbus landed in the New World, ships sailed around the world from here, flying the yellow-and-red flag of Catalonia. These days, they are home to the excellent Museu Marítimo. Across the road, the wooden swing bridge known as the Rambla del Mar takes you across the water to the Maremagnum entertainment and shopping complex.

To the east, the glitzy **Port Vell (Old Port)** was one of the main projects for the city's Olympic renewal scheme. More Miami than Mediterranean, it consists of a marina and large expanses of open recreational areas where people get out and enjoy the sun. It is also home to the city's Aquarium. On one side it is flanked by the **Passeig Joan de Borbón,** the main street of **La Barceloneta (Little Barcelona).** Formerly a fishing district dating from the 18th century, the neighborhood is full of character and is still one of the best places to eat seafood in the city. The blocks here are long and narrow—architects planned them that way so that each room in every building fronted a street. The streets end at Barceloneta beach. This, as in all of the city's beaches, were nonexistent pre-1992. The harborfront was clogged with industrial buildings—many of them abandoned—and *chiringuitos* (beach bars) until the land was reclaimed, sand trawled in from offshore and beach culture returned to Barcelona. Today they are some of the finest urban beaches in Europe. From Barceloneta, they sprawl out northwards to the Vila Olímpica and beyond. The **Olympic Village,** dominated by a pair of landmark, sea-facing skyscrapers (one accommodating the five-star Hotel Arts and the city's casino) boasts yet another marina and a host of restaurants and bars. The entire length of Barcelona's man-made waterfront can be viewed by a stroll along the Passeig Marítim.

L'Eixample To the north of the Plaça de Catalunya is the **Eixample** (Ensanche in Spanish), the section of Barcelona that grew beyond the old medieval walls. In the mid-1800s, Barcelona, as was the case with many European cities, was simply bursting at the seams. The, dank, serpentine streets of the old-walled city were not only breeding grounds for cholera and typhoid, but habitual mass rioting. Rather than leveling the Old Town, the city's authorities had a sloping sweep of land just outside the walls at their disposal and contracted the socialist engineer Idelfons Cerdà to offer a solution. His subsequent 1856 work, *Monograph on the Working Class of Barcelona,* became the first ever attempt to study the living, breathing landscape of a city; urbanization to you and me, a term Cerdà himself coined in the process.

Cerdà actually visited hundreds of Old City hovels before he drew up plans for Barcelona's New City. Needless to say, his fact checking led him to the bowels of human suffering; he found out that life expectancy for the proletariat was half of that of that of the bourgeoisie (while paying double per square meter for their decaying hovels) and mortality rates were lower in the narrower streets. Above all, he concluded that air and sunshine were vital to basic well-being.

Today little remains of Cerdà's most radical plans for L'Eixample, apart from the rigorous regularity of its 20m-wide (67-ft.) streets and famous chamfered pavements. The *modernistas* were the neighborhood's earliest architects, filling the blocks with their labored fantasies, such as Gaudí's La Sagrada Família, Casa Mila, and Casa Batlló. His works aside, L'Eixample is a living, breathing museum piece with an abundance of Art Nouveau architecture and details unfound anywhere in Europe. **La Ruta del Modernismo** (p. 160) is a specially designed walking tour that will guide you to the best of them.

In accordance with Cerdà's basic plans, avenues form a grid of perpendicular streets, cut across by a majestic boulevard—**Passeig de Gràcia,** a posh shopping street ideal for leisurely promenades. L'Eixample's northern boundary is the **Avinguda Diagonal** (or simply the Diagonal) which links the expressway and the heart of the city and acts as Barcelona's business and banking hub.

Gràcia This charming neighborhood sprawls out northwards of the intersection of the **Passeig de Gràcia** and **Diagonal.** Its contained, village-like ambience stems from the fact that it was once a separate village, only connected to central Barcelona in 1897 with the construction of the Passeig de Gràcia. It has a strong industrial and artisan history and many street level workshops can still be seen. Rather than monuments or museum's Gràcia's charm lies in its low-level housing and series of squares—the Plaça del Sol and Plaça Ruis i Taulet with its distinctive clocktower being two of the prettiest. The residents themselves have a strong sense of neighborhood pride and a marked independent spirit and their annual fiestas (p. 20) are some of the liveliest in the city. For the casual visitor, Gràcia is a place to wander through for a slice of authentic *barrio* life.

Montjuïc & Tibidabo Locals call them "mountains" and while there is nothing Alpine in their proportions, the port-side bluff of Montjuïc and Tibidabo to the north of the city are the places to go for fine views and cleaner air. The most accessible, Montjuïc (named the "Hill of the Jews" after a Jewish necropolis that once stood there), gained prominence in 1929 as the site of the World's Fair and again in 1992 as the site of the Summer Olympic Games. Its major attractions are the Joan Miró museum, the Olympic installations, and the **Poble Espanyol (Spanish Village),** a 2-hectare (5-acre) site constructed for the World's Fair. Examples of Spanish art and architecture are on display against the backdrop of a traditional Spanish village. Opposite the village lies the **CaixaForum,** one of the city's newer contemporary art showcases housed in a converted *modernista* textile factory. In a recent push to raise Montjuïc's status even further, new gardens (such as the Jardí Botanic) and parks are being established and a five-star hotel being built on its sea-facing flank. At the base of Montjuïc

is the working class neighborhood of Poble Sec and the Ciutat del Teatre; location of the city's theatrical school and a conglomeration of performing arts spaces. Tibidabo (503m/1,650 ft.) is where you should go for your final look at Barcelona. On a clear day you can see the mountains of Majorca, some 209km (130 miles) away. Reached by train, tram, and cable car, Tibidabo is a popular Sunday excursion in Barcelona when whole families head to the funfair of the same name.

Outer Barcelona

Pedralbes At the eastern edge of El Diagonal, Pedralbes is where wealthy Barcelonans live in either stylish blocks of apartment houses, 19th-century villas behind ornamental fences, or stunning *modernista* structures. Set in a park, the **Palau de Pedralbes,** Av. Diagonal 686, was constructed in the 1920s as a gift from the city to Alfonso XIII, the grandfather of King Juan Carlos. Today it has a new life, housing the Ceramic and Decorative Arts Museums. The Finca Güell is also part of the estate; the country home of Gaudí's main patron Eusebi Güell. Although not open to the public, the main gate and gatehouse, both designed by Gaudí, are visible from the street.

2 Getting Around

GETTING TO BARCELONA FROM THE AIRPORTS

El Prat, Barcelona's main airport is 13kms (8 miles) from the city center and there are several options you can use to get into town.

BY BUS The **Aerobús** leaves just outside all three terminals every 15 minutes from 6am to midnight. Its journey takes about 20 to 25 minutes (leave a few more minutes for the return journey, as the bus takes a slightly different route) and costs 3.60€ ($4.15). The bus stops at Plaça Espanya, Plaça Universitat, and Plaça Catalunya, all major hubs with Metro connections.

BY TRAIN El Prat also has its own train station. While this is convenient for those traveling further afield by train (the journey finishes at Sants, the city's major terminal which also has connections to the Metro) the station itself is a short walk from the airport terminal, which makes it inconvenient for those

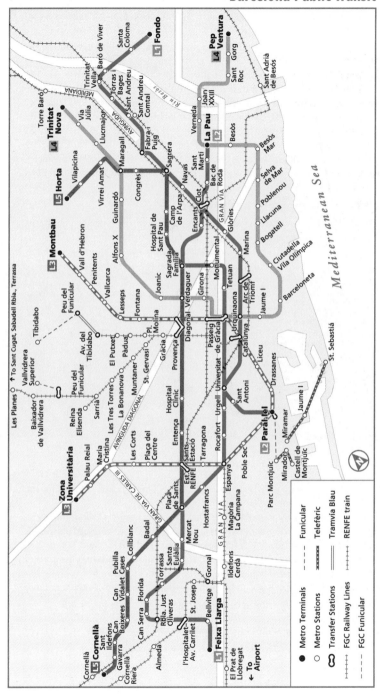

with lots of luggage. Trains leave every 30 minutes from 6:15am to 11:40pm, and the 25-minute journey costs 2.50€ ($2.90).

BY TAXI   There are taxi ranks outside all terminals. The 20-minute journey to the center should cost about 18€ ($21), including the 2.10€ ($2.40) airport surcharge. Luggage that goes in the boot is charged at .85€ ($1) per piece.

Travelers arriving from within the E.U. on budget airlines such as Ryanair may land at **Girona** airport; 97km (60 miles) northeast of Barcelona. Transport into Barcelona is by **Barcelona Bus,** which arrives in Barcelona at Passeig de Sant Joan, 52. Round-trip tickets (which must be purchased inside the terminal) cost 19€ ($22). *Note:* There have been reports of unscrupulous Barcelona taxi drivers waiting for disembarking passengers from this bus. Make sure the meter is on when you hop in, and that you are not being taken the long way round to your destination.

GETTING AROUND IN BARCELONA

BY SUBWAY   Barcelona has an excellent public transport system. The **Metro (subway)** goes pretty much any place in the city you will need to get to. It is run by the TMB (Transports Metropolitans de Barcelona) who also manage the bus network and the FGC (Ferrocarrils de la Generalitat) a pre-Metro, part underground, part over-ground system.

It is the efficient Metro system, however, that most visitors to the city are likely to use. There are five color-coded and numbered lines that fan out from the center of the city. Stations are recognizable by a red diamond-shaped sign with the letter M in the center. Maps are available from the stations themselves and tourist information offices. The stations Catalunya, Sants, and Passeig de Gràcia connect with RENFE or over-ground trains. When you purchase a ticket for another part of Spain or Catalonia (which you can do from RENFE offices at Sants and Passeig de Gràcia stations) make sure you ask which station it leaves from.

All Metro tickets can be bought on the day of journey or beforehand inside the station, either from the ticket office or a touch screen vending machine. Various options are available. A single *(sencillo)* ticket costs 1.10€ ($1.25). More economic options include a T-10 at 6€ ($6.90) which offers 10 journeys that can be shared by two or more people or a T-Día for unlimited 24-hour transport in central Barcelona for 4.60€ ($5.30). Travel Cards of between 2 and 5 days 8.40–18€ ($9.65–$21) are also available. All these tickets are valid for the FGC and bus systems as well as the Metro.

Note that even with a *sencillo* ticket, once it is activated, it is valid for up to 75 minutes on a different form of transport if you need to do a combined Metro/bus journey. The Metro runs 5am to midnight Sunday to Thursday and 5am to 2am Friday and Saturday. TMB's easy to navigate website (**www.tmb.net**) has loads of information on the city's transport system in English, including which Metro stations and buses are equipped to take wheelchairs. The customer service number is ℂ **93-318-70-74;** there are also customer service centers at Universitat, Sagrada Família, Sants, and Diagonal stations. While it's tempting to hop on and off the Metro when seeing the sights remember that Metro stations are only often about a 5- to 10-minute walk apart; a good pair of shoes is the best way to central Barcelona!

BY BUS   Buses are also just as plentiful, but less convenient as they lie at the mercy of the city's infamous traffic snarls. Most bus routes stop at the Plaça Catalunya, also the stop off point for the Aerobús (see "Getting to Barcelona from the Airports," above) and the Bus Turístic (see below). Routes are clearly marked on each stop as are timetables—but most buses stop running well before the Metro closes. One bus service that is particularly useful is the Nitbus, which runs all night and is often the only alternative to the 3am taxi drought. These are bright yellow, clearly marked with an N and most leave from Plaça Catalunya. Note that Travel Cards and other TMB passes are not valid on *nitbuses*. Tickets for this bus (1.50€/$1.70 one-way) are bought directly from the driver.

BY TAXI   Taxis are plentiful and still reasonably priced. Most of the time you simply hail one in the street (a green light denotes their availability). Taxis have meters, but don't make the mistake of confusing the cheaper day rate (Tariff 2) and the more expensive, post-8pm night rate (Tariff 1). A list of prices and surcharges is (by law) on display on the back passenger window. There have been recent reports of some unscrupulous taxi drivers charging exorbitant fares for short distances, but this seems to be mainly be confined to the Ryanair bus drop-off point (see "Getting to Barcelona from the Airports," above). But do make sure that the meter is turned on when you start your journey. If you wish to book a cab, either for the next available or the next day, call the **Institut Metropolità del Taxi** at ℭ **93-223-51-51.** They can also give you information about booking wheelchair adapted taxis.

BY BICYCLE   One growing form of transport in the city is the bicycle. There are a number of bicycle lanes in the center of the city and few firms that rent them, including **Un Coxte Menys,** Esparteria 3 (ℭ **93-268-21-05**), and **Biciclot,** Verneda 16 (ℭ **93-307-74-75**). You are not required by law to wear a helmet.

OTHER FORMS OF TRANSPORT

At some point in your journey, you may want to visit the mountain of Tibidabo for the views and fun fair. A century-old tram called the **Tramvía Blau (Blue Streetcar)** goes from Plaça Kennedy to the bottom of the funicular to Tibidabo. It operates daily from 10am to 8pm from mid-June to mid-September and 10am to 6pm on weekends only the rest of the year.

At the end of the run, you can go the rest of the way by funicular to the top, at 503m (1,650 ft.), for a stunning panoramic view of Barcelona. The funicular

---

Tips **All Aboard!**

The most convenient way to see all of Barcelona, especially if your time is limited, is to hop on (and off) the **Bus Turístic** (ℭ **93-318-70-74**; www. tmb.net/en_US/turistes/busturistic/busturistic.jsp). This double-decker, open topped tourist bus travels to all the major areas and sights; you can either choose to disembark or stay on and continue your journey. There are two routes; the red or Nord (North) route which covers L'Eixample and Tibidabo with Gaudí's main works (including the Sagrada Família) as the highlights or the blue Sur (South) route which allows you to see the Old Town and Montjuïc, both with multilingual commentary along the way. The main hop on point is on Plaça Catalunya outside the El Corte Ingles department store. Cost is 16€ ($18) for the 1-day pass (10€/$12 children 4–12) and 20€ ($23) for the 2-day pass (13€/$15 children 4–12). They can be purchased on board or at the Tourist Information Office at the Plaça Catalunya. The service operates daily from 9am to 9:30 pm. There is no service on Christmas or New Year's days.

operates only when the Fun Fair at Tibidabo is open (p. 174). Opening times vary according to the time of year and the weather conditions. As a rule, the funicular starts operating 20 minutes before the Fun Fair opens, then every half-hour. During peak visiting hours, it runs every 15 minutes. The fare is 2€ ($2.30) one-way, 3€ ($3.45) round-trip.

The **Tibibus** goes from the Plaça de Catalunya, in the center of the city, to Tibidabo at limited times, again depending when the park open and closes. The one-way fare is 2.10€ ($2.40). Call city hall's information hot line (© **010**) for times.

To reach Montjuïc, the site of the 1992 Olympics, take the **Montjuïc funicular.** It links with subway line 3 at the Paral.lel Metro stop. The funicular operates daily from 9am to 8pm in winter, 9am to 10pm in summer. The round-trip fare is 2.10€ ($2.40).

Barcelona's newest form of public transport is the sleek and comfortable Tramvía Baix; a modern cable car that mainly services the outer suburbs. It is handy however for reaching the outer limits of the Diagonal and the Palau de Pedralbes (p. 60). Hop on at Plaça Francesc Macia.

FAST FACTS: Barcelona

American Express There are two American Express Offices in Barcelona: one at Passeig de Gràcia 101 (© **93-415-23-71**), and the other at **Les Ramblas 74** (© **93-301-11-66**).

Area Codes The area code for Barcelona is **93**.

ATM Networks Maestro, Cirrus, and Visa cards are readily accepted at all ATMs.

Business Hours Banks are open Monday through Friday from 8:30am to 2pm. Most offices are open Monday through Friday from 9am to 6 or 7pm. In July this changes from 8pm to 3pm for many businesses, especially those in the public sector. In August, businesses are on skeleton staff if they are not closed altogether. In restaurants, lunch is usually from 2 to 4pm and dinner from 9 to 11:30pm or midnight. There are no set rules for the opening of bars and taverns. Many open at 8am, others at noon and most stay open until midnight or later. Major stores are open Monday through Saturday from 9:30 or 10am to 8pm; smaller establishments, however, often take a siesta, doing business from 9:30am to 2pm and 4:30pm to 8 or 8.30pm. Hours can vary from store to store.

Car Rentals See "Getting Around" in chapter 2.

Currency See "Money" in chapter 2.

Driving Rules See "Getting Around" in chapter 2.

Drugstores To find an open pharmacy outside normal business hours, check the list of stores posted on the door of any drugstore. The law requires drugstores to operate on a rotating system of hours so that there's always a drugstore open somewhere, even Sunday at midnight. Drugstores are called *farmacia* in Spanish and ones open for business are identified by a neon green cross.

Electricity Most hotels have 220 volts AC (50 cycles). Some older places have 110 or 125 volts AC. Carry your adapter with you, and always check at your hotel desk before plugging in any electrical appliance. It's best to travel with battery-operated equipment or just buy a new hair dryer in Spain.

Embassies & Consulates If you lose your passport, fall seriously ill, get into legal trouble, or have some other serious problem, your embassy or consulate can help. These are the Barcelona addresses and hours: The **United States Consulate,** Passeig de Reina Elisenda 23 (© 93-280-22-27; FGC: Reina Elisenda), is open Monday through Friday from 9am to 1pm. The **Canadian Consulate,** Carrer de Elisenda Pinós 10 (© 93-204-27-00; FGC: Reina Elisenda), is open Monday through Friday from 10am to 1pm. The **United Kingdom Consulate-General,** Diagonal 477 (© 93-366-62-00; Metro: Hospital Clinic), is open Monday through Friday from 9:30am and 3pm. The **Republic of Ireland** has a small consulate at Gran Vía Carles III 94 (© 93-491-50-21; Metro: María Cristina); it's open Monday through Friday from 10am to 1pm. In the adjacent building is the **Australian Consulate,** Gran Vía Carles III 98 (© 93-490-90-13; Metro: María Cristina). It is open Monday though Friday from 10am to noon. Citizens of **New Zealand** have a consulate at Travesera de Gràcia 64 (© 93-209-03-99; FGC: Gràcia); it's open Monday through Friday from 9am to 4:30pm and 4 to 7pm.

Emergencies For an ambulance © **061**; or fire © **080.**

Etiquette Contemporary Barcelona is the most relaxed and liberal of all Spanish cities. In Franco's day, many visitors would be arrested for the skimpy, revealing wear worn around the city streets, but these days no one is going to bat an eyelid if you wear a pair of shorts and sandals down Les Ramblas, although in the interest of blending in with the locals consider reserving your resort wear for the beach. Church officials will not stop you visiting churches and cathedrals if scantily clad, but again, try and be as sympathetic as possible to local customs. Women can cover up when needed in the summer months by carrying around a light cardigan or shawl in their bag.

In spite of what you've heard in days of yore, when Spaniards showed up for appointments 2 or 3 hours late, most nationals now show up on time as they do in the rest of the E.U. countries. It's always wise for men to wear a suit for business meetings. The familiar *tú* form is now widely used in Spain, a sign of the country's shaking off of their old-school image. But to be on the safe side foreign Spanish speakers should address strangers, particularly older people, with the formal *usted.* Kissing on both cheeks is reserved for friends, or people your friends introduce you to. Handshakes are more the norm in business transactions. Catalan nationalism is an extremely sensitive subject and often avoided even amongst the Catalans themselves. Unless you are an expert on the topic, stay away from it. If you are invited into a private home for dinner, you are not expected to bring a bottle of wine although a small gift of chocolates or flowers will be appreciated. The Spanish and Catalans are extremely tactile. You should not be offended or feel uncomfortable when people touch you on the back, arms, and so on. I recommend reading *Culture Shock! Spain: a Guide to Customs and Etiquette* (Graphic Arts Centre Publishing).

Holidays See "Barcelona Calendar of Events" in chapter 2.

Hot Lines Call the city hall information service at ℭ **010** for opening and closing times of attractions, special events, and other hard-to-find info.

Information See "Visitor Information," earlier in this chapter.

Internet Access Internet access is plentiful, both in cybercafes and more and more frequently in hotels.

Language Their are two official language in Catalonia; Castilian Spanish *(Castellano)* and Catalan. After years of being outlawed during the Franco dictatorship, Catalan has returned to Barcelona and Catalonia with the language and its derivatives spoken throughout the *Països Catalans* (Catalan Countries), namely Catalonia, Valencia, the Balearic Islands (including Majorca, even though natives there will tell you they speak *Mallorquín*), and pockets of Southern France and Aragon. Although street signs and much of media are in Catalan, no tourist is expected to speak it, although you will be met with delight if you can at least master a few phrases. Descriptions in museums are in both Catalan and Spanish with some also in English. Most restaurants have an English menu.

Laundromats There are a few self-service and serviced laundromats in the Old Town, including **Tigre,** Carrer de Rauric 20, and **Lavamax,** Junta de Comerç 14. Some dry cleaners *(tintorerías)* also do laundry.

Lost & Found Be sure to tell all of your credit card companies the minute you discover your wallet has been lost or stolen and file a report at the nearest police precinct. Your credit card company or insurer may require a police report number or record of the loss. Most credit card companies have an emergency toll-free number to call if your card is lost or stolen; they may be able to wire you a cash advance immediately or deliver an emergency credit card in a day or two. Visa's U.S. emergency number is ℭ **800/847-2911** or 410/581-9994 and emergency number in Spain is ℭ **90-099-11-24.** American Express cardholders and traveler's check holders should call ℭ **800/221-7282** in the U.S. or ℭ **90-237-56-37** in Spain. MasterCard holders should call ℭ **800/307-7309** or 636/722-7111 in the U.S. or ℭ **90-097-12-31** in Spain. For other credit cards, call the toll-free number directory at ℭ **800/555-1212.**

If you need emergency cash over the weekend when all banks and American Express offices are closed, you can have money wired to you via **Western Union** (ℭ **800/325-6000;** www.westernunion.com).

Identity theft or fraud are potential complications of losing your wallet, especially if you've lost your driver's license along with your cash and credit cards. Notify the major credit-reporting bureaus immediately; placing a fraud alert on your records may protect you against liability for criminal activity. The three major U.S. credit-reporting agencies are **Equifax** (ℭ **800/766-0008;** www.equifax.com), **Experian** (ℭ **888/397-3742;** www.experian.com), and **TransUnion** (ℭ **800/680-7289;** www.transunion.com). Finally, if you've lost all forms of photo ID call your airline and explain the situation; they might allow you to board the plane if you have a copy of your passport or birth certificate and a copy of the police report you've filed.

Liquor Laws The legal drinking age is 18. Bars, taverns, and cafeterias usually open at 8am, and many serve alcohol to midnight or later. Generally, you can purchase alcoholic beverages in almost any market.

Mail Airmail letters to the United States and Canada cost 1.30€ ($1.50) up to 20 grams, and letters to Britain or other E.U. countries cost .50€ up to 20 grams; letters within Spain cost .25€ (29¢). As well as post offices, stamps can be bought at *estancos* (tobacconists). Postcards have the same rates as letters. Allow about 8 days for delivery to North America, generally less to the United Kingdom; in some cases, letters take 2 weeks to reach North America. Rates change frequently, so check at your local hotel before mailing anything. As for surface mail to North America, forget it. Chances are you'll be home long before your letter arrives.

Newspapers & Magazines Foreign newspapers and magazines are available on the newsstands along Les Ramblas. *Catalonia Today* is a free newsletter in English published by the Catalan newspaper *El Punt*. *Barcelona Metropolitan* is a monthly magazine in English with loads of information on events as well as features on Barcelona living. You can pick it up in bars and pubs. The *Guía del Ocio* is the most comprehensive "What's On." There is a small section at the back in English.

Passports **For Residents of the United States:** Whether you're applying in person or by mail, you can download passport applications from the U.S. State Department website at **http://travel.state.gov/passport_services.html**. To find your regional passport office, either check the U.S. State Department website or call the **National Passport Information Center** toll-free number (© 877/487-2778) for automated information.

For Residents of Canada: Passport applications are available at travel agencies throughout Canada or from the central **Passport Office,** Department of Foreign Affairs and International Trade, Ottawa, ON K1A 0G3 (© 800/567-6868; www.ppt.gc.ca).

For Residents of the United Kingdom: To pick up an application for a standard 10-year passport (5-year passport for children under 16), visit your nearest passport office, major post office, or travel agency or contact the **United Kingdom Passport Service** at © 0870/521-0410 or search its website at www.ukpa.gov.uk.

For Residents of Ireland: You can apply for a 10-year passport at the **Passport Office,** Setanta Centre, Molesworth Street, Dublin 2 (© 01/671-1633; www.irlgov.ie/iveagh). Those under age 18 and over 65 must apply for a 3-year passport. You can also apply at 1A South Mall, Cork (© 021/272-525) or at most main post offices.

For Residents of Australia: You can pick up an application from your local post office or any branch of Passports Australia, but you must schedule an interview at the passport office to present your application materials. Call the **Australian Passport Information Service** at © 131-232, or visit the government website at www.passports.gov.au.

For Residents of New Zealand: You can pick up a passport application at any New Zealand Passports Office or download it from their website. Contact the **Passports Office** at © 0800/225-050 in New Zealand or 04/474-8100, or log on to www.passports.govt.nz.

Smoking Smoking is not allowed in airports, banks, post offices, and other "public" buildings. Nonsmoking sections in bars and restaurants are rare. Most good hotels have nonsmoking rooms.

Police The national police emergency number is © **091,** although most tourist-related matters are dealt with by the local police force, the Guardia Urbana (© **092**).

Restrooms In Catalonia they're called *aseos, servicios,* or *lavabos,* and are labeled *caballeros* for men and *damas* or *señoras* for women. If you can't find one, go into a bar and order something.

Safety See "Health & Safety," in chapter 2.

Taxes The internal sales tax (known in Spain as *IVA*) ranges between 7% and 33%, depending on the commodity being sold. Food, wine, and basic necessities are taxed at 7%; most goods and services (including car rentals) at 13%; luxury items (jewelry, all tobacco, imported liquors) at 33%; and hotels at 7%.

If you are not a European Union resident and make purchases in Spain worth more than 90€ ($104), you can get a tax refund. To get this refund, you must complete three copies of a form that the store will give you, detailing the nature of your purchase and its value. Citizens of non-E.U. countries show the purchase and the form to the Spanish Customs Office. The shop is supposed to refund the amount due you. Inquire at the time of purchase how they will do so and discuss in what currency your refund will arrive.

Telephones If you don't speak Spanish, you'll find it easier to telephone from your hotel, but remember that this is often very expensive because hotels impose a surcharge on every operator-assisted call. In some cases it can be as high as 40% or more. On the street, phone booths (known as *cabinas*) have dialing instructions in English; although very few actually take coins. Instead, purchase a *tarjeta telefónica* from a newsstand or tobacconist. If you need to make a lengthy overseas call, a *locutorio* (call center) is the best bet. Located throughout the Old Town, these call centers offer the best rates and booths are provided for privacy. *Locutorios* also sell phone cards supplied by private operators. You can purchase as much as three hours of call time to the U.S. for as little as 6€ ($6.90), although you will pay the connection fee (the cost of a local call) on top. These cards can be used from both fixed and mobile phones and must be used within a month of the first call.

When in Spain, the access number for an **AT&T** calling card is © **800/ CALL-ATT.** The access number for **Sprint** is © **800/888-0013.**

More information is also available on the Telefónica website at www.telefonica.es.

For directory assistance: Dial © **11818** for numbers within Spain, and **11825** for the rest of the world.

For operator assistance: If you need operator assistance in making an international call, dial © **1008** for Europe and **1005** for the rest of the world.

Toll-free numbers: Numbers beginning with **900** in Spain are toll-free, but calling a 1-800 number in the States from Spain is not toll-free. In fact, it costs the same as an overseas call.

In Barcelona, most smaller establishments, especially bars, discos, and a few informal restaurants, don't have phones. Further, many summer-only bars and discos secure a phone for the season only, then get a new number the next season. Many attractions, such as small churches or even minor museums, have no staff to receive inquiries from the public.

In 1998 all telephone numbers in Spain changed to a nine-digit system instead of the six- or seven-digit method used previously. Each number is now preceded by its provincial code for local, national, and international calls. For example, when calling within and to Barcelona must dial 93, then the old seven-digit number. If you have a number that does not have a 93 in front of it, add it on and dial before you discount it as erroneous.

To call Spain: If you're calling Spain from the United States:

1. Dial the international access code: **011.**
2. Dial the country code for Spain: **34.**
3. Dial the city code for Spain and then the number. So the whole number you'd dial would be 011-34-93-000-0000.

To make international calls: To make international calls from Spain, first dial 00 and then the country code (U.S. and Canada 1, U.K. 44, Ireland 353, Australia 61, New Zealand 64). Next you dial the area code and number.

Time Spain is 6 hours ahead of Eastern Standard Time in the United States. Daylight saving time is in effect from the last Sunday in March to the last Sunday in October.

Tipping More expensive restaurants add a 7% tax to the bill and cheaper ones incorporate it into their prices. This is NOT a service charge and a tip of 5% to 10% is expected in these establishments. For coffees and snacks most people just leave a few coins or round up to the nearest euro. Taxis do not expect tips.

Although tipping is not mandatory for hotel staff, you should be aware that wages in the hospitality industry are extremely low so any supplement will be more than welcome. Tip hotel porters and doorman between .80€ ($1) and 1€ ($1.15), and maids about the same amount per day.

Useful Phone Numbers **U.S. Department of State Travel Advisory,** © 202/647-5225 (manned 24 hr.); **U.S. Passport Agency,** © 202/647-0518; **U.S. Centers for Disease Control International Traveler's Hot Line,** © 404/332-4559.

Water Although the water in Barcelona is safe to drink, most people find the taste unpleasant and instead buy bottled water.

4

Where to Stay

by Suzanne Wales & Tara Stevens

Barcelona may be one of the most expensive cities in Spain, but prices at its first-class and deluxe hotels can be a bargain compared to other major European cities like Paris and London. This makes Barcelona a good place to splurge, especially with many hotels holding the line on raising their prices (or even pushing them down) because of stiff competition. Be sure to look online for weekend package deals and always ask about any special offers when you call to reserve.

Safety is an important factor when choosing a hotel. Cheaper hotels tend to be in less salubrious parts of town, but have the advantage of being at the heart of the action.

WHICH QUARTER FOR FULL SATISFACTION?

The **Barri Gòtic (Gothic Quarter)** is good for *hostales* (not to be confused with hostels) and cheaper guesthouses, and you can live and eat less expensively here than in any other part of Barcelona and save money on transport as most sights are within walking distance. Hold onto your belongings however, as bag snatching is rife here, in the gentrified El Born area, and in El Raval. While you are unlikely to suffer any bodily harm, be careful when returning to your hotel late at night.

More modern, but more expensive, accommodations can be found north of the Barri Gòtic in the **Eixample district,** centered on the Metro stops Plaça de Catalunya and Universitat. Many buildings are in the *modernista* style, from the last decades of the 19th century. Be aware that sometimes the elevators and plumbing are of the same vintage. However, the Eixample is a desirable and safe neighborhood, especially along its wide boulevards and is excellent for good restaurants. Traffic noise is the only problem you might encounter.

The area around **Sants** and **Plaza Espanya** is the main hub of business hotels and convenient for conferences, meetings and trade shows. It's also convenient for the airport (just 20 min. away by taxi) and the hotels here tend to be quite good if family-sized rooms are needed. However, most leisure travelers will probably find it too far away from the center.

Farther north, above the Avinguda Diagonal, you'll enter the **Gràcia** area, where you can enjoy distinctively Catalan neighborhood life. It has a villagey feel, low-rise buildings, and plenty of sunny plazas populated by students. The main attractions are a bit distant but easily reached by public transportation, still the neighborhood does have a uniquely eclectic feel that makes the barrio worth exploring. Above this the neighborhoods of **Sarrià** and **Sant Gervasi** are mainly upper-class residential areas, with plenty of top-end bars and restaurants.

Barcelona's seafront has never been much of a hotspot for hotels, though after decades of practically ignoring its shoreline, the last few years have seen the area transform into a bustling seaside promenade. The few hotels that do exist tend to be four-or-five star and expensive, although the area of **Poble Nou** (regenerated by the cultural festival Forum2004) is becoming increasingly popular among new developers and is a good choice for anyone looking to get away from the tourist crowds while staying close to the beach.

Another option is to look at **aparthotels** and short-term rented **apartments** (self-catering accommodations), which are becoming increasingly popular. They give you independence, a kitchen to cook for yourself and the sensation of a home-away-from-home. Finally there is a new wave in **bed-and-breakfast** accommodations. Virtually unheard of until two or three years ago, these family-run guesthouses (often no more than two or three rooms) offer a highly personal and cheap alternative.

But whichever option you choose, you *must* book well ahead to secure something on your list of first choices. Don't even think of rolling up into town without a booking in hand or you may find yourself sculling to the outer suburbs or out of Barcelona altogether. This is not just true of the summer months: tourism here is 24/7.

Many of Barcelona's hotels were built before the invention of the automobile, and even the more modern ones rarely have garages. When parking is available at the hotel, the price is indicated; otherwise, the hotel staff will direct you to a garage. Expect to pay upward of 14€ ($16) for 24 hours, and if you do have a car, you might as well park it and leave it there, because driving around the city can be excruciating. If you don't plan to leave the city then there is little point in hiring a car at all.

1 Ciutat Vella (Barri Gòtic, El Raval & La Ribera)

The **Ciutat Vella (Old City)** forms the monumental center of Barcelona, taking in Les Ramblas, Plaça de Sant Jaume, Vía Laietana, Passeig Nacional, the Passeig de Colom, and the full-of-character Raval and La Ribera neighborhoods. It contains some of the city's best hotel bargains. Most of the glamorous, and more expensive, hotels are located in the Eixample and beyond.

VERY EXPENSIVE

Le Meridien Barcelona ★★★   Originally built in 1956, this is the finest hotel in the Old Town, as the roster of famous guests (such as Michael Jackson) can attest. It's superior in comfort to its two closest rivals in the area, the Colón and the Rivoli Ramblas (and also more expensive). Guest rooms are spacious and comfortable, with extra-large beds and heated bathroom floors with tub/shower combos. All rooms have double-glazed windows, but that doesn't fully block out noise from Les Ramblas. The Renaissance Club, an executive floor popular with business people, provides extra luxuries. At the time of writing, the hotel was undergoing extensive renovations of rooms and public areas, but is due to re-open early March 2005.

Les Ramblas 111, 08002 Barcelona. ⓒ 888/250-8577 in the U.S., or 93-318-62-00. Fax 93-301-77-76. www. meridienbarcelona.com. 233 units. 390€–440€ ($449–$506) double; 500€–2000€ ($575–$2300) suite. AE, DC, MC, V. Parking 20€ ($23). Metro: Liceu or Plaça de Catalunya. **Amenities:** Restaurant; bar; health club; limited room service; babysitting; laundry service; dry cleaning. *In room:* A/C, TV, minibar, hair dryer, safe.

EXPENSIVE

Duquesa de Cardona ★★★ *Moments*   This small boutique hotel—popular with honeymooners—is across the road from the harbor of Port Vell, and the rooftop terrace and small plunge pool with Jacuzzi have splendid views of the pleasure and party boats that dock here year round. Recently refurbished, many of the Art Deco features of the 19th-century palace the hotel occupies have been

Ciutat Vella Accommodations

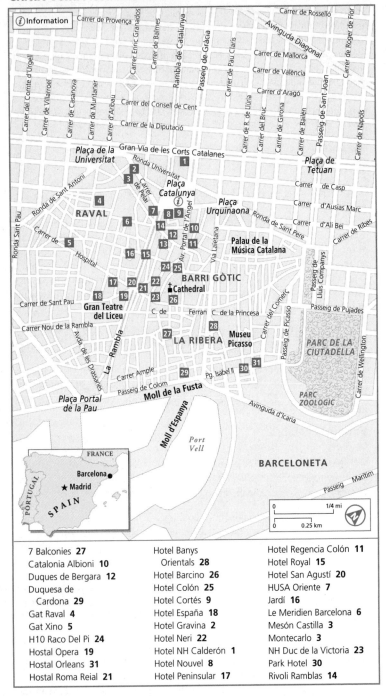

Information

Carrer de Provença · Carrer Enric Granados · Carrer de Balmes · Rambla de Catalunya · Passeig de Gràcia · Carrer de Pau Claris · Carrer de Rosselló · Avinguda Diagonal · Carrer de Roger de Flor · Carrer de Mallorca · Carrer de València · Carrer d'Aragó · Carrer del Comte d'Urgell · Carrer de Villarroel · Carrer de Casanova · Carrer de Muntaner · Carrer d'Aribau · Carrer del Consell de Cent · Carrer de la Diputació · Carrer de R. Llúria · Carrer del Bruc · Carrer de Girona · Carrer de Bailén · Passeig de Sant Joan · Carrer de Nàpols

Plaça de la Universitat · Gran Via de les Corts Catalanes · Plaça de Tetuan · Ronda de Sant Antoni · Ronda Universitat · Plaça Catalunya · Carrer de Casp · Carrer d'Ausias Marc · Carrer d'Ali Bei · Carrer de Pelai · Ronda Sant Pau · Carrer de · Plaça Urquinaona · Ronda de Sant Pere · Carrer de Ribes · RAVAL · Hospital · Carrer de Sant Pau · Av. Portal de l'Angel · Via Laietana · Palau de la Música Catalana · Passeig de Lluís Companys

BARRI GÒTIC · Cathedral · Gran Teatre del Liceu · Carrer Nou de la Rambla · La Rambla · C. de Ferran · C. de la Princesa · Carrer del Comerç · Passeig de Pujades · Passeig de Picasso · PARC DE LA CIUTADELLA · LA RIBERA · Museu Picasso · Carrer de Wellington · Carrer Ample · Pg. Isabel II · PARC ZOOLÒGIC · Plaça Portal de la Pau · Passeig de Colom · Moll de la Fusta · Avinguda d'Icaria · Moll d'Espanya · Port Vell · BARCELONETA · Passeig Marítim

FRANCE · Barcelona · Madrid · PORTUGAL · SPAIN

0 — 1/4 mi · 0 — 0.25 km

7 Balconies **27**	Hotel Banys Orientals **28**	Hotel Regencia Colón **11**
Catalonia Albioni **10**	Hotel Barcino **26**	Hotel Royal **15**
Duques de Bergara **12**	Hotel Colón **25**	Hotel San Agustí **20**
Duquesa de Cardona **29**	Hotel Cortés **9**	HUSA Oriente **7**
Gat Raval **4**	Hotel España **18**	Jardí **16**
Gat Xino **5**	Hotel Gravina **2**	Le Meridien Barcelona **6**
H10 Raco Del Pi **24**	Hotel Neri **22**	Mesón Castilla **3**
Hostal Opera **19**	Hotel NH Calderón **1**	Montecarlo **3**
Hostal Orleans **31**	Hotel Nouvel **8**	NH Duc de la Victoria **23**
Hostal Roma Reial **21**	Hotel Peninsular **17**	Park Hotel **30**
		Rivoli Ramblas **14**

preserved and mixed with elements of modern style to ensure maximum comfort. Communal areas include a stylish living room with deep, cream-colored sofas and a smart Mediterranean restaurant with original marble tiles. The bedrooms have an intimate, romantic feel and all have well-equipped bathrooms with tub/shower combos. If you're used to American style bedrooms however, they might seem a little cramped (especially those at the back), and it is worth paying the extra money to get a front-facing room with views of the harbor.

Passeig Colom 12, Barri Gòtic, 08002 Barcelona. ⓒ 866/376-7831 in the U.S. and Canada or 93-268-90-90. Fax 93-268-29-31. www.hduquesadecardona.com. Double 230€ ($265); jr. suite 345€ ($397); sea-view supplement 35€ ($40). 44 units. AE, DC, MC, V. Public parking nearby 20€ ($23). Metro: Jaume I or Drassanes. **Amenities:** Restaurant; 2 lounges; outdoor swimming pool; solarium; business center; 24-hr. room service; babysitting service; laundry service; dry cleaning; nonsmoking rooms. *In room:* A/C, TV, minibar, hair dryer, safe, Internet access.

Hotel Colón 🐾🐾 *(Kids)*   The Colón is in the heart of Barcelona's Ciutat Vella—a good choice if this is the part of town you've come to see—though it can seem a little old-fashioned, with traditional furniture and fittings and without any concessions to modernity. Situated opposite the main entrance to the cathedral (the best rooms on the sixth-floor have small terraces with splendid views), this hotel sits behind a dignified neoclassical facade. Inside, you'll find conservative and slightly old-fashioned public rooms, a helpful staff, and good-size guest rooms filled with comfortable furniture. Despite recent renovations, the decor remains fairly old-fashioned with heavily patterned drapes and upholstery. All rooms have en suite bathrooms containing a tub/shower combo. Not all rooms have views, however those at the back of the building are quieter. Some of the lower rooms are rather dark. Upon request, families can often be given more spacious rooms and the hotel often has Christmas, New Year, and summer season deals.

Av. de la Catedral 7, 08002 Barcelona. ⓒ 800/845-0636 in the U.S., or 93-301-14-04. Fax 93-317-29-15. www.hotelcolon.es. 145 units. 220€–245€ ($253–$282) double; 350€ ($403) suite. AE, DC, MC, V. Metro: Liceu, Jaume I. **Amenities:** Restaurant; bar; limited room service; babysitting; laundry service; dry cleaning. *In room:* A/C, TV, minibar, hair dryer, safe, Internet access.

Hotel NH Calderón 🐾🐾   Efficient, well maintained, and well staffed with a multilingual corps of employees, this hotel delivers exactly what it promises: safe and comfortable accommodations in a well-conceived, standardized format that's akin to many other modern hotels around the world. Originally built in the 1960s, this 10-story hotel wasn't particularly imaginative then, but was greatly improved in the early 1990s after its acquisition by the NH Hotel Group, with frequent renovations ever since. Accommodations have comfortable, contemporary-looking furnishings with hints of high-tech design, good lighting, lots of varnished hardwood, and colorful fabrics. All units have bathrooms with tub/shower combos.

Rambla de Catalunya 26, 08007 Barcelona. ⓒ 93-301-00-00. Fax 93-412-41-93. www.nh-hoteles.es. 253 units. Mon–Thurs 227€ ($261) double; Fri–Sun 166€ ($191) double. AE, DC, MC, V. Parking 15€ ($17). Metro: Passeig de Gràcia. **Amenities:** Restaurant; bar; indoor and outdoor pool; health club; sauna; limited room service; laundry service; dry cleaning, nonsmoking rooms, business center. *In room:* A/C, TV, minibar, hair dryer, safe, Internet access.

Rivoli Ramblas 🐾   Behind a dignified Art Deco town house on the upper section of the Ramblas, a block south of the Plaça de Catalunya, this recently renovated hotel incorporates many fine examples of avant-garde Catalan design in its stylish interior. The communal areas have acres of polished marble and it's a popular choice for guests in town on business. One of the highlights being the handsome wood decked roof terrace, a pleasant place to start the day. Guest rooms are carpeted, soundproofed, and elegant, but rather cramped. All have neatly kept bathrooms with tub/shower combos.

Les Ramblas 128, 08002 Barcelona. (C) **93-302-66-43**. Fax 93-317-50-53. www.rivolihotels.com. 129 units. 246€ ($283) double; from 300€–696€ ($345–$800) suite. AE, DC, MC, V. Metro: Catalunya or Liceu. **Amenities:** Restaurant; bar; health spa; sauna; solarium; car rental; limited room service; babysitting; laundry service; dry cleaning; nonsmoking rooms. *In room:* A/C, TV, minibar, hair dryer, safe, Internet access (in some).

MODERATE

Catalonia Albioni ★★   Good for shopaholics, the Albioni, is situated halfway up the Portal de l'Angel with its shoulder-to-shoulder Spanish fashion stores like Zara and Mango; El Corte Inglés (Spain's major department store) at one end, boutiques and trinket shops the other. Housed in a former palace dating back to 1876, it was converted into a hotel in 1998. It remains on Barcelona's artistic heritage list and many of the original romantic and baroque features have been beautifully preserved. Not least is the imposing marble lobby and stately interior courtyard where the bar and reception area are located. All 74 of the plush bedrooms have polished wood floors, comfortable beds and en-suite marble bathrooms with tub/shower combos. Breakfast (though overpriced) is served in a wedding-style tent.

Av. Portal de l'Angel 17, Barri Gòtic. 08002 Barcelona. (C) **93-318-41-41**. Fax 93-301-26-31. www.hoteles-catalonia.es. 74 units. 121€–172€ ($139–$198) double. AE, DC, MC, V. Public parking nearby 20€ ($23). Metro: Catalunya. **Amenities:** Cafeteria; car rental; limited room service; babysitting; laundry service; dry cleaning; computers w/Internet. *In room:* A/C, TV, minibar, hair dryer, safe.

Duques de Bergara ★★   This upscale hotel occupies an 1898 town house built for the Duke of Bergara by the architect Emilio Salas y Cortés (a protégée of Gaudí). Lots of elegant *modernista* touches remain including the original wood-molded ceiling with rose dome on the first floor, and a handful of original artworks from the era. In the reception area, look for stained-glass panels displaying the heraldic coat of arms of the building's original occupant and namesake, the Duke of Bergara. In 1998 the original five-story structure more than doubled in size with the addition of a new seven-story tower. Guest rooms throughout have the same conservative, traditional comforts. Each unit has large, comfortable beds with first-rate mattresses, elegant fabrics, and good lighting. The roomy marble bathrooms are equipped with tub/shower combos.

Bergara 11, 08002 Barcelona. (C) **93-301-51-51**. Fax 93-317-34-42. www.hoteles-catalonia.es. 149 units. 171€–235€ ($197-$270) double; 201€–259€ ($231–$298) triple. AE, DC, MC, V. Public parking nearby 18€ ($21). Metro: Catalunya. **Amenities:** Restaurant; cafe/bar; outdoor pool; limited room service; laundry service; dry cleaning; Internet access. *In room:* A/C, TV, minibar, hair dryer, safe.

Hotel Barcino ★ *(Finds)*   For reasons unknown, this smart four-star a stones throw from the Plaza Jaume I, home to Barcelona's regional government and town hall, rarely gets mention in the guide books and yet it must be one of the best located higher-end hotels in town. Everything is a short stroll away, including some of the best spots for tapas (**Taller de Tapas;** p. 118), contemporary Catalan fare (**Café de l'Academia;** p. 108), and cocktails (**Ginger;** p. 207). Staff is courteous and pleasant, bedrooms are classically decorated and all have en suite bathrooms with tub/shower combos. The best rooms have whirlpool baths (big enough for sharing) and private terraces with views over the rooftops and the cathedral, perfect for a predinner drink. They offer a rather expensive buffet breakfast at 14€ ($16). However, there are numerous local cafes serving fresh coffee and pastries a stone's throw from the front door. All in all, a good choice if you want to be at the center of the action.

Jaume I no. 6, Barri Gòtic, 08002 Barcelona. ℂ **93-302-20-12.** Fax 93-301-42-42. www.hotelbarcino.com. 53 units. 216€ ($248) double. AE, DC, MC, V. Public parking nearby 15€ ($17). Metro: Jaume I or Catalunya. **Amenities:** Restaurant; cafe/bar; limited room service; babysitting; laundry service. *In room:* A/C, TV, minibar, hair dryer, safe, Internet access.

Hotel Gravina *(Value)*   Part of the reliable H10 chain, the Gravina is a three-star hotel on a quiet street close to the university. This means it's handy for public transport, sights and shopping, but far enough removed from the main tourist drag to offer some breathing space from the bustle of the Ciutat Vella. The 19th-century facade promises great things to come, but don't get too excited. The interior has been built around the standard H10 model and therefore lacks any real atmosphere. That said, it's good value with friendly, accommodating staff and comfortable, fully equipped bedrooms. It's worth specifying that you want a larger room. Otherwise all have soundproofed windows and en suite bathrooms with tub/shower combos. This is an especially good choice for business travelers on a budget.

Gravina 12, 08001 Barcelona. ℂ **93-301-68-68.** Fax 93-317-28-38 www.hotel-gravina.com. 82 units. 130€–185€ ($150–$213) double; 185€–325€ ($213–$374) suite. AE, DC, MC, V. Public parking nearby 23€ ($26). Metro: Universitat or Catalunya. **Amenities:** Restaurant; cafe/bar; limited room service; laundry service; dry cleaning; nonsmoking rooms, Internet access. *In room:* A/C, TV, minibar, hair dryer, safe.

Hotel Neri ★★★ *(Moments)*   The Barri Gòtic has been crying out for its own boutique hotel for a long time and finally it has one. A gothic palace tucked neatly away on the delightful Plaça Felip Neri near the cathedral. It is fast gaining a reputation as one of the most romantic places in the city with its velvet drapes and soft lit, echoing hallways. Bedrooms are plush with high-thread-count cotton sheets, shot-silk pillowcases, throws and rugs. The minibar has all the usual tipples plus incense and candles and some rooms have a tub as well as a shower. It has just two suites (one of which was occupied by John Malkovich for a month while his play *Hysteria* was done at a local theater), for those who need more space. Space is of the essence in the cramped Barri Gòtic and the Neri has the added advantage of a terrace for coffee and cocktails on the plaza and a rooftop garden overgrown with jasmine plants and creepers. It's a shame they've felt the need to cram in sun loungers and it can feel a bit like a public pool when the place is busy. The somewhat overpriced gourmet "new Catalan cuisine" restaurant here is a further boon to followers of the super chef Ferran Adrià.

Sant Sever 5, Barri Gòtic, 08002 Barcelona. ℂ **93-304-06-55.** Fax 93-304-03-37. www.hotelneri.com. 22 units. 170€–183€ ($196–$210) double; 194€–214€ ($223–$246) suite. AE, DC, MC, V. Public parking nearby 20€ ($23). Metro: Jaume I or Liceu. **Amenities:** Restaurant; cafe/bar; limited room service; babysitting service; laundry service; dry cleaning; nonsmoking rooms; book/CD library. *In room:* A/C, TV, minibar, hair dryer, safe, Internet access.

Hotel Nouvel *(Moments)*   A smart, atmospheric hotel with plenty of its original *modernista* flourishes, the Nouvel makes a charming retreat in the heart of the Old City. It's wonderful for lovers of the Art Deco style with many of the original carved wood panels, smoked glass partitions and elaborate floor tiles. The bedrooms offer a mix of newly renovated accommodations though the rooms with the most character are the more old-fashioned kind with the original tiles. All have newly modernized bathrooms with tub/shower combos. The best have balconies and it's worth asking for a room at the rear if street noise bothers you.

Santa Ana 20, Barri Gòtic, 08002 Barcelona. ℂ **93-301-82-74.** Fax 93-301-83-70. www.hotelnouvel.com. 54 units. 160€ ($184) double. Rate includes breakfast. MC, V. Public parking nearby 22€ ($25). Metro: Catalunya. **Amenities:** Restaurant (lunch daily, dinner Thurs–Sat); babysitting; laundry service; dry cleaning; nonsmoking rooms. *In room:* A/C, TV, minibar, safe in some rooms, Internet access.

Hotel Regencia Colón *Value*   This stately six-story stone building stands directly behind the pricier Hotel Colón and in the shadow of the cathedral. The Regencia Colón attracts tour groups because it's a good value for Barcelona. The formal lobby seems a bit dour, but the well-maintained rooms are comfortable and often roomy, albeit worn at the edges. Rooms are insulated against sound, and 40 have full bathrooms with tubs (the remainder have showers only). All have comfortable beds and piped-in music. The hotel's main draw is its location.

Sagristans 13–17, 08002 Barcelona. ✆ **93-318-98-58.** Fax 93-317-28-22. www.hotelregenciacolon.com. 50 units. 148€ ($170) double; 175€ ($201) triple. AE, DC, MC, V. Public parking 18€ ($21). Metro: Catalunya or Urquinaona. **Amenities:** Restaurant; bar; car rental; babysitting; laundry service; dry cleaning. *In room:* A/C, TV, minibar, hair dryer, safe, Internet access.

Hotel Royal *Value*   The flat-packed front of this hotel with its glassed-in balconies looks rather like an office block compared to the more lavish architecture of the city, but don't let that put you off. Its newness is an asset and recent refurbishments mean it's more comfortable than ever, offering spacious rooms with comfortable beds and furnishings and modern facilities. All have en suite bathrooms with tub/shower combos and the best bedrooms have balconies offering fabulous views over Barcelona's real-life street theatre: the Ramblas.

Ramblas 117, Barri Gòtic, 08002 Barcelona. ✆ **93-304-12-12.** Fax 93-317-31-79. www.hroyal.com. 108 units. 145€–215€ ($167–$247) double. AE, DC, MC, V. Parking 13€ ($15). Metro: Catalunya. **Amenities:** Restaurant; cafe/bar; business center; room service (7am–midnight); babysitting service; laundry service; dry cleaning; nonsmoking rooms. *In room:* A/C, TV, minibar, hair dryer, safe.

Hotel San Agustí   This is arguably the most upmarket hotel in El Raval (though that is likely to change as the neighborhood continues to undergo its gentrification). This tastefully renovated five-story hotel stands in the center of the Old City on a pretty square, near the Boqueria market and overlooking the brick walls of an unfinished Romanesque church. The small guest rooms are comfortable and modern with tiled bathrooms with tub/shower combos. The outdoor cafe is a good place to chill on a hot afternoon and the immediate vicinity full of the funky character that is making El Ravel the current Barcelona hot spot. Some units are equipped for travelers with disabilities.

Plaça de San Agustí 3, El Raval, 08001 Barcelona. ✆ **93-318-16-58.** Fax 93-317-29-28. 76 units. www. hotelsa.com. 95€–140€ ($109–$161) double; 158€–174€ ($182–$210) triple; 174€–183€ ($200–210) quad; 220€–231€ ($253–$266) 2-bedroom family unit. Rates include breakfast. AE, DC, MC, V. Metro: Liceu. **Amenities:** Restaurant; lounge; room service (morning only); laundry service; free Internet. *In room:* A/C, TV, hair dryer, safe, Internet access.

H10 Raco Del Pi ☆   Locations don't get much better than right next to the Old City's prettiest plaza, bustling most days with pavement cafes, weekend produce markets, buskers, and artists. The hotel itself has plenty of character, is small and intimate with helpful staff and some nice touches like serving a glass of *cava* (sparkling wine) to guests on arrival. They also serve a good breakfast buffet offering a range of homemade products. The rooms themselves however can seem a little small and dark (the disadvantage of staying in the Barri Gòtic), but it is very cozy and seems a small price for such a desirable spot in the center of town. All have en suite mosaic tiled bathrooms with tub/shower combos.

Del Pi 7, Barri Gòtic, 08002 Barcelona. ✆ **93-342-61-90.** Fax 93-342-61-91. www.hotelracodelpi.com. 37 units. 165€ ($190) double. AE, DC, MC, V. Public parking nearby 20€ ($23). Metro: Liceu. **Amenities:** Restaurant; cafe/bar; car rental, business center, limited room service; laundry service; dry cleaning; nonsmoking rooms. *In room:* A/C, TV, minibar, hair dryer, safe, Internet access, scale.

HUSA Oriente   Right on the bustling Rambles, this hotel, a government-rated, three-star, was once one of the original "grand hotels" of Barcelona. On the site of a Franciscan monastery, the hotel dates from 1842. It was so prominent in its day that it attracted the likes of Toscanini and Maria Callas. It became part of Hollywood legend when Errol Flynn checked in. He got so drunk he passed out in the bar. The manager ordered two bartenders to carry him upstairs where they were instructed to strip the swashbuckling star. The manager then sent word to guests down below that they could see the star in the nude. They filed in one by one for the viewing all night. When Flynn woke up with a hangover the next morning, he was none the wiser. Renovations have improved the hotel but it lacks the character of its former glory, today attracting mainly frugal travelers. The arched ballroom of yesterday has been turned into an atmospheric lounge, and the dining room still has a certain grandeur. Each simple but comfortable room has a tiled bathroom with shower.

Rambles 45, 08002 Barcelona. ✆ 93-302-25-58. Fax 93-412-38-19. www.husa.es. 142 units. 160€ ($184) double; 180€ ($207) triple. AE, DC, MC, V. Metro: Liceu. **Amenities:** Restaurant (summer only); bar; laundry service. *In room:* A/C, TV, safe.

Mesón Castilla 🐾 *Value*   This government-rated two-star hotel, a former apartment building, has a Castilian facade with a wealth of Art Nouveau detailing on the interior. Indeed, this antiques stuffed hotel is one of the best in town for atmosphere and quirky trinkets to admire. Owned and operated by the Spanish hotel chain HUSA, it is handily located for the hip second-hand stores and record shops of the upper Raval, the MACBA and the CCCB. The midsize rooms are comfortable—beds have ornate Catalan-style headboards—and some open onto large terraces. The tiled bathrooms are equipped with tub/shower combos.

Valldoncella 5, 08001 Barcelona. ✆ 93-318-21-82. Fax 93-412-40-20. hmesoncastilla@teleline.es. 57 units. 122€ ($140) double; 160€ ($184) triple. Rates include breakfast. AE, DC, MC, V. Parking 20€ ($23). Metro: Catalunya or Universitat. **Amenities:** Breakfast room; lounge; room service; babysitting; laundry service; dry cleaning, safe. *In room:* A/C, TV, minibar, hair dryer.

Montecarlo ★★★   The fabulously ornate facade of this Ramblas hotel dates back 200 years to the days when it was an opulent private home and the headquarters of the Royal Artistic Circle of Barcelona. Public areas include some of the building's original accessories, with carved doors, a baronial fireplace, and crystal chandeliers. In the 1930s, it was transformed into the comfortably unpretentious three-star hotel you'll find today and has an excellent reputation verging on the legendary among past guests. It offers a level of comfort superior to that of most competitors. Each of the midsize guest rooms is smartly decorated, with extras that make the difference, such as adjustable beds, large marble bathrooms with Jacuzzi tubs, bathrobes, and slippers. The service is likewise exemplary where nothing is too much trouble from booking winery visits to parking your car.

Les Ramblas 124, 08002 Barcelona. ✆ 93-412-04-04. Fax 93-318-73-23. www.montecarlobcn.com. 55 units. 144€–310€ ($166–$357) double; 384€ ($441) suite. AE, DC, MC, V. Parking 18€ ($21). Metro: Catalunya. **Amenities:** Lounge; bar; limited room service; babysitting; laundry service; dry cleaning; terrace solarium; free Internet. *In room:* A/C, TV, minibar, hair dryer, safe, Internet access.

NH Duc de la Victoria *Value*   Part of the NH Hotel Chain which aims to provide smooth, seamless comfort mid-price accommodations, this smart hotel is well situated on a quiet street in the heart of the Barri Gòtic and makes a great base for exploring the center for those wishing for slightly more upscale accommodations than the standard Barri Gòtic *hostales*. Spotlessly clean throughout, it doesn't have much in the way of communal facilities aside from a breakfast room, but given its location, this hardly matters. Bedrooms are of a decent size with cool parquet floors and all have compact bathrooms with tub/shower combos. Fifth floor rooms with private balconies are the best.

Duc de la Victoria 15, Barri Gòtic, 08002 Barcelona. ℂ **93-270-34-10.** Fax 93-412-77-47. www.nh-hotels-spain.com. 156 units. 170€ double ($196); 236€ ($271) suite. AE, DC, MC, V. Public parking nearby 15€ ($17). Metro: Catalunya. **Amenities:** Restaurant; cafe/bar; limited room service; babysitting service; laundry service; dry cleaning; nonsmoking rooms. *In room:* A/C, TV, minibar, hair dryer, safe, Internet access.

Park Hotel 🏨 A laid-back hotel near the Estació de Franca, the edifice is a unique example of mid-20th-century rationalist architecture: the interior is dominated by a stunning, spiral staircase and the foyer by a sleek, mosaic tiled bar. It also boasts one of the best restaurants in the city, **Abac** (p. 105). Location-wise, it is right on the edge of El Born with numerous bars, restaurants and boutique clothing stores on the doorstep. The Parc de la Ciutadella (central Barcelona's greenest area) is just across the road, and a 10-minute walk will get you to the beach in Barceloneta: All major points in its favor. Bedrooms are stylish (if not slightly small) and comfortably decorated in warm colors and tastefully chosen furnishings. All have en suite bathrooms with tub/shower combos. *Note:* There've been reports of visitors having their luggage stolen on their way in. Take care with your luggage from the taxi to the front door.

Av. Marquès de l'Argentera 11, Born, 08003 Barcelona. ℂ **93-319-60-00.** Fax 93-319-45-19. www.park hotelbarcelona.com. 91 units. 100€–170€ ($115–$196) double. AE, DC, MC, V. Parking 12€ ($14). Metro: Barceloneta or Jaume I. **Amenities:** Restaurant; lounge; limited room service; laundry service; dry cleaning; nonsmoking rooms. *In room:* A/C, TV, minibar, hair dryer, safe, Internet access.

INEXPENSIVE

Gat Raval 🏨🏨 *(Value)* From grim and grungy to green and groovy, the Gat Raval is the first in this extraordinary little chain's mini-empire and has been pioneering in giving *hostal* accommodations a much-needed face-lift. The Gats (Catalan for "cats") are so feverishly cool, that even hipsters who would normally stay at places like the Omm and the Prestige are checking in, and saving themselves a few euros while they're at it. Decorated in bright acid greens with matt black trim, Internet connections in the lobby and neat bedrooms decorated with original works from the local art school give it an upbeat Boho vibe. Only some of the bedrooms have en suite bathrooms (stipulate when booking) and communal arrangements are so clean you could eat your dinner off the floor.

Joaquín Costa 44, 2ª, 08001, Barcelona. ℂ **93-481-66-70.** Fax 93-342-66-97. www.gataccommodation.com. 24 units. 48€ ($55) double with washbasin; 60€ ($69) double with bathroom. MC, V. Metro: Universitat. **Amenities:** Safe; Internet service. *In room:* TV.

Gat Xino 🏨🏨 *(Finds)* Those wishing to experience the same Gat über-coolness with a dash more luxury, can opt instead for the Gat Xino, opened during the second half of 2004 for a slightly more grown-up and affluent visitor. This hip new guesthouse has a sleek breakfast room that gives to a wood-decked terrace and there's a roof terrace for soaking up the rays. All of the rooms have their own, apple green bathrooms with showers and there are a few added extras like flat screen TVs and light boxes above the bedsteads giving abstract photographic views of the city. It's all terribly cool and at just 80€ ($92) a night for a double, affordable enough to make it a regular.

Hospital 149–155, 08001, Barcelona. ℂ **93-324-88-33.** Fax 93-324-88-34. www.gataccomodation.com. 35 units. 80€ ($92) double. Rate includes breakfast. MC, V. Metro: Liceu. **Amenities:** Safe (2€/$2.30 per day); Internet service. *In room:* A/C, TV.

Hostal Opera *(Value)*   Cheap and cheerful, this safe, well-maintained hostal is good for those traveling on a tight budget or alone. Make no mistake, this is basic, no-frills accommodations, the walls are thin (light sleepers might do well to travel with earplugs) and there are no luxuries, but for all that, it's a pleasant little place with a young, upbeat personality. Some rooms are better than others however, and if you arrive without a reservation, ask to look around first. Otherwise, opt for something at the back with a private bathroom (shower only) as the street outside can be noisy until the early hours.

Sant Pau 20, El Raval, 08001 Barcelona. ☎ **93-318-8201.** www.hostalopera.com. 69 units. 58€ ($67) double. MC, V. Metro: Liceu. **Amenities:** Safe; Internet service. *In room:* A/C, phone to receive calls.

Hostal Orleans *(Value)*   Just across the street from Barcelona's prettiest church, Santa María del Mar, this must be one of the most desirable locations in the city so it's a bonus to find something so affordable though it's by no means the smartest option in town. Some of the rooms have been redecorated recently and if this is something that matters to you it's worth asking for a newer one. Otherwise, though spotlessly clean, the Hostal Orleans is filled with objects and color schemes that were last seen in the 1970s. Bedrooms are for the most part small, but the beds are comfortable and all have private bathrooms (also small) with just enough room for a half-sized bath and shower. The best have balconies on to the street, which is great for watching the world go by, not so good for a peaceful nights sleep. The communal sitting room is a nice touch, well stocked with English-language magazines, and a good place to meet other guests. Add to this friendly service, and a genuinely Catalan vibe and it's good value for the price.

Av. Marquès de l'Argentera, 13, 1st floor, El Born, 08003, Barcelona. ☎ **93-319-73-82.** Fax 93-319-22-19. www.hostalorleans.com. 27 units. 51€ ($59) double. MC, V. Metro: Barceloneta or Jaume I. **Amenities:** TV lounge. *In room:* 6€ ($7) supplement for A/C, TV.

Hostal Roma Reial   A good choice for youngsters who want to be out bar-hopping and clubbing long into the night and who don't mind a bit of background noise (the Plaza Reial is a magnet for budding songsters and partygoers unwilling to go home). If these things don't bother you, the Roma Reial is a bargain; friendly, cheap and all of the large rooms have their own bathroom (unusual for an *hostal* of this ilk).

Plaza Reial 11, Barri Gòtic, 08002 Barcelona. ☎ **93-302-03-66.** Fax 93-301-18-39. hotelromareial@ hotmail.com. 61 units. 70€ ($81) double. Rates include breakfast, depending on season. MC, V. Metro: Liceu. **Amenities:** Cafeteria; safe. *In room:* A/C, TV.

Hotel Banys Orientals *(★★ Finds)*   There may not be a pool, gym or minibar in sight, but that hasn't stopped the runaway success of this pioneer boutique hostelry. The reason? Location. The Banys Orientals is the only notable hotel in the El Born district, Barcelona's present haven of hip and party precinct. Set in a 19th-century mansion, the spacious rooms have been relieved of their original adornment and given a soothing, sophisticated make-over that would not be out of place in a hotel four times its room-rate. Also unusual is the fact that the edifice is shared with **Senyor Parellada,** a classic Barcelonese eatery that now partly acts as the hotel's own: a buffet breakfast is served on its mezzanine and guests can run up a tab for lunch/evening meals as well. The catch for all this is the noise factor. The sound of human revelry from the pedestrianized street below reaches a crescendo during the summer months, although this can often be avoided by asking for a room at the back. Of course those who want to be in the thick of it will love having the city's coolest shops and bars right on their doorstep and will possibly be partaking in the nocturnal street activity themselves. Most of the showers are spacious and walk-in; if you really want a bathtub, stipulate at time of booking.

Argenteria 37, 08003 (La Ribera) Barcelona. ✆ **93-268-84-60.** Fax 93-268-84-61. www.hotelbanysorientals. com. 43 units. 95€ ($109) double. AE, DC, MC, V. Public parking nearby 18€ ($21). Metro: Jaume I. **Amenities:** Restaurant; limited room service; laundry service; nonsmoking rooms; free minibar for refreshments. *In room:* A/C, TV, hair dryer, safe, Internet access.

Hotel Cortés   A short walk from the cathedral, the Cortés dates from 1910 and was, like many of its competitors, thoroughly renovated in time for the 1992 Olympics; since then it has been improved again. It competes effectively with the Continental. Midsize to small guest rooms are scattered over five floors. About half overlook a quiet central courtyard, the other half open onto the street. All have private bathrooms, most of which contain tub/shower combos.

Santa Ana 25, Barri Gòtic, 08002 Barcelona. ✆ **93-317-91-12.** Fax 93-412-66-08. 44 units. 103€ ($118) double. Rate includes breakfast. AE, DC, MC, V. Metro: Catalunya. **Amenities:** Restaurant; bar; limited room service; laundry service. *In room:* A/C, TV, safe.

Hotel España *Value*   Although the rooms themselves at this cost-conscious hotel have none of the architectural *modernista* grandeur that characterizes the foyer and splendidly elegant dining room, they're well scrubbed, comfortably sized, and outfitted with functional furniture and neatly kept bathrooms containing tub/shower combos. The building itself is a relic of the city's turn-of-the-20th-century splendor, as it was constructed in 1902 by fabled architect Doménech i Montaner, designer and architect of the Palau de la Música. It was once patronized by the likes of Salvador Dalí. There's an elevator for the building's four floors and a hardworking staff that's comfortable with non-Spanish-speaking visitors. The lower Rambla, near where this hotel sits, evokes either cultural fascination or indignation, depending on how urbanized you are, but overall, it's an acceptable, historically rich and well-managed choice at a relatively reasonable price.

Carrer Sant Pau 11, El Raval, 08001 Barcelona. ✆ **93-318-17-58.** Fax 93-317-11-34. www.hotelespanya.com. 60 units. 98€ ($113) double; 130€ ($150) triple. Rates include breakfast. AE, DC, MC, V. Metro: Liceu or Drassanes. **Amenities:** 3 restaurants. *In room:* A/C, TV, hair dryer, safe.

Hotel Peninsular *Value*   Just off Les Ramblas, this hotel in the Art Nouveau style is a welcoming haven for the budget traveler. Constructed within the shell of a monastery that had a passageway connecting it to Sant Agustí church, the hotel was thoroughly modernized in the early 1990s. Its use of wicker furnishings gives it a colonial air, and its inner courtyard, lined with plants, is its most attractive grace note. In the typical *modernista* style of its era, the Peninsular still has long hallways and high doorways and ceilings. The bedrooms are basic but clean, and the better ones have en suite bathrooms with shower.

Sant Pau 34–36, El Raval, 08001 Barcelona. ✆ **93-302-31-38.** Fax 93-412-36-99. 80 units. 70€ ($81) double; 85€ ($98) triple. Rates include breakfast. MC, V. Metro: Liceu. **Amenities:** Breakfast bar; safe. *In room:* A/C.

Jardí *Value*   Sought out for its location, this little hotel opens onto the tree-shaded Plaça Sant Josep Oriol with its many cafes and the severe Gothic architecture of the medieval church of Santa María del Pi. The building in the heart of Barcelona's Gothic quarter rests on ancient Roman foundations. The five-floor hotel has recently been upgraded and improved, with the installation of an elevator, though many complain that the lighting is over-bright. In the modernization effort, much of the original architectural charm was maintained, and although the rooms themselves are somewhat austere they are comfortable enough with bathrooms with tub and with shower. The quieter units are on top, of course. Five of the accommodations have private terraces, and 26 of them have small balconies. Under separate management, **Bar del Pi,** on the ground floor, is a favorite of artists and students who live nearby

Plaça Sant Josep Oriol 1, 08002 Barcelona. ℭ **93-301-59-00.** Fax 93-342-57-33. hoteljardi@retemail.es. 40 units. 78€–83€ ($90–$95) double; 93€ ($107) triple. MC, V. Metro: Liceu. *In room:* A/C, TV, safe.

7 Balconies ✺ *Finds*   This charmingly old-fashioned three-room guesthouse has been in Natalia's family for over a century and has a snug and inviting feel to it that makes you feel instantly at home. Don't expect any mod cons, rather, a pristinely kept family home filled with heavy antique furniture, faded Art Deco tiling, black and white family photos and crisp, cotton bed linens. The suite has two rooms (one of which has a sofa bed) and the other two share a bathroom. Few places beat it when it comes to atmosphere.

Cervantes 7, Barri Gòtic, 08002 Barcelona. ℭ **65-423-81-61.** Fax 93-302-07-52. www.7balconies.com. 3 units. 75€–110€ ($86–$127). MC, V for room deposit only. Room payment in cash only. Parking nearby 20€ ($23). Metro: Liceu or Jaume I. **Amenities:** Tearoom. *In room:* TV, fridge, safe.

2 L'Eixample

If *modernista* architecture, designer shopping, and high-class restaurants are your bag, then the Eixample (*extension* in Catalan) is the place to be. The area was built in the mid–19th century to cope with the overflow of the Ciudad Vella and has retained its middle-class, residential flavor.

VERY EXPENSIVE

Avenida Palace ✺✺   In an enviable 19th-century neighborhood filled with elegant shops and apartment buildings, this hotel is behind a pair of mock-fortified towers. Despite its relative modernity (it dates from 1952), it evokes an old world sense of charm, partly because of the attentive staff, scattering of flowers and antiques, and 1950s-era accessories that fill its public rooms. The Beatles stayed here after their summer concert in 1965 in the master suite. The more standard rooms are solidly traditional and quiet, with some set aside for nonsmokers. The soundproofed rooms range from midsize to spacious, with comfortable beds, and mostly wood furnishings. Bathrooms are well equipped, with dual basins, tub/shower combos, and heat lamps.

Gran Vía de les Corts Catalanes 605 (at Passeig de Gràcia), 08007 Barcelona. ℭ **93-301-96-00.** Fax 93-318-12-34. www.avenidapalace.com. 160 units. 205€–235€ ($236–$270) double; 314€ ($361) suite. AE, DC, MC, V. Parking 16€ ($18). Metro: Passeig de Gràcia. **Amenities:** 2 restaurants; bar; salon; room service (7am–11pm); babysitting; laundry service; dry cleaning; currency exchange. *In room:* A/C, TV, minibar, hair dryer, safe.

Hotel Casa Fuster ✺✺✺ *Moments*   The Casa Fuster is one of the city's most emblematic *modernista* buildings. In the early 20th century it served as private home for the Fuster family, before being bought by a state electricity company in 1960. Recently acquired by the Spanish hoteliers the Center Group, who invested 68 million euros ($78.2 million) in its ambitious face-lift, the Casa Fuster is now classified as a five star deluxe hotel. The result is a combination of sheer luxury and state of the art amenities. The renovation has been meticulous in the foyer and downstairs Vienna café, once a well-known meeting spot for the city's intelligentsia. A Belle Epoque color scheme in mauve, taupe and magenta has been adopted in the rooms, many with balconies that look onto the elegant Passeig de Gràcia. In keeping with the period architecture, drapery, cushions and padding are abundant, giving the hotel a slightly over-stuffed feel for many-a-taste. But if its out and out indulgence you are after, plus a chance to live like

L'Eixample Accommodations

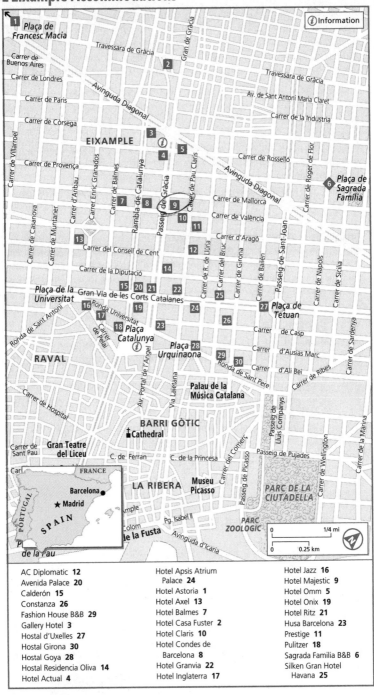

AC Diplomatic **12**
Avenida Palace **20**
Calderón **15**
Constanza **26**
Fashion House B&B **29**
Gallery Hotel **3**
Hostal d'Uxelles **27**
Hostal Girona **30**
Hostal Goya **28**
Hostal Residencia Oliva **14**
Hotel Actual **4**

Hotel Apsis Atrium
  Palace **24**
Hotel Astoria **1**
Hotel Axel **13**
Hotel Balmes **7**
Hotel Casa Fuster **2**
Hotel Claris **10**
Hotel Condes de
  Barcelona **8**
Hotel Granvia **22**
Hotel Inglaterra **17**

Hotel Jazz **16**
Hotel Majestic **9**
Hotel Omm **5**
Hotel Onix **19**
Hotel Ritz **21**
Husa Barcelona **23**
Prestige **11**
Pulitzer **18**
Sagrada Familia B&B **6**
Silken Gran Hotel
  Havana **25**

the turn-of-the-century bourgeoisie, the Casa Fuster offers everything you could possibly desire; from Loewe toiletries to hydro-massage baths and an extremely high staff to guest ratio. Unlike other five star hotels such as the Arts (p. 96) or La Florida (p. 100) the Casa Fuster also has the added advantage of being located in the city center, with some of the best shopping and sightseeing on its doorstep. Opened in June 2004, this is a relatively new hotel, so check their website for special deals.

Passeig de Gràcia 132, 08008 Barcelona. ℂ **90-220-23-45** for reservations, or 93-255-30-00. Fax 93-255-30-02. www.hotelescenter.es/casafuster. 105 units. 360€–450€ ($414–$518) double; 520€–1,750€ ($598–$2,013) suite. AE, DC, MC, V. Valet parking 25€ ($29). Metro: Diagonal. **Amenities:** Restaurant; bar; 11 lounges; pool; health center; Jacuzzi; sauna; solarium, business center; 24-hr. room service; babysitting service; laundry service; dry cleaning; nonsmoking rooms; free newspaper service; audiovisual equipment service. *In room:* A/C, TV, minibar, hair dryer, safe, Internet access.

Hotel Claris ✦✦✦

One of the most unusual hotels in Barcelona, this postmodern lodging is one of the few government-rated five-star deluxe properties in the city center. It incorporates vast quantities of teak, marble, steel, and glass behind the historically important facade of a landmark 19th-century building (the Verdruna Palace). Many hail the Claris as the city's top choice, the only criticism being that the bathrooms can seem poky. Opened in 1992 (in time for the Olympics), it's a seven-story structure with a swimming pool and garden on its roof. There's a small museum of Egyptian antiquities from the owner's collection on the second floor. The blue-violet guest rooms contain state-of-the-art electronic accessories as well as unusual art objects—Turkish kilims, English antiques, Hindu sculptures, Egyptian stone carvings, and engravings. The spacious rooms are among the most opulent in town, with wood marquetry and paneling, custom furnishings, safes, and some of the city's most sumptuous beds. Bathrooms are roomy and filled with deluxe toiletries, and tub/shower combos. If money is no object, book one of the 20 individually designed duplex units.

Pau Claris 150, 08009 Barcelona. ℂ **90-099 00-11** in the U.S., or 93-487-62-62. Fax 93-215-79-70. www. derbyhotels.com. 120 units. 270€–383€ ($311–$441) double; 452€ ($520) suite. AE, DC, MC, V. Self/valet parking 19€ ($22). Metro: Passeig de Gràcia. **Amenities:** 2 restaurants; 2 bars; outdoor pool; fitness center; sauna; business center; limited room service; babysitting; laundry service; dry cleaning; nonsmoking rooms; private museum. *In room:* A/C, TV, minibar, hair dryer, safe, Internet access.

Hotel Condes de Barcelona ✦

Off the architecturally splendid Passeig de Gràcia, this government-rated four-star hotel, originally a private villa (1895), is one of Barcelona's most glamorous. Business was so good it opened a 74-room extension across the street **(Carrer Majorca),** which regrettably lacks the flair of the original. It boasts a unique neo-medieval facade, influenced by Gaudí and recent refurbishments mean it is now possible to have supper on the roof with a live jazz accompaniment. All the comfortable midsize guest rooms contain marble bathrooms, with tub/shower combos, reproductions of Spanish paintings, and soundproofed windows. It continues to be one of the most popular choices in the Eixample.

Passeig de Gràcia 73–75, 08008 Barcelona. ℂ **93-488-22-00.** Fax 93-467-47-81. www.condesdebarcelona. com. 183 units. 150€–325€ ($173–$374) double; 485€ ($558) suite. AE, DC, MC, V. Parking 16€ ($18). Metro: Passeig de Gràcia. **Amenities:** Restaurant; cafe; bar; outdoor pool; business center; limited room service; babysitting; laundry service; dry cleaning; nonsmoking rooms. *In room:* A/C, TV, minibar, hair dryer, safe, Internet access.

Hotel Majestic ✦✦

This hotel is one of Barcelona's most visible landmarks and has been since the 1920s, when it was built in a sought-after location within a 10-minute walk from Plaça de Catalunya. In the early 1990s it was radically renovated and upgraded into five-star status while retaining the dignified state-liness of the public areas, but with an added sense of color and contemporary drama in the bedrooms. Today, each is outfitted in a different, usually mono-chromatic, color scheme, with carpets, artwork, and upholsteries. All units come equipped with bathrooms containing tub/shower combos. Staff is hardworking and conscientious, albeit sometimes swamped with tour buses containing dozens of clients arriving all at once. Its **Drolma** restaurant (p. 121) has a Michelin star.

Passeig de Gràcia 68, 08007 Barcelona. Ⓒ **93-488-17-17**. Fax 93-488-18-80. www.hotelmajestic.es. 303 units. 189€–350€ ($217–$403) double; 439€–600€ ($505–$690) suite. AE, DC, MC, V. Parking 15€ ($17). Metro: Passeig de Gràcia. **Amenities:** 2 restaurants; 2 bars; outdoor pool; fitness center; sauna; business cen-ter; limited room service; laundry service; dry cleaning; courtesy car for guests in suites and apts. *In room:* A/C, TV, minibar, hair dryer, safe, Internet access.

Hotel Omm ★★★   The current darling of the hotel scene is Hotel Omm. Since it opened in 2002, this is where rock stars and architects, actors and media types stay who find classic hotels such as the Ritz or the Majestic just a tad too passé. It is the first hostelry project from the Tragaluz group, Barcelona's most famous restaurateurs, so naturally the in-house restaurant **Moo** (p. 124) is first class and the foyer cocktail bar one of the hottest places around for a pre-dinner drink. Hype aside, the Omm is an outstanding example of intelligent, well-executed design. The striking "wafers of stone" facade has already become a landmark and the crème of the city's design talent was employed for the interior. In contrast to the dark, low-lit halls, the rooms are bathed in natural light and make an incredible use of their size. Predicting that most their guests would be heavy shoppers (and packers) non-intrusive cupboard and wardrobe space is ample. Most of it is built into a modular system that separates the bathroom from the sleeping area without forming a separate room, ensuring a continuous, flowing space rarely seen in urban hotel rooms. Add to that a color-scheme of steel gray and blue, a flat-screen TV, DVD, stereo, and every other state-of-the-art mod con you can think of and you have a hotel that is hard to beat in terms of sheer, streamlined comfort. The rooftop lap pool, with its view over the roof of Gaudí's La Pedrera and chic sun deck, is a privileged spot for to laze away languid Barcelonese evenings.

Rosselló 265, 08008 Barcelona. Ⓒ **93-445-40-00**. Fax 93-445-40-04. www.hotelomm.es. 59 units. 320€–375€ ($368–$431) double; 500€ ($575) suite. AE, DC, MC, V. Parking 22€ ($25). Metro: Diagonal. **Amenities:** Restaurant; cocktail bar; health center (to be installed at end of 2005); business center; room service; babysitting service; laundry service; dry cleaning; nonsmoking rooms. *In room:* A/C, TV, minibar, hair dryer, safe, Internet access.

Hotel Ritz ★★★   Acknowledged by many fans as the most prestigious, and most architecturally distinguished hotel in Barcelona, the Art Deco Ritz dates from 1919. Richly remodeled during the late 1980s, it has welcomed more mil-lionaires, famous people, and aristocrats (and their official and unofficial consorts) than any other hotel in northeastern Spain. One of the finest features is a cream-and-gilt neoclassical lobby, where afternoon tea is served to the strains of a string quartet. The sumptuous guest rooms are as formal, high-ceilinged, and richly fur-nished as you'd expect. Some have Regency furniture, bathrooms accented with mosaics, and showers with bathtubs inspired by those in ancient Rome. You get all the luxuries here: elegant fabrics, deluxe mattresses, and plush towels.

Gran Vía de les Corts Catalanes 668, 08010 Barcelona. Ⓒ **93-318-52-00**. Fax 93-318-01-48. www.ritzbcn.com. 122 units. 380€ ($437) double; from 475€ ($546) suite. AE, DC, MC, V. Parking 21€ ($24). Metro: Passeig de Gràcia. **Amenities:** 3 restaurants; bar; fitness center; car rental; 24-hr. business center; limited room service; babysitting; laundry service; dry cleaning. *In room:* A/C, TV, minibar, hair dryer, safe, Internet access.

Prestige ✦✦✦   Opened in May 2002 in a blaze of glory not dissimilar to a well received couture collection fresh off the catwalk, the Prestige is already well established on the scene of all that is hip and fabulous with some nice touches: the **Zeroom** breakfast bar and library for chilled out mornings—well you wouldn't get up for less, now would you darling? Unless of course you're taking coffee in the Oriental garden with its ivory sun loungers and bamboo planters. There's an "Ask Me" service—really a kind of human-genie-in-a-bottle who vow to hunt down any sort of information on the city you need to know, whether it be the opening hours of a museum or the nearest kosher restaurant. And the Japanese-inspired bedrooms are sleek and spacious with all the added extra's one could possibly need for a good nights sleep. No doubt about it, this is one hotel that takes its name very seriously indeed. The only thing it's lacking is a fancy restaurant with a celebrity chef at the helm.

Passeig de Gràcia 62, 08007 Barcelona. ✆ **93-272-41-80.** Fax 93-272-41-81. www.prestigepaseodegracia. com. 45 units. 185€–254€ ($213–$292) double; from 398€ ($458) suite. AE, DC, MC, V. Valet parking 1€ ($1.15) per hr. Metro: Diagonal. **Amenities:** Cafe/bar; lounge; health and beauty center; Jacuzzi; sauna; business center; 24-hr. room service; babysitting service; laundry service; dry cleaning; nonsmoking rooms; shoeshine; free newspaper service; private garden; Barcelona and music library; "Ask Me service." *In room:* A/C, TV, minibar, hair dryer, safe, Internet access.

Pulitzer ✦✦ *Finds*   Another newcomer to the Barcelona's designer hotel scene, this super-trendy four-star is spitting distance from the Plaça Catalunya. On the whole, hotels in this quarter tend to be of a more uniform, business ilk. Not so the Pulitzer, with its white leather sofas, black marble trim, lounge-area with floor-to-ceiling bookshelves lined with tomes such as *California Homes, Moroccan Interiors,* and *The World's Greatest Hotels.* There's also a chic cocktail bar—just the kind of place you might expect to find the *Sex and the City* ladies—a smart restaurant and a pleasant, candle-lit roof terrace. Bedrooms go after the inky-black and charcoal gray color scheme (some a little on the small side) and are big on sumptuous fabrics: leather, silk, down pillows and showy bathrooms with tub and shower combos that are generous with the toiletries.

Bergara 8, Eixample Esquerra, 08002 Barcelona. ✆ **93-481-67-67.** Fax 93-481-64-64. www.hotelpulitzer.es. 91 units. 145€–215€ ($167–$247) double. AE, DC, MC, V. Public parking nearby 22€ ($25). Metro: Catalunya. **Amenities:** Restaurant; cocktail bar; lounge; external health center; solarium; business center; 24-hr. room service; babysitting service; laundry service; dry cleaning; nonsmoking rooms; library. *In room:* A/C, TV, minibar, hair dryer, safe, Internet access.

Silken Gran Hotel Havana ✦   Opposite the Ritz, the Havana is a little less stuffy than its famous neighbor. It was completely refurbished in 1991 and retains an air of newness that fits pleasingly with the *modernista* architecture and design. The building itself dates back to 1872. In terms of service and quality of

---

(**Kids**) **Family-Friendly Hotels**

Hotel Colón (p. 73)   Opposite the cathedral in the Gothic Quarter, families ask for, and often get, spacious rooms.

Hotel Fira Palace (p. 93)   At the base of the city's most expansive green zone Montjuïc, areas for running wild are only a short distance away.

Citadines (p. 102)   An in-house kitchen and maid service take some of the hassle out of catering to little ones.

accommodations, it is pretty much as one would expect of a four-star hotel: spacious, well-equipped rooms, modern decor with vast, Italian marble bathrooms that have both walk-in shower and tub, and toiletries that are restocked on a daily basis. The best are the executive suites on the sixth floor, which have private terraces with stunning views. One thing to watch out for is rooms on the street; although theoretically soundproofed they can be a little noisy for light-sleepers. The roof-top pool and sun terrace are an added bonus.

Gran Vía de les Corts Catalanes 647, Eixample Dreta, 08010 Barcelona. © **93-412-11-15**. Fax 93-412-26-11. www.silken-granhavana.com. 145 units. 185€ ($213) double; 200€–350€ ($230–$403) suite. AE, DC, MC, V. Parking 17€ ($20). Metro: Passeig de Gràcia, Tetuan, or Girona. **Amenities:** Restaurant; bar; pool; business center; room service; babysitting service; laundry service; dry cleaning; nonsmoking rooms. *In room:* A/C, TV, minibar, hair dryer, safe, Internet access.

EXPENSIVE

Calderón   As business hotels go, the Calderón has two things in its favor. One: Location—it is situated right on the leafy promenade of Rambla de Catalunya with its pavement cafes and tapas bars, and is just minutes from the Barri Gòtic, so when you're not working, leisure time is never far away. Two: Size—it is huge, with plenty of amenities for those who need stay-at-home comforts with gargantuan, bright, airy bedrooms with all mod cons and spacious en suite bathrooms. As places of this ilk go, it offers good value for money.

Rambla de Catalunya 26, 08007 Barcelona. © **93-301-00-00**. Fax 93-412-41-93. www.nh-hotels.com. 253 units. 227€ ($261) double; 528€ ($607) suite. AE, DC, MC, V. Parking 16€ ($18). Metro: Catalunya. **Amenities:** Restaurant; bar; cafeteria; lounge; indoor/outdoor pool sauna; health center; solarium; business center; room service; babysitting service; laundry service; dry cleaning; nonsmoking rooms. *In room:* A/C, TV, minibar, hair dryer, safe, Internet access.

MODERATE

AC Diplomatic ✿   This top-end, glass-fronted, four-star oozes style considering it's predominantly a business hotel. Keeping one eye on its pleasing Zen-like design focus and another on the small details that make a difference, such as 24-hour laundry service, free minibar and nonsmoking rooms, these features alone make it stand out as a cut above most chain hotels. The restaurant also verges on the avant-garde offering a "Sanísimo" (low-fat) menu, rather than the usual steak and chips. Bedrooms are a good size and warmly decorated with wood paneling, parquet floors and a small sitting area. All have en suite bathrooms with shower and/or tub.

Pau Claris 122, 08009 Barcelona. © **93-272-38-10**. Fax 93-272-38-11 www.achoteldiplomatic.com. 211 units. 168€ ($193) double; 280€ ($322) suite. AE, DC, MC, V. Parking 20€ ($23). Metro: Passeig de Gràcia. **Amenities:** Restaurant; bar; lounge; outdoor pool; health center; sauna; limited room service; massage service; babysitting service; laundry service; dry cleaning; nonsmoking rooms; safe. *In room:* A/C, TV, minibar, hair dryer, Internet access.

Constanza ✿✿✿ *(Finds*   A smart boutique hotel with a young vibe located within easy walking distance of good shopping and La Ribera. It combines style with a fair amount of substance for its price range. True it doesn't have a rooftop plunge pool or city views, but it's smart and comfortable with an upbeat, trendy vibe. The lobby is filled with white boxy couches and red trim, and there is a minimalist breakfast room beyond decorated with a continually changing routine of flower prints. The first floor bedrooms are bright and fresh with clean lines and leather-trimmed furniture, throw cushions a-plenty and white, cotton sheets. All have en suite bathrooms with showers. Some are a little on the small side, and those at the front can be noisy, but if you can book a room with its own private terrace the place is a bargain. Note that in early 2005 the rooms will be undergoing renovation, so check for progress before you book.

Bruc 33, 08010 Barcelona. ℂ **93-270-19-10.** Fax 93-317-40-24. www.hotelconstanza.com. 20 units. 90€ ($104) double; 100€ ($115) suite; 120€ ($138) apt. AE, MC, V. Public parking nearby 20€ ($23). Metro: Urquinaona. **Amenities:** Health center; room service; laundry service; dry cleaning; safe. *In room:* A/C, TV, minibar, hair dryer, Internet access.

Gallery Hotel *★ Finds*   This is a winning, modern choice lying between the Passeig de Gràcia and Rambla de Catalunya. In business for a decade, it was completely remodeled in 2002. The name, Gallery, comes from its location close to a district of major art galleries. The stylishly decorated hotel lies in the upper district of the Eixample, just below the Diagonal. Bedrooms are midsize for the most part and tastefully furnished with pleasing touches such as fresh flowers by the bed and crisp bed linens. All have small, en suite bathrooms with tub and shower. The on-site **restaurant** is known for its savory Mediterranean cuisine.

Rosselló 249, 08008 Barcelona. ℂ **93-415-99-11.** Fax 93-415-91-84. www.galleryhotel.com. 115 units. 130€–272€ ($150–$313) double; 155€–319€ ($178–$367) suite. AE, DC, MC, V. Parking: 17€ ($20). Metro: Diagonal. **Amenities:** Restaurant; bar; sauna; fitness center; business center; room service; babysitting; laundry service; dry cleaning. *In room:* A/C, TV, minibar, hair dryer, safe; Internet access.

Hotel Actual *Value*   Situated opposite the achingly hip Omm Hotel (see above), it's no surprise that the Actual is somewhat overshadowed. But, you can save yourself a few euros by staying at this stylish three-star place rather than across the road, and of course you can still make use of the Omm's wonderful bar and restaurant. Small but perfectly formed wood paneling; brushed steel and large windows give it a light, airy feel with a designer edge. Bedrooms are simply but elegantly decorated with chocolate brown soft furnishings and plain white walls and bed linen, and all have compact bathrooms with tub/shower combos.

Rosselló 238, Eixample Esquerra, 08008 Barcelona. ℂ **93-552-05-50.** Fax 93-552-05-55. www.hotelactual. com. 29 units. 190€ ($219) double. AE, DC, MC, V. Public parking 22€ ($25). Metro: Diagonal. **Amenities:** Cafeteria; lounge; outdoor pool; room service; babysitting service; laundry service; dry cleaning; nonsmoking rooms. *In room:* A/C, TV, minibar, hair dryer, safe, Internet access.

Hotel Apsis Atrium Palace *★★★ Finds*   This fabulously modern designer hotel with its sleek lines and oatmeal marble prides itself on its high-tech facilities; Internet is plumbed in throughout the entire building for wireless access (they will even provide you with a Wi-Fi card if you don't have your own) in addition to offering several flat-screen monitors in the library-cum-business center filled with fat, squashy sofas and tea and coffee on tap. Photocopy machines, printers and a selection of international newspapers are also standard here. Indeed, the Atrium Palace is a brave new world when it comes to business facilities, all of which are free. The restaurant is softly lit with wave-rippled ceilings and the indoor swimming pool and Jacuzzi are surrounded by wood decking, which are very stylish and hugely welcome in winter months when even Barcelona gets chilly. Bedrooms are uncommonly spacious (28–32 sq. m/301–344 sq. ft. on average) with quilted throws and small sitting areas, and have added extras that make the world of difference; a free daily quota of mineral water and fruit juice for example. Bathrooms are marble with tub/shower combos. The top floor suites however go for maximum comfort; separate living room, two TVs, a private terrace with deck chairs, temperature controlled hot tub and views. It's a superb value for money and the perfect place to combine business and pleasure.

Gran Vía de les Corts Catalanes 656, Eixample Esquerra, 08010 Barcelona. ℂ **93-342-80-00.** Fax 93-342-80-01. www.hotel-atriumpalace.com. 71 units. 110€–240€ ($127–$276) double; 250€–300€ ($288–$345) suite. AE, DC, MC, V. Parking 22€ ($25). Metro: Passeig de Gràcia or Catalunya. **Amenities:** Restaurant; bar; pool; health center; business center; limited room service; babysitting service; laundry service; dry cleaning; nonsmoking rooms; Barcelona library. *In room:* A/C, TV, minibar, hair dryer, safe, Internet access.

Hotel Axel ✦✦✦ *(Moments)* What began as a hotel that targeted a metropolitan gay audience has become a hot spot for all style-savvy travelers. For now, the Axel is unique, though it's unlikely to be long before copycats jump on the bandwagon following its success. It's the details that make the difference and here you'll find that anything goes, providing it's hip and groovy: there's a cool, scarlet-colored cocktail bar and restaurant in the lobby, and check out Axel's very own men's designer clothing store next door if you should find yourself with nothing suitable to wear; there's free bottled mineral water in refrigerators on every floor, a rooftop pool and sundeck. All bedrooms are soundproofed and have king size beds (there's definitely an emphasis on quality bed time here) strewn with squashy pillows; the art is erotic and the sleek en suite bathrooms are designed for two with tub/shower combos (Jacuzzis in the superior rooms).

Aribau 33, Eixample Esquerra, 08011 Barcelona. ✆ **93-323-93-93**. Fax 93-323-93-94. www.hotelaxel.com. 66 units. 170€–215€ ($196–$247) double; from 300€ ($345) suite. AE, DC, MC, V. Parking 14€ ($16). Metro: Universitat. **Amenities:** Restaurant; bar; lounge; outdoor pool; solarium; health center; massage service; Jacuzzi; sauna; hammam (Arab-style bathhouse); limited room service; laundry service; dry cleaning; nonsmoking rooms; safe; library. *In room:* A/C, TV, minibar, hair dryer, Internet access.

Hotel Balmes Set in a seven-story structure built in the late 1980s, this chain hotel successfully combines conservative decor with modern accessories and well-trained and friendly staff. Bedrooms have a warm color scheme of rich terra cottas and sunset yellows to brighten an otherwise white interior, marble-trimmed bathrooms equipped with tub/shower combos and enough space to allow residents, many of whom are in town on business, to live and work comfortably. If you're looking for a maximum of peace and quiet, rooms at the back of the hotel overlook a small garden and swimming pool and are quieter and calmer than those facing the busy street.

Majorca 216, 08008 Barcelona. ✆ **93-451-19-14**. Fax 93-451-00-49. www.derbyhotels.es. 100 units. 142€–200€ ($163–$230) double; 185€–243€ ($213–$279) triple. AE, DC, MC, V. Parking 15€ ($17). Metro: Diagonal. **Amenities:** Restaurant; bar; outdoor pool; room service; laundry service; dry cleaning. *In room:* A/C, TV, minibar, hair dryer, safe.

Hotel Granvía The Granvía has seen better days, that's for sure, but nevertheless it retains a certain faded grandeur with its glittering chandeliers, marble lobby and sweeping staircase and has a good deal more character than the rather uniform four-star business hotels that have sprung up all over town. Arrive here and it's rather like stepping back in time to the Belle Epoque minus the ladies in bustle dresses and gents in top hat and tails. There is also a handsome communal terrace filled with potted plants. All in all, it's a great place to indulge your aristocratic European fantasies and the bedrooms though likewise a little jaded are stuffed with reproduction antiques and all have en suite bathrooms with tub/shower combos. It is best to avoid front facing rooms if traffic noise disturbs you. Ultimately this atmospheric hotel offers an experience rather than just a place to stay.

Gran Vía de les Corts Catalanes 642, Eixample Esquerra, 08011 Barcelona. ✆ **93-318-19-00**. Fax 93-318-99-97. www.nnhotels.es. 53 units. 115€–125€ ($132–$144) double. AE, DC, MC, V. Public parking nearby 20€ ($23). Metro: Catalunya. **Amenities:** Cafeteria; TV lounge; business center; room service; babysitting service; laundry service; dry cleaning; nonsmoking rooms; garden terrace. *In room:* A/C, TV, minibar, hair dryer, safe, Internet access.

Hotel Inglaterra *(Value)* Despite the name, this sleekly elegant hotel is Japanese-inspired in decor with minimalist, spacious rooms with private bathrooms with tub/shower combos. It was one of the first boutique hotels in town, and makes good use of communal space with comfortable living areas, a snazzy breakfast room and bar and a well-equipped roof terrace for sunbathing and reading. All in all, this is a quality, chilled-out hotel that is amazingly good value for money.

Pelayo 14, Eixample Esquerra, 08001 Barcelona. ✆ 93-505-11-00. Fax 93-505-11-09. www.hotel-inglaterra. com. 55 units. 180€ ($207) double. AE, DC, MC, V. Public parking nearby 23€ ($26). Metro: Catalunya or Universitat. **Amenities:** Restaurant; lounge; room service; laundry service; dry cleaning; safe. *In room:* A/C, TV, minibar, hair dryer, Internet access.

Hotel Onix ⟨Value⟩
Sleek and minimal the Onix Rambla Catalunya opened in 2003 with all the facilities of a more expensive hotel; a large sun terrace and roof-top plunge pool; a pleasant breakfast room and an on-site new-wave snack bar. Filled with discreet works of modern art it's a good choice for anyone who wants to stay in a designer hotel without paying designer prices. Bedrooms are tastefully decorated with natural materials; wood, leather and tiles and all have en suite bathrooms with tub/shower combos.

Rambla Catalunya 24, Eixample Esquerra, 08007 Barcelona. ✆ 93-342-79-80. Fax 93-342-51-52. www. hotelsonix.com. 40 units. 150€ ($173) double. AE, DC, MC, V. Metro: Passeig de Gràcia or Universitat. **Amenities:** Cafeteria; lounge; outdoor pool; health center; solarium; business center; room service; babysitting service; laundry service; dry cleaning; nonsmoking rooms. *In room:* A/C, TV, minibar, hair dryer, safe, Internet access.

HUSA Barcelona
Centrally located, modern and spacious the Husa is a good choice for anyone who just wants a comfortable, functional hotel. Bedrooms are well proportioned (the best have balconies) and all have full bathrooms with tub/ shower combo. Highlights include a rooftop solarium and parking within the building itself—something of a rarity in this city.

Casp 1, Eixample Dreta, 08010 Barcelona. ✆ 93-302-58-58. Fax 93-301-86-74. www.hotelhusabarcelona. com. 72 units. 204€ ($235) double; 280€ ($322) AE, DC, MC, V. Public parking nearby 20€ ($23). Metro: Catalunya. **Amenities:** Cafeteria; bar; TV lounge; solarium; room service; Internet service; laundry service; dry cleaning; nonsmoking rooms. *In room:* A/C, TV, video, minibar, hair dryer, safe.

Hotel Jazz
Calle Pelai has become something of an enclave of design-led hotels and though the Jazz sounds more exciting than it really is, it's nevertheless a slick little three-star in an area predominated by more pricey four-stars, and is just around the corner from Plaça Catalunya. So far so good. It gets better. The bleached wood floors and oatmeal paintwork may be a little generic, but there's nothing offensive about it and the rooms are spacious enough, all en suite and all soundproofed, a bonus on this busy stretch. The highlights however are on the roof, where you'll find a swimming pool and a wood deck terrace, which is more than neighboring four-stars can boast.

Pelai 3, 08001 Barcelona. ✆ 93-552-96-96, 0870-120-1521 (U.K.), or 207/580-2663 (U.S.) Fax 93-552-96-97. www.nnhotels.es. 180 units. 140€–190€ ($161–$219) double; 160€–200€ ($184–$230) suite. AE, DC, MC, V. Parking 19€ ($22) per day. Metro: Catalunya or Universitat. **Amenities:** Cafeteria; lounge; outdoor pool; solarium; business center; room service; babysitting service; laundry service; dry cleaning; nonsmoking rooms. *In room:* A/C, TV, minibar, hair dryer, safe, Internet access.

INEXPENSIVE

Fashion House B&B ⟨Finds⟩
Bed-and-breakfast accommodations are still a relatively new concept in Barcelona, offering good-value and comfortable accommodations for those who prefer a more homey atmosphere. The Fashion House is located in an elegantly restored 19th-century town house decorated with stuccoes and friezes adding an element of class to the overall feel of the place. Bedrooms share one bathroom for two rooms, and all are bright and nicely decorated with bright, pastel colors. The best have verandas. La Suite,

---

ⓘ Tips   Barcelona's Self-Catering Boom

New hotels, particularly in the three and four-star segment, are opening in Barcelona at an astonishing rate, with around 2000 more hotel rooms anticipated within the city between the end of 2004 and the end of 2007. This, despite the fact that during 2004 hotels experienced a slump in visitors checking in, with many opting to keep their prices the same, or even lower than the year before. One of the reasons for this, at least in part, is the trend for quality self-catering accommodations, which allows visitors greater flexibility and independence.

If you've ever been curious about the cute-looking apartments in the Old City with their curved-beamed ceilings and balconies brimming with ferns, or the tiled-entrance apartments with Art Nouveau facades in L'Eixample, now's your chance to get up close and personal. Wander around the Barri Gòtic these days, and many of the residential apartments you see are available for rent at reasonable prices by the day (normally a 3-day minimum) week or month, enabling visitors to get a taste of what its really like to live in the city; to shop in its markets, cook its food, and make merry over glasses of wine around the dinner table.

Google "self-catering accommodations Barcelona" and you'll come up with pages of options, from agencies specializing in holiday rentals to individuals who have bought to let, with something to suit every whim and budget. The array of apartments on offer range from small, practical studios for couples, to luxury apartments and penthouses for families or groups of friends.

If you're looking for something cultural and unconventional one of the most interesting of these is **La Casa de les Lletres (House of Letters; ⓒ 93-226-37-30; www.cru2001.com)**—a thematic collection of apartments that pay homage to writers like George Orwell and the Catalan journalist and food writer Josep Pla, who had a special relationship with the city—mixing state-of-the-art facilities with an intellectual Bohemian vibe. Poetry and prose are literally written on the

---

which doubles as a self-catering apartment, making it a good choice for families who need a little more space and has private access to the communal terrace which is well supplied with shaded tables and chairs and plenty of greenery. Breakfast is served here in the summer.

Bruc 13 Principal, 08010 Barcelona. ⓒ 63-790-40-44. Fax 93-301-09-38. www.bcn-fashionhouse.com. 8 units. 70€ ($81) double; 85€ ($98) double with balcony; 80€ ($92) triple; 100€ ($115) triple with balcony; 120€ ($138) suite. Rates include breakfast. 10€ ($12) supplement in high season. MC, V. Metro: Urquinaona. **Amenities:** Breakfast room. *In room:* A/C, TV (suite only), kitchenette (suite only).

Hostal d'Uxelles ⓐ *Finds*   Cute as a button this one, though it gets mixed reports in terms of the service and the occasionally unhelpful attitude of the staff. It's been recently refurbished and so all rooms are freshly painted and individually decorated with ornate Art Deco wood paneling in places and romantic flourishes such as cupids-bow drapes above the bed, which will not appeal to

walls. Situated in an elegant town house on the handsome Plaza Antonio López, the location couldn't be better, just minutes from Barceloneta and the Barri Gòtic.

More basic accommodations can be found at **www.nivellmar.com**, which offers seaside apartments—or at least those that are no more than 200m (600 ft.) from the beach—all the way from Barceloneta to Poble Nou. The places on their books tend to go after function rather than form, but are reasonably decorated, clean and fairly priced. They are ideal for young travelers, or those with young children, who just want to be close to the sea.

For character apartments that won't break the bank, check out **www.visit-bcn.com** which offers a wide range of different apartments from classic Barri Gòtic town houses, such as the lovely Dos Amigos, in the heart of the Old City with its gorgeous tiles, warm paintwork and small terrace, to minimalist loft-style apartments.

If it's luxury you're after, try **www.friendlyrentals.com** who offer chic, design-led properties at surprisingly good-value prices. Every place on their books is categorized for its artistic personality (for instance, Rembrandt, *modernista*, Impressionist, Romantic, or Art Deco) and is described and photographed in detail. Many have private terraces and/or swimming pools and work out considerably cheaper than a hotel in the same class.

Most self-catering apartments, whether booked through an agency or directly through the owner, require a deposit of one night and possibly a security deposit, both of which are paid via credit card or PayPal. Things to be on the lookout for include "hidden" costs such as cleaning and extra-person charges, although compared to hotels these apartments are extremely cost-effective, especially for longer stays. Don't forget that you are on your own—there is no concierge to help you find a drug store in the middle of the night, or direct you to the Picasso Museum.

those repelled by anything twee. All have their own individually tiled bathrooms with tub/shower combos. The best rooms come with their own balconies big enough to hold a table and two chairs.

Gran Vía de les Corts Catalanes 667 (Hostal 2) and 668 (Hostal 1), Eixample Dreta, 08010 Barcelona. ⓒ **93-265-25-60.** Fax 93-232-85-67. www.hotelduxelles.com. 30 units. 75€–90€ ($86–$104) double; 99€–112€ ($114–$129) triple; 135€–184€ ($155–$212) quadruple. AE, DC, MC, V. Parking nearby 18€ ($21). Metro: Tetuan or Girona. **Amenities:** TV lounge; room service; laundry service; safe. *In room:* TV.

Hotel Astoria ⓐ *Value*   Another quality hotel in the Derby chain (they also own the Balmes and the Claris), this branch is uptown where the Rambles meets the Diagonal, and is exceptionally good value. The Art Deco facade makes it appear older than it is. The high ceilings, geometric designs, and brass-studded detail in the public rooms could be Moorish or Andalusian. The comfortable midsize guest rooms are soundproofed; half have been renovated, with slick louvered closets and glistening white paint. The more old-fashioned units have warm textures of exposed cedar and elegant, pristine modern accessories. All units come equipped with private bathrooms containing showers.

París 203, 08036 Barcelona. ✆ **93-209-83-11.** Fax 93-202-30-08. www.derbyhotels.es. 115 units. 133€–187€ ($153–$215) double; 221€ ($254) suite. AE, DC, MC, V. Parking nearby 18€ ($21). Metro: Diagonal. **Amenities:** Bar; lounge; limited room service; laundry service; dry cleaning. *In room:* A/C, TV, minibar, hair dryer, safe.

Hostal Girona ★★ ⟨Value⟩   One of the most filled-with-character *hostales* in

town, the Girona is decorated with wall hangings and rugs, gilded picture frames and tear-drop chandeliers which offset the old-fashioned *modernista* decor beautifully. The result is a place that feels like home rather than paid accommodations, and unsurprisingly it's become something of a cult figure. It offers a variety of bedrooms from singles without bathrooms to more plush doubles with en suite bathrooms with tub/shower combos and balconies. All are comfortable and freshly painted with plain white linen bedspreads. A bargain.

Girona 24 1-1, Eixample Dreta, 08010 Barcelona. ✆ **93-265-02-59.** Fax 93-265-85-32. www.hostalgirona. com. 19 units. 50€–62€ ($58–$71) double. MC, V. Metro: Girona or Urquinaona. **Amenities:** Safe. *In room:* A/C, TV.

Hostal Goya ★★ ⟨Finds⟩   As hostal accommodations go, this is one of the best

deals in the city: A smart, friendly place that's a cut above the others in terms of decor, cleanliness and service (the newly renovated "Principal" wing is the quietest and has fresh, sleekly decorated rooms). Do remember however that it is an *hostal,* not a hotel, and therefore the clientele tend to be younger and sometimes noisy when coming in late at night. For most, this is no problem and the place itself is good enough to more than compensate for a fun-loving crowd. It offers a variety of different style rooms. The best are doubles with large, sunny balconies; the worst are small, dark, interior rooms (meaning no natural light) for lone travelers, and they come with and without private bathrooms. The prices fluctuate accordingly. Bonuses include a Scandinavian-look comfortable sitting room where free tea, coffee and hot chocolate is available throughout the day giving it a homey feel. Given its central location and good value prices it's unsurprising that it gets booked up quickly, so make your reservation in advance.

Pau Claris 74, Eixample Dreta, 08010 Barcelona. ✆ **93-302-25-65.** Fax 93-412-04-35. www.hostalgoya.com. 19 units. 50€ ($58) double without bathroom; 67€ ($77) double with bathroom; 85€ ($98) suite with bathroom and private terrace. MC, V. Metro: Urquinaona or Catalunya. **Amenities:** TV lounge. *In room:* A/C in some units.

Hostal Residencia Oliva ⟨Value⟩   The thing about staying in the Eixample is

that it can be expensive; not so if you check into the Oliva. At a bit more than 50€ ($58) a night for a double room, you get what you pay for. Don't expect any luxuries (the best rooms overlook Barcelona's smartest shopping street and have their own bathrooms) but its fine if you want to save your money for other things and are simply looking for a place to lay your head. On the upside, it does have plenty of character with high ceilings and tiled floors, but it can be noisy (bring earplugs), and the dark interior rooms are rather grim.

Passeig de Gràcia 32, Eixample, 08007 Barcelona. ✆ **93-488-01-62.** Fax 93-487-04-97. www.lasguias.com/ hostaloliva/homepageingles.htm. 16 units. 55€ ($63) double without bathroom; 65€ ($75) double with bathroom. No credit cards. Metro: Passeig de Gràcia. **Amenities:** Lounge. *In room:* TV.

Sagrada Família B&B ★★ ⟨Finds⟩   A small, family-run bed-and-breakfast with

just three pleasantly decorated rooms with queen size beds and their own balconies. This is a good choice for travelers looking for home-style comforts and what really makes this place special is the large living room with open fireplace, perfect for snuggling up on cold winter evenings.

Nápols 266, Eixample Dreta, 08025 Barcelona. © 65-189-14-13. www.sagradafamilia-bedandbreakfast. com. 3 units. 60€–70€ ($69–$81) double. No credit cards. Metro: Diagonal. **Amenities:** Lounge, kitchen.

3 Sants, Paral.lel & Montjuïc

The place to be for business travelers, this is the hub of Barcelona's out-of-towner meeting district with practical four stars galore, the *Fira* (exhibition centers of Plaça Espanya) and the World Trade Centre at the bottom of Paral.lel. However, it's a bit of a dead zone when it comes to leisure time with little going on aside from the art galleries and parks of Montjuïc.

EXPENSIVE

Catalonia Barcelona Plaza ⭐   Right on the busy plaza, this hotel caters mainly to business travelers attending the various conference and convention halls across the street. It's very convenient for the airport (about 20 min. by cab), and can cater to business meetings of up to 700 people. Aside from which, it is a fairly standard business hotel; big, gleaming and comfortable with all the necessary facilities; various meeting rooms, an in-house travel agency and bank, swimming pool and gym. The rooms likewise are standardized and not wildly interesting and in need of an overhaul but they do provide a comfortable nights sleep and all have en suite bathrooms with tub/shower combos.

Plaça Espanya 6–8, 08014 Barcelona. © 93-426-26-00. Fax 93-426-04-00. www.hoteles-catalonia.com. 338 rooms. 175€–272€ ($201–$313) double; 285€–380€ ($328–$437) suite. AE, DC, MC, V. Parking 16€ ($18). Metro: Plaça Espanya. **Amenities:** Restaurant; lounge; bar; pool; solarium; health center; business center; room service; babysitting; laundry service; dry cleaning; nonsmoking rooms. *In room:* A/C, TV, minibar, hair dryer, safe, Internet access.

Hotel Fira Palace ⭐⭐ *(Kids)*   At the base of Montjuïc this hotel opened for the 1992 Olympics and today is highly popular among business travelers for its plush conference facilities and easy access to the exhibition centers of Plaza Espanya. The main disadvantage for leisure travelers is the hike to the center and the main sights. That said, if you are traveling with kids, the Fira offers some of the best family accommodations around; huge rooms with separate bath and shower facilities and close to Barcelona's green zone, Montjuïc. The Fira has everything one would expect of a four-star offering spacious communal areas, two expensive restaurants (you are better off eating outside of the hotel) and a selection of health and fitness facilities (the swimming pool is closed Sun).

Av. Ruis I Taulet 1–3, 08004 Barcelona. © 93-426-22-23. Fax 93-425-50-47. www.fira-palace.com. 276 units. 212€–282€ ($244–$324) double; 320€–380€ ($368–$437) suite. AE, DC, MC, V. Parking 16€ ($18). Metro: Plaça Espanya. **Amenities:** 2 restaurants; piano bar; indoor pool; sauna; health center; business center; limited room service; massage; babysitting service; laundry service; dry cleaning; nonsmoking rooms; patio garden. *In room:* A/C, TV, minibar, hair dryer, safe, Internet access.

Hotel Torre Catalunya ⭐⭐   A vast skyscraper-style hotel, this brand new four-star is far and away the most deluxe in the area, offering American-style facilities in terms of the size of the bedrooms, excellent service and modern amenities. Added extras include turndown service, chocolates on the pillows and huge marble bathrooms with walk-in showers and deep bathtubs. **Ciudad Condal,** the restaurant on the 23rd floor has awesome views over the city and is worth the visit for these alone. The spa facilities are not due to open until December 2004 but once complete, this hotel looks set to offer five-star luxury at four-star prices.

Sants, Paral.lel & Montjuïc Accommodations

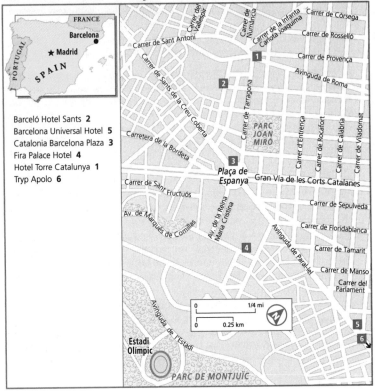

Barceló Hotel Sants **2**
Barcelona Universal Hotel **5**
Catalonia Barcelona Plaza **3**
Fira Palace Hotel **4**
Hotel Torre Catalunya **1**
Tryp Apolo **6**

Av. De Roma 2–4, Sants, 08014 Barcelona. (℃) **93-325-81-00**. Fax 93-325-51-78. www.expogrupo.com. 272 units. 100€–220€ ($115–$253) double; 160€–280€ ($184–$322) suite. AE, DC, MC, V. Free parking. Metro: Sants Estació. **Amenities:** Restaurant; bar; pool; health center; business center; limited room service; laundry service; dry cleaning; nonsmoking rooms. *In room:* A/C, TV, minibar, hair dryer, safe, Internet access.

MODERATE

Barceló Hotel Sants The main reason for staying here is for practical reasons. It's located right on top of Estació de Sants—Barcelona's main train station—and couldn't be more convenient if you're getting in late at night or have an early morning departure. It is what it says it is: a commercial hotel making no attempt to dazzle guests with either history or culture. Ultimately though, the beds are big and comfortable, the rooms well equipped, the bathrooms clean and functional with tub/shower combos.

Plaça dels Països Catalans s/n, 08014 Barcelona. (℃) **93-503-53-00**. Fax 93-490-60-45. www.bchoteles.com. 377 units. 75€–185€ ($86–$213) double; 115€–225€ ($132–$259) suite. AE, DC, MC, V. Parking 13€ ($15). Metro: Sants Estació. **Amenities:** 2 restaurants; bar; pool; sauna; health center; business center; limited room service; massage; babysitting service; laundry service; dry cleaning; nonsmoking rooms. *In room:* A/C, TV, minibar, hair dryer, safe, Internet access.

Barcelona Universal Hotel Predominantly catering to business travelers, the Universal is a practical place for company meetings offering stylish, modern facilities within easy reach of the World Trade Centre and the Exhibition sites at Plaza Espanya. Bonuses include a small rooftop terrace with raised wood decking and a sunken pool. Bedrooms are spacious and comfortable, all have en suite bathrooms with tub/shower combos but although theoretically soundproofed noise from the busy street can be a problem for many guests. If you do stay here ask for something at the rear.

Av. Paral.lel 76–78, 08001 Barcelona. ℂ 93-567-74-47. Fax 93-567-74-40. www.hotelbarcelonauniversal. com. 167 units. 140€–190€ ($161–$219) double; 240€–300€ ($276–$345) suite. AE, DC, MC, V. Parking 19€ ($22). Metro: Paral.lel. **Amenities:** Restaurant; bar; pool; solarium; health center; business center; limited room service; babysitting; laundry service; dry cleaning; nonsmoking rooms. *In room:* A/C, TV, minibar, hair dryer, safe, Internet access.

Tryp Apolo   The Avenida Paral.lel has many business style hotels due to its close proximity to the convention centers on Plaça Espanya. Tryp are the upscale, business orientated hotels of the Sol Meliá chain and often have good value deals. It's pretty much what one expects of four-star formulaic hotel, lots of marble, plenty of space, functional but comfortable rooms (again, ask for something at the rear if traffic noise bothers you) all with en suite bathrooms with tub/shower combos. Where Tryp stands out is in the quality of the service and its exceptional buffet breakfast.

Av. Paral.lel 57–59, 08004 Barcelona. ℂ 93-443-11-22. Fax 93-443-00-59. www.trypapolo.solmelia.com. 314 units. 90€–160€ ($104–$184) double; 120€–210€ ($138–$242) suite. AE, DC, MC, V. Parking 13€ ($15). Metro: Paral.lel. **Amenities:** Restaurant; cafeteria; bar; pool; health center; Jacuzzi; sauna; limited room service; babysitting; laundry service; dry cleaning; nonsmoking rooms; Internet service. *In room:* A/C, TV, minibar, hair dryer, safe, Internet access.

4 Barrio Alto & Gràcia

The Alto represents the *pijo* (posh) part of town with swanky restaurants and cocktail bars, millionaire's mansions and Mercedes, contrasted by the more eclectic, villagey atmosphere of Gràcia with its two-story houses, sunny plazas and student/bohemian vibe.

EXPENSIVE

Hotel Meliá Barcelona Sarrià 🌸   One block from the junction of the Avinguda Sarrià and the Avinguda Diagonal in the heart of the business district, this hotel still earns its five-star government rating, which was granted when it opened back in 1976. Some rooms were renovated in the early to mid-1990s, but others look a bit worn. It offers comfortably upholstered, carpeted guest rooms done in neutral international modern. They have wide beds with firm mattresses and bathrooms with tub/shower combos. A member of the Meliá chain, the hotel caters to both the business traveler and the vacationer.

Av. Sarrià 50, 08029 Barcelona. ℂ 800/336-3542 in the U.S., or 93-410-60-60. Fax 93-410-77-44. www. solmelia.com. 314 units. 197€–273€ ($227–$314) double; 333€–446€ ($383–$513) suite. AE, DC, MC, V. Parking 19€ ($22). Metro: Hospital Clinic. **Amenities:** 2 restaurants; bar; business center; limited room service; babysitting; laundry service; dry cleaning; nonsmoking rooms. *In room:* A/C, TV, minibar, hair dryer, safe, Internet access.

MODERATE

Hotel Wilson   This comfortable hotel in an architecturally rich neighborhood is a member of the HUSA chain. The small lobby isn't indicative of the rest of the building. The second floor opens into a large, sunny lounge. The guest rooms are well kept, generally spacious, and furnished in traditional style. All units contain bathrooms with tub/shower combos.

Av. Diagonal 568, 08021 Barcelona. ℂ 93-209-25-11. Fax 93-200-83-70. www.husa.es. 57 units. 123€–170€ ($142–$196) double; 152€–218€ ($175–$251) suite. AE, DC, MC, V. Public parking 20€ ($23). Metro: Diagonal. **Amenities:** Bar; laundry service; dry cleaning. *In room:* A/C, TV, minibar, hair dryer, iron, safe.

INEXPENSIVE

Acropolis Guest House ⭐ *(Moments)* The Acropolis is nothing if not quirky, and more than a little chaotic, but it has a charm all of its own, with its crumbling columns and peeling paintwork, and is well worth it for lovers of experience hotels. If you plan to travel with your pet, this is also one of the few that welcomes them. The overgrown garden and rustic kitchen are both communal and the bedrooms are simply but comfortably decorated. Half of them have en suite bathrooms but the place is spotlessly clean and sharing shouldn't be a problem. The best room has its own terrace with wonderful views.

Verdi 254, Gràcia, 08024 Barcelona. ℂ/fax **93-284-81-87**. acropolis@telefonica.net. 8 units. 50€ ($58) double with bathroom; 40€ ($46) double without bathroom. No credit cards. Metro: Lesseps. **Amenities:** TV lounge; safe.

5 Barceloneta & Vila Olímpica

VERY EXPENSIVE

Hotel Arts ⭐⭐⭐ Managed by the Ritz-Carlton chain, this hotel occupies 33 floors of one of the tallest buildings in Spain, and one of Barcelona's landmark skyscrapers. The hotel is about 2.5km (1½ miles) southwest of Barcelona's historic core, facing the sea and the Olympic Village. Planned as a key project of the 1992 Olympic Games (but not finished on time), The Arts wore *the* luxury hotel mantle and remained the shining example of "New Barcelona" for over a decade. Realizing that we all need a nip and tuck occasionally, it is currently undergoing a face-lift in all its rooms and new amenities being added such as a luxury spa (p. 98). But don't let the potential noise level put you off; this is being done an entire floor at a time, with two floors situated directly above and below left vacant for the duration. In the meantime, it's business as usual; the privileged clients flock here for the incredible skyline and the Mediterranean views, club rooms with their open bars and free snacks, state-of-the-art executive suites, Aqua de Parma toiletries, and a million other details that makes this hotel top of its class. Its decor is contemporary and elegant. The spacious, well-equipped guest rooms have built-in furnishings, generous desk space, and large, sumptuous beds, flatscreen TVs, DVDs, and B&O sound systems. Clad in pink marble, the deluxe bathrooms have fluffy robes, Belgian towels, dual basins, and phones. The hotel possesses the city's only beachside pool and its new in-house bars and restaurants, such as **Arola** (p. 136), are jumpstarting nightlife into the neglected Olympic Marina. The young staff is polite and hardworking, the product of Ritz-Carlton training.

Carrer de la Marina 19–21, 08005 Barcelona. ℂ **800/241-3333** in the U.S., or 93-221-10-00. Fax 93-221-10-70. www.ritzcarlton.com/hotels/barcelona. 482 units. 325€–475€ ($374–$546) double; 420€–590€ ($483–$679) suite. AE, DC, MC, V. Parking 20€ ($23). Metro: Ciutadella–Vila Olímpica. **Amenities:** 4 restaurants; cafe; 2 bars; outdoor pool; fitness center; business center; limited room service; babysitting; hairdresser; laundry service; dry cleaning; nonsmoking rooms. *In room:* A/C, TV, minibar, hair dryer, iron, safe, Internet access.

Hotel Grand Marina ⭐⭐⭐ Staying here is like being on one of the luxury ocean-going liners you see docked across the port, minus the seasickness. Located in the World Trade Centre, no other hotel in the city gets this close to the sea and few can compare when it comes to design. It was designed by Henry Cobb and I. M. Pei—the man behind the pyramid at the Louvre—and is crammed with artworks and sculpture offset by marble and glass architectural details that give it a distinctly 21st-century feel. A friend to minimalism, the overall look is bright and airy with an overriding feeling of space. Bedrooms are plush without being claustrophobic, and sleekly designed and all have en suite bathrooms. The Presidential Suite on the roof has magnificent views across the port to the city.

World Trade Centre, Moll de Barcelona, 08039 Barcelona. ℂ **93-603-90-00.** Fax 93-603-90-90. www.grand marinahotel.com. 235 units. 240€–290€ ($276–$334) double; 350€–550€ ($403–$633) suite. AE, DC, MC, V. Parking 16€ ($18). Metro: Drassanes. **Amenities:** Restaurant; lounge; piano bar; cafeteria; outdoor pool; health center; Jacuzzi; sauna; business center; room service; massage service; babysitting; laundry service; dry cleaning; nonsmoking rooms. *In room:* A/C, TV, minibar, hair dryer, safe, Internet access.

MODERATE

Hotel Rafael Diagonal Port   Popular with yachties, it's not a bad choice for landlubbers either with its sleek, clean design and chic bar and restaurant. If it were more centrally located, this hotel would no doubt be one of Barcelona's hotspots; as it is, it remains a cool seaside hideaway for those in the know and who don't mind taxiing themselves to the shops, sights and restaurants in the center. Its main disadvantage is that it is rather far out and service can be slow, though if you want to be close to the beach and away from the crowds that could be a bonus. Bedrooms are bright and airy, making use of sea and sandcastles color schemes, perhaps to compensate for the lack of decent views, and all have good-sized bathrooms with tub/shower combos.

Lope de Vega 4, Diagonal Mar, 08005 Barcelona. ℂ **93-230-20-00.** Fax 93-230-20-10. www.rafaelhoteles. com. 115 units. 118€–180€ ($136–$207) double; 216€–230€ ($248–$265) suite. AE, DC, MC, V. Parking 14€ ($16). Metro: Poble Nou. **Amenities:** Restaurant; bar; business center; room service; massage service; babysitting; laundry service; dry cleaning; nonsmoking rooms. *In room:* A/C, TV, minibar, hair dryer, safe, Internet access.

Vincci Marítimo Hotel ⋆⋆ *(Finds)*   A true 21st-century hotel with an emphasis on interior design—lots of glass panels, polished wood and brushed steel—not dissimilar to Glasgow's landmark Lighthouse building. But because it's tucked away in the nether reaches of the city, few people have discovered it. Its advantages, aside from being a design hottie yet to be discovered, are its location along the eastern seaboard (great for hip city beaches like Bogatell and Mar Bella), which is an excellent location if your holiday aim is sunbathe by day, moon bathe and listen to local DJ talent by night. But it could seem a little far out for those wanting to explore the sights and soak of the atmosphere of old Barcelona, though nothing is ever far away by taxi. Bedrooms are sleek and spacious, all with en suite, light-filled bathrooms and many have sea views. Communal facilities include a Japanese garden for relaxing breakfasts and early evening cocktails, and a swanky, avant-garde restaurant. Check the website for deals. With rooms often going for less than 100€ ($115) a night, it's a real bargain.

Llull 340, Poble Nou, 08019 Barcelona. ℂ **93-356-26-00.** Fax 93-356-06-69. www.vinccihoteles.com. 144 units. 130€–180€ ($150–$207) double; 175€–215€ ($201–$247) suite. AE, DC, MC, V. Parking 13€ ($15).

Tips   A Pool with a View

If you're looking for a swim with your hotel, consider the following, which also offer beautiful views:

- **Hotel Balmes** (p. 88) for a garden oasis in the middle of the Eixample
- **Hotel Arts** (p. 96) the city's only beachside hotel
- **Hotel Omm** (p. 84) for unbeatable views of Gaudí's rooftops
- **Hotel Claris** (p. 83) for high-tech design, acres of steel and wood decking
- **Hotel Duquesa de Cardona** (p. 71) for rooftop views over the boats and gin palaces of the Port Vell

Bright Lights, Spa City

Barcelona has never been much of a spa town, though its meteoric rise as an international destination means that hotels are offering ever more luxurious amenities to seduce the city's visitors. First it was gourmet restaurants and movie-star cocktail bars, next came suites with clap-to-control features and rooftop swimming pools, but the latest thing to hit the Barcelona hotel circuit (and it's about time!) are spas.

It seems rather bizarre for a city as cosmopolitan as Barcelona that spas should have been such a long time coming, but somehow, Southern Europeans never seem to have embraced the whole spa therapy thing as passionately as their American neighbors (and northern Europeans). It's still in novelty phase here, and that means anything might, and probably will, happen. Though still light years away from some of the weird and wonderful treatments available in Asia and Switzerland (sheep's placenta body wraps have yet to make an appearance!) the burgeoning market does have a handful of seriously stylish outfits that promise to do more than simply rest and rejuvenate travel weary bodies.

The first on the scene was the **Royal Fitness Center** at the somewhat prim five-star Rey Juan Carlos I Hotel (p. 100), which this year upgraded their look with unfathomable 21st-century fitness technologies and a new line of aphrodisiacal massages in chocolate, honey, or volcanic stone. Who says romance is dead?

For sheer fabulousness, the Spa at the **Gran Hotel La Florida** (p. 100) offers a heavenly, high-class retreat in the clouds high above the hustle and bustle of the city below. Treatments here include beautiful mosaic-tiled Turkish steam rooms, a Finnish sauna, a bubbling hot tub and a

---

Metro: Poble Nou. **Amenities:** Restaurant; bar; room service; laundry service; dry cleaning; nonsmoking rooms; Internet service; garden. *In room:* A/C, TV, minibar, hair dryer, safe, Internet access.

INEXPENSIVE

Marina Folch ⓡ *(finds)*   This small, informal guesthouse is gradually earning itself a loyal following among visitors who want to be close to the sea without paying the earth. Barceloneta (the old fishermen's district) is mysteriously lacking in reasonably priced places to stay, and the friendly Marina Folch is a gem. All 10 rooms have private bathrooms with shower while the bedrooms are simply decorated but fresh, clean and comfortable. It's exactly what cheap, no-nonsense accommodations should be: a genuine retreat from the bustle of daily life minus the sometimes-tiring whistles and bells of more upmarket accommodations. The only drawback is that it is located above a restaurant (same management) so certain times of the day are noisy.

Mar 16, Barceloneta, 08003 Barcelona. (✆) **93-310-37-09.** Fax 93-310-53-27. 10 units. 50€–65€ ($58–$75) double. AE, DC, MC, V. Parking 19€ ($22). Metro: Barceloneta. **Amenities:** Restaurant; room service; laundry service. *In room:* A/C, TV.

Marina View B&B   Just in front of the Port Vell (Old Port) and halfway between the Vía Laietana and Les Ramblas, this new bed-and-breakfast is in a top spot for making the most of the city's prime sights as well as her beaches. Bedrooms are fairly small, but pleasantly decorated and all have private bathrooms

striking 37m-long (121-ft.) half-indoor/half-outdoor L-shaped stainless steel infinity pool that elbows its way across the mountainside. The full range of Natura Bissé beauty treatments are on offer here, including body remolding, mud and algae therapies that promise to shave off the years and excess pounds. Serious spa lovers can check in for a three-night "Relaxation and Beauty" package with prices starting at 900€ ($1,035). Non-guests can make use of La Florida's spa facilities for 100€ ($115) a day.

Hot on the heels of greatness, the Ritz-Carlton–owned **Hotel Arts** (p. 96) is due to open its rooftop sea-view spa on 42nd floor in February 2005, combining hip design with the latest in luxury treatments. They've teamed up with the award-winning Six Senses Spa's to bring clients an exclusive range of holistic, all-natural beauty treatments in half-day, day and weekend packages, including full body wraps, facials, pedicure and manicure as well as a full range of massage therapies. Water facilities include an ice-shower, hammam, sauna and plunge pool while the downstairs treatment rooms (eight in all) are havens of peace where infusions, fresh juices and fruits, are served in relaxation zones or on the deck. The intimate penthouse environment, with views over the sparkling Med, offers one of the most spectacular spots in Spain to pamper and preen. Treatments start from 95€ ($109) an hour.

Meanwhile, the **Hotel Omm** (p. 84) is beavering away readying their spa facilities for completion by the end of 2005. Like the rest of the hotel, expect state-of-the-art design mixed with Mediterranean madness and all the comforts money can buy. Just say sp-*aah!*

with shower, as well as some bonus extras like complimentary tea and coffee. Owner José María is the friendliest and most accommodating host one could hope for, and will even provide breakfast in bed for those who want it.

Passeig de Colom s/n, Barri Gòtic, 08002 Barcelona. ℂ **60-920-64-93.** www.marinaviewbcn.com. 5 units. 95€–110€ ($109–$127) double; 150€ ($173) triple (includes breakfast). MC, V for down payment only. Public parking nearby 20€ ($23). Metro: Drassanes. **Amenities:** Lounge; laundry service. *In room:* A/C, TV, mini-bar, coffee/tea, Internet access.

6 On the Outskirts

VERY EXPENSIVE

Barcelona Hilton ⭐⭐   This government-rated five-star property, on one of the city's main arteries, is a huge 11-floor corner structure. It is part of a huge commercial complex with an adjoining office tower. The lobby is sleek with lots of velvet chairs. Most rooms are rather large and finely equipped. Furnishings are Hilton-standardized, but the rooms are filled with thick carpeting, rich wood furnishings and some of the best combination bathrooms in the city with all the extras, including dual basins and robes. Some units are smoke-free, and others are reserved exclusively for women.

Av. Diagonal 589–591, 08014 Barcelona. ℂ **800/445-8667** in the U.S. and Canada, or 93-495-77-77. Fax 93-495-77-00. www.hilton.com. 287 units. 305€–365€ ($351–$420) double; 320€–435€ ($368–$500) suite. AE, DC, MC, V. Parking 28€ ($32). Metro: María Cristina. **Amenities:** 3 restaurants; cafe; bar; health club; business center; room service; babysitting; laundry service; dry cleaning; nonsmoking rooms. *In room:* A/C, TV, minibar, hair dryer, iron, safe, Internet access.

Gran Hotel La Florida ★★★ If pushed to name Barcelona's finest hotel, the Gran Hotel La Florida would probably have to be it. In fact, this is the second time in its life it would get that title. First opened in the 1920s, it was the hotel of choice for Spanish aristocracy, movie stars and monarchy who sought out the fresher air at the top of Tibidabo mountain. During the Second World War it was used as a hospital, and it didn't welcome guests again until 2003. After a complete overhaul by some of the world's most prolific artists and designers, it is now stuffed with art that would be the envy of many a high profile art gallery and boasts several designer suites. On arrival, guests are offered glasses of rose petal water before being shown to soothing, sand-colored rooms (most of which boast magnificent views) and all have spacious marble bathrooms with separate bath and shower. The 20-minute taxi ride from the center is probably one of the hotel's main disadvantages, though many stay here solely to enjoy the facilities; a world-class restaurant, **L'Orangerie** a spa and infinity pool, terraced gardens and service that really does make you feel like you've died and gone to heaven.

Carretera Vallvidrera (al Tibidabo) 83–93, 08035 Barcelona. ℂ **93-259-30-00.** Fax 93-259-30-01. www. hotellaflorida.com. 74 units. 310€–585€ ($357–$673) double; 650€–870€ ($748–$1,000) suite. AE, DC, MC, V. Parking 18€ ($22) per day. 7km (4miles) from Barcelona. **Amenities:** Restaurant; private nightclub; indoor/outdoor pool; health club; Jacuzzi; sauna; solarium; Turkish bath; business center; room service; babysitting; laundry service; dry cleaning; nonsmoking rooms. *In room:* A/C, TV, minibar, hair dryer, iron, safe, Internet access.

Rey Juan Carlos I ★★★ Named for the Spanish king who attended its opening and has visited several times, this government-rated five-star hotel competes effectively against the Ritz, Claris, and Hotel Arts. Opened just before the Olympics, it rises 17 stories at the northern end of the Diagonal, in a wealthy neighborhood known for corporate headquarters, banks, and upscale stores. Note that it's a bit removed, however, from many of Barcelona's top attractions. The design includes a soaring inner atrium with glass-sided elevators. Midsize to spacious guest rooms contain many electronic extras, conservatively comfortable furnishings, and oversize beds. Many have views over Barcelona to the sea. Thoughtful touches include good lighting, adequate workspace, spacious closets, and blackout draperies, plus marble bathrooms with tub/shower combos.

Av. Diagonal 671, 08028 Barcelona. ℂ **800/445-8355** in the U.S., or 93-364-40-40. Fax 93-364-42-64. www. hrjuancarlos.com. 412 units. 350€ ($403) double; 490€–995€ ($564–$1,144) suite. AE, DC, MC, V. Parking 15€ ($17). Metro: Zona Universitària. **Amenities:** 2 restaurants; 2 bars; indoor pool; outdoor pool; fitness center; car rental; business center; salon; babysitting; room service; laundry/ironing service; dry cleaning; nonsmoking rooms. *In room:* A/C, TV, minibar, hair dryer, safe, Internet access.

EXPENSIVE

Relais d'Orsa ★★★ *Moments* Those looking for a special place to stay need look no further than the Relais d'Orsa; a genuine, romantic hideaway in the tiny village of Vallvidrera, minutes from the better known Gran Hotel La Florida (see above). However, the difference between the two is vast. The d'Orsa occupies a 19th-century mansion that has been renovated to create an intimate space, decorated with antiques and textiles collected from all over Europe by the French owner. Hidden away in a forest with sprawling, lovingly tended gardens filled with shade and flowers and a relaxing pool surrounded by teak decking, it is the perfect place for some quality R&R. And because it has just six bedrooms it has the feel of a private home. The black and white tiled bedrooms with antique beds and French Provençal furniture and linens are sublime, with floor to ceiling windows ensuring plenty of light and fabulous views. Bathrooms meanwhile have tub/ shower combos, fresh flowers, candles and wonderful smelling L'Occitane products also from Provence. A breakfast of local preserves, breads and pastries is served in the dining room, or under a shady pagoda in summer.

Mont d'Orsa 35, 08017 Barcelona. ℂ **93-406-94-11.** Fax 93-406-94-71. www.relaisdorsa.com. 6 units. 215€ ($247) double; 350€ ($403) suite. AE, DC, MC, V. Free parking. Closed Dec 24–Jan 6. From Barcelona take Av. Vallvidrera north of the city; from airport exit 9 (Ronda de Dalt) and then Av. Vallvidrera. **Amenities:** Cafeteria; outdoor pool; room service; babysitting; laundry service; dry cleaning; private gardens. *In room:* A/C, TV, minibar, hair dryer, iron, safe, Internet access.

MODERATE

Abba Garden Hotel   A big, terracotta-red affair at the top of a hill, this newish four-star (opened in 2002) is less than a mile from Barcelona Football Team's Camp Nou, making it a top choice for soccer fans and football tourists. Its distance from the center (6km/3¾ miles) means that it also benefits from space; landscaped gardens, tennis courts and a large outdoor swimming pool, and its well located if you plan to spend your time ferrying to and from golf courses outside of Barcelona. The downside is that it is rather isolated and a taxi ride into town can be expensive. Otherwise it's a fairly standard four-star with sprawling communal areas and a reasonable restaurant and bar. Bedrooms are spacious and freshly decorated with flower print fabrics and all have en suite bathrooms with tub/shower combos. Twenty-nine of the rooms are nonsmoking.

Santa Rosa 33, Esplugues de Llobregat, 08950 Barcelona. ℂ **93-503-54-54.** Fax 93-503-54-55. www.abba hotels.com. 138 units. 85€–150€ ($98–$173) double. AE, DC, MC, V. Parking 12€ ($14). Metro: Zona Universitària; RENFE: Reina Elisenda. From Barcelona take Av. Diagonal out of the center to the Pedralbes area and look out for signs to Hospital St. Jean de Deu next to hotel. **Amenities:** Restaurant; cafeteria; bar; health club; sauna; solarium; tennis courts; car rental; business center; room service; babysitting; laundry service; dry cleaning; nonsmoking rooms; private garden. *In room:* A/C, TV, minibar, hair dryer, safe, Internet access.

Hesperia Sarrià 🎿 (Kids)   This hotel on the northern edge of the city, a 10-minute taxi ride from the center, sits in one of Barcelona's most pleasant residential neighborhoods. Built in the late 1980s, the hotel was last renovated before the 1992 Olympics. You'll pass a Japanese rock formation to reach the stone-floored reception area with its adjacent bar. Sunlight floods the monochromatic guest rooms (all doubles—prices for singles are the same). Although most rooms are medium-size, they have enough room for an extra bed, which makes this a good choice for families. Beds have quality mattresses and fine linen; bathrooms have a generous assortment of good-size towels and tub/shower combos. The uniformed staff offers fine service.

Los Vergós 20, 08017 Barcelona. ℂ **93-204-55-51.** Fax 93-204-43-92. www.hoteles-hesperia.es. 134 units. 142€–198€ ($163–$228) double; 175€–230€ ($201–$265) suite. AE, DC, MC, V. Parking 13€ ($15). Metro: Tres Torres. **Amenities:** Restaurant; bar; business center; room service; laundry service; dry cleaning; non-smoking rooms. *In room:* A/C, TV, minibar, hair dryer, safe, Internet access.

Tryp Barcelona Aeropuerto   As the name suggests, the main reason for staying at this hotel is to be close to the airport. Tryp (part of the Sol Meliá group) is a reliable, four-star chain and excellent in terms of business facilities. This one is brand new and completely modernized in terms of amenities with hardwood floors, comfortable spacious bedrooms all with large, marble bathrooms and tub/shower combos. A buffet breakfast is included in the bargain 80€ ($92) double room price, and there's a free 24-hour airport shuttle bus.

Plaça del Pla De l'Estany 1–2, Polígono Mas Blau II, Prat de Llobregat, 08820 Barcelona. ℂ **93-378-10-00.** Fax 93-378-10-01. www.trypbarcelonaaeropuerto.solmelia.com. 205 units. 90€–132€ ($104–$152) double; 165€ ($190) suite. AE, DC, MC, V. Valet parking 15€ ($17). 1.5km (1 mile) from airport; 10km (6 miles) from

Barcelona. **Amenities:** Restaurant; cafeteria; bar; health center; car rental; airport shuttle service; business center; limited room service; laundry service; dry cleaning; nonsmoking room; safe. *In room:* A/C, TV, minibar, hair dryer, Internet access.

7 Apartments & Aparthotels

Aparthotel Silver ★★ *(Finds* Located in the heart of villagey Gràcia, the appropriately named Silver apartments are a perfect base for those looking to remove themselves a little from the hustle and bustle of the city center. With its low rise houses, cute sunny plazas, eclectic bars and restaurants and Bohemian vibe it is one of Barcelona's least discovered barrio's and one that is worth getting to know. All 49 studio apartments are smartly decorated with plenty of storage space, comfortable beds, and fresh linens. They come with a kitchenette with a small electric stove and a refrigerator, and all have private bathrooms with tub/shower combos. The building also has a private garden and lawn equipped with tables and chairs and parking facilities. This place is a bargain, especially for couples seeking a little independence.

Bretón de los Herreros 26, Gràcia, 08012 Barcelona. ℂ **93-218-91-00.** Fax 93-416-14-47. www.hotelsilver. com. 49 units. 67€–75€ ($77–$86) apt. AE, DC, MC, V. Metro: Fontana. Parking 10€ ($12). **Amenities:** Cafeteria; bar; room service; laundry service; Internet access; private garden. *In room:* A/C, TV, kitchenette w/refrigerator, safe.

Citadines *(Kids* New, modern, clean and bright this apartment hotel is a good choice for those who want to be right on the Ramblas with the option to cook for themselves (the wonderful fresh produce market La Boqueria is just up the street). It's very popular with groups and families with children providing fully equipped kitchens, optional maid service and large, comfortable bedrooms with sofa beds in the living area if you need to accommodate more people. The bathrooms are likewise clean and modern. One of the features that gives the Citadines the edge over many similar hotels in town is the ninth floor roof terrace offering 360-degree views over the whole city.

Les Ramblas 122, 08002 Barcelona. ℂ **93-270-11-11.** Fax 93-412-74-21. www.citadines.com. 115 studios. 16 apts. 145€–170€ ($167–$196) 2-person apt; 230€–250€ ($265–$288) 4-person apt. AE, DC, MC, V. Metro: Plaça Catalunya. Parking 20€ ($23). **Amenities:** Bar; solarium; laundry service; maid service; meeting rooms. *In room:* A/C; TV; hairdryer; safe; Internet access; kitchenette w/microwave, dishwasher, and fridge; stereo.

Hispanos Siete Suiza ★★★ Of all the aparthotels in Barcelona, the Suiza is far and away the most glamorous—a real home-away-from-home combined with the comforts of a luxury hotel. All wood-floored apartments have two bedrooms; two bathrooms; a plush, cozy living room; and a kitchen; continental breakfast included in the price. It's worth knowing that **La Cupula** (the in-house restaurant) is overseen by Carles Gaig, the prestigious Michelin-starred Catalan chef. What makes it truly special is its unexpected history. A Catalan doctor, gynecologist Melchor Colet Torrabadella, originally owned the house. He was also a writer, poet, and philanthropist, and was hugely interested in the arts, as well as fine vintage cars (a collection of seven beautiful 1920s automobiles from which the hotel gets its name decorate the lobby). When his wife died of cancer, Colet set up a foundation in her memory, **Fundación Dr. Melchor Colet,** and part of the hotel's profits go to this cause.

Sicilia 255, Eixample Dreta, 08025 Barcelona. ℂ **93-208-20-51.** Fax 93-208-20-52. www.hispanos7suiza.com. 19 units. 120€–180€ ($138–$207) 2-bedroom apt for 2 with 30€ ($35) supplement for 3 or 4 guests. AE, DC, MC, V. Metro: Sagrada Família. Parking 12€ ($14). **Amenities:** Restaurant; cocktail bar; room service; laundry service; safe; shopping service; DVD/Playstation rental. *In room:* A/C, TV, minibar, safe, Internet access, kitchen w/washing machine and dryer.

5

Where to Dine

Dining out in Barcelona is going to be a very pleasant surprise. Whether it's a hearty nosh-up in an old-style tavern, a late supper in one of the new cutting edge eateries, a tapa or two taken leaning against a bar, or an alfresco paella, Barcelona can accommodate you very nicely. Not only does it have a culinary tradition far and away from the rest of Spain, but its new breed of chefs, led by Ferran Adrià of **El Bulli** fame (p. 245) have taken over the mantle from France as the Continent's new culinary hot spot. The turning point came in 2002 when that year's edition of *Le Guide des Gourmands,* the French foodie bible of where to buy and eat the best products, named Barcelona the most "gourmand" city in Europe, the first time a non-French city has been cited in its 15 years of publication. The criteria for the accolade is a mix of the availability of products; the quality of local wine, market produce, and restaurants; and, in the spirit of the *bon vivant,* the sensibility of the local population as to what goes into their stomachs. Barcelona came up trumps in all areas.

1 Food for Thought

WHAT MAKES IT CATALAN CUISINE?

Much of what these new chefs do is put an avant-garde twist on traditional Catalan cuisine. But what is that exactly? Like its language, what Catalans eat is recognizably different from the rest of Spain, and varies within the region from the Mediterranean coastline and islands to the inland villages and Pyrénées Mountains. Like Catalan culture, its cuisine looks out, towards the rest of Europe (especially France) and the Mediterranean arc rather than inwards towards Castile. Writer Colman Andrews in *Catalan Cuisine,* his definitive English-language book on the subject (Grub Street, 1997) calls it "Europe's Last Great Culinary Secret." Many of the techniques and basic recipes can be traced back to medieval times and, as any Catalan is only too willing to point out, the quality of the produce proceeding from the *Països Catalans* (Catalan countries) is some of the best available. The same goes for the locally produced wine. The D.O.s *(domaines ordinaires)* of the Penedès and Priorat regions are now as internationally renowned as La Rioja and the local *cava* (sparking, champagne-type wine) consumed at celebratory tables from Melbourne to Manchester.

If there is one food item that symbolizes Catalan cuisine, it is the *pa amb tomàquet.* Originally invented as a way of softening stale bread during the lean years of the civil war, there is barely a restaurant in Catalonia, from the most humble workman's canteen to a Michelin-starred palace that does not have it on their menu. In its simplest form, it consists of a slice of rustic white bread that has been rubbed with the pulp of a cut tomato and drizzled with olive oil. Sometimes, especially when the bread is toasted, you are given a tomato to do this yourself and a clove of garlic to add extra flavor if that strikes your fancy. On these occasions, you top the bread with cheese, pâté, chorizo (or any other cured meat), or Iberian ham; the making of what is called a *torrada*. The idea is ingeniously simple and like most ingeniously simple ideas, it works wonderfully, at least in Catalonia. Catalans wax lyrical about it and after a few tries, you too will be hooked and reveling in the fact that you have kicked the high-cholesterol butter habit. But don't try this at home; the tomatoes aren't pulpy enough and the bread never absorbs the pulp (it's just one of those things).

Catalan cuisine is marked by combinations that at first seem at odds with each other; red meat and fish are cooked in the same dish, nuts are pulped for sauces, poultry is cooked with fruit, pulse (bean) dishes are never vegetarian, there is not one part of a pig that is not consumed and imported, salted cod is their favorite fish (although many others are also eaten). Vernacular concoctions that you will see popping up on menus time and time again include *zarzuela* (a rich fish stew), *botifarra amb mongetes* (pork sausage with white beans), *faves a la catalana* (broad beans with Iberian ham), *samfaina* (a sauce of eggplant, peppers, and zucchini), *esqueixada* (a salted cod salad), *fideuà* (similar to a paella, but with noodles replacing the rice), and *miel i mato* (a soft cheese with honey). It's hearty fare, and far more elaborate than the food of Southern Spain. In its most traditional form, it doesn't suit light appetites, which is why many locals have only one main meal a day and that meal is normally lunch, with perhaps a light supper of a *torrada* in the evenings. Breakfast is also a light affair; a milky coffee (*café con leche* in Spanish, *café amb llet* in Catalan) with a croissant or doughnut is what most people survive on till lunchtime. Many bars do fresh orange juice.

WHEN YOU DINE IN BARCELONA

Catalans generally have lunch between 2 and 4pm and dinner after 9pm. Most kitchens stay open in the evenings till about 11pm. It is highly recommended that you make lunch your main meal and take advantage of the *menú del día* (lunch of the day) that is offered in the majority of eateries. It normally consists of three-courses (wine and/or coffee and dessert included) and, at between 8€ and 12€ ($9–$14) per head, is an extremely cost-effective way of trying out some of the pricier establishments. Tipping always seems to confuse visitors, mainly because some restaurants list the 7% IVA (sales tax) separately on the bill. This is *not* a service charge, in fact it is illegal for restaurants to charge for service. As a general rule, tips (in cash) of about 5% should be left in cheap to moderate places and 10% in more expensive ones. In bars, just leave a few coins or round your bill up to the nearest euro. If you are really unhappy with the service or food and think that it warrants following up, you are entitled to ask for a *hoja de reclamación* (complaint form) from the management. These are then perused by independent inspectors.

Vegetarians fare less well here. Vegetarian restaurants are more common than ten years ago, but with some notable exceptions (such as **Organic;** p. 115) "creative cooking" coupled with "meat-free" is a concept that seems to elude many of them. Contemporary places such as **Pla** (p. 112) and **Anima** (p. 108) are a better bet, with always a couple of vegetarian options on offer. Apart from a tortilla, don't expect this in the traditional, old style taverns and always double check; the Catalan word *carn* (*carne* in Spanish) only refers to red meat. Asking for a dish "without" (*sens* in Catalan, *sin* in Spanish) does not guarantee it arrives fish- or chicken-free. Also note that nonsmoking sections in restaurants and bars are, at present, nonexistent. This is set to change in the coming years but don't, as they say, hold your breath; in most cases, it will be left up to the management if they want to implement nonsmoking sections or not. In the meantime there are plenty of outside terraces to enjoy a smoke-free (if not smog free) meal or drink.

Below is only a small selection of the hundreds of Barcelonese restaurants, cafes, and bars. As in many other aspects of a city that is currently one of the most visited in Europe, Barcelona is a victim of its own popularity. The constant influx of tourists means that many places (especially on and around Les Ramblas) now think nothing of offering a microwaved paella or charging 10 times over the average for a coffee. But in the smaller streets of the Barri Gòtic, and the blocks of the L'Eixample area (which has largely escaped the side effects of mass tourism) there are still plenty of value-for-money establishments that take enormous pride in introducing you to the delights of the local cuisine. Around the El Raval, the city's most multicultural neighborhood, you will find dozens of cheap places run by Pakistanis, Moroccans and South Americans should you ever get tired of the local grub. ¡*Bon profit!*

2 Ciutat Vella (Barri Gòtic, El Raval & La Ribera)
EXPENSIVE

Abac ⭑ *Finds* INTERNATIONAL   This is the showcase of a personality chef, Xavier Pellicer, who creates a self-termed *cuisine d'auteur,* meaning a menu of completely original dishes. Inside the 1948 Park Hotel, his minimalist restaurant has even attracted members of the Spanish royal family, eager to see what Pellicer is cooking on any given night. Some of his dishes may be too experimental for most tastes, but I've found his daring palate pleasing. He is a master in balancing flavors, and his dishes perk up the taste buds and even challenge them at times. His plates emphasize color and texture, and his sauces are perfectly balanced. You never know on any given night where his culinary inspiration has led him. Perhaps a mushroom tartare will be resting on your plate, or else a velvety-smooth steamed foie gras. Roasted sea bass appears with sweet pimientos and oyster plant and Iberian suckling pig is cooked and flavored to perfection, as is his fennel ravioli with "fruits of the sea."

Carrer del Rec 79–89 (La Ribera) ℂ **93-319-66-00.** Reservations required. Main courses 23€–33€ ($26–$38); tasting menu 81€ ($93). AE, DC, MC, V. Tues–Sat 1:30–3:30pm; Mon–Sat 8:30–10:30pm. Closed Aug. Metro: Jaume I or Barceloneta.

Agut d'Avignon ⭑ CATALAN   One of our favorite restaurants in Barcelona is in a tiny alleyway near the Plaça Reial. The city's restaurant explosion has toppled Agut d'Avignon from its position as best in the city, but it's still going strong after 40 years and has a dedicated following. It attracts politicians, writers, journalists, financiers, industrialists, and artists—and even the king and cabinet ministers, along with visiting dignitaries. Since 1983 Mercedes Giralt Salinas and her son, Javier Falagán Giralt, have run the restaurant. A small 19th-century vestibule leads to the multilevel dining area, which has two balconies and a main hall evoking a hunting lodge. You may need help translating the Catalan menu. The traditional specialties are likely to include acorn-squash soup served in its shell, fisherman's soup with garlic toast, haddock stuffed with shellfish, sole with *nyoca* (a medley of nuts), large shrimp with aioli, duck with figs, and filet beefsteak in sherry sauce.

Trinitat 3, at Carrer d'Avinyó (Barri Gòtic). ℂ **93-302-60-34.** Reservations recommended. Main courses 11€–21€ ($13–$24); lunch menu 11€ ($13) AE, DC, MC, V. Daily 1–4:30pm and 9pm–12:30am. Metro: Jaume I or Liceu.

Ciutat Vella Dining

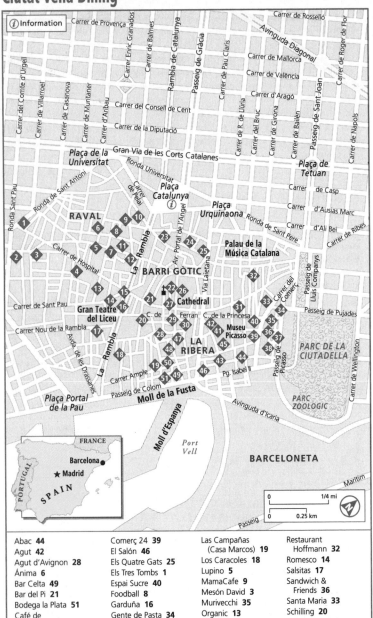

Abac **44**
Agut **42**
Agut d'Avignon **28**
Ánima **6**
Bar Celta **49**
Bar el Pi **21**
Bodega la Plata **51**
Café de
  L'Academia **30**
Cafe de la Òpera **16**
Cal Pep **42**
Can Culleretes **22**
Can Isidre **2**
Casa Leopoldo **4**

Comerç 24 **39**
El Salón **46**
Els Quatre Gats **25**
Els Tres Tombs **1**
Espai Sucre **40**
Foodball **8**
Garduña **16**
Gente de Pasta **34**
Iposa **7**
Kasparo **10**
La Cuineta **26**
La Dentellière **50**
La Paradeta **38**
La Rosca **24**

Las Campañas
  (Casa Marcos) **19**
Los Caracoles **18**
Lupino **5**
MamaCafe **9**
Mesón David **3**
Murivecchi **35**
Organic **13**
Peimong **47**
Pisa Morena **43**
Pla and Re-Pla **29**
Pla de la Garsa **31**
Pucca **37**
Quo Vadis **12**

Restaurant
  Hoffmann **32**
Romesco **14**
Salsitas **17**
Sandwich &
  Friends **36**
Santa Maria **33**
Schilling **20**
Senyor Parellada **41**
Taller de Tapas **45**
Bagel Shop Café **23**
Umita **7**
Venus Delicatessan **48**
Vinissim **27**

Can Isidre ☆ CATALAN   In spite of its seedy location (take a cab at night!), this is perhaps the most sophisticated Catalan bistro in Barcelona. Opened in 1970, it has served King Juan Carlos and Queen Sofía, Julio Iglesias, and the famous Catalan bandleader, Xavier Cugat. Isidre Gironés, helped by his wife, Montserrat, is known for his fresh cuisine beautifully prepared and served. Try spider crabs and shrimp, a foie gras salad, sweetbreads with port and flap mushrooms, or *carpaccio* of veal, Harry's Bar style. The selection of Spanish and Catalan wines is excellent.

Les Flors 12 (El Raval) ℂ **93-441-11-39.** Reservations required. Main courses 15€–42€ ($17-48). AE, DC, MC, V. Mon–Sat 1:30–4pm and 8:30–11pm. Closed Sat–Sun June–July and all Aug. Metro: Paral.lel.

Casa Leopoldo ☆☆ *Finds* SEAFOOD   An excursion through the somewhat seedy streets of the Barrio Chino is part of the Casa Leopoldo experience. At night it's safer to come by taxi. This colorful restaurant founded in 1939 serves some of the freshest seafood in town to a loyal clientele. There's a popular standup tapas bar in front and two dining rooms. Specialties include eel with shrimp, barnacles, cuttlefish, seafood soup with shellfish, and deep-fried inch-long eels.

Sant Rafael 24 (El Raval) ℂ **93-441-30-14.** Reservations recommended. Main courses 25€–38€ ($29–$44); tasting menu 40€ ($46). AE, DC, MC, V. Tues–Sun 1:30–4pm; Tues–Sat 9–11pm. Closed Aug and Easter week. Metro: Liceu.

Quo Vadis ☆ SPANISH/CATALAN   Elegant and impeccable, this is one of the finest restaurants in Barcelona and a favorite with the opera crowd from the Liceu Opera House next door. In a century-old building near the open stalls of the Boqueria food market, it was established in 1967 and has done a discreet but thriving business ever since. The four paneled dining rooms exude conservative charm. Culinary creations include a ragout of seasonal mushrooms, fried goose liver with prunes, filet of beef with wine sauce, and a variety of grilled or flambéed fish. There's a wide choice of desserts made with seasonal fruits imported from all over Spain.

Carme 7 (El Raval) ℂ **93-302-40-72.** Reservations recommended. Main courses 16€–24€ ($18–$28); fixed-price menu 29€ ($33) AE, DC, MC, V. Mon–Sat 1:15–4pm and 8:30–11:30pm. Closed Aug. Metro: Liceu.

Restaurant Hoffmann ☆☆ CATALAN/FRENCH/INTERNATIONAL   This restaurant in the Barri Gòtic is one of the most famous in Barcelona, partly because of its creative cuisine, partly because of its close association with a respected school that trains employees for Catalonia's hotel and restaurant industry. The culinary and entrepreneurial force behind it is German/Catalan Mey Hoffmann, whose restaurant overlooks the facade of one of Barcelona's most beloved Gothic churches, Santa María del Mar. In good weather, three courtyards hold tables. Menu items change every 2 months and often include French ingredients. Examples include a superb *fine tarte* with deboned sardines, foie gras wrapped in puff pastry, baked John Dory with new potatoes and ratatouille, a ragout of crayfish with green risotto, succulent pigs' feet with eggplant, and rack of lamb with grilled baby vegetables. Especially flavorful, if you appreciate beef, is a filet steak cooked in Rioja and served with shallot confit and potato gratin. Fondant of chocolate makes a worthy dessert.

Carrer Argenteria 74–78 (La Ribera) ℂ **93-319-58-89.** Reservations recommended. Main courses 14€–36€ ($16–$42); tasting menu 30€ ($35). AE, DC, MC, V. Mon–Fri 1:30–3:15pm and 9–11:15pm. Closed Aug and Christmas week. Metro: Jaume I.

MODERATE

Agut ★ *(Finds)* CATALAN   In a historic building in the Barrio Chino, 3 blocks from the harborfront, Agut epitomizes the bohemian atmosphere surrounding this fairly seedy area. For three quarters of a century, this has been a family-run business, with María Agut García the current reigning empress. (Don't confuse Agut with the more famous Agut d'Avignon nearby.) The aura is of the 1940s and 1950s, with a cozy little bar to the right as you enter. Paintings on the walls are from well-known Catalan artists from the 1940s to the 1960s. The cuisine is solid and time-tested fare. It is vigorous cookery served at moderate prices. Begin with *mil hojas de botifarra amb zets* or layers of pastry filled with Catalan sausage and mushrooms, or the *terrine de albergines amb fortmage de cabra* (terrine of eggplant with goat cheese gratinée). One of our favorite dishes is *soufle de rape amb gambes* (soufflé of monkfish with shrimp). For gastronomes only, try the *pie de cerdo relleno con foie amb truffles* (pork feet stuffed with duck liver and truffles). Or if you are ravenous, attempt the *chuletón de buey* (loin of ox) for two, which comes thick and juicy and accompanied by a mixture of fresh vegetables. For dessert, if you order *sortido,* you'll get a combination plate with an assortment of the small homemade cakes of the house.

Gignas 16 (Barri Gòtic) ℂ **93-315-17-09.** Reservations required. Main courses 7€–18€ ($8–$21); fixed-price lunch menu Tues–Fri 9€ ($10). AE, DC, MC, V. Tues–Sun 1:30–4pm; Tues–Sat 9pm–midnight. Closed Aug. Metro: Jaume I.

Anima MEDITERRANEAN/FUSION   Located near the MACBA Museum of Modern Art, Anima is yet another of the new breed of Raval eateries. Inside it's all bright colors and minimalism, and a glance at the menu would lead you to think that the cuisine also skimps on the trimmings. But the food here is actually highly satisfying, especially when taken on their outdoor terrace in the summer. Under the plane trees, you may partake in mozzarella balls swimming in gazpacho, ostrich steak with caramelized cranberries with crystallized chocolate truffles for dessert. If all this sounds a bit too risky, take a gamble with the great value set-lunch menu before you leap in.

Angels 6 (El Raval). ℂ **93-342-49-12.** Reservations recommended. Main courses 5€–14€ ($6–$16); fixed-price lunch 9€ ($10). AE, DC, MC, V. Mon–Sat 1–4pm and 9pm–midnight. Metro: Liceu.

Café de L'Academia ★★ *(Value)* CATALAN/MEDITERRANEAN   In the center of Barri Gòtic a short walk from Plaça Sant Jaume, this 28-table restaurant looks expensive but is really one of the best and most affordable in the medieval city. The building dates from the 15th century, but the restaurant was founded only in the mid-1980s. Owner Jordi Casteldi offers an elegant atmosphere in a setting of brown stone walls and ancient wooden columns. At a small bar you can peruse the varied menu and study the wines offered. Dishes of this quality usually cost three times as much in Barcelona. The chef is proud of his "kitchen of the market," suggesting that only the freshest ingredients from the day's shopping are featured. Try such delights as *bacallà gratinado i musselina de carofes* (salt cod gratinée with an artichoke mousse) or *terrina d'berengeras amb fortmage de cabra* (terrine of eggplant with goat cheese). A delectable specialty sometimes available is *codorniz rellena en cebollitas tiernas y foie de pato* (partridge stuffed with tender onions and duck liver). On warm evenings, go for one of the outside, candle-lit tables on the atmospheric square dominated by a Gothic church.

Carrer Lledó 1 (Barri Gòtic), Plaça Sant Just. ℂ **93-315-00-26.** Reservations required. Main courses 8€–13€ ($9–$15); fixed-price lunch menu 12€ ($14). AE, MC, V. Mon–Fri 9am–noon, 1:30–4pm, and 9–11:30pm. Closed 2–3 weeks in Aug. Metro: Jaume I.

Cal Pep ⭐ *(Finds* CATALAN   One of the dining secrets of Barcelona, Cal Pep lies close to the Picasso Museum and is a slice of local life. On a tiny postage-stamp square, it's generally packed, and the food is some of the tastiest in the Old Town. There's actually a Pep himself, and he's a great host, going around to see that everybody is one happy family. In the rear is a small dining room, but most patrons like to occupy one of the counter seats up front. From the pans in the rear emerge a selection of perfectly cooked dishes that might launch you into your meal. Try the fried artichokes or the mixed medley of seafood that includes small sardines. Tiny clams come swimming in a well-seasoned broth given extra spice by a sprinkling of hot peppers. A delectable tuna dish comes with a sesame sauce, and fresh salmon is flavored with such herbs as basil—sublime.

Plaça des les Olles 8. *(C)* **93-310-79-61.** Reservations required. Main courses 12€–20€ ($14–$23). AE, DC, MC, V. Mon 8:30–11:30pm; Tues–Sat 1–4:30pm and 8:30–11:30pm. Closed Aug. Metro: Barceloneta or Jaume I.

Can Culleretes CATALAN   Founded in 1786 as a *pastelería* (pastry shop) in the Barri Gòtic, this oldest Barcelona restaurant retains many original architectural features. All three dining rooms are decorated with tile dadoes and wrought-iron chandeliers. The well-prepared food features authentic dishes of northeastern Spain, including sole Roman style, *zarzuela a la marinera* (shellfish medley), cannelloni, and paella and special game dishes, including *perdiz* (partridge). The service is old-fashioned, and sometimes its filled more with tourists than locals, but it retains enough authentic touches to make it feel like the real McCoy. Signed photographs of celebrities, flamenco artists, and bullfighters who have visited decorate the walls.

Quintana 5 (Barri Gòtic) *(C)* **93-317-64-85.** Reservations recommended. Main courses 5.50€–16€ ($6.40–$18); fixed-price menu Tues–Fri 15€ ($17). MC, V. Tues–Sun 1:30–4pm; Tues–Sat 9–11pm. Closed July. Metro: Liceu. Bus: 14 or 59.

Comerç 24 ⭐⭐ *(Finds* CATALAN/INTERNATIONAL   View a dining visit here as an opportunity to experience the culinary vision of a rare aesthete and artist. The chef is Carles Abellán, who worked with Ferran Adrià of El Bulli fame for a decade. He has given his imaginative, distinctive interpretation to all the long-time favorite dishes of Catalonia. With his avant-garde and minimalist design, he offers a soothing backdrop for his cuisine. The chef uses fresh seasonal ingredients, balanced sauces, and bold but never outrageous combinations, and he believes in split-second timing. Begin perhaps with his freshly diced tuna marinated in ginger and soy sauce, and Abellán will immediately win you over. Perhaps you'll sample his fresh salmon "perfumed" with vanilla and served with yogurt. His baked eggplant with Roquefort, pine nuts, and fresh mushrooms from the countryside is a vibrant and earthy feast. Only the great star Marlene Dietrich could make a better potato omelet than Abellán. Believe it or not, he serves that old-fashioned snack that Catalan children used to be offered when they came home from school, a combination of chocolate, salt, and bread flavored with olive oil. It's surprisingly good!

Carrer Comerç 24 (La Ribera) *(C)* **93-319-21–02.** Reservations required. Main courses 6€–24€ ($7–$28); tasting menu 48€ ($52). AE, DC, MC, V. Tues–Sat 1:30–3:30pm and 8:30pm–12:30am. Closed Christmas week and last 3 weeks in Aug. Metro: Jaume I.

El Salón *(Moments* MEDITERRANEAN/FUSION   Dominated by a huge gilt mirror and low lighting, El Salón has long been a favorite for couples looking for a romantic dinner spot. The menu, which changes daily, pushes the definition of eclectic with Asian, Italian, and especially French influences on local market produce. It's been around long enough to have a firm and faithful following, especially amongst the expat community, but the standard varies. When it's good, it's very, very good. But when it's an off night . . . well, you'll still go back for the sheer charm of the place.

L'Hostal d'en Sol 6–8 (Barri Gòtic). ✆ **93-315-21-59.** Reservations recommended. Main courses 7€–17€ ($8.05–$19); fixed-price dinner 20€ ($23). AE, MC, DC, V. Daily 9pm–midnight. Metro: Jaume I.

Els Quatre Gats ⭐ *(Moments* CATALAN   This has been a Barcelona legend since 1897. The "Four Cats" (Catalan slang for "just a few people") was a favorite of Picasso, Rusiñol, and other artists, who once hung their works on its walls. (Reproductions still adorn them.) On a narrow cobblestone street in the Barri Gòtic, the fin-de-siècle cafe has been the setting for poetry readings by Joan Maragall, piano concerts by Isaac Albéniz and Ernie Granados, and murals by Ramón Casas. It was a base for members of the *modernista* movement and figured in the city's intellectual and bohemian life.

Today the restored cafe-restaurant is a popular meeting place. The fixed-price meal is one of the better bargains in town, considering the locale and dinner dining is a good bet given the overall grandeur. The homespun Catalan cooking here is called *cucina de mercat* (based on whatever looked fresh at the market) but will always include such classics as *suquet de peix* (a fish and potato hot-pot) and *faves a la catalana* (baby broad beans with Serrano ham). The constantly changing menu reflects the seasons.

Montsió 3 (Barri Gòtic) ✆ **93-302-41-40.** Reservations required. Main courses 12€–22€ ($14–$25); fixed-price lunch menu 11€ ($13). AE, DC, MC, V. Daily 1pm–1am. Cafe daily 8am–2am. Metro: Plaça de Catalunya.

Espai Sucre ⭐⭐ *(Finds* DESSERTS   Espai Sucre (Sugar Space) is Barcelona's most unusual dining room, with a minimalist decor and seating for 30. For the dessert lover, it is like entering a heaven created by the sugar fairy himself. The place has a gimmick, and it works. The menu is devoted to desserts. There is a short list of so-called "salty" dishes for those who want to cool it with the sugar. Actually it's quite good and imaginatively prepared, including the likes of ginger couscous with pumpkin and grilled stingray or artichoke cream with a poached quail egg and Serrano ham. The lentil stew with foie gras is first rate, as are the spicy veal "cheeks" with green apples.

Forget all about those tearoom concoctions you'd find in a pastry cafe. The desserts here are original creations. Your "salad" is likely to be small cubes of spicy milk pudding resting on matchsticks of green apple with baby arugula leaves, peppery caramel, dabs of kaffir lime and lemon curd, and a straight line of toffee. Smoky tea cream with chocolate, black sesame, and yogurt appears. Even when your platter holds a tiny phyllo pyramid, no bigger than a pencil eraser, you bite in to discover it's filled with lemon and rosemary marmalade. Ever had a soup of litchi, celery, apple, and eucalyptus? If some of the concoctions frighten your palate, you'll find comfort in the more familiar—vanilla cream with coffee sorbet and caramelized banana. Every dessert comes with a recommendation for the appropriate wine to accompany it.

Princesa 53 (La Ribera) ✆ **93-268-16-30.** Reservations required. Main courses 8.50€–11€ ($9.80–$13); 3-dessert platter 25€ ($29); 5-dessert platter 33€ ($38). MC, V. Tues–Sat 9–11:30pm. Closed mid-Aug and Christmas week. Metro: Arc de Triomf.

Garduña CATALAN   This is the most famous restaurant in Barcelona's covered food market, La Boqueria. Originally conceived as a hotel, it has concentrated on food since the 1970s. Battered, somewhat ramshackle, and a bit claustrophobic, it's fashionable with an artistic set that might have been designated as Bohemian in an earlier era. It's near the back of the market, so you'll

pass endless rows of fresh produce, cheese, and meats before you reach it. You can dine downstairs, near a crowded bar, or a bit more formally upstairs. Food is ultrafresh—the chefs certainly don't have to travel far for the ingredients. You might try "hors d'oeuvres of the sea," cannelloni Rossini, grilled hake with herbs, *rape* (monkfish) *marinera,* paella, brochettes of veal, filet steak with green peppercorns, seafood rice, or a *zarzuela* (stew) of fresh fish with spices.

Jerusalem 18. ☎ 93-302-43-23. Reservations recommended. Main courses 6€–28€ ($6.90–$32); fixed-price lunch 10€ ($12); fixed-price dinner 15€ ($17). DC, MC, V. Mon–Sat 1–4pm and 8pm–midnight. Metro: Liceu.

Gente de Pasta ITALIAN   If you are having trouble finding a table in the trendy Born district, you could do worse than head for this gigantic restaurant that specializes in (as the name suggests) pasta dishes. Just don't expect gingham tablecloths and wicker wine baskets; the industrial, warehouse-like interior has about as much in common with a *trattoria* as a chopstick. The bare walls and floor make the acoustics a nightmare for the audio challenged on busy nights and the sheer size of the place means that waiters are not normally hovering when and where they should. That said, the pastas and other dishes are perfectly passable, with added attraction such as a *caprese* salad with anchovies and a fennel and prawns risotto.

Passeig de Picasso 10 (La Ribera). ☎ 93-268-70-17. Reservations recommended on weekend. Main courses 5€–17€ ($5.75–$19); fixed-price lunch 8.40€ ($9.70). AE, MC, V. Daily 1–4pm and 9pm–midnight. Metro: Barceloneta.

La Cuineta *Value* CATALAN   This restaurant near the Catalan government offices is a culinary highlight of the Barri Gòtic. Decorated in typical regional style, it favors local cuisine. The fixed-price menu is a good value, or you can order a la carte. The most expensive appetizer is *bellota* (acorn-fed ham), but I suggest a market-fresh Catalan dish, such as *favas* (broad beans) stewed with *botifarra,* a tasty, spicy local sausage.

Pietat 12 (Barri Gòtic) ☎ 93-315-01-11. Reservations recommended. Main courses 15€–38€ ($17–$44); fixed-price menu 12€–26€ ($14–$30). AE, DC, MC, V. Daily 1–4pm and 8pm–midnight. Metro: Jaume I.

Los Caracoles *Moments* CATALAN   This restaurant must be one of the easiest to find in Barcelona. As you walk down Escudellers, admittedly one of the city's less-salubrious streets, you are drawn on by the aroma of roasting chickens. This classic restaurant has them on an outside spit, on an open fire built into the side of the edifice and you enter through the main kitchen, with steaming pots and hot-under-the-collar cooks. Inside it's a labyrinth; stairways lead to even more dining rooms and private, one-table nooks are hidden under stairs. The place oozes with atmosphere and the cuisine is Catalan comfort food: *arroz negre* (rice cooked in squid ink), grilled squid, and, of course, roast chicken. There's always a fair share of tourists and the food isn't always up to what it should be, but as an authentic slice of local culture it's definitely worth a visit.

Escudellers 14 (Barri Gòtic). ☎ 93-302-31-85. Reservations recommended. Main courses 6€–28€ ($6.90–$32). AE, DC, MC, V. Daily 1pm–midnight. Metro: Drassanes.

Lupino MEDITERRANEAN FUSION   Lupino was one of the first of the new wave of "cool" Barcelona restaurants. The waitstaff looked like models and dressed in black, there was a DJ in the background, and the decor resembled a catwalk. Three years on, only the latter remains true. Lupino has softened around the edges and has been around long enough to learn that one cannot live by style alone. The food is a mélange of Mediterranean, French, Creole, and North African; grilled entrecote with couscous, cod with ratatouille and coconut emulsion, pork stuffed with goat's cheese with cassava chips on the side . . . you get the picture. It's very good and their lunchtime menu is one of the best deals around. A rear terrace overlooks the back of the Boqueria market (in reality a parking lot, but oversized parasols block out the unsightly bits), and the DJ now only makes an appearance Friday and Saturday nights for late-night cocktails.

Carme 33 (El Raval) ⓒ **93-412-36-97.** Reservations recommended on weekend. Main courses 14€–20€ ($16–$23); fixed-price lunch Mon–Fri 8.50€ ($9.80); Sat–Sun 12€ ($14). AE, MC, V. Mon–Thurs 1–4pm and 9pm–midnight; Sat–Sun 1:30-4:30pm and 9pm–3am. Metro: Liceu.

Mama Cafe MEDITERRANEAN FUSION   In the thick of El Raval's hub of funky eateries, this is one of the more reliable bets where style doesn't give way to substance. The Boho crowd rock in and are greeted by an urban-savvy staff, who churn out the dishes from a frantic open kitchen. The hamburgers here are a rarity in Barcelona (that is, they are very good), the salads (nearly always with a fruit or goat cheese) market fresh, and the pastas (such as salmon and capers) more than acceptable. Mama Café is one of the few inner-city restaurants open on Monday; just don't order the fish (they take it off the menu, anyway)!

Doctor Dou 10 (El Raval) ⓒ **93-301–29-40.** Reservations recommended on weekend. Main courses 5€–17€ ($5.75–$19); fixed-price lunch 19€ ($22). AE, MC, V. Daily 1–4pm and 9pm–midnight. Metro: Liceu.

Pla and **Re-Pla** ⭐⭐ MEDITERRANEAN   Such is the popularity of the original Pla, that the owners opened a second branch which has proven just as hard to get a table at as the first. Popular with locals and visitors alike for its consistently high standard of *carpaccios;* wide selection of market-fresh salads exposing tasty combinations such as spinach, mushrooms, and prawns; and main dishes with Asian and Arabic touches that nearly always include a Thai curry or a Moroccan couscous dish. The waitstaff is amiable, bilingual, and informal, and will take the time to talk you through your selection.

Pla: Bellafila 5 (Barri Gòtic). ⓒ **93-412-65-52.** Reservations required. Main courses 6€–15€ ($6.90–$17). DC, MC, V. Sun–Thurs 9pm–midnight; Fri–Sat 9pm–1am. Closed Dec 25–27. Metro: Jaume I. Re-Pla: Montcada, 2 (La Ribera). ⓒ **93-268-30-03.** Daily 1–4pm and 9pm–midnight. DC, MC, V. Closed Dec 25–27. Metro: Jaume I.

Pucca MEDITERRANEAN/MEXICAN   Run by Mexican-born Fernando Sancheschulz (who also studied architecture) the cool, clean interior is typical of the new wave in Barcelona's restaurant decor. On a trip to Thailand, Fernando found out that the local flavors had a lot in common with his own country, and the imaginative, "Mex-Asian" cuisine of Pucca is the result in dishes such as seared tuna sprinkled with fish flakes, Mediterranean prawns in coconut batter, or avocado-laced gazpacho.

Passeig de Picasso 32 (La Ribera). ⓒ **93-268-72-36.** Reservations recommended on weekend. Main courses 5€–17€ ($5.75–$19); fixed-price lunch 19€ ($22). AE, DC, MC, V. Daily 1–4pm and 9pm–midnight. Metro: Barceloneta.

Senyor Parellada CATALAN/MEDITERRANEAN   The glossy contemporary-looking interior of this place is in distinct contrast to the facade of a building that's at least a century old. Inside, in a pair of lemon–yellow and blue dining rooms, you'll find menu items such as Italian-style cannelloni, stuffed cabbage, cod "as it was prepared by the monks of the Poblet monastery," baked monkfish with mustard and garlic sauce, roasted duck served with figs, and roasted rack of lamb with red-wine sauce. Patrons flock faithfully to this bistro, knowing they'll be served a traditional cuisine of northeast Spain with fine local produce. The chefs seem to know how to coax the most flavor out of the premium ingredients.

Make It Snappy

It had to happen; whether it's because of the tourist demand or a population that has less time to sit down and enjoy a midday meal, fast food establishments are becoming more and more common. McDonald's and Dunkin' Donuts now occupy prime retail real-estate, but unless you don't think you'll see it through the day without a taste of home, why not try some of the local takeout? All over the city, **Pans & Company** and **Bocata** dispense freshly made *bocatas* (crusty rolls) filled with tasty hot and cold combinations. Also everywhere is **La Baguetina Catalana,** a fantastic, franchised fuelling-stop with mountains of carb-ridden cakes and pastries to go. A favorite with health-conscious backpackers, **Maoz** (mainly in the Old Town) churn out freshly made falafels, which you then top up yourself with as much salad as can possibly fit into the pita bread. Along the pedestrian boulevard the **Rambla del Raval** (and the streets to either side) there are dozens of places for enormous sharwamas: giant sandwiches filled with spit-roasted chicken or lamb and salad.

Carrer Argenteria 37 (La Ribera). ✆ **93-310-50-94.** Reservations recommended. Main courses 6€–12€ ($6.90–$14). AE, DC, MC, V. Daily 1–4pm and 8:30pm–midnight. Metro: Jaume I.

Umita SUSHI   Where else but Barcelona would you find designer sushi? Where else but the melting pot Raval would it be made not by natives from Japan but the very un-Nippon region of Peru? There is a reason for this—the thousands of Japanese émigrés to South America had a profound influence on local chefs. Purists will be tempted to pass this place by. But you shouldn't! Lovers of sushi will not be disappointed, as the standard of fresh fish available in Barcelona, plus the creativity of sushi-maestros make for a memorable meal. Seafood, vegetables, avocado, and other fruits in delicate combinations are part of the equation. The place is tiny, so book for a table. Better still, grab a stool at the bar to watch the masters at work.

Pintor Fortuny 15 (El Raval) ✆ **93-301-23-22.** Reservations recommended on weekend. Main courses 5€–17€ ($5.75–$19); fixed-price lunch 19€ ($22). AE, MC, V. Daily 1–4pm and 9pm–midnight. Metro: Catalunya.

INEXPENSIVE

Iposa *Value* FRENCH/MEDITERRANEAN   Iposa is yet another cheap and cheerful Raval hangout with an outside leafy terrace that is coveted on sunny Saturday afternoons. The resident French chef ensures there is always something a little different on offer rather that the usual "Mediterranean Market" fare, but before you ask how they can serve up a main course, drink and coffee at lunchtime for a measly 6€ ($6.90), be warned that the portions are small, so you my need to order an entree as well. The food changes daily and includes things like a vegetable couscous, fresh grilled fish, or a hot "hummus" soup.

Floirestes de La Rambla 14 (Barri Gòtic). ✆ **93-318-60-86.** Main courses 5€–9€ ($5.75–$10); fixed-price lunch 6€ ($6.90). V. Sept–July Mon–Sat 1:30–4pm and 9pm–midnight; Aug daily 9pm–midnight. Metro: Liceu.

La Dentellière ✦ *Finds* FRENCH/INTERNATIONAL   Charming, and steeped in the French aesthetic, this bistro is imbued with a modern, elegant decor. Inside, you'll find a small corner of provincial France, thanks to the dedicated effort of Evelyne Ramelot, the French writer who owns the place. After an aperitif at the sophisticated cocktail bar, you can order from an imaginative menu that includes a lasagna made from strips of salt cod, peppers, and tomato sauce, and a delectable *carpaccio* of filet of beef with pistachios, lemon juice, vinaigrette, and Parmesan cheese. The wine list is particularly imaginative, with worthy vintages mostly from France and Spain.

Ample 26. ℭ 93-218-74-79. Reservations recommended on weekend. Main courses 7€–12€ ($8.05–$14). MC, V. Tues–Sun 8:30pm–midnight. Metro: Drassanes.

La Paradeta *(Value* *(Kids* SEAFOOD   Most *marisco* (seafood) meals can set you back a ton in Barcelona. Not so at this busy restaurant that has more in common with a fish market than the trendy eateries of the El Born district. This could be because of the money they save on waitstaff. The seafood—crabs, prawns, squid, and so on—is displayed in large plastic tubs. You pick out what you want at the counter, it's weighed up, heaved away and you pick it up crisp and steaming on a platter. The same scenario goes for the drinks, which includes some excellent *albariño* whites and other good, reliable local wines. It's loads of fun, but remember to order everything at once as you often have to queue, especially on the weekends.

Comercial 7 (El Born). ℭ 93-268-19-39. Fish charged per kilo (varies). Average price with wine 18€–22€ ($21–$25). No credit cards. Tues–Thurs 8–11:30pm; Fri 8pm–midnight; Sat 1–4pm and 8pm–midnight; Sun 1–4pm. Closed Dec 22–Jan 22. Metro: Arc de Triomf.

La Rosca CATALAN/SPANISH   For more than half a century, owner Don Alberto Vellve has continued to welcome customers into this little Barri Gòtic eatery, close to Plaça de Catalunya. On a short street, the place is easy to miss, except to devotees who have been coming here for decades. Go here if you'd like to see the type of place where people dined inexpensively in the Franco era. A mixture of Catalan and modern Spanish cuisine is served in this house, which is small and in an old rustic style with high ceilings and white walls. The decor has nostalgic touches, such as old bullfighting posters and pictures of Barcelona in the mid–20th century. There are 60 unadorned tables, which diners fill quickly to take advantage of the cheap three-course luncheon menu. Dig into such hearty fare as veal stew or assorted fish and shellfish grilled. Baby squid is cooked in its own ink, and one of the best dishes is white beans sautéed with ham and Catalan sausage. For a true treat, ask for the *rape a la plancha* (grilled monkfish).

Juliá Portet 6 (Barri Gòtic). ℭ 93-302-51-73. Main courses 6€–12€ ($6.90–$14); fixed-price menu 7€–10€ ($8.05–$12). No credit cards. Sun–Fri 9am–9:30pm. Closed Aug 20–30. Metro: Urquinaona and Catalunya.

Mesón David *(Value* SPANISH   Don't come here for a quiet evening. Mesón David is an absolute riot; waiters scream at each other, tips are acknowledged by the ringing of a cowbell, crowds of diners sing and somehow you have to make yourself heard. But the effort is worth it; the food, regional specialties from all corners of Spain, is fast, furious, and excellent: trout stuffed with Serrano ham, Galician-style octopus, and roast suckling pork. As you may have gathered, it isn't the place for a light meal. But it is an enormous amount of fun for a price that's almost unheard of in inner Barcelona. On busy nights you may have to wait for a table at the bar, and be shown the door on your last gulp of coffee.

Carretes 63 (El Raval). ℭ 93-441-59-34. Reservations recommended. Main courses 4€–9€ ($4.60–$10); fixed-price lunch Mon–Fri 7€ ($8.05). AE, DC, MC, V. Thurs–Tues 1–4:30pm and 8pm–midnight. Metro: Paral.lel or Sant Antoni.

Murivecchi *Value* ITALIAN   If this family-run restaurant was just a few hundred meters further in the thick of the El Born neighborhood, you would probably never get a table. The un-alarming decor doesn't do it any favors either, but the food is excellent and good value for money. There is a wood-fired oven for fans of real Neapolitan pizza and the pasta dishes are no less delectable: *tagliatelle al funghi porcini, spaghetti vongole,* and *linguini al pesto* are just a sample. Add to this a list of *antipasti, risotti,* and *carpacci;* daily specials; and a sinful tiramisu—and you have some of the best Italian cuisine this side of Rome.

Princesa 59 (El Born). (C) **93-315-22-97.** Reservations recommended on weekend. Main courses 8€–13€ ($9.20–$15); fixed-price lunch Mon–Fri 10€ ($12). MC, V. Daily 1–4pm and 8–midnight. Metro: Arc de Triomf.

Organic *Value* VEGETARIAN   Hip and hippie, Organic is one of the few vegetarian restaurants in Barcelona that doesn't feel like a convent when you walk in. At lunchtime, a happy wait staff will show you to large communal tables and explain the system; the first course is a help-yourself soup and salad bar, all tasty and organically grown. The second (which you order from them) could be a vegetarian pizza, pasta, or perhaps a stir-fry. The self-serve desserts include apple cake, carob mousse, and fresh yogurt (smaller menus available). At night the menu is a la carte and on the weekends there is live Brazilian music. A small selection of health foods are also available, including their homemade bread, and a local masseuse is there to offer her services to the lunchtime crowd.

Junta de Comerç 11 (El Raval). (C) **93-301-09-02.** Main courses 5€–10€ ($5.75–$12); fixed-price lunch: 5.60€–8€ ($6.40–$9.20). AE, DC, MC, V. Daily 12:30pm–midnight. Metro: Liceu.

Peimong *Value* PERUVIAN   If you have ever wondered what they eat in the Andes, here is your chance to find out. Tucked away behind the City Hall this little restaurant will never win any design awards but the food is very tasty: from a ceviche (chunks of fish marinated in lime juice) to a piquant chicken and coriander soup served with rice and spicy *tamales,* Peimong's tucker is designed to wake up your taste buds. Peruvian beer is a very pleasant way to wash it down—or try Inca Kola, the soft drink of choice in Peru.

Templers 6–10 (Barri Gòtic). (C) **93-318-28-73.** Reservations recommended on weekend. Main courses 5€–17€ ($5.75–$19). AE, MC, V. Daily 1–4pm and 9pm–midnight. Metro: Jaume I.

Pla de la Garsa ⭐ *Value* MEDITERRANEAN/CATALAN   In Barrio Ribera close to the cathedral, this historic building is fully renovated but still retains some 19th-century fittings, such as a cast-iron spiral staircase used to reach another dining area upstairs. The ground floor is more interesting. Here you'll encounter the owner, Ignacio Sulle, an antiques collector who has filled his establishment with an intriguing collection of *objets d'art.* He boasts one of the city's best wine lists, and features a daily array of traditional Catalan and Mediterranean favorite dishes. Begin with one of the pâtés, especially the goose, or a confit of duck thighs. You can also order meat and fish pâtés. One surprise is a terrine with black olives and anchovies. For a main course you can order a perfectly seasoned beef bourguignon or *fabetes fregides amb menta i pernil* (beans with meat and diced Serrano ham). The cheese selection is one of the finest I've found in town, especially bountiful in Catalan goat cheese, including Serrat Gros from the Pyrénées.

Assaonadors 13 (La Ribera). (C) **93-315-24-13.** Reservations recommended on weekend. Main courses 4€–12€ ($4.60–$13). AE, DC, MC, V. Daily 8pm–1am. Metro: Jaume I.

Romesco *Value* CATALAN/MEDITERRANEAN   Frequented by locals and travelers on a budget, Romesco is never going to win any Michelin stars, but it does offer up the sort of homemade food that is rapidly disappearing within the immediate vicinity of the touristy Les Ramblas. The lighting is bright, the tables are laminated and the waiters and food are no-nonsense and generously proportioned. At the top end, you have a hunk of freshly grilled tuna served with a simple salad, at the bottom *arroz a la cubana* (a hangover cure favorite consisting of white rice, tomato sauce, a fried egg, and a fried banana—it's actually very good). Desserts include a creamy *crema catalana* (crème brûlée) or a rice pudding. Finishing it all off with a strong coffee certainly does the trick.

Sant Pau 28 (Barri Gòtic). ✆ **93-318-93-81.** Main courses 5€–12€ ($5.75–$14). No credit cards. Mon–Fri 1pm–midnight; Sat 1–6pm and 8pm–midnight. Closed Aug. Metro: Liceu.

Salsitas MEDITERRANEAN   The pioneer *restauclub* in Barcelona, Salsitas churns out some very good nosh before it morphs into a fun nightclub at 1am. Take a seat on one of the wrought iron chairs amongst the plastic palm trees and you will be served a selection of "lite" cuisine (who wants to see a bulging stomach on the dance floor?), such as a pumpkin soup followed by grilled salmon. There's a DJ spinning dinner music in the background.

Nou de la Rambla 22 (Barri Gòtic). ✆ **93-318-08-40.** Reservations recommended on weekend. Main courses 5€–17€ ($5.75–$20). AE, DC, MC, V. Tues–Sat 8.30pm–midnight. Metro: Liceu.

SNACKS, TAPAS & DRINKS

Bar del Pi TAPAS   One of the most famous bars in the Barri Gòtic, this establishment is midway between two medieval squares opening onto a Gothic church. Typical tapas, canapés, and rolls are available; most visitors come to drink coffee, beer, or local wines, house-sangrias, and *cavas*. In summer you can refresh yourself with a refreshing tigernut milkshake (called an *horchata*) or a slushy ice drink. You can sit inside at one of the cramped bentwood tables, or stand at the crowded bar. In warm weather, take a table beneath the single plane tree on the landmark square. The plaza usually draws an interesting group of young bohemian sorts, travelers, and musicians.

Plaça Sant Josep Oriol 1. ✆ **93-302-21-23.** Tapas 2€–5€ ($2.30–$5.75). No credit cards. Mon–Fri 9am–11pm; Sat 9:30am–10:30pm; Sun 10am–10pm. Metro: Liceu.

Bodega la Plata TAPAS   Established in the 1920s, La Plata is one of a trio of famous bodegas on this narrow medieval street. It occupies a corner building whose two open sides allow aromatic cooking odors to permeate the neighborhood. This bodega contains a marble-topped bar and overcrowded tables. The culinary specialty is *raciones* (small plates) of deep-fried sardines—head and all. You can make a meal with two servings coupled with the house's tomato, onion, and fresh anchovy salad.

Mercé 28. ✆ **93-315-10-09.** Tapas 1.20€–3€ ($1.40–$3.45). No credit cards. Mon–Sat 9am–3:30pm and 6–11pm. Metro: Barceloneta.

Cafe de la Opera CAFE/TAPAS   This is one of the few emblematic cafes in the city that has managed to resist the ravages of modernization. The name comes from the Liceu Opera House, located directly opposite across Les Ramblas and once upon a time patrons would have gathered here for a pre-performance aperitif. Although it has been renovated over the years the interior still retains Belle Epoque details. It's a great place to pull up with a book during its quieter moments during the day, and there is also a terrace if people-watching is more your thing. Tapas are limited, but the cakes are divine. Service is brusque, exuding a jaded formality fitting with the surroundings.

Les Ramblas 74 (Barri Gòtic). ✆ **93-302-41-80.** Tapas from 2€ ($2.30) Cakes from 4€ ($4.60). No credit cards. Mon–Fri 8.30am–2am; Sat–Sun 8.30am–3am. Metro: Liceu.

Els Tres Tombs CAFE/TAPAS   Els Tres Tombs is one of the most versatile bars around: it not only caters to housewives taking a break from shopping at the San Antoní market opposite but also young people stopping off for breakfast after a night out clubbing. The facade is pure '70s, the waiters distinctly old-school, and the placement of the terrace ensures it receives more direct sunlight that just about any bar in Barcelona. Inside there are breakfast pastries to choose from and mounds of tapas to satisfy any daytime hunger pangs. It's a city institution.

Ronda San Antoni 11 (Raval). ℰ **93-443-41-11.** Tapas 2.25€–11€ ($2.60–$12); fixed-price lunch 7€ ($8.05). No credit cards. Daily 6am–2am. Metro: San Antoni.

Foodball ℱ HEALTH FOOD   Foodball is the latest concept from the shoe company **Camper** (p. 198), aiming to transport their wholesome company culture to the food industry. It's a cafe and take-away located near the MACBA museum, and its clientele reflect the neighborhood's neo-hippie vibe. The *foodballs* in question are wholegrain rice balls stuffed with either organic mushrooms, chickpeas, tofu and alga, or chicken. You can either take them way in stylish recycled lunchboxes or choose to park yourself on the grandstand style seating. The interior, with its abundance of organic colors and signage reminiscent of African barbershop imagery is by the quirky Catalan Martí Guixé who is also responsible for many of Camper's shoe shops. Besides the "foodballs," the only other produce available is fresh and dried fruit, juices and purified water. If all this sounds just a bit too contrived don't be put off; healthy fast food is scarcer than hen's teeth in Barcelona, and the foodballs are actually very, very tasty. It's a brilliant concept.

Elisabets 9 (Barri Gòtic). ℰ **93-270-13-63.** Foodballs 1.75€ ($2) each. Menu 5€ ($5.75). Daily noon–11pm. Metro: Liceu.

Kasparo CAFE/TAPAS   This place has one of the all-time favorite terraces; a leafy porticoed affair just a stone's throw from the MACBA (Museum of Modern Art). It's so popular in fact, that you often see people nonchalantly milling around waiting to pounce on the next free table. There is no real reason for this (other than the location) as the tapas are fairly basic, and the daily offerings such as a Greek salad or pasta dish good but a tad overpriced. But if you can spring a table, you will probably find yourself lingering long after you planned to.

Plaça Vicenç Matorell 4 (El Raval). ℰ **93-302-20-72.** Tapas 3€–6.25€ ($3.45–$7.15) No credit cards. Daily 9am–1pm (breakfast) and 1–11pm. Closed Dec 24–Jan 24. Metro: Catalunya.

Las Campañas (Casa Marcos) TAPAS   From the street (there's no sign), Las Campañas looks like a storehouse for cured hams and wine bottles. Patrons flock to the long, stand-up bar for *chorizo* pinioned between two pieces of bread. Sausages are usually eaten with beer or red wine. The place opened in 1952, and nothing has changed since. A tape recorder plays nostalgic favorites, from Edith Piaf to the Andrews Sisters.

Mercé 21. ℰ **93-315-06-09.** Tapas 2€–11€ ($2.30–$13). No credit cards. Thurs–Tues 12:30–4pm and 7pm–2am. Metro: Jaume I.

Pisa Morena CAFE   Underneath this neighborhood's famous porticoes and opposite the inspiring La Llotja (the city's old stock exchange) is this pleasant bar-cafe bereft of the pretension of many of its neighbors. Inside it's tiny, so best to take advantage of its sunny terrace in the morning. Food is limited to hearty *bocadillos* (crusty rolls filled with all the staples such as ham, cheese, and tortilla) and cakes and croissants. As the music and the photos on the inside wall give away, the owner is a die-hard flamenco fan, and it's not unusual for local musicians to roll up in the evening for a spontaneous jam session.

Consolat del Mar 37 (La Ribera). ② **93-268-09-04.** Sandwiches 3€–5€ ($4.60–$5.75). No credit cards. Mon–Fri 9am–1am; Sat–Sun 9am–2am. Metro: Jaume I or Barceloneta.

Sandwich & Friends CAFE   Where else but in El Born would a sandwich be considered cool? On the main drag of the city's hippest quarter, Sandwich and Friends stands out from the rest thanks to its huge wall mural by local but internationally famous illustrator Jordi Labanda. His portrayal of a social gathering of bright young things echoes the clientele itself, who come here to nibble on the cafe's awesome selection of over 50 sandwiches all named after "friends": *Marta* is a pork filet, tomato, and olive oil sandwich; *Daniel* is filled with frankfurter, bacon, and mustard. There is also a selection of salads if you are calorie counting, which going by the size of the waitstaff, is pretty much the norm here.

Passeig del Born 27 (La Ribera). ② **93-310-07-86.** Sandwiches and salads 3.75€–7.35€ ($4.30–$8.45). MC, V. Daily 9:30am–1am. Metro: Jaume I or Barceloneta.

Schilling CAFE   In a street where fast food outlets and franchises are slowly encroaching any of its original flavor, Schilling is a welcome exception. More Brussels than Barcelona, it's all comfy sofas, wooden tables, and newspaper reading during the day, making it a great place to rest your feet and enjoy a sandwich and coffee with some very good cakes. At night the volume goes up and Schilling's Hyde persona takes over as the crowds roll in for a pre or post-dinner drink.

Ferran 23 (Barri Gòtic). ② **93-317-67-87.** Hot and cold sandwiches 4€–8€ ($4.60–$9.20). MC, V. Sept–July daily 10am–2:30am; Aug daily 5pm–2:30am. Metro: Liceu.

Taller de Tapas 🐜🐜 TAPAS   For a foreigner, ordering tapas can be a daunting affair. Making yourself heard of the din is one thing, and then there is the lack of written menus. The Taller de Tapas (Tapas Workshop) has been conceived to take the trouble out of *tapeando*. Amongst a pleasant decor of exposed brick and beams (or the outside terrace) patrons sit at a table and order from a trilingual menu. The tapas are prepared in an open kitchen where there is not a microwave in sight. The owners are always on the lookout for new ingredients that will work in tapas, which means that every week there is a board of specials. The regular menus consists of dozens of tapas delights from all over Spain; marinated anchovies from L'Escala on the Costa Brava, Palamós prawns with scrambled eggs, grilled duck foie, sizzling *chorizo* cooked in cider: it's all here. If you are a large group, this accommodating restaurant will elaborate a special menu for you, and for those that like something a bit more substantial for breakfast, they do a morning *tortilla* menu.

L'Argenteria 51 (La Ribera). ② **93-268-85-59.** Tapas 3€–10€ ($3.45–$12). AE, DC, MC, V. Mon–Thurs 8:45am–midnight; Fri–Sat 8:45am–12:30am; Sun noon–midnight. Metro: Jaume I. There's another location at Plaça Sant Josep Oriol 9, Barri Gòtic (② **93-301-80-20;** Metro: Liceu).

The Bagel Shop CAFE   If you are craving a bagel, head for this simple cafe just off the top end of Les Ramblas. All the staples are here: sesame, poppy seed, blueberry plus a few European versions such as black olive. Fillings go from honey to salmon and cream cheese and they also have a yummy selection of cheesecakes. Take away is available.

Canuda 25 (Barri Gòtic). ② **93-302-41-61.** Bagels 1.45€–5.45€ ($1.70–$6.30). No credit cards. Mon–Sat 9:30am–9:30pm, Sun 11am–4pm Metro: Liceu.

Venus Delicatessan CAFE   This pleasant cafe is on one of the inner-city's alternative fashion shopping streets. It's a good stopping point for tea and coffee and cakes and pastries. The "delicatessen" in the name is a bit misleading (there's not a deli counter in sight) but what it does do very well are light meals such as salads and quiches from midday to midnight. There is a ton of international press to thumb through and work by local artists on the wall to gaze at.

Avinyó 25 (Barri Gòtic). © **93-301–15-85**. Main courses 5€–9€ ($5.75–$10); fixed-price lunch 9€ ($10). No credit cards. Mon–Sat noon–midnight. Metro: Jaume I.

Vinissim *★★* WINE/TAPAS   A warm burgundy and exposed-brick interior is the perfect backdrop for this cozy wine bar on a pretty square in the El Call

More Tapas

Traditionally, Barcelonese don't go for a for a tapas crawl as often as their cousins in Madrid or Andalusia. They prefer to sit down the old fashioned way, over three courses, acres of linen, and a bucket of wine. But the trend for eating in small portions, and the influence of new chefs such as Carles Abellán at **Comerç** 24 (p. 109), has seen heightened interest in this artful cuisine.

For classic Spanish tapas in the heart of the Old City, try **Taller de Tapas,** Calle de l'Argenteria 51 (© **93-268-85-59**). For a 50-strong list of snacks all freshly made on the spot (p. 118) **Cal Pep,** Plaça de les Olles 8 (© **93-310-79-61**), comes close to godliness when you're talking spanking fresh seafood (p. 109); or there's **Bar Celta,** Calle Mercè 16 (© **93-315-00-06**)—one of the oldest tapas joints in town—for purple octopus tentacles, pigs lips and ears, and delightful green peppers known as *pimientos del padrón.* On the same street you can also down rustic farmhouse ciders, flaming chorizo and dark, deeply satisfying slivers of *cecina* (cured beef) at the smattering of *sidrerías* (Asturian tapas bars) that still exist.

In La Ribera and the Born tapas joints have come over all Asian. **Mosquito,** Calle Carders 46 (© **93-268-75-69**), does a well-executed range of Indian, Thai, Malaysian, and Indonesian dishes along with gyoza dumplings and organic beers at unbeatable prices. More upmarket fare can be had from the ever inventive hands of Paco Guzmán at **Santa María,** Calle Comerç 17 (© **93-315-12-27**). Think Spanish–Asian fusion along the lines of local fruits stuffed with Thai spiced peanuts; raw sea bass with passion fruit, tomato, and lime vinaigrettes; and suckling pig with wasabi and soy.

If you're heading up town, avoid the monster barns on the Passeig de Gràcia and opt instead for **Ciudad Condal,** Rambla de Catalunya 18 (© **93-318-19-97**), arguably the city's most visited tapas bar for patatas bravas, fried fish and anchovies. Then, push on up the road to **Cervecería Catalana,** Carrer Majorca 236 (© **93-216-03-68**), for juicy slices of filet beef skewered with peppers, and giant prawn brochettes. (*Note:* These tapas are chalked up on the blackboard, not in the cool chest.)

Finish off with a pudding course courtesy of Jordi Butrón at **Espai Sucre,** Calle Princesa 53 (© **93-268-16-30;** p. 110). Tales of his earthy lapsang souchong tea ice-cream go before him, and for many years his was the only pudding restaurant in the world. Butrón can no longer claim that title, but this is still the ultimate end to a 21st-century tapas crawl.

pocket of the Barri Gòtic. Pull up a stool at one of the high tables and browse their selection of over 50 carefully selected wines—available by glass or bottle—from all regions of Spain. It would be a sin not to order some of their delectable tapas. I noshed on a plate of artisan goat's cheese, a medley of sun-dried tomatoes and caramelized onions, and a potato and cheese *raclette* washed down with an excellent Finca Lobierira *albariño* from Galicia. In the name of research desserts had to be explored; the only thing lacking from the sticky date pudding is a generous splash of runny cream (but it's not readily available in Spain), and the white chocolate cheese cake was superb, especially accompanied by 2001 Etim Moscatel whose sweetness had been derived from its grapes spending no less than 6 months baking under the Valencian sun. All in all, wine bars don't come much better than this, anywhere.

Sant Domenec del Call 12 (Barri Gòtic). ✆ **93-301-45-75.** Tapas 3€–9.40€ ($3.45–$11); tasting menu 20€ ($23); fixed-price lunch 13€ ($15). AE, DC, MC, V. Mon–Sat noon–4pm and 8pm–midnight. Metro: Liceu.

3 Poble Sec & Montjuïc

INEXPENSIVE

La Bella Napoli ITALIAN   Like La Bodegueta below, this Poble Sec eatery has also recently undergone a face-lift, but with more devastating results. Thankfully, there is plenty of character still left in the food, which is authentic Italian from the lasagna to the tiramisu. Most people however come for the thin-crust pizzas, which are hauled out of a wood-fired oven, perfectly crisped and ready to scarf down. Takeaway is available.

Margarit 12. ✆ **93-442-50-56.** Reservations required. Main courses 10€–35€ ($12–$40). AE, DC, MC, V. Tues 8:30pm–midnight; Wed–Sun 1:30–4pm and 8:30pm–midnight. Closed Aug and Christmas week. Metro: Paral.lel or Poble Sec.

La Bodegueta   This bodega is typical (or what was typical) of this working-class neighborhood and a longtime favorite. It's had a recent overhaul, but the period character remains, as does the original rose petal-tiled floor. Owner Eva Amber is on hand to recommend her home cooking, which includes such favorites as lentils with chorizo and Catalan cannelloni. Meat *a al brasa* (grill flamed) and *torrades* (toasted bread with charcuterie) are also on the agenda.

Blai 47. ✆ **93-442-08-46.** Tapas 1.75€–12€ ($2–$14). MC, V. Mon–Fri noon–4pm and 7–10:30pm; Sat noon–4pm. Closed Aug. Metro: Poble Sec.

Quimet & Quimet ⭐ TAPAS/CHEESE   This is a great tapas bar, especially for cheese, of which it offers the finest selection in Barcelona. Built at the turn of the 20th century, the tavern in the Poble Sec sector is still run by the fifth generation of Quimets. Their wine cellar is one of the best stocked of any tapas bar, and their cheese selection is varied. One night I sampled four on the same plate, including *nevat* (a tangy goat cheese), *cabrales* (an intense Spanish blue cheese), *zamorano* (a hardy, nutty sheep's milk cheese), and *torta del Casar* (a soft, creamy farm cheese). If I were a little more adventurous I could have gone for the *tou dels tillers,* a cheese stuffed with trout roe and truffles. Of course, you can also order other delights such as mussels with tomato confit and caviar, razor clams, and even sturgeon.

Poeta Cabanyes 25. ✆ **93-442-31-42.** Tapas 1.75€–12€ ($2–$14). MC, V. Mon–Fri noon–4pm and 7–10:30pm; Sat noon–4pm. Closed Aug. Metro: Paral.lel.

4 L'Eixample
VERY EXPENSIVE

Beltxenea ★★ BASQUE/INTERNATIONAL   In a building originally designed in the late 19th century as an apartment building, this restaurant celebrates Basque cuisine. The Basques are noted as the finest chefs in Spain, and this is indeed grand cuisine. It's served here in one of the most elegantly and comfortably furnished restaurants in the city. Schedule a meal for a special night—it's worth the money. The menu might include hake fried with garlic or garnished with clams and served with fish broth. Roast lamb, grilled rabbit, and pheasant are well prepared and succulent, as are the desserts. There's dining outside in the formal garden during the summer.

Majorca 275. ✆ **93-215-30-24.** Reservations recommended. Main courses 16€–45€ ($18–$52); tasting menu 50€ ($58). AE, DC, MC, V. Mon–Fri 1:30–3:30pm; Mon–Sat 8:30–11:30pm. Closed Easter week, 3 weeks in Aug, and Christmas week. Metro: Passeig de Gràcia and Diagonal.

Drolma ★★★ INTERNATIONAL   In business since 1999, this is one of Barcelona's best haute cuisine restaurants. Fermin Puig is one of Spain's most celebrated chefs, his culinary showcase found in the Hotel Majestic. The restaurant's name is Sanskrit for Buddha's female side. I don't know what this has to do with anything. He might as well have called his restaurant "Majestic," as his food certainly is. Only the freshest of ingredients go into his carefully balanced cookery based on the market's seasonal bounty. I especially like the personal spin he gives to seasonal dishes along with the luxurious foodstuffs presented nightly. What diner could not love the chef who presents pheasant-stuffed cannelloni in a velvety foie gras sauce, the dish delicately sprinkled with the rare black truffle? His wild turbot is enhanced with fresh mushrooms from the Catalan countryside, and his prawns with fresh asparagus tips in a virgin olive oil sauce preserve the natural flavor of each ingredient. Though simple, this dish is in a word divine. The lamb is aromatically grilled with fresh herbs, giving the meat a pungent and refreshing dimension. The baked goat with potatoes and mushrooms is bold yet delicate in flavor.

In the Hotel Majestic, Passeig de Gràcia 68. ✆ **93-496-77-10.** Reservations required. Main courses 35€–109€ ($40–$125). AE, DC, MC, V. Mon–Sat 1–3:30pm and 8:30–11pm. Closed Aug. Metro: Passeig de Gràcia.

Jaume de Provença ★★★ CATALAN/FRENCH   A few steps from the Estació Central de Barcelona-Sants railway station, at the western end of L'Eixample, this is a small, cozy restaurant with rustic decor. Named after its owner and chef, Jaume Bargués, it features modern interpretations of traditional Catalan and southern French cuisine. Examples include gratin of clams with spinach, a salad of two different species of lobster, foie gras and truffles, and pigs' trotters with plums and truffles. Or you might order crabmeat lasagna, cod with saffron sauce, sole with mushrooms in port wine sauce, or an artistic dessert specialty of orange mousse.

Provença 88. ✆ **93-430-00-29.** Reservations recommended. Main courses 9€–37€ ($10–$43). Fixed-price menu 42€ ($48); tasting menu 55€ ($63) AE, DC, MC, V. Tues–Sat 1–4pm and 9–11:15pm; Sun 1–4pm. Closed Easter week and Aug. Metro: Entença.

La Dama ★★★ CATALAN/INTERNATIONAL   This is one of the few restaurants in Barcelona that deserves, and gets, a Michelin star. In one of the

L'Eixample Dining

Alkimia **15**
Bar Turò **1**
Beltxenea **17**
Casa Alfonso **22**
Casa Calvet **21**
Casa Tejada **2**

Cervecería Catalána **10**
Cinc Sentits **9**
Ciudad Condal **19**
Drolma **18**
El Caballito Blanco **11**
Gorría **23**

Il Giardinetto **4**
Jaume de Provença **7**
L'Olive **6**
La Bodegueta **12**
La Dama **5**
Moo **14**

Neichel **1**
Noti **20**
Out of China **8**
Reno **3**
Rosalert **16**
Tragaluz **13**

grand 19th-century buildings for which Barcelona is famous, this stylish and well-managed restaurant serves a clientele of local residents and civic dignitaries. You take an Art Nouveau elevator (or the sinuous stairs) up one flight to reach the dining room. Specialties include salmon steak served with vinegar derived from *cava* (sparkling wine) and onions, cream of potato soup flavored with caviar, a salad of crayfish with orange-flavored vinegar, an abundant platter of autumn mushrooms, and succulent preparations of lamb, fish, shellfish, beef, goat, and veal.

Diagonal 423. ✆ 93-202-06-86. Reservations recommended. Main courses 14€–35€ ($16–$40); fixed-price menu 50€ ($58); tasting menu 70€ ($81). AE, DC, MC, V. Daily 1:30–3:30pm and 8:30–11:30pm. Metro: Provença.

EXPENSIVE

Alkimia ✿✿ MEDITERRANEAN   Jordi Vilà's Alkimia attracts other chefs and fans of his singular style. Vilà is one of the main exponents of New Catalan cuisine; the culinary wave started by Ferran Adrià (p. 245) that is currently sweeping the city. There is nothing in this minimalist eatery that will distract you from the food, which is perhaps just as well as you need to have your taste-buds and wits about you when partaking in his challenging dishes, or better still, set menu. I start off with a deconstructed version of the ubiquitous *pa amb tomàquet* (a slice of white bread rubbed with tomato pulp and olive oil that is to Catalans what vegemite is to Australians). "What I've done here is filter the tomato, or separate the juice from the tomato, which is where all the flavor is, add a little oil, crumbs of toasted bread, and serve it in a shot glass with some *lloganissa* salami," explains Vilà. "This isn't better than the traditional one, just different." Much of what follows is also an offbeat take on traditional Catalan dishes: Tuna belly substitutes for Iberian ham in *faves a la catalana;* truffle is daringly added to a plate of cabbage, potato, and sausage; and fried eggs and Majorcan sausage is served with preserved quinces. The dessert, a convoluted combination of litchi soup, glacé celery, and eucalyptus ice cream was perhaps harder to pigeonhole, but equally as good.

Industria 79. ✆ 93-207-61-15. Reservations required. Main courses 12€–25€ ($14–$29). Tasting menu 40€ ($46) and 54€ ($62). DC, MC, V. Mon–Fri 8am–noon and 1:30–4pm; Sat 8am–noon. Closed Easter week and Aug 8–31. Metro: Sagrada Família.

Casa Calvet ✿✿ MEDITERRANEAN   Probably the most intimate Gaudían experience you can have in Barcelona is eating at this sumptuous dining room. The Casa Calvet, one of the architect's first commissions, was built for the textile magnate Pere Calvet. Now private apartments, the building is off limits to the public, but a restaurant occupies Calvet's former ground-floor offices. Replete with velvet drapery, florid stained glass, Gaudí-designed furniture and other memorabilia, the only thing that jolts you back to the 21st century is the contemporary twist on Miguel Alija's excellent Catalan cuisine, such as giant prawns with rosemary-infused oil or duck liver with oranges. And although the historic setting ensures a fair share of tourists, Casa Calvet is also just as popular with locals. Thankfully, the waitstaff treats everyone that walks over the carved wooden threshold with equal doses of measured hospitality.

Carrer Casp 48. ✆ 93-412-40-12. Reservations recommended. Main courses 13€–28€ ($15–$32); tasting menu 47€ ($54). AE, DC, MC, V. Mon–Sat 1–3:30pm and 8:30–11pm. Metro: Passeig de Gràcia.

Cinc Sentits ✿✿ MEDITERRANEAN   Cinc Sentits is a relatively new kid on the block, but that hasn't stopped it making waves in culinary circles. Chef Jordi Artal spent most of his life in Canada, before coming back to his roots to open this cutting-edge eatery that aims to appease the *cinc sentits* (five senses). He recommends the "Gourmet" tasting menu as "When you sit down to eat and are presented with a big plate of food, the first bite is great, the second is good, but by the time you get to the fifth or sixth, your palate is bored and you have lost interest." There was certainly no chance of waning interest with the eight tapas-size dishes that were subsequently put on our table by Roser and Amy, Jordi's mother and sister (despite its sophistication, Cinc Sentits is a family affair). A *crème fraîche* and caviar soup awoke our curiosity and a sliver of foie with violet petal marmalade set the tone: Artal's cuisine is a combination of Catalan culinary know-how and New World wit. An everyday white garlic soup is graced with pan-seared lobster, a monkfish sprinkled with bacon "dust," or a soft poached egg with tomato jam. Our favorite dish was the smallest: a heavenly shot glass of *cava*, egg yolk, rock salt, and maple syrup. Cinc Sentits is an example of what fusion food can be like with a combination of the finest ingredients and intelligence.

Aribau 58. ✆ **93-323-94-90.** Reservations required. Main courses 10€–23€ ($12–$26); tasting menu 37€ ($43) and 50€ ($58). AE, DC, MC, V. Mon 1:30–3:30pm; Tues–Sat 1:30–3:30pm and 8:30–11pm. Closed Easter week and Aug 8–31. Metro: Passeig de Gràcia.

Gorría ✪ *Finds* BASQUE/NAVARRAN   If you're a devotee of the cookery of Navarre and of the coastal Basque country in northern Spain, as I am, then make a date in Barcelona to head for this quite wonderful discovery. On two levels, this restaurant has been in business since the mid-70s, lying only 200m (656 ft.) from La Sagrada Família and just 50m (164 ft.) from Plaza de Toros, the bullring. Javier Gorría, who learned to cook from his more famous father, the chef, Fermin Gorría, is in charge, and he's as good as his old man. In a location in the Eixample, Gorría holds forth nightly tempting your taste buds with his creations. He pampers his regular clientele, mainly homesick expats from Navarra and the Basque country, with memories of home. No dish is finer than the herb-flavored baby lamb baked in a wood-fired oven. The classic Basque dish, hake, comes in a garlic-laced green herbal sauce with fresh mussels and perfectly cooked asparagus on the side. His grilled turbot is fresh and straightforward, perfection itself with its flavoring of garlic, virgin olive oil, and a dash of vinegar. His braised pork also emerges from the wood-fired oven, and I could make a meal out of his *ponchas* (white beans). Another favorite is a platter of artichokes stuffed with shrimp and wild mushrooms.

Diputació 421. ✆ **93-245-11-64.** Reservations recommended. Main courses 15€–27€ ($17–$31). AE, DC, MC, V. Mon–Sat 1–3:30pm and 9–11:30pm. Closed Aug. Metro: Monumental.

Moo ✪✪✪ MODERN MEDITERRANEAN   Until now, to taste the exquisite cuisine of the famed Roca brothers you had to travel to **El Cellar de Can Roca** (p. 240) their Michelin-starred eatery near Girona. Amidst the cutting-edge surrounds of the applauded **Hotel Omm** (p. 84) they have set up Moo, their second restaurant. Even before the food is on the table, you know you are in for a first class culinary experience by the sculptural table settings, individually hand painted plates (some by well-known local personalities), and the young, yet highly efficient staff, serving the abundance of globe-trotting patrons waiting in smug anticipation. All dishes, from the organic chicken with olives and mango or monkfish with wild mushrooms are available at half-size portions, allowing you to create your own *menú de degustación.* Feeling slightly overwhelmed, I opted for the set menu "Joan Roca," five delightful dishes with wine paring from Moo's talented sommelier Jordi Paronella. I started with a molded crescent of foie embedded with figs and covered with a gelatin of *Pedro Ximénez* sweet wine with a glass of the real thing to wash it down with. Next up was the brilliant lobster, rose, and licorice curry followed by a perfect filet of wild sea bass on a bed of snow peas and pine nuts, both accompanied by two superb local whites. The baby goat roasted in honey and rosemary, resting on a cloud of goat's milk foam, was so tender it could be eaten with spoon. You would be crazy not to go for their trademark desserts designed around a famous fragrance (I "ate" Bvlgari, a blend of Bergamot cream, lemon sorbet, and *pensamiento* flowers), but their trio of chocolate cake, ginger, and 70% chocolate ice cream was just as divine, especially when quaffed with a San Emilio muscatel. Ending on a sweet note (as I had started), I had completed the 360-degree voyage of our taste sensations. With the Roca brothers at the helm, this is indeed a memorable journey and one that is likely to stay with you for time to come.

Rosselló 265. (*C*) **93-445-40-00.** Reservations recommended. Main courses 14€–22€ ($16–$25); Menu "Joan Roca" (with wine pairing) 80€ ($92); midday menu 40€ ($46). AE, DC, MC, V. Daily 1:30–4pm and 8:30–11pm. Metro: Diagonal.

Neichel ★★★ FRENCH/MEDITERRANEAN Alsatian-born owner Jean Louis Neichel is called "the most brilliant ambassador French cuisine has ever had within Spain." Neichel is almost obsessively concerned with gastronomy— the savory presentation of some of the most talked-about preparations of seafood, fowl, and sweets in Spain.

Your meal might include a "mosaic" of foie gras with vegetables, strips of salmon marinated in sesame and served with *escabeche* (vinaigrette) sauce, or slices of raw and smoked salmon stuffed with caviar. The prize-winning terrine of sea crab floats on a lavishly decorated bed of cold seafood sauce. Move on to *escalope* of turbot served with *coulis* (purée) of sea urchins, fricassee of Bresse chicken served with spiny lobsters, sea bass with a mousseline of truffles, Spanish milk-fed lamb served with the juice of Boletus mushrooms, or rack of lamb gratinéed in an herb-flavored pastry crust. The selection of European cheeses and the changing array of freshly made desserts are nothing short of spectacular.

Beltrán i Rózpide 1–5. (*C*) **93-203-84-08.** Reservations required. Main courses 20€–40€ ($23–$46); fixed-price lunch 42€ ($48); tasting menu 55€ ($63). AE, DC, MC, V. Tues–Sat 1:30–3:30pm and 8:30–11pm. Closed Aug. Metro: Palau Reial or María Cristina.

Noti ★ MEDITERRANEAN Slick and ultra sleek without making concessions to comfort, Noti feels more New York than European. The decor is glamorous with capital G: black tables, plush red sofas, and gold panels with dramatic touches of hot pink and electric blue. The power set roll in for lunch, whilst in the evenings the *fashionistas* take over. The menu travels from Japan to Italy; entrees include tuna sashimi or a risotto filled with rocket and monkfish. For mains they do a genuine steak tartare or duck's breast with cherry sauce. The lighting is low and the music is jazz, that is until the kitchen closes and a DJ brings in new patrons for a cocktail or two. The cuisine is very good but falls a tad short of the promises made by the daring surroundings.

Roger de Llúria 35. (*C*) **93-342-66-73.** Reservations required. Main courses 9€–26€ ($10–$30); fixed-price lunch 16€ ($18); tasting menu 52€ ($60). Mon–Fri 1:30–4pm and 8:30pm–midnight; Sat 8:30pm–midnight. Closed Aug 8–22. Metro: Urquinaona.

Reno ★ CATALAN/FRENCH One of the finest and most enduring haute cuisine restaurants in Barcelona, Reno sits behind sidewalk-to-ceiling windows hung with fine-mesh lace to shelter diners from prying eyes on the octagonal plaza outside. The impeccably mannered staff is formal but not intimidating.

Seasonal specialties might include partridge simmered in wine or port sauce, a platter of assorted fish smoked on the premises, hake with anchovy sauce, or filet of sole stuffed with foie gras and truffles or grilled with anchovy sauce. An appetizing array of pastries wheels from table to table on a cart. Dessert might also be crepes flambéed at your table.

Tuset 27. ⓒ 93-200-91-29. Reservations recommended. Main courses 13€–28€ ($15–$32); fixed-price lunch 30€ ($35); tasting menu 45€ ($52). AE, DC, MC, V. Mon–Fri 1–4pm and 9–11:30pm; Sat 9–11:30pm. Closed Aug. Metro: Diagonal.

MODERATE

Il Giardinetto ⓖ *Moments* ITALIAN   This eatery, a perennial favorite of the uptown arts crowd, won a major design award when it was opened in 1973, and the "fantasy forest" surroundings haven't dated one iota. Split into two levels, the space is dominated by columns with painted branch motifs, the walls are covered with naive foliage cutouts, and the low ceilings sport swirls of pretty pale, green leaves. After taking it all in, curl into one of the teal blue velvet banquettes and survey the menu of classic Italian dishes. You may wish to indulge in one of their heady black or white (when in season) truffle risottos or pastas, or a tuna *carpaccio* or tagliatelle with dainty vegetables and strips of Jabugo ham for something lighter. Our salads of rocket and *radicchio* and mixed greens and foie were as good as anything served in the *hosterías* of the Veneto and mains are well executed and generous in size. The only slight letdown was dessert; the tiramisu was lacking in both coffee and amaretto flavors but the sinful "fatty" vanilla ice cream with bitter chocolate sauce more than made up for this lapse. There is a resident pianist in evenings, and the service is old school without being stuffy.

La Granada del Penedès 22. ⓒ 93-218-75-36. Reservations recommended. Main courses 12€–19€ ($14–$22); fixed-price lunch 18€ ($21). AE, DC, MC, V. Mon–Fri 1:30–4:30pm and 8:30pm–1:30am; Sat 8:30pm–2am. Closed Aug. Metro: Diagonal.

L'Olive ⓖ CATALAN/MEDITERRANEAN   You assume that this two-floor restaurant is named for the olive that figures so prominently into its cuisine, but actually it's named for the owner, Josep Olive. You can be born with no more apt a name for a Mediterranean restaurateur. The building is designed in a modern Catalan style with walls adorned with reproductions of famous Spanish painters, such as Miró, Dalí, or Picasso. The tables are topped in marble, the floors impeccably polished. There are sections on both floors where it's possible to have some privacy, and overall the feeling is one of elegance with a touch of intimacy. You won't be disappointed by anything on the menu, especially *bacallà a la llauna* (baked salt cod) or *filet de vedella al vi negre al forn* (veal filets cooked in the oven in a red-wine sauce), and the *salsa maigret* of duck with strawberry sauce. Monkfish flavored with roasted garlic is a palate pleaser, and you can finish with a *crema catalana* or one of the delicious Catalan pastries.

Calle Balmes 47. ⓒ 93-452-19-90. Reservations recommended. Main courses 12€–21€ ($14–$24); *menú completo* 36€ ($41). AE, DC, MC, V. Mon–Sat 1–4pm and 8:30pm–midnight; Sun 1–4pm. Metro: Passeig de Gràcia.

Rosalert ⓖ CATALAN/SEAFOOD   At the corner of Carrer Napols close to La Sagrada Família, this restaurant has been the domain of Jordi Alert for more than 4 decades. He specializes in *comida del mar a la plancha* (grilled seafood), and does so in a typical setting of hardwood floors and tile-covered walls. His seafood and crustaceans are grilled on a heated iron plate without any additives. There is no more awesome glass tank of live shellfish in Barcelona. You choose your meal, and the poor victim is extracted with a net and thrown on the grill.

Of course, you find all the typical offerings, such as tiny octopus, succulent mussels, fat shrimp, squid, fresh oysters, and langoustines. If you're daring, you can order such unusual seafood as *dátiles,* a delicious shellfish whose shape resembles a date (hence the name). Begin with one of the freshly made tapas, such as salt cod in vinaigrette or fava beans laced with garlic and virgin olive oil. Your best bet might be the *parrillada* (assorted fish and shellfish from the grill). One of the best offerings is turbot cooked on the grill with potatoes and fresh mushrooms.

Diagonal 301. ℂ 93-207-10-19. Reservations recommended. Main courses 10€–24€ ($12–$28); fixed-price lunch 18€ ($21); tasting menu 45€ ($52). AE, DC, MC, V. Tues–Sun 9am–5pm and 8pm–2am. Closed Aug 10–30. Metro: Verdaguer/Sagrada Família.

Tragaluz ♣ MEDITERRANEAN   This is the flagship restaurant of the city's most respected group of restaurateurs. It offers three very contemporary-looking dining rooms on separate floors, scattered with eclectic pieces of art and very clever lighting. Menu items are derived from fresh ingredients that vary with the season. Depending on the month of your visit, you might find terrine of duck liver, Santurce-style hake (with garlic and herbs), filet of sole stuffed with red peppers, and beef tenderloin in a Rioja wine sauce. One of the best desserts is a semi-soft slice of deliberately underbaked chocolate cake. Diners seeking low-fat dishes will find solace here, as will vegetarians. The vegetables served are the best and freshest in the market that day. Downstairs you will find Tragarapíd, a faster, more casual version of what's up stairs and across the road is an enormously popular Japanese restaurant that is directed by the same group. The Tragaluz chefs are adept at taking local products and turning them into flavorful, carefully prepared dishes and succeed in this extremely well.

Passatge de la Concepció 5. ℂ 93-487-06-21. Reservations recommended. Main courses 15€–28€ ($17–$32); fixed-price lunch 20€ ($23); tasting menu 50€ ($58). AE, DC, MC, V. Sun–Wed 1:30–4pm and 8:30pm–midnight; Thurs–Sat 1:30–4pm and 8:30pm–1am. Metro: Diagonal.

INEXPENSIVE

El Caballito Blanco SEAFOOD/INTERNATIONAL   This is a Barcelona standby famous for seafood and popular with the locals. The fluorescent-lit dining area does not offer much atmosphere, but the food is good, varied, and relatively inexpensive (unless you order lobster or other expensive shellfish). The "Little White Horse," in the Passeig de Gràcia area, features a huge selection, including monkfish, mussels marinara, and shrimp with garlic. If you don't want fish, try the grilled lamb cutlets. Several different pâtés and salads are offered. There's a bar to the left of the dining area.

Mallorca 196. ℂ 93-453-10-33. Main courses 8€–30€ ($9–$35). AE, DC, MC, V. Tues–Sat 1–3:45pm and 9–10:45pm; Sun 1–3:45pm. Closed Aug. Metro: Hospital Clinic and Diagonal.

Out of China CHINESE   Unless you have somehow lost all your taste buds, the majority of Chinese restaurants in Barcelona, with their soulless, order-by-numbers version of Chinese food which for some reason is deemed more suitable to Latin taste, are not worth considering. One exception is Out of China. They claim to serve "homemade" Chinese food, and they are not far off the mark. The decor, with its brightly colored Mao kitsch and cigarette girl posters, is certainly a change from the normal snarling dragons and sad fish tanks. They are also one of the only Chinese restaurants to serve dim sum and other exotic (at least for Barcelona) dishes such as green tea noodles with grilled shrimp tails.

Muntaner 100. ℂ 93-451-55-55. Main courses 5€–9€ ($5.75–$10); Fixed-price lunch menu 8.50€ ($9.80). AE, MC, V. Daily 1–4pm and 8:30pm–midnight. Metro: Diagonal.

> ### (Kids) Family-Friendly Restaurants
>
> **Dulcinea** This longtime favorite cafe/snack bar, at Petrixol 2 (© **93-302-68-24**), makes a great refueling stop any time of the day—guaranteed to satisfy any chocoholic. Lots of other sweet treats and drinks are on offer.
>
> **Poble Espanyol** (p. 165)   A good introduction to Spanish food. All the restaurants in the "Spanish Village" serve comparable food at comparable prices—let the kids choose what to eat.
>
> **La Paradeta** (p. 114)   Fish and chip fun; fish-loving kids get to choose what they want and see it being cooked.
>
> **Mesón David** (p. 114)   You don't have to worry about them making a noise here, the rest of the patrons and staff are just as ear bursting.
>
> **Murivecchi** (p. 115)   Friendly, family-run Italian place with plenty of pasta dishes to suit the young ones.

SNACKS, TAPAS & DRINKS

Bar Turò TAPAS/CATALAN   In an affluent residential neighborhood north of the Old Town, Bar Turò serves some of the best tapas in town. In summer you can sit outside or retreat to the narrow confines of the bar. You select from about 20 kinds of tapas, including Russian salad, fried squid, and Serrano ham.

Tenor Viñas 1. © **93-200-69-53**. Tapas 2€–12€ ($2.30–$14); main courses 4€–18€ ($4.60–$21). MC, V. Mon–Sat 8:30am–midnight; Sun 10am–4pm. Closed weekends in Aug. Metro: Hospital Clinic.

La Bodegueta TAPAS   Founded in 1940, this old wine tavern is one of the more authentic options in this ritzy boulevard of franchised eateries. It specializes in Catalan sausage *(botifarra)*, salamis, and cheeses. Wash them all down with inexpensive Spanish wines from the barrel. It's loud, no-nonsense, and a favorite with students.

Rambla de Catalunya 100. © **93-215-48-94**. Tapas from 1.40€–15€ ($1.60–$17). No credit cards. Mon–Sat 7am–1:30am; Sun 7pm–1am. Closed Aug 8–22. Metro: Diagonal.

Casa Alfonso TAPAS   Spaniards love their ham, which comes in many forms. The best of the best is *jamón Jabugo,* the only one sold at this traditional establishment. Entire hams hang from steel braces. They're taken down, carved, and trimmed before you into paper-thin slices. This particular form of cured ham, generically called *jamón Serrano,* comes from pigs fed acorns in Huelva, in deepest Andalusia. Devotees of all things porcine will ascend to piggy-flavored heaven. Also serve salads and grilled meat dishes.

Roger de Llúria 6. © **93-301-97-83**. Tapas 4€–9€ ($4.60–$10); tasting menu 15€ ($17). AE, DC, MC, V. Mon–Tues 9am–midnight; Wed–Sat 9am–1am. Metro: Urquinaona.

Casa Tejada TAPAS   Covered with rough stucco and decorated with hanging hams, Casa Tejada (established in 1964) offers some of the best tapas. Arranged behind a glass display case, they include such dishes as marinated fresh tuna, German-style potato salad, ham salad, and five preparations of squid (including one that's stuffed). For variety, quantity, and quality, this place is hard to beat. There's outdoor dining in summer.

Tenor Viñas 3. © **93-200-73-41**. Tapas 3€–17€ ($3.45–$20). MC, V. Daily 7am–1:30am. Closed Aug 8–21. Metro: Hospital Clinic.

5 Gràcia

EXPENSIVE

Botafumeiro ★★★ SEAFOOD   Although the competition is strong, this classic *marisquería* consistently puts Barcelona's finest seafood on the table. Much of the allure comes from the attention of the white-jacketed staff. If you like, you can eat at the bar. If you venture to the rear, you'll find a series of attractive dining rooms noted for the ease with which business deals seem to be arranged during the lunch hour. International businesspeople often rendezvous here, and the King of Spain is sometimes a patron.

Menu items include fresh seafood prepared in a glistening modern kitchen visible from parts of the dining room. The establishment prides itself on its fresh and saltwater fish, clams, mussels, lobster, crayfish, scallops, and several varieties of crustaceans that you may never have seen before. Stored live in holding tanks or in enormous crates near the entrance, many of the creatures are flown in daily from Galicia, home of owner Moncho Neira. With the 100 or so fish dishes, the menu lists only four or five meat dishes, including three kinds of steak, veal, and a traditional version of pork with turnips. The wine list offers a wide array of *cavas* from Catalonia and highly drinkable choices from Galicia.

Gran de Gràcia 81. ℂ 93-218-42-30. Reservations recommended for dining rooms. Main courses 22€–40€ ($25–$46). AE, DC, MC, V. Daily 1pm–1am. Metro: Fontana.

Jean Luc Figueras ★★★ CATALAN   For a *Kama Sutra*–like dining experience, head for this hip Gràcia town house that was once the studio of Balenciaga. Even if food critics narrowed the list of Barcelona restaurants down to five, the chef and owner, Jean Luc Figueras, would likely appear on the list. The setting is modern and refined, and the cookery is both traditional and innovative, as Figueras stamps every dish with his own personal touch. Highly dedicated to staying on top, Figueras is a seeker of the finest raw materials on the Barcelona market, and his menu is adjusted to take advantage of the best produce in any season. The emphasis is on fresh seafood, although his meat dishes are also sublime. His fried prawn and ginger-flecked pasta in a mango and mustard sauce would make the gods weep, and his sea bass with cod and blood sausage was no less brilliant. Your tongue will fall in love with you if you're wise enough to select such nouvelle-inspired dishes as shrimp with a velvety smooth and golden pumpkin cream sauce or the pork with a zesty goat cheese enlivened with peach honey. The desserts are homemade and inevitably sumptuous, and I took particular delight in the seven varieties of freshly made bread.

Santa Teresa 10. ℂ 93-415-28-77. Reservations required. Main courses 20€–36€ ($23–$41); tasting menu 75€ ($86). AE, DC, MC, V. Mon–Sat 1:30–3:30pm and 8:30–11:30pm. Metro: Diagonal.

Roig Robí ★ INTERNATIONAL   This restaurant—the name means "ruby red" (the color of a perfectly aged Rioja) in Catalan—serves excellent food from an imaginative kitchen with a warm welcome. Although I'm not as excited about this restaurant as I once was, it does remain one of the city's most dependable choices. Order an aperitif at the L-shaped oak bar, then head down a long corridor to a pair of flower-filled dining rooms. In warm weather, glass doors open onto a verdant walled courtyard. Menu items include fresh beans with pine nut sauce, *hake al Roig Robí,* fresh mushroom salad with green beans and fresh tomatoes, and shellfish from Costa Brava. Monkfish comes with clams and onion confit, ravioli stuffed with spring herbs, and chicken stuffed with foie gras. Cockscomb salad is available for those with adventuresome palates.

Gràcia Dining

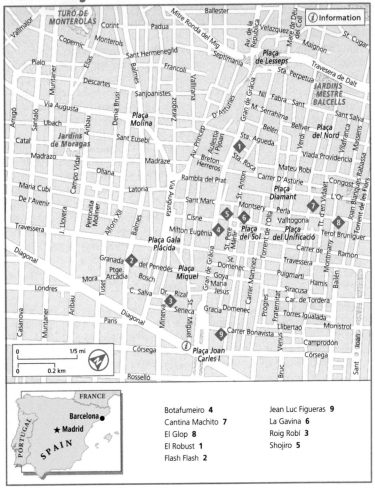

FRANCE

Barcelona •

★ Madrid

SPAIN

PORTUGAL

Botafumeiro **4**	Jean Luc Figueras **9**
Cantina Machito **7**	La Gavina **6**
El Glop **8**	Roig Robí **3**
El Robust **1**	Shojiro **5**
Flash Flash **2**	

Séneca 20. ☏ **93-218-92-22.** Reservations required. Main courses 12€–36€ ($14–$41); tasting menu 56€ ($64); fixed-price menu 44€ ($51). AE, DC, MC, V. Mon–Fri 1:30–4pm; Mon–Sat 9–11:30pm. Closed Aug 8–21. Metro: Diagonal.

MODERATE

El Glop CATALAN   This place has been a Gràcia institution for decades. It offers affordable, local cuisine at great prices and in a highly agreeable setting in a corner building with exposed beams and an interior patio. Many pop in for some quick *torrades,* toasted rustic bread rubbed with tomato and topped with all manner of cheese, salamis, and hams. More substantial fare includes *botifarras* (Catalan sausages), chops, chicken, and other carnivore fare cooked over an open flame and served up with creamy aioli and snails cooked in the oven. It's bright, informal, and always busy, and a good place to bring the kids.

Montmany 46. ☏ **93-213-70-58.** Reservations recommended. Main courses 3€–20€ ($3.45–$23); fixed-price menu 7€ ($8.05); tasting menu from 22€ ($25). MC, V. Mon–Sun 1–4pm and 8pm–1am. Metro: Joanic. Another branch is located at Caspe 21 (☏ **93-318-75-75;** Metro: Catalunya).

Flash-Flash Tortillería *Moments* OMELETS/HAMBURGERS   Hamburgers, steaks salads, and over 70 types of *tortillas* are served up in a pop-art setting of funky black-and-white murals and white leather banquettes. It's completely authentic; Flash-Flash was opened in 1970 and the interior hasn't been altered since. The Twiggy-like model adorning the walls was the wife of Leopoldo Pomés, a well-known fashion photographer of the time and part owner. Decor aside, the food is very good; the tortillas fly out fresh and fluffy and the bunless burgers are some of the best in town. It's a favorite with uptown business types, some who have been coming here since the place opened.

Granada de Penedès 25. ℂ **93-237-09-90.** Reservations recommended. Main courses 8€–25€ ($9.20–$29). AE, DC, MC, V. Daily 1pm–1:30am. FGC: Gràcia

Shojiro ✿ ASIAN FUSION   With Japanese restaurants now the norm in Barcelona, it was only a matter before Nippon cuisine was fused with the local one. This quirky restaurant, led by Shojiro Ochi, a native of Japan who arrived in Barcelona in 1979, does just that. Ochi presents it to you in set-price four- and five-course menus. These delectable morsels include *bonito* (a type of A-grade tuna) preserved in a Catalan *escabeche,* tuna with a sherry reduction, or duck's breast with shitake mushrooms. Desserts include more unconventional delights such as a foie bon-bon and ostrich *tataki.*

Ros de Olano 11. ℂ **93-415-65-48.** Fixed-price lunch 16€ ($18); fixed-price dinner 30€–40€ ($35–$46). AE, DC, MC, V. Mon–Sat 1:30–3:30pm; Tues–Sat 9pm–12:30am. Metro: Fontana and Joanic.

INEXPENSIVE

Cantina Machito MEXICAN   This is generally considered to be the best Mexican restaurant in Barcelona. It's hard to get a table, especially when the cinema crowd from next door rolls in, but it's worth the wait. What they serve is far from the rudimentary Tex-Mex fare. The tacos and tortillas and a tangy guacamole are all present and correct but so is a chicken mole and *sopa malpeña,* a warming soup of chickpeas, tomato, and chicken, plus an unusual lime and tequila mousse for dessert. The margaritas are renowned as are their parties on Mexican national days and *fiestas.*

Torrijos 47. ℂ **93-217-34-14.** Reservations recommended. Main courses 6€–12€ ($6.90–$14). MC, V. Daily 1–4:30pm and 7pm–1:30am. Metro: Fontana and Joanic.

La Gavina PIZZAS   This place is hugely popular for pizzas, from your basic tomato and mozzarella type to a more lavish version with seafood and caviar. Well worth trying is the *payes,* paper-thin slices of potato, rosemary, and olive oil. The owner is obviously obsessed with heavenly bodies as thousands of angels, virgins, and other religious deities are hung everywhere for a chic, junk-shop affect.

Ros de Olano 17. ℂ **93-415-74-50.** Reservations recommended. Main courses 6€–11€ ($6.90–$13). No credit cards. Daily 1pm–1am; July–Sept daily 6pm–1am. Metro: Fontana.

El Robust CATALAN   Locals wishing to escape the evening heat clamor for El Robust's pretty patio garden replete with lemon and pine trees. The fare here is solid Catalan: organic meat *a la brasa* (flame grilled) and charcuterie from Vic, the inland town famed for its cured meats. Vegetarians will be appeased by a good selection of salads and other tidbits such as deep-fried Camembert.

Gran de Gràcia 196. ℂ **93-237-90-46.** Main courses 6€–12€ ($6.90–$14). MC, V. Mon–Sat noon–4pm and 8.30pm–midnight. Closed Aug 8–31. Metro: Fontana.

Eating Alfresco

Finding a great terrace to sit out on in Barcelona is a feat easier said than done. There are literally hundreds of sidewalk cafes where you can drink your cappuccino to the roar of passing traffic, and tourist-filled plazas lined by restaurants serving the same old microwaved paellas. But a tucked away garden, a tranquil terrace, or a hideaway by the sea . . . that's another matter altogether.

The **Café de L'Academia,** Calle Lledó 1 (© **93-319-82-53**; p. 108), is located on the one of the prettiest plazas in Barcelona, Plaza Sant Just. Presided over by a church of the same name, it is reputedly Barcelona's oldest, and according to lore, if you believe your life to be in mortal danger you can still make a legally binding will at the altar with a friend as a witness. It was also on this square that the Romans executed the first Christians. Ghosts of the past aside, today it is one of the most peaceful and unspoiled plazas in the Old City. In the Born, the **Tèxtil Café,** Calle Montcada 12 (© **93-268-25-98**), is an oasis of calm enclosed within the courtyard of an 18th-century palace. Providing you're not in a hurry (service is notoriously laidback) it's an idyllic place in the inner city to fuel up on tea, coffee, and hearty, wholesome lunches in the shade of large, white parasols or the warmth of outdoor gas fires in winter.

Barcelona's seafront has restaurant terraces a-plenty, but for something a little more clandestine continue along to the so-called Parc del Port Olímpic, which straddles two busy highways. Here, sunk from view and traffic noise, is the gorgeous **Anfiteatro,** Av. Litoral 36 (© **65-969-53-45;** p. 133)—a smart restaurant serving creative Mediterranean dishes—with a spacious terrace that wraps around an ornamental pool. Another way to escape the crowds is to get up onto the rooftops; namely at **La Miranda del Museu,** Museu d'Història de Catalunya, Plaça Pau Vila 3 (© **93-225-50-07**), which has fabulous views over the yachts in Port Vell. Frustratingly the terrace is for drinks only, so go in time for an aperitif and linger over coffee.

Heading a little further out and halfway up the hill to Montjuïc, **La Font del Gat,** Passeig Santa Madrona 28 (© **93-289-04-04**), is a secret garden and lunch spot chiseled out of the mountainside beneath the better known Joan Miró Foundation. Like anywhere though, the further out you go, the prettier the surroundings, and if its real tranquillity you're seeking (not to mention exclusivity), the restaurants in the suburbs are what really shine. In Horta, **Can Travi Nou,** Jorge Manrique, Parc de la Vall d'Hebron (© **93-428-04-34**), is a converted 14th-century farmhouse with sprawling grounds, two or three ample terraces and gardens for strolling. It's great for long Sunday lunches or evenings under the stars, and serves decent, if pricey, roast meats, fish dishes, and paella.

Finally, if you're looking to treat yourself (or somebody else) **L'Orangeriek** Gran Hotel La Florida, Carretera de Vallvidrera al Tibidabo 83–93 (© **93-259-30-00**), is situated on the highest peak of the Collserola with stunning views over Barcelona. Its scented gardens and terraces make it one of the most spectacular dining destinations in the city.

6 Barceloneta & Vila Olímpica

EXPENSIVE

Anfiteatro ★ *(Moments* MEDITERRANEAN   As chic as it is, it's amazing how this restaurant manages to elude so many. This could be because it's tucked away on an underground level of a boulevard in the Olympic Village. It was designed by the studio of Oriol Bohigas, one of the city's leading architects who also responsible for the Olympic Village itself. Its rationalist lines are softened by an abundance of mosaics and a central pond, which is surrounded by tables. Amongst this unique setting of urban romanticism you can partake in wild sea bass with grapes and a port sauce or cuttlefish and crab ravioli. If there is room for dessert, go for the mascarpone and vanilla ice cream with a mango purée.

Parc del Port Olímpic, Av. Litoral 37 (opposite Calle Rosa Sensat). ✆ **65-969-53-45.** Reservations recommended on weekend. Main courses 15€–30€ ($17–$35); fixed-price lunch menu 30€ ($35); tasting menu 38€ ($44) and 50€ ($58). AE, MC, V. Tues–Sat 1–4pm and 8.30pm–midnight; Sun 1–4pm. Closed Easter week. Metro: Port Olímpic.

Can Costa ★ SEAFOOD   This is one of the oldest seafood restaurants in this seafaring town. Established in the late 1930s, it has two busy dining rooms, a practiced staff, and an outdoor terrace, although a warehouse blocks the view of the harbor. Fresh seafood prepared according to traditional recipes rules the menu. It includes the best baby squid in town—sautéed in a flash so that it has a nearly grilled flavor, almost never overcooked or rubbery. A longstanding chef's specialty is *fideuà de peix,* a relative of the classic Valencian shellfish paella, with noodles instead of rice. Desserts are made fresh daily.

Passeig de Joan de Borbón 70. ✆ **93-221-59-03.** Reservations recommended. Main courses 16€–30€ ($18–$35). MC, V. Thurs–Tues 12:30–4pm and 8–11:30pm; Wed 12:30–4pm. Metro: Barceloneta.

Can Solé ★ CATALAN   In Barceloneta at the harbor, Can Solé still honors the traditions of this former fishing village. Many of the seafood joints here are too touristy for our tastes, but this one is authentic and delivers good value. The decor is rustic and a bit raffish, with wine barrels, lots of noise, and excellent food. Begin with the sweet tiny clams or the cod cakes, perhaps some bouilla-baisse. Little langoustines are an eternal but expensive favorite, and everything is aromatically perfumed with fresh garlic. You might also sample one of the seafood-rich dishes. Desserts are so good they're worth saving room for, especially the orange pudding or the praline ice cream.

Carrer Sant Carles 4. ✆ **93-221-50-12.** Reservations required. Main courses 9€–40€ ($10–$46). AE, DC. MC, V. Tues–Sat 1–4pm and 8:30–11pm; Sun 1–4pm. Metro: Barceloneta.

Els Pescadors ★★ SEAFOOD   Out of all the fish restaurants in Barcelona, it is generally agreed that this is one of the best. It's located slightly out of the main drag, in the working-class beach side suburb of Poble Nou, but that doesn't stop foodies from making the trip. The restaurant is divided into two *ambientes;* one is old school—with marble tabletops and wooden beams—while the other is modern Mediterranean. But no one has come to gawk at the surroundings. What they have to come to do (and have been doing so for generations) is enjoy the freshest fish in Barcelona, cooked in classical ways with surprising touches. Local prawns will be served with steaming chickpeas, or a baked fish, whatever has been trawled in that day, with clams and small white beans.

Plaça Prim 1. ✆ **93-225-20-18.** Reservations recommended on weekend. Main courses 13€–32€ ($15–$37). AE, DC, MC, V. Daily 1–3:45pm and 8.30pm–midnight. Closed Easter week. Metro: Poble Nou.

Barceloneta Dining

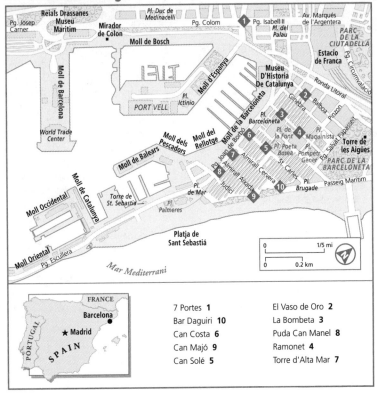

7 Portes **1**

Bar Daguiri **10**

Can Costa **6**

Can Majó **9**

Can Solé **5**

El Vaso de Oro **2**

La Bombeta **3**

Puda Can Manel **8**

Ramonet **4**

Torre d'Alta Mar **7**

7 Portes ★ *Moments* CATALAN Festive and elegant, 7 Portes been going since 1836, making it one of the oldest restaurants in Barcelona. Pretty much anybody who is anybody has dined here over the years. While these days it's more touristy than aristocratic, there is still enough authentic charm left in the decor (and patrons) to make it well worth the visit. The kitchen is continuous, and the white-aproned staff members are constantly on the go, which in some ways makes it feel like an up-market canteen. There is nothing slap-dash about the food though; regional dishes include fresh herring with onions and potatoes, a different paella daily (sometimes with shellfish, for example, or with rabbit), and a wide array of fresh fish, expertly deboned and skinned at the table. You might order succulent oysters or an herb-laden stew of black beans with pork or white beans with sausage. Portions are enormous. The restaurant's name means "Seven Doors," and it really does have seven doors, underneath some charming porticoes that are typical to this portside pocket of Barcelona.

Passeig d'Isabel II 14. ☎ **93-319-30-33**. Reservations required. Main courses 18€–32€ ($21–$37). AE, DC, MC, V. Daily 1pm–1am. Metro: Barceloneta.

Torre d'Alta Mar MEDITERRANEAN Altamar is sort of a mile high gastro club. Its unique setting is the 75m-high (246 ft.) Torre de Sant Sebastián, one of the three towers that serves the port-crossing, tourist carrying cable car (p. 166). But don't worry about rubbing shoulders with back-packers when you enter this exclusive eatery; patrons are whisked up in a private high-tech glass lift

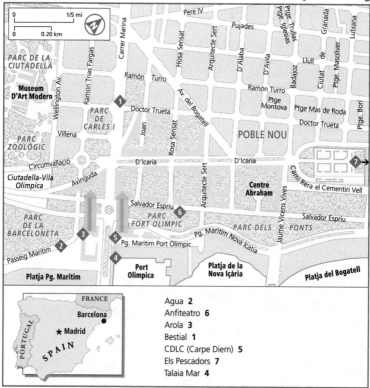

Agua **2**
Anfiteatro **6**
Arola **3**
Bestial **1**
CDLC (Carpe Diem) **5**
Els Pescadors **7**
Talaia Mar **4**

to be greeted by a simply breathtaking 360-degree view of the city and sea. Once your jaw finally stops dropping and you are settled in the plush decor, you can dine in style from a predominantly fish menu that includes such inventions as a hake, porcini and artichoke stir-fry, stewed monkfish in *romesco* sauce, or salt-roasted bream.

Passeig de Joan de Borbón 88. ⓒ **93-221-00-07.** Reservations recommended. Main courses 20€–30€ ($23–$35). Daily 1–3:30pm and 8.45–11:30pm. Metro: Barceloneta.

MODERATE

Agua ⓖ MEDITERRANEAN   It bustles, it's hip, and it serves well-prepared fish and shellfish in a hyper-modern setting overlooking the beach. A terrace beckons anyone who wants an in-your-face view of the water, but if the wind is blowing with a bit too much chill, you can retreat into the big-windowed blue-and-yellow dining room. Here, amid display cases showing the catch of the day, you can order heaping portions of meats and fish to be grilled over an open fire. Excellent examples include grilled versions of chicken, fish, shrimp, crayfish, and an especially succulent version of stuffed squid. Most of them are served with as little culinary fanfare, and as few sauces, as possible, allowing the freshness and flavor of the raw ingredients to shine through the chargrilled coatings. Risottos, some of them studded with fresh clams and herbs, are usually winners, with many versions suitable for vegetarians. The only problem here is its popularity; make sure you book on the weekends.

Passeig Marítim de la Barceloneta 30 (Vila Olímpica). © 93-225-12-72. Reservations recommended. Main courses 5€–15€ ($5.75–$17). AE, DC, MC, V. Daily 1:30–4pm and 8:30pm–midnight (until 1am Fri–Sat). Metro: Ciutadella–Vila Olímpica.

Arola ⭐ CATALAN/SPANISH   Blessed with two Michelin stars and good-looking to boot, Sergi Arola is one of the rising young stars of Spain's culinary world. He hails from Catalunya, but this is his first restaurant in Barcelona (his other, La Broche, is in Madrid) and the setting is no less than the luxury Hotel Arts in the Olympic Village. What Arola aims to do amidst a quirky, pop-art decor in purple and lime green, is to give the *pica-pica* modern makeover. *Pica-pica* can be best translated as "nibbles." It's not tapas exactly, as tapas usually involve some form of labor-intensive preparation. Pica-pica on the other hand could be bite-sized pieces of Manchego cheese, Iberian ham, preserved shellfish, or high-end canned tuna. Thus your meal at Arola is likely to start with *patatas bravas* cut and arranged on plate to look like dozens of tiny female breasts, tinned cockles that meticulously fan out from a dainty bowl of piquant dressing, and perfect asparagus spears that lay languidly on a bed of romesco sauce. Main courses include Mediterranean standards with a touch of Arola magic: steamed mussels with citrus juice and saffron, Gorgonzola cheese croquettes, grilled prawns with cold potato cream, and sea bass with an emulsion of watercress to name just a few. The dessert of goat's cheese, macadamia nuts, tomato jam, and quince cream should convince you of his talent.

Hotel Arts, Marina 19–21. © 93-483-80-90. Reservations required. Main courses 8€–29€ ($9.20–$33); tasting menu 45€ ($52). AE, DC, MC, V. Tues 8:30–11pm; Wed 1:30–3:30pm; Thurs–Fri 1:30–3:30pm and 8.30–11:30pm; Sat–Sun 2–4pm and 8:30–11pm. Closed Jan (month closed can vary each year). Metro: Ciutadella–Vila Olímpica.

Bestial MEDITERRANEAN/ITALIAN   One of the latest conquests of the Tragaluz group (p. 6) is the modern Mediterranean eatery Bestial. Mercifully unrecognizable from the location's previous tenant Planet Hollywood, it brings some well-needed class to the gastronomically pedestrian Olympic Marina and the menu has been designed as an Italian-influenced alternative to the dozens of packet-paella restaurants in the immediate vicinity. What sounds good on paper often doesn't transfer well to table. Our *caprese* salad was promising; a hearty mound of *buffala* surrounded by plump red tomato slices, but my following *carbonara* measly in size and slap-dash in execution. My companion's seared tuna with black olive risotto proved a better choice; nothing measly about the size of the fish chunks here. That said, the outdoor setting, with its meters of noise-absorbing wooden decking and oversized umbrellas, is highly stylish (and functional), but the inside dining room is like sitting in a sci-fi bus station.

Ramón Trias Fargas 30 (Vila Olímpica). © 93-224-04-07. Main courses 8€–18€ ($9.20–$21). AE, DC, MC, V. Mon–Fri 1:30–4pm and 8.30pm–midnight (until 1am on Fri); Sat 1:30–5pm and 8.30pm–1am; Sun 1:30–5pm and 8.30pm–midnight. Metro: Ciutadella–Vila Olímpica.

Can Majó ⭐⭐ SEAFOOD   This is one of the best seafood restaurants in Barcelona, lying close to the harbor life. In summer one of the most desirable tables at the port is found on the terrace of this restaurant. The decoration inside is in the rustic tavern style, most inviting. Art lines the walls, and the staff exudes a hospitable, friendly aura as they give excellent, sometimes rushed service. The food plows fairly familiar ground, but when it's good, it's good, and it can be very good indeed. The fish is very fresh tasting, as it was just brought in that morning. Now almost into its fourth decade, the restaurant still serves some of the best *sopa de pescado y marisco* (fish and shellfish soup) in the area. Its sautéed squid is a heavenly meal in itself, or in the words of one diner: "A day without calamari is a day in hell." *Bacalao* (dried cod) appears in a savory green sauce with little baby clams in their shells. Its paellas are as good as those served in the restaurants of Valencia, and their lobster bouillabaisse is extremely gratifying.

Almirall Aixada 23. ℭ **93-221-54-55**. Reservations required. Main courses 12€–24€ ($14–$28). AE, DC, MC, V. Tues–Sat 1–4pm and 8:30–11:30pm; Sun 1–4pm. Metro: Barceloneta.

CDLC (Carpe Diem) MEDITERRANEAN FUSION

Before it turns into a club for *gente guapa* (beautiful people; see p. 211), CDLC functions as a restaurant. Rather than the food or impeccable service, the attraction here is its sea-facing terrace. Not that the cuisine, with its strong Thai and Japanese influence, is in anyway unacceptable, but true foodies may be suspect as to how a plate of sushi can make it to your table in just under 30 seconds. Perhaps better stick to the lunchtime fare, which includes very reasonably priced salads, sandwiches, and burgers. In true show-off style, the wine list includes some offerings priced to impress; treat your date to a 306€ ($352) bottle of Cristal champagne, and if that doesn't do the trick go for the 496€ ($570) Sant Emilion Cheval Blanc from 1996 with the mains.

Passeig Marítim 32. ℭ **93-224-04-70**. Reservations required. Main courses 9€–22€ ($10–$25); fixed-price lunch 15€ ($17). AE, DC, MC, V. Daily noon–3am. Metro: Ciutadella–Vila Olímpica.

Puda Can Manel ⊛ MEDITERRANEAN/SPANISH

One of the more annoying aspects of walking down Barceloneta's main boulevard are waiters trying to coax you into their often over-priced and ordinary outdoor restaurants. You will notice that none of this goes on at Puda Can Manel because it is none of the above but rather one of the best bets along this touristy stretch. On Sunday afternoons you see locals waiting patiently for a table while its neighbors remain empty. They are lining up for succulent, tasty paellas and *fideuàs* (which replace rice for thin noodles), rich *arroz negre* (rice cooked in squid ink) and calamari fried to perfection, all at excellent prices considering the overall standard.

Passeig de Joan de Borbón 60 (Barceloneta). ℭ **93-221-50-13**. Reservations required. Main courses 8€–15€ ($9.20–$17). AE, DC, MC, V. Tues–Sun 1–4pm and 7–11pm. Metro: Ciutadella–Vila Olímpica.

Ramonet ⊛ SEAFOOD

In a Catalan-style villa near the seaport, this rather expensive restaurant serves a large variety of fresh seafood and has done so since 1763. The front room, with stand-up tables for seafood tapas, beer, and regional wine, is often crowded. In the two dining rooms, you can choose from a variety of seafood—shrimp, hake, and monkfish are almost always available. Other specialties include pungent anchovies, grilled mushrooms, black rice, braised artichokes, tortilla with spinach and beans, and mussels "from the beach."

Carrer Maquinista 17. ℭ **93-319-30-64**. Reservations recommended. Main courses 10€–25€ ($12–$29). DC, MC, V. Daily noon–midnight. Metro: Barceloneta.

Talaia Mar ⊛⊛ MEDITERRANEAN

This is not only the best restaurant at Olympic Port, but has one of the most innovative menus in Catalonia. Javier Planes, the chef, devises unique menus and turns out food that is both amusing and savory. The presentations are often simple yet always elegant. To discover this chef's talent, sample his set menu, which he calls, quite appropriately, *festival gastronómico*. For a main course, sample his tuna tartare with guacamole and salmon eggs or his brochettes of lobster. The increasingly rare black truffle appears in some of his smooth and velvety risottos. He does a marvelous steamed hake in a balsamic reduction as well as a grilled sea bass with shrimp, which is flavored with asparagus juice among other delights. Fresh fish arrives from the market daily and is grilled to perfection, as is the aromatically roasted rack of lamb. I could return here night after night and always find some new dish to tempt the palate. Rising above the port, the restaurant is beside two towers, Hotel Arts and Torre Mapfre.

Marina 16. (C) **93-221-90-90**. Reservations required. Main courses 15€–27€ ($17–$31); fixed-price menu 51€ ($59). AE, DC, MC, V. Tues–Sun 1–4pm and 8pm–midnight. Metro: Ciutadella–Vila Olímpica.

SNACKS, TAPAS & DRINKS

Bar Daguiri CAFE   This bar-cafe with a bohemian vibe is right on the beach, an enviable location for many a restaurateur. They serve up light meals such as salads, dips, and sandwiches, plus coffee and drinks to a reggae beat, and outside on the terrace there is always a street musician doing his or her thing. The service can be infuriatingly inept, but it's all part of the laid-back beach culture in this neck of the woods. A plus is the free Internet access—bring in your laptop and they will wire you up, and there is free live gig (mainly jazz and Latin) music on Thursday evenings. The large selection of daily foreign newspapers is also a welcome touch.

Grau i Torras 59. (C) **93-221-51-09**. Snacks 5€–8€ ($5.75–$9.20). MC, V. Daily 10am–midnight. Metro: Barceloneta.

El Vaso de Oro ⭐ TAPAS   Another very good Barceloneta tapas bar that also makes its own beer. Inside the place is not so much small but ridiculously narrow, making it a challenge not to elbow your neighbor as you raise your glass. Most people consider this part of the fun though as they tuck into the juiciest *solomillo* served with *pimientos del padrón* (miniature green peppers), the lightest croquettes, or a creamy Russian salad. If you are on a budget watch what you eat as the potions here are quite small, and the bill tends to add up unexpectedly.

Balboa 6 (Barceloneta). (C) **93-319–30-98**. Tapas 4€–15€ ($4.60–$17). MC, V. Daily 9am–midnight. Metro: Barceloneta.

La Bombeta ⭐ TAPAS   This place is a real slice of local life and one of the best tapas bars in the city. It looks like a slightly modernized version of a *taverna,* and its

---

Moments **A Wine Taster's Secret Address**

It doesn't get much better in Barcelona than an afternoon spent on the terrace of **La Vinya del Senyor,** Plaça Santa María 5 ((C) **93-310-33-79**), taking in the glorious Gothic facade of Santa María del Mar. You could even take a wine connoisseur like Mel Brooks (when not counting his take on *The Producers*), and I think even this hard-to-please man would be pleased. The wine list will inspire awe. Imagine, for example, 13 Priorats, 31 Riojas, and more than a dozen vintages of the legendary Vega Sicilia. In all, there are more than 300 wines and selected *cavas,* sherries, and *moscatells,* and the list is constantly rotated so you can always expect some new surprise on the *carte.* If you don't want a bottle, you'll find some two dozen wines offered by the glass, including a sublime 1994 Jané Ventura Cabernet Sauvignon. To go with your wine, tantalizing tapas are served, including walnut rolls drizzled in olive oil, cured Iberian ham, and French cheese. Tapas cost from 1.65€–5.85€ ($1.90–$6.70). American Express, Diners Club, MasterCard, and Visa are accepted. Hours are Tuesday through Saturday from noon to 1:30am and Sunday from noon to midnight. Metro: Jaume I or Barceloneta.

---

house specialty is *bombas,* deep-fried balls of fluffy mashed potato served with a spicy *brava* sauce. Other tapas include succulent mussels, either steamed or with a marinara sauce, giant grilled prawns, plates of paper-thin Serrano ham, and small chunks of deep fried calamari called *rabas.* Needless to say, when washed down with a jug of their excellent in-house sangria, this is a highly satisfying meal-in-itself.

Maquinista 3 (Barceloneta). © **93-319-94-45.** Tapas 4€–12€ ($5–$14). MC, V. Thurs–Tues 10am–midnight. Metro: Barceloneta.

7 Barrio Alto

MODERATE/EXPENSIVE

La Balsa INTERNATIONAL   On the uppermost level of a circular tower built as a cistern, La Balsa offers a view over most of the surrounding cityscape. To reach it, you climb to the structure's original rooftop where you're likely to be greeted by owner and founder Mercedes López. Food emerges from a cramped but well-organized kitchen several floors below. (The waiters are reputedly the most athletic in Barcelona, because they must run up the stairs carrying steaming platters.) The restaurant serves such dishes as a *judías verdes* (broad beans) with strips of salmon in lemon-flavored vinaigrette, stewed veal with wild mushrooms, a salad of warm lentils with anchovies, and pickled fresh salmon with chives. Undercooked maigret (breast) of duck is served with fresh, lightly poached foie gras, and baked hake (flown in from Galicia) is prepared in squid-ink sauce. The restaurant is 2km (1¼ miles) north of the city's heart—you'll need a taxi—in the Tibidabo district, close to the Science Museum (Museu de la Ciéncia). It's often booked several days in advance.

Infanta Isabel 4. © **93-211-50-48.** Reservations required. Main courses 12€–27€ ($14–$31). AE, DC, MC, V. Mon 9–11:30pm; Tues–Sat 2–3:30pm and 9–11:30pm. Aug buffet only 9–11:30pm. Closed Easter week.

Via Veneto ★★★ CATALAN   Given its consistently well-prepared cuisine and overall class, this uptown restaurant mysteriously tends to fall under the radar. Not that this in anyway worries the management, who are busy catering to regulars and visiting sports stars to make a noise about what they do. Opened 38 years ago, the name alludes to the *glamoor* that was signified by the famous Roman boulevard in the mid-1960s and nothing to do with the style of food, which has its roots firmly in Catalonia. It has a reputation for serving the finest *caza* (game) and fungi around, so I timed my trip for early autumn. After whetting our appetite on a prawn served on crispy brioche with greens, I was presented with a silky plate of *rovellons* and *ceps,* both wild mushrooms from the Catalan forests, cooked to perfection in olive oil and rock salt. I then partook of a filet of hare stuffed with foie and served on a bed of baked apples while I watched the expert waiters serving Via Veneto's signature duck dish. A whole baby duck is slow roasted, brought to the table and deboned. The bones are then put through an antique silver press, extracting the flavorsome juice, which accompanies the flesh in a culinary ceremony that seems to belong to another era. The wine list is legendary (and the size of an encyclopedia) so ask José, the amiable sommelier, to recommend one of their covetable Vega Sicilias or another of the 10,000 or so bottles they have in their underground bodega. Meals may be finished with a cheese platter or heady dessert combinations such as chocolate mouse spiced with mixed peppers and cinnamon ice cream.

Ganduxer 10. © **93-200-72-44.** Reservations required. Main courses 18€–40€ ($21–$46); tasting menu 60€ ($69). AE, DC, MC, V. Mon–Fri 1:15–4pm and 8:30–11:30pm; Sat 8:30–11:30pm. Closed Aug 1–20. Metro: La Bonanova.

8 On the Outskirts

VERY EXPENSIVE

El Racó de Can Fabes ★★★ MEDITERRANEAN   This is one of the greatest restaurants of Spain—maybe the greatest. If you don't mind the 30-minute drive or the 45-minute train ride from Barcelona, a distance of 52km (32 miles), you will be transported to a gourmet citadel, housed in a 3-century-old building in the center of the Catalan village of 1,700 people. Santi Santamaría, who founded the restaurant in the '80s, seemed rather immune to press acclaim, continuing to show their discipline and craftsmanship in spite of all the raves. They don't let a single platter reach their dining room without getting their keen-eyed sense of approval. This Michelin three-star restaurant (its highest rating) is run with exquisite care and dedication. The restaurant is refined and elegant yet retains a rustic aura. Recent strokes of their inspiration included hot and cold mackerel with cream of caviar and tender pigeon with duck tartare. A heavenly concoction is spicy foie gras with Sauterne and a *coulis* (purée) of sweet red and green peppers. Two different preparations of crayfish, each one a delight, come both raw and cooked. Roast pigeon is prepared in ways that correspond to the seasons and the "mood of the chef." For dessert, there's nothing finer than their "Festival de chocolate."

Sant Joan 6 (Sant Celoni). ℂ **93-867-28-51**. Reservations required. Main courses 29€–55€ ($33–$63); tasting menu 120€ ($138). AE, DC, MC, V. Tues–Sat 1:30–3:30pm and 8:30–10:30pm; Sun 1:30–3:30pm. Closed Jan 28–Feb 11 and June 24–July 8. Take any RENFE train from the Passeig de Gràcia station, heading for France, disembarking at Sant Celoni.

EXPENSIVE

Gaig ★★★ MODERN CATALAN   One of the shining culinary showcases of Barcelona, Gaig was founded some 130 years ago by the great-grandmother of present owner Carlos Gaig. Back then it was an out-of-town *fonda,* or small inn for travelers. Now it has a new downtown locale with a sleek and luxurious interior. The restaurant is celebrated locally for the quality and freshness of its food. If you order a meal with eggs, those eggs will have been contributed by the chickens seen wandering about the patio where customers often dine alfresco in the summer months. The cuisine of Gaig centers on traditional Catalan recipes transformed and altered to suit lighter and more modern palates. Among the stellar dishes to order are *arroz del delta con pichón y zetas* (rice with partridge and mushrooms), *rape asado a la catalana* (grilled monkfish with local herbs), and *els petits filet de vedella amb prunes i pinyons* (small veal filets with prunes and pine nuts). One of the tastiest dishes is marinated roast pork thigh. Desserts include *crema de Sant Joseph* (a warm flan with wild strawberries on top), homemade chocolates, and a selection of tarts.

Aragó 214. ℂ **93-429-10-17**. Reservations recommended. Main courses 25€–40€ ($29–$46); tasting menu 74€ ($85). AE, DC, MC, V. Mon–Sat 1:30–3:30pm and 9–11pm; Sun 9–11pm. Closed 3 weeks in Aug and Easter week. Metro: Passeig de Gràcia.

6

Exploring Barcelona

Long a Mediterranean center of commerce, Barcelona is also one of the focal points of European tourism, a role sparked by the 1992 Olympic Games. Spain's second-largest city is also its most cosmopolitan and avant-garde.

Because of its rich history, Barcelona is filled with landmark buildings and world-class museums. These include Antoni Gaudí's famed Sagrada Família, the Museu Picasso, the Gothic cathedral, and Les Ramblas, the tree-lined promenade cutting through the heart of the old quarter.

You can also branch out from Barcelona to one of the sites of interest in its environs, including the beaches of Sitges, the monastery at Montserrat, and the Penedès vineyards (see chapter 9).

To begin, however, you'll want to take in the artistic and intellectual aura of this unique seafaring city. Residents take justifiable pride in their Catalan heritage, and are eager to share it. Many of these sights can be covered on foot, and this chapter includes a walking tour of the Old Town.

1 Sightseeing Suggestions for First-Time Visitors

If You Have 1 Day   Spend the morning exploring the Barri Gòtic. In the afternoon visit Antoni Gaudí's unfinished masterpiece, La Sagrada Família, before returning to the heart of the city for a walk down Les Ramblas. To cap your day, take the funicular to the top of Montjuïc or Tibidabo, the two mountains overlooking the metropolis, for a panoramic view of Barcelona and its harbor.

If You Have 2 Days   On Day 2, visit the Museu Picasso then stroll through the surrounding district, La Ribera, which is filled with Gothic mansions and is the site of the gorgeous church Santa María del Mar. Pick up a knick-knack to take home in one of the many eclectic shops in the area. Follow this with a ride to the top of the Columbus Monument for a panoramic view of the harborfront. Have a seafood lunch at the old maritime quarter La Barceloneta and in the afternoon, stroll up Les Ramblas again. Explore some of the museums at Montjuïc such as the Museu d'Art de Catalunya if time remains.

If You Have 3 Days   On Day 3, spend some time exploring the L'Eixample district and some of the *modernista* (Art Nouveau) architecture that resides there such as Gaudí's Casa Mila or Casa Batlló. Pop into Vinçon, the city's famed design emporium. Have lunch or dinner in Casa Calvet, a restaurant housed in an early work of Gaudí's.

If You Have 4 or 5 Days   On Day 4, take a morning walk along the harborfront, finishing at the Vila Olímpica. In the afternoon visit Montjuïc again to tour the Fundació Joan Miró and walk through the Poble Espanyol, a miniature village with reproductions of representative regional architecture, created for the 1929 World's Fair. On Day 5, take another excursion from the city. If you're interested in history, visit the former Roman city of Tarragona to the south. If

Barcelona Attractions

Plaça de
Francesc Macià

Carrer de Buenos Aires ❸

Carrer de Londres

Carrer de Paris

Travessara de Gràcia

Avinguda Diagonal

Gran de Gràcia

❹

0   1/4 mi
0   0.25 km

ⓘ Information

Travessara de Gràcia

Av. de Sant Antoni Maria Claret

Carrer de la Industria

Carrer de Còrsega

EIXAMPLE   ⓘ

Carrer de Rosselló

Carrer de Provença

Carrer Enric Granados

Carrer de Balmes

Rambla de Catalunya

Passeig de Gràcia

❼

Avinguda Diagonal

Carrer de Roger de Flor

Plaça de la
Sagrada
Família ❺

Carrer de Pau Clarís

❾

❽

Carrer de Mallorca

Carrer de València

Carrer del Comte d'Urgell

Carrer del Comte Borrell

Carrer de Villarroel

Carrer de Casanova

Carrer de Muntaner

Carrer d'Aribau

❿ ⓫

⓬

Carrer del Consell de Cent

Mançana de la Discòrdia

⓭

Carrer d'Aragó

Carrer de R. de Llúria

Carrer del Bruc

Carrer de Girona

Carrer de Bailén

Passeig de Sant Joan

Carrer de Nàpols

Carrer de Sicília

❻➔

Carrer de la Diputació

Plaça de la
Universitat

Gran Via de les Corts Catalanes

Ronda Universitat

Ronda de Sant Antoni

Carrer de Pelai

Plaça
Catalunya

ⓘ

Plaça
Urquinaona

Ronda de Sant Pere

Plaça de
Tetuan

Carrer   de Casp

Carrer   d'Ausias Marc

Carrer   d'Ali Bei

Carrer de Ribes

Carrer de Sardenya

Plaça de la
Universitat

Plaça
Catalunya

RAVAL

⓯
⓰
⓱

Carrer de Hospital

⓲

BARRI GÒTIC

⓳

Av. Portal de l'Angel

Via Laietana

⓴

Passeig de Lluís Companys

Carrer de la Marina

❹⓪
㉕

㉖

㉔

㉑

㉒

Carrer de Sant Pau

㊵

㉗ ㉘ Ferran

C. de la Princesa

㉓

Passeig de Picasso

Passeig de Pujades

PARC DE LA
CIUTADELLA

Carrer de Wellington

Ronda Sant Pau

㊶

⓷⓽

La Rambla

C. de

㉙

Carrer del Comerç

Carrer Nou de la Rambla

㊳

Avda. de les Drassanes

La Rambla

LA RIBERA

㉚ ㉛

㊱

㉟

Carrer Ample

Passeig de Colom
Moll de la Fusta

Pg. Isabel II

Plaça Portal
de la Pau

㊲

㉞

㉝

Avinguda d'Icaria

Villa
Olímpica ➔

Moll d'Espanya

Port
Vell

㉜

BARCELONETA

Passeig   Marítim

143

you want to unwind on a beach, head south to Sitges. Or make a pilgrimage to the monastery of Montserrat, about 45 minutes outside of Barcelona, to see the venerated Black Virgin and a host of artistic and scenic attractions. Try to time your visit to hear the 50-member boys' choir.

2 Ciutat Vella (Old City)

The Ciutat Vella (Old City) is where the top attractions are and if you are short of precious time this is where you will want to spend most of it. The Gothic Cathedral, the Roman foundations, the funky Raval and Ribera districts are all located within this large chunk of the city's landscape that, die to its abundance of one-way and pedestrianized streets is best visited on foot. It seems a little daunting at first but striking landmarks such as the city's cathedral, the MACBA (Museum of Modern Art) and the Plaça del Rei will help you navigate your way around the maze. To make it easier, I have divided the attractions up into three subareas: the Barri Gòtic (east of Les Ramblas), El Raval (west of Les Ramblas), and La Ribera (west of Vía Laietana). For more information on these neighborhoods, see chapter 3.

BARRI GOTIC ✸✸✸

One of Barcelona's greatest attractions is not a single sight but an entire neighborhood, the **Barri Gòtic (Gothic Quarter)**. This is the oldest quarter, parts of which have survived from the Middle Ages. Spend at least 2 or 3 hours exploring its narrow streets and squares (see the walking tour on p. 177), which continue to form a vibrant, lively neighborhood. A nighttime stroll takes on added drama. The buildings are austere and sober for the most part, the cathedral being the crowning achievement. Roman ruins and the vestiges of 3rd-century walls add further interest. This area is intricately detailed and filled with many attractions that are easy to miss.

Catedral de Barcelona ✸✸✸ Barcelona's cathedral is a celebrated example of Catalan Gothic architecture. Its spires can be seen from almost all over the Barri Gòtic and the large square upon which it resides, the Plaça de la Seu, one of the neighborhood's main thoroughfares. The elevated site has always been Barcelona's center of worship; before the present cathedral there was a Roman temple and then later a mosque. Construction on the cathedral began at the end of the 13th century under the reign of Jaume II (on the exterior of its southern transept, on the Plaça de Sant Lu, there is a portal commemorating beginning of the work). The bishops of the time ordered a wide, single nave, 28 side chapels, and an apse with an ambulatory behind a high altar. Work was finally completed in the mid–15th century (although the west facade dates from the 19th c.). The nave, cleaned and illuminated, has some splendid Gothic details. With its large bell towers, blending of medieval and Renaissance styles, high altar, side chapels, handsomely sculptured choir, and Gothic arches, it ranks as one of the most impressive cathedrals in Spain. The most interesting chapel is the Cappella de Sant Benet, behind the altar with its magnificent 15th-century interpretation of the crucifixion by Bernat Matorell. It is the cloister however that enthralls most visitors. Consisting of vaulted galleries enhanced by forged iron grilles, it is filled with orange, medlar, and palm trees and features a mossy central pond and fountain, and is (inexplicably) home to a gaggle of white geese. Underneath the well-worn slabs of its stone floor, key members of the Barri Gòtic's ancient guilds are buried. The historian Cirici called this "the loveliest oasis in Barcelona." On its northern side, the cathedral's chapter house occupies

---

(Fun Fact How the Egg Dances

During the feast of Corpus Christi in June, a uniquely Catalan tradition can be seen in the cathedral's cloister. *L'ou com balla* (the egg that dances) consists of an empty egg shell that is placed on top of the fountain's gushes of water and left to "dance." Its origins go back to 1637, although its significance is disputed. Some say that the egg simply represents spring and beginning of a new life cycle, others that its form represents the Eucharist.

---

the museum whose highlight is the 15th-century *La Pietat* of Bartolomé Bermejo. Another pocket of the cathedral that is worth seeking out is the alabaster sarcophagus of Santa Eulàlia, the co-patroness of the city. The martyr, allegedly a virgin daughter of a well-to-do Barcelona family, was burnt at the stake by the Roman governor for refusing to renounce her Christian beliefs. You can take an elevator to the roof where you can see a wonderful view of Gothic Barcelona but only Monday through Saturday from 10:30am to 1:30pm and 5 to 6pm, price 2€ ($2.30). At noon on Sunday, you can see the *sardana*, a Catalonian folk dance, performed in front of the cathedral.

Plaça de la Seu s/n. (*C*) 93-315-15-54. Free admission to cathedral; museum 1€ ($1.15). Global ticket for 1–4:30pm guided visit to museum, choir, rooftop terraces, and towers 4€ ($4.60). Cathedral daily 9am–1pm and 5–7pm; cloister museum daily 10am–1pm and 4–6:30pm. Metro: Jaume I and Liceu.

Conjunt Monumental de la Plaça del Rei (Museu d'Història de la Ciutat and Palau Reial Major) ✦✦✦   These two museums are viewed as a double act, and both reside in Plaça del Rei, which is nestled underneath a remaining section of the old city walls. Visitors enter through the Casa Clariana Padellàs, a Gothic mansion that was originally located on the nearby Career Mercaders and was moved here when the construction of the Vía Laietana ripped though the Barri Gòtic in the early 1930s. The ground floor is dedicated to temporary exhibitions on Iberian and Mediterranean culture with a permanent virtual-reality display on the history of the city. The highlight however lies underground, underneath the Plaça del Rei itself. Excavation work carried out for the relocation of the Casa Clariana Padellàs unearthed a large section of Barcino, the old Roman city. Workers unearthed a forum, streets, squares, family homes, shops, and even laundries and huge vats used for wine production. A clever network of walkways has been built over the relics, allowing you to fully appreciate the ebb and flow of daily life in old Barcino. Be on the lookout for a handful of beautiful mosaics, in situ, of what is left of family homes.

The visit continues above ground in the medieval Royal Palace. The complex dates back to the 10th century when it was the palace of the counts of Barcelona, then later became the residence of the kings of Aragon. The top step of its sweeping entrance is supposedly where King Ferdinand and Queen Isabella received Columbus after he returned from the New World. Immediately inside, the palace's chapel, the Capella de Santa Agüeda, is also used for temporary exhibitions. Adjacent to the chapel is the Saló del Tinell, a key work of the period featuring the largest stone arches to be found anywhere in Europe. Another palace highlight is the Mirador del Rei Martí (King Martin's Watchtower). Constructed in 1555, it is a later addition to the palace but in many ways one of its most interesting. King Martin was the last of the line of the city's count-kings and this five-story tower was built to keep an eye on foreign invasions and peasant uprisings that often took place in the square below.

Plaça del Rei s/n. ℂ **93-315-11-11**. Admission 4€ ($4.60) adults, 2.50€ ($3) students, free for children under 16. June–Sept Tues–Sat 10am–8pm; Oct–May Tues–Sat 10am–2pm and 4–8pm; year-round Sun 10am–3pm. Metro: Liceu, Jaume I, or Urquinaona.

La Mercè The church of La Mercè is dear to the heart of the people of Barcelona. Our Lady of Mercy (La Mercè) is the city's patron saint; she earned the privilege after supposedly diverting a plague of locusts in 1637. Thus, the city's main fiesta (Sept 24) is named in her honor and many Barcelona-born females are called Mercè (among males there is an abundance of Jordis—or George—Catalonia's patron saint).

The church itself is the only one in the city with a baroque facade. Perched on top is a statue of the lady herself, a key feature of the city's skyline. The edifice resides on an elegant square with a central fountain of Neptune.

Plaça de la Mercè 1. ℂ **93-315-27-56**. Free admission. Daily 10am–1pm and 6–8pm. Metro: Drassanes.

Mirador de Colón This monument to Christopher Columbus was erected at the Barcelona harbor on the occasion of the Universal Exhibition of 1888. It consists of three parts, the first being a circular structure raised by four stairways (6m/19½ ft. wide) and eight iron heraldic lions. On the plinth are eight bronze bas-reliefs depicting Columbus's principal feats. (The originals were destroyed; these are copies.) The second part is the base of the column, consisting of an eight-sided polygon, four sides of which act as buttresses; each side contains sculptures. The third part is the 50m (164-ft.) column, which is Corinthian in style. The capital boasts representations of Europe, Asia, Africa, and America—all linked together. Finally, over a princely crown and a hemisphere recalling the newly discovered part of the globe, is a 7.5m (25-ft.) high bronze statue of Columbus—pointing, ostensibly, to the New World—by Rafael Ataché. Inside the iron column, a tiny elevator ascends to the *mirador*. From here, a panoramic view of Barcelona and its harbor unfolds.

Portal de la Pau s/n. ℂ **93-302-52-24**. Admission 2€ ($2.30) adults, 1.30€ ($1.50) children 4–12, free for children under 4. June–Sept 9am–8:30pm; Oct–May 10am–6:30pm. Metro: Drassanes.

Museu de la Cera *Kids* Madame Tussaud's it may not be, but Barcelona's Wax Museum still has plenty of appeal. Located in a 19th-century building that used to be a bank, the winding staircase and frescoes are a fitting setting for the array of Catalan and Spanish historical and cultural personages plus Dracula, Frankenstein, and the usual suspects. Next door, the museum's cafe El Bosc de les Fades is fitted out "fairy forest" style with magic mirrors, bubbling brooks, and secret doors, further adding to the fantastical experience.

Passatge de la Banca 7. ℂ **93-317-26-49**. Admission 6.65€ ($7.65) adults; 3.75€ ($4.30) children 5–11, students, and seniors. Oct–Jun Mon–Fri 10am–1:30pm and 4–7:30pm, Sat–Sun and holidays 11am–2pm and 4:30–8:30pm; July–Sept daily 10am–10pm. Metro: Drassanes.

Museu Frederic Marés ✦✦ One of the biggest repositories of medieval sculpture in the region is the Frederic Marés Museum, just behind the cathedral. Marés was a sculptor and obsessive collector and the fruit of this passion is housed in an ancient palace with beautiful interior courtyards, chiseled stone, and soaring ceilings. He amassed a simply mind-boggling collection of religious sculpture and imagery. Downstairs, the pieces date from the 3rd and 4th centuries then travel through to the fixating polychromatic crucifixes and statues of the Virgin Mary of the Romanesque and Gothic periods. Upstairs, the collection continues into the baroque and Renaissance before becoming the so-called Museu Senti-mental, a collection of everyday items and paraphernalia that illustrate life in Barcelona during the past two centuries. The "Entertainment Room" features toys and automatons, and the "Women's Quarter" has Victorian fans, combs, and other objects deemed for "feminine use only." Outside, the **Café d'Estiu** in the courtyard is an agreeable place to rest before moving on.

Plaça de Sant Iú 5–6. 🕐 **93-310-58-00.** Admission 3€ ($3.45) adults, free for children under 12. Tues–Sat 10am–7pm; Sun 10am–3pm. Metro: Jaume I.

Plaça Sant Jaume ✮

The Plaça Sant Jaume is the political nerve center of Barcelona. Separated by a wide expanse of polished flagstones, the Casa de la Ciu-tat, home to the *ajuntament* (town hall) faces the Palau de la Generalitat, seat of Catalonia's autonomous government. The square itself frequently acts as a stage for protest gatherings, rowdy celebrations (such as when a local team wins a sporting event), and local traditions like the spectacular *castellers* (human towers).

The buildings themselves are only infrequently open to the public, but if you do happen to coincide they are well worth visiting, especially the **Palau de la Generalitat** ✮✮. Although the governing body of Catalonia has its origins in 1283, under the reign of Pere II, it wasn't until the 15th century that it was given a permanent home. The nucleus spreads out from the **Pati de Tarongers (Courtyard of Orange Trees),** an elegant interior patio with pink renaissance columns topped with gargoyles of historical Catalan folkloric figures.

Another highlight is the **Capella de Sant Jordi (Chapel of St. George),** which is resplendent with furnishings and objects depicting the legend of Catalonia's patron saint, whose image is a recurring theme throughout the Generalitat. The walls of the Gilded Hall are covered with 17th-century Flemish tapestries.

Across the square is the late-14th-century **Casa de la Ciutat** ✮, corridor of power of the *ajuntament.* Behind its neoclassical facade is a prime example of Gothic civil architecture in the Catalan Mediterranean style. The building has a splendid courtyard and staircase. Its major architectural highlights are the 15th-century Salón de Ciento (Room of the 100 Jurors) with gigantic arches sup-porting a beamed ceiling and the black marble Salón de las Crónicas (Room of the Chronicles). The murals here were painted in 1928 by Josep Maria Sert, the Catalan artist who went onto decorate the Rockefeller Center in New York.

Capella de Sant Jordi: Plaça de Sant Jaume s/n. 🕐 **93-402-46-17.** Free admission. 2nd and last Sun of each month, Apr 25, and Sept 24 10:30am–1:30pm. Casa de la Ciutat: Plaça de Sant Jaume s/n. 🕐 **93-402-70-00.** Free admission. Sun 11am–3:30pm. Metro: Jaume I or Liceu.

Sant Maria del Pi

This church takes its name from the huge pine tree out-side its main entrance. The church, built over a period of nearly two hundred years between the early 14th and late 16th centuries, resides on one of the most charming squares (of the same name) in the Barri Gòtic. There is always some-thing happening on the square (or rather the trio of squares) whether it is an art market (Sun), local cheese and artisan food hawkers (Thurs–Sat), street musi-cians strutting their stuff, or people milling around the plentiful outdoor cafes.

The church itself is a typical, if not the most complete, example of Catalan Gothic. Its wide, single nave spans nearly two thirds of the building's length, lending the church its squat appearance. Above the main entrance is placed a gigantic rose window. Inside it's just as austere, although worth inspecting for the ingenious stone arch that has supported the structure's width for centuries.

Plaça del Pi 7. 🕐 **93-318-47-43.** Free admission. Daily 9am–1pm and 4–9pm. Metro: Liceu.

LA RIBERA

Smaller than the Barri Gòtic, the top attractions in the La Ribera district are the Picasso Museum and the soaring Gothic church Santa María del Mar. But smaller treasures abound in its atmospheric streets in the form of cafes, artisan workshops, and small boutiques laden with home and fashion booty. It's a wonderful place to stroll around window shopping and grabbing a bite in its many outdoor cafes and compact enough to cover in an afternoon. At night the bars and *coctelerías* open their doors and crowds roll in.

El Palau de la Música Catalana *ααα*   Not strictly within the borders of La Ribera but north of the Calle Princesa in the La Pere district, the Palau de la Música is, for many, the most outstanding contribution of the *modernista* movement. Declared a UNESCO World Heritage site in 1997, it was designed by

El Call: the Jewish Quarter

Before the "Catholic Kings" Ferdinand and Isabella systematically set about persecuting all Jewish communities in Iberia in the late 15th century, Barcelona's Jews had lived harmoniously for centuries alongside Christians and enjoyed special status under the city's autonomous rule. Barcelona's Sephardic Jews flourished in the Middle Ages, reaching a population of four million people in the 13th century, 15% of the total population of the city. They were respected for their financial expertise, understanding of the law, and learned figures, including poet Ben Ruben Izahac and the astronomer Abraham Xija. The community resided in the city neighborhood El Call (pronounced "kye") reputedly from the Hebrew word *kahal*, which means "community" or "congregation." The area was bordered by the old walls to the west and east, and its entrance was through the Plaça Sant Jaume. Today this tiny, ancient neighborhood is marked by atmospheric, narrow streets with 14th- to 16th-century buildings, some with vestiges of its former residents. The largest and most complete is the main synagogue in Calle Marlet, no. 5. Consisting of two cellar-like rooms below street level, the space was virtually unknown, serving as a warehouse until 1995 when the building with its four floors added on top was put up for sale. It was acquired by the Associación Call de Barcelona (see below) who embarked on a meticulous process of renovation.

On the same street, in the direction of the Arc de Sant Ramon is a wall plaque dating from 1314 bearing the inscription (in Hebrew) "Holy Foundation of Rabbi Samuel Hassardi, whose life is never ending." The remains of the female Jewish public baths can be seen nearby in the basement of the pleasant Café Caleum at the intersection of the streets Banys Nous (which means "New Baths") and Palla. The men's baths are hidden in the rear of the furniture shop S'Oilvier (Banys Nous 10) although you will need to ask permission from the owner to take a peek.

Old Synagogue and Asociación Call de Barcelona: Marlet 5. © **93-317-07-90.** Free admission. Hours are Tuesday through Sunday 11am to 2:30pm and 4 to 7:30pm. Metro: Jaume I or Liceu.

Lluis Domènech i Montaner, a contemporary of Gaudí's also responsible for the magnificent Hospital Sant Pau (p. 155).

In 1891 it was decided that the Orfeó Catalan (Catalan Coral Society) needed a permanent home. The Orfeó was a key player in La Renaixença, a heady political and cultural climate of renewed Catalan nationalism and artistic endeavor (with the two closely intertwined). The Orfeó, which still regularly performs at the Palau, had been touring Catalan rural areas, performing *catalanismo*-charged folk songs to much acclaim. The general opinion was that they deserved their own "Palace of Music." Domènech i Montaner obliged.

A riot of symbolism, the Palau de la Música Catalana, constructed between 1905 and 1908, is a feast for the senses. The facade features a rippling sculpture representing popular Catalan song and is crowned by an allegorical mosaic of the Orfeó underneath which reside busts of composers such as Bach, Beethoven, and the period's most popular composer, Wagner. The foyer, or vestibule, is linked to the street by an arcade and features dazzling columns of mosaic. It is the first-floor auditorium however where the excesses of *modernisme* run wild. Using the finest craftsmen of the day, Domènech i Montaner ordered almost every surface embellished with the most extraordinary detail. The ceiling features a stained glass inverted dome, the auditorium's main light source, surrounded by 40 female heads, representing a choir. On the stage's rear wall are the *Muses del Palau,* a series of dainty, instrument-bearing maidens in terra cotta and *trencadis* (broken mosaic collage). The *pièce de résistance* is the masterpiece proscenium that frames the stages. Executed by Pau Gargallo, on the left it features the Orfeó's director Josep Clavé bursting forth from the "Flowers of May," a tree representing a popular Catalan folk song. On the opposite side Beethoven peeks through a stampede of Wagner's Valkyries.

In 2003 local architect Oscar Tusquets completed his sensitive extension of El Palau, providing extra rehearsal space, a library and another, underground auditorium. It is worth checking their program when in town; concerts range from international orchestras and soloists to jazz and sometimes world music. Tickets for local acts are often very reasonably priced. If not, there are daily tours of the building, see below. Advance purchase for these is recommended.

Career de Sant Francesc de Paula 2. (Ⓒ 93-295-72-00 for information, or 902-442-882 to buy tickets. Tour 8€ ($9) adults, 7€ ($8) students. Tickets can be bought up to 1 week in advance from the gift shop adjacent to the building. Guided tours daily, every half-hour 10am–3:30pm. Metro: Urquinaona.

Mercat del Born
At the end of the Passeig del Born the pretty promenade that is the heart of the neighborhood is the Mercat del Born, the city's steel and glass ode to the industrial age. Inspired by Les Halles in Paris, it acted as the city's wholesale market until 1973 and its closing marked the beginning of the neighborhood's decline before its currant renaissance. Having lain abandoned for over three decades, a decision was taken in 2003 to turn the edifice into a library and cultural center. When the renovation work started, the remains of entire streets and homes from Phillipe V's demolition orders (see Parc de la Ciutadella, above) were discovered underneath. Work continues and in the future visitors will be able to see these significant remains via glass flooring.

Carrer Comerç s/n. Interior closed to public.

Museu Barbier-Mueller Art Precolombí ✦
Inaugurated in 1997, this museum is a smaller cousin to the museum of the same name in Geneva; one of the most important collections of pre-Columbian art in the world. In the

restored Palacio Nadal, which was built during the Gothic period, the collection contains almost 6,000 pieces of tribal and ancient art. Josef Mueller (1887–1977) acquired the first pieces by 1908. The pre-Columbian cultures represented created religious, funerary, and ornamental objects of great stylistic variety with relatively simple means. Stone sculpture and ceramic objects are especially outstanding. For example, the Olmecs, who settled on the Gulf of Mexico at the beginning of the 1st millennium B.C., executed notable monumental sculpture in stone and magnificent figures in jade. Many exhibits focus on the Mayan culture, the most homogenous and widespread of its time, dating from 1000 B.C. Mayan artisans mastered painting, ceramics, and sculpture. Note the work by the pottery makers of the Lower Amazon, particularly those from the island of Marajó, and the millennium-old gold adornments from northern Peru.

Carrer de Montcada 12–14. ⓒ **93-310-45-16**. Admission 3€ ($3.45) adults, 1.50€ ($1.70) students, free for children under 16. Tues–Sat 10am–6pm; Sun 10am–3pm. Metro: Jaume I.

Museu de Ciències Naturals de la Ciutadella (Geologia and Zoologia)

These two museums, which can be viewed with the same ticket, reside inside the elegant Parc de la Ciutadella (see below). The most crowd-pleasing is the **Museu de Zoologia** ⓐ, which is housed in a whimsical building designed by the *modernista* architect Lluis Domènech i Montaner. It was created (but not finished in time) as a cafe for the 1887–88 World's Fair, which was largely centered around the park. Known at the time as the **Castell de Tres Dragons (Castle of the Three Dragons),** it is a daring example of medieval-inspired *modernisme* with fortress-like towers featuring ceramic heraldry, Mudéjar windows, and walls of exposed brick. Inside, although extremely altered, exhibits are displayed in Victorian-style wooden and glass cabinet. Specimens include Goliath frogs, giant crabs, and a section on Catalan flora. Located in a colonnaded neoclassical structure, the setting for the Geological Museum is slightly less inspiring. It was however the first building in the city to be constructed specifically for a museum, first Scientific Museum in Spain, and it still holds the largest geology collection in the whole country, fruit of a passionate collector and man of science by the name of Francesc Martorell. The left wing displays various granites, quartzes, and naturally radioactive rocks. The more interesting right wing is the area of fossils with some nostalgic Jules Verne–type illustrations made in the 1950s, which depict prehistoric life.

Parc de la Ciutadella, Passeig Picasso 1. ⓒ **93-319-68-95** (Museu de Geologia) or ⓒ **93-319-69-12** (Museu de la Zoologia). Admission (for both) 3.50€ ($4) adults, children under 16 free. Tues–Sat 10am–7pm; Sun 10am–3pm. Metro: Barceloneta, Arc de Triomf.

Museu de la Xocolata ⓐ ⓚⁱᵈˢ

Opened in 2000 in a former convent, this museum is an initiative from the city's chocolate and pastry makers. More like a giant, hands-on textbook, the exhibition takes you through the discovery of the cocoa bean by New World explorers, its commercialization, and chocolate as an art form. Every Easter, the museum is the venue for the annual *mona* competition. *Monas,* a Catalan invention, are elaborate chocolate sculptures, often of famous buildings, people, or cartoon characters. Chocolate makers display them in their windows during Easter week and try to outdo each other with sheer creativity and inventiveness. Once your appetite has been whetted, you can enjoy a cup of hot chocolate or pick up some bonbons at the museum's cafe.

Antic Convent de Sant Augustí, Comerç 36. ⓒ **93-268-78-78**. Admission 3.80€ ($4.40), children under 7 free. Mon–Sat 10am–7pm; Sun 10am–3pm. Metro: Jaume I or Arc de Triomf.

Museu d' Textil i d' Indumentària   Located in the stunning Palau del Marquès de Llió, a gothic mansion adjacent to the Museu Barbier-Mueller Art Precolombí (see above) the city's textile museum is a slightly slapdash but overall interesting permanent display of fabric and lace-making techniques and costumes. The first floor covers periods from the Gothic through to Regency; the latter consisting of crinoline skirts with bone-crushing bodices plus a wonderful selection of fans and opera glasses. Upstairs you arrive at the 20th century with ensembles from the Basque-born creator Cristóbel Balenciaga, Paco Rabanne, and Barcelona's own Pedro Rodríguez. Temporary exhibitions have ranged from Catalan jewelry to the outfits of Australian *enfant terrible* performer Leigh Bowery. There is a great cafe in the courtyard and above-average gift shop.

Montcada 12–14. ✆ **93-319-76-03**. Admission 3.50€ ($4) adults, free for children under 16. Tues–Sat 10am–6pm; Sun 10am–3pm. Metro: Jaume I.

Museu Picasso ✰✰✰   Five medieval mansions on this street contain this museum of the work of Pablo Picasso (1881–1973). The bulk of the art was donated by Jaume Sabartés y Gual, a lifelong friend of the artist's. Although born in Malaga, Picasso moved to the Catalan capital in 1895 after his father was awarded a teaching job at the city's Fine Arts Academy in La Llotja. The family settled in the Calle Merce and when Picasso was a bit older, he moved to the Nou de Les Ramblas in the Barrio Chino. Although he left Spain for good at the outbreak of the Civil War—and refused to return while Franco was in power—he was particularly fond of Barcelona, where he spent his formative years painting its seedier side and hanging around with the city's Bohemians. As a sign of his love for the city, and adding to Sabartés enormous bequest, Picasso donated some 2,500 of his paintings, engravings, and drawings to the museum in 1970. All of these were executed in his youth (in fact, some of the paintings were done when he was only 9), and the collection is particularly strong on his Blue and Rose Periods. Many works show the artist's debt to van Gogh, El Greco, and Rembrandt.

The highlight of the collection is undoubtedly *Las Meninas,* a series of 59 interpretations of Velázquez's masterpiece. Another key work is *The Harlequin,* a painting clearly influenced by the time the artist spent with the Ballet Russes in Paris. It was his first bequest to Barcelona. Key works aside, many visitors are transfixed by his notebooks containing dozens of sketches of Barcelona street scenes and characters, proof of his extraordinary and often overlooked drawing talents. Because the works are arranged in rough chronological order, you can get a wonderful sense of Picasso's development and watch as he discovered a trend or had a new idea, mastered it, grew bored with it, and then was off to something new. You'll learn that Picasso was a master portraitist and did many traditional representational works before his flights of fancy took off. The exhibits in the final section ("The Last Years") were donated by his widow Jacqueline and include ceramic and little-known collage work.

Montcada 15–23. ✆ **93-319-63-10**. Admission 5€ ($5.75) adults, 2.50€ ($2.90) students and people under 25, free for children under 16. Tues–Sat 10am–8pm; Sun 10am–3pm. Metro: Jaume I, Liceu, or Arc de Triomf.

Parc de la Ciutadella ✰✰   Barcelona's most formal park is also the most seeped in history. The area was formerly a loathed citadel, built by Phillip V after he won the War of the Spanish Succession (Barcelona was on the losing side). He ordered that the "traitorous" residential suburb be leveled. Between 1715 and 1718, over 60 streets and residences were torn down to make way for the structure, without any compensation to the owners (although many were relocated to the purpose-built neighborhood of Barceloneta). It never really functioned as a citadel, but was used a political prison during subsequent uprisings and occupations. Once the decision to pull down the old city walls was made in 1858, the government decided that the citadel should too go. Work on the park began in 1872, and in 1887–88 the World's Fair was held on its grounds, with the nearby Arc de Triomf acting as the event's grandiose main entrance.

Today lakes, gardens, and promenades fill most of the park, which also holds a **Zoo** (see below). Gaudí contributed to the monumental, Italianate fountain in the park when he was a student; the lampposts are also his. Other highlights include the Hivernacle, an elegant, English style hot-house with an adjacent cafe and the unusual Umbracle, a glasshouse that contains no glass but whose facades are of bare brick with wooden louvers. Both these structures are on the Passeig de Picasso flank of the park. On the opposite side bordering Calle Wellington is the old arsenal, which now accommodates the parliament of Catalonia.

Entrances on the Passeig de Picasso and Passeig Pujades. Daily sunrise–sunset. Metro: Arc de Triomf.

Parc Zoològic 🐾 *Kids*   A large hunk of the Parc de la Ciutadella is taken up with the city's zoo. Until recently, the main attraction was Copito de Nieve (Snowflake), the only albino gorilla in captivity in the world. He died of skin cancer in 2003, but left behind a large family of children and grandchildren, none of whom fortunately (or unfortunately for the scientific world) inherited his condition. Despite losing its star attraction, there are still plenty of other reasons to visit Barcelona's Zoo, and one is the pleasant (at least for humans) leafy garden setting itself. Many of the enclosures are barless and the animals kept in place via a moat. This seems humane until you realize how much running space the creatures actually have at their disposal on their "islands." To be fair, Barcelona's Zoo is probably a lot more progressive than many other zoos on the continent and unless you are of the firm belief that there is no such thing as a "good" zoo, you, and especially children, will delight at the mountain goats, llamas, lions, bears, hippos, huge primate community, and dozens of other species. There are also a dolphin show and sizable reptile enclosure and an exhibition on the extinction of gorillas in Snowflake's memory; from the time he was captured in Equatorial Guinea in 1966 through his rise to celebrity status and the city's mascot.

Parc de la Ciutadella. 📞 **93-225-67-80**. Admission 13€ ($15) adults, 8.20€ ($9.40) students and children 3–12. Summer daily 10am–7pm; off season daily 10am–6pm. Metro: Ciutadella or Arc de Triomf.

EL RAVAL

El Raval is a neighborhood of contrasts. Here, cutting edge new architecture and urban projects are being built in the streets of the city's largest inner city hood. Historically working class, gentrification is evident in many parts, while others still retain a marked down trodden air. For many, El Raval represents 21st-century Barcelona with signs of Catalan, Arabic, Middle Eastern, and South American culture at every turn.

Centre de Cultura Contemporània (CCCB) 🐾   Adjacent to the MACBA (see below), the CCCB is a temporary exhibition space located in what was a 19th-century poorhouse. The building has been ingeniously adapted to its current function; the extension is an impressive structure with sheer glass exterior walls supporting a large mirror that reflects the surrounding rooftops. You enter it via a pretty courtyard, and there is an exterior garden that has an outside cafeteria.

Exhibitions here tend to focus on writers and the world of literature or cultural/political movements such as situationism or the Parisian surrealism. The setting is inundated in mid-June when **Sonar,** the annual dance music festival, stages its daytime events here, and other mini festivals such as alternative film and the plastic arts are also part of its vibrant calendar.

Montalegre 5. ℂ **93-306-41-00.** Admission 5.50€ ($6.30) adults, 4€ ($4.60) students, free for children under 14. Tues and Thurs–Fri 11am–2pm and 4–8pm; Wed and Sat 11am–8pm, Sun and holidays 11am–7pm. Metro: Catalunya or Universitat.

Forment d'les Arts Decoratives (FAD)

FAD is the 100-year-old engine that drives the city's active design culture, in charge of dishing out design and architecture awards and grants and promoting its artists to Spain and the rest of the world. Its headquarters, easily identifiable by the huge steel letters spelling its name outside the main entrance, are in a converted Gothic convent opposite the MACBA, and continuous exhibitions are held in the exposed brick nave. These range from the winners of their various competitions to more didactic shows such as pirating in the design world to everyday, utilitarian objects from around the world. Fun stuff includes the Tallers Oberts, where artisans of the Raval throw open their workshops to the public, and *mercadillos* where young designers sell their wares at cut prices.

Plaça dels Angels. ℂ **93-443-75-20.** Free admission. Mon–Sat 11am–8pm. Metro: Catalunya or Universitat.

Gran Teatre del Liceu ★★

Barcelona's opera house El Liceu opened to great fanfare in 1847 and again in 2000 when a new and improved version was finished after a devastating fire destroyed the original 6 years before. During its first life, El Liceu had been a symbol of the city's bourgeoisie, often provoking the wrath of the proletariat (a telling note is that in 1893, an anarchist threw two bombs from a first floor balcony into the audience, killing 22 people). It was the principal venue for the Wagnerian craze that swept the city in the late 19th century. During its second life, El Liceu consolidated its reputation as one of the finest opera houses in the world. The original design was based on La Scala in Milan with a seating capacity of almost 4,000. The 1994 fire (started by sparks from the blowtorch of a stage worker) destroyed everything but the facade and members' room. The subsequent renovation saw the demolition of neighboring buildings (much to the horror of neighborhood action groups, provoking further backlash) for new rehearsal space and workrooms, and the auditorium returned to its former gilt, red velvet, and marble glory. Tickets to the concerts, at least the evening performances, are quite expensive but, like the Palau de la Música, tours of the edifice are available.

Les Ramblas 51–59. ℂ **93-485-99-00.** Guided tours depend on season. Information available at the Espai Liceu, the theater's bookshop and cafe in the foyer. Metro: Liceu.

Museu d'Art Contemporani de Barcelona (MACBA) ★★

A soaring white edifice in the once-shabby but rebounding Raval district, the Museum of Contemporary Art is to Barcelona what the Pompidou Center is to Paris. Designed by the American architect Richard Meier, the building is a work of art itself, manipulating sunlight to offer brilliant, natural interior lighting. The permanent collection, which is expanding all the time, exhibits the work of modern international luminaries such as Broodthaers, Klee, Basquiat, and many others. The majority of the museum however, has been allotted to Catalan artistic movements. The **Grup del Treball** were a bunch of reactionaries producing conceptual art criticizing Franco's dictatorship via enormous documents promoting independence for Catalonia. On a social level, photographs by Oriol Maspons and Leonardo Pómes illustrate Barcelona street life and the bohemians of the Gauche Divine (Divine Left) in the '70s. **Dau al Set,** a surrealist movement led by the brilliant "visual poet" Joan Brossa provokes thought and reflection through the juxtaposition of everyday items. Catalonia's most famous contemporary artists, Tàpies and Barceló are both represented. Temporary exhibitions highlight international artists or a monographic show on a particular city or political movement. The museum has a library, bookshop, and cafeteria. Outside, the enormous square has become a meeting place for locals and international skate boarders who make use of the MACBA's sleek ramp, presumably with the management's blessing.

Plaça dels Angels 1. ⓒ 93-412-08-10. Admission 7€ ($8) adults, 5.50€ ($6.30) students, free for children under 14. Wed only 3€ ($3.45). Mon and Wed–Fri 11am–7:30pm; Sat 10am–8pm; Sun 10am–3pm. Metro: Catalunya or Universitat.

Palau Güell 🖈🖈   This mansion is an important earlier work of Antoni Gaudí's. Built between 1885-89, it was the first major commission the architect received from Eusebi Güell, the wealthy industrialist who went onto become Gaudí's life-long friend and patron.

A plot was chosen just off Les Ramblas in the lower Raval district, more for its close proximity to Güell's father's residence than anything else, and Gaudí given a *carte blanche*. Although much of the marble for the town house was supplied by Güell's own quarry, it is said that his accountants criticized the architect on more than one occasion for his heavy-handed spending. Sr. Güell himself however, as much a lover of the arts as Gaudí, wished to impress his family and Barcelona's high society with an extravagant showpiece. He got his wish. Sometimes heavy-handed in detail, the work's genius lies in its layout and inspired interconnected spaces.

The facade of the building is Venetian in style and marked by two huge arched entrances protected by intricate forged iron gates and a shield of Catalonia, lending it a fortress-like appearance. The interior of the Palau Güell can only be viewed by guided tour. First you'll see the basement-stables, which feature the nature-obsessed architect's signature columns with mushroom capitals, then you ascend again to view the interconnected floors. The first, the anteroom, is in fact four salons. Most of the surfaces are dark, lending the rooms a heaviness, with Moorish-style detailing predominant throughout. Lightness comes in the form of an ingenious system that filters natural light via a constellation of perforated stars inlaid in a parabolic dome above the central hall. Also outstanding is the screened, street-facing gallery that sweeps the entire length of the facade, also letting light into all salons except the "ladies room" where female visitors did their touchups before being received by Sr. Güell. The ceilings of the first floor, in oak and bulletwood, are beautifully decorated with foliage, starting off as buds in the first room and in full bloom by the fourth. The dining room and the private apartments contain some original furniture, a sumptuous marble staircase, and a magnificent fireplace designed by architect Camil Oliveras, a regular collaborator with Gaudí. But visitors are usually most impressed by the roof, with its army of centurion-like, *trencadis*-covered chimneys. These chimneys, along with the rest of the building, were given an overhaul in the mid-1990s, and their tilework was restored; see if you can spot the one bearing a fragment of the Olympic mascot Cobi.

Nou de la Rambla 3–5. ⓒ 93-317-39-74. Admission 3€ ($3.45), free for children under 7. Mon–Sat 10am–6:15pm. Metro: Drassanes.

Palau de la Virreina   Built in the 1770s, this building was the former home of Manuel d'Amat, a wealthy viceroy who had made his fortune in the Americas. Set slightly back from the street, this grand structure is marked by typically Spanish topheaviness. Inside there is a patio featuring columns and a staircase to the right leads to the interior, most of which is not open to the public as it is home to the city's cultural events committee. On the left, a large space is lent to a changing calendar of exhibitions, predominantly on some aspect of Barcelona. One of the best, held in September, is the Fotomercé, amateur photographs of the previous year's Mercé festival. On the ground floor there are an excellent gift shop and a cultural information point.

Les Ramblas 99. ✆ **93-316-10-00**. Admission varies. Tues–Sat 11am–8:30pm, Sun 11am–3pm. Metro: Catalunya or Liceu.

Sant Pau del Camp ★★ Architecture from the Romanesque period is rich in rural Catalonia, which only makes the presence of this church in an inner-city street even more surprising. Its name ("Saint Paul of the countryside") stems from the fact that the church was once surrounded by green fields outside the city walls and is the oldest church in Barcelona. Given its grand old age, Sant Pau is remarkably intact. Remains of the original 9th-century structure can be seen on the capitals and bases of the portal. The church was rebuilt in the 11th and 12th centuries and is shaped in the form of a Greek cross with three apses. The western exterior door features a Latin inscription referring to Christ, Saint Peter, and Saint Paul. In the 14th-century chapter house is the tomb of Guífre Borrell, count of Barcelona in the early 10th century. The small cloister however is the highlight, with its Moorish arches and central fountain.

Sant Pau 99. ✆ **93-441-00-01**. Free admission. Mon–Fri 6–7:45pm. Metro: Paral.lel.

3 L'Eixample

Barcelona's "new town," its extension beyond the old city walls, actually contains a glorious grid of 18th- and 19th-century buildings, including the most vibrant examples of the *modernista* movement. The famous **Quadrat d'Or (Golden Triangle),** an area bordered by the streets Bruc, Aribau, Aragó, and the Diagonal, has been named the world's greatest living museum of turn-of-the-20th-century architecture. Most of the key buildings are within these hundred-odd city blocks, including Gaudí's **La Pedrera** and the ultimate *modernista* calling card, the **Manzana de la Discordia** (see below). Many of these still serve their original use: luxury apartments for the city's 19th-century nouveau riche. Others are office buildings and even shops (the Passeig de Gràcia, the neighborhood's main boulevard, is the top shopping precinct). In case you were wondering, marine-colored, hexagonal tiles on the footpaths are reproductions of ones used by Gaudí for La Pedrera and the Casa Batlló.

L'EIXAMPLE DRETA

L'Hospital de la Santa Creu i San Pau ★★★ The elegant pedestrianized boulevard, the Avenida Gaudí, stretches northwards from the Sagrada Família, and at the opposite end sits another key work of the *modernista* movement, almost equal in vitality to that of Gaudí's. The Hospital San Pau (as it's more commonly known) is a remarkable work by the architect Domènech i Montaner. He is often quoted as being the second most important *modernista* architect after Gaudí, and his magnificent Palau de la Música Catalana (p. 148) is one of the movement's most emblematic pieces.

The Hospital San Pau was commissioned by Pau Gil i Serra, a rich Catalan banker who wished to create a hospital based on the "garden city" model. While patients languished in turn-of-the-20th-century prisonlike edifices, Gil i Serra had the then-revolutionary idea to make their surroundings as agreeable as possible. He conceived a series of colored pavilions, each (like a hospital ward) serving a specific purpose, scattered among parkland. He only achieved half his vision. Although the first stone was laid in 1902, by 1911 funds ran out, and only 8 of the 48 projected pavilions were completed. Domènech died in 1930; after work carried out by his son and economic intervention from another city medical institution, the Hospital San Pau was opened.

The Hospital San Pau is an inspiring place to wander around. The interiors of the pavilions are off-limits, but their gorgeous Byzantine and Moorish-inspired facades and decoration, from gargoyles and angels to fauna and blossoming flora greet you at every turn. The largest, the **Administrative Pavilion,** can be entered and explored. Its facade glows with mosaic murals telling the history of hospital care, and in the interior there are beautiful columns with floral capitals and a luxurious, dusty pink tiled ceiling.

Sant Antoni María Claret 167–171. ✆ 93-488-20-78. Admission 4.20€ ($4.80) adults, 3€ ($3.45) students, children under 15 free. Free to walk around discreetly. Guided tours Sat–Sun 10am–2pm. Metro: Hospital San Pau.

La Pedrera ✪✪✪   Commonly known as La Pedrera (The Quarry), the real name for this spectacular work of Antoni Gaudí's is the Casa Milà. The nickname stems from its stony, fortress-like appearance, much ridiculed at the time, but today it stands as the superlative example of *modernista* architecture. The entire building was restored in 1996, the Espai Gaudí—a didactic museum—installed in the attic and one of the apartments refurbished to how it would have looked at the time of its early-20th-century residents.

The building was commissioned by Pere Mila i Camps, a rich developer who had just married an even richer widow. He wanted the most extravagant showpiece on the fashionable Passeig de Gràcia so Gaudí, having just completed the Casa Batlló (see below), was the obvious choice.

La Pedrera occupies a corner block, and its sinuous, rippling facade is in sharp contrast to its neoclassical neighbors. In fact, it is unlike any piece of architecture anywhere in the world. La Pedrera seems to have been molded rather than built. Its massive, wave-like curtain walls are of Montjuïc limestone and the balconies' iron balustrades look like masses of seaweed. Inside as out, there is not one straight wall or right angle in the edifice, further adding to La Pedrera's cave-like appearance (in a well known anecdote, after the French president Georges Clemenceau visited the building, he reported that in Barcelona they make caves for dragons). The apartments (many still private homes) are centered on two courtyards whose walls are decorated with subtle, jewel-like murals. The highpoint of the visit (literally!) is the spectacular roofscape. It features clusters of centurion-like chimneystacks, artfully restored and residing on an undulating surface, mirroring the arches of the attic below with outstanding views of the neighborhood, the Sagrada Família, and the port. In the summer months, jazz and flamenco concerts are held in this unique setting. The entire first floor has been handed over as an exhibition space (past shows have included artists of the caliber of Dalí and Chillida). Admission is included in the La Pedrera entry.

Provença 261–265 (on corner of Passeig de Gràcia). ✆ 93-484-59-80 or 93-484-59-00. Admission 7€ ($8.05) adults, 3.50€ ($4) students, free for children under 12. Daily 10am–7:30pm; English tours Mon–Fri 6pm. Metro: Diagonal.

La Sagrada Família ✪✪✪ *(Moments*   Gaudí's incomplete masterpiece is one of the city's more idiosyncratic creations—if you have time to see only one Catalan landmark, you should make it this one. Begun in 1882 and incomplete at the architect's death in 1926, this incredible temple—the Church of the Holy Family—is a bizarre wonder. The languid, amorphous structure embodies the essence of Gaudí's style, which some have described as Art Nouveau run wild.

The Sagrada Família became Gaudí's all-encompassing obsession towards the last years of this intensely religious man's life. The commission came from the Josephines, a right-wing, highly pious faction of the Catholic Church. They were of the opinion that the decadent city needed an expiatory (atonement) temple where its inhabitants could go and do penance for their sins. Gaudí, whose view of Barcelona's supposed decadence largely coincided with that of the Josephines, by all accounts had a free hand; money was no object, nor was there a deadline to finish it. As Gaudí is known to have said, "My client [God] is in no hurry."

Literally dripping in symbolism, the Sagrada Família was conceived to be a "catechism in stone." The basic design followed that of a Gothic church, with transepts, aisles, and a central nave. Apart from the riot of stone carvings, the grandeur of the structure is owed to the elongated towers: four above each of the three facades (representing the apostles) at 100m (329 ft.) high with four more (the evangelists) shooting up from the central section at a lofty 170m (558 ft.). The words SANCTUS, SANCTUS, SANCTUS, HOSANNA IN EXCELSIUS (Holy, Holy, Holy, Glory to God in the Highest) are written on these, further embellished with colorful geometric tilework. The last tower, being built over the apse, will be higher still and dedicated to the Virgin Mary. It is the two completed facades however that are the biggest crowd pleasers. The oldest, and the only one to be completed while the architect was alive, is the **Nativity Facade** on the Carrer Marina. So abundant in detail, upon first glance it seems like a wall of molten wax. As the name suggests, the work represents the birth of Jesus; its entire expanse is crammed with figurines of the Holy Family, flute-bearing angels, and an abundance of flora and fauna. Nature and its forms were Gaudí's passion; he spent hours studying its forms in the countryside of his native Reus, south of Barcelona, and much of his work is inspired by nature. On the Nativity Facade he added birds, mushrooms, even a tortoise to the rest of the religious imagery. The central piece is the "Tree of Life," a Cyprus tree scattered with nesting white doves.

On the opposite side, the **Passion Facade** is a harsh counterpart to the fluidity of the Nativity Facade. It is the work of Josep M. Subirachs, a well-known Catalan sculptor who, like Gaudí, has set up a workshop inside the church to complete his work. His highly stylized, elongated, figures are of Christ's passion and death, from last supper to the crucifixion. The work, started in 1952, has been highly criticized. In the book *Barcelona,* art critic Robert Hughes called it "the most blatant mass of half-digested *modernista* clichés to be plunked on a notable building within living memory."

Despite his and dozens of other voices of dissent, work ploughs on. In 1936 anarchists attacked the church (as they did many others in the city) destroying the plans and models Gaudí had left behind. The present architects are working from photographs of them aided by modern technology. The central nave is starting to take shape and the Glory Facade is limping along. It is estimated that the whole thing will be completed by 2026 (the centenary of Gaudí's death), funded entirely by visitors and private donations.

Admission includes a 12-minute video on Gaudí's religious and secular works and entrance to the museum where fascinating reconstructions of Gaudí's original models are on show.

Moments Gaudí's Resting Place

Before you leave the Sagrada Família, make sure you pay a visit to the crypt, Gaudí's resting place. The architect spent the last days of his life on the site, living a hermitlike existence in a workroom and dedicating all of his time to the project. Funds had finally dried up, and the *modernisme* movement fallen out of fashion. In general, the Sagrada Família was starting to be viewed as a monumental white elephant.

In 1926 on his way to vespers, the old man did not see the no. 30 tram hurtling down the Gran Vía. He was taken to a hospital for the poor (in his disheveled state, no one recognized the great architect) where he lay in agony for three days before dying and was laid to rest under a simple tombstone in the Sagrada Família's crypt.

In contrast to the rest of the Sagrada Família, the crypt is built in neo-Gothic style. Being the first part of the building to be completed, it is the work of Francesc de Villar, the architect who was originally commissioned for the project until Gaudí took over (Villar quit for unknown reasons). During 1936's "Tragic Week," when anarchists went on an anti-clerical rampage in the city, the crypt was ransacked. The only thing left intact was Gaudí's tomb.

Mallorca 401. ✆ **93-207-30-31**. Admission 8€ ($9.20) adults, 5€ ($5.75) students, guide/audio-guide 3€ ($3.45), elevator to the top (about 60m/197 ft.) 2€ ($2.30). Nov–Mar daily 9am–6pm; Apr–Sept daily 9am–8pm. Metro: Verdaguer or Sagrada Família.

L'EIXAMPLE ESQUERRA

Casa Amatller ★★   Constructed in a cubical design with a Dutch gable, this building was created by Puig i Cadafalch in 1900 and was the first building on the *manzana*. It stands in sharp contrast to its neighbor, the Gaudí-designed Casa Batlló (see below). The architecture of the Casa Amatller, imposed on an older structure, is a vision of ceramic, wrought iron, and sculptures. The structure combines grace notes of Flemish Gothic—especially on the finish of the facade—with elements of Catalan architecture. The gable outside is in the Flemish style. Look out for the sculptures of animals blowing glass and taking photos, both hobbies of the architect. They were executed by Eusebi Arnau, an artist much in demand by the *modernistas*.

Passeig de Gràcia 41. ✆ **93-216-01-75**. Ground floor open to public Mon–Sat 10am–7pm. Metro: Passeig de Gràcia.

Casa Batlló ★★★   Next door to the Casa Amatller, Casa Batlló was designed by Gaudí in 1905 and is hands-down the superior of the three works in the *manzana*. Using sensuous curves in iron and stone and glittering, luminous *trencadis* (collage of broken tiles and ceramic) on the facade, the Casa Batlló is widely thought to represent the legend of Saint George (the patron saint of Catalonia) and his dragon. The balconies are protected by imposing skull-like formations and supported by vertebrae-like columns representing the dragon's victims, while the spectacular roof is the dragon's humped and glossy scaled back. St. George can be seen in the turret, his lance crowned by a cross. The building was opened to the public in 2004 and although its admission price is steep (16€/$18) compared to many other Gaudí attractions, the interior of the building is no less spectacular than the exterior with sinuous staircases, flowing wood paneling, and a stained-glass gallery supported by yet more bone-like columns. Custom-made Gaudí-designed furniture is scattered throughout.

Passeig de Gràcia 43. ℭ **93-488-06-66.** Admission 16€ ($18) adults, 13€ ($15) children and students, free for children under 5. Mon–Sun 9am–8pm. Metro: Passeig de Gràcia.

Casa Lleó Morera ★★   The last building of the trio, on the corner of Carrer del Consell de Cent stands the Casa Lleó Morera. This florid work, completed by Doménech i Montaner in 1906, is perhaps the least challenging of the three, as it represents a more international style of Art Nouveau. One of its quirkier features is the tiered wedding cake-type turret and abundance of ornamentation: comb the facade for a lightbulb and telephone (both inventions of the period) and a lion and mulberry bush (after the owner's name: in Catalan, lion is *lleó,* and mulberry is *morera*). Tragically, the ground floor has been mutilated by its tenant, who stripped the lower facade of its detail and installed plate glass. The shop's interior, which fared no better, is the only part of the building open to the public.

Passeig de Gràcia 35. Metro: Passeig de Gràcia.

Fundació Antoni Tàpies ★   When it opened in 1990, this became the third Barcelona museum, after Miró and Picasso, devoted to the work of a single, prolific artist. In 1984 the Catalan artist Antoni Tàpies set up a foundation bearing his name, and the city of Barcelona donated an ideal site: the old Montaner i Simon publishing house. One of the city's landmark buildings, the brick-and-iron structure was built between 1881 and 1884 by that important exponent of Catalan *modernista* architecture, Lluis Doménech i Montaner, also perpetrator of the Casa Lleó Morera around the corner (see above). The core of the museum is a collection of works by Tàpies (most contributed by the artist), covering stages of his career as it evolved into abstract expressionism. Here, you can see the entire spectrum of media in which he worked: painting, assemblage, sculpture, drawing, and ceramics. His associations with Picasso and Miró are apparent. The largest of the works is on top of the building: a controversial gigantic sculpture, *Cloud and Chair,* made from 2,700m (8,858 ft.) of metal wiring and tubing. The lower floor is used for temporary exhibitions, nearly always on contemporary art and photography and upper floor a library with an extremely impressive section on oriental art, one of the artist's inspirations.

Aragó 255. ℭ **93-487-03-15.** Admission 4.20€ ($4.80) adults, 2.10€ ($2.40) students, free for children under 16. Tues–Sun 10am–8pm. Metro: Passeig de Gràcia.

La Manzana de la Discordia

The superlative showcase of the *modernista* architecture is the so-called **Manzana de la Discordia (Illa de la Discordia).** The "Block of Discord," which is on the Passeig de Gràcia between Consell de Cent and Aragó, consists of three works by the three master architects of the movement; Josep Puig i Cadafalch, Lluis Domènech i Montaner, and Antoni Gaudí. Although they are all quite different in style, they offer a coherent insight into the stylistic language of the period. The Casa Amatller houses the Centro del Modernismo, an information point on the *modernistas* and the movement (see below).

Tips **Doing the *Modernista* Walk**

As most of Barcelona's *modernista* legacy is in the L'Eixample neighborhood, it makes sense to see it on foot. The **Centre del Modernisme** at the Casa Amatllet, Passeig de Gràcia 41 (© **93-488-01-39;** Mon–Sat 10am–7pm, Sun 10am–2pm; Metro: Gràcia), is a one-stop information point on the movement. They have devised the "modernism route," a tour of the city's 100 most emblematic Art Nouveau buildings. You can either pick up a free map or buy a well-produced, explanatory book (12€/$14), which includes a book of coupons offering discounts of between 15% and 50% on attractions that charge admission, such as Gaudí's Casa Batlló and La Pedrera.

If you wish to explore *modernisme* beyond the boundaries of Barcelona, the center can also supply you with information on towns such as Reus (Gaudí's' birthplace) and Terrassa, which has an important collection of *modernista* industrial buildings. Tours are also offered.

In early 2005, the Centre del Modernisme will be opening branches at the Hospital Sant Pau and the Finca Güell in Pedralbes.

Fundació Francisco Godia *Finds* In the heart of Barcelona, this new museum showcases the famous art collection of Francisco Godia Sales, the Catalan art collector and entrepreneur. He amassed one of the great private collections of art in the country. Godia (1921–90) combined a love of art with a head for business and a passion for motor racing. When he wasn't driving fast ("the most wonderful thing in the world"), he was amassing his art collection. As a collector, he showed exquisite taste and great artistic sensibility.

He gathered a splendid array of medieval sculpture and ceramics but showed a keener instinct for purchasing great paintings. Godia acquired works by some of the most important artists of the 20th century, including Julio González, María Blanchard, Joan Ponç, Antoni Tàpies, and Manolo Hugué, the latter a great friend of Picasso. From its earliest stages, Godia realized the artistic importance of Catalan *modernisme* and collected works by sculptors like Josep Llimona and celebrated *modernista* painters Santiago Rusiñol and Ramon Casas. Godia also dipped deeper into the past, acquiring works, for example, of two of the most important artists of the 17th century: Jacob van Ruysdael and Luca Giordano.

Carrer Valencia 284. © **93-272-31-80.** Admission 4.50€ ($5.15) adults, 2.10€ ($2.40) students and seniors, free for children under 5. Wed–Mon 10am–8pm. Metro: Passeig de Gràcia.

Museu Egipci de Barcelona Spain's only museum dedicated to Egyptology contains more than 250 pieces from the personal collection of founder Jordi Clos (owner of the Hotel Claris). On display are sarcophagi, jewelry, hieroglyphics, sculptures, and artwork. Exhibits focus on ancient Egyptians' everyday life, including education, social customs, religion, and food. The museum has its own lab for restorations. A library with more than 3,000 works is open to the public.

Valencia 284. © **93-488-01-88.** Admission 5.50€ ($6.30) adults, 4.50€ ($5.15) students and children. Mon–Sat 10am–8pm; Sun 10am–2pm. Guided tours Sat. Metro: Passeig de Gràcia.

4 Montjuïc

For many visitors, and certainly those who arrive by sea, the mountain of Montjuïc is their first glimpse of Barcelona. Jutting out over the port on one side and facing the monumental Plaça Espanya on the other, Montjuïc is strategically placed as a pleasure ground and a fortunate lack of a constant water source has deterred residential development. Instead it became the focal point of two of the city's key international events: first the World Fair of 1929, of which many structures still remain, and second the 1992 Olympic Games.

The largest "green zone" in the city, the forests and parks of Montjuïc have always been popular with joggers, cyclists, and strollers. In the past couple of years, the city's council has embarked on a project to spruce these up, install walkways and connecting escalators, and reclaim some forgotten gems in the process. One of these is the **Font del Gat,** Passeig Santa Madrona 28 (② **93-289-04-04**), a once-fashionable cafe built by *modernista* architect Josep Puig i Cadafalch that now acts as a Montjuïc information point and restaurant. Add to that some of the city's top flight museums such as the Miró Foundation and the MNAC and there are more than enough reasons to leave the bustle of city behind and head for the hills.

CaixaForum ★★   This is one of the city's more exciting contemporary art spaces, both in term of its setting and what's inside. It opened in 2002 in the Casaramona, an old *modernista* textile factory designed by Puig i Cadalfach that was used as police barracks in the '30s. The vibrant edifice features a red brick facade and singular turret, to which the Japanese architect Arata Isozaki added a daring walkway, courtyard, and entrance. (Isozaki is the designer responsible for the Palau St. Jordi, a major music and meeting venue, further up the hill of Montjuïc.) Inside, after passing the huge abstract mural by Sol de Witt, the elevator whisks you up to three exhibition spaces, connected by exterior halls. These are changing constantly, meaning that three, normally very diverse, shows can be viewed at the same time. Some recent ones have included Rodin's sculpture, a didactic show on Confucius, Turner's Venice, and an installation by Cuban artist Jorge Pardo, who created a baroque setting for minimalist pieces from the CaixaForum's permanent collection. The foundation puts on a lively calendar of related events and performances, the latter focusing on world music and modern dance. There is an excellent bookshop in the foyer.

Av. Marquès de Comillas 6–8. ② **93-476-86-00.** Free admission. Tues–Sun 10am–8pm. Metro: Espanya. FGC: Espanya.

Fundació Joan Miró ★★★   Born in 1893, Joan Miró was one of Spain's greatest artists, and along with Tàpies, the undisputed master of contemporary Catalan art. His work is known for its whimsical abstract forms, brilliant colors, and surrealism. Some 10,000 works, including paintings, graphics, and sculptures, are collected here. The building, constructed in the early 1970s, was designed by Catalan architect Josep Lluis Sert, a close friend of Miró's (he also designed the artist's workroom in Majorca). Set among the parkland of Montjuïc, the museum consists of a series of white, rationalist style galleries with terracotta floors. *Claraboias* (skylights) ensure that the space is bathed in natural light. Its hilltop setting affords some wonderful views of Barcelona, especially from the rooftop terrace that also serves as a sculpture garden.

The collection, donated by the artist himself, is so huge that only a portion of it can be shown at any one time. There is also a gallery put aside for temporary exhibitions, being either on an aspect of Miró's work or a contemporary artist or movement. Concerts are held in the gardens in the summer months.

The first gallery holds two of the collection's treasures; the magnificent 1979 **Foundation Tapestry,** which Miró executed especially for the space and the extraordinary **Mercury Fountain,** a work by his friend the American sculptor Alexander Calder. In contrast to Miró's painting, which was nearly always carried out in a primary color palette, there is a huge collection of drawings from his days as student. Even as a young man, you can tell his deep sense of national identity and Catalanism which (logically) later led to an extreme horror at the civil war. The key work representing this sentiment is the powerful *Man and Woman in Front of a Pile of Excrement* (1935) in the Pilar Juncosa Gallery, one of the so-called "Wild Paintings." Much of Miró's work though is dreamlike and uplifting, with the sun, moon and other celestial bodies represented again and again. Note the poetic *The Gold of the Azure* (1967) in the same gallery; a transfixing blue cloud on a golden background with dots and strokes for the planets and stars.

Even if you are already familiar with Miró's work, the excellent commentary provided via the audioguide (available at the ticket office) will supply you with special insight into this fascinating artist.

Parc de Montjuïc s/n. ✆ 93-443-94-70. Admission 7.20€ ($8.30) adults, 3.90€ ($4.50) students, free for children under 14. July–Sept Tues–Wed and Fri–Sat 10am–8pm; Oct–June Tues–Wed and Fri–Sat 10am–7pm; year-round Thurs 10am–9:30pm and Sun 10am–2:30pm. Bus: 50 at Plaça d'Espanya or 55; Funicular de Montjuïc.

Galería Olímpica   An enthusiastic celebration of the 1992 Olympic Games, this is one of the few museums in Europe devoted to sports. Exhibits include photos, costumes, and memorabilia, with heavy emphasis on the events' pageantry, the number of visitors who attended, and the fame the events brought to Barcelona. Of interest to statisticians, civic planners, and sports buffs, the gallery contains audiovisual information about the building programs that prepared the city for the onslaught of visitors. There are conference facilities, an auditorium, video recordings of athletic events, and archives. In the cellar of the Olympic Stadium's southeastern perimeter, the museum is most easily reached by entering the stadium's southern gate (Porta Sud).

Passeig Olímpic s/n, Estadí Olímpic. ✆ 93-426-06-60. Admission 2.70€ ($3.10) adults, 1.50€ ($1.70) children and seniors. Apr–Sept Mon–Fri 10am–2pm and 4–7pm; Oct–Mar Tues–Sat 10am–1pm and 4–6pm. Metro: Espanya, then 15-min walk, or take bus nos. 13 or 50 from Plaça Espanya.

Museu d'Arqueologia de Catalunya ✮   The Museu d'Arqueologia occupies the former Palace of Graphic Arts built for the 1929 World's Fair. It has been attractively restored, with some rooms retaining their Art Deco flavor. The artifacts, which are arranged chronologically, reflect the long history of this Mediterranean port city and surrounding province, beginning with prehistoric Iberian artifacts. The collection includes articles from the Greek, Roman, and Carthaginian periods. Some of the more interesting relics were excavated in the ancient Greco-Roman city of L'Empúries in Northern Catalonia. The Greeks in particular developed a strategic trading post here with other Mediterranean peoples and the vessels, urns, and other everyday implements they left behind make fascinating viewing.

But undoubtedly the high point of the collection is the Roman artifacts. The Roman empire (using Empúries as their entry point) began their conquest of Iberia in 218 B.C., and the glassware, lamps, grooming aids, and utensils here are truly outstanding. The mosaics, many of them outstandingly intact, have been laid into the floor and visitors are invited to tread on them, the curators believing that their use provokes better preservation.

Passeig de Santa Madrona 39–41, Parc de Montjuïc. ✆ **93-424-65-77**. Admission 2.40€ ($3) adults, 1.80€ ($2.50) students, free for children under 16. Tues–Sat 9:30am–7pm; Sun 10am–2:30pm. Metro: Espanya.

Museu Militar de Montjuïc ⊛

Although the collection at the city's museum is interesting enough, most people head up here for the views. Perched on the sea-facing side of Montjuïc, this fortress (Castell de Montjuïc) dates back to 1640 and was rebuilt and extended during the mid–1800s. Its gloomy cells served as a military prison during the Civil War, earning it an indifferent, if not hostile, reputation among the people of Barcelona. While there have been noises from the local government to change the focus of the museum to a more peaceful and reflective tone, it remains pretty much the same as when it was opened, shortly after the army moved out in 1960.

The collection itself contains the usual assortment of paintings marking military events and dozens of rooms of armor, uniforms, weapons, and the instruments of war. One of the more entertaining exhibits (Room 8) contains thousands of miniatures forming a Spanish division, which first went on show during the 1929 World's Fair.

The terraces and highest points of the star-shaped fortress-castle, and the walkways that surround it, offer some breathtaking views of the Barcelona skyline and Mediterranean. The parkland around the castle is currently being dug up to make it more accessible and easier to walk around. If you don't mind an uphill stroll, note that the most spectacular way to get here is via the port-crossing cable car (see below). On the walk from the drop-off point, you will pass the famous statue of La Sardana, the traditional Catalan dance, which is featured on many postcards of the city. Otherwise, grab the funicular from Paral.lel Metro station, which drops you off pretty much at the door.

Parc de Montjuïc s/n. ✆ **93-329-86-13**. Admission museum and castle 2.50€ ($2.90), 1€ ($1.15) castle and grounds, free for children under 14. Nov to mid-Mar Tues–Sun 9:30am–5:30pm; mid-Mar to Oct Tues–Sun 9:30am–8pm. Transbordador Aeri (cable car; p. 166) from Barceloneta to Montjuïc, then uphill walk. Bus: PM (Parc Montjuïc); departs from Plaça Espanya 8am–9:20pm Sat–Sun and public holidays. Metro: Paral.lel, then funicular (tram) to top 9am–8pm (until 10pm July–Sept).

Museu Nacional d'Art de Catalunya (MNAC) ⊛⊛⊛

This museum, which recently underwent massive renovations and expansion, is the major depository of Catalan art. Although its mammoth collection also covers the Gothic period and 19th and 20th centuries, the MNAC is perhaps the most important center for Romanesque art in the world. The majority of the sculptures, icons, and frescoes were taken from dilapidated churches in the Pyrénées, restored, and mounted as they would have appeared in the churches in expertly reproduced domes and apses. Larger works are shown with a photograph of the church and a map pointing out its location, drawing you further into this fascinating and largely underexposed 11th- to 13th-century movement. Simplistic yet mesmerizing, Romanesque art is marked by elongated forms, vivid colors, and expressiveness. Most outstanding is the **Apse of Santa María de Taüll** (in Ambit [Gallery] V) with a serene, doe-eyed Christ surrounded by the apostles. Lapis lazuli was used to create the intense blue in the piece. Also look out for a series of ceiling paintings from an Aragonese chapter house. In a more subtle color scheme, they echo Tudor miniature painting (Ambit XI). The entire collection is in sequential order, giving the viewer a tour of Romanesque art from its beginnings to the more advanced late Romanesque and early Gothic eras.

A Bicycle Built for Two

One of the star pieces of the MNAC's *modernista* collection is a self-portrait of Ramón Casas and fellow painter Pere Romeu riding a tandem. This iconic work was originally done for **Els Quatre Gats** (p. 110), essentially a tavern that served as a fraternity house for *modernista* movers and shakers, bohemians, intellectuals, and poets. A young Picasso designed the menu (and held his first-ever exhibition there), and various other works donated to the owners still adorn the walls, although now most, such as Casas' peddling portrait, are reproductions of the originals. The colorful Casas, who had spent many years in the artistic circles of Montmarte, was a perpetrator of the city's newfound modernity and a notable artist in his own right. His interpretations of *fin-de-siècle* Barcelona provide a valuable insight to this heady time.

Sensory overload withstanding, the next section you visit deals with the Gothic period, made up of pieces from the 13th to 15th centuries. All styles that were adopted in Catalonia are represented: Italianate Gothic, Flemish Gothic, and a more linear, local Gothic style. Look out for *retablos* by Jaume Huguet (Room XIII). The primary artist in the Catalan School, Huguet mixed Flemish and Italian influences with local Romanesque conventions. The Gothic collection also holds some Barcelonese Gothic quarter artifacts such as giant object-signs (made for an illiterate population) that used to hang outside workshops (shoes, scissors, and such) and other decorative pieces. The Gothic section finishes with the Cambó collection. A bequest from a local businessman the selection of 14th- to 19th-century paintings includes works by Rubens, El Greco, and Goya.

Thanks to the MNAC's most recent acquisitions—pieces of 19th- and 20th-century decorative art and painting, most stemming from the city's all-important *modernista* movement—the collection now spans a millennium. While *modernista* architecture in the city is abundant, most buildings interiors have been stripped bare of their mirrors, chandeliers, sculptures, and furnishings, many designed by the architects themselves such as Gaudí. Until mid-2004 they were on display at the Museu d'Art Modern in the Parc de la Ciutadella. At the MNAC they have a stunning new home.

Highlights of this collection, which spans the neoclassical, Art Nouveau (or *modernista*), and subsequent *nou-centista* (or *fin-de-siècle*) movements are too numerous to mention. Look out for the marquetry pieces by Gaspar Homar (a master *modernista* carpenter) and the Rodin-influenced sculptor Josep Clara. The superb private oratory by Joan Busquets will leave you breathless at the Art Nouveau movement's excesses and craftsmanship. There are also many pieces taken from the interiors of homes of the Manzana de Discordia (earlier in this chapter).

Palau Nacional, Parc de Montjuïc. 🕐 **93-622-03-60.** Admission 4.80€ ($5.50) adults, 3.30€ ($3.80) students and youths 7–21, free for children under 7. Temporary exhibits: 4.20€ ($4.80). Tues–Sat 10am–7pm; Sun 10am–2:30pm. Metro: Espanya.

Pavelló Mies van der Rohe 🖈🖈   Directly across the road from the CaixaForum, this serene building stands in welcome contrast to the *modernista* style of the Casaramona and the faux traditionalism of the Poble Espanyol. Designed by German architect Mies van der Rohe, it was originally built as the German

Pavilion for the 1929 World's Fair, and was the last of the architect's works before he emigrated to the United States. It is considered a key work of both his and the "International Style" movement for which van der Rohe, and others, like Frank Lloyd Wright, became famous. The simple, horizontal structure contains his trademarks: precision, fluidity of space, and abundance of "pure" materials, in this case different kinds of marble and glass. The structure is built around a shallow pool featuring a statue by Georg Kolbe, the German sculptor known for his female nudes. Inside is the original **Barcelona Chair** designed by van der Rohe and seen (mainly in reproduction form) throughout the city in reception areas. Although the pavilion now stands on its original location, this wasn't always the case. After the World's Fair, it was banished to an outer suburb, only to be rescued and reconstructed in 1985 thanks to an initiative by a group of the city's prominent architects.

Av. Marquès de Comillas s/n. © **93-423-40-16.** Admission 3.40€ ($3.90) adults, free for children under 18. Daily 10am–8pm. Metro: Espanya. FGC: Espanya.

Poble Espanyol ★★ (Kids)   This recreated Spanish village, built for the 1929 World's Fair, provokes mixed feelings: purists see it as the height of kitsch, while others delight in its open spaces and period-Disneyland type feel. But the question remains; where else would you find over 100 styles of Spanish vernacular architecture crammed into one very pleasant spot? From the Levante to Galicia, Castilian high Gothic, humble whitewashed dwellings of the south and colorful Basque homes, it's all here. At the entrance, for starters, stands a facsimile of the gateway to the grand walled city of Avila. This leads you to the center of the village with an outdoor cafe where you can sit and have drinks, and there are various other venues throughout, including the excellent flamenco taberna the **El Tablao de Carmen** (p. 203) and a couple of other trendy nightspots. The big names of July's El Grec festival also play here, in the main plaza just inside the gates. As was its original purpose, numerous shops still sell provincial crafts and souvenir items, and in some of them you can see artists at work, printing fabric,

---

(Moments **The Magic Fountain**

Without a doubt, the most popular attraction for young and old alike in the Montjuïc area is the **Font Màgica (Magic Fountain).** During the day, the grandiose fountain at the base of the staircase to the MNAC seems like any other, but at night it takes on a different personality. At regular intervals, the fountain puts on a spectacular show: Music, a range of pop songs to popular classical, belts out from loudspeakers, and different colored lights are beamed from inside the fountain itself. The gushes of water, controlled externally, "dance" to the mixture of light and sound. Supposedly the only one of its kind in the world, the fountain was designed by the visionary engineer Carles Buïgas for the 1929 World's Fair, pre-dating similar Vegas-type attractions by decades. It's free and never fails to enthrall. Grab a seat at one of the nearby outdoor cafes and enjoy. It's at Plaça Carles Buïgas 1. Metro: Espanya. The sound and light shows run from May to early October, Thursday through Sunday at 9:30, 10pm, 10:30, 11, and 11:30pm. The rest of the year, they are held on Friday and Saturday at 7, 7:30, 8, and 8:30pm.

Tips **Swinging over the Port**

Unless you suffer from vertigo, the most spectacular way to reach the Castell de Montjuïc and the other attractions on the sea-face of the mountain of Montjuïc is via a cable car that crosses the port. The **Transbordador Aeri** starts at Torre de Sant Sebastián at the very end of the Passeig de Joan de Borbó in Barceloneta (bus: 17, 64, or 39), stops at the World Trade Centre on the way, and finishes at the ascent to the peak of Montjuïc. The cable car runs every 15 minutes daily from 10:30am to 7pm. Cost is 6€ ($6.90) one-way, 7.20€ ($8.30) round-trip.

---

making pottery, and blowing glass. If you are lucky, your visit may coincide with a wedding at the faux Sant Miquel monastery, one of the more popular places in the city to get married. A sign that the Poble Espanyol is on a mission to up its cultural ante is a recent addition: **Fundació Fran Daural** (daily 10am–7pm); a collection of contemporary Catalan arts boasting works by Dalí, Picasso, Barceló, and Tàpies. As said, many families delight in the faux-Spanish atmosphere, but the more discriminating find it a bit of a tourist trap.

Av. Marquès de Comillas s/n, Parc de Montjuïc. ⓒ **93-508-63-00**. Admission 7€ ($8.05) adults, 3.90€ ($4.50) children 7–12, free for children under 7; 14€ ($16) family ticket; 2€ ($2.30) guided tours. Mon 9am–8pm; Tues–Thurs 9am–2am; Fri–Sat 9am–4am; Sun 9am–midnight. Metro: Espanya, then 10-min walk uphill, or take bus no. 13 or 50 from Plaça Espanya.

Jardí Botànic ⭐   Just behind the Castell de Montjuïc, the city's Botanical Garden opened in 1999, but has already gathered international praise for its cutting-edge landscaping and concept. The foliage focuses on Mediterranean species, or plants, flowers, and trees that flourish in a Mediterranean-type climate. These include such far-flung destinations as Australia and California, and the park is divided up into sections representing each of these regions. The sci-fi telecommunications aerial you see a short distance away was designed by the Valencia-born architect Santiago Calatrava for the Olympic Games. This ingenious structure has a base decorated with broken tiles (a homage to Gaudí, one of the architect's main influences), and its position, leaning at the same angle as the hill's inclination, means that it also acts as a sundial.

Doctor Font i Quer s/n, Parque de Montjuïc. ⓒ **93-426-49-35**. Admission 3€ ($3.45), children under 16 free. Mon–Sat 10am–5pm; Sun 10am–3pm; July–Sept Mon–Sat 10am–8pm. Transbordador Aeri (cable car; see above) from Barceloneta to Montjuïc, then an uphill walk. Bus: PM (Parc Montjuïc) departs from Plaça Espanya 8am–9:20pm Sat–Sun and public holidays. Metro: Paral.lel, then funicular (tram) to top 9am–8pm (until 10pm July–Sept).

5 The Harborfront

For a city that for centuries "lived with its back to the sea," Barcelona now sports a spectacular harborfront, the busiest leisure port in the Mediterranean, and kilometers of urban beaches. The relocation of the commercial port and coastal freeway and the demolition of industrial buildings and eyesores that blocked the view of the sea were pushed ahead for the 1992 Olympic Games. Without a doubt, the reclaiming of the city's coast has been the most life-enhancing change Barcelona has seen in the last century. Starting at the Columbus Monument, you can follow the city's coastal stretch via boardwalks and esplanades to the Olympic Village and beyond. Along the way you will pass through the modern marina the Port Vell, the old fisherman's district of La Barceloneta, and end at Frank Gehry's famous fish sculpture at the Olympic Port.

L'Aquarium de Barcelona ★★   One of the most impressive testimonials to sea life anywhere opened in 1996 in Barcelona's Port Vell, a 10-minute walk from the bottom of the Rambles. The largest aquarium in Europe, it contains 21 glass tanks positioned along either side of a wide curving corridor. Each tank depicts a different marine habitat, with emphasis on everything from multicolored fish and corals to seagoing worms to sharks. The highlight is a huge "oceanarium" representative of the Mediterranean as a self-sustaining ecosystem. You view it from the inside of a glass-roofed, glass-sided tunnel that runs along its entire length, making fish, eels, and sharks appear to swim around you. Kids can let off some steam in the **Explora** section, a collection of touchy-feely educational exhibits on Catalonia's Costa Brava and Ebro Delta.

Moll d'Espanya-Port Vell. 🕐 **93-221-74-74.** Admission 14€ ($16) adults, 9.25€ ($11) children 4–12 and students, free for children under 4. July–Aug daily 9:30am–11pm; Sept–June Mon–Fri 9:30am–9pm, Sat–Sun: 9:30am–9:30pm. Metro: Drassanes or Barceloneta.

Museu d'Història de Catalunya ★   The Catalan History Museum is located in the Palau del Mar, a huge warehouse dating from the late 19th century. Many similar buildings stood alongside it before this flank of the port was re-developed for the 1992 Olympic Games, creating the marina and recreational area that now surrounds it.

The museum, divided into eight sections, aims to provide a stroll through history and that pretty much sums up what it does. It's a sometimes exhausting, highly didactic tour of the country. **"Roots," "Birth of a Nation,"** and **"Our Sea"** look at Catalonia's ancient ancestors, the flourishing Romanesque period, and the Catalan-Aragonese sea trade. **"On the Periphery of an Empire," "Bases of the Revolution,"** and **"Steam and Nation"** study Catalonia's decline under the Hapsburg rule and subsequent economic and cultural recovery in the industrial age. Finally **"The Electric Years"** (which is, by far, one of the more entertaining parts of the exhibit) and **"Defeat and Recovery"** deal with the 20th century, the Civil War, Catalonia during Franco's dictatorship, and the first democratic elections after his death.

It's a lot of area to cover and the museum uses a mixture of multimedia, recreations, models and other interactive devices as their medium, most of the time with effective results. As all of the accompanying explanations are in Catalan, you are provided with a translation (in book form) at the entrance.

The temporary exhibitions on the ground floor are less heavy going, and have included some excellent shows on the Mediterranean cultures, and the relationship between the famed poet Federico García Lorca and Salvador Dalí.

After all this you may need a break. The museum's **cafe** offers great food and an excellent view of the port; also on the port side are a handful of outdoor seafood restaurants.

Plaça de la Pau Vila 3. 🕐 **93-225-47-00.** Admission 3€ ($3.45) adults, 2.10€ ($2.40) children 7–18 and students. Tues–Sat 10am–7pm (until 8pm Wed); Sun 10am–2:30pm. Metro: Barceloneta.

Museu Marítim ★★★ *Kids*   In the former Royal Shipyards (Drassanes Reials), the city's Maritime Museum is the finest of its kind in Spain and possibly the world. The seafaring cities of Venice, Genoa, and Valencia all had impressive arsenals, but only vestiges remain. In contrast, Barcelona's shipyards with their majestic arches, columns, and gigantic vaults are a preciously intact example of medieval civic architecture. This complex, which before the coastline receded sat right on the water's edge, was used to dry-dock, construct, and repair ships for the Catalan–Aragonese rulers. During the 18th century, the place went into decline, mainly due to the dissolution of naval construction. Right up until the Civil War, it served as an army barracks until it opened as a museum in the 1970s.

Its collection titled **The Great Adventure of the Sea** is homage to Catalonia's maritime history. The most outstanding exhibit occupies an entire bay. It is a reconstruction of La Galería Real of Don Juan of Austria, a lavish royal galley. In 1971 following extensive documentation, this model was built in celebration of the vessel's most glorious achievement 400 years earlier. The ship headed an alliance of Spanish, Venetian, Maltese, and Vatican vessels in a bloody battle against a Turkish squadron. The so-named "Holy League" won, effectively ending Ottoman rule in the Mediterranean. There is an excellent film recreating the battle which you watch onboard, and you can view the galley's elaborate hull, hold, and deck where each of its 59 oars were manned by the sailors.

Other exhibits chart the traditional fishing techniques and sailing as sport through neat little caravels and draggers, snipes, and sloops. The art of wooden shipbuilding, the charting of the oceans, and launch into the steam age are also covered. Particularly fine is the collection of late 19th-century mastheads, navigational instruments and models of the Compañía Trasmediterránea's fleet (this local company still operates the Barcelona–Balearic islands route). The collection also boasts a model of *Ictíneo,* one of the world's first submarines designed by the Catalan visionary Narcís Monturiol.

Av. de les Drassanes s/n. ✆ **93-342-99-20.** Admission 5.40€ ($6.20) adults, 2.70€ ($3.10) children 7–16. Daily 10am–7pm. Metro: Drassanes.

GRACIA

Located above the Diagonal, Gràcia is a large neighborhood that has a unique character, product from when it was a separate town altogether. Although notable attractions here are not abundant, Gràcia is well worth visiting for a taste of authentic *barri* life. Shopping and cafe society are particularly good around the Calle Verdi and Plaça del Sol and nocturnal activity here is lively, particularly in the summer at the famous **Fiestas de Gràcia** (p. 20). Gràcia boasts a unique mixture of proud locals that have lived all their lives and young, progressive urbanites. This melting pot is reflected in its street life.

Casa Vicens ★★   Although this early work of Gaudí's can only be viewed from the exterior, the exuberance of its facade and form make the trip well worth it. The architect accepted the commission for a summer residence from the tile manufacturer Manuel Vicens i Montaner in 1883, making the Casa Vicens not only one of the first architectonic examples of Art Nouveau in Barcelona but the whole of Europe.

Since the home was designed to be an exponent of Sr. Vicen's business, the entire facade is covered with florid, vividly colored tiles. At the time Gaudí was deeply influenced by North African and Middle Eastern architecture, and this can be seen in the home's form. Its overall opulence and exoticism, with minarets and corbels, is reminiscent of the Indian Raj style. Inside Ottoman, Koranic, and Andalusian influences can also be seen in eccentric touches such as the Turkish-style smoking room. The residence, on a narrow Graciàn street, is owned by descendants of Sr. Vicens and still a private home (although they seem to have no objections to camera-flashing tourists). The interior however has been well-photographed, and is always featured in books on the architect.

Carrer de les Carolines 18–24. Metro: Fontana.

Parc Güell ★★★   After the abundant religious symbolism of the Sagrada Família and the heavy-handedness of the Palau Güell, Gaudí's whimsical Parc Güell often seems like light relief and is for many his favorite and most accessible work. Although it's now officially a public park, in 1900 the Parc Güell began as a real estate venture for a friend, the well-known Catalan industrialist Count Eusebi Güell (see below), who planned to make this a model garden city community of 60 dwellings with its own market and church. It was never completed and the city took over the property in 1926.

Spread over several acres of woodland high above central Barcelona, with wonderful views at every turn, the Parc Güell is one of the most unique manmade landscapes on the planet. It is abundant with the architect's unique vision and expertise at finding creative solutions posed by the demands of the project.

Arriving at the main entrance in the Carrer Olot, you are greeted by two gingerbread-style gatehouses. At the time they were built, Gaudí was working on some set designs for the opera *Hansel and Gretel* at the Liceu Opera House, so it is presumed that the inspiration for these whimsical structures came from that. Both shimmer with broken mosaic collage and are topped with chimneys in the shape of wild and toxic mushrooms. Much has been made of the Parc Güell's symbolism and it has even been suggested that these toadstool-chimneys reflect Gaudí's penchant for hallucinogenic substances. The fact is that mushroom gathering is a national pastime and the work, as in most of Gaudí's cache, reflects a deep-rooted nationalism and respect for nature and Catalonia's history.

The main steps to the **Sala Hipóstila (marketplace)** feature a spectacular tiled lizard, the park's centerpiece. The covered would-be market supports a large platform above with 86 Doric columns connected by shallow vaults. This paganlooking space is largely thought to be inspired by Barcelona's Roman foundations. The roof is embellished with four sun-shaped disks representing the seasons. Above in the elevated square, a sinuous bench, said to be the longest in the world, snakes its way around the perimeter. The decoration on this elaborate piece was carried out by architect and craftsman Josep Marià Jujol. The story

---

⌐ Fun Fact Gaudí's Patron

Eusebi Güell i Bacigalupi, the man who launched Gaudí's career and went on to become a lifelong friend, was a product of the city's new, wealthy elite. He studied art, poetry, and theology in Paris and London and upon returning to Barcelona, put his acute business sense into practice in the shipping, banking, railroad, and textile sectors—all the industries that drove Catalonia's industrial revolution in the late 1800s.

Enormously well respected, Güell was high-minded and took civic duty extremely seriously. He felt bound to improve the lives of his city's inhabitants (of all classes) through art and better working conditions. It seems Güell's first meeting with Gaudí was in a carpentry workshop Gaudí had designed as a showcase for a Barcelona glove shop and shortly afterwards Güell saw the work displayed at the 1878 International Exhibition in Paris. The fruit of the relationship materialized in such marvels as the Parc Güell, the Palau Güell, and the church for the ambitious Colònia Güell in outer Barcelona. Just before his death in 1918, Güell was made a count by King Alfonso XIII.

goes that all the workers on the park were ordered to bring Jujol all the shards of broken crockery and glass they could lay their hands on, which accounts for the work's extraordinary mixture of colors and textures. Palm trees and vistas of the skyline add to the moment.

Three kilometers (2 miles) of more rustic inspired paths and porticoes using material taken from the land itself weave through the rest of the park, which is filled with Mediterranean vegetation. In typical Gaudí style, sculptures and figurines pop up in the most surprising places. Worth hunting out is the **Closed Chapel** at the highest point of the park, in reality an archaic six-lobed structure crowned by a cross that seems to have taken inspiration from the ancient stone watchtowers or druid temples not uncommon in the Balearic Islands.

Only two homes were ever built in the colony and neither of them by Gaudí. One of them, designed by the architect Ramón Berenguer became Gaudí's residence in the latter part of his life. It is now the **Casa-Museu Gaudí** Carrer del Carmel 28 (© **93-219-38-11**) and contains furniture designed by the architect, drawings, and other personal effects, many of them arranged the same way as when the architect lived his reclusive life there. Admission to the house is 4€ ($4.60); open daily from 10am to 6pm.

Carrer del Carmel 28. © **93-424-38-09**. Free admission. Daily 10am–sunset. Metro: Lesseps (then a 15-min. walk). Bus: 24.

6 Outer Barcelona

Barcelona's outer suburbs are largely residential. Once they were considered to be country areas, annexed over the years by the city's continuing sprawl. Thus there are a handful of notable buildings that once stood in a village or country estate. The *barri* of Sarrià, easily reached by the FGC station of the same name, has retained a particularly authentic villagey feel. Located at the foot of Tibidabo, it's a pleasant place to wander around and take in some clean air.

Colònia Güell ★★   For many, Gaudí's most prolific work lies not within Barcelona but outside. He designed the church for the Colònia Güell, an ambitious plan of Eusebi Güell's that lies 20 minutes by train inland from the city. Güell was a progressive man and wished to set up a colony for the workers of his textile mill, which was being transferred here from central Barcelona. The colony would contain a hospital, library, residences, a theater, and a church. Only the crypt was completed before Güell's death.

The haunting grottolike structure stands on an elevated part of the *colònia* surrounded by a pine forest. Its cavelike dimensions and stone-forest interior are due to an ingenious method that the architect employed in the planning stages, one that is on display in the museums both the Sagrada Família and La Pedrera. Gaudí devised the models for his work using lengths of string attached to weights, with the weights taking the tension, photographed the pieces, then inverted the photos. What was concave became a convex, as in an arch. Thus he was able to measure the angles, build the scaffolding and envisage the forms, and predate three-dimensional computer drawing by a hundred years. The work is one of Gaudí's most organic: walls bend and curve at impossible angles and windows open out like beetles' wings.

It's also worth taking a walk around the rest of the colony. The red-brick *modernista* buildings were designed by architects Francesc Berenguer and Joan Rubió Bellver. Most of these are now private residences. Many of the other buildings, the factory and warehouses, have been abandoned, which gives the place a ghost town–like ambience.

Claudi Güell s/n, Santa Coloma de Cervelló. © **93-630-58-07.** Admission 4€ ($4.60), free for children under 10. Mon–Sat 10am–2pm and 3pm–7pm; Sun 10am–3pm (Mass at 11am and 1pm). FGC: Colònia Güell. Lines S33, S34, S8, and S7 (all leave from Plaça Espanya).

CosmoCaixa (Museu de la Ciència) ★★★ (Kids)

This spectacular new Science Museum is an enlarged, much improved version of the 1980 original. Funded by a major bank (La Caixa) the Museu de la Ciència closed in 1998 and embarked on a 6-year overhaul. The result is the best, most high tech, and certainly most hands-on Science Museum in Europe.

Like the original, El Museu de la Ciència occupies a *modernista* building (originally a poorhouse) at the foot of Tibidabo, but with a daring underground extension and renovation of the original edifice, effectively quadrupling its exhibition space to 3,700 sq. m (39,826 sq. ft.).

As well as the additional new bioresearch center, the permanent collection has been completely overhauled and through an imaginative combination of original material and multimedia takes the novice on a comprehensive tour of the scientific principals. Divided into four separate categories, **"Inert Material"** deals with the Big Bang up to the first signs of life, **"Living Material"** to the birth of mankind, **"Intelligent Materials"** looks at the development of human intelligence, and **"Civilized Materials"** history and science from pioneers to the computer age.

The biggest crowd pleaser is **"The Flooded Forest,"** a living, breathing Amazonian rain forest *inside* the museum with over 100 species of animal and plant life. Kids come into close contact with animal life in the *Toca Toca* section, which has rats, frogs, spiders, and other natives from diverse ecosystems, some which can be picked up and touched. There is a 3-D planetarium and the extraordinary "Geological Wall" that explains, through an interactive route, the history of the world from a geological perspective. All in all, the new Science Museum is a unique and highly entertaining window to the world of science.

Teodor Roviralta 55. © **93-212-60-50.** Free admission. Planetarium 2€ ($2.30), Toca Toca (children come into contact with animals) 2€ ($2.30). Tues–Sun 10am–8pm. FGC: Avinguda Tibidabo (then 10-min. walk). Bus: 17, 22, 58, or 73.

Finca Güell ★

The Finca Güell, or country estate of Eusebi Güell, features three works by Antoni Gaudí, the industrialist's favorite architect. Still on a private estate, they can only be viewed from the street but that doesn't detract from the impact they have upon the viewer. Eusebi Güell asked Gaudí to create an entrance gate, a gatehouse, and stables. The first is probably one of the most stunning pieces of wrought-iron work in the world. Locally known as the Drac de Pedralbes (the Dragon of Pedralbes) a huge reptile literally jumps out at you, his tongue extended and ready to attack. The dwellings are no less powerful; like the **Casa Vicens** (p. 168) they were designed early in Gaudí's career when he was influenced by Islamic architecture and feature turrets and white walls contrasted with brightly colored tiles. The pavilion on the right houses a library and Gaudían research center.

Gaudí took inspiration for the *finca* from the Greek myth of Hesperides. The ominous dragon is a metaphor for the beast that Hercules battled, and although they are a tad run down, the gardens behind the gate used to be lush and full of citrus trees—the legendary gardens of Hesperides themselves.

Av. Pedralbes 7. Metro: Palau Reial.

Museu de les Arts Decoratives/Museu de Ceràmica ★

The city's museums of decorative arts and ceramics occupy the Palau de Pedralbes and can be seen together. The palace is set in an elegant garden that once belonged to the Finca Güell, the country estate of Gaudí's patron and friend Eusebi Güell.

Mes Que un Club (More Than a Club)!

Next to the Picasso, the most visited museum in the city is the **Museu FC Barcelona,** or the museum of the city's beloved football team Barça. It's inside their home ground Camp Nou, the largest stadium in Europe, with a capacity of 120,000. Despite its size, tickets to matches are scarce as hen's teeth. Most of the seats are taken by *socis* (members) of the richest soccer club in the world. As their slogan goes, Barça is *Mes que un club* (More than a club). Membership, which is often handed down through the generations, is a mark of Catalanismo (Catalan identity). During the dictatorship, the war was played out on the football field with the capital's team seen as representative of the loathed central government. Madrid is still Barça's archenemy (old grudges die hard in soccer) and when the two meet at Camp Nou, the whole city stops.

Along with the museum, you can choose to see the (empty) stadium, the chapel where players say a prayer before a big match, the club and pressrooms, and the tunnel via which players enter the field. The collection consists of photos, trophies, documents, kits, and other paraphernalia telling the dramatic and emotive history of the club from its beginnings in 1899 to the present. It's fun, makes for some light relief from other heady cultural offerings, and is not just for die-hard soccer fans.

Camp Nou stadium, access doors 7 and 9. Arístides Maillol s/n. ℂ **93-496-36-09.** Admission Museum and stadium: 9.50€ ($11) adults, 6.50€ ($7.50) children under 13. Museum only: 6.50€ ($7.50) adults, 3.70€ ($4.25) children under 13. Monday through Saturday 10am to 6:30pm; Sunday 10am to 2pm. Metro: Collblanc.

The neoclassical residence was taken over by King Alfonso XIII (who hardly ever used it) in 1920, then 10 years later handed over to the local government who turned it into an exhibition space for the decorative arts. During the dictatorship, General Franco made it his Barcelona abode, before it finally regained its status as a museum again in 1960.

Inside, the lavish halls with their gilt, marble, and frescoes make a picturesque backdrop for both these collections. By far the superior of the two is the Ceramic Museum, whose collection, arranged regionally, spans from the 11th century to the present day. Particularly striking are the mudéjar and metallic inlay work from the South and the baroque and Renaissance pieces from Castile. One extraordinary exhibit from Catalonia is an enormous plaque from the 18th century depicting a chocolate feast in the countryside.

Compared with the collection of decorative arts at the MNAC (p. 163), the small exhibition here is a slight let down. The name is somewhat deceiving, as the focus here, at least in the latter part of the collection, is really on design, as opposed to decorative objects that may or may not be functional. That said, Catalonia's design heritage is an important one, and there are many pieces here from the city's design boom of the '80s and early '90s featuring top names such as Javier Mariscal and Oscar Tusquets. In the future, this collection may form part of the projected Design Museum, a project that is currently on the drawing board.

Av. Diagonal 686. (℃) **93-280-16-21.** Admission (for both) 3.50€ ($4) adults, 2€ ($2.30) students, free for children under 16. Tues–Sat 10am–6pm; Sun 10am–3pm. Metro: Palau Reial.

Monestir de Pedralbes ★★   The oldest building in Pedralbes (the city's wealthiest residential area) is this monastery founded in 1326 by Elisenda de Montcada, queen of Jaume II. It housed the nuns of the Order of Saint Clare (who are now taking up residence in a much smaller adjacent building), and after the king's death Queen Elisenda took up residence in the convent. She is

---

Tips **Small but Good: Other Barcelona Museums**

There are dozens of small private museums in Barcelona, some the fruit of a collector's obsessive passion, others that display an ancient guild's craft. Many are free; others charge a minimal entrance fee or ask for a donation. The charming **Museu de Calçat,** Plaça Sant Felip Neri 5 ((℃) **93-301-45-33;** Tues–Sun 11am–2pm; Metro: Liceu), is housed in the ancient headquarters of the city's shoemaker guild. The collection spans from Roman sandals to the boots of the famous Catalan cellist Pau Casals. The **Museu de Carrosses Fúnebres (Museum of Funeral Carriages),** Sancho d' Avilla 2 ((℃) **93-484-17-00;** Mon–Fri 10am–1pm and 4–6pm, Sat–Sun 10am–1pm; Metro: Marina), also has an unusual location: the basement of the city's morgue.

Although bullfighting is not popular in Catalonia except among a handful of diehard *aficionados,* Monumental, Barcelona's bullring, is an exotic structure that also houses **Museu Tauri,** Gran Vía 749 ((℃) **93-310-45-16;** Apr–Sept Tues–Sat 10:30am–2pm and 4–7pm, Sun 10am–1pm; Metro: Monumental), a small museum of memorabilia, costumes and other bull-ish items. The taboo and the sacred of cultures around the world are explored in the **Museu Etnológic,** Passeig de Santa Madrona s/n ((℃) **93-424-64-02;** Tues–Sun 10am–2pm; Metro: Espanya). In a similar vein, ethnographic pieces collected by Capuchin nuns in the Amazon region can be viewed in their convent at the **Museu Etnogràfic Andino-Amazónic,** Cardenal Vives i Tutó 2–16 ((℃) **93-204-34-58;** by appointment only; Metro: María Cristina). In 1982 the prominent Barcelonese doctor Melcior Colet donated his home, a *modernista* dwelling designed by Puig i Cadafalch, and amassed sporting memorabilia to the city. The result, the **Museu de L'Esport Dr. Melcior Colet,** Buenos Aires 56–58 ((℃) **93-419-22-32;** Mon–Fri 10am–2pm and 4–8pm; bus: 7, 15, 33, 34, or 59) is a collection of objects relating to Catalan sporting achievements.

In an outer Barcelona park, an extraordinary collection of period carriages, adornments, and uniforms worn by coachmen is at the **Museu de Carruatges,** Plaça Josep Pallach 8 ((℃) **93-427-58-13;** Mon–Fri 10am–1pm; Metro: Mundet). One of the prettiest of all the city's private museums is at the rear of a perfume shop. **The Museu del Perfum,** Passeig de Gràcia 39 ((℃) **93-216-01-21;** Mon–Fri 10:30am–1pm and 5–8pm, Sat 11am–1:30pm; Metro: Passeig de Gràcia) holds over 5,000 examples of perfume bottles, vials, and paraphernalia from Egyptian times to the present day. Watch out for the Dalí-designed Le Roi de Soleill.

buried in the Gothic church next door (where the nuns still sing their vespers) in a beautiful tomb surrounded by angels.

After passing over the threshold, you come to the serene cloister with a central fountain, well, herb gardens, and other greenery. There are nearly two dozen elegant arches on each side, rising three stories high. Immediately to your right is a small chapel containing the chief treasure of the monastery, the incredibly intact Chapel of St. Michael. Inside, it is decorated with murals by Ferrer Bassa, a major artist of Catalonia in the 1300s, depicting the Passion of Christ.

The original nuns' residence houses an exhibition recreating the monastic life of the 14th century; what they ate, how they dressed, the hours of prayer, and their general coming and goings. Some of the day chambers contain original artifacts of the *monestir,* although the most evocative rooms are the kitchen and refectory and the communal dining room where the Mother Superior broke her vow of silence with mealtime Bible readings from the wooden pulpit.

Baixada del Monestir 9. ✆ **93-203-92-82.** Admission 5€ ($5.75) adults, 3.50€ ($4) students and seniors, free for children under 16. Tues–Sun 10am–2pm. FGC: Reina Elisenda.

Parc d'Atraccions Tibidabo ★★ *Kids*   On top of the mountain of Tibidabo, this amusement park combines tradition with modernity—rides from the beginning of the century compete with cutting-edge novelties such as the hair-raising Dragon Khan. In summer, the place takes on a carnival-like atmosphere and in fact the peak of the mountain has been a popular retreat for Barcelonese since 1868 when a road was built connecting it to the city. Most of the credit goes to a wealthy pill manufacturer by the name of Dr. Andreu. Believing the fresh, mountain air to be good for the health, he created the Sociedad Anónima de Tibidabo, which promoted the slopes as a public garden and was instrumental in installing both the blue tram and funicular which get you there (p. 63). Some of the attractions in the park date back from Andreu's time. L'Avio is a quaint replica of the first plane that served the Barcelona–Madrid route. In the Tibidabo version you are treated to a whisk over the summit in a toy-like version suspended from a central axis. There is also a charming museum of period automatons. There are plenty of other rides and attractions designed to scare you out of your wits, many enhanced by the elevated position of the park itself.

The church next door to the amusement park (and which can be seen from all over the city) is **Temple de Sagrat Cor,** an ugly and highly kitschy building dating from 1902 that was meant to provide Barcelona with its own Sacré Cour.

Plaça Tibidabo 3. ✆ **93-211-79-42.** 22€ ($25) for all rides, 11€ ($13) for 6 rides, 9€ ($11) children under 1.2m (4 ft.), free for children under 3. Summer daily noon–10pm; off season Sat–Sun noon–7pm. Bus: 58 to Avinguda Tibidabo Metro, then take the Tramvía Blau, which drops you at the funicular. Round-trip 3.10€ ($3.60).

7 Parks & Gardens

Barcelona isn't just museums and contrary to first impressions, it is not solely a city of concrete squares and stone streets. In a fine Mediterranean climate, life takes place outside, in unique parks and gardens, many of which were designed by the city's top architects for the Olympic renewal frenzy. The most popular ones are the leafy and formal **Parc de la Ciutadella** (p. 151), Gaudí's visionary **Parc Güell** (p. 169), and the mountain of **Montjuïc** (p. 161). But there are plenty more parks, gardens, wide-open spaces, and leafy hideaways for a bit of solitude or one-on-one with nature. Most parks are open 9am to sunset.

Not strictly a park but a large open square, one of the city's most famous "hard plazas," the **Parc de Joan Miró,** Aragó 1 (Metro: Espanya) occupies an entire L'Eixample block, once the city's slaughterhouse. Its main features are an esplanade and a pond from which a towering sculpture by Miró, *Woman and Bird*, rises. Palm, pine, and eucalyptus trees, as well as playgrounds and pergolas, complete the picture. Nearby, the enormous Parc de L'Espanya Industrial, next to the Sants train station (access Plaça dels Països Catalans) is a surrealist landscape of amphitheater type seating, watchtowers, and postmodern sculpture juxtaposed with a more vegetated parkland at the rear. On the opposite side of L'Eixample, the **Parc de L' Estació del Nord,** Nápoles 70 (Metro: Arc de Triomf or Marina) is a whimsical piece of landscape gardening featuring sculptures and landart by the U.S. artist Beverly Pepper.

Another daring urban space is the **Parc de la Crueta del Coll** near the Parc Güell, Castellterçol 24 (Metro: Penitents). Located in a former quarry, this urban playground features a man-made pool and an enormous oxidized metal sculpture the *Elogia del Agua* by Basque sculptor Eduardo Chillida. Looking somewhat like a huge claw, it is theatrically suspended from a cliff face. Even further north is Collserola, a natural parkland of nearly 1,800 hectares (4,446 acres). Urbanites come up here in droves on the weekend to cycle, stroll or have a picnic. The best way to get here is to take the FGC from Catalunya to either Baixador de Vallvidrera (which has an information office on the park) or Les Planes.

For those that like their parks more traditional, the romantic **Parc del Laberint** (Passeig de Castanyers s/n; Metro: Mundet) in the outer suburb of Horta is the oldest, and therefore most established, in the city. As the name suggests, there is central maze of Cyprus trees and the rest of the site is laid out over terraces with Italianate-style statues and balustrades.

8 Outdoor & Sporting Pursuits

GOLF

One of the city's best courses, **Club de Golf Vallromanes,** Afueras s/n, Vallromanes, Barcelona (☎ **93-572-90-64**), is 20 minutes north of the center by car. Nonmembers who reserve tee times in advance are welcome to play. The greens fee is 75€ ($86) on weekdays, 125€ ($144) on weekends. The club is open Wednesday through Monday from 9am to 9pm. Established in 1972, it is the site of Spain's most important golf tournament.

Reial Club de Golf El Prat, El Prat de Llobregat (☎ **93-379-02-78**), is a prestigious club that allows nonmembers to play under two conditions: They must have a handicap issued by the governing golf body in their home country; and they must prove membership in a golf club at home. The club has two 18-hole par-72 courses. Greens fees are 60€ ($69) Monday through Friday. Weekends are for members only. From Barcelona, follow Avinguda Once de Septiembre past the airport to Barrio de San Cosme. From there follow the signs along Carrer Prat to the golf course. For more information on golfing around Barcelona, see p. 41.

Tips **Act Like an Olympian**

One of the city's most prestigious fitness centers, **Piscina Bernardo Picornell** (see "Swimming," below), is adjacent to the Olympic Stadium in an indoor/outdoor complex whose main attractions are its two beautifully designed swimming pools. Built for the 1992 Summer Olympics, the facility contains a health club and gym. It's open to the public; a day pass costs 8€ ($9.20).

Kids **Happy, Happy, Joy, Joy!**

Happy Park is the perfect solution for kids who need to let off a little steam. It's a huge covered labyrinth-type set-up full of bouncy, touchy, feely, jumpy, rubbery contraptions for the little darlings to romp around on. Monitors are on hand and there is a special enclosed area for tiny tots. There are two in Barcelona: one at Comtes de Bell-lloc 74–78 (© **93-490-08-35**; Metro: Sants) and the other at Pau Claris 97 (© **93-317-86-60**; Metro: Urquinaona). Both are open Monday to Friday 5pm to 9pm and weekends 11am to 9pm. Cost is 4€ ($4.60) per hour for children, free for adults.

SWIMMING

Swim where some Olympic events took place, at **Piscina Bernardo Picornell,** Av. de Estadí 30–40, on Montjuïc (© **93-423-40-41**). Adjacent to the Olympic Stadium, it incorporates two of the best swimming pools in Spain (one indoors, one outdoors). Custom-built for the Olympics, they're open to the public Monday through Friday from 7am to midnight, Saturday from 7am to 9pm, and Sunday from 7am to 4pm. Admission costs 8€ ($9.20) for adults and 4€ ($4.60) for children and allows full use throughout the day plus the gymnasium, the sauna, and the whirlpools. Bus no. 61 makes frequent runs from the Plaça d'Espanya.

TENNIS

The **Centre Municipal de Tennis,** Passeig Vall d'Hebron 178 (© **93-427-65-00;** Metro: Montbau), has been the training ground for some of the country's top players. It has 17 clay and 7 grass courts set over beautiful grounds, but you will need to supply your own racket and balls.

HORSEBACK RIDING

Set high above the city on the mountain of Montjuïc, this is a top setting for a riding school. The **Escola Municipa d' Hípica,** Av. Muntayans 14–16 (© **93-426-10-66;** Metro: Espanya), imparts classes to all ages from 15€ ($17) per hour.

SURFING & WINDSURFING

When the wind blows, Barcelona's beaches offer good conditions for wind and kite surfing and regular surfing, and the latter is really taking off. **Wind 220º,** on the corner of Passeig Marítimo and Pontevedra (© **93-221-47-02**; Metro: Barceloneta), right on the beach at Barceloneta, has all the equipment you need for rent, plus storage facilities, a cafe, information, and courses.

THE SWALLOW BOATS

Las Golondrinas (Swallow Boats) (© **93-442-31-06**) are pretty little double-deckers that take you on a leisurely cruise of the city's port or port and northern coast combined. Boats depart from the port side of the Plaça Portal de la Pau, directly in front of the Columbus statue. The port-only tour leaves every hour (weekends only) between 11:45am and 6pm and the port and coast excursion daily at 11am and 12:20, 1:15, and 3:30pm. Prices for adults are 3.70€ ($4.25) for port-only and 8.80€ ($10) for port and coast; children 4 to 14 pay 1.90€ ($2.30).

WALKING TOUR THE GOTHIC QUARTER

Start:	Plaça Nova (Metro: Jaume I).
Finish:	Same point at Plaça Nova or the Vía Laietana opposite Port Vell (Metro: Barceloneta).
Time:	2 to 3 hours.
Best Times:	Any sunny day or early evening.

Begin at the:
❶ Plaça Nova

Set within the shadow of the cathedral, this is the largest open-air space in the Gothic Quarter. Behind you, the facade of the **Collegi de Architects,** the city's Architecture school, features a frieze designed (but not executed by) Picasso. From Plaça Nova, climb the incline of the narrow asphalt-covered street (Carrer del Bisbe).

At the approach of the first street on the right, the Carrer de Montjuïc del Bisbe de Santa Llúcia, turn right and follow this winding street to the:

❷ Plaça de Sant Felip Neri

This small square is often cited as the most charming in the Barri Gòtic. Although none of the buildings are in fact Gothic (and some have been moved from other parts of the city, the central fountain, majestic trees, and overall tranquillity more than qualify it for the status of "urban oasis." The holes you see in the stonework of the lower facade of the 17th century church (which unfortunately lost many of its baroque features in the late 18th c.) were caused by a bomb dropped by Fascist troops that killed 20 children from the adjoining school. On the opposite side, the oldest building is Renaissance in style and serves as the headquarters of the shoemakers guild with a Shoe Museum inside.

Walk back to the Carrer del Bisbe. Backtrack left, then take the immediate right Carrer de Santa Llúcia. This will lead you to:

❸ Casa de L'Ardiaca (Archdeacon's House)

Constructed in the 15th century as a residence for Archdeacon Despla, the Gothic building has sculptural reliefs with Renaissance and early 20th-century motifs. In its cloister-like courtyard are a fountain and a palm tree. Notice the mail slot, designed by the *modernista* architect Domènech i Montaner, where five swallows and a turtle carved into stone await the arrival of important messages. This beautiful setting now holds the city's archives, but you are free to inspect the courtyard and exterior.

As you exit the Archdeacon's House, continue in the same direction several steps until you reach the:

❹ Plaça de la Seu

From this square in front of the main entrance to the **Catedral de Barcelona** (p. 144). If you are here in the first couple of weeks of December, you will be lucky to coincide with the lively Mercat de Santa Llúcia; an outdoor market selling Christmas trees, decorations, and figurines such as the pooping Catalan the *caganer* (p. 21).

After touring the cathedral, exit from the door you entered and turn right onto Carrer dels Comtes, admiring the gargoyles along the way. After about 100 paces on the left, you'll approach the:

❺ Museu Frederic Marés

This wonderful museum holds an extraordinary collection of Romanesque and Gothic religious artifacts (p. 146). Even if you don't go in, the courtyard of this 13th-century former Bishop's palace is worth taking in. The outdoor cafe is a soothing spot to take a break.

Exit through the same door you entered and continue your promenade in the same direction. You'll pass the portal of the cathedral's right side, where the heads of two rather

Barri Gòtic Walking Tour

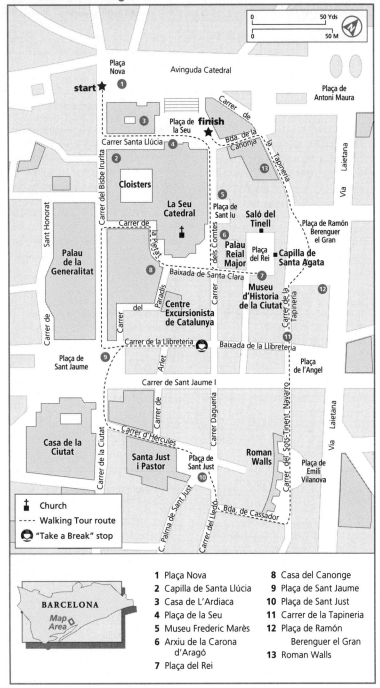

1 Plaça Nova
2 Capilla de Santa Llúcia
3 Casa de L'Ardiaca
4 Plaça de la Seu
5 Museu Frederic Marès
6 Arxiu de la Carona
    d'Aragó
7 Plaça del Rei
8 Casa del Canonge
9 Plaça de Sant Jaume
10 Plaça de Sant Just
11 Carrer de la Tapineria
12 Plaça de Ramón
    Berenguer el Gran
13 Roman Walls

abstract angels flank the throne of a seated female saint. A few paces farther, on the left, notice the stone facade of the:

⑥ Arxiu de la Carona d'Aragó

This is the former archives building of the crown of Aragon and Catalunya. Formerly called **Palau del Lloctinent (Deputy's Palace),** this Gothic building was the work of Antonio Carbonell. It is not open to the public but you can get a glimpse of its patios and upper arcades, admiring the century-old grapevines.

As you exit from the courtyard, you'll find yourself back on Carrer dels Comtes. Take the street in front of you, the Carrer de la Pietat which follows the rear facade of the cathedral and then the first street on your left, the Carrer del Paradis. At no. 10 is one of the Barri Gòtic's best kept secrets, the:

⑦ Temple d'Augustus

Inside the courtyard of this medieval building, these four majestic Corinthian columns are all that remains of Roman Barcelona's main temple. Most historians believe that it was dedicated to the emperor Caesar Augustus, hence its name. What is certain is that on the highest point of the city, it was once the prominent feature of the Roman Forum. June through September, the temple is open Tuesday to Saturday from 10am to 8pm, Sunday from 10am to 2pm; the rest of the year, it's open Tuesday to Saturday from 10am to 2pm and 4 to 8pm, Sunday from 10am to 2pm.

Retrace your steps back along the Carrer de la Pietat to the Palau del Lloctinent. Continue in the same direction on the same street and it will bring you to the most famous squares of the Gothic Quarter:

⑧ Plaça del Rei

The Great Royal Palace, an enlarged building of what was originally the residence of the counts of Barcelona, dominates this square. Here you can visit both the **Palau Reial** and the **Museu d'Història de la Ciutat** (p. 145). On the right side of the square stands the **Palatine Chapel of Santa Agata,** a

14th-century Gothic temple that is part of the Palau Reial. In this chapel is preserved the altarpiece of the Lord High Constable, a 15th-century work by Jaume Huguet.

TAKE A BREAK
Mesón del Café, Llibretería 16 (*②* **93-315-07-54**), founded in 1909, specializes in coffee and cappuccino. It is one of the oldest coffeehouses in the neighborhood, sometimes crowding 50 people into its tiny precincts. Some regulars perch on stools at the bar and order breakfast. Coffee costs .80€ (90¢), and a cappuccino goes for 1.75€ ($2). The cafe is open Monday to Saturday from 7am to 9:30pm.

Exit the Plaça de Rei on its southern side. Turn left into the steep Baixada de Llibretería. At no. 7 you will see the beautiful candle shop the Cereria Subira, the oldest continuous retail establishment in Barcelona. A few paces on turn left, crossing over the busy Carrer Ferran. Continue along the Career de la Dagueria. This will lead you to:

⑨ Plaça de Sant Just

The square is dominated by the entrance to the **Església dels Sants Just i Pastor.** Above the entrance portal, an enthroned Virgin is flanked by a pair of protective angels. The Latin inscription hails her as VIRGO NIGRA ET PULCHRA, NOSTRA PATRONA PIA (Black and Beautiful Virgin, Our Holy Patroness). This church dates from the 14th century, although work continued into the 16th. Some authorities claim that the church, in an earlier 4th-century manifestation of the present structure, is the oldest in Barcelona. You'll find that its doors are usually closed except during Sunday mass.

Opposite the church, at Plaça de Sant Just 4, is the 18th-century **Palau Moixó,** an aristocratic town house covered with faded but still elegant frescoes of angels cavorting among garlands. At its base is a public well, the oldest water source in the city.

Continue walking in the same direction down the Carrer de la Dagueria, which changes its name to the Carrer de Lledó. If you like, take a detour to the street parallel to you on your left, the Carrer del Sorts-Tinent Navarro; here you will see the remains of the old Roman walls. If not, take the second street on your right, the Carrer Cometa (so named for a sighting of comet here in 1834) Turn right again into the Career del Regomir. At no. 3 is the:

❿ Pati de Llimona

This lively community center named after its interior patio and lemon tree has a beautiful 15th-century gallery and vestiges of the old Roman sewerage system displayed underneath glass in the floor. Next door, the tiny 16th-century open **chapel of St. Christopher** is protected from the street by an iron gate. It's worth checking out what exhibitions are on in the center, normally by local artists and photographers.

Continue walking up the Carrer Regomir (which changes its name to the Carrer de la Ciutat) until you reach the:

⓫ Plaça de Sant Jaume

In many ways, this plaza is the political heart of Catalan culture. Across this square, constructed at what was once a major junction for two Roman streets, race politicians and bureaucrats intent on Catalonian government affairs. On Sunday evenings you can witness the *sardana,* the national dance of Catalonia. Many bars and restaurants stand on side streets leading from this square.

Standing in the square, with your back to the street you just left (Carrer de la Ciutat), you'll see, immediately on your right, the Doric portico of the **Palau de la Generalitat,** the parliament of Catalonia. Construction of this exquisite work, with its large courtyard and open-air stairway, along with twin-arched galleries in the Catalonian Gothic style, began in the era of Jaume I. A special feature of the building is the Chapel of St. George,

constructed in flamboyant Gothic style between 1432 and 1435 and enlarged in 1620 with the addition of vaulting and a cupola with hanging capitals. The back of the building encloses an orange tree courtyard begun in 1532. In the Gilded Hall, the Proclamation of the Republic was signed. Across the square are the Ionic columns of the **Casa de la Ciutat/ Ayuntamiento,** the Town Hall of Barcelona. Both these buildings are only periodically open to the public (p. 147).

With your back to the Casa de la Ciutat, cross the square to the right and turn left, once again into the Carrer del Bisbe. On your immediate right is the:

⓬ Casa del Canonge (House of the Canon)

This series of buildings, once a group of canon's houses, dates from the 14th century and restored in 1925; escutcheons from the 15th and 16th centuries remain. Notice the heraldic symbols of medieval Barcelona on the building's stone plaques—twin towers supported by winged goats with lion's feet. On the same facade, also notice the depiction of twin angels. The building today is used as the town residence of the President of the Generalitat.

Connecting it to the Palau de la Generalitat across the road is a charming **bridge** carved into lacy patterns of stonework also dating from the 1920s.

Continue walking until Carrer del Bisbe until you reach your starting place the Plaça Nova. If you wish to continue your walk, cross the square to the right to the busy Vía Laietana. Here you will see:

⓭ Plaça de Ramón Berenguer el Gran

An equestrian statue dedicated to this hero (1096–1131) is ringed with the gravel of a semicircular park, whose backdrop is formed by the walls of the ancient Roman fort and, nearby, a

Gothic tower. Keep walking down the Vía Laietana towards the port and you will see more of these. Known as Las Murallas in Spanish, they were constructed between A.D. 270 and 310. The walls followed a rectangular course, and were built so that their fortified sections would face the sea.

By the 11th and 12th centuries, Barcelona had long outgrown their confines. Jaume I ordered the opening of the Roman Walls, and the burgeoning growth that ensued virtually destroyed them, except for the foundations you see today.

7

Shopping

Even for the most demanding consumer, the shopping panorama in Barcelona is a very pleasant surprise. Many visitors arrive with a mental picture of a few dusty old establishments and department stores, only to find glittering avenues of top-name boutiques, polished and well-kept specialty stores, cutting-edge designer showcases, fascinating markets, and modern malls. Many are also surprised to know that some of the leading global fashion names (Zara and Camper, to name a couple) are, in fact, Spanish and, therefore, stock a larger range at more competitive prices.

Often, travelers blow their credit cards in London or Paris and kick themselves for not waiting to arrive in the city where the euro goes a lot further. A lot of people are surprised to see that in the fashion scene, Barcelona's shops are on par with the major style cities. Barcelona's *fashionistas* have a tendency to look outwards for trend inspiration, rather than toward the rest of Spain. In short, you may find you spend more time shopping here than gallery-hopping and not feel guilty about it.

1 The Shopping Scene

The elegant Passeig de Gràcia contains some of the most expensive retail space in Spain. Along its wide octagon-tiled footpaths, the big guns of fashion have set up shop in gorgeous 19th- and 20th-century buildings; Chanel, Max Mara, and Loewe jostle for your attention alongside Benetton, Zara, and Diesel. All along the avenue there are dozens of outdoor cafes to rest up, enjoy a tapa or two, and examine your booty. The Rambla de Catalunya, which runs parallel to the Passeig de Gràcia, has lesser internationally known but equally as glitzy establishments with less of a focus on fashion and more on housewares, books, and beauty. Don't bypass the cross streets that run between the two, they are also scattered with some of the city's top shopping, particularly Valencia, Provença and Consell de Cent, the latter renowned for its expensive antique shops and art galleries. The top end of the Passeig de Gràcia meets El Diagonal, one of the city's main arteries. Here you will find the housewares giant Habitat, the mega mall L'Illa and various other boutiques in between. The Metro does not service this part of town and the shops are spread out but don't despair: The *tombus* is a comfortable minibus that does the "shopping line" along the Diagonal; hop on at any regular bus stop.

The throngs hit the Portal d'Angel and Portaferrisa at the top end of the Barri Gòtic on Friday evenings and Saturdays, seeking out new arrivals in fashion from the top High Street names such as H&M, Levis, Benetton, and other global fashion labels. With the major department store El Corte Ingles in the immediate vicinity, these two streets (which cross each other) make up the city's most central, convenient, and popular shopping hub.

Further into the old quarter (El Raval, El Born, and the Barri Gòtic) is where you will find more one-of-a-kind retailers. One promising new hub is around the MACBA, the city's museum of contemporary art in the Raval. Smaller galleries come (and go) here at various intervals, and there are fashion and design shops springing up all the time. In the direction of the port, shops on the streets running off Les Ramblas (particularly Carme and Hospital) reflect the melting-pot nature of the neighborhood; wine shops sit side by side with *halal* butchers and others seemed to have survived for centuries selling scissors. This is where you see the dusty, old school emporiums of yesteryear, ones that have sadly disappeared from cities like London and New York. While not enough is done here to protect their heritage, many do survive the onslaught of the mall, at least for the moment.

Catalonia has resisted the lure of Sunday trading, mainly at the insistence of the trade unions. The good news is that most shops in the center (Passeig de Gràcia, Portal d'Angel, and Portaferrisa) stay open through the lunch hour and generally don't close until 9pm, even on Saturdays with department stores extending this to 10pm. As a general rule of thumb, smaller shops are open Monday through Saturday 9:30 or 10am to 1:30 or 2pm then open again in the afternoon 4 or 4:30pm to 8:30pm. You will always find exceptions to this, especially as the tourist trade fans out over the city. You may come across some that frustratingly take Monday morning off, or decide to take a three-hour afternoon break, but even that adds to the unique experience of Barcelona being a modern city that has retained its quaint retro feel.

Credit cards are accepted nearly everywhere, even for smallish purchases. Note however that you (along with everyone else) must show a form of photo ID (passport or driver's license) when making a purchase with your credit card. Don't be offended when the assistant asks for this; it is an effective guard against fraudulent credit card use.

Sales tax is called IVA; for food items it is generally charged at 7%, rising to 16% for most other goods. Cash register receipts will show this as a separate charge (if not, ask). If you see a "Tax-Free Shopping" sticker displayed in a shop, and are a non-E.U. resident, you can request a tax-free check on purchases of over 90€ ($104). Present this to the Cash Refund counter at the airport (Terminal A) when you depart the E.U. and you will be issued a cash refund. Refunds can also be made to your credit card or by check. For more information see www.globalrefund.com.

Sales (*rebajas* or *rebaixes*) start early July and early January, slightly later than northern Europe as the shops hang out until after the Día de los Reyes (Jan 6) the Christmas gift-giving date. Discounts at the sales are extraordinary, often starting at 50%, but surprisingly you never see the mad rushes that fill the news programs in other countries at the onslaught of the sales. On the whole shopping in Barcelona is a genteel affair; small business and trading has historically been a major backbone of its economy and many establishments here, in terms of both service and presentation, still feel like a piece of living history.

WHAT TO BUY

Stylish clothing and shoes and leatherwear are the items to go for in Barcelona. Leather shoes, belts, jackets, and coats are particularly good buys; whether you go for a top of the range brand such as Loewe or succumb to the leather hawkers on Les Ramblas, the quality and value of leather goods is superb. Barcelona has always been renowned for its expertise in design and has a vibrant design culture supported by the local government. Decorative objects and housewares here are original and well made and can be found in the shops around the MACBA and Picasso Museums. Artisan pieces, such as ceramic tiles and gifts and earthenware bowls and plates are cheap, cheerful, and plentiful. Cookware, crockery, wine glasses, and utensils in general are a great buy; a poke around a humble hardware store can unearth some great finds.

What follows is only a limited selection of some of the hundreds of shops in Barcelona.

2 Shopping A to Z

ANTIQUES

Serious collectors should check out the maze of streets around the Calle Palla near the Plaça de Pi the Barri Gòtic; while there are few bargains to be had you will find everything from bric-a-brac to old posters and lace. Consell de Cent in the Eixample houses a range of shops selling fine antiques and antiquities. Every Thursday, many of these traders set up stalls outside the cathedral, transferring to Port Vell (the port end of Les Ramblas) at the weekend.

Angel Batlle ★★ *Finds* This shop has an unbeatable collection of old posters, from travel to advertising and music to sport, postcards, engravings, maps, prayer cards, anything that's printed. Some of them make a wonderful souvenir or memento; consider a 1950s sherry poster to take home rather than a Picasso or Miró print. Palla 23. ⓒ **93-301-58-84.** Metro: Liceu.

El Bulevard des Antiquaris This 70-unit indoor market just off one of the town's most aristocratic avenues has a huge collection of art, antiques, bric-a-brac, and just plain junk assembled in a series of stands and small shops. It's great for browsing, although the erratic opening hours (stall owners set their own hours) may drive you mad. Passeig de Gràcia 55. No phone. Metro: Passeig de Gràcia.

L' Arca de l' Aviva ★★ *Moments* Like stepping back into Grandma's glory-box, this gorgeous shops sells lace and linen bedspreads and curtains, petticoats and handkerchiefs, and other assorted textiles from the 18th- to early 20th-centuries. Some of the sequined numbers worn by Kate Winslet in the film *Titanic* were snapped up here from their exquisite collection of period clothing. Prices aren't cheap but the quality of their collection is unsurpassable. Banys Nous 20. ⓒ **93-302-15-98.** Metro: Liceu.

Sala d'Art Artur Ramón ★★ One of the finest antiques and art dealers in Barcelona can be found at this three-level emporium. Set on a narrow flagstone-covered street near Plaça del Pi (the center of the antiques district), it stands opposite a tiny square, the Placeta al Carrer de la Palla. The store, which has been operated by four generations of men named Artur Ramón, also operates branches nearby and is known for its 19th- and 20th-century painting and sculpture, 19th- and 20th-century drawings and engravings, and 18th- and 19th-century decorative arts and *objets d'art* along with rare ceramics, porcelain, and glassware. Prices are high, as you'd expect, but the items are of high quality and lasting value. Palla 23. ⓒ **93-302-59-70.** Metro: Jaume I.

Urbana *Finds* Urbana sells an array of architectural remnants (usually from torn-down mansions), antique furniture, and reproductions of brass hardware. There are antique and reproduction marble mantelpieces, wrought-iron gates, and garden seats, even carved wood fireplaces with the *modernisme* look. It's an impressive, albeit costly, array of merchandise. Còrsega 258. ⓒ **93-218-70-36.** Metro: Hospital Sant Pau.

BOOKS

Buffet y Ambigú *(Finds* In among the deli stalls at the back of the Boqueria market is a unique book outlet. The stall sells cookbooks catering to most tastes; from the best tapas recipes to manuals for chefs and special editions such as El Bulli's encyclopedia explaining techniques of the Catalan super-chef Ferran Adrià. Many of the books are in English. Mercat de la Boqueria, Parada 435. No phone. Metro Liceu.

Casa del Llibre *(Value* Huge book barn covering all the genres from novels to self-help, travel to technical. There are sections of foreign language books, including English, and cover prices here tend to be the same as you would pay back home. Passeig de Gràcia 62. ℂ 93-272-34-80. Metro: Passeig de Gràcia.

Cooperativa d'Arquitectes Jordi Capell For books on Spain's architects and interior designers, head to the basement of the city's architecture school. This bookshop has a huge range of technical books for architects as well as monographs and photographic books of the work of leading architects, from Gaudí to Gehry. Plaça Nova 5. ℂ 93-481-35-62. Metro: Liceu.

FNAC *(Value* The Plaça Catalunya branch of this music and entertainment megastore has a solid section of English-language books. Most of the novels are bestsellers (or recent bestsellers), and a large range of the current travel guides to Barcelona and the rest of Spain are available. If you are here to learn Spanish, there is also a bilingual dictionary and language textbook section. El Triangle, Plaça Catalunya. ℂ 93-344-18-00. Metro: Catalunya.

LAIE *(★★* A good selection of English-language books, including contemporary literature, travel maps, and guides, is at LAIE. The bookshop has an upstairs cafe with international newspapers and a terrace. It serves breakfast, lunch (salad bar), and dinner. The cafe is open Monday through Saturday from 9am to 1am. The shop also schedules cultural events, including art exhibits and literary presentations. Pau Claris 85. ℂ 93-318-17-39. Metro: Catalunya or Urquinaona.

CHOCOLATES & CAKES

Cacao Sampaka *(★★* If there were such a thing as *haute chocolat,* this establishment would be the Christian Dior. Using only the finest cacao available, a mind-boggling selection of sweetmeats is categorized into "collections": "flowers and herbs," "liquors and digestives," "gastronomic innovations," and "spices of the Americas" to name just a few. The sleek packaging turns them into true objects of desire, and there is a bar-cafe where you can enjoy a cup of creamy hot chocolate, pastries, and high-cholesterol sandwiches, all made of the highest quality ingredients at prices not dissimilar to more pedestrian places. Consell de Cent 292. ℂ 93-272-08-33. Metro: Passeig de Gràcia.

Escribà *(★ (Finds* You may have already seen the glittering facade of this beautiful Art Nouveau shop on postcards. But far from a curious relic, it sells the goods of one of the city's finest families of chocolate and cake makers. You can pop in for a coffee and croissant (outside tables in the summer) or pick up a box of bonbons or a bottle of dessert wine to take home. At Easter, the windows display *monas,* elaborate chocolate sculptures decorated with jewels and feathers. Les Ramblas 83. ℂ 93-301-60-27. Metro: Liceu.

Xocoa *(★* Brothers Marc and Miguel Escurell have managed to thoroughly modernize their century-old family business, by employing top graphic artists to design their packaging and some novel ideas such as chocolate candles, incense, even a CD for chocolate lovers. Try the house specialty, the *Ventall,* a scrumptious cake of almond pastry and chocolate truffle. There's also a branch at Roger de Lluria 87 (no phone; Metro: Girona). Petritxol 11. ℂ **93-301-11-97.** Metro: Liceu.

DEPARTMENT STORES

El Corte Inglés   The main Barcelona branch of the largest department store chain in Spain, this branch sells a wide variety of merchandise. It ranges from Spanish handicrafts to high-fashion items, from Spanish records to food. The store has restaurants and cafes and offers consumer-related services, such as a travel agent. It has a department that will mail your purchase. Not only that, but you can have shoes reheeled, hair and beauty treatments, and food and drink in the rooftop cafe. The basement supermarket (Plaça Catalunya branch only) is the best place to pick up wines and other foodstuffs to take back home. Open Monday through Saturday from 10am to 10pm. El Corte Inglés has two other Barcelona locations at Av. Diagonal 617–619 (ℂ **93-366-71-00;** Metro: María Cristina) and Av. Diagonal 471 (ℂ **93-493-48-00;** Metro: Hospital Clinic). Plaça de Catalunya 14. ℂ **93-306-38-00.** Metro: Catalunya.

DESIGNER HOMEWARES

BD Ediciones de Diseño ★★★   Started by a group of prominent Catalan architects, this gorgeous gallery-shop, housed in a sumptuous *modernista* edifice, offers only the best contemporary pieces along with reproductions by the likes of Gaudí, Dalí, and Mackintosh. Oscar Tusquets, one of the shop's founders and a leading Catalan designer, should also be sought out. Goodies range from furniture, fittings, and rugs, to smaller easily packed items such as kitchenware and decorative objects. Sleek and serious, BD is Barcelona's bastion of design culture. Mallorca 291. ℂ **93-458-69-09.** Metro: Passeig de Gràcia.

Dom   The pop esthetic well and truly lives on in this housewares/objects store. Beaded curtains, bubble furniture, plastic stools, chrome lamps, and kitchenware in bold colors, plus an informed selection of international design magazines and knick-knacks ensure there is something on offer for all budgets. The result is either extremely hip or horribly kitsch, depending on your taste and age. The shop is open Monday to Saturday from 10:30am to 9pm; there's another branch at Avinyó 7 (ℂ **93-342-55-91;** Metro: Jaume I). Provença 249–251. ℂ **93-487-11-81.** Metro: Passeig de Gràcia.

Gotham *(Finds)*   Although the fad for retro design pieces has been well and truly established in Spain, this shop was a pioneer. Furniture from the '50s through '60s plus ceramics, crockery, vases, lights, and other items hailing from the same epoch. Prices aren't cheap, but most objects have either been restored or are in faultless condition. Cervantes 7. ℂ **93-412-46-47.** Metro: Jaume I.

Ici Et Là ★   Craftsmanship and quirky design characterize the pieces on display in this corner shop in the heart of the El Born shopping strip. Most pieces are one-off or limited editions by local artists, but they also receive regular shipments of say Nepalese chairs, African baskets, or Indian textiles. Glass is also featured strongly, from candleholders to delicately embossed wine glasses. Nearly everything in this shop could be described as a "conversation piece." Plaça Sant Maria 2. ℂ **93-268-11-67.** Metro: Jaume I and Barceloneta.

Vinçón ★★   Fernando Amat's Vinçón is the best design emporium in the city, with 10,000 products—everything from household items to the best in Spanish contemporary furnishings. Its mission is to purvey good design, period. Housed in the former home of artist Ramón Casas—a contemporary of Picasso's during his Barcelona stint—the showroom is filled with the best Spain has. The always-creative window displays alone are worth the trek: Expect *anything*. Passeig de Gràcia 96. (C) **93-215-60-50**. Metro: Diagonal.

Vitra ★★ The famed Swiss contemporary design company has a formidable, two-story showcase in Barcelona, featuring unique pieces by Charles and Ray Eames and Phillipe Starck, Alväro Siza and Frank Gehry to name but a few. The prices may be restrictive and the size of most of their items mean they will not fit into your hand luggage, but it's okay to dream isn't it? Plaça Comercial 5. (C) **93-268-72-19**. Metro: Jaume I and Arc de Triomf.

FABRICS, TEXTILES & TRIMMINGS

Antiga Pasamaneria J. Soler *(Finds)* If fringes, ribbons, braids, tassels, and cords is your thing, then look no further. This place has been selling them since 1898, and has a wall-to-wall display of everything from dainty French grosgrain ribbons to thick tapestry braids and borders. Plaça del Pi 2. (C) **93-318-64-93**. Metro: Liceu.

Coses de Casa ★ Appealing fabrics and weavings are displayed in this 19th-century store, called simply "Household Items." Many are hand-woven in Majorca, their boldly geometric patterns inspired by Arab motifs of centuries ago. The fabric, for the most part, is 50% cotton, 50% linen; much of it would make excellent upholstery material. Cushions, spreads, and throws can be made to order. Plaça de Sant Josep Oriol 5. (C) **93-302-73-28**. Metro: Jaume I or Liceu.

Gastón y Daniella ★★ This century-old company originally hails from Bilbao, although these days, its name is synonymous with fine fabrics for upholstery and drapery all over Spain. Every one of their damasks, polished cottons, brocades, and tapestries is extremely lush, more suited to a time when children's fingerprints and cat hair was not an issue. It's great to browse in, even if it's just for an end-piece for a new cushion cover. Pau Claris 171. (C) **93-215-32-17**. Metro: Diagonal.

FASHION

Adolfo Domínguez ★ This shop, one of many outlets across Spain and Europe, displays fashion that has earned for the store the appellation of "The Spanish Armani." There's one big difference: Domínguez's suits for both women and men, unlike Armani, are designed for those with hips and limited budgets. And they cover all ages at their stores, including the youth market. As one fashion critic said of their latest offerings, "They are austere but not strict, forgivingly cut in urbane earth tones." Passeig de Gràcia 32. (C) **93-487-41-70**. Metro: Passeig de Gràcia.

Antonio Miró ★ This shop is devoted exclusively to the clothing design of Miró, but without the Groc label (see below). It carries fashionable men's and women's clothing. Before buying anything at Groc, survey the wares at this store, which seems even more stylish. Consell de Cent 349. (C) **93-487-06-70**. Metro: Passeig de Gràcia.

Comité *(Finds)* This store is typical of the fashion startups in the streets around the MACBA. Inside a charmingly naive decor of pastel colors and meters of white curtains, much of clothing is made of recycled items: an embroidered sheet or tablecloth is transformed into a wrap skirt or dress or a striped men's shirt is retouched and tucked into a blouse. The overall affect is one of "the dressing-up box meets *Vogue*." Notariat 8. (C) **93-317-68-813**. Metro: Catalunya and Liceu.

Commercial Woman ★ This French-owned boutique stocks beautifully detailed and highly feminine clothing for day and evening by the likes of

Cacharel, Paul&Joe, Comme des Garçon, and Spain's own Jocomomola. There is also a selection of artisan Parisian perfumes and accessories by the bijoux jewelry brand Scooter. A men's wear outlet is located across the street. Calle Rec 52. ℂ **93-319-34-63**. Metro: Jaume I and Barceloneta.

Custo-Barcelona ⭐ First it was Hollywood, with the likes of Julia Roberts and Drew Barrymore seen sporting Custo t-shirts. Now they have taken over the world, with stores from Chicago to Perugia to Shanghai. As the name suggests, however these tops and shirts, skirts, and pants in mad mixes of fabrics and emblazoned with '60s retro motifs are a homegrown product and have become a symbol of "Cool Barcelona." There's another location at Calle Ferran 36 (ℂ **93-342-66-98;** Metro: Jaume I and Barceloneta). Plaça de les Olles 6. ℂ **93-268-78-93**. Metro Jaume I and Liceu.

El Mercadillo This is Barcelona's temple to alternative culture, with in house DJs, piercing salons, and dozens of stalls selling urban and club wear, leather and suede jackets, records and second hand clothes. The kids love it but you may have a hard time of it if you have a post-30 or post-teenage body size. Portaferrisa 17. ℂ **93-301-89-13**. Metro Liceu.

Giménez & Zuazo ⭐ Quirky, colorful and very Barcelonese, Giménez & Zuazo's creations are characterized by daring prints and unusual fabrics. Their skirts may have the silhouette of a svelte female splashed across the front, or a shirt collar may be bordered in contrasting cross-stitch. Their Boba T-shirts, with hand-painted imagery have become something of a cult item. There's another location at Rec 42 (ℂ **93-310-67-43;** Metro: Jaume I and Barceloneta). Elisabets 20. ℂ **93-412-33-81**. Metro: Catalunya and Liceu.

Jean-Pierre Bua ⭐⭐ Another pioneer, this boutique was the first to import big-name Parisian fashion houses to Barcelona. There is a large stock of Gaultier (the French enfant terrible and Bua are personal friends); Comme des Garçon; Spain's most international designer, Sybilla; and Brussels is represented with Dries van Noten. Despite the price tags, the staff are laid back and no one seems to mind if you spend time simply looking. Diagonal 469. ℂ **93-439-71-00**. Bus: 5, 7, 15, 33, or 34.

Josep Font ⭐⭐ With a masterful eye for fabrics and attention to detail that recalls vintage St. Laurent, Catalan designer Josep Font is in class of his own. His sumptuous shop has retained many of its original Art Nouveau features customized with Font's inherent quirkiness. Bold, yet feminine, with only a slight nod to the current trends, his designs remain timeless. Provença 30. ℂ **93-487-21-10**. Metro: Passeig de Gràcia.

La Boutique del Hotel In the lobby of Hotel Axel, Barcelona's "Gay Hotel" (p. 88), the Boutique stocks (as one would perhaps expect) the best and brightest names in menswear: John Richmond, Helmut Lang, and Rykiel Homme to name just a few. In a city that is somewhat lacking in cutting edge menswear stores, this one is frequented by homo-, hetero-, and metrosexuals alike. Aribau 33. ℂ **93-323-93-98**. Metro: Passeig de Gràcia.

Loft Avignon This emporium was largely responsible for converting this shabby Barri Gòtic street into the fashion hub that it is today. The clothes for men and women feature labels such as Vivienne Westwood, Gaultier, and Bikkembergs. Be warned, however, that the staff members are merciless, and you may find yourself handing over your credit card for a micromini you never intended to purchase. Avinyó 22. ℂ **93-301-24-20**. Metro: Jaume I or Liceu.

The Zaravolución

Many visitors to Spain are already familiar with the **Zara** clothing label. Now with over 600 (1,900, counting the Zara offshoot brands) outlets in 49 countries, including megastores in the fashion capitals of Milan, Paris, London, and New York, Zara is hard to ignore. But many are not aware, and probably surprised to know, that Zara is Spanish-owned.

Zara was started back in the early '70s by an industrious young Galician by the name of Amancio Ortega, now the richest man in Spain. He saw a necessity for stylish housecoats for the women in his rural village and out of that an empire grew. Today, Zara is one of the few fashion empires in the world that vertically controls the entire process, from textile manufacture to design to retail. Using a global network of buyers and trend-spotters, they interpret (many within the industry use the word "plagiarize") hot-off-the-catwalk pieces for men, women, and children at astoundingly affordable prices. They appeal to the full, cross-generational, demographic gamut, from urban tribes to executives. Zara's calendar doesn't just consist of four seasons; they produce and distribute clothing all year round in their behemoth headquarters in Ortegas's native Galicia and Zaragoza. New, never-to-be-repeated models arrive every day, meaning converts return again and again and again . . .

A revolution needs a charismatic leader and Ortega is no exception. Until he took the company public in 2001, the press possessed only one photo of a man estimated to be worth $10.3 billion. He imposes a strict "no-press" policy to his staff and never gives interviews. He never accepts any of the dozens of accolades awarded to him in person. What he has done is, in less than a generation, democratized fashion and made it possible to dress like a film star for a song. *¡Viva la revolución!*

Located at Pelayo 58 (© **93-301-09-78**; Metro: Catalunya), Passeig de Gràcia 16 (© **93-318-76-75**; Metro: Passeig de Gràcia), and all over the city.

Mango *(Value)*   Apart from Zara (see below) Spain's other main fashion export is Mango, which in foreign countries often goes under the name MNG. Young, trendy, and mid-priced is the deal here, and although the range isn't quite as extensive as their main competitors (nor do they do men's or children's wear), it's a sad day in Retailand when you won't find at least something to pop on for that special evening out. If your visit coincides with the winter season, their suede and leather coats and jackets are definitely worth considering. There are branches all over Barcelona, including the one at Passeig de Gràcia 65 (© **93-215-75-30;** Metro: Passeig de Gràcia). Portal de l'Angel 7. © **93-317-69-85**. Metro: Catalunya.

On Land *(Value)*   Although On Land is surrounded by hyper-trendy boutiques, the men's and women's clothing here is highly wearable; it's cross-generational without forfeiting a cutting edge. Their own label produces some well-cut trousers and jackets, and when complemented by one of Monte Ibáñez's hand-painted T-shirts you have a distinctive outfit. Prices are good and sizes (mercifully) generous. Princesa 25. © **93-310-02-11**. Metro: Jaume I.

Textil i d'Indumentaria   Operated as a showcase for Catalonian design and ingenuity by Barcelona's Museum of Textile and Fashion, and set on a medieval street across from the Picasso Museum, this shop proudly displays and sells clothing and accessories for men, women, and children, all of which is either designed or at least manufactured within the region. Inventories include shoes, men's and women's sportswear and formal wear, jewelry, teddy bears, suitcases and handbags, umbrellas, and towels, each shaped and cut by up-and-coming Catalans. Two of the most famous designers include menswear specialist Antonio Miró (no relation to the 1950s and 1960s artist Joan Miró) and women's clothing designer Lydia Delgado. Montcada 12. ✆ **93-310-74-04.** Metro: Jaume I.

FINE FOOD & WINE

Caelum *(Finds)*   Everything in this shop has been produced in monasteries and nunneries throughout Spain: jams and preserved fruit, quality cakes and biscuits, marzipan and liquors. The ornate, ecclesial packaging makes them great gifts, and there is a cafe downstairs where you can sample before you buy. Palla 8. ✆ **93-302-69-93.** Metro: Liceu.

E & A Gispert   If you have trouble finding this shop behind the Santa María del Mar church, then simply follow your nose. Coffee and nuts are roasted here daily (go for the almonds straight out of the oven), and are sold alongside dried and candied fruit of all descriptions: Turkish figs, apricots, currants, and raisins, and even French *marron glacé*. Sometimes the queues spill out onto the street, such is the quality of everything this century-old shop sells. Sombrerers 23. ✆ **93-319-75-35.** Metro: Jaume I.

La Botifarreria de Santa María *(*   If you haven't already noticed that when faced with a rib eye filet and a *botifarra* (sausage), Catalans will opt for the latter, then visit the shop opposite the Gothic Santa María del Mar church. As well as making their own *botifarras* (reputed to be the finest in the land) on the premises, they sell the richest *jamón Jabugo* (acorn-fed ham), rare cheeses, sweet *fuet* (a thin salami) from central Catalonia, and other meaty delicacies. They will vacuum pack your edibles for traveling (check if you can bring it back to your home country), or take some of their produce to the nearby Parc de Ciutadella for a picnic. Santa María 4. ✆ **93-319-91-23.** Metro: Jaume I and Barceloneta.

Lavinia *(**   Sort of like a wine megastore, Lavinia makes selection easy as all their products are displayed according to country of origin; from Germany to Uruguay, Australia to California. As expected, the Spanish section is the most numerous, bulging with Riojas, Priorats, *cavas*, albariños, and sherries. There is a pack-and-send service, which is handy as most bottles come cheaper by the dozen (check your country's laws about what/how much you can send back). Diagonal, 605. ✆ **93-363-44-45.** Metro: María Cristina.

Origins 99.9% *(*   Purveyors of fine, exclusively Catalan foodstuffs (.1% being the margin of error presumably). Olive Oils from Llerida, *mato* (a fresh, ricotta-like cheese) from the mountains, and wines from the Penedès and Priorat regions. There is a cafe next door where you can try before you buy. This a good place to pick up presents for foodies back home. (Check regulations on what you can legally bring back to your country!) Vidrería 6–8. ✆ **93-310-75-31.** Metro: Jaume I and Barceloneta.

Vina Viniteca *(**   This awesome wine shop in the heart of the El Born neighborhood supplies most of the restaurants in the area. The selection here can be frightening for the non-vinicultured amongst us, but those in the know rave about it. There are 4,500 different wines, sherries, *cavas,* liquors, and spirits from all over Spain, many of which are exclusive to the shop. Check out the bargain basket at the counter, where the last in the crates are sold for a song. Agullers 7–9. ✆ 93-310-19-56. Metro: Jaume I and Barceloneta.

GALLERIES

Despite producing some of the world's great artists, small galleries have a notoriously hard time surviving in Barcelona. This could be due to the fickleness of the scene. At the moment, gallery hubs include the streets around the Picasso Museum, the MACBA museum, and Calle Petritxol in the Barri Gòtic.

Art Picasso   Here you can get good lithographic reproductions of works by Picasso, Miró, and Dalí, as well as T-shirts emblazoned with the masters' designs. Tiles often carry their provocatively painted scenes. Tapinería 10. ✆ 93-310-49-57. Metro: Jaume I.

Iguapop *(Finds*   The Iguapop company is one of the leading promoters of contemporary music in Barcelona. Hardly surprising then, that the emphasis is firmly on youth culture in their first gallery. Graffiti and video artists, magazine design, and contemporary photography by young people from both Spain and abroad can be seen in their airy, white space located near the Ciutadella Park. There is an adjoining shop that sells cult streetwear and accessories. Comerç 15. ✆ 93-310-07-35. Metro: Jaume I.

Sala Parés 🌟🌟   Established in 1840, this is a Barcelona institution. The Maragall family recognizes and promotes the work of Spanish and Catalan painters and sculptors, many of whom have gone on to acclaim. Paintings are displayed in a two-story amphitheater, with high-tech steel balconies supported by a quartet of steel columns evocative of Gaudí. Exhibitions of the most avant-garde art in Barcelona change about every 3 weeks. Petritxol 5. ✆ 93-318-70-20. Metro: Plaça de Catalunya.

HATS

Sombrería Obach *(Finds*   Reassuringly old-fashioned hat shop in the Call (old Jewish quarter) district. It stocks the largest color-range of berets on earth, as well as panamas, Kangol flat caps, straw sun hats, and a host of other headgear for men and women. Check out the classic Spanish sombrero; wide-brimmed, black, and very stylish. Carrer del Call 2. ✆ 93-318-40-94. Metro: Jaume I and Liceu.

HERBS & HEALTH FOODS

Comme-Bio   Comme-Bio is one-stop shopping for organic fruit and vegetables, health foods, tofu and other meat substitutes, and natural cosmetics. Don't get a shock at the prices; demand here for whole foods is just starting to take off, so expect to pay more than in the U.K. or U.S. Next to the supermarket is a juice bar and restaurant open for lunch and dinner, although the food here is a bit pedestrian. Vía Laietana 28. ✆ 93-319-89-68. Metro: Jaume I.

Mantantial de Salud   This period shop has dried medicinal herbs, aromatic pills and potions, and its own range of natural beauty products all displayed in pretty pale and green glass cabinets or large ceramic urns. Many locals pop in here for a natural cure to what ails them. The staff is extremely knowledgeable and used to dealing with foreigners, although you should look up a few key words in your dictionary beforehand. Xucla 23. ✆ 93-301-14-44. Metro: Liceu.

JEWELRY

Forvm Ferlandina 🌟🌟   Contemporary jewelry and accessories from over 50 designers are on show here in tiny cubist cases that give the shop the feel of a

La Boqueria: One of the World's Finest Food Markets

The **Boqueria market,** Les Ramblas 91–101 (✆ **93-318-25-84;** Mon–Sat 8am–8pm; Metro: Liceu), is the largest market in Europe (and probably the greatest in the world) and a must-see in the Catalan capital. The Boqueria is located right in the middle of any visitor's top destination: the famous boulevard Les Ramblas. While many markets have little to offer a visitor in terms of practical shopping, the Boqueria boasts some of the best bars and cafes in the city, and a chance to rub shoulders with the people who are helping put the city at the forefront of Mediter-ranean cuisine.

The Boqueria's central location is owed to a historical twist of fate. In the mid-1800's, the demolition of the city's medieval walls began. *Pageses* (Catalan peasants) had been touting their bounty roughly on the spot of the present market (originally one of the city's gates) and around the parameter of the neighboring Convent de Sant Josep for centuries, and the authorities saw no reason to move them when the work began. When the convent burnt to the ground in 1835, the mar-ket expanded, and thirty years later, the engineer Miquel de Bergue fin-ished his plans for a grandiose, wrought-iron market of five wings supported by metal columns, a project that wasn't finished until 1914. The official name of the market is Mercat de Sant Josep (a reference to the Capuchin nuns' old dwelling) although the term *boqueria* (meaning *abattoir,* or butcher shop, in Catalan) has stuck since the 13th century, when the site was a slaughterhouse.

The Boqueria's 330 stalls are a living testament to the fertility of the peninsula (Spain produces the widest variety of farm produce in all Europe) and its surrounding seas. What lies inside is a gastronomic

contemporary gallery. Silversmithing, enamel work, beading, and most of the disciplines are featured. Particularly lovely are felt-flower bouquet brooches, rings, and hair ornaments which are produced in the rear workroom. Ferlandia 31. ✆ **93-441-80-18.** Metro: Liceu and Catalunya.

Platamundi *Value* The string of Platamundi stores offer highly affordable, high quality pieces in silver, both imported and by local designers such as Ricardo Domingo, head of the jewelry wing of FAD, the city's design council. Seek out the pieces that combine silver with enamel work in Mediterranean shades. There are other branches at Montcada 11 (Metro: Jaume I), Plaça Santa María 7 (Metro: Jaume I), and Portaferrisa 22 (Metro: Liceu). Hospital 37. ✆ **93-317-13-89.** Metro: Liceu.

Tous Depending on your point of view, the jewelry and objects made by this Catalan family are either must-have or too twee to contemplate. Tous's leifmotif is the teddy bear, and the little fellow features in everything from earrings to key rings to belts and bracelets. They are adored by the city's VIP set and their pop-ularity grown to such an extent that you now see pirated versions. Everything in Tous is produced to a very high standard in precious metals and semiprecious stones. Passeig de Gràcia 75. ✆ **93-488-15-58.** Metro: Passeig de Gràcia.

cornucopia that changes its palette from season to season. Early autumn sees the hues of burnt yellow, orange, and brown in the cluster of stalls selling the dozens of varieties of *bolets,* wild mushrooms from the hills and forests of Catalonia. In spring, the candy colors of fresh strawberries and plump peaches and in early summer the greens of a dozen different lettuces, from curly bunches of escarole to pert little heads of endives and *cogollos* (lettuce hearts) make an appearance. The fish and seafood section takes prime place in a central roundabout known as the Isla del Pescado (Island of Fish), a pretty marble and shiny steel affair that was given priority in the Boqueria's recent overhaul. The variety here is awesome, like an exotic aquarium on ice. From giant carcasses of tuna that send Japanese tourists into a camera flashing frenzy, to the ugly but tasty scorpionfish, prawns the size of bananas, live crawfish making a dash across their frozen beds, octopi, bug-eyed grouper, and countless other species. Other stalls range from game and delicatessens to bewildering businesses that survive by specializing in one product, whether it be lettuces, potatoes, or smoked salmon.

If you are up early enough, the best time to visit the Boqueria is the early morning as it is being hurled into life. Able-bodied men drag cart-loads of produce to the stalls, while women arrange it into patterns and combinations that border on food art. Have breakfast at Pinotxo on the immediate right of the main entrance. Here you will rub shoulders with the city's main chefs before they embark on their daily sourcing spree. If you wish to do a bit of shopping yourself, avoid the stalls at the front unless you want to pay "tourist" prices.

LEATHER

Acosta ⚝ Started in the '50s, this chain of stylish, Spanish leather belts and bags now has 37 shops all over Spain and one in both Lisbon and Brussels. It's still a family-run affair, which is perhaps why everything sold has the air of being lovingly and meticulously produced. Prices are excellent, given the overall quality. Diagonal 602. © 93-414-32-78. Bus: 5, 7, 15, 33, or 34.

Loewe ⚝⚝⚝ Barcelona's biggest branch of this prestigious Spanish leather-goods chain is in one of the best-known *modernista* buildings in the city. Everything is top-notch, from the elegant showroom to the expensive merchandise to the helpful salespeople. The company exports its goods to branches throughout Asia, Europe, and North America. With designer José Enrique Ona Selfa now at the helm, their clothing line is looking better than ever. Passeig de Gràcia 35. © 93-216-04-00. Metro: Passeig de Gràcia.

Lupo ⚝⚝ The current name in luxe leather goods is Lupo. Trading from a minimalist silver and white shop in the L'Eixample, their bags and belts stretch the limits of the craft by molding and folding leather into incredible shapes and using new dyeing techniques to create the most vivid colors. The world is now taking notice, and the company is now exporting to the U.S., the rest of Europe, and Japan. Majorca 257, bajos. © 93-487-80-50. Metro: Passeig de Gràcia.

LINEN & TOWELS

El Indio *(Finds)* Established in 1870 and easily recognizable from the florid facade and arched windows, this emporium sells all sorts of textile goods, from sheets to tea towels to tablecloths. The service and wood-lined surrounds are charmingly old school and the range mind-boggling; from cheap polyester sheets to the finest linen napkins. If they don't have it, it probably doesn't exist. Carme 24. © **93-317-54-42.** Metro: Liceu.

Ràfols *(★)* Beautiful, made to order and hand-embroidered bed linen, towels, tablecloths, and other items for your trousseau. The nimble-fingered staff will whip up any design you like, and the pure cottons and linens used are pure heaven. Bori i Fontestà 4. © **93-200-93-52.** Metro: Diagonal.

LINGERIE

Le Boudoir *(Finds)* This may look like an upmarket sex shop (and in many ways it is) but in reality, the scarlet red walls house a gorgeous collection of silk and lace lingerie and racy bedroom accessories: from furry handcuffs to music CDs designed to "get you in the mood" and other objects for intimate moments. In summer, they bring in an exclusive range of swimwear. Naughty, but very, very nice. Canuda 21. © **93-302-52-81.** Metro: Catalunya.

To Market, to Market . . .

There are a variety of outdoor markets held around the streets of Barcelona. Practice your bartering skills before heading for **El Encants flea market,** held every Monday, Wednesday, Friday, and Saturday in Plaça de les Glòries Catalanes (Metro: Glòries). Go anytime during the day to survey the selection of new and used clothing, period furniture, and out-and-out junk (although the traders will try to convince you otherwise). **Coins** and **postage stamps** are traded and sold in Plaça Reial on Sunday from 10am to 8pm. It's off the southern flank of Les Ramblas (Metro: Drassanes). A **book** (mainly Spanish language) and **coin market** is held at the Ronda Sant Antoni every Sunday from 10am to 2pm (Metro: Universitat) with a brisk trade in pirated software and DVDs taking place around the periphery. All types of fine quality **antiquarian** items can be found at the Mercat Gòtic every Thursday. 9am to 8pm, on the Plaça Nova outside the city's main cathedral (Metro: Liceu) although don't expect any bargains. More like a large **car-boot sale** is the Encants del Gòtic, Plaça George Orwell. Saturdays 11am to 4pm (Metro. Drassanes). The wide promenade the Rambla del Raval (Metro: San Antoni) is taken over by hippie-type traders all day, every Saturday hawking **handmade clothing, jewelry,** and other objects. Nearby, the **vintage and retro clothing traders** of the Riera Baixa (Metro: San Antoni) drag their goods on the street (some real bargains are to be found here). Over fifty painters set up shop every weekend in the pretty Plaça del Pi (Metro: Liceu) in a **Mostra d' Art** that is of a surprisingly high standard. If food is more your thing, over a dozen purveyors of artisan cheese, honey, biscuits, olives, chocolate, and other **Catalan delicacies** can also be found in the Plaça del Pi, on the first and third weekend of every month from 10am to 10pm.

Women'Secret *(Value)*   This chain of lingerie, underwear, and sleepwear stores will make you wish you had one in your hometown. The prints are hip and colorful, the designs funky, and the prices highly palatable. From their basics range of pure cotton bras and nighties to striped PJs and panty sets with matching slippers and toiletry bags, this is concept retailing at its cleverest. There are several shops in the center; the biggest are at Portaferrisa 7–9 (© **93-318-92-42**; Metro: Liceu), Puerta de l'Angel 38 (© **93-301-07-00**; Metro: Catalunya), Diagonal 399 (© **93-237-86-14**; Metro: Diagonal), and Fontanella 16 (© **93-317-93-69**; Metro: Urquinaona).

MAPS

Llibreria Quera *(Finds)*   This establishment was started in 1916 by the legendary adventurer Josep Quera, who pretty much covered every square inch of Catalonia and Andorra in his lifetime. Whether you are going hiking in the Pyrénées, motoring along the coast, or rock-climbing in the interior you can plan your trip here with their selection of specialized books and maps. Petritxol 2. © **93-318-07-43**. Metro: Liceu.

MUSIC

Casa Beethoven *(Finds)*   Established in 1920, this store carries the most complete collection of sheet music in town. The collection naturally focuses on the works of Spanish and Catalan composers. Music lovers might make some rare discoveries. Les Ramblas 97. © **93-301-48-26**. Metro: Liceu.

Discos Castelló   With six shops over Barcelona, Castelló pretty much has the CD market sewn up. Half of them are located in the Calle Tallers, a street of door-to-door music and vinyl shops. Opened in 1934, their flagship store at no. 7 is mainly pop rock. Next door, "Overstocks" has more of the same plus sections on jazz, world, Spanish, and country music. Classical music is sold at no. 3. Calle Tallers. © **93-318-20-41**. Metro: Catalunya.

FNAC *(Value)*   In central Barcelona, and if you don't want anything too far out of the mainstream, the best place to pick up music is the FNAC megastore. The second floor has CDs of all kinds, rock, pop, jazz, classical, and a tempting selection that consists of mostly not-quite-current releases of current artists at rock-bottom prices. You can ask to listen before buying, which is handy for making purchases of Spanish music and flamenco. It's open 10am to 10pm Monday through Saturday. Plaça de Catalunya 4. © **93-344-18-00**. Metro: Catalunya.

OUTLETS & SECONDS

Contribución y Moda *(Finds)*   Large split-level store selling men's and women's designer clothing from last season and beyond. It's the sort of place where you may pick up a pair of Vivienne Westwood woolen trousers for as little as 80€ ($92), or wonder if that Gaultier skirt was really worth 200€ ($230) at full price. That said, you can normally find at least one item to your taste and budget (especially at the beginning of the season) although the different size ranges can make you want to scream. Riera de Sant Miquel 30. © **93-218-71-40**. Metro: Diagonal.

La Roca Village   Only true bargain hunters will perhaps be bothered to make the trip to this outer Barcelona "outlet village." But those that do will be rewarded with up to 60% off over 50 brands, from high fashion labels such as Roberto Verino, Versace, and Carolina Herrera, shoes from Camper, luxury leatherware from Loewe and Mandarina Duck, and even sportswear from the likes of Billabong and Timberland. The setting is actually quite pleasant with a playground for the kids, cafes, and the like and the savings here are legendary. Open daily from 11am to 9pm. La Roca del Vallès. © **93-842-39-00**. **By car:** Take the

AP-7 to Exit 12, head to Cardedeu and then to the Centre Comercial. **By train:** Take the train from Sants Station to Granollers Center (trains leave every half-hour; trip time: 35 min.). From the station, a bus leaves for La Roca Village every hour at 23 min. past; a taxi will cost you 10€ ($12). **By bus:** Sagalés (✆ 93-870-78-60) runs buses directly to La Roca Village from the Fabra i Puig Bus Terminal (Passeig Fabra i Puig, next to the Metro entrance). Buses (4€/$4.60 round-trip) leave Mon–Fri at 9am, noon, and 4 and 8pm (trip time: 50 min.).

MNG Outlet *Value*   MNG is Mango, one of the biggest chains in Spain for young fashion. Their outlet store has items with *taras* (faults—of varying dimensions) and last season's stock at the silliest of prices. It's not unusual to pick up a pair of jeans here for 10€ ($12) or a T-shirt for as low as 5€ ($5.75). There is also a good selection of shoes and bags at rock bottom prices. It gets frustratingly busy Saturdays. A few other outlet stores are located in the immediate vicinity. Girona 37. No phone. Metro: Tetuan and Urquinaona.

112   People with a foot fetish will love this Barrio Alto shop selling last year's shoes, boots, and bags at 50% off. Marc Jacobs, Givenchy, Emma Hope, Emilio Pucci, Robert Clegerie, and Rossi are just some of the names. Laforja 105. ✆ 93-414-55-13. FGC: Gràcia.

PERFUME & COSMETICS

La Galería de Santa María Novella *Finds*   This is the Barcelona outlet of the famed Officina Profumo-Farmaceutica di Santa Maria Novella in Florence, the oldest and possibly most luxurious apothecary in the world. The perfumes and colognes are unadulterated scents of flowers, spices, and fruits; the soaps handmade; and the packaging seemingly unchanged since the 18th century. Prices are high. Espasería 4–8. ✆ 93-268-02-37. Metro: Jaume I and Barceloneta.

Regia 🌟   This high-end perfume and cosmetics shop has a secret: wander through the racks stacked with Dior and Chanel and you reach a small door that leads to a unique museum (free admission). There are over 5,000 examples of perfume bottles and flasks from Grecian times to the present day. The star of the collection is the dramatic "Le Rei Soleil" by Salvador Dalí. Passeig de Gràcia 39. ✆ 93-216-01-21. Metro: Passeig de Gràcia.

Sephora   Cosmetics addicts may be forgiven for thinking they have died and gone to heaven when they enter this beauty megastore. All the desired brands are here: Clarins, Dior, Arden, Chanel, et al—plus hard-to-finds such as Urban Decay and Phytomer. The house brand's range of makeup is a great value and Sephora claims not to be knowingly undersold. El Triangle, Pelayo 13–37. ✆ 93-306-39-00. Metro: Catalunya.

PORCELAIN

Kastoria   This large store near the cathedral is an authorized Lladró dealer, and stocks a big selection of the famous porcelain. It also carries many kinds of leather goods, including purses, suitcases, coats, and jackets. Av. Catedral 6–8. ✆ 93-310-04-11. Metro: Plaça de Catalunya.

POTTERY

Artesana i Coses   If you are in the vicinity of the Picasso Museum, pop into this jumble sale of a shop selling pottery and porcelain from every major region of Spain. Most of the pieces are heavy and thick-sided, and you can pick up a coffee mug for a little as a couple of euros. Placeta de Montcada 2. ✆ 93-319-54-13. Metro: Jaume I.

Specialty Stores in the Barri Gòtic

The streets around the Barri Gòtic are packed with traditional establishments specializing in everything from dried cod to dancing shoes, some of them remnants from when mercantile activity and trading was Barcelona's lifeblood. If you see a shop window that entices don't be shy; most of the shop keepers welcome curious tourists, and a brief exchange with one of them just may be one of those fleeting traveler's experiences you cherish long after its over.

Dating from 1761, the **Cereria Subira,** Baixada de Llibreteria 7 (© **93-315-26-06**) has the distinction of being the oldest, continuous shop in Barcelona. It specializes in candles, from long and elegant white ones used at Mass to more fanciful creations. It's worth popping in to see the two torch-bearing blackamoor figures alone. Magicians and illusionists love the **Rei de la Magia,** Princesa 11 (© **93-319-39-20**), a joke and magic shop dating from 1881. Behind the ornate Art Nouveau facade of **Alonso,** Santa Ana 27 (© **93-317-60-85**), lie dozens of gloves, from dainty calf skin to more rugged driving gloves plus pretty fans and lace *mantillas* (Spanish shawls). More traditional Spanish garb is to be found at **Flora Albaicín,** which specializes in flamenco dancing shoes and spotty, swirly skirts and dresses. The **Herbolisteria del Rei,** del Vidre 1 (© **93-318-05-12**), is another shop seeped in history; it has been supplying herbs, natural remedies and cosmetics and teas since 1823. **Casa Colmina,** Portaferrisa 8 (© **93-412-25-11**), makes its own *turrones,* slabs of nougat and marzipan that are a traditional Christmas treat. Nimble fingers will love the **Antiga Casa Sala,** Call 8 (© **93-381-45-87**), which has an enormous range of beads and trinkets just begging to be turned into an original accessory. In the old Born food hub, **Angel Jobal,** Princesa 38 (© **93-319-78-02**), is the city's most famed spice merchant, from Spanish saffron to Indian pepper and oregano from Chili. **Ganiveteria Roca,** Plaça del Pi 3 (© **93-302-12-41**), has an enormous range of knives, blades, scissors, and all sorts of special-task cutting instruments. **Xancó Camiseria,** Les Ramblas 78–80 (© **93-318-09-89**), is one of the few period shops remaining on Les Ramblas: they have been making classic men's shirts in cottons, wools, and linens since 1820. If you get caught in the rain, head to **Paraguas Rambla de Las Flores,** Les Ramblas 104 (© **93-412-72-58**), which stocks all manner of umbrellas and walking sticks. And finally, you never know when you may need a chicken feather; the **Casa Morelli,** Banys Nous 13 (© **93-302-59-34**), has sacks of them, for simple stuffing or decorating a party outfit.

Art Escudellers   This is one-stop shopping, unashamedly aimed at the tourist market but in reality it contains a great range of pottery and ceramics from all over Spain. You'll see the more colorful, hand-painted pieces of the south to the earthy, brown and green earthenware of the north, everyday utilitarian objects, and more spectacular conversation pieces. It has a shipping service and hundreds of Spanish wines to taste and buy. Escudellers 23–25. © **93-412-68-01.** Metro: Drassanes.

Baraka Baraka's owner regularly raids the *souks* of Morocco and brings back the booty to this small shop in the trendy Born area. There is a lovely range of brightly colored and patterned pottery and ceramics, plus traditional *dhurries* (woven rugs), *bubucha* slippers, earthenware *tagines*, lamps, and other North African paraphernalia. Canvis Vells 2. © **93-268-42-20.** Metro: Jaume I.

Itaca *(Finds* Here you'll find a wide array of handmade pottery from Catalonia and other parts of Spain, plus Portugal, Mexico, and Morocco. The merchandise has been selected for its basic purity, integrity, and simplicity. There is a wide range of Gaudí-esque objects, inspired by trademark *trencadís* (broken tile) work. Ferran 26. © **93-301-30-44.** Metro: Liceu.

SCARVES, SHAWLS & ACCESSORIES

Rafa Teja Atelier *⋆⋆* This shop has a sublime collection of wool, cotton, and silk scarves and shawls from India, Asia, and Spain, all neatly hung on wooden rails or folded into glorious, multicolored stacks. Whether it's a pashmina wrap, a mohair collar, or an extravagant shawl to match an evening dress, you are bound to unearth it here. They also do their own limited range of clothing, such as evening coats in Chinese brocades or sarong-style skirts in Indonesian batiks. Passeig del Born 18. © **93-310-27-85.** Metro: Jaume I or Barceloneta.

SHOES

Camper *⋆⋆* Made on the island of Majorca, Camper shoes have now well and truly conquered the world. Their distinctive molded shapes in unusual colors are seen treading the streets of New York and Sydney. But Barcelona has the biggest range at better prices. The shop interiors, often done by the quirky Catalan designer Martí Guixe, reflect the brand's wholesome yet hip culture. There are several locations throughout the city. Valencia 249. © **93-215-63-90.** Metro: Passeig de Gràcia.

Casas *⋆⋆* If you are serious about footwear, then this is the only name you need to know. With three shops in central Barcelona, Casas is a one-stop shoe shop for the most prominent Spanish brands (Camper, Vialis, Dorotea, and so on) and coveted imports from Clergerie, Rodolfo Zengari, and Mare, plus sports and walking shoes. Three locations: Les Ramblas 125 (© **93-302-75-52),** Portaferrisa 25 (© **93-302-11-32),** and Portal de l'Angel 40 (© **93-302-11-12).** Metro: Catalunya and Liceu.

Czar If sports shoes and trainers are your thing then look no further than Czar. From the Converse, Le Coq Sportif, and Adidas classics to more bizarre creations by Diesel, W&LT, Asics, and other cult labels. Passeig del Born 20. © 93-310-72-22. Metro: Jaume I and Barceloneta.

La Manual Alpargatera *(Finds* The good people at this Old Town shop have been making espadrilles on the premises for nearly a century. As well as the classic, slip on variety, you will find the Catalan *espadenya* which has ribbon ankleties, wedge-heeled versions in fashion colors, toasty lambs wool slippers, and other "natural" footwear. Clients have included Michael Douglas and the Pope. Avinyó 7. © **93-301-01-72.** Metro: Jaume I and Liceu.

Lotusse These Majorcan cobblers are revered for their extraordinary quality. The brogues, loafers, T-bars, and other classic styles for men and women actually look and feel handmade. They won't make you stand out in a crowd, but are liable to last you a lifetime. Lotusse also sells bags, wallets, and belts. Rambla de Catalunya 103. © **93-215-89-11.** Metro: Passeig de Gràcia.

Muxart ✸✸   Hermenegildo Muxart knows how to make heels that appeal, offering sexy, cutting-edge shoes and handbags from his Eixample shop. A pair of black stilettos may feature a red disc on the toe, for example, or metallic sliver and electric blue leather plaited together with straw to form an intricate tapestry. Whilst this may sound a bit faddy, Muxart knows when to draw in the reins, making a pair of his shoes an investment buy rather than an expensive whim. There's another location at Rambla de Catalunya 47 (📞 **93-467-74-23;** Metro: Passeig de Gràcia). Rosselló 230. 📞 **93-488-10-64.** Metro: Diagonal.

SHOPPING CENTERS & MALLS

Shopping malls are a bit of a contentious topic in Catalonia. Many small traders feel they are squeezing them out of the market. The local government has reacted by limiting their construction, especially in central Barcelona. But there are still enough in existence to appease any mall fan.

Centre Comercial Glòries   Built in 1995, part of a huge project to rejuvenate a down-trodden part of town, this is a three-story emporium based on the California model. It has more than 230 shops, few posh and others far from it. Most people head here for the Carrefour department stores, the cheaper cousin of El Corte Ingles that mainly sells electrical and home goods. Although there's a typical shopping mall anonymity to some aspects of this place, it's great for kids, with lots of open spaces and bouncy things to jump on. Open Monday through Saturday from 10am to 10pm. Av. Diagonal 208. 📞 **93-486-04-04.** Metro: Glòries.

Diagonal Mar   This is the newest of the malls, part of a huge urban project that is breathing residential and commercial life on the city's northern coastline. Reflecting the surrounding property prices, shops here tend to be mid- to high-end. All the fashion staples are here, plus a branch of the music and entertainment megastore FNAC, and even a cinema. Open Monday to Saturday from 10am to 10pm. Av. Diagonal s/n. 📞 **902-530-300.** Metro: Maresme/Forum, Selva de Mar, or Besós-Mar.

L'Illa Diagonal   Located in an expensive part of town, shopping here is mainly high end. Thus, this two-story mall has stores mainly devoted to fashion and luxury products; Benetton, Mandarina Duck, Zara, Diesel, Miss Sixty, as well as a scattering of home, gift, and toy boutiques. The first level has a huge supermarket and food hall selling everything from handmade chocolates to dried cod. Open Monday through Saturday 10am to 9:30pm. Av. Diagonal 557. 📞 **93-444-00-00.** Metro: María Cristina.

Pedralbes Centre   This two-story arcade focuses mainly on fashion. Check out the street and club wear from E4G and ZasTwo, frou-frou party frocks by Puente Aereo, and the brightly colored quirky cloths of Agata Ruiz de la Prada. Diagonal 609–615. 📞 **93-410-68-21.** Metro: María Cristina.

SPORTING GOODS

Decathlon *Value*   If in Barcelona you plan to do some physical activity beyond a stroll down the Les Ramblas, Decathlon is really the only name you need to know. Every single sport is covered in this French-owned megastore, from football and tennis to *ja-kai* (Basque handball) and ping-pong. There is swimwear, clothing for jogging, aerobics, cycling hats (and cycles), ski gear, hiking boots, and wet suits. Their prices are pretty much unbeatable, especially on their house items. There's another location at Diagonal 557 (📞 **93-444-01-65;** Metro: María Cristina). Canuda 20. 📞 **93-342-61-61.** Metro: Catalunya and L'Illa.

8

Barcelona After Dark

Barcelona is a great nighttime city, and the array of after-dark diversions is staggering. There is something to interest almost everyone and to fit most pocketbooks. Fashionable **bars** and **clubs** operate in nearly every major district of the city, and where one closes, another will open within weeks.

Locals sometimes opt for an evening in the *tascas* (**taverns**), or perhaps settling in for a bottle of wine at a cafe, an easy and inexpensive way to spend an evening people-watching. The official legal age for drinking is 18, but is rarely enforced with much vigor if you look the part. It is extremely rare for any bar to have a nonsmoking section; cigarettes are part of the culture here, so expect to have to air out your clothes when you get back from a night out.

If the weather is good (which is most of the time) this is a city filled with outdoor squares, with at least half of the space filled with as many tables and chairs as they can reasonably fit in. Beware where two tables are squeezed next to each other: the occupants of each will be fiercely protective of its chairs and won't like it if you drag a chair from one place to make an extra seat at the table of another. Alfresco drinking has become so popular that the local government has been forced by complaining neighbors to restrict its hours in some areas—around midnight, it's usual to be asked to finish your drinks or to go inside. Particularly good places to sit and see the world go by are **Plaça del Sol** in Gràcia and **Passeig del Born, Plaça del Pi,** and **Plaça Reial** in the Old Town. The squares are also popular drinking haunts for groups of teenagers, but their tipple tends to be more of the supermarket-bought variety. The old Spanish tradition of the *botellón,* whereby groups of young people sit around on the cement swilling beer or wine, is treated as a nuisance by the local government and noise-sensitive neighbors. Despite cracking down on the practice it persists, especially in the summer.

People-watching of a more flesh-exposed nature can be done down at the beach in the summer. Between May and October, a line of *chiringuitos* (beach bars) opens for nighttime frivolity in the sands along Barcelona's urban beaches (Barceloneta to Poble Nou). Each one has its own flavor—some play chill-out music, others have live DJs/bands. Owners, names, and styles change from year to year, but generally they open at lunchtime (or late breakfast) and stay open until 2 or 3am.

Also down near the sands, there are plenty of bars and restaurants around the Olympic marina and port. Both here and Maremagnum, the entertainment and leisure complex, and the port end of Les Ramblas offer more foreigner-focused spots for those looking for strong drinks and fellow English speakers.

Other areas filled with bars include the **Carrer Avinyó** in the Barri Gòtic, the **Rambla del Raval** in El Raval and the in streets of **El Born** in La Ribera—just walk around and see where the noise is coming from. There are plenty of local secrets to uncover, if you just follow the crowd for a while.

JOINING IN BARCELONA NIGHTLIFE

Nightlife will begin for many Barcelonese with a **promenade** *(paseo)* from about 8 to 9pm. Then things quiet down a bit until a second surge of energy brings out the post-dinner crowds from 11pm to midnight. Serious drinking in the city's pubs and bars usually begins by midnight. For the most fashionable places, Barcelonese will delay their entrances until at least 1am—meeting friends for the first drink of the evening after midnight certainly takes some getting used to. If you want to go on to a club, you should be prepared to delay things even longer—most of them won't open until around 2am, and then be mostly empty for the first half-hour or so, until the bars close at 3am. Many clubs stay open to as late as 6am. Most of them will have free entrance or discount flyers available in bars or given out on the streets, saving yourself between 5€ and 10€ ($5.75–$12), which is the normal club entrance price, if there is one; this will largely depend on the night, the DJ and what the doorman thinks you look like. The price of a mixed drink (such as a *cuba libre,* which is a rum and coke) hovers between 5€ and 10€ ($5.75–$12). This may seem pricey but drinks here are *strong.* If you are charged an admission, ask if its *amb consumició* (drink included). If so, take your ticket to the bar to get the first drink free.

Barcelona is a trendy town and the clubbing scene is notoriously fickle. New things come up and others disappear. Although I've recommended places that have been around for a while, don't be too surprised if names and styles of the places have changed from what is printed here when you roll up.

A lot of famous international names, from the Rolling Stones to Anastasia include Barcelona in their tours. The biggest concerts take place at the **Palau Sant Jordi** on Montjuïc, a flexible and cavernous space that's also used to house the city's basketball games. In a city where the cult of the DJ reigns, Barcelona is short of small and midsize exclusively live music venues (although some clubs do both, with a concert taking place before the club kids roll in).

One of the best places to see people playing instruments (as opposed to spinning records) is the street. In the summer you'll see plenty of free entertainment—everything from opera to Romanian gypsy music—by walking around the Barri Gòtic. Festivals such as **El Grec** (July–Aug) and **La Mercè** (late Sept) are when the biggest musical offering tends to take place.

If you want to find out what's going on in the city, the best source of local information is a little magazine called *Guía del Ocio,* which previews "La Semana de Barcelona" (This Week in Barcelona). It's in Spanish, but most of its listings will be comprehensible. Every news kiosk along Les Ramblas carries it. If you have Internet access, *Le Cool* magazine (www.lecool.com) also carries an English summary of some of the more alternative options each week.

If you've been scared off by press reports about Les Ramblas between the Plaça de Catalunya and the Columbus Monument, know that the area's been cleaned up in the past decade. Still, you will feel safer along the Rambla de Catalunya, in the Eixample, north of the Plaça de Catalunya. This street and its offshoots are lively at night, with many cafes and bars.

The main area where things feel a little uneasy is in El Raval, or the Barrio Chino, that is, the lower half of the right-hand side as you go towards the port. But despite (or because of?) this, a lot of the new trendy bars are appearing there. The area is still known for occasional nighttime muggings—there are some great bars and strange venues down there (such as Bar Pastis; see p. 211), but do use caution if you go there, especially when withdrawing money from a cash machine (although more and more of these are locked at night anyway).

1 The Performing Arts

Culture is deeply ingrained in the Catalan soul, and the performing arts are strong. Long a city of the arts, Barcelona experienced a cultural decline during the Franco years, but now it is filled once again with the best opera, symphonic, and choral music. At the venues listed here, unless otherwise specified, ticket prices depend on the event. Tickets can be bought at the venues, but it's often more convenient and easier to use one of the special ticket services. The bank Caixa Catalunya sells *entradas* for many events and it also has the wondrous **Servicaixa**—an automated machine that dispenses theatre and cinema tickets—in many of its branches. *Tel-entrada* (© **902-33-22-11**) lets you buy over the phone with your credit card.

CLASSICAL MUSIC

Gran Teatre del Liceu 🎭🎭🎭   This monument to Belle Epoque extravagance, a 2,700-seat opera house, is one of the grandest theaters in the world—and it's very easy to find, as it's halfway down Les Ramblas. It was designed by the Catalan architect Josep Oriol Mestves. On January 31, 1994, a huge fire gutted the opera house, shocking Catalans, many of whom regarded this place as the very citadel of their culture. The government immediately vowed to rebuild, and were helped by the proceeds of a spectacular open-air concert in the burnt-out shell of the old building. The new Liceu was reopened in 1999, well before the millennium deadline set by the cultural czars. Included in the rebuild were a quiet cafe and an extensive shop in the basement, open during the day. Each show will offer a couple of reduced rate performances, where ticket prices are half-price (or close to it). Guided tours of the edifice (lasting about an hour) are also available daily 10am to 6pm. Rambla dels Caputxins 51–59. © **93-485-99-13**. Metro: Liceu.

La Casa dels Músics   Pianist Luis de Arquer has established a small chamber company in his 19th-century Gràcia home. They now call it the smallest opera house in the world, and they're probably not wrong as the performers are almost sitting on your lap as they perform small-scale productions of *opera buffa* and *bel canto*. Shows usually begin at 9pm, but you must call to confirm if presentations will go on and to make reservations. For the true music lover, this could be your most charming evening in Barcelona. Encarnació 25. © **93-284-99-20**. Tickets 20€ ($23). Metro: Fontana.

L'Auditori 🎭🎭   This is the newest of the city's classical music bastions, designed as a permanent home for the Orfeó Catala choral society and the OBC (Barcelona's Symphony Orchestra) although top-flight international names perform here as well. The edifice was designed by the award-winning Spanish architect Rafael Moneo, and its acoustics are said to be state-of-the-art. Lepant 150. © **93-247-93-00**. Metro: Glòries.

Palau de la Música Catalana 🎭🎭🎭   In a city chock-full of architectural highlights, this one stands out. In 1908 Lluis Doménech i Montaner, a Catalan architect, designed this structure as a home for the choral society the Orfeó Catala, using stained glass, ceramics, statuary, and ornate lamps, among other elements. It stands today as the most lush example of *modernisme*. Concerts (mainly classical but also jazz, folk, and other genres) and leading recitals take place here, as do daily guided tours of the buildings (p. 202). But they say you only really appreciate it when enjoying a concert. A new extension called Petit Palau, including a luxury restaurant, recently opened. Open daily from 10am to

3:30pm; box office open Monday through Saturday from 10am to 9pm. Sant Francesc de Paula 2. ℭ 93-295-72-00. Metro: Urquinaona.

THEATER

The majority of theater in Barcelona is presented in the Catalan language with the Spanish production. Avant-garde theater and comedy is particularly strong; La Fura dels Baus is an internationally renowned troupe whose work never fails to confront, El Comedients and La Cubana draw on local folklore and popular culture to make us laugh, and El Tricicle is a well-loved trio of comedians whose medium is mime. The Catalan director Calixto Bieito is one of the world's leading directors, renowned for his contemporary and often violent versions of Shakespeare.

Institut del Teatre ⋆⋆⋆   This grand new theatrical complex is where the city's theater and dance schools are located. There are three auditoriums of varying capacities and performances range from student showcases, to cutting-edge international companies such as New York's Wooster Group to 24-hour circus "marathons." Plaça Margarida Xirgú s/n. ℭ 93-227-30-00. Metro: Espanya.

L'Antic Teatre *(Finds)*   This is a real avant-garde small theatre near the Palau Musica Catalana, which hosts both touring companies and locals. It's only been open for a couple of years, when an old venue was "rediscovered," after being left to ruin for decades. You never know what to expect, so it's worth reading through the schedules on the door, if you can understand them—one night it's Belgian mime, the next South American circus skills, the next a Jamaican documentary. Prices are always excellent value, whatever you end up seeing. Verdaguer i Callis 12. ℭ 93-315-23-54. Tickets around 6€ ($6.90). Metro: Urquinaona.

Mercat de Los Flors ⋆⋆   Housed in a building constructed for the 1929 International Exhibition at Montjuïc, this is the other major Catalan theater. Peter Brook first used it as a theater for a 1983 presentation of *Carmen*. The theater focuses on innovators in drama, dance, and music, as well as European modern dance companies. It also often features in avant-garde art festivals. The 999-seat house has a restaurant overlooking the city rooftops. Lleida 59. ℭ 93-426-18-75. Metro: Espanya.

Teatre Nacional de Catalunya   Josep Maria Flotats heads this major company in a modern, mock-Roman building a little out of the center near L'Auditori (see above). The actor-director trained in the tradition of theater repertory, working in Paris at Théâtre de la Villa and the Comédie Française. His company presents both classic and contemporary plays. Plaça de les Arts 1. ℭ 93-306-57-06. Metro: Plaza de las Glorias.

Teatre Victoria   Situated in the west of the city, this unpretentious large-capacity theater hosts big-scale productions, usually musical spectaculars or comedies. Last year it even hosted *Hysteria,* a comedy production in Spanish that's directed (with the help of a translator) by John Malkovich. Paral.lel 65. ℭ 93-329-91-89. Metro: Paral.lel.

FLAMENCO

Flamenco isn't the rage here that it is in Seville and Madrid, but it still has its devotees. It's not a Catalan tradition, but Barcelona has an active Andalusian population and dancers with as much verve and color as any you'd find further south.

El Tablao de Carmen ⋆⋆⋆   This club presents a highly rated flamenco cabaret in the re-created imitation "typical Spanish artisan village" of Poble

---

⟨*Moments*⟩ I Could Have Danced All Day

Although the city caters to music lovers of most tastes, the really big thing here is electronic dance music. DJs are the new rock heroes, and the Woodstock of this generation is called **Sonar (www.sonar.es)**. The festival began 10 years ago in a small, outside venue, as a way of showcasing some of the more unusual experimental music coming out of different parts of Europe. Now it takes over a significant part of the city for a long weekend in mid-June, drawing in people from far and wide. It's now really two festivals, held in two separate locations. During the day, it's held at a number of stages around the MACBA and CCCB museums in El Raval. At night, it moves to a huge congress and trade fair hall outside the center, with a special bus shuffling punters in between. For the day and night gigs, tickets are sold separately, although you can buy a pass to the whole thing. Recent Sonar nighttime headliners have included Massive Attack and Björk, but the daytime music is much more open and eclectic, often accompanied by strange visuals. Of course, this being Barcelona, there's also a string of unofficial festivals running at the same time, all of which are much cheaper (or sometimes free) and can be read about on walls and from flyers in bars. This, claim the purists, is where you find the true experimental music, Sonar having sold out to the big sponsors years ago. The best thing is probably to enjoy both—but if you want to go to the official Sonar festival, you should buy your tickets (and book your accommodations) well beforehand.

Espanyol on the side of the Montjuïc hill. You can go early and explore the village, and even have dinner there as the sun sets. This place has long been a tourist favorite. The club is open Tuesday through Sunday from 8pm to past midnight—around 1am on weeknights, often until 2 or 3am on weekends, depending on business. The first show is always at 9:30pm; the second show is at 11:30pm on Tuesday, Wednesday, Thursday, and Sunday, and midnight on Friday and Saturday. Reservations are recommended. Poble Espanyol de Montjuïc. ℂ **93-325-68-95**. Dinner and show 53€–78€ ($61–$90); drink and show 29€ ($33). Metro: Espanya.

Los Tarantos ⟨★★⟩ Established in 1963, this is the oldest flamenco club in Barcelona, with a rigid allegiance to the tenets of Andalusian flamenco. Its roster of artists changes regularly. If you are lucky, they often come from Seville or Córdoba, stamping out their well-rehearsed passions in ways that make the audience appreciate the arcane nuances of Spain's most intensely controlled dance idiom, or otherwise it could be a lesser-known local artist or a percussion show. No food is served. The place resembles a cabaret theater, where up to 120 people at a time can drink, talk quietly, and savor the nuances of a dance that combines elements from medieval Christian and Muslim traditions. Shows are sporadic, so check before you roll up. Plaça Reial 17. ℂ **93-318-30-67**. Cover (includes 1 drink) normally around 20€ ($23). Metro: Liceu.

Tablao Flamenco Cordobés ⟨★⟩ At the southern end of Les Ramblas, a short walk from the harborfront, you'll hear the strum of the guitar, the sound of hands clapping rhythmically, and the haunting sound of the flamenco, a tradition here since 1968. Head upstairs to an Andalusian-style room where performances take place with the traditional *cuadro flamenco*—singers, dancers, and guitarist. Cordobés is said to be the city's best flamenco showcase. Three shows are offered nightly with dinner, at 7pm and 8:30pm and 10pm. Reservations are required. Les Ramblas 35. ℂ 93-317-57-11. Dinner and show 50€–60€ ($58–$69); 1 drink and show 28€–30€ ($32–35). Metro: Drassanes.

Tirititran A flamenco restaurant run by genuine *gitanos*, the background music, the pictures on the wall and the menu all sing of the same passionate musical tradition. In the basement they have a small stage, music and, late on weekends, groups of Andalusians often come by to strum a guitar and drink some hard liquor. The atmosphere is friendly and, although you won't see many beautifully dressed dancers or roses between the teeth, they know their flamenco as good as anyone. Buenos Aires 28. ℂ 93-363-05-91. Metro: Urgell.

CABARET, JAZZ & MORE

Espai Barroc ✦✦✦ One of Barcelona's most culture-conscious (and slightly pretentious) nightspots occupies some of the showplace rooms of the Palau Dalmases, a stately gothic mansion in the La Ribera. In a room lined with grand art objects, flowers, and large platter of fruit, you can listen to recorded opera arias and sip glasses of beer or wine. The most appealing night is Thursday—beginning at 11pm, 10 singers perform a roster of arias from assorted operas, one of which is invariably *Carmen*. Since its establishment in 1996, the place has thrived. Almost everyone around the bar apparently has at least heard of the world's greatest operas, and some can even discuss them more or less brilliantly. Montcada 20. ℂ 93-310-06-73. Metro: Jaume I.

Harlem Jazz Club ✦✦ On a quiet street in the Ciutat Vella, and although its recent, rather soulless makeover would suggest otherwise, this is one of Barcelona's oldest and finest jazz clubs. It's also one of the smallest, with just a handful of tables that get cleared away when the set ends so that people can dance. No matter how many times you've heard "Black Orpheus" or "The Girl from Ipanema," they always sound new again here. Music is viewed with a certain reverence; no one talks when the performers are on. Live jazz, blues, tango, Brazilian funk, Romanian gypsy music, African rhythms—the sounds are always fresh. Most gigs start around 10pm, slightly later on the weekends. Comtessa de Sobradiel 8. ℂ 93-310-07-55. Admission (if any) 5€–10€ ($5.75–$12). 1-drink minimum. Closed 2 weeks in Aug. Metro: Jaume I.

Jamboree ✦✦ Amongst the boisterous revelry of the Plaça Reial just off Les Ramblas, this has long been one of the city's premier locations for good blues and jazz, although it doesn't feature jazz every night. Sometimes a world-class performer will appear here, but most likely it'll be a younger group. The crowd knows its stuff and demands only the best talent. On our last visit, I was entertained by an evening of Chicago blues. Or you might find that a Latin dance band has been scheduled. As it gets late, the music changes totally and the place opens up as a nightclub for a young crowd, with hip-hop featuring downstairs and a more world music vibe upstairs. Most shows begin about 10pm to midnight. Plaça Reial 17. ℂ 93-301-75-64. Shows 5€–10€ ($5.75–$12). Metro: Liceu.

Luz de Gas ✦✦ This theater is renowned for Latino jazz. The place itself is a turn-of-the-20th-century delight, with colored glass lamps, red drapery and other details, but enough mod-cons to make it a world-class live music venue. It was once a theater, and its original seating has been turned into different areas each with its own bar. The lower two levels open onto the dance floor and stage. If you'd like to talk, head for the top tier, which has a glass enclosure. Call to see what the lineup is on any given night: jazz, pop, soul, rhythm and blues, salsa, bolero, whatever. Be warned that the management can be somewhat snooty, so go with attitude. Montaner 246. ☎ **93-209-77-11.** Cover (includes 1 drink) usually 18€–22€ ($21–$25). Bus: 6, 27, 32, or 34.

2 Bars, Cafes, Pubs & Clubs

CIUTAT VELLA

BARS, CAFES & PUBS

Almirall ✪ Quiet and dimly lit, if you're finding trouble imagining Barcelona as late-19-century bohemian artists' hangout, this bar might help you. A huge Art Nouveau mirror behind the bar completes the picture. The crowd is still bohemian and it's a good place to pop in for a pre-club drink. Joaquín Costa 33 (El Raval). No phone. Metro: Sant Antoni.

Barcelona Rouge *Finds* Hidden in deeply unfashionable Poble Sec, this scarlet red bar serves unique cocktails (including some with absinthe) and has an overstuffed collection of furniture to cozy up in, making the overall look one of a of a turn-of-the-century bordello. There are sporadic performances (of the legal nature) of anything from Argentine tango to acrobats. The music is more of the old-school variety and regulars tend to shimmy up and ask you to dance. Poeta Cabanas 21 (Poble Sec). ☎ **93-442-49-85.** Metro: Poble Sec.

Borneo The name is a pun on the area it's in, known as El Born, but the only concession to the historical theme is a slideshow straight from the pages of *National Geographic*. Otherwise what you have is a spacious, relaxed bar with an upstairs area for those who want to escape for a while. Rec 49 (La Ribera). ☎ **93-268-23-89.** Metro: Jaume I.

Café Bar Padam One of the new breed of chic bars in a down-at-heel part of town, the clientele and decor here are modern and hip. The only color in the black-and-white rooms comes from fresh flowers and modern paintings. French music is sometimes featured as well as art expositions. Rauric 9 (El Raval). ☎ **93-302-50-62.** Metro: Liceu.

Café Zurich *Overrated* At the top of the Ramblas, this is a traditional meeting point in Barcelona, and it's also great for the passing parade around Catalonia's most fabled boulevard. If the weather is fair, opt for an outdoor table, enjoying a cold beer, and the gaiety, which often includes live music. Launched in the early 1920s, the cafe was moved out as they built the Triangle shopping center, and then swiftly moved back in. Despite the high-ish prices, grumpy waiters, and rudimentary tapas, it's been going strong ever since. Location says it all. Plaça de Catalunya 1. ☎ **93-317-91-53.** Metro: Catalunya.

Cocktail Bar Boadas ✪ This intimate, conservative bar is usually filled with regulars. Established in 1933, it is the city's oldest cocktail bar. Located at the

---

Is It a Bar, Cafe, Pub, or Club?

In Barcelona, it's not unusual for places to have several personalities. During the day, that peaceful cafe is the perfect place to sit and read a book or enjoy a fresh croissant. Then, as night falls, the staff change, the music is turned up and suddenly you might look up from your book and find yourself in a cool bar surrounded by a loud group of trendy young things. If you wait longer, you might find yourself moved from your table as the furniture is stored away so that the DJ can turn it up louder and people can dance.

top end of Les Ramblas, many visitors stop in for a pre-dinner drink and snack before wandering to one of the areas' many restaurants. It stocks a wide array of Caribbean rums, Russian vodkas, and English gins, and the skilled bartenders know how to mix them all. You won't regret trying a daiquiri. Tallers 1 (El Raval). © 93-318-95-92. Metro: Catalunya.

Eat, Drink, Life   This bar combines the best of all the atmospheres a homesick tourist could want. Comfortable seats, low lighting, friendly English-speaking staff, and TVs showing English-language news and sports. They do good food, although in small portions, all day, while at night things get more lively. A great place to go with friends if you want somewhere that mixes local with English in the best way. Princesa 23. © 93-268-86-19. Metro: Jaume I.

El Born   Facing a rustic-looking square, this former fish store has been cleverly converted. There are a few tables near the front, but our preferred spot is the inner room decorated with rattan furniture and modern paintings. The music might be anything from Louis Armstrong to classic rock 'n' roll. The upstairs buffet serves dinner. The room is somewhat cramped, but you'll find a simple, tasty collection of fish, meat, and vegetable dishes, all carefully laid out. Passeig del Born 26 (La Ribera). © 93-319-53-33. Metro: Jaume I or Barceloneta.

El Bosc de las Fades _(Finds_   This is the most bizarre bar-cafe in Barcelona, evoking a fairy-tale forest, or at the least trying to. It's brought to you by the same people who created Museu de Cera (Wax Museum), which is next door. Expect "unreal trees" and the whispering sound of waterfalls, plus a "gnome" or two—and a magic mirror that merits 30 seconds' closer inspection. At night the place attracts essentially a young crowd who enjoy the faux woodland dell, the loud background music, and the drinks. Pasaje de la Banca 7 (Barri Gòtic). © 93-317-26-49. Metro: Drassanes.

El Café Que Pone Muebles Narvarro _(Finds_   A strange little bar that likes to feel trendy about itself. The name means "The bar where they put Narvarro Furniture." It's an old furniture storeroom and it does feel a little like drinking alcohol while sitting in an old-fashioned IKEA. Good music though. Riera Alta 4–6 (El Raval). © 60-718-80-96. Metro: San Antoni.

Fonfone   A great example of a bar that fits as many in as it can when the music gets them dancing. The colorful, lighting-based decor is particularly original and the dance music is always of high quality for those that like modern, accessible electronica. This isn't a place to stand and talk, but rather a good place to fill in those awkward hours when you're ready to go out but it's still too early to hit the clubs. The location is perfect for finding your way anywhere in the Old Town later on. Escudellers 24 (Barri Gòtic). © 93-317-14-24. Metro: Drassanes.

Ginger ★★   A stylish, split-level cocktail, wine, and tapas bar on a pretty Barri Gòtic square. The well-mixed cocktails (including a rarity—a traditional Pimms) makes it worth hunting out, as do the tasty snacks which include imaginative morsels such as sausages flamed-cooked in _orujo_ and grilled foie. It's the sort of place you pop in for one and stay for three. Lledó 2 (Barri Gòtic). © 93-310-53-09. Metro: Jaume I.

Hivernacle _(Finds_   This is an airy bar-cafe luring a young, hip crowd to a setting of towering palms in a 19th-century greenhouse. The location is just inside the gates of the city's most centrally located park, but it stays open after the park is closed (entrance is down one side, on Passeig Picasso). A fashionable crowd likes to come here to "graze" upon the tapas. A restaurant adjoins and there is live music during the summer months. Parc de la Ciutadella s/n (La Ribera). ✆ 93-295-40-17. Metro: Arc de Triomf.

La Concha *(Finds)* There aren't many bars that have that Moroccan gay kitsch feeling, but this place does and it's also great fun to go there and hang out while staring at the walls filled with color-treated photos of Spain's starlet from the 1960s, Sara Montiel. One part of the bar becomes a tiny dance floor at weekends. This bar is a Barrio Chino institution and it's still a bit hairy, but perfect to experience an authentic slice of bohemia. Guàrdia 14 (El Raval). ✆ 93-302-41-18. Metro: Drassanes.

La Fianna A place with a Moroccan feel that's perfect to lie back and relax if it's raining or when you don't want a night that's too wild. The place is international and is a real find. It houses a restaurant at the back and some normal tables and barstools, but the best thing is to get there early or to wait for a platform to come free–with cushion-filled platforms at different levels, it's the coziest place to curl up with a few drinks and a friend or three. They also do big American-style Sunday brunches. Banys Vells 15 (La Ribera). ✆ 93-315-18-10. Metro: Jaume I.

La Oveja Negra *(Value)* An Old City classic, "the black sheep" is like a hidden beer hall. The crowd is young—it's a student favorite—and the drinks are great value. Noisy, friendly, with a beer-stained pool table and a remarkable cave-like setting, this is a fun place for young people to order some jugs of cheap sangria and meet some people. There will almost certainly be a queue at the foosball table, so that's not a bad place to start. Sitges 5 (El Raval). No phone. Metro: Catalunya.

L'Ascensor *(★)* "The Elevator" has an entrance just like you'd think—you pass through (rather than go up or down in) an old European sliding door style elevator to get into this very local bar that is so well known for its *mojitos* (Cuban rum cocktails) that it has a line of mint-and-sugared glasses waiting to be filled on order. Bellafila 3 (Barri Gòtic). ✆ 93-318-53-47. Metro: Jaume I.

Margarita Blue *(★)* They may try to cram in a few too many tables in the Mexican restaurant part, but if you can find a corner to stand in then the bar is well worth visiting. The music's good, the crowd lively, and the cocktails very good, especially the namesake Blue Margarita. Josep Anselm Clavé 6 (Barri Gòtic). ✆ 93-317-71-76. Metro: Drassanes. They also have a sister club called Rita Blue, Plaça Sant Agustí 3 (Barri Gòtic). ✆ 93-342-40-86. Metro: Liceu.

Molly's Fair City The hangout of expats, plus visiting Brits and Irishmen, and like all of Barcelona's beer halls it is incredibly popular. The sound of English voices is heard throughout the pub, growing louder as the evening wears on, and that can be very late. Expect blaring music, loud voices, and beer flowing like a river. Plus, if there's a major soccer game, a lot of friendly shouting. Ferran 7 (Barri Gòtic). ✆ 93-342-40-26. Metro: Liceu.

Nao Colón *(★)* Though really a designer restaurant, on Thursdays to Sundays it becomes a club playing funk, soul, and house. If you dine there on a Thursday, they also serve up live jazz from 10pm with the meal. It sounds more pretentious than it actually is. Marquès de l'Argentera 19 (La Ribera). ✆ 93-268-76-33. Metro: Barceloneta.

Pitin Bar Easy to spot thanks to the lit-up stars over the door, this is a great place to sit with friends. The bar downstairs may not look anything special, and the patio, though nice, is fairly standard . . . but if you can brave the small spiral staircase, upstairs is a cozy beamed old-town room with some funky little decorations. It's a great place to sit and talk while watching people through the

Dancing with the Green Fairy

If you're feeling adventurous, there's good reason to go to **Bar Marsella,** Sant Pau 65 (no phone; Metro: Liceu), and that's its specialty: absinthe *(absenta).* Picasso and Dalí are reputed to have been regulars here and it looks like they haven't dusted the bottles since. The bar's been here more than 150 years serving the homemade drink that gives it its fame. Absinthe is an impossibly strong aniseed-tasting drink made, in part, with the herb wormwood. Some countries still ban it for its alleged hallucinogenic qualities, which led to it being called "the green fairy." Here they serve it the traditional way: with a fork, a small bottle of water, and a sugar cube. You place the sugar on the fork prongs up, and balance it over the rim of your glass. Then slowly drip a little of the water (not too much!) over the sugar so that it slowly dissolves into the drink. Wait for it to sink in, and then keep adding drips of water so that the sugar has nearly all dripped into your glass. Then mix the last of the sugar into your glass with the fork, and then drink. One glass won't do you much harm, but you can see those around the bar who've had at least a few by their glassy expressions and loose jaws.

windows—but tall people may have trouble with the low roof. Passeig del Born 34 (La Ribera). (C) **93-319-50-87.** Metro: Jaume I.

So_Da If just the thought of shopping makes you thirsty, this bar has the perfect concept. At the back of a trendy clothes store is a cute little bar where you can have a drink and look enviously at the outfits. If you're not careful, you might find yourself agreeing to return the next day, when the shop section is open, to try some of it on. Music is of the electronic variety. Avinyó 24 (Barri Gòtic). (C) **93-342-45-29.** Metro: Jaume I.

The Black Horse This is where many of the neighborhood expats hang out. It has a traditional old pub feel and offers classic British beers on draft. It also shows all the major soccer games and even has a bilingual pub quiz on Sundays. A good place to hear what the situation in the city is from those who've been living here for years. Allada Vermell 16 (La Ribera). (C) **93-268-33-38.** Metro: Jaume I.

Travel Bar The place for the solo backpacker to start. This friendly place is built entirely to help introduce the city to those who are passing through. It's a convenient bar to get a sandwich or a beer, to find out what you need to know— or to hook up with others for a night of exploring. If you need some guidance in where to go, the bar also runs its own nightly bar crawls around local haunts. Boqueria 27 (Barri Gòtic). (C) **93-342-52-52.** Metro: Liceu.

CLUBS

Apolo A genuine multi-tasking venue located in a turn of the century ballroom—Tuesdays it's an alternative cinema, Thursdays it's a funk club, sometimes they have rock concerts, Sundays they have a hugely popular gay night, and on Fridays and Saturdays it's a dance club called Nitsa. Check out listings to find out what's going on when you're in town. Nou de la Rambla 113 (Poble Sec). (C) **93-318-99-17.** Metro: Poble Sec.

Café Royale ⭐⭐ Right next to Plaça Real, this trendy bar is a place for beautiful people—grungy students may have problems getting past the bouncer. But if you can, it's worth it for the subtle gold lighting, the in-house DJs, and the comfortable seating all around the small dance floor. A classic central location for local trendies and models. Nou de Zurbano 3 (Barri Gòtic). © **93-412-14-33.** Metro: Drassanes.

Club 13 ⭐⭐ This new addition to Barcelona's night scene has quickly made itself a favorite of the trendy set. The meeting point for those who like to see and be seen in the heart of Plaça Reial, it gets a few tourists strolling in so the majority of those striking a pose are local. Don't be fooled by how small it looks upstairs—all the real action, and the very loud music, happens in the basement where two rooms—one small, one large—house the dancing masses and the cool cats until late. The music is usually electronic dance. Plaça Reial 13 (Barri Gòtic). © **93-317-23-52.** Metro: Drassanes.

Dot Anyone who's both a hardcore dance music fan and a Star Trek geek will love this small bar/club. The music is loud and rhythmical but by far the best thing about the place is the transporter-style doorway between bar and dance floor. Beam me up. Nou de Sant Francesc 7 (Barri Gòtic). © **93-302-70-26.** Metro: Drassanes.

La Luz de Luna ⭐ For lovers of music a little more Latin, La Luz de Luna ("the light of the moon") is a friendly place that specializes in salsa. Don't worry about making a fool of yourself on the dance floor if you don't know the moves—but if you do, you'll find no end of partners who also really know where to put their feet and at what point to twirl you around. Comerç 21 (La Ribera). © **93-272-09-10.** Admission after 2am 5€ ($5.75). Metro: Jaume I.

Magic Make devil horns with your hands and rock your sweaty mullet at this hard rock/metal club. It's all harmless fun though, and tourists are more than welcome, as long as they can mosh with the best of them. Passeig Picasso 40 (La Ribera). © **93-310-72-67.** Metro: Barceloneta.

Moog ⭐ The place where lovers of techno music and hard pumping beats gather to crash heads. The music is heavy but the people are friendly. Upstairs is a much smaller space where, strangely, 1980s disco (including a wide selection

---

Old-Time Dancing

Plenty of nightclubs claim to be "classics" but none can beat **La Paloma,** Tigre 27 (© **93-301-68-97;** Metro: Universitat)—more than 101 years young and still going strong. The name means "the pigeon" and it opened as a ballroom in 1903, with its famous murals and chandelier added in 1919. It's a part of Barcelona's history—Pablo Picasso met one of his long-term girlfriends here, and Dalí used to sit in a box by the long balcony and sketch the people who came in. During the religiously strict time of Franco, someone called "El Moral" was employed to make sure that couples didn't get too close to each other. But there's none of that now. During the early evening, it opens as before for lovers of the fox-trot, tango, bolero, and so forth, accompanied by live orchestras. But, late at night from Thursday to Sunday, the place undergoes a transformation and becomes a hip and happening nightclub from 2:30am to 5am. From its incredible decor to the mimes that stand outside trying to keep people quiet, this place is a true original. Admission is 7€ ($8.05)—more on special nights.

Moments Piaf, Drag Queens & a Walk on the Wild Side

Do you long to check out the seedy part of Barcelona that writers such as Jean Genet brought so vividly to life in their books? Much of it is gone forever, but *la Vida* nostalgically lives on in pockets like the **Bar Pastis,** Carrer Santa Mónica 4 (*C* **93-318-79-80;** Metro: Drassanes).

Valencianos Carme Pericás and Quime Ballester opened this tiny bar just off the southern end of Les Ramblas in 1947. They made it a shrine to Edith Piaf, and her songs still play on an old phonograph in back of the bar. The decor consists mostly of paintings by Ballester, who had a dark, rather morbid vision of the world. The house special, naturally, is the French aniseed-flavored drink pastis (to be drunk straight or with a mixer) and you can order four kinds of pastis in this dimly lit so-called "corner of Montmartre"—the district of Paris that contains the famous Sacre Coeur church.

Outside the window, check out the view—often a parade of transvestite hookers. The bar crowd is likely to include almost anyone, especially people who used to be called bohemians. The bar also features live music of the French, tango, and folk variety, squeezed into one corner.

of Abba) is played and the DJ himself is part of the experience. Arc del Teatre 3 (El Raval). *C* **93-301-72-82.** Metro: Drassanes.

New York   Talk about late, late night life in Barcelona. The gang of 20-something patrons who like this club don't show up until 3am. It's a former strip joint, and the red lights and black walls still evoke its heyday when the women bared all. Recorded music—mainly hip hop and soul/funk—is heard in the background. Carrer Escudellers 5 (Barri Gòtic). *C* **93-318-87-30.** Cover after 2am (includes 1 drink) 9€ ($10). Metro: Drassanes.

Sidecar   Upstairs is an international restaurant and bar but when it gets late, they open downstairs—a lively and fun dance club with an indie feel in a brick-lined sizeable basement. Sometimes there's live music too. Plaça Reial 7 (Barri Gòtic). *C* **93-302-15-86.** Admission 6€ ($6.90). Metro: Drassanes.

BEACH CLUBS, PORT CLUBS & BEACH BARS

Baja Beach Club   If you want to dance to classic disco tracks, there's no place quite like Baja. It can feel a bit of a meat market and it's as far from the sophisticated trendy club or upmarket cocktail bar as you can possibly go, but if you don't mind topless waiters and bikini-clad waitresses, and want a night dancing to cheesy songs you can sing along to from the '80s and '90s, then this is probably the place to head. You probably won't find many other places where the entrance is a giant beach ball and the DJ is standing in a speedboat on the dance floor! It's located right on the beach and also does reasonably priced food during the day. Paseo Marítimo 34. *C* **93-225-91-00.** Metro: Vila Olímpica/Ciutadella.

Carpe Diem Lounge Club ★★   People on a budget should avoid the dress-code conscious CDLC. Prices are high and so is the snob factor at this achingly cool bar on the edge of the beach. The VIP section is a favorite of famous soccer players but if you want to join them on the comfortable looking white chill-out beds, you'll have to buy a 120€ ($138) bottle of spirits. It has a fairly large outside terrace for passers-by to gawk at the beautiful people. The new trendy night is Sunday, when chill-out music plays early (around 11pm) for those cool

Twisting by the Port

At the bottom end of the Ramblas, and over the wooden swing bridge known as the Rambla del Mar, lies the entertainment/shopping mall **Maremagnum.** Touted as a one-stop drink and dance venue when it opened in 1988, the Barcelona City Council hoped that it would attract millions of punters (especially tourists) for its privileged surrounded-by-water position and swinging selection of restaurants, bars, and clubs. It did, and was perhaps a little unprepared (and under-trained) for its popularity. Over the next couple of years Maremagnum hit the head-lines for the wrong reasons; namely the aggressiveness of its security staff towards ethnic minorities. This left a sour taste in the mouth of many and clients started to stay away in droves. Recently taken over by new management, they plan to put less of an emphasis on nightlife and develop more the complex's shopping and cultural potential. In the meantime however, Maremagnum still has a good number of bars and clubs, and is incredibly handy for a post-dinner bop if you find yourself anywhere near Les Ramblas and don't mind a more sanitized, slightly soulless version of a Latin nightclub (this is a shopping mall after all). A couple of the better venues here include **Irish Winds** (Local 202), which often has live music of the rock/pop variety, and **Mojito** (Local 58), which serves up some mean Brazilian cocktails to a bossa nova beat.

enough to not have to wake up first thing on Monday. Paseo Marítimo 32. ℂ **93-224-04-70.** Metro: Vila Olímpica/Ciutadella.

Le Kashba ⍟   Situated next to the Olympic port in the old Palau del Mar building now occupied by the Museu de Catalunya, this cool little bar/dance floor plays projections on the wall, has cushions on the benches, and offers good dance music both inside and outside on the terrace. Great place to head to on a hot evening. Plaça Pau Vila 1. ℂ **62-656-13-09.** Metro: Barceloneta.

Shoko ⍟   A relatively new addition to the bars by the beach, this Asian restaurant-come-club has an annoying faux spiritual decor that doesn't sit well with its high drink prices and fashionable clientele, many of whom spill over from the neighboring über-trendy nightspot CDLC. That said, it's a nice place to boogie amongst the bright young things and the VIP lounge is open to anyone willing to splash out on champagne. Passeig Marítim 36. ℂ **93-225-92-03.** Metro: Vila Olímpica/Ciutadella.

The Fastnet Bar ⍟⍟   Out of the dozens of Irish pubs and bars in the city, this is the only one that seems to have realized that it is situated in Mediterranean climes and not wet and windy Dublin. Located on a boulevard overlooking the marina, the bar has an ample outside terrace, which fills up on soccer on rugby days when the large-screen TV is turned out onto the street. The rest of the time it is frequented by Anglo-Saxon yachters, who pop in for a Guinness and hearty bacon-and-egg breakfast. Passeig Juan de Borbón 22. ℂ **93-295-30-05.** Metro: Barceloneta.

L'EIXAMPLE

The bars and clubs of the L'Eixample tend to attract a slightly more mixed age group than those of the Old City, and more of a classic nature. They are also more spread out, so you may find yourself hopping in and out of cabs if you plan to bar hop.

Antilla Latin Club ★★★ Catering to Barcelona's sizable Latin American and Caribbean community, this is the city's biggest salsa club. Since it opened its doors over 10 years ago, some of the biggest names in salsa, merengue, mambo rumba, son, and all their derivatives have passed through and when there's not live music the recorded variety is just as stomping. If you are unsure of how to shake your booty, the club runs a dance school on Monday and Wednesday to Friday between 9 and 11:30pm (cost 60€–110€/$69–$127 per week) and on Tuesday, classes are free when you've paid your entrance fee. Open late at weekends. Aragó 141. ☎ 93-451-21-51. Cover (include 1 drink) 9€ ($10). Metro: Urgell.

City Hall ★ A dark, busy club with a small, cool VIP room upstairs and a reasonably sized dance floor downstairs. The music is usually the standard electronic dance music fare, but it also has a small, urban chill-out garden with a bar outside at the back. If you get one of the comfortable seats out there, it can be difficult to get up. The other big advantage of this place is that it's situated very close to Plaça Catalunya—very convenient for taxis and many hotels. Discount flyers can be found in many bars. Rambla Catalunya 2–4. ☎ 93-317-22-77. Cover (includes 1 drink) 8€ ($9.20). Metro: Catalunya.

The Village People

During the day it's dedicated to small artisan shops, market stalls and street theater (see chapter 7), but at night **Poble Espanyol**, Av. Marquès de Comillas s/n (☎ 93-5 08-63-30; Metro: Espanya), turns into a party town. Built as a "typical Spanish village" for the Universal Exhibition in 1929, it may look old but the whole place—right down to the huge fortified towers that dominate the entrance—is fake. At night, that makes it the perfect location to party, as no one actually lives inside and the gates can be strictly guarded. You have a couple of options: one is to buy a 3€ ($3.45) ticket and enter the village to pass the night in three or four small bars which offer drinks, Spanish pop music, and outside tables to watch the party-goers pass by and leave it at that. The other more expensive option is to pay for a ticket (18€–20€/$21–$23) *outside* to one of the clubs that lie *inside* the walls (entrance to the village is included in your ticket price). There are two main venues: **Discotheque**, a self-consciously trendy location for dance music fans, and the venue of choice for many of the big-name visiting DJs and, during the summer, **La Terrazza**, an outdoor-only club that's open from May to October—again, trendy dance music and a great place to dance the night away until the sun comes up (but not so much when it's raining). Due to a falling out between the owners of the two, the ticket lines and entrances to the two clubs are separate, so check which is which before you start to queue. If you stay the distance (until 6am on a weekend), there are flyers and sometimes even buses to take you to "after parties," situated a little out of town and open until noon, if your dancing feet can take it.

Costa Breve ⚐   Sitting uptown this is a decent disco playing a mixture of Spanish and European commercial music, with the odd surprise thrown in such as a stripper or live gig. Hugely popular with office workers in the area, and young *picos* (yuppies), the vibe is different from the Old Town clubs but its tourist-free clientele makes for a nice change. Aribau 230. ℂ **93-441-427-78.** Cover 10€ ($12). FGC: Gràcia.

Nick Havanna ⚐⚐   Started in 1987, this was one of the first of the city's "designer bars," that is, post-modern drinking palaces that spent more on decor than practicalities (such as plumbing). It's still very stylish, although in a more retro sort of way with projections, a dome over the dance floor, uncomfortable metal seating, and some of the most highly designed toilets in the city. Rosselló 208. ℂ **93-215-65-91.** Metro: Diagonal.

Toscano Anticuo ⚐   A noisy Italian cocktail bar that's a million miles away from the slickness you might expect. They serve all the cocktails in the same style of glass, the music is loud and the decor very rough and ready. But the drinks are excellent and they even offer free Italian food on the bar before 10:30pm. The place is all staffed and owned by Italians (the name means "Old Tuscany") and is so Italian that it even has its own ice cream shop a few blocks down—that stays open until 1am on summer weekends. For directions, ask at the bar for the *cremería.* Aribau 167. ℂ **93-532-15-89.** Metro: Diagonal.

GRACIA

Though the area is filled with small squares and hidden corners, the center of the Gràcia world is Plaça del Sol. In the summer, it's the best place to head to meet young Catalans and to watch people on their way to party. Just as many take their own cans of beer as buy from the bars around the square—the atmosphere is noisy and fun and drives the neighbors mad.

Alfa   A great club if you like indie and rock music. The walls are filled with framed covers of classic albums from bands like U2 and the Smiths, which gives you a good idea of the music. It's as local as you can get (its location in a quiet, shop-filled street means there aren't many passing tourists) and the enormous candles dripping wax onto the bar just add to the atmosphere. It's not a big place, nor a particularly clean one, but it does what it does just fine. Mayor de Gràcia 36. ℂ **93-415-18-24.** Metro: Fontana.

Café del Sol   The center of the young Catalan scene, this bar is filled with bohemians, pro-independence Catalan youth, and just people who go to enjoy the tapas and the view over the plaza and its people from the large collection of outside tables. Plaça del Sol 16. ℂ **93-415-56-63.** Metro: Fontana.

Cibeles ⚐⚐   Similar to La Paloma (see above), although not quite as spectacular, Cibeles morphs every Friday from a dance hall for tango and paso doble lovers into **The Mond Club**—the dance music venue of choice in this part of town. Around the corner, **The Mond Bar,** Plaça del Sol 21 (ℂ **93-457-38-77**) has the same music without the dance floor. Còrsega 363. ℂ **93-457-38-77.** Cover 9€ ($10). Metro: Diagonal.

KGB   If the dance music is getting you down, KGB is the place where independent pop acts (metal, reggae, hip-hop) come to find people of their own kind—and to play at them, very loudly. Gigs are normally Thursday through Saturday. The rest of the time, it's a more standard club. Alegre de Dalt 55. ℂ **93-210-59-06.** Cover 9€ ($10). Metro: Lesseps.

Tips Finding Munchies!

After a long night out, the one thing you need is food—and the greasier the better. If you're out of the center, you might come across a traveling *churros* stand, selling fresh potato chips, long strips of greasy fried donut dough, and sometimes cups of hot chocolate to dip them in to. Some tapas bars are open late or very early, such as El Reloj (Vía Laietana 47). If it's any early morning but Sunday, the markets usually have bars open too— the local favorite is Bar Pinotxo in the Boqueria Market on Les Ramblas. Also open very early is the real local secret: the croissant factory hidden on the small Carrer Lancaster on the Raval side of Les Ramblas near the corner of Nou de la Rambla. It opens about 5am and, for 2€ ($2.30), you can buy a box of greasy, chocolate cream-filled doughy croissants that you'll be hard pressed to finish.

BARRIO ALTO

Barrio Alto is sometimes seen as a world of its own. Here is where all the rich families live, in houses no less (something unheard of down in the city), and many of them never leave the Alto enclave. The same applies to going out—rich kids aplenty, alongside some more normal types, throughout the area. The main bars and clubs are concentrated around a street called Marie Cubí, near the María Cristina Metro stop. They're all very quiet during the week, though. *Note:* The Metro system doesn't serve this part of town.

Bikini A classic of the Barcelona nightlife scene, this place opened first as an outdoor bar and minigolf place in the 1950s, then re-opened in the mid-1990s. It is now a venue both for live music and for lively dancing. One room is Latin rhythms, another disco/punk/rock/whatever's going, plus a chill-out cocktail bar tucked away as well. It's also one of the better places to hear live music; when the gig's over, the walls roll back and disco rules. Deu i Mata 105. ℂ 93-322-00-05. Cover (if no concert) 8€ ($9.20).

Gimlet A stylish uptown cocktail bar with a smaller sister bar downtown. The lights are low, the music is jazz, and the measures are generous. Sit at the tables or head for the bar at the back and chat with the waitstaff as they shake and mix the drinks, pour them into retro glasses, and place them on the cute little coasters. There's nothing they can't whip up, and everything they do they do with admirable style. There's a branch at Rec 24. Santaló 46 (La Ribera). ℂ 93-201-53-06.

Otto Zutz If you're anyone who's anyone in Barcelona, you'll have one of the gold VIP cards to Otto Zutz, which allows you access to the bar/small dance floor on the top floor, where you can watch all of the trendy wannabes down below strutting their stuff and, if the whim takes you, go down and invite one of them up to join you at the balcony. For mere mortals and those from out of town, the dance floor is a good size and the small stage often features club dancers who pose and pout almost as much as those upstairs. There's no short-age of discount cards in bars all over town, but its location means that it can be hard to get back home afterwards if you're staying in the Old Town. Lincoln 15. ℂ 93-238-07-22. Cover 10€ ($12).

Up and Down The chic atmosphere here attracts elite Barcelonans of all ages. The more mature patrons, specifically the black-tie, post-theater crowd, head upstairs, leaving the downstairs section to loud music and flaming youth.

Up and Down is the most cosmopolitan disco in Barcelona, with impeccable service, sassy waiters, and a welcoming atmosphere. Technically, this is a private club—you can be turned away at the door. Numància 179. ✆ **93-205-51-94.** Cover (includes 1 drink) 12€–17€ ($14–$20). Metro: María Cristina.

Universal   Uptown fun for the rich set, Universal's name is apt as it's the place where two generations of nighttime revelers go—while the 20-somethings bop around downstairs, those of a more sedate age can be found upstairs with the jazz DJ. Marià Cubí 182. ✆ **93-201-35-96.**

OUTER BARCELONA

Danzatoria   Dress up reasonably smart for Danzatoria, for this is far from the grungy student scene. The setting is a mansion house on the hillside and it's a great place to go, especially in the summer when the three-tier garden with three bars opens up. Inside, from the bottom up, there's a chill-out room with a sofa suspended from the roof, a small dance floor bathed in ultraviolet light, a grand bar in the entrance hall, and an upstairs restaurant until around midnight when it turns into a bar playing modern music. There isn't a view of the city as the place is hidden away in the trees, but it's a great experience. The only way to get there is by taxi. If you're relying on a taxi home, though, you should leave at least a half-hour before it closes (which is at 3am) and walk down the hill to find one. Drinks are pricey. Av. Tibidabo 61. ✆ **93-268-74-30.**

Mirablau   It's all about the location at Mirablau. Although there are worse disco/bars in the city, there are certainly better ones too. But you don't go for the music, the bar prices or the crowd—you go for the view, as Mirablau is situated right next to the funicular near the top of Tibidabo hill and has a huge window overlooking the twinkling lights of the entire city from the hill to the sea. It's open during the day for coffee, but the view at night is something else entirely. If it's pretty enough to help tune out the music, all the better. Plaça Doctor Andreu 2. ✆ **93-418-58-79.**

Razzmatazz   Five clubs in one, each with their own style of music. The venue is an enormous multi-leveled warehouse, and its not unusual to have a big name chill-out DJ playing the main stage while upstairs, oblivious, a group of goths and rock chicks mosh themselves into a frenzy. If you can't find music you like here, you probably don't like music very much. The crowd can be quite studenty but it depends very much on the night. One ticket gets you entry to all the venues, so intrepid dancers can spend the night trying them all. Almogàvers 122. ✆ **93-320-82-00.** Cover (except for special concerts) 12€ ($14).

CHAMPAGNE BARS

The Catalans call their own version of sparkling wine *cava* and it comes from the nearby Penedès region (p. 233). In Catalan, champagne bars are called *xampanyerias*. With more than 50 Catalan companies producing *cava,* and each bottling up to a dozen grades of wine, the best way to learn about Catalan "champagne" is to sample the products at a *xampanyeria.*

Champagne bars usually open at 7pm and stay open till midnight or later. They serve a small range of tapas, from caviar to smoked fish to frozen chocolate truffles. The traditional local time to go is late-morning on a Sunday, when entire families will have a pre-lunch sip. Most establishments sell only a limited array of house *cavas* by the glass, and more esoteric varieties by the bottle. You'll be offered a choice of *brut* (slightly sweeter), *brut nature,* or *rosat* (rosé, or pink champagne).

Can Paixano (Value   If you want to sample the cheapest *cava* in town alongside a bewildering selection of sandwiches, this is the best place to go. It's a rowdy *cava* bar where a *copa* is about 50 céntimos and the most expensive own-label bottle a little over 4€ ($4.60). There are no seats though. If you go at lunchtime, you'll be able to find some space to enjoy your drink—but if you go at night, expect the place to be crammed full. It's a good way to get tipsy early, but don't say I didn't warn you about the evenings—any time after 7pm will start to get very, very full. It's compulsory to order two mini sandwiches with the first bottle you buy. Open 10:30am to 10pm. Reina Cristina 7. No phone. Metro: Barceloneta.

El Xampanyet ✿✿✿   This little champagne bar, our favorite in Barcelona, has been operated by the same family since the 1930s. When the Picasso Museum opened nearby, its popularity was assured. On this ancient street, the tavern is adorned with colored tiles, antique curios, marble tables, and barrels. With your sparkling wine, you can order fresh anchovies in vinegar, impressively fat green olives, or other tapas. If you don't want the *cava,* you can order fresh cider at the old-fashioned zinc bar. Closed in August. Montcada 22. ✆ **93-319-70-03**. Metro: Jaume I.

Xampanyeria Casablanca   Someone had to fashion a champagne bar after the Bogart-Bergman film, and this is it. It serves four kinds of house *cava* by the glass, plus a good selection of tapas, especially pâtés. Bonavista 6. ✆ **93-237-63-99**. Metro: Passeig de Gràcia.

Xampú Xampany   At the corner of the Plaça de Tetuan, this *xampanyeria* offers a variety of hors d'oeuvres in addition to wine. Abstract paintings, touches of high tech, and bouquets of flowers break up the pastel color scheme. Gran Vía de les Corts Catalanes 702. ✆ **93-265-04-83**. Metro: Girona.

GAY & LESBIAN BARS

The city has a vibrant, active gay nightlife, with bars and clubs to suit all tastes. The best thing to do is to walk around the area known locally as "Gayxample"— a part of the left side of the Eixample area, more or less between Carrer Sepulveda and Carrer Aragon, and Carrer Casanova and Plaça Urquinaona. By no means every bar there is gay, but many are—and all of the trendy-looking ones almost certainly will be. Most bars welcome people of any persuasion—but hetero couples should be prepared to be discreet.

Aire—Sala Diana   Lesbians aren't so well served by the city, but this is the classic club of note for everyone from fashionable young things to older women. It's a large venue with a big dance floor and a buzzing bar. Carrer Valencia 236. ✆ **93-487-83-42**. Metro: Passeig de Gràcia.

Café Dietrich   As if you didn't already know by its namesake, this cafe stages the best drag strip shows in town, a combination of local and foreign divas "falling in love again" like the great Marlene herself. It remains Barcelona's most popular gay haunt. The scantily clad bartenders are hot, and the overly posh decor lives up to its reputation as a "divinely glam musical bar/disco." Many of the drag queens like to fraternize with the handsomest of the patrons, to whom they offer deep kisses on the mouth. Consell de Cent 255. ✆ **93-451-77-07**. Metro: Gràcia or Universitat.

Caligula   A kitsch bar which is fun for people of all persuasion. Though the decor is attractive, the most stunning feature is the occasional nightly floor show, where a series of transsexuals mime to international diva hits. No nudity, nothing seedy—just great entertainment with its tongue firmly in its cheek. Consell de Cent 257. No phone. Metro: Universitat.

Medusa This minimalist decorated bar draws a trendy young crowd, mainly of cute boys. "The cuter you are, the better your chances of getting in if we get crowded as the night wears on," I was assured by one of the staff members. A super trendy place, Medusa draws the fashionistas. I prefer its DJs to all others in town. The place gets very cruisy after 1am. Casanova 75. ℭ **93-454-53-63.** Metro: Urgell.

Metro Still one of the most popular gay discos in Barcelona, Metro attracts a diverse crowd—from young fashion victims to more rough-and-ready macho types. One dance floor plays contemporary house and dance music, and the other traditional Spanish music mixed with Spanish pop. This is a good opportunity to watch men of all ages dance the sevillanas together in pairs with a surprising degree of grace. The gay press in Barcelona quite accurately dubs the backroom here as a "notorious, lascivious labyrinth of lust." One interesting feature appears in the bathrooms, where videos have been installed in quite unexpected places. Sepulveda 185. ℭ **93-323-52-27.** Cover 10€ ($12). Metro: Universitat.

New Chaps Gay Barcelonese refer to this saloon-style watering hole as Catalonia's premier leather and denim bar. In fact, the dress code usually is leather of a different stripe: more boots and jeans than leather and chains. Behind a pair of swinging doors evocative of the old American West, Chaps contains two different bar areas. Some of Barcelona's horniest guys flock to the downstairs darkroom in the wee hours. Diagonal 365. ℭ **93-215-53-65.** Metro: Diagonal.

Punto BCN Barcelona's largest gay bar attracts a mixed crowd of young "hotties" and foreigners. Always crowded, it's a good base to start out your evening. There is a very popular happy hour on Wednesday from 6 to 9pm. Montaner 63–65. ℭ **93-453-61-23.** Metro: Eixample.

Salvation This leading gay dance club has been going strong since 1999. It's still the flashiest dive on the see-and-be-seen circuit, and a good place to wear your see-through clothing, especially as the hour grows late. There are two rooms devoted to a different type of music, the first with house music and DJs and the other with more commercial and "soapy" themes. An habitué told me, "I come here because of the sensual waiters," and indeed they are the handsomest and most muscular in town. Look your most gorgeous, buffed self if you want to get past the notoriously selective doorman. Ronda de Sant Pere 19–21. ℭ **93-318-06-86.** Metro: Urquinaona.

9

Side Trips in Catalonia

About six million people live in Catalonia, and twice that many visit every year, flocking to the beaches along the Catalan *costas* (coasts), the area of Spain that practically invented package tourism. This sounds more ominous that it actually is and there are many unspoiled little seaside spots still to be found, the best being the whitewashed fishing village Cadaqués in the far northern **Costa Brava (Rocky Coast),** near the French border.

The capital of this region is Girona, an ancient town seeped in history. Art lovers will also be enthralled with Figueres, birthplace of the father of surrealism, Salvador Dalí, and home to his mad museum. To the south, along the **Costa Daurada (Golden Coast)**

the beaches are wider and sandier. Sitges, a fine resort town that has a huge gay following and Tarragona, the UNESCO classified capital of the region, are the two destinations to visit here, the latter for its concentration of Roman vestiges and architecture.

A hugely popular day excursion from Barcelona is to the Benedictine monastery of **Montserrat,** to the northwest. The serrated outline made by the sierra's steep cliffs led the Catalonians to call it *montserrat* (sawtoothed mountain). Today it remains the religious center of Catalonia. Thousands of pilgrims annually visit the monastery-complex to see its Black Virgin.

1 Montserrat ★★

56km (34 miles) NW of Barcelona, 592km (368 miles) E of Madrid

The monastery at **Montserrat,** which sits atop a 1,200m (3,937-ft.) high mountain, 11km long (7 miles) and 5.5km (3½ miles) wide, is one of the most important pilgrimage spots in Spain. It ranks alongside Zaragoza and Santiago de Compostela in Galicia, at the end of the pilgrimage route of Saint James. Thousands travel here every year to see and touch the medieval statue of La Moreneta (The Black Virgin), the most important religious icon in Catalonia. Many newly married couples flock here for her blessing.

Avoid visiting on Sunday, especially if the weather is nice, as thousands of locals pour in. At all times, remember to take along warm sweaters or jackets, since it can get cold.

ESSENTIALS

GETTING THERE   The best and most exciting way to go is via the Catalan railway. **Ferrocarrils de la Generalitat de Catalunya** to Montserrat-Aeri leaves every hour from the Plaça d'Espanya in Barcelona. The train connects with a high-tech funicular (Aeri de Montserrat), which leaves every 15 minutes.

The train, with its funicular tie-in, has taken over as the preferred and cheapest means of transport. However, long-distance **bus** service is also provided by **Autocar Julià** in Barcelona. Daily service from Barcelona to Montserrat is generally available, with departures near the Estació de Sants on the Plaça de Països

Catalans. Buses leave at 9:15am, returning at 5pm and at 6pm in July and August; the round-trip ticket costs 9.30€ ($11) on weekdays and 11€ ($13) on weekends. Contact the Julià company (© **93-490-40-00**).

To drive here, exit via the Avinguda Diagonal, then take the A-2 (exit Matorell). The signposts and exit to Montserrat will be on your right. From the main road, it's 15km (9 miles) up to the monastery through eerie rock formations and dramatic scenery.

VISITOR INFORMATION   The **tourist office** is at the Plaça de la Creu (© **93-877-77-77**), open daily from 8:50am to 7:30pm. This office can provide you with various maps for walks around the mountain.

EXPLORING MONTSERRAT

One of the monastery's noted attractions is the 50-member **Escolanía** ✸✸, one of the oldest and most renowned boys' choirs in Europe, dating from the 13th century. At 1pm daily (noon on Sun) you can hear them singing "Salve Regina" and the "Virolai" (hymn of Montserrat) in the basilica. The basilica is open Monday to Friday from 7:30am to 7:30pm and Saturday to Sunday from 7:30pm to 8:30pm. Admission is free. To view the Black Virgin, a statue from the 12th or 13th century, enter the church through a side door to the right. She was found in one of the mountain caves (see below) in the 12th century and is said to be have been carved by the hands of Saint Luke himself.

At the Plaça de Santa María you can also visit the **Museu de Montserrat** (© **93-877-77-77**), known for its collection of ecclesiastical paintings, including works by Caravaggio and El Greco. Modern Spanish and Catalan artists are also represented (see Picasso's early *El Viejo Pescador,* 1895). Works by Dalí and such French Impressionists as Monet, Sisley, and Degas are shown. The collection of ancient artifacts is quite interesting. Be sure to look for the crocodile mummy, which is at least 2,000 years old. The museum is open Monday through Friday from 10am to 6pm, and Saturday and Sunday from 9:30am to 6:30pm, charging 4.50€ ($5.20) adults and 3€ ($3.45) for children and students.

The 9-minute **funicular ride** to the 1,236m (4,005-ft.) high peak, Sant Joan, makes for a panoramic trip. The funicular operates about every 20 minutes daily from 11am to 6pm. The cost is 6.10€ ($7) round-trip. From the top, you'll see not only the whole of Catalonia but also the Pyrénées and the islands of Majorca and Ibiza.

You can also make an excursion to **Santa Cova (Holy Grotto),** the alleged site of the discovery of the Black Virgin. The grotto dates from the 17th century and was built in the shape of a cross. You go halfway by funicular but must complete the trip on foot. The grotto is open year-round daily from 10am to 1pm and 2pm to 5:45pm. The funicular operates every 20 minutes daily from 11am to 6pm at a cost of 2.50€ ($2.90) round-trip.

WHERE TO STAY & DINE

Few people spend the night here, but most visitors want at least one meal. There is only one restaurant on Montserrat and it is expensive (see below). Consider bringing a picnic lunch from Barcelona instead.

Abat Cisneros   This modern hotel on the main square of Montserrat offers few pretensions and a history of family management from 1958. The small rooms are simple and clean, each with a comfortable bed, and the bathrooms come with tub/shower combos. Rudimentary regional dishes are served in the in-house restaurant. The hotel's name is derived from a title given to the head of any Benedictine monastery during the Middle Ages.

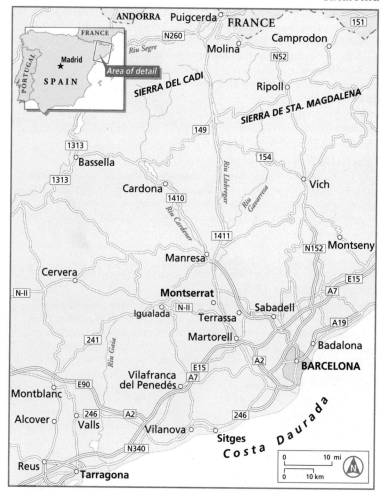

Plaça de Montserrat s/n, 08199 Montserrat. **93-877-77-00.** Fax 93-877-77-24. interhotel.com/spain/es/ hoteles/1829.html. 56 units. 50€–88€ ($58–$101) double. Rates include breakfast. AE, DC, MC, V. Parking 5€ ($5.75). Bus: Autobuses Julià from Plaça Espanya in Barcelona. Train: Montserrat line from Estació Sants and then Ferrocarril. **Amenities:** Restaurant; bar; lounge; laundry service. *In room:* TV, safe.

2 Tarragona ★★

97km (60 miles) S of Barcelona, 554km (344 miles) E of Madrid

The ancient Roman port city of **Tarragona,** on a rocky bluff above the Mediterranean, is one of the grandest but most neglected sightseeing centers in Spain. Honoring its abundance of Roman and medieval remains, UNESCO named Tarragona a world heritage city in 2000.

The Romans captured Tarragona *(Tarraco)* in 218 B.C., and during their rule the city sheltered one million people behind 64km (40-mile) long city walls. One of the four capitals of Catalonia when it was an ancient principality and once the home of Julius Caesar, Tarragona today consists of an old quarter filled with interesting buildings, particularly the houses with connecting balconies. The upper walled town is mainly medieval; the town below is newer.

In the new town, walk along the **Rambla Nova,** a fashionable wide boulevard that's the city's main artery. Running parallel with Rambla Nova to the east is the **Rambla Vella,** which marks the beginning of the Old Town. The city has a bullring, good hotels, and even some beaches, particularly the Platjes del Miracle and del Cossis.

After seeing the attractions listed below, cap off your day with a stroll along the **Balcó del Mediterráni (Balcony of the Mediterranean),** where the vistas are especially beautiful at sunset.

ESSENTIALS

GETTING THERE   Daily, there are **trains** every 15 to 45 minutes making the 1-hour trip to and from the Barcelona-Sants station. In Tarragona, the RENFE office is in the train station, the Plaza Pedrera s/n (✆ **90-224-02-02**).

From Barcelona, there are eight **buses** per day from Monday to Saturday and two on Sunday and Bank holidays to Tarragona (1½ hr.) run by the company La Hispania (✆ **97-775-41-47**). Buses leave from outside the María Cristina Metro station and cost 7.90€ ($9.10) one-way.

To **drive,** take the A-2 southwest from Barcelona to the A-7, via Vilafranca. The route to Tarragona is well marked.

VISITOR INFORMATION   The **tourist office** is at Carrer Major 39 (✆ **97-725-07-95;** www.costadaurada.info), open July to the end of September; Monday through Friday from 9am to 9pm, Saturday 9am to 2pm and 4 to 9pm and Sunday10am to 2pm. The rest of the year, it's open Monday to Saturday 10am to 2pm and 4 to 7pm, and Sunday 10am to 2pm.

EXPLORING THE TOWN

Amfiteatre Romà ⊛   At the foot of Miracle Park and dramatically carved from a cliff that rises from the beach, this Roman amphitheater recalls the days in the 2nd century when thousands gathered here for amusement.

Parc del Milagro s/n. ✆ **97-724-25-79**. Admission 2€ ($2.30) adults; 1€ ($1.15) students and seniors. Mar–Sept Tues–Sat 9am–9pm, Sun 9am–3pm; Oct–Feb Tues–Sat 9am–5pm, Sun 10am–3pm. Closed Dec 25, Jan 1, and Jan 6. Bus: 2.

Catedral ⊛⊛   At the highest point of Tarragona is this 12th-century cathedral, whose architecture represents the transition from Romanesque to Gothic. It has an enormous vaulted entrance, fine stained-glass windows, Romanesque cloisters, and an open choir. In the main apse, observe the altarpiece of Santa Tecla, the patron of Tarragona, carved by Pere Joan in 1430. Two flamboyant doors open into the chevet. The east gallery is the **Museu Diocesà,** with a collection of Catalan art.

Plaça de la Seu s/n. ✆ **97-723-72-69**. Admission to cathedral and museum 2.40€ ($2.75) adults; 1.50€ ($1.70) students and seniors; free for children under 16. Mar–May daily 10am–12:30pm and 4–7pm; June–Sept daily 10am–5pm; Oct–Feb daily 10am–2pm. Bus: 1.

Museu Nacional Arqueològic ⊛   Overlooking the sea, the Archaeology Museum houses a collection of Roman relics—mosaics, ceramics, coins, silver, sculpture, and more. The outstanding attraction here is the mosaic *Head of Medusa* ⊛⊛, with its penetrating stare.

Plaça del Rei 5. ✆ **97-723-62-09**. Admission for museum and Museu i Necròpolis Paleocristians 2.40€ ($2.75) adults; 1.20€ ($1.40) students; free for seniors and children under 18. June–Sept Tues–Sat 10am–8pm, Sun 10am–2pm; Oct–June Tues–Sat 10am–1:30pm and 4–7pm, Sun 10am–2pm. Bus: 8.

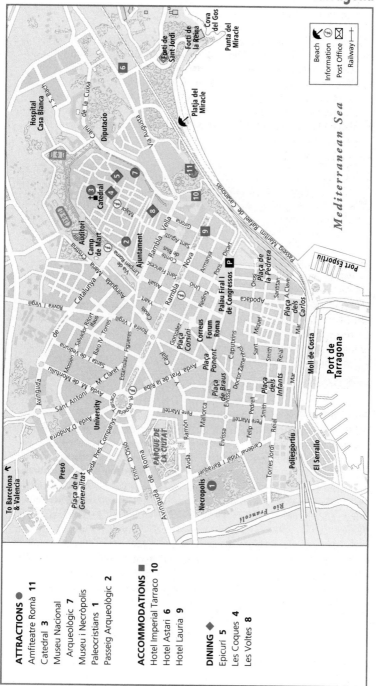

Tarragona

ATTRACTIONS ●
Amfiteatre Romà **11**
Catedral **3**
Museu Nacional
Arqueològic **7**
Museu i Necròpolis
Paleocristians **1**
Passeig Arqueològic **2**

ACCOMMODATIONS ■
Hotel Imperial Tarraco **10**
Hotel Astari **6**
Hotel Lauria **9**

DINING ◆
Epicuri **5**
Les Coques **4**
Les Voltes **8**

Beach
Information
Post Office
Railway

Mediterranean Sea

Port de
Tarragona

223

Catalonia Remembers Pablo Casals

Fleeing from Franco and the fascist regime, the world's greatest cellist, Pablo Casals, left his homeland in 1939. Today his body has been returned to El Vendrell, 72km (45 miles) south of Barcelona, where he is remembered with a museum in his honor. The museum is installed in the renovated house where he lived until he went into self-imposed exile.

Seventeen rooms are filled with Casals memorabilia, including his first cello, photographs and films of his performances, the Peace Medal awarded by the United Nations in 1971, and photographs of the artist with such famous men as John F. Kennedy, who awarded him the Medal of Freedom.

Casals died in Puerto Rico in 1973 at the age of 96, and he was finally returned to his beloved Catalonia in 1979, where he is buried at the El Vendrell graveyard.

Casa Pau Casals lies at Av. Palfuriana 59–61, in Sant Salvador-El Vendrell (ⓒ **97-768-42-76**). From September 16 to June 14 it is open Tuesday through Friday from 10am to 2pm and 4 to 6pm, Saturday from 10am to 2pm and 4 to 7pm, and Sunday from 10am to 2pm. From June 15 to September 15 it's open Tuesday through Saturday from 10am to 2pm and 5 to 9pm, and Sunday from 10am to 2pm. Admission is 5€ ($5.75) for adults, 3€ ($3.45) for children, students, and seniors, and free for children under 8. Allow 1 hour.

To reach El Vendrell from Barcelona, head south along C-32 until you come to the El Vendrell exit just past Calafell.

Museu i Necròpolis Paleocristians 🏛️   This is one of the most important burial grounds in Spain, used by the Christians from the 3rd to the 5th century. It stands outside town next to a tobacco factory whose construction led to its discovery in 1923. While on the grounds, visit the **Museu Paleocristià,** which contains a number of sarcophagi and other objects discovered during the excavations.

Av. de Ramón y Cajal 80. ⓒ **97-723-62-09.** Admission to museum, necropolis, and Museu Arqueològic 2.40€ ($2.75) adults; 1.20€ ($1.40) students; free for seniors and children under 18. June–Sept Tues–Sat 10am–1:30pm and 4–7pm, Sun and holidays 10am–2pm; Oct–May Tues–Sat 10am–1:30pm and 3–5:30pm, Sun and holidays 10am–2pm. Bus: 4.

Passeig Arqueològic 🏛️🏛️   At the far end of the Plaça del Pallol, an archway leads to this .8km (½-mile) walkway along the ancient ramparts, built by the Romans on top of gigantic boulders. The ramparts have been much altered over the years, especially in medieval times and in the 1600s. There are scenic views from many points along the way.

El Portal del Roser s/n. ⓒ **97-724-57-96.** Admission 2€ ($2.30) adults; 1€ ($1.15) students and seniors; free for children under 16. Oct–Mar Tues–Sat 9am–7pm, Sun and holidays 10am–3pm; Apr–Sept Tues–Sat 9am–9pm, Sun and holidays 9am–3pm. Bus: 2.

THEME PARK THRILLS

A 10-minute ride from the heart of Barcelona, the **Port Aventura Amusement Park,** Port Aventura (ⓒ **97-777-90-90**), is Spain's biggest theme park. Universal Studios has acquired a prime stake in it and has plans to make it even larger.

On a vast 809 hectares (1,998 acres), it'll be expanded to become Europe's largest entertainment center. Since its inauguration in 1995, it has already become one of the Mediterranean's favorite family destinations.

The park is a microcosm of five distinct worlds, with full-scale re-creations of classic villages ranging from Polynesia to Mexico, from China to the old American West. It also offers a thrilling variety of roller coaster and white-water rides, all centered on a lake you can travel to via the deck of a Chinese junk.

The park is open daily March 18 to June 19 from 10am to 8pm; June 20 to September 13 from 10am to midnight; September 14 to January 11 from 10am to 8pm. It's closed January 9 to March 18. Admission costs 34€ ($39) adults, 27€ ($31) children. Nighttime admission, available only in summer months, is 23€ ($26) adults, 19€ ($22) children. The fee includes all shows and rides.

WHERE TO STAY
EXPENSIVE
Hotel Imperial Tarraco ★★ About .4km (¼ mile) south of the cathedral, atop an oceanfront cliff whose panoramas include a sweeping view of both the sea and the Roman ruins, this hotel is the finest in town. It was designed in the form of a crescent and has guest rooms that may angle out to sea and almost always include small balconies. The accommodations, all with bathrooms containing tub/shower combos, contain uncomplicated plain modern furniture. The public rooms display lots of polished white marble, Oriental carpets, and leather furniture. The staff responds well to the demands of both traveling businesspeople and art lovers on sightseeing excursions.

Paseo Palmeras s/n, 43003 Tarragona. ℂ 97-723-30-40. Fax 97-721-65-66. www.fut.es/~imperial. 170 units. 109€–150€ ($125–$173) double; 160€–203€ ($184–$233) suite. AE, DC, MC, V. Free parking on street; Mon–Fri parking lot 13€ ($15) per day. Bus: 1. **Amenities:** Snack bar; outdoor pool; tennis court; limited room service; babysitting; laundry service; dry cleaning. *In room:* A/C, TV, minibar, hair dryer, safe.

MODERATE/INEXPENSIVE
Hotel Astari *(Value* Travelers in search of peace and quiet on the Mediterranean come to the Astari, which opened in 1959. This resort hotel on the Barcelona road offers fresh and airy though rather plain accommodations. Most rooms are small, but each comes with a good bed and a bathroom with a tub/shower combo. The Astari has long balconies and terraces, one favorite spot being the outer flagstone terrace with its umbrella-shaded tables set among willows, orange trees, and geranium bushes. This is the only hotel in Tarragona with garage space for each guest's car.

Vía Augusta 95, 43003 Tarragona. ℂ 97-723-69-00. Fax 97-723-69-11. www.gsmhoteles.es. 81 units. 64€ ($74) double; 89€ ($102) business suite. AE, DC, MC, V. Parking 7€ ($8.05). Bus: 9. **Amenities:** Restaurant; bar; pool; room service; laundry service; dry cleaning. *In room:* A/C, TV, minibar, hair dryer, safe.

Hotel Lauria ★ Less than half a block north of the town's popular seaside promenade (Passeig de les Palmeres), beside the tree-lined Rambla, this government-rated three-star hotel offers unpretentious clean rooms, each of which has been recently modernized. Rooms range from small to medium, and each bathroom is equipped with a tub/shower combo. Long considered the leading hotel in town until the arrival of some newcomers, it still draws loyal repeat visitors. The rooms in back open onto a view of the sea.

Rambla Nova 20, 43004 Tarragona. ℂ 97-723-67-12. Fax 97-723-67-00. www.hlauria.es. 72 units. 56€–66€ ($64–$76) double. AE, DC, MC, V. Parking 9€ ($10). Bus: 1. **Amenities:** Bar; outdoor pool; business center; limited room service; laundry service; dry cleaning. *In room:* A/C, TV, hair dryer, safe.

The Beaches of the Costa Daurada

Running along the entire coastline of the province of Tarragona, for some 211km (131 miles) from Cunit as far as Les Cases d'Alcanar, is a series of excellent beaches and impressive cliffs, along with beautiful pine-covered headlands. In the city of Tarragona itself is **El Milagre** beach, and a little farther north are the beaches of **L'Arrabassade, Savinosa, dels Capellans,** and the **Llarga.** At the end of the latter stands **La Punta de la Mora,** which has a 16th-century watchtower. The small towns of **Altafulla** and **Torredembarra,** both complete with castles, stand next to these beaches and are the location of many hotels and urban developments.

Farther north again are the two magnificent beaches of **Comarruga** and **Sant Salvador.** The first is particularly cosmopolitan; the second is more secluded. Last come the beaches of **Calafell, Segur,** and **Cunit,** all with modern tourist complexes. You'll also find the small towns of **Creixell, Sant Vicenç de Calders,** and **Clarà,** which have wooded hills in the background.

South of Tarragona, the coastline forms a wide arc that stretches for miles and includes **La Piñeda** beach. **El Recó** beach fronts the Cape of Salou where, in among its coves, hills, and hidden-away corners, many hotels and residential centers are located. The natural port of **Salou** is nowadays a center for international, family-oriented package tourism but is pleasant enough if you don't mind the crowds and noisy night scene.

Continuing south toward Valencia, you next come to **Cambrils,** a maritime town with an excellent beach and an important fishing port. In the background stand the impressive Colldejou and Llaberia mountains. Farther south are the beaches of **Montroig** and **L'Hospitalet,** as well as the small town of **L'Ametlla de Mar** with its small fishing port.

After passing the Balaguer massif, you eventually reach the delta of the River Ebro, a wide lowland area covering more than 483km (300 miles), opening like a fan into the sea. This is an area of rice fields crisscrossed by branches of the Ebro and by an enormous number of irrigation channels. There are also some lagoons that because of their immense size are ideal as hunting and fishing grounds. Moreover, there are some beaches over several miles in length and others in small hidden estuaries. Two important towns in the region are **Amposta,** on the Ebro itself, and **Sant Carles de la Ràpita,** a 19th-century port town favored by King Carlos III.

The Costa Daurada extends to its most southwesterly point at the plain of **Alcanar,** a large area given over to the cultivation of oranges and other similar crops. Its beaches, along with the small hamlet of **Les Cases d'Alcanar,** mark the end of the Tarragona section of the Costa Daurada.

WHERE TO DINE

Epicuri ★★ *(Value)* CATALAN/CONTINENTAL   In 2002 this long-established restaurant was bought by chef Javier Andrieu, who poured years of experience into a site in the heart of town, a very short walk from the archaeological treasures of medieval Tarragona. Within a cozy dining room whose decor falls midway between the organic *modernisme* of Gaudí and the Art Nouveau opulence of turn-of-the-20th-century Paris, you'll be presented with a choice of two set menus, one at 17€ ($20) that includes three courses; and a much more lavish one, priced at 35€ ($40), that features an aperitif plus six courses. Cuisine is based on securing the best market-fresh ingredients in town. The most intriguing dishes include half-cooked foie gras served with grapes, a succulent entrecôte of veal with artichokes, steamed veal cutlets with lemon or Madeira sauce, maigret of duckling with tiny Catalan mushrooms known as *moixernons,* and a heaven-sent filet of turbot with an almond-flavored saffron sauce. If the ingredients are available in the market, you might find other such dishes as a ragout of squid cooked in black beer.

Mare de Deú de la Mercè s/n. © **97-724-44-04.** Reservations required. Main courses 6€–12€ ($6.90–$14); set dinner menu 22€–36€ ($25–41). AE, DC, MC, V. Mon–Sat 8–12:30pm. Closed Dec 25–Jan 2.

Les Coques ★ *(Finds)* MEDITERRANEAN   This is a real discovery in the historic core of old Tarragona. Sophisticated Les Coques specializes in fare from both land and sea and does so exceedingly well. For example, they prepare the best grilled octopus (the miniature variety) in town. I tasted virgin olive oil and garlic, but the chef prefers to keep his other flavors "secret." They also offer marvelously tender and succulent lamb chops flavored with rich burgundy sauce. The specialties depend on whatever is good in any season. Their selection of wild mushrooms (*seta*) can be prepared in almost any style without losing their marvelously woodsy taste.

Sant Lorenzo 15. © **97-722-83-00.** Reservations required. Main courses 17€–21€ ($20–24). AE, DC, MC, V. Mon–Sat 1–3:45pm and 9–10:45pm. Closed 1 week in Feb and July 24–Aug 14.

Les Voltes ★ *(Finds)* MEDITERRANEAN   This excellent restaurant lies within the vaults of the Roman Circus Maximus. Chiseled stone from 2,300 years ago abides harmoniously with thick plate glass and polished steel surfaces. A large 250-seat restaurant, Les Voltes offers a kitchen of skilled chefs turning out a flavorful and well-seasoned Mediterranean cuisine. The menu features time-tested favorites such as a succulent baked lamb from the neighboring hills. *Rape* (monkfish) deserves special billing, served with roasted garlic in a cockle and mussel sauce. Showing sure-handed spicing, the loin of veal is peppery and served with broiled eggplant.

Carrer Trinquet Vell 12. © **97-723-06-51.** Reservations recommended. Main courses 6€–18€ ($6.90–$21). DC, MC, V. Tues–Sun 1–4pm; Tues–Sat 8:30–11:30pm. Closed Dec 25–Jan 2.

3 Sitges ★★

40km (25 miles) S of Barcelona, 596km (370 miles) E of Madrid

Sitges is one of the most popular resorts of southern Europe and the brightest spot on the Costa Daurada. It's especially crowded in summer, mostly with affluent young northern Europeans, many of them gay. Throughout the 19th century, the resort largely drew prosperous middle-class industrialists and traders (known as *indios* since they made their fortunes in the Americas) and many of their stately homes still stand along the sea-facing promenade, the Passeig Marítim. Today,

Sitges easily accommodates a mixed crowd of affluent residents, vacationing families and couples and swarms of day-trippers from Barcelona.

Sitges has long been known as a city of culture, thanks in part to resident artist, playwright, and Bohemian dandy Santiago Rusiñol. The 19th-century *modernisme* movement was nurtured in Sitges, and the town remained the scene of artistic encounters and demonstrations long after the movement waned. Sitges continued as a resort of artists, attracting such giants as Salvador Dalí and poet Federico García Lorca. The Spanish Civil War (1936–39) erased what has come to be called the "golden age" of Sitges. Although other artists and writers arrived in the decades to follow, none had the impact of those who had gone before.

ESSENTIALS

GETTING THERE   RENFE runs **trains** from Barcelona-Sants and Passeig de Gràcia to Sitges, a 30 to 40 minute trip. Call ℂ **90-224-02-02** in Barcelona for information about schedules. If you plan to stay late, check what time the last train leaves once in Sitges as they vary.

Sitges is a 45-minute **drive** from Barcelona along the C-246, a coastal road. There is also an express highway, the A-7, which passes through the Garraf Tunnels. The coastal road is more scenic, but it can be extremely slow on weekends because of the heavy traffic, as all of Barcelona seemingly heads for the beaches.

VISITOR INFORMATION   The **tourist office** is at Carrer Sínea Morera 1 (ℂ **93-894-42-51;** www.sitges.org). From June to September 15, it's open daily from 9am to 9pm; from September 16 to May, hours are Monday through Friday from 9am to 2pm and 4 to 6:30pm, and Saturday from 10am to 1pm.

SPECIAL EVENTS   The **Carnaval** at Sitges is one of the outstanding events on the Catalan calendar and frankly makes all other carnival celebrations in the region look lame. For more than a century, the town has celebrated the days

Where the Boys Are

Along with Ibiza, Key West, and Mikonos, Sitges has established itself firmly on the "A" list of gay resorts. It's a perfect destination for those who want a ready-made combination of beach and bars, all within a few minutes' walk of each other. It works well as a temporary, calmer alternative to Barcelona, which is about 30 minutes away by train, and so is great for a day trip or a few days out of the city. In the off season, it's pretty quiet on the gay front apart from the carnival in February, when hordes of gays and lesbians descend from Barcelona and the party really begins.

Summer, however, is pure hedonistic playtime, and the town draws males in from all over Europe. Sitges is never going to tax the intellect, but it might well exhaust the body. There's a gay beach crammed with the usual overload of muscles and summer accessories in the middle of the town in front of the Passeig Marítim. The other beach is nudist and farther out of town, between Sitges and Vilanova. The best directions are to go as far as the L'Atlántida disco and then follow the train track to the farther of the two beaches. The woods next to it are unsurprisingly packed with playful wildlife sporting short hair and deep tans.

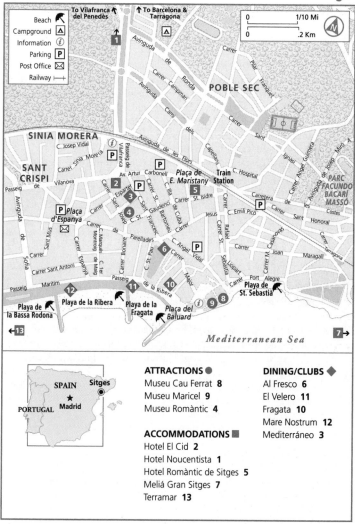

ATTRACTIONS ●
Museu Cau Ferrat **8**
Museu Maricel **9**
Museu Romàntic **4**

ACCOMMODATIONS ■
Hotel El Cid **2**
Hotel Noucentista **1**
Hotel Romàntic de Sitges **5**
Meliá Gran Sitges **7**
Terramar **13**

DINING/CLUBS ◆
Al Fresco **6**
El Velero **11**
Fragata **10**
Mare Nostrum **12**
Mediterráneo **3**

before the beginning of Lent. Fancy dress, floats, feathered outfits, and sequins all make this an exciting event. The party begins on the Thursday before Lent with the arrival of the king of the Carnestoltes and ends with the Burial of a Sardine on Ash Wednesday. Activities reach their flamboyant best on Sant Bonaventura, where gay people hold their own celebrations. During the week of Corpus Christi in June blankets of flowers are laid in the streets of the Old Town, and on the night of June 23, the feast of Sant Joan, the beach lights up with fireworks and bonfires.

FUN ON & OFF THE BEACH

The old part of Sitges used to be a fortified medieval enclosure. The castle is now the seat of the town government. The local parish church, called **La Punta (The**

Point) and built next to the sea on top of a promontory, presides over an extensive maritime esplanade, where people parade in the early evening. Behind the side of the church are the Museu Cau Ferrat and the Museu Maricel (see "Museums," below).

Most people are here to hit the beach. The beaches have showers, bathing cabins, and stalls; kiosks rent motorboats, watersports equipment, beach umbrellas, and sun-beds. Beaches on the eastern end and those inside the town center are the most peaceful—for example, **Aiguadolç** and **Els Balomins. Playa San Sebastián, Fragata Beach,** and the **"Beach of the Boats"** (below the church and next to the yacht club) are the area's family beaches. A young, happening crowd heads for the **Playa de la Ribera** to the west.

All along the coast, women can and certainly do go topless. Farther west are the most solitary beaches, where the scene grows racier, especially along the **Playas del Muerto,** where two tiny nude beaches lie between Sitges and Vilanova i la Geltrú. A shuttle bus runs between the church and the Hotel Terramar. From here, go along the road to the club L'Atlántida, then walk along the railway. The first beach draws nudists of every sexual persuasion, and the second is almost solely gay. Be advised that lots of action takes place in the woods in back of these beaches.

MUSEUMS

Beaches aside, Sitges has some choice museums, which really shouldn't be missed.

Museu Cau Ferrat ★★ (Moments) The Catalan artist Santiago Rusiñol combined two, charming 16th-century cottages to make this house, where he lived and worked; upon his death in 1931 he willed it to Sitges along with his art collection. More than anyone else, Rusiñol made Sitges a popular resort. The museum's immense and cluttered collection includes two paintings by El Greco and several small Picassos, including *The Bullfight*. A number of Rusiñol's works are on display, along with his prolific collection of wrought-iron objects and a dazzling display of Mediterranean tilework. The edifice, with its dramatic sea views from tiny windows, is worth the visit alone.

Carrer Fonollar s/n. (C) **93-894-03-64.** Admission 3€ ($3.45) adults; 1.50€ ($1.70) students; free for children under 12; combination ticket for the 3 museums listed in this section is 5.40€ ($6.20) adults, 3€ ($3.45) students. June 15–Sept Tues–Sun 10am–2pm and 5–9pm; Oct–June 14 Tues–Fri 10am–1:30pm and 3–6:30pm, Sat 10am–7pm, Sun 10am–3pm.

Museu Maricel ★ Opened by the king and queen of Spain, the Museu Maricel contains art donated by Dr. Jesús Pérez Rosales. The palace, owned by American Charles Deering when it was built right after World War I, is made up of two parts connected by a small bridge. The museum has a good collection of Gothic and Romantic paintings and sculptures, as well as many fine Catalan ceramics. There are three noteworthy works by Santiago Rebull and an allegorical painting of World War I by José María Sert.

Carrer del Fonollar s/n. (C) **93-894-03-64.** Admission 3€ ($3.45) adults; 1.50€ ($1.70) students; free for children under 12; admission included in combination ticket (see Museu Cau Ferrat, above). Same hours as Museu Cau Ferrat.

Museu Romàntic ("Can Llopis") This museum re-creates the daily life of a Sitges land-owning family in the 18th and 19th centuries. The family rooms, furniture, and household objects are most interesting. Upstairs, you'll find wine cellars and an important collection of antique dolls.

Sant Gaudenci 1. ℂ **93-894-29-69.** Admission (including guided tour) 3€ ($3.45) adults; 1.50€ ($1.70) students; free for children under 12; admission included in combination ticket (see Museu Cau Ferrat, above). All museums have the same hours and dates.

WHERE TO STAY

In spite of a building spree, Sitges just can't handle the large numbers of tourists who flock here in July and August. By mid-October just about everything—including hotels, restaurants, and bars—slows down considerably or closes altogether.

EXPENSIVE

Meliá Gran Sitges ⭐   Designed with steeply sloping sides reminiscent of a pair of interconnected Aztec pyramids, this hotel dates from 1992, when it housed spectators and participants in the Barcelona Olympics. The hotel has a marble lobby with what feels like the largest window in Spain, overlooking a view of the mountains. Each midsize room comes with a large furnished veranda for sunbathing, and each bathroom has a tub/shower combo. Many guests are here to participate in the conferences and conventions held frequently in the battery of high-tech convention facilities. It's about a 15-minute walk east of the center of Sitges, near the access roads leading to Barcelona.

Joan Salvat Papasseit 38, Puerto de Aiguadolç, 08870 Sitges. ℂ **800/336-3542** in the U.S., or 93-811-08-11 (hotel) or 90-214-44-44 (reservations). Fax 93-894-90-34. www.solmelia.com. 307 units. 84€–213€ ($97–$245) double; 250€ ($288) suite. Some rates include breakfast. AE, DC, MC, V. Parking 8€ ($9). **Amenities:** Restaurant; bar; indoor pool; outdoor pool; health club; sauna; business center; limited room service; babysitting; laundry service; dry cleaning. *In room:* A/C, TV, minibar, hair dryer, safe.

Terramar ⭐⭐ *(Finds*   Facing the beach in a residential area of Sitges, about half a mile from the center, this resort hotel, one of the first "grand hotels" along this coast, is a Sitges landmark. Its balconied front evokes a multi-decked yacht and the interior, renovated in the 1970s is a near-perfect example of retro design. The foyer has a quirky marine-theme, the floors and wall panels are lined with different marbles, and the ladies restroom is hot pink. The spacious and comfortable guest rooms contain the same sort of eccentric detailing.

Passeig Marítim 80, 08870 Sitges. ℂ **93-894-00-50.** Fax 93-894-56-04. www.hotelterramar.com. 209 units. 100€–155€ ($115–$178) double; 140€–170€ ($161–$196) suite. Rates include breakfast buffet. AE, DC, MC, V. Closed Nov–Mar. **Amenities:** 2 restaurants; 2 bars; outdoor pool; 2 outdoor tennis courts; children's center; business center; limited room service; babysitting; laundry service; dry cleaning. *In room:* A/C, TV, minibar, hair dryer, safe.

Hotel Romàntic de Sitges ⭐ *(Finds*   Made up of three beautifully restored 19th-century villas, this hotel is only a short walk from the beach and the train station. The romantic bar is an international rendezvous, and the public rooms are filled with artworks. You can have breakfast in the dining room or in a garden filled with mulberry trees. The rooms, reached by stairs, range from small to medium and are well maintained, with good beds and bathrooms with shower stalls. Overflow guests are housed in a nearby annex, the Hotel de la Renaixença.

Sant Isidre 33, 08870 Sitges. ℂ **93-894-83-75.** Fax 93-894-81-67. www.hotelromantic.com. 60 units. 77€–94€ ($89–$108) double without bathroom; 87€–107€ ($100–$123) double with shower/bathroom. Rates include breakfast. AE, MC, V. Closed Nov–Mar 15. **Amenities:** Bar; babysitting. *In room:* Hair dryer, safe.

MODERATE

Hotel Noucentista ⭐ *(Value*   Owned by the same family that owns the popular Hotel El Xalet across the street, this is a winning choice. After undergoing 3 years of renovation, it is now better than ever. The name, Noucentista, means

1900, the year of the building's original construction. The interior is quite stunning, a statement of *modernisme* with much use of antiques. The small to mid-size bedrooms are stylishly and comfortably furnished with ample closet space and bathrooms, each with a shower. Some of the accommodations open onto small private balconies. The inn is a 10-minute walk from the beach. The hotel is also graced with a small courtyard garden, and guests have access to Xalet's swimming pool and restaurant.

Isla de Cuba 21, 08870 Sitges. ✆ 93-811-00-70. Fax 93-894-55-79. www.elxalet.com. 12 units. 60€–90€ ($69–$104) double; 110€ ($127) suite. AE, DC, MC, V. *In room:* A/C, TV, minibar, hair dryer, safe.

INEXPENSIVE

Hotel El Cid 🏛 El Cid's exterior suggests Castile and inside, appropriately enough, you'll find beamed ceilings, natural stone walls, heavy wrought-iron chandeliers, and leather chairs. The same theme is carried out in the rear dining room and in the pleasantly furnished rooms, which, though small, are still quite comfortable, with fine beds and bathrooms containing shower stalls. Breakfast is the only meal served. El Cid is off the Passeig de Vilanova in the center of town.

San José 39 bis, 08870 Sitges. ✆ 93-894-18-42. Fax 93-894-63-35. 77 units. 40€–65€ ($46–$75) double. Rates include continental breakfast. MC, V. Closed Oct–Apr. **Amenities:** Bar; outdoor pool; babysitting. *In room:* No phone.

WHERE TO DINE
EXPENSIVE

El Velero 🏛 SEAFOOD   This is one of Sitges's leading restaurants, positioned along the beachside promenade. The most desirable tables are found on the glass greenhouse terrace, opening onto the esplanade, though there's a more glamorous restaurant inside. Try a soup, such as clam and truffle or whitefish, followed by a main dish such as paella marinara (with seafood) or suprême of salmon in pine-nut sauce.

Passeig de la Ribera 38. ✆ 93-894-20-51. Reservations required. Main courses 18€–36€ ($21–41); tasting menu 36€ ($41); gastronomic menu 48€ ($55). AE, DC, MC, V. Tues–Sun 1:30–4pm and 8:30–11:30pm. Closed Dec 22–Jan 6.

MODERATE

El Fresco 🏛🏛 *(Finds)* FUSION   Many people, especially the gay community, reckon this is the best bet in Sitges, perhaps something to do with the fact that it is more like an eatery you would encounter in Sydney. Owned by an Australian couple, the eclectic menu draws heavily on Asian influences. Upstairs there is a cheaper cafe, an enormously popular breakfast spot; here, you can feed your hangover on such un-Spanish fare as blueberry pancakes, fresh muesli, and muffins, or choose from a selection of salads such as Thai beef or Caesar for lunch.

Pau Barrabeitg 4. ✆ 93-894-06-00. Reservations recommended. Main courses 8€–20€ ($9–$23). MC, V. May–Sept Tues–Sun 8:30am–midnight; Oct–Apr Wed–Sun 8:30am–midnight. Closed Dec 20–Jan 20.

Fragata 🏛 SEAFOOD   Though its simple interior offers little more than well-scrubbed floors, tables with crisp linens, and air-conditioning, some of the most delectable seafood specialties in town are served here, and hundreds of loyal customers come to appreciate the authentic cuisine. Specialties include seafood soup, a mixed grill of fresh fish, cod salad, mussels marinara, several preparations of squid and octopus, plus some flavorful meat dishes, such as grilled lamb cutlets.

Passeig de la Ribera 1. ✆ 93-894-10-86. Reservations recommended. Main dishes 12€–24€ ($14–$28). AE, DC, MC, V. Daily 1–4:30pm and 8:30–11:30pm.

Cava **Country**

The Penedès region is Catalonia's wine country; the place where the crisp whites, hearty reds, and sparkling *cava* that you've tried in Barcelona's restaurants are produced. After years of being thought of solely as an agrarian region, wine tourism is starting to take off in the villages and rolling vineyards of this delightful destination.

The capital is Vilafranca, a bustling provincial town that has a fine outdoor market on Saturday mornings and is famous for its local *castellers* (human towers) team. The **Museu del Vi,** Plaça Jaume I 1 (© **93-817-00-36**), has a collection of viniculture equipment and memorabilia considered to be the best of its kind in Europe. If you are curious to know more, the Museu de Vilafranca located next door has a collection of works by artists on wine-related themes and a gorgeous collection of Spanish and Catalan ceramic work from the 15th century onwards. If you have time, the Basílica de Santa María (also located in the Plaça Sant Jaume) is a gothic church dating from the 15th century. Ascend the 52m (171 ft.) bell tower for a panoramic view of the town and surrounding area.

Nothing, however, beats the hands on-experience of seeing the process of winemaking from start to finish. A handful of bodegas (wineries) are open to the public, the best being the estate of **Codorníu** (© **93-818-32-32**) the top *cava* maker in Catalonia. Their magnificent winery is located 10km (6 miles) from Vilafranca in the village of Sant Sadorni d'Anoia. Designed at the end of the 19th century by Josep María Puig i Cadafalch (a master architect of the *modernisme* movement) his beautiful project reflects the luxurious product made within; the complex is replete with Art Nouveau touches and details and 15km (9 miles) of sinuous underground tunnels where the product is aged. Another highlight is a museum containing gorgeous past advertising posters of the product, many by renowned artists of the period. Codorníu is open to the public Monday through Friday 9am to 5pm and Saturday 9am to 1pm. A mini train whisks you around the estate, including the vineyards, and a *cava* tasting nicely rounds off your visit.

Another sumptuous *modernista* wine palace is that of **Freixenet,** Av. Casetas Mir s/n (© **93-891-70-25**), Codorníu's main competition. Freixenet's landmark bodega, located right beside the train station of Sant Sadorni d'Anoia, also gives tours of its headquarters (by previous appointment) on Saturday from 10am to 1pm. Its colorful, florid facade is one of the area's landmarks.

The tourist office in Vilafranca del Penedès is located at Carrer de la Cort 14 (© **93-892-03-58;** www.turismevilafranca.com). It's open Tuesday to Friday from 9am to1pm and 4:30 to 7pm, and Saturday 10am to 1pm. **RENFE** (© **90-224-02-02;** www.renfe.es) runs dozens of trains a day (trip time: 55 min.) from Barcelona to Vilafranca del Penedès and Sant Sadorni d'Anoia, leaving from Catalunya station. If you're driving, head west out of the city via the A-7. Follow the signs to Sant Sadorni d' Anoia and then stay on the same highway to Vilafranca.

Mare Nostrum 🐟🐟 SEAFOOD   This landmark dates from 1950, when it opened in what had been a private home in the 1890s. The dining room has a waterfront view, and in warm weather tables are placed outside. The menu includes a full range of seafood dishes, among them grilled fish specialties and steamed hake with champagne. The fish soup is particularly delectable. Next door, the restaurant's cafe serves ice cream, milkshakes, sandwiches, tapas, and three varieties of sangria, including one with champagne and fruit.

Passeig de la Ribera 60. (𝄋 **93-894-33-93.** Reservations required. Main courses 9€–20€ ($10–$23). AE, DC, MC, V. Thurs–Tues 1–4pm and 8–11pm. Closed Dec 15–Feb 1.

SITGES AFTER DARK

One of the best ways to pass an evening in Sitges is to walk the waterfront esplanade, have a leisurely dinner, then retire at about 11pm to one of the dozens of open-air cafes for a nightcap and some serious people-watching.

If you're straight, you may have to hunt to find a late night bar that isn't predominantly gay in the center of town. For the locations of Sitges's gay bars, look for a pocket-size map that's distributed in most of the gay bars—you can pick it up in the Parrot's Pub (in the Plaza de la Industria) or it can be downloaded on **www.gaymap.info**. Nine of these bars are concentrated on **Carrer Sant Bonaventura,** a 5-minute walk from the beach (near the Museu Romàntic). If you grow bored with the action in one place, you just have to walk down the street to find another. Drink prices run about the same in all the clubs.

Mediterráneo, Sant Bonaventura 6 (no phone), is the largest gay disco/bar. It sports a formal Iberian garden and sleek modern styling. And upstairs in this restored 1690s house just east of the Plaça d'Espanya are pool tables and a covered terrace. On summer nights, the place is filled to overflowing.

4 Girona ★★

97km (60 miles) NE of Barcelona, 90km (56 miles) S of the French city of Perpignan

Founded by the Romans, **Girona** is one of the top ten important historical sites in Spain. Later, it became a Moorish stronghold and later still, it reputedly withstood three invasions by Napoleon's troops in the early 1800s. For that and other past aggressions, Girona is often called the "City of a Thousand Sieges." These days, residents go about their daily business smug in the knowledge that their city is constantly rated the best in the country in terms of quality of life.

Split by the Onyar River, this bustling, provincial city often only gets a nod from the crowds of tourists who use its airport as a springboard for the resorts and beaches of the nearby Costa Brava. When you arrive, make your way to the narrow lanes and hidden staircases of the Old City and the Call, the remains of the sizable Jewish community, via the ancient stone footbridge across the Onyar. From here, you'll have the finest view of ochre-colored town houses flanking each side, instantly recalling Venice. Bring good walking shoes, as you will want to circumnavigate the old city walls to fully take in the splendid stone edifices and lush countryside of its surrounds. Much of Girona can be appreciated from the outside, but it does contain some important attractions you'll want to see on the inside.

ESSENTIALS

GETTING THERE   More than 26 **trains** per day run between Girona and Barcelona-Sants or Passeig de Gràcia stations. Trip time is 1 to 1½ hours, depending on the train. Trains arrive in Girona at the Plaça Espanya (𝄋 **97-220-70-93** for information).

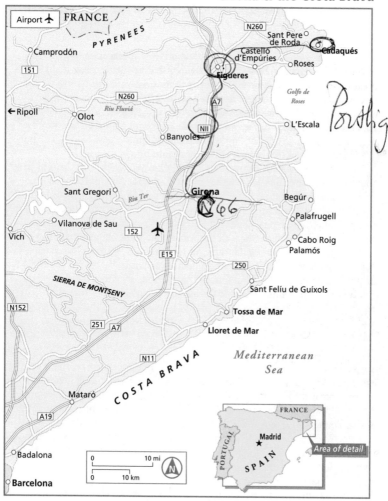

By **car** from Barcelona, take the A-7 at Ronda Litoral and head north via the A-7.

VISITOR INFORMATION   The **tourist office** at Rambla de la Libertat 1 (© **97-222-65-75;** www.ajuntament.gi) is open Monday through Friday from 8am to 8pm, Saturday from 8am to 2pm and 4 to 8pm, and Sunday from 9am to 2pm.

EXPLORING THE MEDIEVAL CITY

Banys Arabs ⊛   These 12th-century Arab baths, an example of Romanesque civic architecture, are in the old quarter of the city. Visit the **caldarium (hot bath),** with its paved floor, and the **frigidarium (cold bath),** with its central octagonal pool surrounded by pillars that support a prism-like structure in the overhead window. Although the Moorish baths were heavily restored in 1929, they'll give you an idea of what the ancient ones were like.

Carrer Ferran el Catolic s/n. ✆ **97-221-32-62.** Admission 1.50€ ($1.70) adults; .75€ (85¢) students; free for seniors and children under 16. Apr–Sept Mon–Sat 10am–7pm, Sun 10am–2pm; Oct–Mar Tues–Sun 10am–2pm. Closed Jan 1, Jan 6, Easter, and Dec 25–26.

Catedral ★★★ Girona's major attraction is its magnificent cathedral, reached by climbing a 17th-century baroque staircase of 90 steep steps. The 14th-century cathedral represents many architectural styles, including Gothic and Romanesque, but it's most notably Catalan baroque. The facade you see as you climb those long stairs dates from the 17th and 18th centuries; from a cornice on top rises a bell tower crowned by a dome with a bronze angel weather vane. Enter the main door of the cathedral and go into the nave, which, at 23m (75 ft.), is the broadest example of Gothic architecture in the world.

The cathedral contains many works of art, displayed for the most part in its museum. Its prize exhibit is a **tapestry of the Creation,** a unique piece of 11th- or 12th-century Romanesque embroidery depicting humans and animals in the Garden of Eden. The other major work displayed is one of the world's rarest manuscripts—the 10th-century *Códex del Beatus,* which contains an illustrated commentary on the Revelation. From the cathedral's **Chapel of Hope,** a door leads to a **Romanesque cloister** from the 12th and 13th centuries, with an unusual trapezoidal layout. The cloister gallery, with a double colonnade, has a series of biblical scenes that are the prize jewel of Catalan Romanesque art. From the cloister you can view the 12th-century **Torre de Carlemany (Charlemagne's Tower).**

Plaça de la Catedral s/n. ✆ **97-221-44-26.** Free admission to cathedral; cloister, and museum 3€ ($3.45). Cathedral daily 9am–1pm and during cloister and museum visiting hours. Cloister and museum: July–Sept Tues–Sat 10am–8pm, Sun 10am–2pm; Oct–Feb Tues–Sat 10am–2pm and 4–6pm, Sun 10am–2pm; Mar–June Tues–Sat 10am–2pm and 4–7pm, Sun 10am–2pm.

Església de Sant Feliu ★ This 14th- to 17th-century church was built over what may have been the tomb of Feliu of Africa, martyred during Diocletian's persecution at the beginning of the 4th century. Important in the architectural history of Catalonia, the church has pillars and arches in the Romanesque style and a Gothic central nave. The **bell tower**—one of the Girona skyline's most characteristic features—has eight pinnacles and one central tower, each supported on a solid octagonal base. The main facade of the church is baroque. The interior contains some exceptional works, including a 16th-century **altarpiece** and a 14th-century alabaster *Reclining Christo.* Notice the eight pagan and Christian **sarcophagi** set in the walls of the presbytery, the two oldest of which are from the 2nd century A.D. One shows Pluto carrying Persephone off to the depths of the earth.

Pujada de Sant Feliu s/n. ✆ **97-220-14-07.** Free admission. Daily 8am–7:45pm.

Museu Arqueològic ★ Housed in a Romanesque church and cloister from the 11th and 12th centuries, this museum illustrates the history of the region from the Paleolithic to the Visigothic periods, using artifacts discovered in nearby excavations. The monastery itself ranks as one of the best examples of Catalan Romanesque architecture. In the cloister, note some Hebrew inscriptions from gravestones of the old Jewish cemetery.

Sant Pere de Galligants, Santa Llúcia 1. ✆ **97-220-26-32.** Admission 1.80€ ($2.10) adults; 1.25€ ($1.45) students, and free for seniors and children under 16. Oct–May Tues–Sat 10am–2pm and 4–6pm, Sun 10am–2pm; June–Dec Tues–Sat 10am–1:30pm and 4–7pm, Sun 10am–2pm.

Museu d'Art ★ In a former Romanesque and Gothic Episcopal palace (Palau Episcopal) next to the cathedral, this museum displays artworks spanning 10 centuries (once housed in the old Diocesan Museum and the Provincial

El Call

The Jewish diaspora made an indelible mark on the city of Girona. A sizable chunk of the Old Town is taken up with the remains of **El Call,** once Spain's most sizable Jewish ghetto. From 20-odd families who arrived at the end of the 9th century, the community grew to nearly 2,000, with three synagogues, butchers, bakers, and other mercantile activity taking place in the neighborhood's cobbled streets. In 1492, along with other Jewish communities on the Peninsula (including Barcelona and Majorca), they were blamed for the spread of the plague and unceremoniously ousted by Catholic powers. The **Centre Bonastruc Ca Porta,** Calle La Força 8 (*(C)* **97-221-67-61),** in the heart of El Call, contains exhibitions on medieval Jewish life and customs, with an emphasis on the co-habitation of Jews and Christians, as well as exhibitions by contemporary Jewish artists. It also conducts special-interest tours of the area and courses on Jewish culture and history. It's open Monday to Saturday 10am to 8pm, Sunday 10am to 3pm.

Museum). Stop in the throne room to view the **altarpiece of Sant Pere of Púbol** by Bernat Martorell and the **altarpiece of Sant Miguel de Crüilles** by Luis Borrassa. Both of these works, from the 15th century, are exemplary pieces of Catalan Gothic painting. The museum is also proud of its **altar stone** of Sant Pere de Roda, from the 10th and 11th centuries; this work in wood and stone, depicting figures and legends, was once covered in embossed silver. The 12th-century *Crüilles Timber* is a unique piece of Romanesque polychrome wood. *Our Lady of Besalù,* from the 15th century, is one of the most accomplished depictions of the Virgin carved in alabaster.

Pujada de la Catedral 12. *(C)* **97-220-38-34.** Admission 2€ ($2.30) adults; 1.50€ ($1.70) students; free for seniors and children. Mar–Sept Tues–Sat 10am–7pm, Sun 10am–2pm; Oct–Feb Tues–Sat 10am–6pm, Sun 10am–2pm. Closed Jan 1, Jan 6, Easter, and Dec 25–26.

Museu de Cinema ⚑⚑   Film buffs flock to this film museum, the only one of its kind in Spain. It houses the Tomàs Mallol collection of some 25,000 cinema artifacts, going all the way up to films shot as late as 1970. Many objects are from the "pre-cinema" era, plus other exhibits from the early days of film. The museum even owns the original camera of the pioneering Lumière brothers. Fixed images such as photographs, posters, engravings, drawings, and paintings are exhibited along with some 800 films of various styles and periods. There's even a library with film-related publications.

Sèquia 1. *(C)* **97-241-27-77.** Admission 3€ ($3.45) adults; 1.50€ ($1.70) students and seniors; free for children under 16. May–Sept Tues–Sun 10am–8pm; Oct–Apr Tues–Fri 10am–6pm, Sat 10am–8pm, Sun 11am–3pm. Closed Dec 25–26, Jan 1, and Jan 6.

WHERE TO STAY
MODERATE
Hotel Carlemany ⚑   In a commercial area only 10 minutes from the historic core, this 1995 hotel is often cited as the best in town. A favorite of business travelers, the facilities are top class. Overall, it's contemporary with a modern (though slightly lacking in character) design. That said, the midsize to spacious rooms are soundproofed and airy, and the bathrooms contain tub/shower combos.

Plaça Miquel Santaló s/n, 17002 Girona. ℂ **97-221-12-12.** Fax 97-221-49-94. www.carlemany.es. 90 units. 110€ ($127) double; 150€ ($173) suite. AE, DC, MC, V. Parking 12€ ($14). **Amenities:** Restaurant; 2 bars; limited room service; laundry service; nonsmoking rooms. *In room:* A/C, TV, hair dryer, safe.

Hotel Ciutat de Girona 🌟   This hip and hi-tech four-star hotel is located right in the town center, and is a good choice for people who prefer mod cons to rustic charm. Opened in 2003, all the classy rooms are decked out in *diseño catalán* style in tones of taupe and cream with dramatic swathes of red, and all have Internet connections (you can even get your own PC upon request). The classy cocktail bar in the foyer clinches the stylish deal.

Nord 2, 17001 Girona. ℂ **97-248-30-38.** Fax 97-248-30-26. www.hotel-ciutatdegirona.com. 44 units. 124€ ($143) double; 154€ ($177) triple. AE, DC, MC, V. Parking 14€ ($16). **Amenities:** Restaurant; bar; limited room service; laundry service. *In room:* A/C, TV, free minibar, dataport, hair dryer.

Hotel Ultonia   Restored in 1993 and now better than ever, this small hotel lies a short walk from the Plaça de la Independencia. Since the late 1950s it has been a favorite with business travelers, but today it attracts more visitors, as it's close to the historical district. The rooms are compact and furnished in a modern style, with comfortable beds and bathrooms, most of which have tub/shower combos. Double-glazed windows keep out the noise. Some of the rooms opening onto the avenue have tiny balconies. In just 8 to 12 minutes, you can cross the Onyar into the medieval quarter. Guests can enjoy a breakfast buffet (not included in the rates quoted below), but no other meals are served.

Av. Jaume I no. 22, 17001 Girona. ℂ **97-220-38-50.** Fax 97-220-33-34. 45 units. 78€–95€ ($90–109) double. AE, DC, MC, V. Parking 9€ ($10) nearby. **Amenities:** Laundry service. *In room:* A/C, TV, minibar.

INEXPENSIVE

Bellmirall 🌟🌟 *Moments*   Across the Onyar River, this little discovery lies in the heart of the old Jewish ghetto. It's one of the best values in the Old Town. The building itself, much restored and altered over the years, dates originally from the 14th century. Christina Vach took control of the venerated old building and proceeded to restore it and convert it to a hotel. She has succeeded admirably in her task. Bedrooms are small to midsize and are decorated in part with antiques set against brick walls. Some of these walls are adorned with paintings, others come with carefully selected ceramics. Each room comes with a small bathroom with shower. In summer, it's possible to order breakfast outside in the courtyard.

Carrer Bellmirall 3, 17004 Girona. ℂ **97-220-40-09.** 7 units. 58€ ($67) double; 75€ ($86) triple. Rates include breakfast. No credit cards. Free parking (hotel provides permit). Closed Jan–Feb. *In room:* No phone.

Hotel Peninsular 🌟   Devoid of any significant architectural character, this modest hotel provides clean but uncontroversial accommodations near the cathedral and the river. The small rooms, which benefited from a 1990 renovation, are scattered over five floors. All units contain neatly kept bathrooms with showers. The hotel is better for short-term stopovers than for prolonged stays. Breakfast is the only meal served (and is not included in the rates quoted below).

Nou 3, 17001 Girona. ℂ **97-220-38-00.** Fax 97-221-04-92. www.novarahotels.com. 47 units. 58€–63€ ($67–72) double. AE, DC, MC, V. Parking 6€ ($6.90) nearby. **Amenities:** Breakfast bar; laundry service. *In room:* TV, hair dryer, safe.

NEARBY PLACES TO STAY

Hostal de la Gavina 🌟🌟🌟   This is the grandest address in the northeast corridor of Spain. Since it opened in the early 1980s, the Hostal de la Gavina has attracted the rich and glamorous, including King Juan Carlos, Elizabeth Taylor, and a host of celebrities from northern Europe. It's on a peninsula jutting seaward from the center of S'Agaro, within a thick-walled Iberian villa built as the home of the Ansesa family (the owners of the hotel) in 1932. Most of the accommodations are in the resort's main building, which has been enlarged and modified. The spacious rooms are the most sumptuous in the area, with elegant appointments, deluxe fabrics, plush towels, toiletries, and tub/shower combos.

Plaça de la Rosaleda s/n, 17248 S'Agaro (Girona). ✆ **97-232-11-00.** Fax 97-232-15-73. www.lagavina.com. 72 units. 245€–305€ ($282–$351) double; 265€–820€ ($305–$943) suite. AE, DC, MC, V. Parking 19€ ($22) garage; free outside. Closed Nov–Mar. 34km (21 miles) from Girona. Take direct road to Llagostera/S'Agaró. **Amenities:** 2 restaurants; 2 bars; outdoor pool; tennis courts; health club; Jacuzzi; sauna; limited room service; massage; babysitting; laundry service; dry cleaning. *In room:* A/C, TV, minibar, hair dryer, safe.

Mas de Torrent ★★★ An hour's drive north of Barcelona and a 15-minute drive from the beaches of Costa Brava, this is a Relais & Châteaux member that was elegantly created from a 1751 farmstead *(masía)*. In the hamlet of Torrent, Mas de Torrent is one of the most artsy and best hotels in Spain. Try for one of the 10 rooms in the original farmhouse, with its massive beams and spacious bathrooms with deep tubs and power showers. The rooms in the more modern bungalow-style annex are just as comfortable but lack the mellow old atmosphere. From the stone balconies of the rooms, vistas of the countryside come into view with Catalonian vineyards in the distance. In the restaurant, the chef focuses mainly on the classic dishes of Catalonia, including monkfish in saffron or fine noodles simmered in fish consommé and served with fresh shellfish.

Afores s/n, Torrent 17123 Girona. ✆ **97-230-32-92.** Fax 97-230-32-93. www.mastorrent.com. 39 units. 380€–550€ ($437–633) suite. AE, DC, MC, V. Free parking. 37km (23 miles) from Girona. Take the N-11 northbound and then take the 1st right onto the Gi652 road to Torrent/Pals/Begur. **Amenities:** Restaurant; bar; outdoor pool; limited room service; babysitting; laundry. *In room:* A/C, TV, minibar, safe.

WHERE TO DINE

Bronsoms ★ CATALAN In the heart of the Old Town, within an 1890s building that was once a private home, this restaurant is one of the most consistently reliable in Girona. Praised by newspapers as far away as Madrid, it has been under its present management since 1982. It's perfected the art of serving a Catalan-based *cocina del mercado*—that is, cooking with whatever market-fresh ingredients are available. The house specialties include fish paella, *arroz negro* (black rice, tinted with squid ink and studded with shellfish), white beans, and several preparations of Iberian ham.

Sant Francesc 7. ✆ **97-221-24-93.** Reservations recommended. Main courses 6€–14€ ($6.90–$16); fixed-price menu 7€ ($8.05). AE, MC, V. Mon–Sat 1–4pm and 8–11:30pm; Sun 1–4pm.

Cal Ros CATALAN In the oldest part of Girona, near the Plaza de Cataluña, this restaurant thrives as a culinary staple and has done so since the 1920s. It was named after a long-ago light-haired owner, although exactly who that was, no one today seems to remember. You'll be seated in one of four rustic dining rooms, each with heavy ceiling beams, exposed stone and plaster, and a sense of old Catalonia. Menu items include savory *escudilla,* made with veal, pork, and local herbs and vegetables; at least four kinds of local fish, usually braised with potatoes and tomatoes; tender fried filets of veal with mushrooms; and flaky homemade pastries, some of them flavored with anise-flavored cream. Kosher and halal dishes are also prepared.

Cort Reial 9. ✆ **97-221-73-79.** Reservations recommended. Main courses 4€–28€ ($4.60–$32). AE, DC, MC, V. Nov–Mar Tues–Sun 1–4pm, Tues–Sat 8–11pm; Apr–Oct Sun–Mon 1–4pm and 8–11pm.

El Cellar de Can Roca ✦✦✦ CATALAN   Just 2km (1¼ miles) from the center of Girona, El Cellar de Can Roca is the best of the new spate of Catalonian restaurants and represents the success of the campaign to transform Girona into one of the more fashionable cities in Spain. Run by three young brothers (one of whom now heads the achingly fashionable Moo Restaurant in Barcelona) the restaurant is intimate, with only 12 tables. The cuisine is an interesting combination of traditional Catalan dishes creatively transformed into contemporary Mediterranean fare. Start with an avocado purée, and for dessert you can't pass up the mandarin orange sorbet with pumpkin compote.

Taiala 40. ② **97-222-21-57.** Reservations recommended. Main courses 17€–35€ ($20–$40); fixed-price menus 57€ ($66). AE, DC, MC, V. Tues–Sat 1–4pm and 9–11pm. Closed Dec 22–Jan 6 and June 23–July 14. Bus: 5.

SHOPPING

There are some interesting shops to be found around El Call and the Old Town. Look out for little specialty shops selling local wares such as beige and yellow-colored ceramic cookware and more upmarket designer joints. The famous Barcelonese design and furniture emporium BD has a branch here at Calle La Força 20 (② **97-222-43-39**) one of a handful of design and object stores on the same medieval street in El Call. There are also a couple of open-air, artisan markets on Saturdays; the first at the Pont de Pedra (stone bridge) and the second in the Plaça Miquel Santaló and Plaça de les Castanyes.

GIRONA AFTER DARK

Central Girona has a good number of tapas bars and cafes. Many of them are scattered along **Les Ramblas,** around the edges of the keynote **Plaça de Independencia,** and within the antique boundaries of the **Plaça Ferran el Católic.** Moving at a leisurely pace from one to another is considered something of an art form. Some animated tapas bars in the city center are **Bar de Tapes,** Carrer Barcelona 13 (② **97-241-01-64**), near the rail station, and **Tapa't,** Plaça de l'Oli s/n (no phone), which is noteworthy for its old-fashioned charm. Also appealing for its crowded conviviality and its impressive roster of shellfish and seafood tapas is **Bar Boira,** Plaça de Independencia 17 (② **97-220-30-96**). In a street that is the hub of Girona's bar culture, **Zanpanzar,** Cort Real 10–12 (② **97-221-28-43**), pulls in the crowds for its mouth-watering Basque-style *pintxos.* **La Sala del Cel,** Pedret 118 (② **97-221-46-64**), Girona's "palace of techno," is located in an old convent with outdoor gardens. The DJs, both local and international, are top class. Be prepared for lines and a *very* late night out. Slightly more subdued is the **Sala de Ball,** Carretera de la Deversa 21 (② **97–220-14-39**), an elegant, old style dance hall that aims to please most tastes from hip-hop to house and salsa, depending on the night.

5 Figueres

219km (136 miles) N of Barcelona, 37km (23 miles) E of Girona

In the heart of Catalonia, **Figueres** once played a role in Spanish history. Philip V wed María Luisa of Savoy here in 1701 in the church of San Pedro, thereby paving the way for the War of the Spanish Succession. But that historical fact is nearly forgotten today: The town is better known as the birthplace of surrealist artist Salvador Dalí in 1904. In view of the lack of other worthy sights in the town, most people stay only a day in Figueres using Girona, Cadaqués, or any of the other towns along the Costa Brava as a base.

ESSENTIALS

GETTING THERE   RENFE, the national railway of Spain, has hourly **train** service between Barcelona and Figueres, stopping off at Girona along the way. All trains between Barcelona and France stop here as well.

Figueres is a 1½- to 2-hour **drive** from Barcelona. Take the excellent north–south A-7 and exit at the major turnoff to Figueres.

VISITOR INFORMATION   The **tourist office** is at the Plaça del Sol s/n (© **97-250-31-55;** www.figueresciutat.com). From November until Easter, hours are Monday through Friday from 8:30am to 3pm. From Easter to the end of June and October, the office is open Monday through Friday from 8:30am to 3pm and 4:30 to 8pm, Saturday 9:30am to 1:30pm and 3:30pm to 6:30pm. From July to August, it's open Monday to Friday 8:30am to 9pm, Saturday 9am to 9pm and Sunday 9am to 3pm. In September, it's open Monday to Friday 8:30am to 8pm and Saturday 9am to 8pm.

VISITING DALI

Casa-Museu Castell Gala Dalí ★★ *Finds*   For additional insights into the often bizarre aesthetic sensibilities of Spain's most famous surrealist, consider a 40km (25-mile) trek from Figueres eastward along highway C-252, following the signs to Parlava. In the village of Púbol, whose permanent population almost never exceeds 200, you'll find the Castell de Púbol. Dating from A.D. 1000, the rustic stone castle was partially in ruin when bought by Dalí as a residence for his estranged wife, Gala, in 1970, on the condition that he'd come only when she invited him. (She almost never did.) After her death in 1982, Dalí moved in for 2 years, moving on to other residences in 1984 after his bedroom mysteriously caught fire one night. Quieter, more serious, and much less surrealistically flamboyant than the other Dalí buildings in Port Lligat and Figueres, the castle is noteworthy for its severe Gothic and Romanesque dignity and for furniture and decor that follow the tastes of the surrealist master. Don't expect a lot of paintings—that's the specialty of the museum at Figueres—but do expect a fascinating insight into one of the most famous muses of the 20th century.

Carrer Gala Salvador Dalí s/n. © **97-248-86-55.** Admission 5.50€ ($6) adults; 4€ ($4.60) students; free for children under 9. June 15–Sept 15 Tues–Sun 10:30am–8pm; Mar 13–June 14 and Sept 16–Nov 1 Tues–Sun 10:30am–6pm; Nov 2–Dec 31 10am–4:30pm.

Teatre-Museu Dalí ★★★   The internationally known artist Dalí was as famous for his surreal and often erotic imagery as he was for his flamboyance and exhibitionism. At the Figueres museum, in the center of town beside the Rambla, you'll find his paintings, watercolors, gouaches, charcoals, and pastels, along with graphics and sculptures, many rendered with seductive and meticulously detailed imagery. His wide-ranging subject matter encompassed such repulsive issues as putrefaction and castration. You'll see, for instance, *The Happy Horse,* a grotesque and lurid purple beast the artist painted during one of his long exiles at Port Lligat. A tour of the museum is an experience. When a catalog was prepared, Dalí said with a perfectly straight face, "It is necessary that all of the people who come out of the museum have false information."

Plaça de Gala Dalí 5. © **97-267-75-00.** Admission 9€ ($10) adults; 6.50€ ($7.50) students and seniors; free for children under 9. July to mid-Sept daily 9am–7:45pm; mid-Sept to June and Oct–Dec Tues–Sun 10:30am–5:45pm. Closed Jan 1 and Dec 25.

The Mad, Mad World of Salvador Dalí

Salvador Dalí (1904–89) became one of the leading exponents of surrealism, depicting irrational imagery of dreams and delirium in a unique, meticulously detailed style. Famous for his eccentricity, he was called "outrageous, talented, relentlessly self-promoting, and unfailingly quotable." At his death at age 84, he was the last survivor of the three famous *enfants terribles* of Spain (the poet García Lorca and the filmmaker Luis Buñuel were the other two).

For all his international renown, Dalí was born in Figueres and died in Figueres. Most of his works are in the eponymous Theater-Museum there, built by the artist himself around the former theater where his first exhibition was held. Dalí was also buried in the Theater-Museum, next door to the church that witnessed both his christening and his funeral—the first and last acts of a perfectly planned scenario.

Salvador Felipe Jacinto Dalí i Domènech, the son of a highly respected notary, was born on May 11, 1904, in a house on Carrer Monturiol in Figueres. In 1922 he registered at the School of Fine Arts in Madrid and went to live at the prestigious Residencia de Estudiantes. There, his friendship with García Lorca and Buñuel had a more enduring effect on his artistic future than his studies at the school. As a result of his undisciplined behavior and the attitude of his father, who clashed with the Primo de Rivera dictatorship over a matter related to elections, the young Dalí spent a month in prison.

In the summer of 1929, the artist René Magritte, along with the poet Paul Eluard and his wife, Gala, came to stay at Cadaqués, and their visit caused sweeping changes in Dalí's life. The young painter became enamored of Eluard's wife; Dalí left his family and fled with Gala to Paris, where he became an enthusiastic member of the surrealist movement. Some of his most famous paintings—*The Great Masturbator, Lugubrious Game,* and *Portrait of Paul Eluard*—date from his life at Port

6 Cadaqués ★★

196km (122 miles) N of Barcelona, 31km (19 miles) E of Figueres

Cadaqués is still unspoiled and remote, despite the publicity it received when Salvador Dalí lived in the next-door village of Port Lligat in a split-level house surmounted by a giant egg. The last resort on the Costa Brava before the French border, Cadaqués is reached by a small winding road, twisting over the mountains from Rosas, the nearest major center. When you get to Cadaqués, you really feel you're off the beaten path and miles from anywhere. The village winds around half a dozen small coves, with a narrow street running along the water's edge.

Scenically, Cadaqués is a knockout: crystal-blue water, fishing boats on the sandy beaches, old whitewashed houses, narrow twisting streets, and a 16th-century parish up on a hill.

Lligat, the small Costa Brava town where he lived and worked off and on during the 1930s.

Following Dalí's break with the tenets of the surrealist movement, his work underwent a radical change, with a return to classicism and what he called his mystical and nuclear phase. He became one of the most fashionable painters in the United States and seemed so intent on self-promotion that the surrealist poet André Breton baptized him with the anagram "Avida Dollars." Dalí wrote a partly fictitious autobiography titled *The Secret Life of Salvador Dalí* and *Hidden Faces,* a novel containing autobiographical elements. These two short literary digressions earned him still greater prestige and wealth, as did his collaborations in the world of cinema (such as the dream set for Alfred Hitchcock's *Spellbound,* 1945) and in those of theater, opera, and ballet.

On August 8, 1958, Dalí and Gala were married according to the rites of the Catholic Church in a ceremony performed in the strictest secrecy at the shrine of Els Angels, just a few miles from Girona.

During the 1960s, Dalí painted some very large works, such as *The Battle of Tetuán.* Another important work painted at this period is *Perpignan Railway Station,* a veritable revelation of his paranoid-critical method that relates this center of Dalí's mythological universe to his obsession with painter Jean-François Millet's *The Angelus.*

In 1979 Dalí's health began to decline, and he retired to Port Lligat in a state of depression. When Gala died, he moved to Púbol, where, obsessed by the theory of catastrophes, he painted his last works, until he suffered severe burns in a fire that nearly cost him his life. Upon recovery, he moved to the Torre Galatea, a building he had bought as an extension to the museum in Figueres. Here he lived for 5 more years, hardly ever leaving his room, until his death in 1989.

ESSENTIALS
GETTING THERE   There are three **buses** per day that run from Figueres to Cadaqués (11am, 1pm, and 7:15pm). Trip time is 1¼ hours. The service is operated by SARFA (© **97-225-87-13**).

VISITOR INFORMATION   The **tourist office,** Cotxe 2 (© **97-225-83-15**), is open Monday through Saturday from 10:30am to 1pm and 4:30 to 7:30pm.

SEEING THE SIGHTS
Casa-Museu Portlligat ★★ *Moments*   This fascinating private home turned museum completes (along with the Teatre-Museu Dalí and the Casa-Museu Castell Gala Dalí) the touted "Dalían Triangle" of northern Catalonia. The structure, home to the Dalís for over forty years, lies in the tiny fishing port of Port Lligat and is surrounded by the eerie rock and coastal formations that feature heavily in his work. If walking from the town center, 15 minutes away, your

first glimpse of the museum will be of the oversize white eggs that adorn the roof. Inside the home has been pretty much left as it was when it was inhabited, with the expected eclectic collections of Dalían objects, art, and icons thrown together in surrealist fashion. The swimming pool and terrace, where Dalí threw many of his legendary parties in the '70s, is the highlight. The museum doesn't have a proper address, but you can't miss it.

© 97-225-10-15. Admission 8€ ($9.20) adults; 6€ ($6.90) students and seniors; free for children under 9. Mid-Mar to mid-June Tues–Sun 10:30am–6pm; mid-June to mid-Sept 10:30am–9pm; mid-Sept to Jan 6 10:30am–6pm.

WHERE TO STAY

Hotel Playa Sol ✿   In a relatively quiet section of the port along the bay, this 1950s hotel offers a great view of the stone church that has become the town's symbol; it's located at the distant edge of the harbor and overlooks the bay of Cadaqués. Many of the rooms have balconies looking right onto the bay (specify when booking) and the smallish rooms are comfortably furnished. Most of the bathrooms have tub/shower combos. The hotel doesn't have an official restaurant, but it does offer lunch from June 15 to September 15 and breakfast all year round. The swimming pool is a definite plus.

Platja Planch 3, 17488 Cadaqués. © 97-225-81-00. Fax 97-225-80-54. www.playasol.com. 50 units. 95€–150€ ($109–$173) double. AE, DC, MC, V. Parking 7€ ($8.05). Closed Jan–Feb. **Amenities:** Bar; outdoor pool; outdoor tennis court; bike rental; limited room service. *In room:* A/C, TV.

Llane Petit ✿✿ *Value*   This is a little inn of considerable charm lying below the better known Hotel Rocamar opening right onto the beach. A hospitable place, it offers decent-sized and well-maintained bathrooms with both tubs and showers. All accommodations open onto a little terrace. The owners keep the hotel under constant renovation during the slow months so it's always fresh again when the summer hordes descend. Try to patronize the hotel's little dinner-only restaurant, as the cuisine is well prepared and most affordable.

Platja Llane Petit s/n, 17488 Cadaqués. © 97-225-10-20. Fax 97-225-87-78. 37 units. 70€–115€ ($81–$132). AE, DC, MC, V. Rates include breakfast in off season. Free parking. Closed Jan 9–Feb 21. **Amenities:** Restaurant; bar; limited room service; laundry; dry cleaning. *In room:* A/C, TV, safe.

Rocamar ✿✿   On the beach, this government-rated three-star hotel is one of the better choices in town, attracting a fun-loving crowd of young northern Europeans in the summer. All the accommodations are well furnished, with rustic yet comfortable pieces, along with small and neatly kept bathrooms with both tubs and showers. The rooms in front have balconies opening onto the sea; those in back have balconies, with views of the mountains and beyond. The hotel is known for its good food served at affordable prices.

Doctor Bartomeus s/n, 17488 Cadaqués. © 97-225-81-50. Fax 97-225-86-50. www.rocamar.com. 71 units. 88€–176€ ($101–$202) double; 140€–259€ ($161–$298) suite. Rates include breakfast. DC, MC, V. Free parking. **Amenities:** Restaurant; bar; indoor pool; outdoor pool; tennis court; sauna; morning room service; massage; babysitting; laundry; dry cleaning. *In room:* A/C, TV, safe.

WHERE TO DINE

Es Trull *Value* SEAFOOD   On the harbor side street in the center of town, this cedar-shingled cafeteria is named for the ancient olive press dominating the interior. A filling fixed-price meal is served. According to the chef, if it comes from the sea and can be eaten, he'll prepare it with that special Catalan flair. You might try mussels in marinara sauce, grilled hake, or natural baby clams. Rice dishes are a specialty, not only paella but also black rice colored with squid ink and rice with calamari and shrimp.

The Most Famous Chef in the World

Ferran Adrià has been hailed not just as the most exciting chef in Spain, but also in the entire world. The press has dubbed him the "Salvador Dalí of the kitchen" because of his creative, wholly high-tech approach to cookery that challenges the concept of food as we know it. He operates his *luxe* **El Bulli,** Cala Montjoi ((C) **97-215-04-57;** fax 97-215-07-17; www.elbulli.com), out of an old farmhouse in the little hamlet of Roses near Cadaqués, but that doesn't stop hoards of discerning international palates from seeking him out, having waited perhaps a year for the privilege. Michelin grants it three stars, an accolade most often reserved for the top restaurants of Paris.

Your only option is to order the 30-course set menu, which changes each season. You never know what's going to appear, but anticipate the most delightful surprises, based on what's the finest produce in any given month. Adrià is an alchemist in the kitchen. Originally hailed for his array of savory "foams," an idea that has now been pirated by top restaurants from Miami to Melbourne, he is constantly experimenting with the composition of food; thus, a pea soup is made into tiny, solid droplets through a process using calcium chloride and basil, pulped into an edible "paper," and served with calamari "seeds" and a mandarin concentrate. You anticipate you're in for a delightful evening at the beginning when you're given addictive little dishes of polenta chips and caramelized sunflower seeds. Your *amuse-bouche* might be a "cappuccino" of guacamole. One dish alone should give Adrià culinary immortality: his lasagna of calamari.

Reservations for next season are by fax or e-mail (bulli@elbulli.com) on a first-come, first-served basis. The *menú de degustación* is 145€ ($167) per person. American Express, MasterCard, and Visa are accepted. The restaurant is open from Easter to the end of September. To get there from Girona, take N-1 north to Figueres, then Route 260 east to Roses, for a total of 56km (35 miles).

Port Ditxos s/n. (C) **97-225-81-96.** Reservations recommended in high season. Main courses 10€–26€ ($12–$30). AE, DC, MC, V. Daily 12:30–4pm and 7–11pm. Closed Nov–Easter.

La Galiota (★★) CATALAN/FRENCH   Dozens of surrealist paintings, including some by Dalí, adorn the walls of this award-winning restaurant, the finest in town. On a sloping street below the cathedral, the place has a downstairs sitting room and a dining room converted from what was a private house. Dalí himself was a patron (his favorite meal was cheese soufflé and chicken roasted with apples) and the chef's secret is in selecting only the freshest of ingredients and preparing them in a way that enhances their natural flavors. The roast leg of lamb, flavored with garlic, is a specialty. The marinated salmon is also excellent, as are the sea bass and the sole with orange sauce.

Carrer Narciso Monturiol 9. (C) **97-225-81-87.** Reservations required. Main courses 18€–26€ ($21–$31). AE, DC, MC, V. Daily 1:30–3:30pm and 8:30–10:30pm. Closed Oct to mid-June.

10

Majorca

by Suzanne Wales & Tara Stevens

"The Pearl of the Mediterranean," Majorca (pronounced "mah-*yohr*-kah") is Spain's most popular island and the largest of the Balearics that include Menorca and Cabrera in the North, and Ibiza and Formentera in the South. Palma (the capital) has the busiest airport in the country, attracting millions of visitors each year, and yet, the island can be remarkably peaceful and remote.

About 209km (130 miles) from Barcelona and 145km (90 miles) from Valencia, Majorca has a coastline 500km (311 miles) long. The exterior is an explorer's paradise of ragged cliffs and lush canopy, although horribly overbuilt along certain coastal regions including parts of the Bay of Alcúdia and the central block of the East coast. The north is mountainous, and the fertile southern flatlands offer a tranquil landscape of olive and almond groves, occasionally interrupted by lime-washed windmills.

The golden sands of Majorca are famous, with pleasure beaches such as **Ca'n Pastilla** and **El Arenal** spreading out along the East Bay of Palma, but they tend to be overcrowded with sun worshippers on package tours. Playa Magaluf may boast the longest beach on the Calvía coast, but it's also the most densely packed with high-rise apartment blocks and every tourist gimmick imaginable lining the strand. More secluded beaches can be found dotted all around the island and it is worth hiring a car to explore these properly. Cala de San Vicente, 6.5km (4 miles) north of Pollença, is a pretty beach with rudimentary facilities save for one massive hotel, bordered by a pine grove and towering cliffs. The Cala Mesquida, Cala Mitjana, and Cala Torta (the latter only accessible on foot), on the tip of the eastern coast, offer sublime turquoise water and almost total seclusion.

ISLAND ESSENTIALS

GETTING THERE　At certain times of the year the trip by boat or plane can be pleasant, but in August the routes to Palma must surely qualify as the major bottleneck in Europe. Don't travel without advance reservations, and be sure you have a return plane ticket if you come in August—otherwise you may not get off the island until September! Package tours, which combine airfare, car rental, and accommodations, can save you a ton of money.

Iberia (© **90-240-05-00**) flies to Palma's Aeroport Son San Joan (© **97-178-90-00**) from Barcelona seven times daily and even more frequently in summer. **Spanair** (© **90-292-91-91**) flies into Palma from Barcelona up to seven times a day. **Air Europa** (© **90-240-15-01**) also has regular, daily flights to Palma. The budget airline Vueling (© **93-378-78-78;** www.vueling.com) only has one flight a day, but you can get there for as low as 20€ ($23) one-way.

Countless charter flights also make the run. Bookings are very tight in August, and delays of at least 24 hours, sometimes more, are common. If you're flying— say, Iberia—on a transatlantic flight from New York to Madrid or Barcelona, have

Majorca

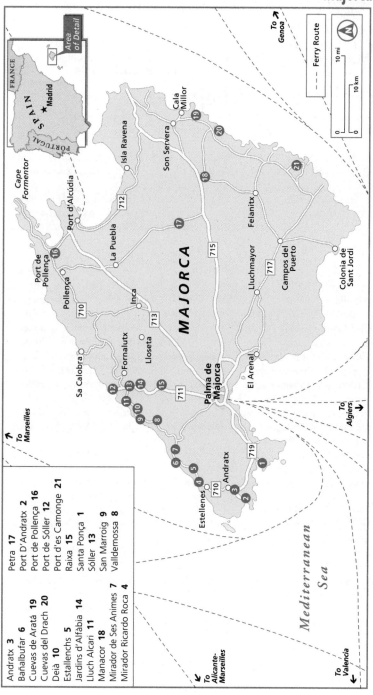

Andratx **3**
Bañalbufar **6**
Cuevas de Aratá **19**
Cuevas del Drach **20**
Deià **10**
Estallenchs **5**
Jardins d'Alfàbia **14**
Lluch Alcari **11**
Manacor **18**
Mirador de Ses Animes **7**
Mirador Ricardo Roca **4**

Petra **17**
Port D'Andratx **2**
Port de Pollença **16**
Port de Sóller **12**
Port d'es Camonge **21**
Raixa **15**
Santa Ponça **1**
Sóller **13**
San Marroig **9**
Valldemossa **8**

--- Ferry Route

Tips Not an Island for All Seasons

July and August are high season for Majorca; don't even think of coming then without a reservation. It's possible to swim comfortably from June to October; after that it's too cold except for the hardcore.

Majorca written into your ticket before your departure if you plan to visit the Balearics as part of your Spanish itinerary.

From Palma de Majorca-Son Sant Joan airport, bus no. 1 takes you to the center of Palma, leaving every 15 to 20 minutes, from 6:10am to 2:10am daily. The trip takes about 30 minutes and costs 2€ ($2.35). A metered cab costs 16€ ($18) for the 25-minute drive into the city center.

Transmediterránea, Estació Marítim 2, Muelle de Pelaires in Palma (© **90-245-46-45** for schedules and reservations), operates one to three **ferries** a day from Barcelona depending on the time of year, taking 8 hours and costing from 50€ ($58) for one-way passage. Tickets can be booked at the Transmediterránea office in Barcelona, Moll Sant Bertran 1–3 (© **93-295-91-00**), and in Valencia at the office at Terminal Transmediterránea Estación Marítima, Puerto de Valencia (© **96-376-10-62**). Any travel agent in Spain can also book you a seat. Schedules and departure times are subject to change and should always be checked and double-checked.

GETTING AROUND At the tourist office in Palma, you can pick up a **bus** schedule that explains island routes. Or call **Emprese Municipal de Transportes** (© **97-121-44-44**). This company runs city buses from Estació Central D'Autobus, Plaça Espanya, the main terminal. The standard one-way fare is 1€ ($1.15) within Palma; at the station you can buy a booklet good for 10 rides, costing 7.50€ ($8.65).

The most popular destination routes on the island (Valldemossa, Deià, Sóller, and Port de Sóller) are offered by **Darbus,** Carrer Estada s/n (© **97-175-06-22**) in Palma.

Ferrocarril de Sóller, Carrer Eusebio Estada 1 (© **97-175-20-51**), off Plaça Espanya, is a **train** service operating between Palma and Sóller and makes for an unforgettable journey passing through majestic mountain scenery. Trains run from 8am to 7:15pm, and a one-way ticket costs 5€ ($5.75). A "tourist train" leaves daily at 10:50am and costs 7.40€ ($8.50), so-named because it makes a 10-minute stop at the Mirador del Pujol d'en Banya for photos. In itself, it is a worthy sightseeing trip. Privately owned, this cute choo-choo was constructed by orange growers in the early 1900s and still uses carriages from the Belle Epoque days.

Another train runs to Inca; it's often called "the leather express" because most passengers are on board to buy inexpensive leather goods in the Inca shops and to visit the Camper Factory Shop. This line is the **Servicios Ferroviarios de Majorca,** and it, too, leaves from Plaça Espanya (© **97-175-22-45** for more information and schedules). The train ride is only 40 minutes, with 40 departures per day Monday through Saturday and 32 per day on Sunday. A one-way fare costs 1.80€ ($2.10). For a radio taxi, call © **97-176-45-45** or 97-140-14-14.

If you plan to stay in Palma, you don't need a car. The city is extremely traffic-clogged, and parking is scarce. If you'd like to take a driving tour (described later in this chapter), you can rent cars at such companies as the Spanish-owned

Atesa at Passeig Marítim (© **97-145-66-02**), where rentals range from 44€ ($51) to 87€ ($100) per day. **Avis** at Passeig Marítim 16 (© **97-173-07-20**) is well stocked with cars; its rates range from 54€ ($62) to 168€ ($193) per day. Both Atesa and Avis maintain offices at the airport. Reservations should always be made in advance.

1 Palma de Majorca ★★

Palma, on the southern tip of the island, is the seat of the autonomous government of the Balearic Islands, as well as the center for most of Majorca's hotels, restaurants, and nightclubs. Founded by the Romans in 123 B.C., Palma was later reconstructed by the Moors in the style of a casbah, or walled city. Its roots are still visible, if obscured a bit by the high-rise hotels that have cropped up.

Old Palma has a wonderfully bohemian flavor with winding alleys and narrow cobblestone streets echoing back to the time when Palma was one of the chief ports in the Mediterranean.

Today Palma is a bustling city whose massive tourist industry has more than made up for its decline as a major seaport. It's estimated that nearly half the population of the island lives in Palma. The islanders call Palma simply *Ciutat* (City), and, as the largest of the Balearic ports, its bay is often clogged with yachts. Arrival by sea is the most impressive way to travel here, with the skyline characterized by Bellver Castle and the bulk of the cathedral, known locally as La Seu (Catalan for "cathedral" or "headquarters").

ESSENTIALS

VISITOR INFORMATION   The **National Tourist Office** is in Palma at Plaça Reina 2 (© **97-171-22-16**). It's open Monday through Friday from 9am to 8pm, and Saturday from 10am to 2pm.

GETTING AROUND   Palma is the perfect strolling city and it is easy to get around by foot. Several bus routes skirt the bay itself, and taxis are reasonably priced. But if you want to get out and about elsewhere on the island, buses or rental cars are your only option.

FAST FACTS   The **U.S. Consulate,** Calle Puerto Pi 8 (© **97-140-37-07**), is open from 10:30am to 1:30pm, Monday through Friday. The **British Consulate,** Plaça Mayor 3 (© **97-171-24-45**), is open from 9am to 3pm, Monday through Friday.

In case of an **emergency,** dial © **112.** If you fall ill, head to the **Centro Médico,** Av. Juan March Ordinas 8, Palma de Majorca (© **97-121-22-00**), a private facility.

Majorca observes the same **holidays** as the rest of Spain but also celebrates June 29, the Feast of St. Peter, the patron saint of fishermen.

The central **post office** is at Carrer Paseo Bornet 10 (© **90-219-71-97**). Hours are Monday through Friday from 8:30am to 8:30pm, and Saturday from 9:30am to 2pm.

Tips Where to Get Those Phone Cards

Local newsstands and tobacco shops sell phone cards valued between 3€ ($3.45) and 15€ ($17). They can be used in any public telephone booth, and allow you to make both domestic and international calls.

FUN ON & OFF THE BEACH

With so many good beaches within stone's throw of the city center it would be madness to bathe on the beach in front of the cathedral. Head instead for the quiet fishing neighborhoods turned hip hang-outs of **Portixol** ✶✶ and **Ciutat Jardí,** where there are a handful of tiny shingle beaches as well as the main sand strand, and numerous trendy bars and eateries. The closest public beach is **Playa Nova,** a 35-minute bus ride, west from downtown Palma, which has a couple of chiringuitos (beach bars) and good swimming, or opt for the upmarket marina resort of Portals Nous—good for ogling the jet set. Heading east you will hit the fun-loving beaches of **Ca'n Pastilla** and **El Arenal,** both well equipped with tourist facilities and hubs of summer beach parties. If it's isolation you seek, head south to the diminutive **Cala Pi** and walk along the cliff tops until you find a space to call your own, or west to **Cap de Cala Figuera** for nude bathing and grilled fish lunches.

You can swim from June to October; Majorcan winters are an ideal time to escape the masses and discover the delights of the city. Be sure to bring warm clothes to wrap up in. Majorcan weather in the spring and fall can be ideal, and in summer the coastal areas are pleasantly cooled by sea breezes.

BIKING   The best places for biking on the island are Ca'n Picafort, Alcúdia, and Port de Pollença, all along the north coast, and across the central plains. These can get choked with Tour de France wannabees in training, because they are relatively flat. Most city roads have special bike lanes on the island, but be on guard for fast-moving cars once you're out in the country. For rentals, go to **Belori Bike,** Edificio Pilari, Marbella 22, Playa de Palma (✆ 97-149-03-58). Depending on their model, and how many gears they have, pedal bikes rent for around 10€ ($12) per day.

GOLF   Majorca is a golfer's dream. The best course is the Son Vida Club de Golf, Urbanización son Vida, about 13km (8 miles) east of Palma along the Andrade highway. This 18-hole course is shared by guests of the island's two best hotels, the Arabella Golf Hotel and the Son Vida. However, the course is open to all players who call for reservations (✆ 97-178-71-00). Greens fees are 66€ ($76) for 18 holes.

HIKING   Because of the hilly terrain in Majorca, this sport is better pursued here than on Ibiza or Minorca. The mountains of the northwest, the Serra de Tramuntana, are best for exploring or there are plenty of rugged cliff top walks for those who prefer to stop for swims. The tourist office (see "Visitor Information," above) will provide you with a free booklet called *20 Hiking Excursions on the Island of Majorca.*

HORSEBACK RIDING   The best stables on the island are at **The Riding School of Majorca,** on the Palma-Sóller road. Call ✆ **97-161-31-57** to make arrangements and get directions from wherever you are on the island.

WATERSPORTS   Most beaches have outfitters who will rent you windsurfers and dinghies. The best diving operation is **Planet Escuba,** Pont Adriano (✆ **97-123-43-06** or 97-752-68-81). Divers here are highly skilled and will take you to the most intriguing sights underwater if you are a qualified diver.

SHOPPING

Stores in Palma offer handicrafts, elegant leather goods, Majorcan pearls, colorful linens, and fine needlework. The best shopping is on the following streets: San Miguel, Carrer Sindicato, Jaume II, Jaume III, Carrer Plateria, Vía Roman,

Palma de Majorca

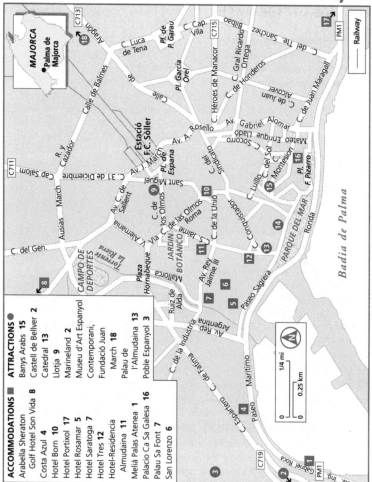

and Passeig des Borne, plus the streets radiating from the Borne all the way to Plaça Cort, where the city hall stands. There are also craft markets in the evenings from May through October on the Plaça de les Meraviles. Most shops close on Saturday afternoon and Sunday.

The famous **Casa Bonet,** Plaça Federico Chopin 2 (© **97-172-21-17**), founded in 1860, sells finely textured needlework. All of the sheets, tablecloths, napkins, and pillowcases are made in Majorca from fine linen or cotton (and less expensively, from acrylic). Many are hand-embroidered, using ancient designs and floral motifs popularized by this establishment. For beautiful olive wood salad bowls, salt and pepper grinders and the like, try **El Olivo,** Calle Pescateria Vella 4 (© **97-172-70-25**).

Loewe, Av. Jaume III no. 1 (© **97-171-52-75**), offers fine leather, elegant accessories for men and women, luggage, and chic apparel for women. For funkier leather items, head for **Pink,** Av. Jaume III no. 3 (© **97-172-23-33**). **Passy,** Av. Jaume III no. 6 (© **97-171-33-38**), offers high-quality, locally made shoes, handbags, and accessories for men and women. There's another branch, not as well stocked, at Carrer Tous y Ferrer 8 (© **97-171-73-38**).

Fashionistas need look no further than the Passeig d'es Borne for sumptuous designer togs by **Carolina Herrera** or high street basics and accessories from Spanish mega-stores; **Zara, Mango** and **Massimo Dutti.**

Perlas Majorica, Av. Jaume III no. 11 (© **97-172-52-68**), is the authorized agency for authentic Majorcan pearls, offering a 10-year guarantee for their products. The pearls come in varied sizes and settings and if baubles are your thing, you can pick up some good deals here. Better still, go see how they are made at the factory in Manacor, Calle Pere Riche s/n (© **97-155-09-00**).

SEEING THE SIGHTS

It may not have the cultural richness of Seville or Barcelona, but Palma is well worth dedicating some time to getting lost in.

Viajes Sidetours, Passeig Marítim 19 (© **97-128-39-00**), offers numerous full- and half-day excursions throughout Palma and the surrounding country-side. The full-day excursion to Valldemossa and Sóller takes visitors through the monastery where former island residents Chopin and his lover, George Sand, spent their winter and scandalized locals by residing together out of wedlock. After leaving the monastery, the tour explores the peaks of the Sierra Ma-llorquina, then makes its way to the seaside town of Sóller. A visit to the Arabian gardens of Raixa or Alfàbia is included in the 32€ ($37) cost of the tour, on Wednesday only.

Another full-day tour of the mountainous western side of the island is con-ducted by train and boat, including a ride on one of Europe's oldest railways to the town of Sóller and the Monasterio de Lluch, as well as a boat ride between the port of Sóller and La Calobra. Daily tours cost 45€ ($52). The eastern coast of Majorca is explored in the Caves of Drach and Hams tour. A concert on the world's largest underground lake (Lake Martel), tours through the caves, a stop at an olive-wood works, and a visit to the Majorica Pearl Factory are all covered daily in the 33€ ($38) cost. Times of departure may vary.

Banys Arabs　These authentic Moorish baths are located in pleasant gardens and date from the 10th century. They represent the only complete Moorish building in Palma. The main room has striking archways and columns support-ing a dome that is pierced with skylights to represent the stars.

Can Serra 7. © **97-172-15-49**. Admission 1.50€ ($1.70) adults, free for children under 10. Apr–Nov daily 9am–8pm; Dec–Mar 9am–7pm. Bus: 15.

Castell de Bellver ⚜　Erected in 1309, this hilltop round castle was once the summer palace of the kings of Majorca—during the short period when there were kings of Majorca. By the 18th century it had become a military prison, and today it is fun to wander around. The castle, which was a fortress with a double moat, is well preserved and now houses the Museu Municipal, which is devoted to archaeological objects, old coins, and a small collection of sculpture. It's really the view, however, that is the chief attraction. In fact, the name, Bellver, means beautiful view.

Camilo José Cela s/n. © **97-173-06-57**. Admission 1.75€ ($2) adults; .85€ ($1) children, students, and sen-iors. Apr–Sep Mon–Fri 8am–9pm, closed Sun and bank holidays; Oct–Mar Mon–Fri 8am–8pm, Sun and bank holidays 10am–5pm. Bus: 3, 4, 20, 21, or 22 to Joan Miró (Gomila) then 20-min walk.

Catedral ⚜⚜　This Catalonian Gothic cathedral, called La Seu, stands in the old town overlooking the seaside. It was begun during the reign of Jaume II

(1276–1311) and completed in 1601. Its central vault is 43m (141 ft.) high, and its columns rise 20m (66 ft.). There is a wrought-iron *baldachin* (canopy) by Gaudí over the main altar. The treasury contains supposed pieces of the True Cross and relics of San Sebastián, patron saint of Palma. Museum and cathedral hours often change; call ahead to make sure they're accepting visitors.

Plaça Almoina 1, Almoyna. ℂ 97-172-31-30. Free admission to cathedral; museum and treasury 3.50€ ($4). Apr 1–May 31 and Oct Mon–Fri 10am–5:15pm; Jun–Sept Mon–Fri 10am–6:15pm; Nov 2–Mar Mon–Fri 10am–3:15pm; year-round Sat 10am–2:15pm. Bus: 15.

Llotja ⭐   This 15th-century Gothic structure is a leftover from the wealthy mercantile days of Majorca. La Lonja (its Spanish name) was, roughly, an exchange or guild. Exhibitions here are announced in local newspapers.

Passeig Sagrera. ℂ 97-171-17-05. Free admission. Tues–Sat 11am–2pm and 5–8pm; Sun 11am–2pm. Bus: 15.

Marineland *(Kids)*   Eighteen kilometers (11 miles) west of Palma, just off the coast road en route to Palma Nova, Marineland is a great one for the kids with dolphin and sea lion shows, as well as a Polynesian pearl-diving demonstration and a small zoo. You'll find a cafeteria, picnic area, and children's playground, as well as beach facilities.

Costa d'en Blanes s/n, Calviá. ℂ 97-167-51-25. Admission 17€ ($20) adults, 15€ ($17) seniors, 11€ ($13) children 3–12, free for children under 3. July–Aug daily 9:30am–6:45pm; Sept–June 9.30am–5:15pm. Closed Dec 16–Jan 31. Bus: Direct, marked MARINELAND, from Palma rail station.

Museu d'Art Espanyol Contemporani, Fundació Juan March ⭐   The Juan March Foundation's Museum of Spanish Contemporary Art reopened in 1997, with a series of newly acquired modern paintings. The works represent one of the most fertile periods of 20th-century art, with canvasses by Picasso, Miró, Dalí, and Juan Gris, as well as Antoni Tàpies, Carlos Saura, Miquel Barceló, Lluis Gordillo, Susana Solano, and Jordi Teixidor. A room devoted to temporary exhibits was added to the restored museum. One series, for example, featured 100 Picasso engravings from the 1930s. The oldest and best-known work in the museum is Picasso's *Head of a Woman,* from his cycle of paintings known as Les Demoiselles d'Avignon. These works form part of the collection that the Juan March Foundation began to amass in 1973.

Sant Miquel 11. ℂ 97-171-35-15. Admission 3€ ($3.45) adults, 1.50€ ($1.70) students and seniors. Mon–Fri 10am–6:30pm; Sat 10:30am–2pm. Closed Sun and bank holidays. Bus: 1.

Palau de l'Almudaina   Long ago, Muslim rulers erected this splendid fortress surrounded by Moorish-style gardens and fountains opposite the cathedral. During the short-lived reign of the kings of Majorca, it was converted into a royal residence evocative of the Alcázar at Málaga. Now it houses a museum displaying antiques, arts, suits of armor, and Gobelin tapestries. Panoramic views of the harbor of Palma can be seen from here.

Palau Reial s/n. ℂ 97-121-41-34. Admission 3.20€ ($3.70) adults, 2.30€ ($2.65) children, free for all Wed. Apr–Sept Mon–Fri 10am–5:45pm, Oct–Mar Mon–Fri 10am–1:15pm and 4–5:15pm. Closed Sun and Jan 1, Jan 6, Jan 20, Apr 12, May 1, Dec 24–25, and Dec 31. Bus: 15.

Poble Espanyol   Spain in miniature, this toy town–like curiosity represents buildings from all over the country (rather like the Daddy Poble Espanyol in Barcelona). Included is the Alhambra in Granada, the Torre de Oro in Seville, and El Greco's House in Toledo. As part of the "authentic" experience, bullfights are held in its *corrida* on summer Sundays.

Poble Espanyol 39. ℂ 97-173-70-70. Admission 5€ ($5.75) adults, 4.50€ ($5.20) children. Apr–Nov daily 9am–6pm; Dec–Mar daily 9am–5pm. Bus: 4 or 5.

WHERE TO STAY

Majorca has a staggering number of hotels, but it's still not enough to hold the crowds in August. If you go in high season, reserve well in advance. Some of our hotel recommendations in Palma are in the El Terreno section, the heart of "la vida loca" (the local nightlife). Don't book into one of these hotels unless you like plenty of action, continuing until late at night. More conservative readers may find it unsavory. If you want peace and quiet, check our other suggestions. The old quarter is particularly good for smart, high-quality boutique hotels.

Palma's suburbs, notably Cala Mayor, about 4km (2½ miles) from the center, and San Agustín, about 5km (3 miles) from town, continue to sprawl. In El Arenal, part of Playas de Palma, there is a huge concentration of hotels. The beaches at El Arenal are quite good but have a Coney Island atmosphere. I've included a number of hotel recommendations in these suburbs for those who don't mind staying outside the city center.

VERY EXPENSIVE

Arabella Sheraton Golf Hotel Son Vida ★★   In 1992 the German-based Arabella chain bought this hotel, as well as the Son Vida Hotel (which can be reached after a brisk 10-min. walk) elevating both into the realms of grand luxury. The natural environment surrounding this hotel has been fiercely protected, despite its close proximity 5km (3 miles) northwest of the center of Palma. Don't come here expecting raucous good times on the beach; the resort is elegant but rather staid and is better suited to an older, golf-playing crowd. There's no health club and no shuttle to the beach; many visitors drive to one of several nearby beaches. But it does boast one of the only hotel bullrings in Spain!

The complex is low-rise, intensely landscaped, and offers views over the lush green grounds (not of the sea) from many of its good-size rooms. Bedrooms and suites are fresh and white with dark wood furniture, wall-to-wall carpeting, bathrooms with tub/shower combos, and in all but the least expensive accommodations, a balcony or veranda.

De la Vinagrella s/n, E-07013 Palma de Majorca. (✆ **97-178-71-00.** Fax 97-178-72-00. www.arabellasheraton. com. 93 units. 320€–380€ ($368–$437) double; 471€–565€ ($542–$650) suite. Rates include breakfast. AE, DC, MC, V. Parking free outside or 15€ ($17) in garage. Bus: 7. **Amenities:** 2 restaurants; bar; outdoor pool; 18-hole golf course; tennis courts; fitness center; sauna; business center; salon; 24-hr. room service; babysitting; laundry service; dry cleaning. In room: A/C, TV, minibar, hair dryer, iron, safe.

Palacio Ca Sa Galesa ★★★ (Moments   This five-star boutique hotel is a delight and far more personal than the bigger chains. For generations this 15th-century town house languished as a decaying apartment building facing the side of the cathedral. But in 1993, an entrepreneurial couple from Cardiff, Wales, restored the place, salvaging the original marble floors and stained-glass windows, sheathing the walls of the public areas with silk, and adding modern amenities. Today, the setting is the most alluring in all of Palma, a labyrinthine space loaded with English and Spanish antiques and paintings. It also has a grand dining room available for private dinner parties, a cozy lounge with open fireplace adjoining a parlor where English teas are served in the afternoons, and a sunny roof terrace from which you can almost touch the cathedral. Honor bars are conveniently dotted about the place. The rooms themselves are sumptuous with antiques and Persian rugs, comfortable beds and high-quality linens. All have neat bathrooms with tub/shower combos. There's no restaurant, but a hearty Majorcan buffet is served each morning (for an extra charge).

Miramar 8, 07001 Palma de Majorca. (✆ **97-171-54-00.** Fax 97-172-15-79. www.palaciocasagalesa.com. 12 units. 292€ ($336) double; 349€–422€ ($401–$485) suite. AE, DC, MC, V. Parking 12€ ($14). 7km (4 miles) from airport. Call in advance for directions. **Amenities:** Lounge; sauna; plunge pool; limited room service (noon–10pm) w/free tea/coffee; massage; babysitting; laundry service; dry cleaning. *In room:* A/C, TV, mini-bar, hair dryer, safe.

EXPENSIVE

Meliá Palas Atenea 🐾   A member of the Sol Meliá chain, this modern hotel offers extensive leisure facilities for vacationers, while still catering to business travelers. It overlooks the Bay of Palma, within walking distance of the town's major restaurants and shops. Spacious guest rooms have terraces, many over-looking the harbor or Bellver Castle. Furnishings are standardized and somewhat characterless but the rooms are comfortable, ranging from medium-size to spa-cious. All are fitted with gleaming tile bathrooms equipped with tub/shower combos. An entire floor has been designed with business travelers' needs in mind.

Passeig Ingeniero Gabriel Roca 29, 07014 Palma de Majorca. ✆ **97-128-14-00.** Fax 97-145-19-89. www. solmelia.com. 361 units. 190€ ($219) double; from 210€ ($242) suite. AE, DC, MC, V. Parking 10€ ($12). Bus: 1. 8km (5 miles) from airport. **Amenities:** 2 restaurants; cafe; bar; nightclub; indoor pool; outdoor pool; Jacuzzi; sauna; business center; salon; 24-hr. room service; massage; laundry service; dry cleaning. *In room:* A/C, TV, minibar, hair dryer, coffeemaker, safe.

Palau Sa Font 🐾   Housed in a Majorca 16th-century palace successfully con-verted into a hotel, this funky boutique hotel is popular among a younger crowd; especially hip weekenders from London. Jellybean colors update the dis-tressed iron and island stone features giving it a pleasantly old-meets-new feel. The bedrooms have been fully modernized and have plump comforters, linen curtains, rustic iron furnishings, and plain, soothing walls. Bathrooms are shiny and new, with either a tub or shower. Breakfast is a good enough reason to stay; the hotel offers a bounteous feast of smoked salmon, Serrano ham, tortillas, and fresh fruits.

Apuntadores 38, 07017 Palma de Majorca. ✆ **97-171-22-77.** Fax 97-171-26-18. www.palausafont.com. 19 units. 140€–190€ ($161–$219) double; 205€ ($236) junior suite. Rates include buffet breakfast. AE, MC, V. Closed Jan. 8km (5 miles) from airport. **Amenities:** Breakfast lounge; bar; outdoor pool; babysitting; laundry service. *In room:* A/C, TV, minibar, hair dryer.

Hotel Portixol 🐾🐾🐾 *(Finds)*   Locations don't get much better than this achingly hip portside hotel. It has buckets of Scandinavian trim—big white airy bedrooms, most with fabulous sea views contrasted cleverly with cute features like zebra print rugs and the odd splash of Mediterranean color. But it's the added extras that make the difference: binoculars in all the rooms for, say, bird watching; bicycles to hire; spa treatments; top notch food; cocktails to rival any in New York; and the best swimming pool in town. The only danger at the Por-tixol is that you might never want to leave.

Sirena 27, 07006 Palma de Majorca. ✆ **97-127-18-00.** Fax 97-127-50-25. www.portixol.com. 24 units. 190€–350€ ($219–$403) doubles. Rates include breakfast. AE, MC, V. Bus: 15. **Amenities:** Restaurant; out-door pool; business center; salon; limited room service; massage; laundry service; dry cleaning. *In room:* A/C, TV, minibar, hair dryer, safe.

Hotel Tres 🐾🐾   A spectacular newcomer to Palma's burgeoning boutique hotel scene, the Hotel Tres is situated in two palaces dating back to 1576, and many of the original features have been preserved. Two roof terraces (connected by a bridge) offer an unusual space where guests can enjoy an infinity splash pool, sauna, and superb panoramic views of the city. Combining contemporary design with rustic charm, all 41 rooms and one suite are extremely comfortable with a tub or shower, fresh cotton sheets, and splashes of color in the form of plush sofas, throw cushions, and drapes. The suite has its own terrace and

Jacuzzi. The handsome patio, shaded by a magnificent palm, serves as a breakfast area and is open to the public for snacks, wine, and cocktails in the evening.

Apuntadores 3, 07012 Palma de Majorca. ℰ **97-171-73-33**. Fax 97-171-73-72. www.hoteltres.com. 42 units. 160€–195€ ($184–$224) double; 225€–325€ ($259–$374) suite. Rates include breakfast. AE, DC, MC, V. 8km (5 miles) from airport. **Amenities:** Wine and cocktail bar; splash pool; sauna. *In room:* A/C, TV/DVD, minibar, dataport, hair dryer, safe, CD player.

MODERATE

Hotel-Residencia Almudaina
Located on the main commercial street in Palma, this simple hotel offers comfortable, clean, basic rooms. Although small, the units are well maintained and have neatly kept bathrooms, most with tub/shower combos. Because of its location, many of the rooms can be noisy; the quietest are in the rear. Some have terraces and glass doors that let in ample sunlight.

Av. Jaume III no. 9, 07012 Palma de Majorca. ℰ **97-172-73-40**. Fax 97-172-25-99. 77 units. 95€–120€ ($109–$138) double. AE, DC, MC, V. Public parking nearby 20€ ($23). Bus: 13, 15, or 21. **Amenities:** Bar; limited room service; laundry service; dry cleaning. *In room:* A/C, TV, hair dryer, safe.

Hotel Saratoga ⋆
Under the arches of an arcade beside the old city's medieval moat stands the entrance to the Hotel Saratoga. Constructed in 1962 and renovated in 1992, the hotel features bright, well-furnished guest rooms, many with balconies or terraces with views of the bay and city of Palma. The typically midsize rooms have well maintained, tiled bathrooms, most with tub/shower combos.

Passeig Majorca 6, 07012 Palma de Majorca. ℰ **97-172-72-40**. Fax 97-172-73-12. www.hotelsaratoga.es. 187 units. 135€–150€ ($155–$173) double; 215€ ($247) suite. Rates include breakfast. AE, DC, MC, V. Parking 10€ ($12). Bus: 1, 3, 7, or 15. **Amenities:** Restaurant; bar; 2 pools (1 rooftop); spa; sauna; limited room service; babysitting; laundry service; dry cleaning. *In room:* A/C, TV, minibar, hair dryer, safe.

San Lorenzo ⋆⋆ *(Finds*
This pint-sized antique hotel has just six rooms and is set in the middle of the maze of winding streets that form the old city of Palma. The building is 17th century and the decor is a pleasant mixture of traditional Majorcan and modern. The rooms are airy, painted white, and have bathrooms that include tub/shower combos. All rooms have beamed ceilings and while some have only balconies, the more luxurious offer fireplaces and a private terrace. This hotel is perfect for relaxing after a day of sightseeing or shopping.

San Lorenzo 14, 07012 Palma de Majorca. ℰ **97-172-82-00**. Fax 97-171-19-01. www.hotelsanlorenzo.com. 6 units. 120€–170€ ($138–$196) double; 210€ ($242) suite. AE, DC, MC, V. 8km (5 miles) from airport. **Amenities:** Bar; outdoor pool; limited room service; babysitting; laundry service; dry cleaning. *In room:* A/C, TV, minibar, hair dryer, iron, safe.

INEXPENSIVE

Costa Azul *(Value*
Head here for a bargain—despite the reasonable rates, you'll get views of the yachts in the harbor. This place isn't glamorous, but it is a good value. A short taxi ride will deposit you at night on the Plaça Gomila in El Terreno with its after-dark diversions. Barren, well-worn rooms are clean, but modestly furnished, each with an en suite bathroom equipped with a tub/shower combo.

Passeig Marítim 7, 07014 Palma de Majorca. ℰ **97-173-19-40**. Fax 97-173-19-71. www.fehm.es/pmi/costa. 126 units. 88€ ($101) double. AE, DC, MC, V. Bus: 1 or 3. **Amenities:** Restaurant; bar; indoor pool; sauna; limited room service; babysitting; laundry service; dry cleaning. *In room:* A/C, TV, safe.

Hotel Born ⋆ *(Value*
If you want to be in the heart of the old city, and don't want to pay through the nose, there is no better bargain than this government-rated two-star hotel. A 16th-century palace, it once belonged to the Marquis of Ferrandell. It was vastly altered and extended during the 18th century with the addition

of a Majorcan courtyard shaded by a giant palm tree (this is where breakfast is served in the summer). It still retains much of its original architecture, such as Romanesque arches, though amenities have been modernized. Bedrooms are generally spacious and well equipped, with neatly tiled bathrooms with a shower. Off Plaça Rei Juan Carlos, the hotel opens onto a tranquil side street.

Sant Jaume 3, 07012 Palma de Majorca. (*) **97-171-29-42.** Fax 97-171-86-18. www.mallorcaonline.com/hotel/bornu.htm. 30 units. 93€ ($107) double; 114€ ($131) suite. Rates include breakfast. AE, DC, MC, V. **Amenities:** Bar; bike rentals. *In room:* A/C, TV.

Hotel Rosamar   Hotel Rosamar, right on the main road in the boomtown El Terreno district, is popular with Germans and Scandinavians. Fresh and clean small rooms have bathrooms with tub/shower combos and balconies overlooking a front patio surrounded by tall palm trees. It is peopled by a young, lively crowd that comes here to party.

Av. Joan Miró 74, 07015 Palma de Majorca. (*) **97-173-27-23.** Fax 97-128-38-28. www.rosamarpalma.com. 40 units. 58€ ($67) double; 70€ ($81) triple; 80€ ($92) suite. Rates include breakfast. AE, MC, V. Closed Nov–Feb. Bus: 3, 4, 21, or 22. **Amenities:** Bar; lounge.

AT ILLETAS

This suburb of Palma lies immediately west of the center.

Hotel Bonsol *(Kids)*   Set across from the beach, about 6.5km (4 miles) west of Palma, this government-rated four-star hotel was built in 1953 and has been well maintained ever since. It charges less than hotels with similar amenities, and the nearby beach makes it quite popular with vacationing families, who dine within the airy if spartan dining room. The core is a four-story, white-sided masonry tower, with some of the suites clustered into a simple collection of outlying villas. The hotel overlooks a garden adjacent to the sea. The midsize rooms are larger than you might expect, efficient but comfortable and well suited to beachside vacations.

Paseo de Illetas 30, 07181 Illetas. (*) **97-140-21-11.** Fax 97-140-25-59. www.mallorcaonline.com/hotel/bonsolu.htm. 147 units. From 98€ ($113) double. Rates include breakfast. AE, DC, MC, V. Free parking. Closed Nov 20–Jan 2. Bus: 108, 109, or 3. **Amenities:** 2 restaurants; lounge; outdoor pool; 2 tennis courts; fitness center; sauna; limited room service; babysitting; laundry service; dry cleaning. *In room:* A/C, TV, minibar, hair dryer, safe.

Hotel Meliá de Mar   Originally built in 1964, and still in excellent shape, the Meliá de Mar is one of the most comfortable (albeit expensive) hotels in Palma. This seven-story hotel is close to the beach and has a large, shady garden. The marble-floored lobby and light, summery furniture offer a cool refuge from the hot sun and a calm, deliberately uneventful setting that's evocative of some of the spa hotels of central Europe. Rooms, mainly midsize, have many fine features, including original art, terra-cotta-tiled balconies, marble or wrought-iron furnishings, excellent beds, and marble-clad bathrooms with deluxe toiletries, tub/shower combos, and dual basins.

Paseo Illetas 7, 07015 Palma de Majorca. (*) **97-140-25-11.** Fax 97-140-58-52. www.solmelia.com. 144 units. 257€ ($296) double; from 650€ ($748) suite. AE, DC, MC, V. Free parking. Closed Nov 1–Apr 15. Bus: 108, 109, or 3. **Amenities:** Restaurant; bar; heated outdoor pool; health spa; limited room service; massage; babysitting; laundry service; dry cleaning. *In room:* A/C, TV, minibar, hair dryer, safe.

AT PORTOCOLOM

This hotel is on the eastern coast, reached by going east from Palma along C-717, then cutting north at the signposted directions.

Hotel Villa Hermosa/Restaurant Vista Hermosa   This is one of the most creative government-rated five-star hotels on Majorca—a 1993 adaptation of a 19th-century farm. But it's not rustic; the building and outbuildings were recently reconstructed to take advantage of the soaring views available from the high-altitude hillside. Evocative of a severe, dignified monastery, this building is set on elaborate terraces cut into the rocky hillside. Rooms come in various shapes and sizes and each is exceedingly well furnished, with excellent beds and immaculately kept bathrooms with tub/shower combos.

Carretera Felanitx-Portocolom Km 6, PM 401, 07200 Felanitx. ℰ **97-182-49-60.** Fax 97-182-45-92. www. hotel-villahermosa.com. 10 units. 245€ ($282) double; 325€ ($374) suite. Rates include breakfast. AE, DC, MC, V. From Portocolom follow signs to direct road leading to Felanitx. **Amenities:** Restaurant; lounge; 2 outdoor tennis courts; 2 pools; health club; Jacuzzi; sauna; babysitting; laundry service. *In room:* A/C, TV, minibar, hair dryer, safe.

AT SANTA MARIA DEL CAMI

Read's Hotel ★★★ *Moments*   Peacefully located in beautiful countryside, this hotel is only 18km (11 miles) from Palma on the way to Inca Alcudia. The 16th-century Majorcan villa is now run by a British family and is a favorite spot for well-heeled northern Europeans and the occasional celebrity. The building has been lovingly renovated, original details intact, and furnished with a combination of good-quality reproduction furniture as well as genuine antiques. An unspoiled view of the Tramuntana Mountains forms the backdrop to the hotel, with well-manicured lawns rolling out to the surrounding fields. Beamed ceilings and wooden shutters add an authentic touch to the rooms, which have all been recently refurbished and painted in a variety of subtle Mediterranean colors. They are decorated with prints of classical architecture and Turkish rugs on traditional stone floors. There are various categories of rooms; the four deluxe doubles and 10 suites have French doors opening onto terraces with stunning views. The beds are all extremely comfortable, and the bathrooms are well stocked and contain tub/shower combos. Four reception rooms include an extraordinary blue room with *trompe l'oeil* clouds painted on the walls and what was previously the olive pressing room, the *tafona*, in which the original fittings have been preserved. The Michelin-starred restaurant is one of the island's best, with chef Marc Fosh serving up ingenious dishes that are both healthy and satisfying.

Ca'n Moragues, 07320 Santa María. ℰ **97-114-02-61.** Fax 97-114-07-62. www.readshotel.com. 23 units. 290€ ($334) double; 375€–540€ ($431–$621) suite. Rates include breakfast. AE, DC, MC, V. Free parking. Take Santa María exit off Inca/Alcudia motorway. In village turn left at Bodega Marcià Batle and then right at sign to hotel. **Amenities:** 2 restaurants; bar; indoor pool; outdoor pool; outdoor tennis court; health club; Jacuzzi; sauna; 24-hr. room service; babysitting; laundry service; dry cleaning. *In room:* A/C, TV, hair dryer, safe.

AT PUIGPUNENT

Gran Hotel Son Net ★★★   For those wanting to combine total relaxation and luxury, this is the perfect destination. This 17th-century manor house is next to a nature reserve and nestles in a lush mountain valley 15km (9 miles) from Palma. It was converted from a private residence in 1998 by David Stein, a California tycoon and art collector (who also owns the Gran Hotel La Florida in Barcelona). The result is one of Europe's finest hotels. Apart from the glorious setting, the hotel boasts works by artists such as Hockney, Stella, and Christoph, and there's even a small Chagall on the walls. A classical Majorcan aristocratic sense of decoration has been followed faithfully, with white walls, stone floors, and dark wood beams and shutters. The rooms are spacious, the largest being 250 sq. m (820 sq. ft.), and all have satellite television. The most idyllic rooms are the corner units on the top floor with southern exposure. The bathrooms are fully equipped with deep tubs, power showers, and glamorous novelties such as anti-steam mirrors. There are several reception rooms and an immense terrace with a seductive swimming pool of equally grandiose proportions. On Sunday, Mass is held in the hotel's private chapel.

Castillo Son Net s/n, 07194 Puigpunent. ℂ **97-114-70-00.** Fax 97-114-70-01. www.sonnet.es. 25 units. 230€–490€ ($265–$564) double; from 590€ ($679) suite. AE, DC, MC, V. Free parking. Take direct road from airport or Palma de Majorca to Puigpunent. **Amenities:** 2 restaurants; bar; outdoor pool; clay tennis court; health club; sauna; whirlpool; salon; limited room service; babysitting; laundry service; dry cleaning. *In room:* A/C, TV, minibar, hair dryer, safe.

AT LA BONANOVA
This magnificently situated hotel is directly west of Palma and south of the sprawling grounds of Castell de Bellver, the round hilltop castle crowning Palma.

Valparaíso Palace 🏚🏚 Only minutes from the center of Palma and 2km (1¼ miles) from a good beach, this is a seven-story luxury property that opened in 1976. The architecture is sleek and elegant with clean lines set among pretty landscaped gardens with an artificial lake. The lobby is impressive with its marble floors and pristine decor, and staff members are efficient and helpful. The rooms are spacious and handsomely furnished, all with fully equipped bathrooms with tub/shower combos.

Francisco Vidal Sureda 23, 07016 Palma de Majorca. ℂ **97-140-03-00.** Fax 97-140-59-04. www.grupotel. com. 174 units. 252€ ($290) double; 320€–950€ ($368–$1,093) suite. Rates include buffet breakfast. AE, DC, MC, V. Free parking. Bus: 6. **Amenities:** 2 restaurants; 2 bars; 3 outdoor pools (1 heated); artificial grass tennis court; minigolf; Jacuzzi; sauna; salon; limited room service; massage; babysitting; laundry service; dry cleaning. *In room:* A/C, TV, minibar, hair dryer, safe.

AT PALMANOVA
On the western coast, and west of Palma, this hotel enjoys a privileged position in Costa d'en Blanes. Count on a 10-minute drive from the center of Palma.

Hotel Punta Negra 🏚🏚 In an exclusive area, this two-story hotel is flanked by two golden sand beaches and numerous golf courses. Elegant and refined, it is classically Majorcan with Majorca white walls, antique furnishings, carpeted floors, and panoramic views of either the sea or pine forests. The hotel is only 1.5km (1 mile) from the yachting port of Puerto Portals. Spacious and beautifully furnished rooms are equipped with elegant bathrooms containing tub/shower combos.

Carretera Andaitz Km 12, Costa d'en Blanes, 07181 Majorca. ℂ **97-168-07-62.** Fax 97-168-39-19. www. h10.es. 137 units. 108€ ($124) double; 128€ ($147) suite. Rates include continental breakfast. AE, DC, MC, V. Free parking. Take exit 4 off direct road to Palma Nova/Portals Nous. **Amenities:** 2 restaurants; bar; 2 outdoor pools; indoor pool; 7 clay tennis courts; sauna; salon; limited room service; babysitting; laundry service; dry cleaning. *In room:* A/C, TV, minibar, hair dryer, safe.

AT BINISSALEM
Scott's Hotel 🏚🏚🏚 *(Finds* This is a handsomely restored 18th-century mansion lying in the little town of Binissalem in the center of Majorca and has gradually earned itself a reputation as one of the most memorable places to stay on the island. It's not for beach buffs, but if you have a car and want to get away from the hoards, you'll find this gem situated a short 20km (12½ miles) from Palma and a 20-minute drive to the beach. The beautifully furnished and rather elegant bedrooms come in a wide variety of sizes from singles to two full suites, with units "in between" consisting of king-size doubles, twins, queen-size doubles, or junior suites. Each comes with a well-kept bathroom with tub or shower. With its welcoming atmosphere, it really does feel like staying at a private home rather than at a hotel, and the owners are extremely accommodating when it

comes to doling out insider tips: As one visitor put it: Scott's is "aggressively not touristy." The antiques, handmade beds, Persian rugs, and flower filled terraces make a superb backdrop to this wonderfully tranquil, hospitable island retreat. A second branch of Scott's opened in Galilea on the southwest of the island in 2003.

Plaza de la Iglesia 12, 07350 Binissalem. (℡) **97-187-01-00.** Fax 97-187-02-67. www.scottshotel.com. 18 units. 175€–205€ ($201–$236) double; 235€–330€ ($270–$380) suite. AE, MC, V. Take exit to Binissalem off motorway to Inca and Port Alcudia, and head for church steeple. **Amenities:** Nearby restaurant; indoor pool; laundry service; nonsmoking rooms. *In room:* A/C, hair dryer.

WHERE TO DINE

The most typical main dish of Majorca is pork and it appears in a myriad of styles: cured, roasted, and made into sausages and meatballs, steaks, chops, and loins. The specialty in any restaurant offering typical Majorcan cuisine, *lomo con col,* is a typical dish where pork loin is wrapped in cabbage leaves, cooked in its own juices, and served with a sauce of tomatoes, grapes, pine nuts, and bay leaves.

The local sausage, *sabrosada,* is a soft, spreadable pork pâté mixed with paprika, giving it its characteristic bright red color. *Sopas mallorquinas* can mean almost anything, but usually involves mixed greens in a soup flavored with olive oil and thickened with bread. When *garbanzos* (chickpeas) and meat are added, it becomes a hearty meal in itself.

The best-known vegetable dish is *el tumbet,* a kind of cake with a layer of potato and another of lightly sautéed eggplant. Everything is covered with a tomato sauce and peppers, then boiled for a while. Eggplant, often served stuffed with meat or fish, is one of the island's vegetable mainstays. *Frito mallorquín* is essentially a peasant dish of fried onions and potatoes, mixed with red peppers, diced lamb liver, "lights" (lungs), and fennel. It's still hugely popular on the island and, like Scottish haggis, can be delicious in the right hands.

Majorcan wine is slowly gaining the recognition it deserves, and the region produces better quality wine each year. The red wine bottled around Binissalem tends to be the best and Macià Batle has won several awards for its rich, spicy reds. Most of the restaurants' wine, however, comes from Spain. *Café carajillo—* coffee with cognac—is another Spanish drink particularly enjoyed by Majorcans.

EXPENSIVE

Koldo Royo ✿✿✿ BASQUE This one Michelin star restaurant is a top spot to enjoy world-class New Basque Cuisine, which has recently enjoyed the spotlight in the international food pages. Staff members are attentive and helpful in deciphering the sometimes unusual dishes on the menu, including baked hake cheeks, tripe, and lamprey eel. This big-windowed establishment lies about a half-kilometer (¾ mile) south of Palma's cathedral, adjacent to a marina and one of the island's most popular beaches.

Av. Ingeniero Gabriel Roca 3, Paseo Marítimo. (℡) **97-173-24-35.** Reservations required. Main courses 16€–29€ ($18–$33); tasting menu 53€ ($61). AE, DC, MC, V. Tues–Sat 1:30–3:30pm and 8:30–11:15pm. Closed 2 weeks in Nov. Bus: 1.

Porto Pí ✿ MODERN MEDITERRANEAN This favorite of King Juan Carlos and other royals occupies an elegant 19th-century mansion above the yacht harbor at the west end of Palma. Contemporary paintings complement the decor, and there is an outdoor terrace. The food has a creative Mediterranean influence. Specialties change with the season but might include house-style fish *en papillote,* angelfish with shellfish sauce, and quail stuffed with foie gras cooked in a wine sauce. Game is a specialty in winter.

Finds **A Special Treat**

Dating from 1700, **Can Juan de S'aigo,** Carrer Sans 10 (© 97-171-07-59), is the oldest ice-cream parlor on the island. Correspondingly elegant and old world, it serves its homemade ice creams (try the almond), pastries, cakes, *ensaimadas* (light-textured and airy specialty cakes of Palma), fine coffee, and several kinds of hot chocolate amid marble-top tables, beautiful tile floors, and an indoor garden with a fountain.

Joan Miró 174. © **97-140-00-87.** Reservations required. Main courses 12€–25€ ($14–$29); fixed-price menu 50€–55€ ($58–$63); tasting menu 60€ ($69). AE, DC, MC, V. Mon–Fri 1–3:30pm; daily 7:30–11:30pm. Bus: Palma-Illetas.

Tristán ★★ NOUVELLE CUISINE   Several miles southwest of Palma, Tristán overlooks the marina of Port Portals and is one of the best restaurants in the Balearics, boasting a coveted two Michelin stars. This is very much a place to see and be seen, attracting well-heeled yachties and British B-list celebrities. Expect a refined, elegant menu of market fresh produce with dishes ranging from juicy pigeon in rice paper to simply cooked. Mediterranean vegetables, or the catch of the day, are usually prepared in Majorcan style.

Port Portals, Portals Nous. © **97-167-55-47.** Reservations required. Main courses 31€–43€ ($36–$49); fixed-price menu 94€ ($108); tasting menu 112€ ($129). AE, DC, MC, V. Daily 1–3:30pm and 8–11pm. Closed Oct 31–Mar 1. Bus: 22.

MODERATE

Arroseria Sa Cranca SEAFOOD   This sophisticated eatery specializes in rice dishes offering a huge diversity of flavors and styles from traditional Valencian paella (with rabbit and snails) to the Majorcan favorite of *arroz a banda* (a particularly succulent version with spider crabs, clams, and mussels) or *arroz negre* (black rice cooked in squid ink and served with a hearty dollop of aioli—garlic mayonnaise). Kick off with a platter of finger-lickin' grilled baby sardines or a well-seasoned version of *buñuelos de bacalau* (minced and herb-laden cod formed into rounded patties). Either of these might be followed with a *parrillada*—an array of grilled fish and shellfish—or any of the above-mentioned rice casseroles. Other variations include vegetables, roasted goat, or hake with tomatoes and garlic.

Passeig Marítim 13. © **97-173-74-47.** Reservations recommended. Main courses 9€–20€ ($10–$23); fixed-price menu 18€ ($21). AE, DC, MC, V. Tues–Sun 1–4pm; Tues–Sat 8pm–midnight. Closed Sept 1–20. Bus: 1.

Caballito del Mar (Little Seahorse) SEAFOOD   Although there are several outdoor tables, many guests prefer to dine inside because of the lively spirit of this popular place along the seafront. The decor is vaguely nautical, and service can be frenzied, but that's part of its charm. The food is well prepared from fresh ingredients; specialties include a Majorcan version of bouillabaisse, *zarzuela,* the ubiquitous assorted grilled fish (our favorite), briny oysters in season, red bream baked in salt, or sea bass with fennel.

Passeig de Sagrera 5. © **97-172-10-74.** Reservations recommended. Main courses 10€–26€ ($12–$30). AE, DC, MC, V. Tues–Sun 1–4pm and 8pm–midnight. Bus: 5.

INEXPENSIVE

Ca'an Carlos *Value* MAJORCAN   Something of a Palma institution, this old-school restaurant is set in two dining rooms of a much-renovated stone-sided house that's at least a century old. Owner and cook, Carlos turns out wonderfully authentic dishes with buckets of charm. The well-executed menu includes plenty of traditional fare including Majorca *sabrosada,* a soft pork sausage flavored with pepper and paprika; chicken or fish croquettes; stuffed squid; eggplant stuffed with pulverized shellfish; and a version of the Majorcan national dish, *cocida mallorquina,* a succulent stew.

De S'Aigua 5. ℂ **97-171-38-69.** Reservations recommended. Main courses 12€–21€ ($14–$24). AE, MC, V. Mon–Sat 1–4pm and 8–11pm. Closed 3 weeks in Aug. Bus: 3, 7, or 15.

La Bóveda ⭒ SPANISH   Located in the oldest part of Palma, just a few steps from the cathedral, this lively little bar is widely agreed to serve the best tapas in town. With just 14 tables set near the bar and a tiny basement, it gets crowded and raucous but the food is well worth the jostling. Choose from juicy roasted veal, pork, chicken, and fish, lip-smacking seafood, maple-sweet *jamón,* fava beans with strips of ham, spinach tortillas, grilled or deep-fried calamari, and shrimp with garlic sauce washed down with bottles of full-bodied red or more delicate white wines. Finish off with a refreshing, freshly made sorbet, garnished with a shot of vodka or bourbon.

Boteria 3. ℂ **97-171-48-63.** Reservations required for a table, not for the tapas bar. Main courses 7€–23€ ($8.05–$26); tapas selection 11€ ($13). AE, DC, MC, V. Mon–Sat 1–4pm and 8:30pm–12:30am. Closed Feb. Bus: 7 or 13.

Sa Caseta ⭒ *Finds* MAJORCAN   Those inclined towards something a little more gourmet will find tasty regional cooking in this old style hacienda with its warren of smartly decorated dining rooms. But it's the salt cod dishes that made it famous, offering at least 10 intriguingly different preparations. If you're traveling with friends, you might want to order some of the best suckling pig or roast baby lamb in Majorca. Perhaps it's not quite as tantalizing as the versions served in Old Castile, but it's a rewarding dish, especially when the weather is cool. On hotter days, you may prefer one of the local fish dishes, including (our favorite) monkfish in a shellfish sauce. Paella served with meaty salt cod and plump vegetables makes an unusual variation on this classic dish. *Sopas mallorquinas* (the island's famed vegetable soup) begin many a meal here. A series of homemade desserts, including ice cream, is a special feature.

Alférez Martínez Vaquer 1, Gènova. ℂ **97-140-42-81.** Reservations recommended. Main courses 15€–30€ ($17–$35); tasting menu 35€ ($40). AE, DC, MC, V. Daily 1pm–midnight. Bus: 4.

PALMA AFTER DARK

Majorca is packed with bars and dance clubs. Sure, there are some fun hangouts along the island's northern tier, but for a rocking, laser- and strobe-lit club, you'll have to hit Palma.

Set directly on the beach, close to a dense concentration of hotels, **Tito's,** Passeig Marítim (ℂ **97-173-00-17**), charges a cover of 15€ ($17), including the first drink. If you only visit one nightclub during your time on the island, this should be it; this club is the most popular, panoramic, and appealing disco on Majorca. A truly international crowd gathers here to mingle on a terrace overlooking the Mediterranean. Between June and September, it's open every night of the week from 11pm to at least 6am. The rest of the year, it's open only Thursday through Sunday, from 11pm to 6am.

Bar Barcelona, Carrer Apuntadores 5 (ℂ **97-171-35-57**), is a popular jazz club attracting a more grownup crowd that can enjoy live jazz, blues, and occasionally flamenco with a body of local aficionados. Open every night from 11pm to 3am, there is no cover charge, and drinks are reasonably priced, making this one of Palma's best value nights out.

B.C.M., Av. Olivera s/n, Magaluf (© **97-113-15-46**), is the busiest, most lighthearted, and most cosmopolitan disco in Majorca. Boasting high-tech strobe lights and lasers, this sprawling, three-story venue offers a different sound system on each floor, giving you a wide variety of musical styles. If you're young, eager to mingle, and like to dance, this place is for you. The cover charge of 12€ ($14) includes your first drink and entitles you to party till 4am.

Come and enjoy a Caribbean cocktail with one of Palma's more charismatic bar owners, Pasqual, who just might invite you to dance a bit of salsa at **Bodeguida del Medio,** Paseo el Mar, Cala Ratjada (no phone). The music is Latin inspired and the crowd is a mix of locals and visitors from almost everywhere. Try their delicious mojito cocktail, more potent than it tastes. The inside is rustic in tone; the outside is more intimate and romantic, with Chinese lanterns illuminating a garden that overlooks the sea.

ABACO ★★, Carrer Sant Joan 1 (© **97-171-59-11**), just might be the most opulently decorated nightclub in Spain—a cross between a harem and a czarist Russian church. The bar is decorated with a trove of European decorative arts. The place is always packed, with many customers congregating in a beautiful courtyard, which has exotic caged birds, fountains, more sculptures than the eye can absorb, extravagant bouquets, and hundreds of flickering candles. All this exoticism is enhanced by the lushly romantic music (Ravel's *Boléro,* at our last visit) piped in through the sound system. Whether you view this as a bar, a museum, or a sociological survey, be sure to go. The bar is open daily from 9pm to 2:30am, from February to December only. Wandering around is free; however, drinks cost a whopping 10€ ($12) to 15€ ($17).

At the end of the Andratx motorway, adjacent to the Cala Figuera turnoff, the **Casino de Majorca,** Urbanización Sol de Majorca s/n, Costa del Calviá (© **97-113-00-00**), is the place to go in search of lady luck. The cover charge is 4€ ($4.60); dinner with no drinks is 55€ ($63); the floor show without dinner but with two drinks is 40€ ($46). Children under 12 get discounts of 50%. If you bring your passport, you can indulge in American or French roulette, blackjack, or dice, or simply pull the lever on one of the many slot machines. A glittery cabaret show, styled in Monte Carlo fashion, is accessible through a separate entrance from the section of the casino devoted to gambling. It's presented every Tuesday through Saturday at 10:30pm. You might want to precede it with dinner, which is served from 8pm. The casino's gambling facilities are open Monday through Thursday from 6pm to 4am (Sun until 3am), and Friday and Saturday from 8pm to 5am.

Although Majorca is generally a permissive place, it doesn't have the gay scene that Ibiza does. Still, one of Palma's most noteworthy gay bars is **Baccus,** Carrer Lluis Fábregas 1 (© **97-145-77-89**), catering to both gays and lesbians. It is open nightly from 9pm to at least 3am, and often later. There is no cover, and beers begin at 3.50€ ($4). If you feel like dancing, the largest and most popular disco in Palma is the **Black Cat,** Av. Joan Miró 75 (no phone), which attracts a mixed crowd of young locals as well as visitors from Spain and the rest of the world. There are nightly shows at 3:30am. It is open daily from midnight to 6am but doesn't begin to get crowded until 2am. It is closed on Mondays during the winter. Admission is 7€ ($8.05).

2 Exploring Majorca by Car: The West Coast

Mountainous Majorca has the most dramatic scenery in the Balearics. It's best appreciated if you have your own car to explore it at will. Below is an outline of an enjoyable but long daytrip of about 142km (88 miles) that begins and ends in Palma. If you want a more relaxing trip, arrange to stay overnight in Deià (if you have a hefty budget) or Sóller (if your purse strings are tight).

Head west out of Palma on the C-719, passing through some of the most beautiful scenery in Majorca. Just a short distance from the sea the Sierra de Tramontana rises majestically from the plains. The road passes the heavy tourist development of Palma Nova before coming to **Santa Ponça,** a town with a fishing harbor divided by a promontory. A fortified Gothic tower and a watchtower are evidence of the days when this diminutive harbor suffered repeated raids and attacks. And it was in a cove here that Jaume I's troops landed on September 12, 1229, to begin the reconquest of the island from the Muslims.

From Santa Ponça, continue along the highway, passing Paguera, Cala Fornells, and Camp de Mar, all beautiful spots with sandy coves. Between Camp de Mar and Port D'Andratx are corniche roads, making for a twisting journey to **Port D'Andratx.** Summer vacationers mingle with fishers in this natural port, which is set against a backdrop of pines. It was once a haven for smugglers.

Leaving the port, continue northeast along C-719 to reach **Andratx** ✦, 5km (3 miles) away. Because of frequent raids by Turkish pirates, this town moved inland. Lying 31km (19 miles) west of Palma, Andratx is one of the loveliest towns on the island, surrounded by fortifications and boasting a Gothic parish church and the mansion of Son Mas.

After leaving Andratx, take the C-710 north, a winding road that runs parallel to the island's jagged northwestern coast. It's the highlight of the trip; most of the road is perched along the cliff edge and is shaded by pine trees, but keep your eyes on the road and stop at the **Mirador Ricardo Roca** for a panoramic view of a series of coves. These coves can only be reached from the sea.

The road continues to **Estallenchs,** a town of steep slopes surrounded by pine forests, olive and almond groves, and fruit orchards (especially apricot). Estallenchs sits at the foot of the Galatzo mountain peak. Stop and explore some of its steep, winding streets on foot. From the town, you can walk to the Cala de Estallenchs cove, where a spring cascades down the high cliffs.

The road winds on to **Bañalbufar,** 8km (5 miles) from Estallenchs and about 26km (16 miles) west from Palma—one of the most scenic spots on the island. Set 100m (328 ft.) above sea level, it seems to perch directly over the sea. **Mirador de Ses Animes** ✦, a belvedere constructed in the 17th century, offers a panoramic view of the coastline.

Many small excursions are possible from here. You might want to venture over to **Port d'es Canonge,** reached by a road branching out from the C-710 to the north of Bañalbufar. It has a beach, a simple restaurant, and a handful of fisherman's cottages. The same road takes you inland to **San Granja,** a mansion that was originally constructed by the Cistercians as a monastery in the 13th century.

Back on C-710, continue to **Valldemossa,** the town where the composer Frédéric Chopin and the French writer George Sand spent their now-famous winter. After a visit to the **Cartuja (Carthusian monastery),** where they lived, you can wander at leisure through the steep streets of the old town. The cloister of **Ses Murteres** provides a romantic garden, and there is a pharmacy where Chopin, who was ill a lot during that winter, spent much of his time. The **Carthusian Church** is from the late 18th and early 19th centuries. Goya's father-in-law, Bayeu, painted the frescoes of the dome.

Beyond Valldemossa, the road runs along cliffs some 395m (1,296 ft.) high until they reach **San Marroig,** the former residence of Archduke Lluis Salvador (see "Valldemossa & Deià [Deyá]," below), which is actually within the town limits of Deià. He erected a small neoclassical temple on a slope overlooking the sea to give visitors a panoramic vista. Son Marroig, his former mansion, has been turned into a museum. From an arcaded balcony, you can enjoy a view of the famous pierced rock, the Foradada, rising out of the water.

By now you have reached **Deià** 𝄞𝄞, where a series of small tile altars in the streets reproduces scenes from Calvary. This was the home for many years of the English writer Robert Graves. He is buried at the **Campo Santo,** the cemetery, which you may want to visit for its panoramic view, if nothing else. Many other foreign painters, writers, and musicians have found inspiration in Deià. For living and dining, this is the choice spot on Majorca, a virtual Garden of Eden and a second home for many a Hollywood star including Michael Douglas and Catherine Zeta-Jones.

Continue north along the highway and you'll come to **Lluch Alcari.** The Archduke Salvador considered it to be one of the most beautiful spots on earth, and Picasso holed up here for a short period during the 1950s. Like so many parts of the coast, it was easy prey for pirate raids and the ruins of several defense towers can still be seen.

C-710 continues to **Sóller,** just 10km (6 miles) from Deià. The urban center has five 16th-century facades, an 18th-century convent, and a parish church from the 16th and 17th centuries. It sprawls on a picturesque basin amid citrus and olive groves (known as the Valle de los Naranjos—Valley of the Oranges) where many painters, including Rusiñol, found inspiration.

Travel 5km (3 miles) north on the C-711 to reach the coast and **Port de Sóller,** one of the best of the natural shelters along the island. It lies at the back of a bay that forms an almost complete circle. Today it is home to a submarine base, as well as pleasure craft, and it has a lovely beach. The **Sanctuary of Santa Catalina** dominates one of the best views of the inlet. This is also a good place to break for lunch, with fish and paella restaurants galore.

If you can't make it that far and prefer to stop in high-priced Deià, **Restaurante Jaime,** Carrer Archiduque Lluis Salvador 24 (© **97-163-90-29**), attracts a healthy mix of locals and tourists. Unpretentious, family-run, and open since 1964, they offer a value menu of grilled meats and fish, and make superlative homemade desserts such as almond cake with almond ice cream. It is open Tuesday through Sunday from 1 to 4pm and 7:30 to 10:30pm.

After leaving the Sóller area, you have two choices: you can cut the tour in half and head back along C-711 to Palma with two stops along the way, or you can continue north, following the C-710 and local roads, to **Cape Formentor,** where still more spectacular scenery awaits you. Among the highlights of this coastal detour are **Fornalutx** 𝄞𝄞𝄞, a lofty mountain village with steep cobbled streets, Moorish-tiled roofs, and groves of almond trees; the splendid, hair-raising road to the harbor village of **Sa Calobra,** plunging to the sea one minute,

---

⌒Tips Take the Train

If you're not driving, you can still reach Sóller aboard a turn-of-the-20th-century narrow-gauge railroad train from Palma. It's a spectacularly scenic 3-hour ride. You can catch the train at the Palma Terminal on Calle Eusebio Estada, near Plaça d'Espanya. It runs five times a day from 8am to 8pm, and the fare is 4.80€ ($5.50) each way. Call © **97-175-20-51** for information.

then climbing arduously past olive groves, oaks, and jagged boulders; and the 13th-century **Monasterio de Lluch,** some 45km (28 miles) north of Palma, which is home to the Black Virgin of Lluch, the island's patron saint. The well-known "boys' choir of white voices" sings there daily at noon and again at twilight.

Those not taking the coastal detour can head south along the C-711, stop-ping at **Jardins d'Alfàbia,** Carretera Palma–Sóller Km 17 (© **97-161-31-23**), a former Muslim residence. This estate is in the foothills of the sierra, and visitors can access both the palace and romantic gardens. Richly planted, it is a glorious place to wander among the pergolas, a pavilion, and ponds. The palace has a decent collection of Majorcan furniture in contrast to the Arabic coffered ceil-ing. The gardens are open from June to August, Monday through Friday from 9:30am to 6:30pm, Saturday from 9:30am to 1pm; from September to May, Monday through Friday from 9:30am to 5:30pm, Saturday from 9:30am to 1pm. Admission is 4.50€ ($5.20).

From Alfàbia, the highway straightens, out and Palma is just 18km (11 miles) away. But before reaching the capital, consider a final stop at **Raixa,** another charming place, built on the site of an old Muslim hamlet. The present build-ing was once the estate of Cardinal Despuif and his family, who constructed it in the Italian style near the end of the 1700s, and the estate also boasts some Roman ruins. Rusiñol came here, and painted the place several times. It keeps the same hours as Jardins d'Alfàbia (see above).

After Raixa, the route leads directly to the northern outskirts of Palma.

3 Valldemossa & Deià (Deyá)

Valldemossa is the site of the **Cartoixa Reial** ☆, Plaça de las Cartujas s/n (© **97-161-21-06**), where George Sand and the tubercular Frédéric Chopin wintered in 1838 and 1839. The monastery was founded in the 14th century, but the present buildings are from the 17th and 18th centuries. After monks abandoned the dwelling, their cells were rented to guests, which accounts for the appearance of Sand and Chopin, who managed to shock the conservative locals with their unorthodox (unmarried) living arrangements. They occupied cells two and four. The only belongings that remain are a small painting and a French piano. The peasants burned most of it after the couple returned to the mainland, fearing they'd catch Chopin's tuberculosis. It may be visited Monday through Saturday from 9:30am to 6pm, Sunday from 10am to 1pm for 6€ ($6.90) adults, free for children under 10. Out of season, it shuts down an hour earlier.

It is also possible to visit the **Palau del Rei Sancho,** next door to the monastery, on the same ticket. This is a Moorish retreat built by one of the island kings. Tours are given by guides in traditional dress.

From Valldemossa, continue through the mountains following the signposts for 11km (6½ miles) to Deià. But before you approach the village, consider a stopover at **San Marroig** (© **97-163-91-58**), at Km 26. Now a museum, this was once the estate of Archduke Lluis Salvador. Born in 1847, he tired of court life in his early 20s and found refuge here with his young bride in 1870. Many of his personal furnishings and mementos, such as photographs and his ceramic collection, are still here, as is a turret that dates back to the 1500s. The estate is surrounded by lovely gardens, leading to the cliffs' edge and offering endless views of the blue horizon. Here, you can also glimpse Sa Foradada, a monolithic rock noted for its keyhole gap through the middle, rising from a nearby sea bed. The museum is open from April to October, Monday through Saturday from 9:30am to 2pm and 3 to 8pm (closing at 6pm in winter). Admission is 3€ ($3.45).

> **Moments** **Just Ask a Painter Where the Sun Sets Best**
>
> After walking through the old streets, stand on a rock overlooking the sea and watch the sun set over a field of silvery olive trees and orange and lemon groves. It won't take long to figure out why painters and artists were so enamored with the place.

Set against a backdrop of olive-green mountains, **Deià (Deyá)** is peaceful and serene, with its sandstone houses and creeping bougainvillea. It has long had a special meaning for artists. Robert Graves, the English poet and novelist (*I, Claudius* and *Claudius the God*), lived in Deià, and died here in 1985. He is buried in the local cemetery. These days the mountainside cluster of exclusive residences, pricey restaurants, and luxury hotels is very much a haunt of the rich and/or famous.

Valldemossa lacks basic services, including a tourist office, but it does have a bus service from Palma. **Darbus** (© 97-175-06-22) goes to Valldemossa five times daily for a one-way fare of 1.10€ ($1.25). Buses leave from the bar at Carrer Archiduque Lluis Salvador 1.

WHERE TO STAY

Deià offers some of the most tranquil and stunning retreats on Majorca—La Residencia and Es Molí—but it is possible to find somewhere cheaper if you head a bit out of town.

EXPENSIVE

Hotel Es Molí ★★   One of the most spectacular hotels on Majorca originated in the 1880s as a severely dignified manor house in the rocky highlands above Deià, home of the landowners who controlled access to the town's freshwater springs. Indeed, the hotel still has a private spring that now feeds the swimming pool. In 1966 two annexes were added turning it into a fabulous four-star hotel. Rooms are beautifully furnished and impeccably maintained, often with access to a private veranda overlooking the gardens or the faraway village. All units have neatly kept bathrooms with tub/shower combos. Hardy souls make it a point to hike for 30 minutes to the public beach at Deià Bay; but there is a shuttle bus that delivers the less energetic to the hotel's private beach, 6km (4 miles) away.

Carretera Valldemossa s/n, 07179 Deià. © **97-163-90-00.** Fax 97-163-93-33. www.esmoli.com. 87 units. 182€–242€ ($209–$278) double; 367€–400€ ($422–$460) suite. Rates include breakfast; half-board 18€ ($21) extra per person per day. AE, DC, MC, V. Free parking. Closed early Nov to early Apr. Take exit to Deià off direct road .5km (¾ mile) after going through Valldemossa. **Amenities:** Restaurant; bar; outdoor pool; outdoor tennis court; limited room service; babysitting; laundry service; dry cleaning. *In room:* A/C, TV, minibar, hair dryer, safe.

La Residencia ★★★   This is the most stylish, hip, elegant hotel on Majorca, which really came into its own during the early 1990s when it was acquired by British businessman and founder of Virgin Airlines Richard Branson. Since Branson took over, the hilltop property, affectionately dubbed "La Res," quickly became a celebrity haven, proclaiming itself "your revenge on everyday life." Guests have included everyone from Queen Sofía and the emperor of Japan to America's sweethearts and rock 'n' roll elite. It was taken over by Orient Express in 2002 but has retained its air of laid-back glamour. Surrounded by 5.3 hectares (13 acres) of rocky Mediterranean gardens, the hotel's two sprawling stone 16th-century mansions offer guests every conceivable luxury. Spacious rooms are outfitted with rustic antiques, terra-cotta floors, romantic four-poster beds, and in some cases, beamed ceilings, all with luxurious appointments, including bathrooms with tub/shower combos. Open hearths, deep leather sofas, wrought-iron candelabra, and a supremely accommodating staff make this hotel internationally famous. Several newly opened luxury suites even have private swimming pools. Although it's technically defined as a four-star resort and a member of Relais & Châteaux, only Spanish technicalities prevent it from reaching deserved government-rated five-star status.

San Canals s/n, 07179 Deià. ℂ **97-163-90-11.** Fax 97-163-93-70. www.hotel-laresidencia.com. 63 units. 440€–575€ ($506–$661) double; from 710€ ($817) suite. Rates include breakfast. AE, DC, MC, V. Free parking. Take direct road to Deià turning off after Valldemossa. **Amenities:** 3 restaurants; 3 bars; 2 indoor pools; 1 outdoor pool; 2 lit composition tennis courts; fitness center; sauna; spa; limited room service; babysitting; laundry service; dry cleaning. *In room:* A/C, TV, hair dryer, safe.

INEXPENSIVE

Hotel Costa d'Or ✦ 〈Value〉 This good-value former villa, 1.5km (1 mile) north of Deià on the road to Sóller, offers beautiful views of the vine-covered hills and the rugged coast beyond. Surrounded by lush gardens filled with fig trees, date palms, and orange groves, this old-fashioned hotel is furnished with odds-and-ends furniture. Although rooms by the pool can get a little noisy, all rooms are clean and comfortable. Most are simple but have decent views, and all come with good beds and neat bathrooms, most of which are equipped with tub/shower combos.

Lluch Alcari s/n, 07179 Deià. ℂ **97-163-90-25.** Fax 97-163-93-47. www.hoposa.es. 41 units. 179€ ($206) double; 259€ ($297) suite. Rates include breakfast. DC, MC, V. Closed Nov–Mar 21. Take direct road to Deià turning off after Valldemossa. **Amenities:** Restaurant; health club; tennis court; outdoor pool; limited room service; laundry service; dry cleaning. *In room:* A/C; TV, hair dryer, minibar; safe.

WHERE TO DINE

Ca'n Quet ✦ INTERNATIONAL If you fancy something a little more gourmet, this restaurant is part of the Hotel Es Molí (see above), and is one of the most sought-after dining spots on the island. Set on a series of terraces above a winding road leading out of town, and festooned with pink geraniums, this is a delightful spot for a romantic lunch or dinner. Wander along the sloping pathways, and you'll find scented groves of citrus trees, roses, and a swimming pool ringed with neoclassical balustrades. In summer, you can sit at the sunny bar or shady terrace and, in winter, relax by the blazing fire in the elegant dining room. The food is meticulously prepared and makes good use of local produce: spanking fresh marinated fish ceviches, flavorful vegetable terrines, sumptuous seafood stews, tender duck with sherry sauce, and an ever-changing catch-of-the-day.

Carretera Valldemossa–Sóller. ℂ **97-163-91-96.** Reservations required. Main courses 18€–22€ ($21–$25); tasting menu 40€ ($46). AE, DC, MC, V. Tues–Sun 1–4pm and 8–11pm. Closed Nov–Mar. Bus: Sóller line from Palma de Majorca.

El Olivo ✦✦ 〈Moments〉 INTERNATIONAL/MEDITERRANEAN The best of the bunch, La Residencia's upscale restaurant regularly counts kings, queens, and A-listers among the diners who come to enjoy its superlative Mediterranean cooking, candlelit decor, and occasional live classical music. If you're not staying at the hotel, the 30- to 40-minute drive north of Palma is well worth it for a really special evening. Offering regularly changing seasonal dishes to surprise and delight the senses, El Olivo is a must for traveling gourmands. Expect subtle, creative cuisine that excites the palette but goes easy on the stomach. The tasting menu is well worth the money to sample such joy-inducing dishes as foie gras soup infused with calvados, lightly roasted red mullet with baby spring veg-etables, tender pink rack of lamb delicately scented with herb and tomato sauce, and prawns with pork belly confit.

In La Residencia Hotel, San Canals. (C) **97-163-93-92.** Reservations recommended. Main courses 30€–57€ ($35–$66); fixed-price menu 75€ ($86). AE, DC, MC, V. Daily 1–3pm and 8–11pm.

4 Inca

About 27km (17 miles) north of Palma lies Inca, the island's second-largest city and Majorca's market and agricultural center.

Thursday is market day for farming equipment and livestock, but visitors will be more interested in the variety of low-priced leather goods—shoes, purses, jackets, and coats—sold here. In general, stores in Inca selling these leather goods are open Monday through Friday from 9:30am to 7pm, and Saturday from 9:30am to noon. The cult Majorcan shoemaker, **Camper,** has a factory outlet on the outskirts of town, which makes a visit to Inca worth it just to pick up a bargain or two.

Modernization has deprived Inca of its original charm, but the parish church of Santa María la Mayor and the convent of San Jerónimo hold some interest, as does the original Son Fuster Inn, a reminder of an earlier, simpler era. The only other thing the town is notable for, is its "cellar" restaurants; cavernous din-ing rooms located in old wine cellars.

From Palma, **trains** ((C) **97-150-00-59**) run Monday through Friday at the rate of 40 per day and 34 on Saturday and Sunday. Trip time is only 40 min-utes. A round-trip ticket costs 3.25€ ($3.75).

Inca lies on C-713, the road leading to the Pollença–Formentor region.

WHERE TO DINE

Cellar Ca'n Amer *(Finds* MAJORCAN   This is probably Inca's most famous restaurant, housed in one of the town's old fashioned bodegas dating back to the 1850s. Barrels of country wine line the vaults' stone walls, waiting to be decanted into diners' carafes. Rustic and sometimes a bit rough, it nevertheless manages the old-fashioned and sometimes heavy local cooking very well (unless you order a la carte). *Lechona frit* (a mélange of minced pork offal fried and sea-soned), bread and vegetable soup, Majorcan cod, quail cooked in honey, and the chef's version of roast suckling pig with a bitter but tasty sauce are just some of the Majorcan specialties dished out in large portions. There's also a decent selec-tion of fresh seafood and fish.

Carrer Pau 39. (C) **97-150-12-61.** Main courses 15€–25€ ($17–$29). AE, MC, V. Mon–Sat 1–4:30pm and 7pm–midnight.

5 Port de Pollença & Formentor

Beside a sheltered bay and between Cape Formentor to the north and Cape del Pinar to the south lies the pretty **Port de Pollença,** flanked by two hills: **Cal-vary** to the west and **Puig** to the east. From the town, the best views of the resort and the bay are from Calvary Chapel. The bay is a haven for water sports, par-ticularly windsurfing, water-skiing, scuba diving, and sailing. It's located 65km (40 miles) north of Palma.

A series of low-rise hotels, private homes, restaurants, and snack bars lines the attractive beach, which is somewhat narrow at its northwestern end but has some of the island's finest, whitest sand and warmest, clearest water. The sand at the southeastern end of Pollença Bay was imported to create a broad ribbon of sunbathing space that stretches for several miles along the bay. Wrapping around its entirety is a pleasant pedestrian promenade as well as a hiking trail inland along the **Vall de Boquer** (6kms/3¾ miles). There is only one luxury hotel in the area, the Hotel Formentor (see below), out on the Formentor Peninsula.

Cabo de Formentor ✪, "the devil's tail," can be reached from Port de Pollença via a spectacular road, twisting along to the lighthouse at the cape's end. Formentor is Majorca's fjord country—a dramatic landscape of mountains, pine trees, rock, and sea, plus some of the best beaches in Majorca—studded with *miradores,* convenient cliff-top terraces providing panoramic views of the area.

ESSENTIALS

GETTING THERE **Autocares,** at Villalonga (✆ **97-153-00-57,** www.auto caresmallorca.com), has five daily **buses** leaving the Plaça Espanya in Palma, passing through Inca, and continuing on to Port de Pollença. Fares are 4.45€ ($5.10) one-way. You can continue on from Deià (see above) along C-710, or from Inca on C-713, all the way to Pollença.

VISITOR INFORMATION The **tourist information office** (✆ **97-189-26-15**), on Carretera de Artá, is open from May to October, Monday through Saturday from 9am to 7pm. It's closed off season. From November to March, another office can answer telephone queries (✆ **97-154-72-57**). Hours are Monday through Saturday from 9:30am to 8pm.

EXPLORING THE COAST

The plunging cliffs and rocky coves of Majorca's northwestern coast are a stunning prelude to Port de Pollença. The **Mirador de Colomer** provides an expansive view of the striking California-like coast that stretches from Punta de la Nau to Punta de la Troneta and includes El Colomer (Pigeon's Rock), named for the nests in its cave.

But it is the 20km (12½-mile) stretch of winding, at times vertiginous, road leading from Port de Pollença to the tip of the **Formentor Peninsula** that delivers the island's most intoxicating scenic views. Soaring cliffs more than 197m (646 ft.) high and spectacular rock-rimmed coves embrace intense turquoise waters. About halfway along this road is the **Cala de Pi de la Posada,** where you will find a lovely bathing beach. Continuing on to the end, you'll come to the lighthouse at **Cabo de Formentor.**

Market days are on Sunday (in Pollença) and Wednesday in Port de Pollença. Head for the main town square between 8am to 1pm to browse for farm fresh produce, local wines and olive oils, leather goods, embroidered tablecloths, ceramics, and olive wood bowls, plates, and salad servers. **Alcúdia Bay** is a long stretch of narrow, sandy beach with beautiful water backed by countless hotels, whose crowds rather overwhelm the area in peak season. The walled old town is charming for an amble, though there's not a great deal to see. Should you chose to stay in the area, the surrounding resorts offer the kind of brash beachside nightlife characteristic of heavily touristy destinations and atypical of the majority of the country.

Between Port de Alcúdia and Ca'n Picafort is the lovely **Parc Natural de S'Albufera** ✪, Carretera Alcúdia–Artá Km 27, 07458 Ca'n Picafort (✆ **97-189-22-50;** www.Majorcaweb.net/salbufera). A pristine wetlands area of lagoons, dunes, and canals covering some 800 hectares (1,976 acres), this attracts bird-watchers and other nature enthusiasts. To date, more than 200 species of birds have been sighted here, among them herons, owls, ospreys, and warblers. The best times to visit are in spring and fall, when migratory birds abound and endemic flower and grasses are in full bloom. The park is open daily (except Christmas) from October 1 to March 30 from 9am to 5pm, and from April 1 to September 30 from 9am to 7pm. Visits are free, but you must get a permit at the reception center, where you can also pick up maps, information about the flora and fauna that surrounds you, and rent binoculars. All motorized vehicles must be left at the park entrance.

For cultural sights, the pretty town of Pollença, about 6km (4 miles) from Port Pollença, has a number of places of interest for visitors, including a Roman stone bridge and an 18th-century stairway leading up to an *ermita* (hermitage). It's a grueling climb up 365 steep, stone stairs, known locally as the **Monte Calvario (Calvary),** but you can also reach the top by car via Carrer de las Cruces, which is lined with 3m (10 ft.) high concrete crosses.

Cala San Vicente, between Pollença and Port de Pollença, is a pleasant, small sandy cove with some notable surf, which is dotted with several suitable small hotels and restaurants.

Various companies offer tours of Pollença Bay, and many provide glass-bottomed boats for viewing the varied aquatic creatures and plants. Many of these boats leave from Port de Pollença's Estació Marítim several times daily during the summer months, with less frequent departures in winter. Your hotel concierge or the marina can provide you with a schedule.

Part of the allure of a trip to the Balearics is boating in the Mediterranean; if you're in the market to rent either a small sailing craft or a glamorous yacht that comes with a full complement of staff and crew, Associación Provinciale d'Empresarios de Actividades Marítimas de Baleares, Muelle Viejo 6, in Palma (© 97-172-79-86), can steer you in the right direction. Chances are they'll direct you to one of two well-respected maritime charter companies, both based in Palma. These are **Moorings Formentor,** Contramuelle 12 (© 97-121-42-31), and **Alga Charter,** Contramuelle Mollet s/n (© 97-171-64-28). Both lease boats of different sizes by the day, week, or month.

For parasailing, head for **Deportes Náuticos,** Carrer Estornell 2, Sonferrer/Calvia (© 97-123-03-28), which is about 15km (9 miles) southeast of Palma.

WHERE TO STAY

Hotel Illa d'Or ⚘ Originally built in 1929, and enlarged and improved several times since then, this handsome four-star hotel sits at the relatively isolated northwestern edge of Pollença Bay—far from the heavily congested, touristy region around the port. Decorated in a mixture of colonial Spanish and English reproductions, it has a seafront terrace that juts out over the gently lapping waves with a view of the mountains behind and airy, simply furnished rooms. Rooms are midsize to spacious, each with comfortable furnishings, including good beds and bathrooms with tub/shower combos. The beach is just a few steps away.

Passeig Colón 265, 07470 Port de Pollença. (© **97-186-51-00.** Fax 97-186-42-13. www.hoposa.es. 119 units. 154€–197€ ($177–$227) double; 315€–435€ ($362–$500) suite. Rates include breakfast. AE, DC, MC, V. Free parking. Closed Nov–Feb. Take direct road to Inca/Pollença. **Amenities:** Restaurant; 2 bars; 2 outdoor pools; tennis court; fitness center; Jacuzzi; sauna; bike rental; business center; limited room service; massage service; laundry service; dry cleaning. *In room:* A/C, TV, minibar, hair dryer, safe.

Hotel Miramar *Value* This centrally located hotel was the first hotel to be built on the beach here and retains an old-fashioned charm with its ornately carved columns supporting a formal balustrade, tiled eaves, and several gardens. The lobby is furnished with antiques and filled with photos from its golden age. All the small to midsize rooms are comfortably furnished and well maintained, each with a firm bed and a bathroom equipped with a tub/shower combo. The best rooms have private verandas overlooking the flower-filled courtyard in back.

Passeig Anglada Camarasa 39, 07470 Port de Pollença. ☏ **97-186-64-00.** Fax 97-186-40-75. 84 units. 75€–132€ ($86–$152) double. Rates include breakfast. AE, DC, MC, V. Closed Nov to Easter week. Take direct road to Inca/Pollença. **Amenities:** Restaurant; lounge; limited room service; babysitting; laundry service; dry cleaning. *In room:* A/C, TV, hair dryer, safe.

Hotel Pollentia ⭐   This hotel is .8km (½ mile) from the commercial center of the resort, tucked away behind a screen of verdant foliage. Cool and spacious with a genial staff, the formal lobby is overflowing with plants and glittering Majorcan glass chandeliers. Many of the small but comfortable rooms have private terraces—a major bonus—and all have bathrooms with tub/shower combos. Guests also have access to a private terrace overlooking the Mediterranean. The hotel is booked only through Thomson Tours or by e-mailing the hotel directly.

Passeig de Londres s/n, 07470 Port de Pollença. ☏ **97-186-52-00.** Fax 97-186-60-34. www.thomson.co.uk. huyal-pollentia@hoposa.es. 70 units. 60€–70€ ($69–$80) double. Rates include breakfast. AE, DC, MC, V. Closed Nov–Apr. **Amenities:** Bar; lounge; bike rental; laundry service; dry cleaning. *In room:* Hair dryer, safe.

Hotel Formentor ⭐⭐   This historic property dates back to 1231, but it didn't become a hotel until 1929. Since its inception, it's seen a string of high-powered politicos and spiritual leaders, including Winston Churchill and the Dalai Lama, as well as various literary luminaries and screen goddesses like Liz Taylor. There is virtually nothing this hotel, an old school five-star, doesn't have, from plush rooms filled with every imaginable comfort, antiques, and heavily brocaded fabrics, to amenities like a cinema, hairdresser, and boutique shopping. Marble bathrooms come with a shower and/or tub and abundant toiletries, and the sprawling grounds run right down to the beach.

Platja de Formentor s/n, 07470 Port de Pollença. ☏ **97-189-91-00.** Fax 97-186-51-55. www.hotelformentor. net. 274€–410€ ($315–$472) double; 450€–694€ ($518–$798) suite. AE, DC, MC, V. **Amenities:** 2 restaurants; outdoor pool; minigolf nearby; 5 tennis courts (2 lit); sauna; car-rental desk. *In room:* A/C, TV/DVD, minibar, hair dryer, safe.

WHERE TO DINE

Restaurant Clivia ⭐ MAJORCAN/SPANISH   This is one of the most appealing restaurants in Pollença, attracting clientele from all over the island. It comprises two antique filled dining rooms built around an outdoor patio in a century-old house in the heart of town. The menu is short, sharp, and well executed and offers mouthwatering veal, chicken, and pork dishes along with a more wide-ranging roster of seafood. The salt cod, monkfish, dorado, eel, squid, and whitefish, either baked in a salt crust or prepared as part of a succulent *parrillada* (platter) of shellfish, are all unbeatable. The restaurant, incidentally, takes its name from the bright red flowers *(las clivias)* that are planted profusely beside the patio and that bloom throughout the summer.

Av. Pollentia 4760. ☏ **97-153-46-16.** Reservations recommended. Main courses 12€–21€ ($14–$24). AE, DC, MC, V. May–Oct Tues and Thurs–Sun 1–3pm and 7–11pm, Mon and Wed 7–11pm; Nov 1–14 and Dec 16–Apr Thurs–Tues 1–3pm and 7–11pm. Closed Nov 15–Dec 20.

---

6 Majorca's East Coast: The *Cava* Route

In general, the East Coast of Majorca does not have the dramatic scenery of the West Coast and the endless white-concrete resort towns that have gobbled up much of the middle of this stretch of coast are rather dreary. The north and south tips of the coast, however, have some pleasant seaside towns, and the region does have some gems; namely the Majorca intricate network of caves that bore into its coastline.

Leave Palma on the freeway but turn onto Carretera C-715 in the direction of Manacor. About 56km (35 miles) east of Palma, you'll come to your first stop, Petra.

PETRA

Petra was founded by Jaume II over the ruins of a Roman settlement. It was the birthplace of Father Junípero Serra (1713–84), the Franciscan priest who founded the missions in California that eventually evolved to become San Diego, Monterey, and San Francisco. A statue commemorates him at the Capitol building in Washington, D.C., and its twin can be seen here, in his native village.

Museo Beato Junípero Serra, Carrer Barracar s/n (ℂ **97-156-11-49**), reflects life on the island during the 18th and 19th centuries, and was presented as a gift to the citizens of Petra in 1972 by the San Francisco Rotary Club. The museum, 457m (1,499 ft.) from the center of the village, is open every day of the year but doesn't keep regular hours. Visits are by appointment only. Admission is free, but donations are encouraged.

MANACOR

The C-715 continues east to Manacor, the town where the famous artificial pearls of Majorca are manufactured. Avoid such knock-offs as "Majorca," faux-pearl jewelry (made to resemble the sheen of real pearls using fish scales). The official manufacturer is "Perlas Majorica," (ℂ **97-155-09-00**) and these pearls can be purchased here at 5% to 10% cheaper than at most retail outlets in Barcelona. It's located at Pedro Riche s/n, conveniently situated on the road to Palma at the edge of town, and offers guided tours of its premises. Watching the 300 or so artisans shaping and polishing the pearls can be fascinating, and it's worth a stop if jewelry making interests you. It is open Monday through Friday from 1pm to 7pm, and on Saturday and Sunday from 9:45am to 1pm. Admission is free. Perlas Majorica products carry a 10-year guarantee.

CUEVAS DEL DRACH ✦✦✦

From Manacor, take the road southeast to the sea—about 12km (7½ miles)—to the town of **Porto Cristo,** 61km (38 miles) east of Palma. Go .8km (½ mile) south of town to **Cuevas del Drach (Caves of the Dragon)** ✦✦✦ (ℂ **97-182-07-53**), which boast a fairy-tale underground forest of stalactites and stalagmites as well as five subterranean lakes, with cheesy piped music as well as the occasional concert. Regardless, boating here is a magical experience and arguably one of Majorca's top outings. Martel Lake, 176m (578 ft.) long, is the largest underground lake in the world. E. A. Martel, a French speleologist who charted the then mysterious caves in 1896, described the area better than anyone: "As far as the eye can see, marble cascades, organ pipes, lace draperies, pendants or brilliants, hang suspended from the walls and roof." From mid March to October tours depart daily, every hour from 10am to 5pm (Nov–Mar 10:45am, noon, 2, and 3:30pm). Admission is 7.50€ ($8.60).

Four daily buses leave the railroad station in Palma. Inquire at the tourist bureau in Palma for times of departure (p. 249). Buses stop in Manacor on the way to Porto Cristo if you want to organize a combined trip.

CUEVAS DE ARTÁ ★★★

Near Platja de Canyamel (Playa de Cañamel on some maps), the **Cuevas de Artá** (② **97-184-12-93**) burrow into the northernmost tip of Canyamel Bay to the north and are said to be the inspiration for Jules Verne's novel, *Journey to the Center of the Earth,* published in 1864. (Verne may have heard or read about the caves; it is not known if he ever actually visited them.) They are undeniably impressive, carved out of the soft limestone by the pounding sea over millennia, and situated about 32m (105 ft.) above sea level. Some of the cathedral-esque caverns have domes more than 46m (151 ft.) from the floor.

You enter an impressive vestibule into smooth stone corridors eerily blackened by the torches carried by tourists in the 1800s. From here, things get increasingly theatrical with the dramatically lit Reina de las Columnas (Queen of the Columns), a stalactite rising about 22m (72 ft.) tall, pointing the way to a lower cavern named after Dante's "Inferno" for its hellish appearance. Beyond this the "purgatory rooms"—fields of stalagmites and stalactites—eventually lead to a functioning "theater" and on into "paradise."

These caves once provided a safe house for pirates' loot, and centuries ago provided a haven for Spanish Moors fleeing the persecution of Jaume I. The stairs that lead up to the cave's entrance were built in honor of Isabella II for her visit in 1860. The caves have received numerous important visitors since then, including Alexandre Dumas, Victor Hugo, and Sarah Bernhardt. Tours depart daily, every half-hour from 10am to 6pm May through June, daily from 10am to 7pm July through September, and daily from 10am to 5pm off season. Admission is 8€ ($9.20).

WHERE TO STAY

Hotel Restaurante S'Abeurador ★★ *(Finds* Basic but oozing with character, this charming town house built around rambling garden terraces, a small patio, and a goldfish pond has individually decorated rooms with a Moorish bent, including one inside a converted chapel. It's a great spot for getting off the beaten track a little and recuperating. All bedrooms have en suite bathrooms with a shower or tub.

Calle Abeurador 21. ② **97-183-52-30.** Fax 97-186-60-34. 70€ ($81) double. Rates include breakfast. AE, DC, MC, V. Closed Dec–Mar. **Amenities:** Restaurant. *In room:* A/C.

11

Bilbao

The **Basque** people are the oldest traceable ethnic group in Europe. Their language, Euskera, predates any of the Romance languages; its origins, like that of the Basque race itself, are lost in obscurity. One theory is that the Basques descended from the original Iberians, who lived in Spain before the arrival of the Celts some 3,500 years ago. Conqueror after conqueror, Roman to Visigoth to Moor, may have driven these people into the Pyrénées, where they stayed and carved out a life for themselves—filled with tradition and customs practiced to this day.

The region is called Euskadi, which in Basque means "collection of Basques." In a narrow sense it refers to three provinces of Spain: Guipúzcoa (whose capital, **San Sebastián,** is the #1 sightseeing destination in Euskadi and features La Concha, one of Spain's best-loved stretches of sand); Viscaya (whose capital is **Bilbao**); and Alava (whose capital is **Vitoria**). But to Basque nationalists who dream of forging a new nation, Euskadi also refers to the northern part of Navarra and three provinces in France, including the famed resort of Biarritz.

The three Spanish Basque provinces occupy the eastern part of the Cantabrian Mountains, between the Pyrénées and the valley of the Nervión. They maintained a large degree of independence until the 19th century, when they finally gave in to control from Castile, which continued to recognize their ancient rights and privileges until 1876.

Geographically, the Basque country straddles the western foothills of the Pyrénées, so the Basque people live in both France and Spain—but mostly in the latter. During the Spanish Civil War (1936–39), the Basques were on the Republican side defeated by Franco. Oppression during the Franco years has led to deep-seated resentment against the policies of Madrid. The Basque separatist movement, ETA (Euskadi ta Askatasuna, or "Freedom for the Basque Country") and the French organization Enbata (Ocean Wind) engaged unsuccessfully in guerrilla activity in 1968 to secure a united Basque state.

Many Basque nationalists still wish that the Basque people could be united into one state instead of being divided between France and Spain.

The riddle of the Basque language has puzzled linguists and ethnologists for years; its grammar, syntax, and vocabulary are unrelated to those of any other European language. The language is known as **Euskera.** Although on the wane in the 20th century, the Basque language is now enjoying a renaissance; it's widely taught in schools, and autonomous TV and radio stations in the region broadcast in the language.

Many older Basques still wear a *boina* (Spanish for beret; *txapela* in Euskera) of red, blue, black, or white woolen cloth as a badge of pride and as a political statement. You are likely to see photos of political prisoners as you travel and nationalist graffiti painted everywhere. Although the separatist issue is still a hot one, you'll find most of the people friendly, hospitable, and welcoming. Politics rarely intrudes on vacationers in this beautiful corner of Spain.

1 Bilbao ★★

396km (246 miles) N of Madrid, 100km (62 miles) W of San Sebastián

Bilbao (**Bilbo** in Euskera) is Spain's sixth-largest city and biggest and busiest port. Once accurately described as an "ugly, gray, decaying, smokestack city," the city is fast becoming one of the must-see destinations in Spain. Taking a leaf out of Barcelona's book, and with Frank Gehry's spectacular **Guggenheim Museum** as the catalyst, Bilbao is undergoing some radical urban changes; its old quarter getting cleaned up, and daring new architecture rising along the Nervión River (in reality an estuary) where decaying warehouses and factories once stood. The overriding feeling of the city is one of optimism, and visitors who have previously visited say Barcelona or Madrid will notice a less jaded and more eager-to-please attitude to tourists. Like the rest of the Basque Country, Bilbao is also renowned for its cuisine and conveniently serves as a rail and bus hub for exploring some of the best attractions located in its vicinity.

Bilbao is the industrial hub of the north and the political capital for the Basques. Shipping, shipbuilding, and steel have made it prosperous, so there's no shortage of bankers or industrialists. BBVA, one of the biggest banks in Spain, was founded by Bilbao's merchant classes in the mid-1800s to finance the bustling trading industry. After surviving a devastating flood in 1983, which covered much of the city in water, Bilbao is now bursting with cranes and humming with activity. Among cities of the Basque region, it has the highest population (around 450,000); the metropolitan area, including the suburbs and many surrounding towns, is home to over a million inhabitants.

Bilbao has a wide-open feeling, extending more than 8km (5 miles) across the valley of the Nervión River, one of Spain's most polluted waterways. Because of its commercial and industrial character (and its historical connections to British industrialists) Bilbaínos often compare their city to post-industrial towns of Northern Britain. However, the extravagant Guggenheim Museum is cast as a symbol of Basque economic revival, and has undoubtedly led to a revitalization of their city. Bilbao was badly hit by the 1970s economic crisis, resulting in a closure of shipyards and steelworks. It has benefited greatly from a $1.5-billion grant, of which the Guggenheim project is one of the main beneficiaries. Signs of revitalization are also seen in a flashy new Metro system and a spectacular new airport terminal, the work of Spanish architect Santiago Calatrava.

Most of the city's sights can be viewed in a day or two. Many visitors flock here to see the $100-million Guggenheim Museum and for that alone, the trip is well worth taking. Designed by Canadian architect Frank Gehry (and called "the beast" by some locals because of its bizarre shape), from afar it resembles a gargantuan, glittering sculpture, with a tumbling boxes profile and a 131m-long (430-ft.) ship gallery. Perhaps no other modern building has transformed a city the way this astonishing work has. Gehry even incorporated an ugly bypass into the design, thus fusing the new and old Bilbao with one masterly stroke.

Bilbao was established by charter on June 15, 1300, which converted it from a village *(pueblo)*, ruled by feudal duke Don Diego López de Haro, into a city. Until then, it was a prosperous fishing and trade port. Basque fishermen and *marineros* were renowned for their expertise, with accounts of early Basque fisherman sailing as far as Greenland. Aided by waterpower and the transportation

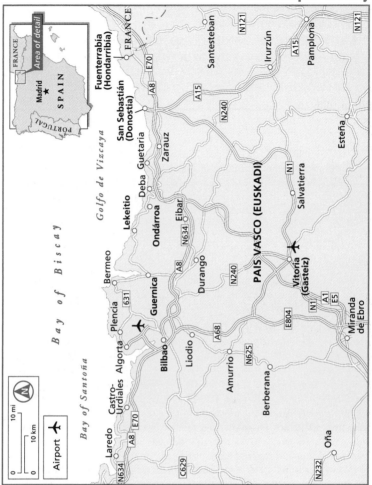

potential of the Nervión River plus the prosperous exportation of wine and wool to Northern Europe, it grew and grew. Most of its fame and glory came during the industrial expansion of the 19th century. Many of the city's grand homes and villas for industrialists were constructed then, particularly in the wealthy suburb of Neguri, part of the Ensanche (extension) which saw the city break out of the confines of the old town and over to the southern side of the River.

ESSENTIALS

GETTING THERE **Bilbao Airport** (© 94-471-03-01 or 94-453-23-06) is 8km (5 miles) north of the city, near the town of Erandio. There are 10 daily flights from Barcelona served by both **Iberia** (© 90-240-05-15) and **Spanair** (© 90-292-91-91). **Iberia**'s main booking office in Bilbao is at the airport (© 94-486-98-30), open daily from 5am to 10pm. From the airport into town, take red bus A-3247 to the heart of the city for 1€ ($1.15). A taxi to the center should cost about 20€ ($23).

Tips **Blame It on the Rain**

Basques claim that *txirrimirri* (pronounced "chi-rry-*mi*-rry"), a special type of rain, is theirs and theirs alone. Perhaps just as well, as its appearance is mis(t)leading. It may look like a light mist but unless you have an umbrella or raincoat, you will find your clothes soaked once you get back to the hotel.

The **RENFE** station, the Estación de Abando (© **90-224-02-02**), is on Plaza Circular 2, just off the Plaza de España. From here, you can catch short-distance trains within the metropolitan area of Bilbao and long-distance trains to most parts of Spain. Two trains per day run to and from Barcelona (the journey takes about 9 hr.). The nifty **EuskoTren** services the coast and various inland destinations, Atxuri 6 (© **90-254-32-10**).

PESA, at the Estación de Buses de Garillano (© **94-439-50-77**), operates more than a dozen buses per day to and from San Sebastián (1¼ hr.). **Continental,** Calle Gurtubay s/n (© **94-439-50-77**) has four buses per day to and from Barcelona (7 hr.).

Bilbao is beside the A-8, linking the cities of Spain's northern Atlantic seacoast to the western edge of France. It is connected by a superhighway to both Barcelona and Madrid.

VISITOR INFORMATION   There is a tourist office at Bilbao Airport arrivals (© **94-453-23-06**), open daily from 7:30am to 11:30pm. The main **tourist office** in town at Plaza del Ensanche 11 (© **94-479-57-60;** www.bilbao.net) is open Monday to Friday from 9am to 2pm and 4 to 7:30pm, Sunday and holidays from 9:30am to 2pm. There is a smaller office outside the entrance to the Guggenheim Museum. **Bilbao's Tourist Board**'s website (www.bilbao.net) is loaded with information (in English).

SPECIAL EVENTS   Festivals often fill the calendar, the biggest and most widely publicized being **La Semana Grande,** dedicated to the Virgin of Begoña and lasting from mid-August until early September. During the celebration, the Nervión River is the site of many flotillas and regattas. Fireworks light up the sky most nights and the old town is a mass of revelry as locals bar hop until the early hours. Bilbao lies on the famous **Camino de Santiago (Route of Saint James)** the city's patron Saint. On July 25 they honor him and July 31 is the holiday devoted to the region's patron saint, St. Ignatius.

FAST FACTS: **Bilbao**

Area Code The area code for Bilbao is © **94.**

Car Rentals **Budget,** Doctor Achucarro 8 (© **94-415-08-70**); **Avis,** Doctor Alameda Areilza 34 (© **94-427-57-60**).

Emergencies For an **ambulance,** © 092; **police,** © 091; **fire,** © 080; **medical emergencies,** © 90-221-21-24.

Information Call the **City Hall Information Service** at © **010.**

Post Office The post office is at Alameda Urquijo 19 (© **94-422-05-48**).

Taxis Recommended taxi companies include **Radio Taxi** (© **94-444-88-88**), **Tele-Taxi** (© **94-410-21-21**), and **Radio Taxi Bizkaia** (© **94-426-90-26**).

Trains Call **RENFE** (© **90-224-02-02** or 94-423-86-23) or **Eusko Tren** (© **90-254-32-10** or 94-433-80-08).

EXPLORING BILBAO

The **Nervión River** meanders through Bilbao, whose historic core was built inside one of its loops, with water protecting it on three sides. The charming Casco Viejo (Old Town) is where most of the historic buildings are conglomerated, including the city's main Cathedral and old Stock Exchange. It is also the place to head after dark for the dozens of eateries and bars. Most of the swankiest shops, banks, upmarket hotels, and tourist facilities lie in the Ensanche, on the southern side of the River. Built on a grid system and easy to navigate, its main artery is the **Gran Vía Don Diego López de Haro,** a wide boulevard with an almost-impossible-to-remember name (thankfully, everyone just calls it the Gran Vía). If you have a bit more time, the area to the west of the Guggenheim on the southern side of the River is also worth exploring. This is where most of the more dramatic architectural changes are taking place, including a brand new Sheraton (see "Where to Stay" below), seen as a sign of confidence in Bilbao's future.

THE TOP ATTRACTIONS

Euskal Museoa/Museo Vasco   Devoted to Basque archaeology, ethnology, and history, this museum is in the center of the old quarter, south of Calle Esperanza Ascao, in a centuries-old Jesuit cloister. Some of the exhibits showcase Basque commercial life during the 16th century. You can see everything from ship models to shipbuilding tools, along with reconstructions of rooms illustrating political and social life. Basque gravestones are also on view. In addition, you'll see the equipment used to play the Basque game of *pelota* (jai alai).

Plaza Miguel de Unamuno 4. © **94-415-54-23**. Admission 3€ ($3.45) adults, 1.50€ ($1.70) children and students, free for seniors and children under 10. Tues–Sat 11am–5pm; Sun 11am–2pm. Closed public holidays. Metro: Casco Viejo.

Guggenheim Museum 🕮🕮🕮   The newest and biggest attraction in Bilbao is the Guggenheim Museum, at the intersection of the bridge called Puente de la Salve and the Nervión River. The 104,700 sq. m (1,126,980 sq. ft.) colossus is the focal point of a $1.5-billion redevelopment plan for the city. The internationally acclaimed Frank Gehry design features a 50m-high (164-ft.) atrium—more than 1½ times the height of the rotunda of Frank Lloyd Wright's Guggenheim Museum in New York. Stretching under the aforementioned

Value **The Bilbao Card**

Depending on the amount of sightseeing you plan to do, it may be worth purchasing the **Bilbao Card.** The card offers unlimited access to the city's public transport system and discounts of up to 50% in most museums (except the Guggenheim) and between 10% and 50% off in selected in shops and restaurants. It costs 6€ ($6.90) for 1 day, 10€ ($12) for 2 days, and 12€ ($14) for a 3-day pass. The Bilbao Card is available at all tourist offices.

bridge and incorporating it in its design, the museum reanimates the promenade with a towering roof reminiscent of a blossoming metallic flower. The result is simply breathtaking and still Gehry's best work to date.

The Guggenheim isn't an encyclopedic museum, such as the Met in New York City. This museum features the works of some of the most towering artists of the latter half of the 20th century—including Picasso, Robert Motherwell, Robert Rauschenberg, Clyfford Still, Antoni Tàpies, Andy Warhol, Ives Klein, and (my personal favorite) Willem de Kooning. The beginning of the collection is marked by a 1952 Mark Rothko work, *Untitled,* and the behemoth central hall features work of equally humbling proportions, the best being Richard Serra's *Snake* sculpture which was specially made for the space. Recent European art is also exhibited (including some paintings from the 21st c.) along with the work of an array of young Basque and Spanish artists. Artwork lent by the Guggenheims in New York and Venice will rotate, and Bilbao will also host temporary exhibits traveling here from New York.

Although some disgruntled Basque locals still call the museum "the colossal Californian cauliflower" or "a cheese factory," many architectural critics from around the world, including Paul Goldberger of the *New York Times,* have hailed Gehry's unique structure as the first great building of the 21st century. The structure is said to have been inspired by the Fritz Lang film classic *Metropolis* and is viewed as a homage to Bilbao's industrial past and commitment to its future. The massive museum is clad in shimmering titanium, which many observers find sexy and unmistakably elegant. The building takes up 24,000 sq. m (258,333 sq. ft.) in the former dockyards beside the Nervión River, and about half of that space is devoted to the exhibition halls. The museum has virtually abolished right angles and flat walls. As one critic put it, "it was as if Gehry were working in pastry rather than concrete or steel."

Calle Abandoibarra 2. ℂ **94-435-90-80.** Admission 10€ ($12) adults, 6€ ($6.90) seniors and students, free for children under 13. Free guided tours Tues–Sun 11am–12:30pm and 4:30-6:30pm; July–Aug Mon–Sun 10am–8pm; Sept–June Tues–Sun 10am–8pm. Closed Dec 25 and Jan 1. Bus: 1, 10, 13, or 18 stopping at the Fine Arts Museum Square; 27, 38, 46 or 38 at Alameda de Recalde; and 11 or 71 stopping at La Salve Sq. RENFE: Bilbao–Abando station.

Museo de Bellas Artes ★★ This is another one of Spain's important art museums, containing both medieval and modern works, including paintings by

---

⸢Fun Fact *La Pelota Vasca*

As you travel around the Basque country, chances are you will happen upon a *pelota* match (Americans may know the game as jai alai). Often referred to as the fastest ball game in the world, it is enormously popular in both the Spanish and French Basque country and has become a symbol of Basque strength and resistance. Slightly similar to squash, there are several versions of the game, some using bare hands to propel the ball and others using a racquet or canoe-shaped baskets. Basque filmmaker Julio Medem used the *pelota vasca* as a metaphor in his highly controversial 2004 documentary: *The Basque Ball: Skin Against Stone.* The film attempts to explain the Basque situation from early history to the beginnings of ETA and beyond, ultimately urging for dialogue between Basque extremists and the Spanish state. Members of Spain's ruling government of the time refused to be interviewed for Medem's work and then tried to ban it.

Bilbao

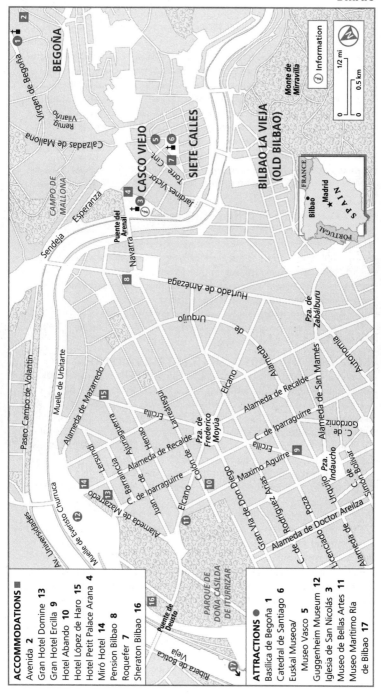

ACCOMMODATIONS ■
Avenida **2**
Gran Hotel Domine **13**
Gran Hotel Ercilla **9**
Hotel Abando **10**
Hotel López de Haro **15**
Hotel Petit Palace Arana **4**
Miró Hotel **14**
Pension Bilbao **8**
Roquefer **7**
Sheraton Bilbao **16**

ATTRACTIONS ●
Basílica de Begoña **1**
Catedral de Santiago **6**
Euskal Museoa/
  Museo Vasco **5**
Guggenheim Museum **12**
Iglesia de San Nicolás **3**
Museo de Bellas Artes **11**
Museo Marítimo Ria
  de Bilbao **17**

ⓘ Information

0   1/2 mi
0   0.5 km

BEGOÑA

CASCO VIEJO

SIETE CALLES

BILBAO LA VIEJA
(OLD BILBAO)

Monte de
Miravilla

FRANCE
Bilbao ★
Madrid ●
SPAIN
PORTUGAL

Velázquez, Goya, Zurbarán, and El Greco. The sheer size and quality of the collection—unusual for a town of Bilbao's size—is thanks to donations and bequests made by the city's rich 19th-century industrialists and merchants. Among the works of non-Spanish artists are *The Money Changers* by the Flemish painter Quentin Massys and *The Lamentation Over Christ* by Anthony Van Dyck. In its modern wing, the museum contains works by Gauguin, Picasso, Léger, Sorolla, and Mary Cassatt. The gallery is particularly strong in 19th- and 20th-century Basque artists, the foremost of which is the modern sculptor Eduardo Chillida, who created a massive piece titled *Monument to Iron.* Once you tire of looking at art, relax in the adjoining Doña Casilda de Iturriza park, a veritable slice of tranquillity in bustling downtown Bilbao.

Plaza del Museo 2. ✆ **94-439-60-60**. Admission 4.50€ ($5.15) adults, 3€ ($3.45) seniors and students, free for children under 12, free for all Wed. Tues–Sat 10am–8pm and Sun 10am–2pm. Closed Dec 25 and Jan 1. Metro: Moyúa.

Museo Marítimo Ría de Bilbao   Discover Bilbao's rich maritime history in this museum located at the old dockyards. Old boating equipment, all manner of vessels (originals, reproductions, and models), documentation, and photographs paint a vivid picture of this great seafaring nation and the wealth the estuary has brought it. Divided into three sections—the port, the river as a marketplace, and factory and naval dockyards, there is also an outside section where you can watch period boats being repaired.

Muelle Ramón de la Sota 1. ✆ **90-213-10-00**. Admission 7€ ($8.05) adults; 4€ ($4.60) children, students, and seniors. Tues–Fri 10am–2pm and 4–6pm; Sat–Sun 10am–2pm and 4–8pm. Closed Dec 25 and Jan 1. Metro: Sabino Arana.

EXPLORING THE CASCO VIEJO (OLD QUARTER) ⊛

Despite the fact that Bilbao was established around 1300, it has few medieval monuments. It does have an intriguing old quarter, however, on the east side of Nervión River and the site of its most interesting bars and restaurants. The custom is to go here at night and barhop, filling up on *pintxos* (the Basque version of tapas) and washing them down with the local white wine *txakoli.* On Saturday mornings it buzzes with life, with people darting around exploring its specialty shops and meeting for lunch afterwards.

The old quarter of Bilbao is connected to the much larger modern section on the opposite bank by four bridges. A few paces north of the old quarter's center are **graceful arches,** 64 in all, enclosing the Plaza Nueva, also called the Plaza de los Mártires, completed in 1830.

The entire *barrio* has been declared a national landmark. It originally defined an area around seven streets, but it long ago spilled beyond that limitation. Its most important church is the **Iglesia de San Nicolás.** Behind this church you'll find an elevator on Calle Esperanza Ascao, which, if working, carries sightseers to the upper town. You can also climb 64 steps from the Plaza Unamuno. From here it's a short walk to the **Basílica de Begoña,** built largely in the early 1500s. Inside the dimly lit church is a brightly illuminated depiction of the Virgin, dressed in long, flowing robes. She's the patroness of the province. Also displayed are some enormous paintings by Luca Giordano. While in the old town, you might visit the **Catedral de Santiago,** Plaza Santiago, which was built in the 14th century and then restored in the 16th century after a fire. The cathedral's facade was rebuilt in the 19th century. These three churches are open daily from 9am to 5pm. On Sundays you may take in the **flea market,** starting at 8am, on the streets of the old quarter or the old books and coins stalls on the Plaza Nueva.

Moments **Crossing the Bridge When You Come to It**

Bilbao's **Puente Colgante (Transporter Bridge;** *©* **94-463-88-54** or 94-480-10-12; Metro: Areeta), 15km (9 miles) from the city center where the Nervión River meets the sea, was the first of its kind in the world and a living treasure. Designed by engineer and architect Alberto Palacio in 1890, its maze of iron cross bars makes it a sort of horizontal Eiffel Tower (Gustav Eiffel was a friend of Palacio's). You can choose to walk it on foot, or take the more thrilling *gondala*, a transporter that slides underneath the walkway offering spectacular views 50m (164 ft.) above sea level of the city, the sea, and the marina in a 2-minute journey. The bridge is open around the clock daily; admission is 24€ to 90€ (30¢–$1.05), depending on the time of day.

To reach the old town on foot, the only way to explore it, take the Puente del Arenal from the Gran Vía, the main street of Bilbao.

TOURS

Bilbao's Tourist Office runs some excellent walking tours of both the Old Town and the Ensanche. Groups leave from outside the main tourist office Plaza de Ensanche 11 (*©* **94-479-57-60**) every Saturday and Sunday at 10am for the Old Town and at noon for the modern areas. Both tours last about 1½ hours, are conducted in either English or Spanish (or both), and cost 3€ ($3.45). These are highly recommended.

Another alternative for the more active is to see the main sights by bike. Bilbao has a solid network of bicycle lanes and the Tourist Office has produced a map called *Bici&Arte*, which shows the routes and attractions along the way. From the first of June to mid-September, bikes can be borrowed for free on a first-come, first-served basis (10:30am–2pm) underneath the Euskalduna Bridge (next to the entrance of the Maritime Museum), for more information *©* **94-420-51-30.** More and more hotels are also participating in the "Clients on Wheels" plan, which allows guests free use of bicycles.

SHOPPING

The big name boutiques can be found along the Gran Vía, as can the department store **El Corte Inglés,** Gran Vía 7–9 (*©* **94-425-35-00**), where most items can be picked up, from camera equipment to hosiery. Seek out more specialized shops in the narrow streets of the Caso Viejo. Fashion is strong along the Calle Bidebarrieta, with **Zara, Women'Secret,** and all the Spanish High Street stores. **La Palma,** Correo 3, is a two-story, shoe-lover's idea of heaven.

Many visitors like to return from the Basque country with a chic beret, which locals call *txapelas*. The best selection is found at **Sombreros Gorostiada,** Calle Victor 9 (*©* **94-416-12-76**), a family-owned business since 1857. They also sell woolen caps, various hats, and also hunting caps. Another great souvenir is *turrones*, slabs of nougat in wonderful flavors. The best are sold at **Turronería Iváñez,** Correo 23 (*©* **94-479-24-07**).

If you'd like to purchase Basque artisan products, head for **Basandere,** Calle Iparraguirre 4 (*©* **94-423-63-86**), near the Guggenheim Museum. Their crafts are of high quality, and every three months they stage art exhibitions from local artists. In addition, the shop also sells gourmet Basque food items. At the opposite end of the scale but also just near the Guggenheim is **Kartell,** Alameda Mazarredo 67 (© **94-423-60-80**), a sleek establishment selling contemporary design objects and furniture.

WHERE TO STAY
EXPENSIVE

Gran Hotel Domine ★★★ Opposite the Guggenheim and embellishing the city's new craze for contemporary design, the Gran Domine reaches beyond where many design hotels fall short and offers first-rate service *and* facilities in highly creative surroundings. This is the first interiors project of graphic design wunderkind Javier Mariscal, and the quirkiness that marks his illustrative work is present in the hotel throughout. A sinuous stone-laden column curls up through the central light well and the foyer is dotted with organically shaped pop-style furniture in bold colors. The rooms are fitted out in more subdued shades of browns and grays, with Mariscal's artwork adorning the walls. Breakfast is taken in the atrium with a spectacular view of the Guggenheim Museum through the sheet glass walls. Opened in 2002, the Gran Domine is at the top of the list of Spain's Best Urban Hotels, and for once you can believe the hype.

Alameda de Mazarredo 61, 48009 Bilbao. © **94-425-33-00**. Fax 94-425-33-01. www.silken-granhoteldomine. com. 145 units. 140€–170€ ($161–$196) double; 275€–400€ ($316–$460) suite. AE, DC, MC, V. Parking 12€ ($14). Metro: Moyúa. **Amenities:** Restaurant; cafeteria; bar; business center; limited room service; babysitting; laundry service; dry cleaning. *In room:* A/C, TV, minibar, hair dryer, safe.

Gran Hotel Ercilla ★ Soaring high above the buildings surrounding it in the heart of Bilbao's business district, this is a tastefully decorated bastion of attentive service and good living. The midsize to spacious guest rooms are conservative and comfortably furnished, all with roomy bathrooms with tub/shower combos. The Ercilla is one of Bilbao's most desirable hotels, usually the preferred choice of Spanish politicians, movie stars, and journalists.

Ercilla 37–39, 48011 Bilbao. © **94-470-57-00**. Fax 94-443-93-35. www.hotelercilla.es. 333 units. 98€–196€ ($113–$225) double; 187€–370€ ($215–$426) suite. AE, DC, MC, V. Parking 14€ ($16). Metro: Indautxu. **Amenities:** Restaurant; bar; cafe; car rental; business center; limited room service; babysitting; laundry service; dry cleaning. *In room:* A/C, TV, minibar, hair dryer, safe.

Hotel Abando ★ This government-rated four-star hotel isn't in the same class as the López de Haro, but it's a first-class property achieving a sudden fame. This new hotel lies in the city center, offering an array of well-furnished rooms with comfortable beds. The rooms also have roomy tiled bathrooms with tub/shower combos. If you don't want to go out at night, you can enjoy top Basque and international cuisine at the restaurant.

Colón de Larreautegui 9, 48001 Bilbao. © **94-423-62-00**. Fax 94-424-55-26. www.aranzazu-hoteles.com. 143 units. 94€–149€ ($108–$171) double; 123€–175€ ($141–$201) suite. AE, DC, MC, V. Parking 12€ ($14). Metro: Abando. All buses to Estación de Abando. **Amenities:** Restaurant; cafe; health club; business center; room service; babysitting; laundry service; dry cleaning. *In room:* A/C, TV, minibar, hair dryer, safe.

Hotel López de Haro ★★★ This refined palace of pleasure is the ultimate in luxury living in the greater Bilbao area. Behind a discreet facade of chiseled gray stone, this 1990 hotel is filled with English touches and features marble flooring, hardwood paneling, and a uniformed staff. The comfortable midsize guest rooms contain flowered or striped upholstery, modern bathrooms with tub/shower combos, and wall-to-wall carpeting or hardwood floors.

Obispo Orueta 2–4, 48009 Bilbao. © **94-423-55-00.** Fax 94-423-45-00. www.hotellopezdeharo.com. 53 units. 128€–255€ ($147–$293) double; 329€ ($378) suite. AE, DC, MC, V. Parking 15€ ($17). Metro: Moyúa. **Amenities:** Restaurant; bar; business center; limited room service; babysitting; laundry service; dry cleaning. *In room:* A/C, TV, minibar, hair dryer, safe.

Miró Hotel ★★ *Finds* Named not after the famous Catalan artist, but rather the well-known fashion designer Antonio Miró, who makes his foray into interior design in the well-equipped boutique hotel near the Guggenheim. From its functional black and beige rooms, generous use of marble and leather throughout, and classy spa (with massage service, a Jacuzzi, *and* a Turkish bath) the Miró is the true definition of an "urban" hostelry. Modern art, the new leitmotif for Bilbao is hung throughout the library and cocktail/meeting areas and foyer.

Alameda Mazarredo 77, 48009 Bilbao. © **94-661-18-80.** Fax 94-425-51-82. www.mirohotelbilbao.com. 50 units. 160€–180€ ($184–$207) double; 230€–260€ ($265–$299) suite. AE, DC, MC, V. Parking 13€ ($15). Metro: Moyúa. **Amenities:** Snack bar; health club; Jacuzzi; limited room service; babysitting service; laundry service; dry cleaning; laptop rental. *In room:* A/C, TV, minibar, hair dryer, safe, Internet access.

Sheraton Bilbao ★★★ This dramatic new addition to Bilbao's accommodations offerings is next to the Congress Hall in a slice of the city that is being touted as a new destination for trade fairs and big business. Opened in July 2004, the design was influenced by the Basque sculptor Eduardo Chillida and the pinky rust colored facade and cavernous lobby are reminiscent of one of his overpowering works. All features expected with the Sheraton name are present, from plasma TV screens to king-size beds and hydromassage baths in the suites. The only downside is that much of the surrounding area is under construction, so request a riverside room unless you want to wake up to a view of a crane.

Lehendakari Leizaola 29, 48001 Bilbao. © **94-428-00-00.** Fax 94-428-00-06. www.sheraton.com/bilbao. 190 units. 100€–240€ ($115–$276) double; 180€–500€ ($207–$575) suite. AE, DC, MC, V. Parking 12€ ($14). Metro: Moyúa. **Amenities:** Restaurant; cafeteria; bar; outdoor pool; health club; sauna; business center; 24-hr. room service; babysitting; laundry service; dry cleaning; nonsmoking rooms. *In room:* A/C, TV, minibar, hair dryer, safe.

MODERATE

Avenida For those who want to be away from the center and don't mind a bus or taxi ride or two, this is a welcoming choice. It's in the Barrio de Begoña, near one of the major religious monuments of Bilbao, the Basílica de Begoña. The hotel was built in the late 1950s, and its small rooms, furnished in a functional modern style, are well kept and maintained. All units contain bathrooms with tub/shower combos. During special fairs in Bilbao, rates increase by at least 10%.

Zumalacárregui 40, 48006 Bilbao. © **94-412-43-00.** Fax 94-411-46-17. www.bchoteles.com. 189 units. 78€–140€ ($90–$161) double; 115€–158€ ($132–$182) suite. Rates include breakfast. AE, DC, MC, V. Parking 12€ ($14). Metro: Santutxu. **Amenities:** Restaurant; bar; health club; business center; limited room service; laundry service; dry cleaning; nonsmoking rooms. *In room:* A/C, TV, minibar, hair dryer, safe.

Hotel Petit Palace Aranal ★★ *Value* Dating from the mid–18th century, this hotel is the oldest in the city. It spent most of its life as a humble inn, then a backpackers' hostel until a recent renovation turned it into one of the city's better mid-range options. On the threshold of the Casco Viejo and opposite the Arriaga Theater, the hotel is a mixture of ancient stone and high tech. Rooms have been re-fitted with dark wood paneling and floors and pure white linen and curtains. Black and white photographs of Basque sporting heroes complete the monochrome effect. The more timid among us will find the sheer glass bathroom walls and doors a little uncomfortable, but points are scored with a very cozy attic lounge with free Internet access.

Bidebarrieta 2, 48005 Bilbao. (©) 94-415-64-11. Fax 94-416-12-05. www.hthoteles.com. 64 units. 70€–150€ ($81–$173) double. Metro: Casco Viejo. **Amenities:** Restaurant; bar; room service; laundry service; dry cleaning; nonsmoking rooms; computer access. *In room:* A/C, TV, minibar, hair dryer, safe, exercise bicycle.

INEXPENSIVE

Roquefer   If you'd like to stay in the old quarter and avoid the high prices of business hotels, this is a very basic choice, suitable if your main concern is only a place to lay your head. The small rooms are simple and furnished in a functional style, each with a good bed. If you're looking for any kind of amenities or extras, try another location. You'll be in the center of the *tasca* and restaurant district for nighttime prowls. To reach the hotel, take the bridge, Puente del Arenal, across the river to the old town.

Lotería 2, 2nd Floor, 48005 Bilbao. (©) 94-415-07-55. Fax 94-423-18-16. hotelripa@teleline.es. 18 units (6 with bathroom). 35€ ($40) double without bathroom; 45€ ($52) double with bathroom. MC, V (through Hotel Ripa next door). Parking 6€ ($6.90). Metro: Casco Viejo. *In room:* TV.

Pensión Bilbao ⟨★⟩   Very well thought of pension within a stone's throw of the Casca Viejo and main train station. Opened in 2000, all rooms are spacious, all with bathrooms, wooden floors, and those little extras rarely associated with budget accommodations. Some rooms have balconies. Management is friendly and helpful.

Amistad 2–4° izda., 48001 Bilbao. (©)/fax **94-424-69-43**. www.pensionbilbao.com. 9 units. 45€ ($52) double. MC, V. Metro: Abando. **Amenities:** Safe, laundry service. *In room:* TV, hair dryer.

WHERE TO DINE

Basque cuisine is generally considered to be the finest on the Peninsula, and the good news is you needn't spend a fortune to eat well. *Pintxos* (pronounced "*peen*-chohs"), the Basque version of tapas, can be a meal on their own. The versions are endless, but basically they consist of tiny rounds of rustic bread topped with combinations of cured meats, seafood, cheeses, and vegetables such as asparagus and tiny green peppers.

The Basques take their food *seriously* and although you may pay a little more for eating out than in other parts of Spain, the overall quality and care taken in preparation is infinitely better. The abundance of fishing villages along the coast ensures a constant supply of seasonal fresh fish such as anchovies *(anchoas),* hake *(merluza),* and the delicate red bream *(salmonettes).* The lush interior is a breeding ground for wild mushrooms and fungi, and a rich soil ensures high quality vegetables. Some local specialties include *bacalao al pil-pil* (salt cod with garlic and emulsion), *chipirones rellenos de su tinta* (stuffed baby squid in ink), and *pimientos verdes rellenos de rabo* (green peppers stuffed with vegetables and steak with a rich wine gravy). Small eaters note that portions here are large, so you may wish to skip, or at least share, entrees.

EXPENSIVE

Bermeo ⟨★★★⟩ BASQUE   One of the best hotel restaurants in all of Spain and one of the finest representatives of Basque cuisine anywhere in the world, Bermeo caters to the Basque world's most influential politicians, writers, and social luminaries. Within the modern walls of one of Bilbao's tallest hotels, the restaurant is decorated with glowing wood panels, crisp linens, and copies of 19th-century antiques. Service from the formal uniformed staff is impeccable. Menu items change with the seasons but might include a salad of lettuce hearts in saffron dressing with smoked salmon, homemade foie gras with essence of bay leaves, fresh thistles sautéed with ham, five preparations of cod, stewed partridge with glazed shallots, and duckling filets with green peppercorns. For dessert, try the truffled figs or a slice of bilberry pie with cream.

In the Gran Hotel Ercilla, Ercilla 37. ✆ **94-470-57-00.** Reservations required. Main courses 14€–27€ ($16–$31); fixed-price menu 36€ ($41); tasting menu 46€ ($53). AE, DC, MC, V. Sun–Fri 1–3:30pm; Mon–Sat 8:30–11:30pm. Closed Sat–Sun July–Sept. Metro: Indautxu.

Club Náutico ★★★ BASQUE/FRENCH   One of the top restaurants in the Basque world, the elegant Club Náutico is in the Hotel López de Haro (p. 284). Chef Alberto Velez is the former protégé of Alberto Zuluaga, who ran the kitchen here for years and was one of the most publicized culinary luminaries of northern Spain. The restaurant offers formal tables set with some of the finest china, crystal, and silverware. Specialties include local artichokes stuffed with foie gras, poached eggs with beluga caviar and oyster sauce, lobster sautéed with artichokes and balsamic vinegar, baked sea bass with béarnaise sauce, sautéed scallops with truffle sauce, and roast beef with a purée of radishes. A superb selection of Spanish and international wines is available by the glass or the bottle.

In the Hotel López de Haro, Obispo Orueta 2. ✆ **94-423-55-00.** Reservations recommended. Main courses 18€–28€ ($21–$32); fixed-price menus 29€–50€ ($33–$58). AE, DC, MC, V. Mon–Fri 1–3:30pm and 8:30–11:30pm; Sat 8:30–11:30pm; July 15–Aug 15 buffet only. Metro: Moyúa.

Etxanobe ★★ BASQUE/INTERNATIONAL   In the gleaming postmodern Palacio Euskalduna (the congress and music hall) this restaurant is one of the hottest dining spots in Bilbao. Sporting a terrace with a waterfront view and faux period decor that frankly doesn't sit well with its location, this bastion of grand cuisine is a showcase for the culinary talents of Fernando Canales. I opted for the gastronomic set menu, starting off with a memorable cold lasagna of anchovies in a creamy tomato sauce and things got better from then on. From the fungi and octopus risotto to the giant crab and potato salad, everything was made from the freshest of ingredients and handled with precision and skill. The chocolate "bomb" with mango ice cream finished me off at the end of the meal. The only drawback was the slightly stuffy air of the waitstaff. If Canales's approach to service and decor were as spot-on as his cuisine, Etxanobe would be truly world class.

Av. de Abandoibarra 4. ✆ **94-442-10-23.** Reservations required. Main courses 17€–28€ ($20–$32); tasting menu 47€ ($54). AE, DC, MC, V. Mon–Sat 1:30–3:30pm and 8:30–11:30pm. Closed Aug 1–14. Metro: San Mamés.

Guría ★ BASQUE   One of Bilbao's most venerable restaurants, Guría is expensive and worth it. The chef serves only market-fresh ingredients. He's celebrated for his *bacalao* (cod), which he prepares many ways. Try the sea bass with saffron or loin of beef cooked in sherry as an alternative. A slightly caloric but divine dessert is the *espuma de chocolat.* Guría is on the southern edge of one of the most monumental traffic arteries in town, 6 blocks west of Bilbao's most prominent square, the Plaza de Federico Moyúa, a block south of the sprawling Parque de Dr. Casilda Iturriza. Inside you'll find a modern decor of dark-stained wood, two dining rooms, and a monochromatic color scheme.

Gran Vía de López de Haro 66. ✆ **94-441-85-64.** Reservations required. Main courses 18€–60€ ($21–$69); tasting menu 41€–59€ ($47–$68). AE, DC, MC, V. Mon–Sat 12:30–4pm and 9pm–midnight; Sun 12:30–4pm. Metro: Indautxu.

Restaurante Guggenheim Bilbao ★★ INTERNATIONAL/BASQUE   This museum is home not only to a world-class art collection but to a world-class restaurant carved out of this architectural curiosity. The chef de cuisine,

Bixenta Arrieta, is a master of *nueva cocina vasca,* and his fisherman's stew in an herb-laced green broth is award winning, as is his white salt cod with tomatoes stuffed with baby squid and black rice (colored by the squid's ink). Diners make a selection from the menu of the sea or the menu from the countryside *(del campo).* Begin perhaps with a lobster salad or duck-stuffed cannelloni. A wide selection of Basque wines is served.

Abandoibarra Etorbidea 2. ⓒ **94-423-93-33.** Reservations recommended as far in advance as possible. Main courses 12€–28€ ($14–$32). AE, DC, MC, V. Tues–Sun 1:30–3:15pm; Wed–Sat 9–10:30pm. Closed Dec 24–Jan 9. Metro: Moyúa.

Zortziko ⭐⭐⭐ BASQUE/CONTINENTAL   This is a bastion of refined cuisine and ranks near the top in Basque country. It's convenient to the Guggenheim, which is a few steps away. In a multiroomed, vaguely French setting furnished in late Victorian style, you'll find a formal environment. Lunches tend to focus on business discussions among clients; dinners tend to be more leisurely and recreational. One of the most unusual dining areas is the wine cellar, where diners who appreciate the sense of being surrounded by valuable vintages reserve the only table, sometimes many days in advance. It's more likely, however, that your table will be on the restaurant's street level. In a city where competition is fierce, this kitchen emerges at the very top. Menu items include most of the traditional Basque staples, like pigeon breast or sea bass marinated and roasted in red Rioja wine. The tasting menu presents a wide variety of Basque specialties.

Alameda de Mazarredo 17. ⓒ **94-423-97-43.** Reservations recommended. Main courses 15€–29€ ($17–$33); tasting menu 70€ ($81). AE, DC, MC, V. Mon–Sat 1–3:30pm; Tues–Sat 8–11pm. Closed Aug 24–Sept 14. Metro: Abando.

MODERATE

El Perro Chico ⭐ *Finds* BASQUE   This may be the most unappreciated restaurant in Bilbao. It's true that the decor won't win any *Architectural Digest* awards. It could easily be turned into a gypsy den for telling fortunes. But patrons come here for the cuisine, an array of Basque classics. Many discerning celebrities have already found the place: Antonio Banderas, Dennis Hopper, and Jeremy Irons. Frank Gehry, architect of the Guggenheim, considers it his favorite Bilbao dining room. Start, perhaps, with the grilled fresh anchovies with a green sauce or long green peppers, which are fried and perfectly salted. Fresh tuna comes with a black, squid ink sauce that's rich and delectable. The dish of clams and artichokes would keep me coming back again and again. The hake *(merluza)* has a natural sweetness only enhanced by the topping of a velvety béchamel sauce and scoops of freshly mashed potatoes.

Aretxaga 2. ⓒ **94-415-05-19.** Reservations required. Main courses 10€–21€ ($12–$24). DC, MC, V. Tues–Sat 1:30–3pm; Tues–Sat 9:15–11:15pm. Closed July 21–Aug 15 and Easter week. Tramvía: Rivera.

Matxinbenta ⭐ BASQUE   Serving some of the finest Basque food in the city since the 1950s, this restaurant is popular for business lunches or dinners. Specialties include fresh tuna in piquant tomato sauce and a local version of ratatouille known as *piperada.* You can order veal cutlets cooked in port wine and finish with a mint-flavored fresh-fruit cocktail. The service is excellent. Matxinbenta has three dining rooms, each with contemporary furniture, potted plants, and lots of exposed wood. It's a block north of the Gran Vía, in the center of the city, adjacent to Bilbao's most visible department store, El Corte Inglés.

Ledesma 26. ⓒ **94-424-84-95.** Reservations recommended. Main courses 15€–21€ ($17–$24); Fixed-price lunch menu 30€ ($35); tasting menu from 42€ ($48). AE, DC, MC, V. Daily 1–4pm; Mon–Sat 8–11:30pm. July–Sept closed Sun. Metro: Moyúa.

Bilbao has three beautifully kept period cafes. Dating from the mid-1920s, **Café La Granja** (© **94-423-08-13;** Metro: Abando) is a high-ceilinged, wood and leather affair right on Plaza Circular in the shopping and business district. The turn-of-the-20th-century **Café Iruña** (© **94-423-70-21;** Metro: Abando) is in the pretty park Jardines de Albia and boasts Andalusian–style decor and extravagant wall murals. The **Café Boulevard,** Arenal 3 (© **94-415-31-28;** Metro: Casco Viejo), is the eldest of the trio and has the honor of being mentioned by the city's man of letters Miguel de Unamuno. "There in the Boulevard," he wrote in 1891, "Brokers, businessmen and merchants. They meet because they are stuck there and are stuck there because they meet." You may find it hard to leave the confines of its gilt mirrors, marble, and stained glass as well. All cafes serve coffee and breakfast, a substantial lunchtime menu, and snacks throughout the day.

INEXPENSIVE

Aitxiar *(Value* BASQUE   Respected for its good food, low prices, and lack of pretension, this restaurant in the Casco Viejo serves Basque cuisine in two dining rooms in a house built in the 1930s. Expect a decor that includes lots of exposed stone and wood, a hardworking waitstaff, strong flavors, and lots of regional pride. Menu items include potato soup with chunks of fresh tuna and an array of fish hauled in that morning from nearby waters. Two of the most appealing are hake, which tastes marvelous in an herb-infused green sauce, and cod, prepared in at least two versions. Baby squid is a savory choice, as are the spicy sausages *(chuletas),* which taste best when consumed as an appetizer.

Calle María Muñoz 8. © 94-415-09-17. Main courses 11€–24€ ($13–$28); fixed-price lunch menu 8€ ($9). AE, DC, MC, V. Tues–Sun 1–3:30pm and 8–11pm. Closed Aug 15–Sept 15. Metro: Casco Viejo.

Urbieta *★★ (Finds* BASQUE/TAPAS   This bar-restaurant specializes in *cazuelitas* (hot, homemade casseroles) and other concoctions served in earthenware dishes. This may sound rather pedestrian but one taste of their *albóndigas* (bite-size meatballs), *chipirones en su tinta* (baby squid in ink), *tigres* (mussels topped with béchamel sauce), or any number of their other lovingly prepared recipes, and you will be hooked (I went back three times in 2 days). This is Basque comfort food at its most authentic and makes a more satisfying alternative to the plethora of *pintxo* bars in the surrounding streets.

Perro 4. © 94-415-02-43. Reservations recommended for tables. Main courses 8€–18€ ($9–$21); fixed-price lunch menu 10€ ($12). MC, V. Daily 1–4pm and 8–11pm. Metro: Casco Viejo.

Víctor Montes *(Finds* BASQUE/SPANISH   In the heart of Bilbao's oldest neighborhood, this restaurant maintains a handful of battered dining rooms—some upstairs—where closely packed tables, racks of wine, and frantic waiters create a sense of good-natured hysteria, especially at lunchtime. Expect copious portions of old-fashioned roasts, stews, soups, and salads, usually with an emphasis on fresh vegetables and seafood such as grilled squid or fresh broad beans with nuggets of cod. Many locals, especially those in a hurry, tend to bypass a dining table altogether, opting for one or more *raciones* of tapas. They're lined up atop the bar, served to patrons on small plates, and taste wonderful when accompanied with sherry, wine, or beer.

Tips   *Tapeando:* A Tapas Bar Crawl

The best places to *tapear* (do a tapas bar crawl) are around **Calle Licenciado Poza**, between Alameda del Doctor Areilza and Calle Iparraguirre. Favorites include **Atlanta**, Calle Rodríguez Arias 28 (© **94-427-64-72**), famous for its *jamón Serrano* (cured ham) sandwiches, and **Busterri**, Calle Licenciado Poza 43 (© **94-441-50-67**), well known for its grilled anchovies and *jamón Jabugo* (a regional ham). **Gatz**, Calle Santa María 10 (© **94-415-48-61**), serves Bilbao's finest cod tartlets and their unique version of a Basque-style ratatouille. The young Riojas and the crisp Navarran whites will help you wash everything down. **Café Bar Bilbao**, Plaza Nueva 6 (© **94-415-16-71**), has the silkiest anchovies (fresh, of course) curled around green olives. **Berton**, Calle Jardines 11 (© **94-416-70-35**), does a delectable slice of crusty bread topped with a ribeye filet and truffle paste and **Xukela**, Perro 2 (© **94-415-97-72**), has a memorable range of all manner of *pintxos* and walls covered with interesting movie memorabilia.

Plaza Nueva 8. © **94-415-70-67**. Reservations recommended for full meals, not tapas bar. Tapas from 1.50€ ($1.70); main courses 12€–22€ ($14–$25). MC, V. Mon–Sat 1–3:30pm and 7:30pm–midnight. Metro: Casco Viejo.

BILBAO AFTER DARK
PERFORMING ARTS

The two major cultural venues in Bilbao are the **Teatro Arriaga**, Plaza Arriaga s/n (© **94-479-20-56**) and the **Palacio Euskalduna**, Abandoibarra 4 (© **94-431-03-10**), both on the banks of the Nervión River. These are the setting for world-class opera, classical music concerts, ballet, and even *zarzuelas* (comic operas). Announcements of cultural events at the time of your visit are available at the tourist office (see "Visitor Information," earlier in this chapter).

BARS & CLUBS

Bilbao has a lively nightlife. Wandering around the bars and bodegas of the old town's narrow alleyways, you will see bands of *cuadrillas*, lifelong friends out on a pub crawl. Inside a bar, you may be suddenly invaded by a troupe of *Txikiteros*, middle-aged men who spend their evening singing for a *txixi* (small glass of red wine). If you are still standing after midnight there many venues that are open late into the night. The queen of the night is **La Tramoya**, Calle Elanko 26 (© **94-421-71-32**), a venue that often has live entertainment, from comedy to theme nights. On Friday and Saturday nights from 6:30pm to 6:30am, the bar that's jumping is **Cotton Club**, Simón Bolívar s/n (© **94-410-49-51**), named after its early ancestor in New York's Harlem. More than 30,000 beer bottle caps form part of the decor. A DJ spins the latest tunes for the mingling throngs in their 20s and 30s. The atmosphere is less hectic on Sunday from 6:30pm to 3am and Monday and Thursday from 4:30pm to 3am. If Latin dancing is more your thing, then head to **Cache Latino**, Muelle de Ripa 3 (© **94-423-43-23**). **Bullit Groove**, Dos de Mayo 3 (© **61-578-05-78**), has a younger crowd grooving on soul, funk, and dub while **Bilbaína Jazz Club**, Calle Navarra 1 (© **94-423-51-58**), has gigs every Thursday. For details on live music in Bilbao, whether it be jazz, pop, or classical, pick up a copy of the weekly guide **La Ría del Ocio** in any news kiosk.

If it's a gay bar you are after, the boys of Bilbao (sounds like a film, doesn't it?) gather at **Kasko,** Calle Santa María 16 (© **94-416-03-11**), a popular restaurant that after midnight turns into a cocktail bar/dance club, or the **New High Club,** Calle Naja 5 (no phone), the city's most visible gay club. Mostly young males show up here, but some women appear nightly as well. In the main room, Spanish dance music is played, and in a small theater upstairs, XXX-rated films are shown. There's a hyperactive "dark room" in the back.

2 Side Trips From Bilbao

by Suzanne Wales & Tara Stevens

SAN SEBASTIAN ⭐

21km (13 miles) W of the French border, 483km (300 miles) N of Madrid, 100km (62 miles) E of Bilbao

San Sebastián (**Donostia** in Euskera) is the summer capital of Spain, and here the Belle Epoque lives on. Situated on a choice spot on the Bay of Biscay, it's surrounded by green mountains. From June to September, the population swells as swarms of Spanish bureaucrats escape the heat and head for this tasteful resort—it has few of the tawdry trappings associated with major beachside cities. San Sebastián is an ideal base for trips to some of the Basque country's most fascinating towns.

Queen Isabella II put San Sebastián on the map as a resort when she spent the summer of 1845 there. In time, it became the summer residence of the royal court. On July 8, 1912, Queen María Cristina inaugurated the grand hotel named after her, and the resort became very fashionable. In what's now the city hall, built in 1887, a casino opened, and European aristocrats gambled in safety here during World War I.

San Sebastián is the capital of the province of Guipúzcoa, the smallest in Spain, tucked in the far northeastern corner bordering France. It's said that Guipúzcoa has preserved Basque customs better than any other province. Half of the Donostiarras (residents of San Sebastián) speak Euskera. The city is a major seat of Basque nationalism, so be advised that protests, sometimes violent, are frequent.

San Sebastián contains an old quarter, **La Parte Vieja,** with narrow streets, hidden plazas, and medieval houses, but it is primarily a modern city of elegant shops, wide boulevards, sidewalk cafes, and restaurants.

La Concha is the city's most famous beach—especially in July and August, when it seems as though half the population of Spain and France spends its days under striped canopies or dashing into the refreshingly cool waters of the bay. The shell-shaped La Concha is half-encircled by a promenade, where crowds mill during the evening. At one end of the beach where the sand gives way to dramatically shaped rocks lies the monumental *Comb of the Wind,* a dramatic steel structure by the famous Basque sculptor Eduardo Chillida (see the listing for Museo Chillida-Leku, below) At the opposite end, the adjoining beach is the **Playa de Ondarreta.** The climate here is decidedly more Atlantic than Mediterranean so it's best to bring a light jacket and be prepared for rain, even during summer months.

San Sebastián has a good, though insufficient, choice of hotels in summer, plus many excellent restaurants, most of which are expensive. Its chief drawback is overcrowding in July and August. Bullfights, art and film festivals, sporting events, and cultural activities keep San Sebastián hopping during summer.

ESSENTIALS

GETTING THERE   From Bilbao, the bus company Pesa has more than a dozen buses a day to San Sebastián, which leave from the main bus terminal, Estación de Buses de Garillano (© **94-439-50-77**). Duration: 1¼ hr.

San Sebastián is well linked by a **bus** network to and from many of Spain's major cities. The Barcelona route (7 hr.) is serviced by Vivasa (© **90-210-13-63**), which runs four buses a day. Taking the train from Barcelona is longer, but infinitely more picturesque. There are two trains, one day (8 hr.) and one overnight (also 8 hr.). Contact the national train network RENFE (© **902-24-02-02**).

From Barcelona by **car,** take the AP-2 toll road to Zaragoza, then just before city the AP-68 to Corella. After that the A-15 will take you via Irutzun to San Sebastián.

VISITOR INFORMATION   The **tourist office** is at Calle Reina Regente 3 (© **94-348-11-66**). From June to September, it's open Monday through Saturday from 8am to 8pm, Sunday from 10am to 2pm; off-season hours are Monday through Saturday from 9am to 1:30pm and 3:30 to 7pm, Sunday from 10am to 2pm.

EXPLORING & ENJOYING SAN SEBASTIAN

San Sebastián means beach time, excellent Basque food, and strolling along the Paseo de la Concha. The monuments, such as they are, can easily be viewed before lunch.

Museo de San Telmo ⭐, Plaza Zuloaga 1 (© **94-342-49-70**), housed in a 16th-century Dominican monastery, contains an impressive collection of Basque artifacts from prehistoric times. The museum includes works by Zuloaga (*Torreillos en Turégano,* for example), golden age artists such as El Greco and Ribera, and a large number of Basque painters. In the old town at the base of Monte Urgull, the museum is open Tuesday through Saturday from 10:30am to 1:30pm and 4 to 8pm, Sunday from 10:30am to 2pm. Admission is free.

The wide promenade **Paseo Nuevo** almost encircles Monte Urgull, one of the two mountains between which San Sebastián is nestled (Monte Igueldo is the other one). A ride along this promenade opens onto panoramic vistas of the Bay of Biscay. The paseo comes to an end at the **Palacio del Mar** ⭐, Muelle 34 (© **94-344-00-99**), an oceanographic museum/aquarium. Like most modern aquariums, it boasts a mesmerizing collection of huge tanks containing myriad marine species. A transparent underwater walkway allows a 360-degree view of sharks, rays, and other fish as they swim around you. A maritime museum upstairs presents a fascinating synopsis of mankind's precarious relationship with the sea down through the ages through historical displays of fishing gear, naval artifacts, and marine fossils. Here you can also see the skeleton of the last whale caught in the Bay of Biscay, in 1878. The museum is open January to April daily from 10am to 7pm (extended to 8pm on weekends), May to June and September daily 10am to 8pm (to 9pm on weekends) and July and August daily 10am to 9pm. Admission is 10€ ($12) adults, 8€ ($9.20) students, 6€ ($6.90) for children ages 3 to 12.

Other sights include the **Palacio de Miramar (Paseo de Miraconcha;** © **94-321-90-22**), which stands on its own hill opening onto La Concha. In the background is the residential district of Antiguo. Queen María Cristina, after whom the grandest hotel in the north of Spain is named, opened this palace in 1893, but by the turbulent 1930s, it had fallen into disrepair. The city council took it

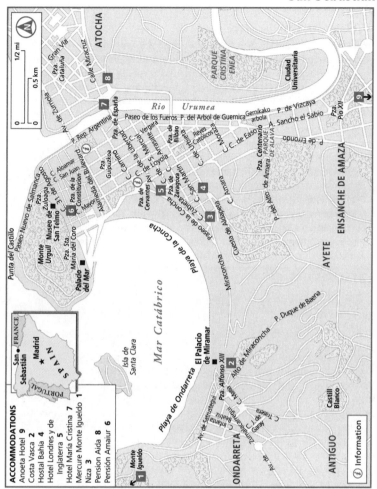

ACCOMMODATIONS
Anoeta Hotel **9**
Costa Vasca **2**
Hostal Bahía **4**
Hotel Londres y de Inglaterra **5**
Hotel María Cristina **7**
Mercure Monte Igueldo **1**
Niza **3**
Pensión Aida **8**
Pensión Amaiur **6**

ⓘ Information

over in 1971 and it is now a conference center. You can visit it year-round from 9am to 8:30pm. Because you can't go inside the palace, you must settle for a look at the lawns and gardens. The palace stands on land splitting the two major beaches of San Sebastián: Playa de la Concha and Playa de Ondarreta.

Palacio de Aiete was constructed by the duke of Bailén in 1878 and became the summer home of King Alfonso XIII and his queen, María Cristina, until their own Palacio de Miramar (see above) was completed. With 75,000 sq. m (807,293 sq. ft.) of parkland, the palace served as the summer home of Franco from 1940 until 1975. The residence remains closed to the public, but you can wander through the grounds daily: in summer from 8am to 8:30pm, in the off season from 8am to 5:30pm. To reach it, take bus 19 to Ayete from Plaza de Guipúzcoa.

Museo Chillida-Leku, Caserío Zabalaga 66, Jáuregui Barrio, Hernani (℃ **94-333-53-08**), is devoted to the artwork of Eduardo Chillida, a sculptor legendary in the Basque world and one whose work appears in many world museums. A 10-minute drive from the heart of San Sebastián, the museum lies

Moments   Festival Time

San Sebastián is the location for two prestigious events that draw visitors from around the world. The first, in late July is **Jazzaldia,** a jazz (in all its genres) festival that takes place in both private venues and public spaces around the city and in the past has featured top musicians such as Ricki Lee Jones, Roy Ayers, and Rubén Blades. The second is the **San Sebastián International Film Festival,** which takes place in mid-September. Started in the mid-1950s, the festival antagonized Franco and he ordered his cronies to keep a close eye on the films for anything "immoral." After his death, the festival flourished and now has a reputation for previewing the year's most disquieting and avant-garde releases. Every year the Donostia Prize is awarded to an industry professional (over the last couple of years Sean Penn, Woody Allen, and Isabel Huppert have been handed the accolade), ensuring the festival enjoys its fair share of glamour. For more local color, San Sebastián stages its annual carnival, **Aste Nagusia** in mid-August: a joyous celebration of traditional Basque music and dance, along with fire-works, cooking competitions, and sporting events.

in the little mountain town of Hernani. The hillside around the museum is studded with some 40 Chillida monoliths set amongst beech trees, oaks, and magnolias.

In the center of the property is a farmhouse from the 1500s, which the artist designed to display some of his smaller pieces. These include hanging paper "grav-itations" (not quite a collage, but not a mobile either), translucent alabaster sculp-ture, stone blocks that evoke the Mayan culture, as well as "jigsaw" sculptures of metal and marble. The aging sculptor refers to his museum as a "cathedral." Sur-prisingly and virtually unheard of in an art museum, he invites visitors to touch his sculpture, as he firmly believes that sculpture "should be touched." Hours in July and August are Wednesday through Monday from 10:30am to 7pm; Sep-tember through June from 10:30am to 3pm. Admission is 7€ ($8.05) for adults; 5€ ($5.75) for children over 8, students, and seniors; and free for children under 8. Closed December 25 and January 1. Take bus G2 from San Sebastián.

The **Fundación Balenciaga,** another out-of-town museum, is dedicated to the influential couturier Cristobel Balenciaga. Although more associated with Parisian haute couture, Balenciaga was born in Getaria, a small town 30kms (19 miles) west of San Sebastián on the coast. Over his long career, Balenciaga was known for masterful draping (Givenchy called him the "architect" of haute cou-ture), use of intricate fabrics, and extravagant evening gowns. The foundation's collection consists of forty hats and ensembles, plus photographic material. Par-que Aldamar 3, Getaria (© **94-300-47-77**). Open Tuesday through Saturday 10am to 2pm and 4pm to 7pm, Sunday 10am to 2pm. Admission is 2€ ($2.30). Take the Getaria bus from San Sebastián's main bus terminal.

Finally, to get the best view of the city, take the funicular to the top of **Monte Igueldo** ⋆⋆⋆, where, from a gazebo, you get a panoramic view of the bay and the Cantabrian coastline. October to March, the funicular runs from 11am to 6pm Monday, Tuesday, Thursday, and Friday; from 11am to 8pm Saturday and Sunday. April to September, it runs 10am to 10pm Thursday to Tuesday. A round-trip fare costs 1.20€ ($1.40). It's also possible to drive up (about 45 min. to reach the top). In spring, the air is rich with the scent of honeysuckle.

SHOPPING

Your immersion into Basque culture will probably prompt you to buy some of the handicrafts and accessories from the region. Two of the best outlets are **Txapela,** Calle Puerto 3 (© **94-342-02-43**), and **Arriluzea,** Calle 31 de Agosto 13 (© **94-342-41-35**). Both sell souvenirs and the rough cotton shirts for which the Basques are famous. And if you're looking for a *boina* (typical Basque beret) or any other form of headgear, consider a visit to the venerable shelves of San Sebastián's oldest hat manufacturer, **Ponsol,** Calle Narrica 4 (© **94-342-08-76**). *Boinas* run about 9€ to 21€ ($10–$24); other styles can go up to and over the 100€ ($115) mark.

For other knickknacks, the streets of the Parte Vieja are the place to pick up ceramics, leather wares, and postcards. If you have the luggage space, the squat Basque wine glasses that you may have been eyeing in tapas bars are incredibly cheap and can be picked up in most hardware stores. The street wear of local designer **Loreak Mendian,** Calle Hernani 27 (© **94-343-41-76**), enjoys cool status throughout Spain (and as far away as Australia).

WHERE TO STAY

Try to book accommodations (of any category) as far in advance as possible in San Sebastián.

Very Expensive

Hotel María Cristina ✰✰✰   One of the most spectacular Belle Epoque hotels in Spain, enviably positioned in the heart of town midway between the bay and Río Urumea, this is the town's top choice. The Cristina opened in 1912 behind a facade of chiseled stone and ornate ironwork. The crowd is likely to include movie stars, film directors, and newly moneyed moguls; this is where the glitterati stay during San Sebastián's film festival. The hotel was richly remodeled in 1987. The public rooms are opulent with ormolu, mahogany, onyx and exotic marbles, and rosewood marquetry. The spacious guest rooms are appropriately lavish, with luxury beds and bathrooms with tub/shower combos.

Oquendo 1, 20004 San Sebastián. © **800/221-2340** in the U. S., or 94-343-76-00. Fax 94-343-76-76. www. starwoodhotels.com. 136 units. 235€–415€ ($270–$477) double; 350€–900€ ($403–$1,035) suite. AE, DC, MC, V. Parking 22€ ($25). **Amenities:** Restaurant; bar; health club; car rental; business center; 24-hr. room service; babysitting; laundry service; dry cleaning. *In room:* A/C, TV, minibar, hair dryer, safe.

Expensive

Costa Vasca ✰✰   A large red-brick hotel rated four stars by the government, the Costa Vasca is 10 minutes from Ondarreta Beach and a 5-minute drive (or

---

Tips **Pamper Yourself**

A truly great way to unwind in San Sebastián is a visit to **La Perla,** Paseo de La Concha s/n (© **94-345-88-56**). Right on the waterfront in an elegant Belle Epoque building, this spa offers treatments such as massages, facials, skin scrubs, and all manners of ways to rejuvenate your tired self. Most people however simply go for the "circuit" (18€/$20), which consists of an array of water therapies, including a Jacuzzi, a saltwater pool, a cold freshwater pool, massage jets, and a sauna. Sea views are to be enjoyed throughout your visit, which last 1 hour and 45 minutes, just enough to make you feel like new again. Other treatments range from 13€ to 80€ ($15–$92). The spa is open from 8am to 10pm year-round.

10 min. on foot) from the center of town. The interior of the hotel is modern and businesslike with plenty of space for conferences and banquets; however, it's ideal for the individual traveler, too. The rooms are a good size and comfortably furnished, their bathrooms equipped with tub/shower combos. Many of the accommodations have balconies. The decoration is tasteful but discreet.

Av. de Pío Baroja 15, 20008 San Sebastián. ⓒ **94-321-10-11.** Fax 94-321-24-28. www.aranzazu-hoteles. com. 203 units. 125€–140€ ($144–$161) double; 310€–330€ ($357–$376) suite. AE, DC, MC, V. Free parking. **Amenities:** Restaurant; bar; outdoor pool; limited room service; babysitting; laundry service; dry cleaning. *In room:* A/C, TV, minibar, hair dryer, safe.

Hotel de Londres y de Inglaterra 🌟🌟
Beside the northern edge of the town's most popular beach, Playa de la Concha, this 19th-century hotel is one of the most stylish in town. It's not as plush as the María Cristina but is significantly more affordable. The views from many of the balconies encompass the beach and some rocky offshore islands. The traditional-style public rooms contain deep armchairs and big windows. Renovated in the past few years, the hotel has good-size guest rooms with a vaguely English decor and modern bathrooms with tub/shower combos.

Zubieta 2, 20007 San Sebastián. ⓒ **94-344-07-70.** Fax 94-344-04-91. www.hlondres.com. 148 units. 175€–202€ ($201–$232) double; 220€–246€ ($253–$283) suite. AE, DC, MC, V. Parking 15€ ($17) nearby. **Amenities:** Restaurant; bar; limited room service; babysitting; laundry service; dry cleaning; nonsmoking rooms. *In room:* A/C, TV, minibar, hair dryer, safe.

Moderate

Anoeta Hotel
Close to the sports arena and a 5-minute drive from the town center, this government-rated three-star hotel is named for the village that once stood here but was long ago absorbed by the growing boundaries of San Sebastián. Anoeta features cherrywood, marble fittings, and a modern decor behind its brick facade. With a welcoming atmosphere, it's one of the better choices in the moderate range. The rooms are generally small but inviting, with comfortable beds, wooden furniture, and bathrooms with tub/shower combos.

Paseo de Anoeta 30, 20014 San Sebastián. ⓒ **94-345-14-99.** Fax 94-345-20-36. www.hotelanoeta.com. 26 units. 77€–95€ ($89–$109) double; 95€–125€ ($109–$144) suite. AE, DC, MC, V. Parking 7.50€ ($8.60). Bus: 26 or 28. **Amenities:** Restaurant; bar; babysitting; laundry service; dry cleaning. *In room:* A/C, TV, minibar, hair dryer, safe.

Mercure Monte Igueldo 🌟
This first-class hotel is perched like a castle on the top of the mountain overlooking San Sebastián, a 10-minute drive from the center of town. The public rooms, guest rooms, and main terrace all boast panoramic coast views. Each of the streamlined modern rooms has a private balcony. The furnishings are standardized but reasonably comfortable; each room has a well-kept bathroom with a tub/shower combo.

Paseo del Faro 134, Monte Igueldo, 20008 San Sebastián. ⓒ **94-321-02-11.** Fax 94-321-50-28. www.monte igueldo.com. 125 units. 88€–120€ ($101–$138) double; 154€–160€ ($177–$184) triple. AE, DC, MC, V. Free parking. Bus: 16 Igueldo. **Amenities:** Restaurant; bar; outdoor pool; limited room service; babysitting; laundry service; dry cleaning. *In room:* A/C, TV, minibar, hair dryer, safe.

Niza 🌟 *Finds*
This little hotel, opening onto the Playa de la Concha, offers real character and a great location. It has modern furnishings in the small rooms and antiques in the public lounges. The petit salon, for example, contains an Oriental rug, Directoire chairs, a tall grandfather clock, and a rosewood breakfront. In

direct contrast are the rather basic rooms, with wooden headboards, white walls, and wall-to-wall carpeting. All units have bathrooms with tub/shower combos.

Zubieta 56, 20007 San Sebastián. ℂ **94-342-66-63.** Fax 94-344-12-51. www.hotelniza.com. 40 units. 98€–112€ ($113–$ 129) double. AE, DC, MC, V. Parking 12€ ($14), reservations required. Bus: 5 or 6. **Amenities:** Restaurant/pizzeria; cafeteria; babysitting; laundry service; dry cleaning; safe. *In room:* A/C, TV, hair dryer.

Inexpensive

Pensión Amaiur 🅐🅐 *Finds*   This charming place is a bit of an institution. Such is its popularity that it has now spread over two floors of a 19th-century building and each room has a character all its own, from chintzy to "palm and cane" to purple feature walls and bold colors. Bathrooms are shared (one to every three rooms) as is a kitchen on the second floor that the highly congenial owner put in for the sole purpose of encouraging fellow travelers to get to know one another. The front rooms sport the archetypal geranium-filled balconies, but can be noisy at night time. But that's a small price to pay for this A-grade type, homespun accommodations that is sadly (and at least in the cities) disappearing.

Calle 31 de Agosto, 20003 San Sebastián. ℂ **94-342-96-54.** www.pensionamaiur.com. 13 units. 45€–52€ ($52–$60) double; 85€ ($98) family room. MC, V. *In room:* TV (in 10 units).

Hostal Bahía *Value*   A good-value hotel a block from the beach, the Bahía features guest rooms of varying sizes: Some are large enough to contain sofas and armchairs; others fall into the cubicle category. Each comes with a little bathroom with a shower stall. Many North Americans stay here and take public transportation to Pamplona for the running of the bulls.

Calle San Martín 54B, 20007 San Sebastián. ℂ **94-346-92-11.** Fax 94-346-39-14. www.hostalbahia.com. 55 units. 60€–90€ ($69–$104) double; 60€–95€ ($69–$109) family room. Rates include breakfast. MC, V. Parking nearby 12€ ($14). Bus: 5, 6, 7, 8, or 9. **Amenities:** Bar; laundry service; dry cleaning. *In room:* A/C (in 25 units), TV, hair dryer, safe.

Pensión Aida *Value*   The resort's best bargain is this recently discovered nugget with a certain charm. *Travel & Leisure* called its rates "ridiculously low." At the film festival, Robert DeNiro won't be seen checking in here, heading for María Cristina instead. But struggling filmmakers who haven't made a distribution deal are likely to be found here. It is simply but comfortably decorated. Bedrooms are small to midsize, each with a little tiled bathroom with shower. Although the little boardinghouse itself is short on amenities, many facilities are just outside its doors, including a dry cleaning and laundry establishment across the street and several cafeterias and inexpensive restaurants nearby.

Calle Iztueta 9, 20001 San Sebastián. ℂ **94-332-78-00.** Fax 94-332-67-07. www.pensionesconencanto. com. 9 units. 48€–72€ ($55–$83) double. MC, V. **Amenities:** Breakfast bar, safe, Internet access. *In room:* TV, hair dryer, iron.

WHERE TO DINE
Expensive

Akelare 🅐🅐🅐 BASQUE   Akelare (which means "Witches' Sabbath" in Euskera) does indeed have an air of magic about it. Not only is it one of the finest dining experiences in the gourmet mecca San Sebastián, it is one of the finest restaurants in Spain and a must on the list of serious foodies. Together with Juan Mari Arzak (see below), Pedro Subijana's preparations helped shape the phenomenon of *la nueva cocina vasca* (modern Basque cuisine) and have influenced and inspired whole generations of Basque chefs, many of whom have gone on to

---

⌒ *Value* **Relish the Experience**

San Sebastián is known as the gastronomic pulse of Spain, and there are more Michelin-starred restaurants per head here than Paris. But prices are well below their French cousins, especially for a *menú de degustación* (multicourse fixed-price meal of small dishes). Anyone serious about food should book a table in advance at one of San Sebastián's fine restaurants; the experience will be relished for years to come.

---

become stars in their own right. Opened in 1974, the restaurant is perched high on a cliff-top on the western edge of San Sebastián and boasts one desirable view, yet despite an expansive terrace out front, alfresco dining is a no-no. They don't really do it that way in Basque country. Instead a bank of picture windows surrounds a formal dining hall giving sweeping vistas of the Bay of Biscay.

Subijana's constantly changing repertoire of dishes inspired by the Basque *caseríos* (farmsteads) is as good a place as any to start a foray into the world of high-end Basque cookery. Like many of the chefs his connection to land and sea is tantamount; he grows many of his own vegetables and uses mainly local ingredients to produce lively, yet down to earth dishes. Depending on the season these may include fat Cantabrian anchovies washed down with briny manzanilla sherry, *kokotzas* (hake cheeks) with clams in a delicate herbal bath, and the local catch with nothing more complicated than a scrap of garlic and pinch of parsley. His more racy dishes include snails with watercress sauce; a highly modernized version of pigs trotters on a light yogurt foam; and Subijana's landmark dessert, cubes of gin and tonic jelly with lemon sorbet.

Paseo del Padre Orkolaga 56. ⓒ **94-321-20-52.** Reservations strongly recommended. Main courses 28€–42€ ($32–$48); tasting menu 95€ ($109). AE, DC, MC, V. Jan–June Wed–Sat 1–3:30pm and 8:30–11pm, Sun 1–3:30pm; July–Dec Tues–Sat 1–3:30pm and 8:30–11pm, Sun 1–3:30pm. Closed Feb and Oct 1–15. Bus: Igueldo.

Arzak ⊛⊛⊛ *Moments* BASQUE   In a nutshell, Arzak is the difference between good cooking and really great cooking, especially since the legendary owner/chef Juan Mari Arzak joined forces with his daughter, Elena, who has refined the menu considerably, placing greater focus on single ingredients and more minimal dishes. Together they form a formidable team, hatching culinary breakthroughs in the laboratory kitchen: a space age den where the glass drawers that line the walls are filled with every imaginable flavor from pink peppercorns to shriveled Tasmanian lemons. The restaurant itself dates back to 1897, when it was still the family home, and while more old-school plush these days, the family atmosphere still shines through.

The menu changes and evolves almost on a daily basis often dictated by something Arzak has seen or heard in the market on his daily rounds. Expect such delights as fruity, salty, spicy appetizers of pineapple and pepper; melon and anchovy; a crunchy banana cone oozing fluffy tuna mousse; cherry and tomato gazpacho; mango dim sum stuffed with foie; poached egg "graffiti"; pink *chipirones* (baby squid) in a "sea beaten" sauce; spring lamb encased in a gossamer thin sheet of coffee, then melted to produce a subtle and highly pleasing gravy; chocolate omelets; cheese in a spinach cloak and magical, fizzing, strawberry milkshakes.

Alto de Miracruz 21. ℭ **94-327-84-65**. Reservations required. Main courses 35€–43€ ($40–$49); fixed-price menu 110€ ($127). AE, DC, MC, V. Jan–June Wed–Sat 1–3:30pm and 8:30–11:30pm, Sun 1–3:30pm; July–Dec Tues–Sat 1–3:30pm and 8:30–11:30pm, Sun 1–3:30pm. Closed June 13–30 and Nov 7–Dec 1. .2km (⅛ mile) from San Sebastián.

Martín Berasategui ★★★ BASQUE   Just when you thought the dining situation in San Sebastián couldn't stand any more starred chefs, along comes Martín Berasategui, whose cooking excites food critics throughout Europe. His family still owns a restaurant in the old part of San Sebastián (Bodegón Alejandro Jatetxea, see below) where he spent most of his time growing up, learning the ropes from his aunt and mother. He still occasionally puts in an appearance. For the most part however he's based at his handsome suburban restaurant just outside the city limits where an army of chefs turn out dishes that are constantly evolving. "Ninety-eight percent of my guests eat whatever the tasting menu is that day," he says. It's also one of the few top-end restaurants that has a terrace for outdoors dining.

The kind of dishes you can expect to have include a shot glass of beetroot and *txakoli* (the local white wine) infusion, a lozenge of sweet onion topped with a slice of raw anchovy, smoked eel with caramelized foie, salad set in an intensely flavored tomato jelly, a simply grilled scallop on a heap of braised celeriac, fatty tuna eaten with a teaspoon to accentuate its softness, ruby red pigeon breast with tea cheese and cherry confit, green apple ice cream, and lemon granita to finish. All in all, extraordinary food paired with perfect wines.

Loidi Kalea 4, Lasarte. ℭ **94-336-64-71**. Reservations required. Main courses 26€–36€ ($30–$41); tasting menu 94€ ($108). AE, MC, V. Wed–Sat 1–3pm and 8:30–11pm; Sun 1–3pm. Closed Dec 14–Jan 15. 8km (5 miles) from San Sebastián: Take N-1 towards Tolosa, continue for 5km (3 miles) then exit Lasarte.

Mugaritz ★★★ *Finds* BASQUE   Of the young chefs making their mark on the San Sebastián dining scene, one name seems to resonate clearer than the rest: Andoni Luis Aduritz. He opened Mugaritz nearly 7 years ago—in a barn-like farmhouse set in rolling countryside about 20 minutes outside of San Sebastián—and offers a lighter, more organic style of cooking than many of the townies.

The tasting menu offers a balanced range of dishes, building from light starters like poached egg with three truffled consommé and flower and herb salad (from his own garden out back), to roasted purple tomatoes with black rice and mollusk jus; raw, irony sea urchins and velvety tuna *marmitako* (a typical Basque marinade) surrounded by edible lily flowers; and on to heavier meat dishes such as roasted foie gras with date stone broth and meltingly tender stewed beef with vegetable tears: every single dish beautifully conceived and presented. Aduritz incidentally is also the purveyor of a superb regional cheese board, something that still seems to be struggling to make a comeback elsewhere.

Aldura Aldea, Errenteria, San Sebastián. ℭ **94-352-24-55**. Reservations required. Main courses 60€–90€ ($69–$104); tasting menu 100€–180€ ($115–$207). AE, DC, MC, V. Wed–Sun 1–3pm and Tues–Sat 8:30–11pm. Closed Dec 22–Jan 14 and Easter week. 8km (5 miles) from San Sebastián.

Panier Fleuri ★ BASQUE/INTERNATIONAL   This citadel is a long established favorite on the San Sebastián dining circuit serving French-style Basque dishes with elegance and flair. And it makes a change from the more aggressively creative cooking of other Michelin-starred places. The third generation of a family of chefs who helped put the city on the map as a gastronomic treasure, Chef Tatus Fombellida keeps things fairly simple, offering a strong selection of classic dishes with a focus on prime, seasonal ingredients. Her *faisan* (pheasant) and *becada asada* (roast woodcock) have been hailed as among the finest game dishes anywhere in the Basque country, as are her market fresh fish dishes including a delectable sole baked with spinach and enveloped in a freshly prepared hollandaise sauce. Puddings contrast nicely with the fairly rich mains; a light palette cleanser such as lemon sorbet with champagne makes a suitably elegant end to a meal. The wine cellar is also worthy of mention. As a collector, Fombellida offers an interesting list of wines, many of which are more unusual vintages, but rest assured you are in safe hands. The sommelier is happy to advise on the often perplexing selection, including mellow versions of such wines as Remelluri, Barón de Oña, and Viña Albina.

Paseo de Salamanca 1. © **94-342-42-05.** Reservations required. Main courses 22€–52€ ($25–$60); fixed-price menu 55€ ($63). AE, DC, MC, V. Mon–Sat 1–3:30pm and 6:30–11pm; Sun 1–3:30pm. Closed June 1–24 and Dec 24–31.

Moderate

Bodegón Alejandro Jatetxea ⭐ *(Value* BASQUE   Few places come with greater pedigree (Martín Berasategui grew up here and was born upstairs), but you'll find not airs and graces here. The custard colored dining rooms accented with tiles have barely changed over the years and still breathe an air of quiet refinement. Few places are more pleasing for a cozy lunch, and the focus here is on a set-price market menu that changes every day. Menu items are based on old family recipes and include local sweet red peppers stuffed with salt cod and herbs, seafood stews with rice, artichokes with clams, and roasted veal or braised pork in wine sauce. Any of a rotating series of pastries and cakes offer highly caloric but eminently satisfying desserts.

Calle Fermín Calbetón 4B. © **94-342-71-58.** Reservations recommended. Set-price menu 25€ ($29). AE, MC, V. Tues–Sat 1–4pm and 9–11pm; Sun 1–4pm.

Agorregi ⭐ *(Value* CONTEMPORARY BASQUE   A newcomer to the scene, the food cooked here by Agorregi Gorka Arzelus is unapologetically modern while sticking within the confines of what constitutes real food. This is a super lunch spot that proudly shows off the superiority of local produce. Dishes may include a salad of mixed leaves, topped with *boquerones* (anchovies "cooked" in vinegar) and shards of *bonito* (a member of the tuna family), drizzled with well-aged (as opposed to reduced) balsamic vinegar. Local filet of steak on a layer of oozing Brie and topped with sweet pimientos *piquillo* (small, pointed red peppers), or catch of the day, with light desserts and cheeses to finish. It's the perfect antidote to the Michelin-starred tour, but offers something more substantial than a *pintxo* crawl.

Puerto 14. © **94-342-01-80.** Reservations required. Main courses 15€–20€ ($17–$23); fixed-price menu 22€ ($25). AE, DC, MC, V. Tues–Sat 1–3:30pm and 8:30–11:30pm; Sun 1–3:30pm.

Urepel ⭐ BASQUE/INTERNATIONAL   Close to its major competitor, Panier Fleuri (see above), Urepel is near the mouth of the Urumea River, at the edge of the old town. Its interior isn't as elegant as those of the restaurants above, but that doesn't bother fans of this place at all. They come for the food. The restaurant is the domain of Tomás Almandoz, one of the outstanding chefs in the north of Spain. Seafood dominates the menu and is deftly handled, either served with delicate, traditional sauces or nothing at all. The main courses are made even better by an emphasis on perfectly prepared vegetables and *rape, dorada* (gilthead sea bream), and *cigalas* (crayfish) are all likely to turn up on the menu, as well as more seasonal fishes. A local food critic got so carried away with the dessert cart and its presentation that she claimed, "It would take Velázquez to arrange a pastry so artfully"—an indication of how highly regarded this place is. It's preferable for dinner when the ambience is less business oriented.

Paseo de Salamanca 3. ✆ **94-342-40-40.** Reservations required. Main courses 16€–37€ ($18–$43); tasting menu 55€–75€ ($63–$86). AE, DC, MC, V. Mon and Wed–Sat 1–3:30pm and 8:30–11pm. Closed Easter week, July 1–23, and Dec 24–Jan 6.

Inexpensive

La Cuchara de San Telmo *Value* TAPAS   The team of young chefs here all trained under the mighty, but lacking sufficient funds to set up a "real" restaurant they opted instead for a classic tapas bar serving hearty, "peasant food" with a twist. Where decades ago folks would have been perfectly happy with some *morro de ternera* (cow lips) chef/owner Alex and his pals make robust stews and more palatable patties out of every part of the beast; trotters, cheeks and ears as well as the more conventional beef in Rioja wine. Lighter dishes include *ventresca* (belly tuna) stuffed into a whole tomato and doused with parsley oil, and a luxury rice pudding flecked with cinnamon. Unlike the other pintxo bars in town, you'll find no food on the bar tops; instead, everything is chalked up on the blackboard. You'll need two or three dishes each to make a substantial main course.

Corredor de San Telmo s/n. ✆ **94-343-54-46.** Main courses 7€–12€ ($8.05–$14). Tues–Sat 1–3pm and 6:30–11pm; Sun 1–3pm.

Bodega Gambara ★★ *Finds* TAPAS   Tiny but perfectly formed, Gambara is one of a rare breed of places that specializes in one thing; wild mushrooms from the fields and forests of the Basque country on both the French and Spanish sides of the border. The bar is heaped with baskets piled high with bulbous, caramel-covered *bolets;* golden, trumpet-shaped *rovellós;* truffles; morels; and milk caps, depending on the season. Most are sautéed and served with a freshly cracked quails egg at the center. It's also a good spot for breakfast, when the bar is laden with hot, mini croissants stuffed with *jamón*, eggs, and velvety black pudding.

San Jerónimo 21. ✆ **94-342-25-75.** *Pintxos* around 2€ ($2.30); main courses 9€ ($10); fixed-price menu 24€ ($28). AE, DC, MC, V. Tues–Sun 11am–3:15pm and 6:30-11:45pm. Closed July 15–31 and Nov 15–30.

SAN SEBASTIAN AFTER DARK

The best evening entertainment in San Sebastián is to go **tapas-tasting** in the old quarter. Even the Bilbaínos reluctantly admit that the *pintxos* here beat their own. Certainly in terms of quantity, quality, and variety the tapas of San Sebastián is unequalled.

Groups of people often spend their evenings on some 20 streets in the old town, each leading toward Monte Urgull, the port, or La Brecha marketplace. **Alameda del Bulevar** is the most upscale of these streets and **Calle Fermín Calveton** one of the most popular. You'll find plenty of these places on your own, but here are some to get you going. Keep in mind that most bars stop making *pintxos* after 9pm, so start early.

The tasty tapas served at **Casa Alcalde,** Mayor 19 (✆ **94-342-62-16**), just a 5-minute walk from the Parque Alderdi Eder, are thinly sliced ham, cheese, and shellfish dishes. The different varieties are all neatly displayed. You can also have full meals in a small restaurant at the back. It's open daily from 10am to 11pm. The variety of tapas and wines offered at **Casa Vallés,** Reyes Católicos 10 (✆ **94-345-22-10**), seems endless. Go to hang out with the locals and feast on tidbits guaranteed to spoil your dinner. Casa Vallés, in the center of town behind the cathedral, is open daily from 8:30 to 11:30pm (closed the last 2 weeks of Dec).

Many locals say that **La Cepa,** 31 de Agosto 7–9 (© **94-342-63-94**), on the northern edge of the old town, serves perhaps the best tapas, and the Jabugo ham is one proof of this claim. Try the grilled squid or the salt-cod-and-green pepper omelet. You can also order dinner here. It's open Wednesday through Monday from 11am to midnight. At **Aloña/Berri,** Bermingham 24, Nuevo Gros (© **94-329-08-18**), you can feast on the delights of silky salt cod *bran-dade,* pigeon in pastry, and anchovies in red pepper cream. At **Oñatz,** Urdaneta 22 (© **94-345-55-47**), they serve the city's most exquisite morsels, none better than a "haystack" of foie gras and apples. You can go on to the mussel-and-gar-lic flan or braised oxtail. At the family-run **Bar Juli,** Viteri 27, Renteria (© **94-351-28-87**), Igor, a graduate of Arzak (see "Where to Dine," above), lures and satisfies the most demanding palates of San Sebastián. Try his sushi-like tuna salad and what have been called "the best seafood *croquetas* on the northern shore of Spain."

San Sebastián has other nightlife possibilities, but they dim when compared to a *tapeo.* Nevertheless, if disco isn't too retro for you, head for **La Kabutzia,** Paseo de la Concha (© **94-342-97-85**), where a cover and one drink cost 12€ ($14). The club opens at 8pm, with variable closing times, depending on busi-ness. The best live jazz is found at **Altxeri,** Calle Reina Regente 2 (© **94-342-16-93**), where a cover charge may or may not be imposed, depending on the group. It's open Tuesday through Sunday from 4pm to 2:30am.

San Sebastián's only venue for gambling is the **Casino de San Sebastián,** Mayor 1 (© **94-342-92-14**). The casino requires minimum bets of 1€ ($1.15) to 2.50€ ($2.90) for the roulette tables and 5€ ($5.75) for the blackjack tables. Jackets and ties for men aren't required. The casino is open daily from 5pm to 5am. It is closed on Christmas and New Year's Eve.

The big cultural center is the concert hall, **Auditorio Kursaal,** Av. de Zurriola 1 (© **94-300-30-00**), a daringly modern avant-garde building strategically posi-tioned on the Bay of Concha. It is a cultural, sporting, and leisure center, which is the venue for almost any major event: "Basque Dixieland" band, a big salsa band from Madrid, or gospel singers from America's Deep South. The designer was famed Spanish architect Rafael Moneno, who created what's been compared to two mammoth Noguchi lantern lamps.

Kursaal, along with the Guggenheim museum in Bilbao, has helped put the Basque country on the cultural maps of Europe. Many tradition-minded locals objected to the glaringly modern structure, feeling that it was out of style with the city's essential Belle Epoque architecture.

All the major festivals of San Sebastián, including the September film festival, are staged here. There is a 1,800-seat theater for plays, music, dance, and *zarzuela* performances. Even if there is no major event staged here during your visit to San Sebastián, you can take a guided tour from Monday through Friday at noon and weekends at noon and 1:30pm, costing 2.05€ ($2.35). Reserva-tions are recommended.

MUNDAKA

640km (399 miles) NW of Barcelona, 105km (65 miles) E of San Sebastián, 40km (25 miles) E of Bilbao

The coastline between Bilbao and San Sebastián is some of the most beautiful in Spain, characterized by dramatic rock formations, hidden coves, and the crashing blue waters of the Cantabrian Sea. Mundaka, 40km (25 miles) east of Bilbao, is the archetypal Basque fishing village with an unusual claim to fame; it is also one of the top ten surfing spots on the planet. Located at the mouth of the river of the same name, Mundaka's waters are reputed to produce the longest wave in Europe. Hardly surprising then that the World Surf Championship is located here every October when its tiny population of 1,700 is invaded by camper vans full of American, Australian, South African, and other surfers from all over the world. But even if diving into 3m (10-ft.) waves with a long piece of fiberglass is not your idea of a holiday, Mundaka is the ideal place to relax for a day or two, walking along the breathtaking coastline and observing the ebb and flow of Basque rural life. Of cultural interest is the 11th-century church that dominates the village and the 19th-century Hermitage of Saint Catherine, once part of the old fort's walls.

GETTING THERE   From Bilbao: The EuskoTren (destination: Bermeo) runs every half-hour (every 10 min. in peak hours) from the Atxuri station, Calle Atxuri 6 (© **90-254-32-10**). Alternately, the Bizkaibus runs an hourly service (destination: Bermeo) from the terminal outside the Abando train station, Bailén 2 (© **94-448-40-80**). By car, take the BI-635 road towards Guernika from Bilbao.

From San Sebastián: There is no direct public transportation from San Sebastián to Mundaka. Your best bet it to head back to Bilbao and take the transport stated above.

WHERE TO STAY

Hotel El Puerto ✪   In terms of location, the Hotel El Puerto has the Mundaka accommodations market covered, which is why it is best to book well ahead. Sitting right on the small harbor, where a fleet of fishing boats can be seen making its way out to the open sea, rest assured that you will fall asleep with the gentle sounds of rolling waves in the distance. For a view however, state you want a front room, which they charge extra for. The rooms themselves are functional and comfortable enough, if not a bit under par with what you would normally get for the price. Downstairs there is lounge with free Internet access, and the adjoining bar serves some excellent tapas and is quite the village meeting point. The hotel also has various apartments located around the village, one that (according to management) is a favorite retreat of the artist Julian Schabel.

Portu Kalea 1, 48360 Mundaka. © **94-687-67-25.** Fax 94-687-67-26. www.hotelelpuerto.com. 11 units. 45€–75€ ($52–$86) double. AE, DC, MC, V. Parking 6€ ($6.90). **Amenities:** Cafeteria; room service; laundry service; dry cleaning. In room: TV.

Hotel Kurutziaga Jauregia *(Value)*   This ancient inn is in the center of the village, on the old route to Santiago as signified by the cross that adorns the pretty square outside. Until 1648 it was known as "The House of Pirates," but these days there is nothing dishonest about its prices or amenities. Rooms have been lovingly restored in shades of white and mauve, while retaining rustic touches in the forms of exposed brick walls and beams. There is a restaurant (with adjoining terrace) downstairs where breakfast is served.

Kurtzio Kalea 1, 48360 Mundaka. © **94-687-69-25.** Fax 94-617-70-12. www.kurutziagajauregia.com. 22 units. 48€–79€ ($55–$91) double. AE, DC, MC, V. Free public parking. **Amenities:** Cafeteria; room service; laundry service. In room: A/C, TV.

WHERE TO DINE

El Casino ✪ *Moments* BASQUE   Confusingly named, as there are no games of chance around (save for the domino-playing locals), this restaurant-private club is generally considered to be the finest dining on this stretch of the coast. After ascending a wooden staircase, you are greeted by a spacious ante-chamber before being led to the magnificent dining room with sea vistas from every angle. When the waitress says that the fish on offer "depends on the sea" you know you are in for a real treat (if she offers *lubina,* take it; this delicate fish is a renowned in these waters). And indeed the salad of lettuce hearts and anchovies, the fish soup with hearty chunks of the day's catch, grilled clams, monkfish and hake were all top class. Desserts consist of tried and true classics such as flan and homemade cakes. The only disappointment was the slightly rudimentary wine list.

Calle San Pedro 2. ℂ **94-687-60-05.** Reservations required. Main courses 18€–25€ ($21–$29). AE, DC, MC, V. Mon–Sat 1–3:30pm and 8:30–11pm.

Appendix A:
Barcelona Past & Present

Once called Spain's "second city," Barcelona no longer deserves that appellation. Long suppressed by the dominance of Madrid, Barcelona has well and truly found its own personality. Barcelona, like Milan, is both industrious and pleasure seeking, serious but playful, and image conscious without losing its inherent grittiness. Warlords, kings, and dictators have all tried to mold the city to suit their interests, but Barcelona is nothing if not resilient, re-inventing itself time and time again and refusing to renounce its culture, language, and identity. Today, with a booming economy and arts scene, plus an enviable lifestyle largely facilitated by a people-oriented local government, Barcelona seems to epitomize modern Europe and continues to seduce with its special charms.

1 Barcelona Today

As Catalonia moves on its journey into the millennium, tourism continues to boom and to dominate the economy—it remains a hot, hot industry with yearly arrivals in Barcelona bypassing the 4.5 million mark and the Old City, at least in the summer, bustling with tour groups and buses.

Visitors from pre-1992, that pivotal year when Barcelona presented a new-and-improved city to the rest of the world at the Summer Olympics, sometimes barely recognize the place. After the gray years, during which the Franco-dominated central government withheld much-needed funds for public infrastructure and let package tourism eyesores blight the coastline, Catalonia is no longer interested in the "lager lout" image. Although it's still possible to find bargains in rural areas and the coast, tourism of the $5-a-day variety is now a distant memory as prices have skyrocketed, especially since the introduction of the euro in 2002. The media has baptized Barcelona the coolest city in Europe with the city's restaurants, bars, shops, and hotels among the most cutting-edge on the Continent. But despite its chic image, Barcelona remains steeped in tradition, where history plays an important part in its *fiestas* (celebrations) and in everyday life.

If there is one fact you should have perfectly clear before arriving, it's that for an overwhelming majority of Catalans, their homeland is *not* Spain (in high season you maybe even handed a leaflet or two telling you as much). Most consider themselves Catalan first and Spanish second, so bemoaning the lack of sangria and bullfights will only be met with the coldest of receptions. Historically robbed of its status as an independent nation, autonomy was returned to Catalonia via the 1978 Spanish constitution, and politicians have pretty much been at the negotiating table ever since, pushing for even greater self-rule. After more than 20 years as head of the **Generalitat (Catalan Regional Government),** the conservative Jordi Pujol lost to the socialist Pasqual Maragall (who served as mayor of Barcelona during the Olympic years) in 2003. In coalition with the left-wing ERC party (whose aim is *total* independence for Catalonia), Maragall has been accused of placing more emotive issues of a nationalist nature before policy-making. But the fact remains that Catalonia contributes more to the central government's tax coffers than any other region—and receives less in paybacks. Despite a largely restored identity and culture, the dream of a fully self-governing Catalonia remains a long way off for the Catalanistas.

Barcelona reinvented itself yet again in the mid-1980s after the city had time to digest its newfound, post-Franco freedom. A pent-up creative and political force was let loose. Shameless in its self-promotion, it affected all aspects of society, from politics to culture and the arts. Its achievements have resulted in what *Newsweek* recently described as "one of Europe's most dynamic and innovative cities."

Immigration is now the region's biggest challenge. Apart from Spanish and Latin communities, Catalonia remained a monocultural society for centuries before the current wave of immigration. Immigrants now make up 5% of the total population of just over six million, rocketing to 50% in some inner-Barcelona pockets. Providing a good education, emphasizing religious tolerance, regulating the foreign workforce, and the immersion of Catalan language and culture are all now high on the agenda, amid a backdrop of hysterical cries from the right that the latter will be lost if Catalonia is to absorb any more foreigners.

Immigrants are essential, however, for Catalonia's primary industry. South Americans and North Africans are now employed in the vast acres of vineyards, olive groves, and other agrarian pursuits. Secondary industry sectors include chemical, car, and textile manufacturing, with a mushrooming dot-com and technology sector attracting foreign investment and startups. Tourism employs a huge amount of temporary workers during the summer, but unemployment still hovers, as it does in the rest of the country, at around 10%.

2 History 101

ORIGINS, INVASIONS & THE BIRTH OF NATION

Before the arrival of the Romans, the plains surrounding what is now defined as Barcelona were populated by peaceful, agrarian people known as the Laetani, while other parts of the Catalonia were settled by the Iberians. The Greeks were the region's first immigrants, setting up a sizable trading colony on the northern coast at Empúries, the remains of which can still be seen today. Empúries was also the entry point for the Romans, who were at war with Carthage, a northern African power, for dominance over the western Mediterranean. Their base on the Peninsula was New Carthage (Cartagena), a city rich in silver and bronze mines that the Romans saw as prime booty. In response to an attack on Rome led by Hannibal, the Romans started their subjugation of the Peninsula using Tarraco (Tarragona) as a base. Barcino (Barcelona),

Dateline

- **550 B.C.** Greeks settle at Empúries in northern Catalonia.
- **218 B.C.** The Romans, using Empúries as an entry point, subjugate Spain. Barcino, principally a trading port, is founded.
- **A.D. 415** Barcelona occupied by the Visigoths.
- **719** The Muslim invasion of the Peninsula reaches Barcelona.
- **801** Barcelona taken by the Franks.
- **878** Guifré el Pilós (Wilfred the Hairy) defeats the Moors and becomes Count of Barcelona, the first in the line of a 5-century-long autonomous rule.
- **1064** The Usatges, the first Catalan Bill of Rights, is drafted.
- **1137** A royal marriage unites Catalonia and neighboring region of Aragon.
- **1213–35** Jaume I conquers Majorca, Ibiza, and Valencia.
- **1265** Barcelona forms the Consell de Cent, its own municipal government.
- **1282–1325** Catalonia conquers Corsica and Sicily.

with its lack of a harbor, served merely as port of call between Tarraco and Narbonne in France—but out of that, a town grew. It mushroomed out from Mons Taber, the highest point of the city, where the cathedral now stands. Traces of Roman civilization can still be seen in Barcelona and to a much greater extent in Tarragona.

When Rome fell in the 5th century, the Visigoths pounced, taking a broad swath stretching from the eastern Pyrénées to Barcelona. The chaotic rule of the Visigoth kings, who imposed their sophisticated set of laws on existing Roman ones, lasted about 300 years. The Visigoths were prolific church builders, and Visigothic fragments still survive in Barcelona and, more vividly, in Tarragona's cathedral.

In A.D. 711, Moorish warriors led by Tarik crossed over into Spain and conquered the country. By 714, they controlled most of it, except for a few mountain regions around Asturias. Their occupation of Barcelona was short-lived, which accounts for why the city has virtually no vestiges of Moorish architecture compared with *al-Andalús,* or Andalusia, where their culture flourished.

In the Pyrénées, Catalonia's heartland, the Moors clashed head on with the Franks, who, led by Charlemagne, drove them back south. In 801, Louis the Pious, son of Charlemagne, took Barcelona and set up a buffer state, marking the territorial boundaries (known as the Marcha Hispánica) of what was to become medieval Catalonia and endowing the local language with elements of his own (Provençal). Counts were awarded various territories. Guifré el Pilós (Wilfred the Hairy; 878–97) acquired several (including Barcelona) and managed to unite the area through a bloody battle that history has deemed the birth of the Catalonia. In the 9th century, mortally wounded from a battle against the Moors, the Frankish

- 1347–59 The Black Plague halves the city's population. The Generalitat (autonomous government) is founded.
- 1479 Fernando II, monarch of the crown of Catalonia-Aragon marries Isabel, queen of Castile, therefore uniting all of Spain. Catalonia falls under Castilian rule.
- 1492 Columbus discovers America. The "Catholic Kings" expel all remaining Jews and Muslims.
- 1522 Under the rule of Charles V, Catalans are refused permission to trade in the New World.
- 1640–50 Catalan revolt known as the Guerra dels Segadors (Harvesters' War).
- 1702 The War of Succession begins.
- 1759 Barcelona falls to Franco-Spanish army. Catalan language banned.
- 1808–14 French occupy Catalonia.
- 1832 The Industrial Revolution begins in Barcelona with the first steam-driven factory.
- 1833–39 The Carlist wars begin. Trade unions and collectives form in Barcelona.
- 1859 Work begins on the "new city," L'Eixample.
- 1873 First Spanish Republic.
- 1888 First International Exhibition in Barcelona held at the Ciutadella Park.
- 1892–93 Collectives demand Catalan autonomy. Anarchist throws bombs in the Liceu Opera House.
- 1909 Setmana Tràgica; anarchists go on anticlerical rampage in Barcelona.
- 1923 Dictatorship led by General Primo de Rivera starts in Spain.
- 1929 Second International Exhibition, this time on Montjuïc.
- 1931 Francesc Macià negotiates autonomy for Catalonia during the Second Republic and declares himself president.
- 1939 Anarchist-occupied Barcelona is taken by Franco's army.
- 1953 Defense treaty between Spain and the U.S. signed.
- 1960s The package tourism boom takes off on Catalonia's Costa Brava.
- 1975 Franco dies. Barcelonese drink the city dry in celebration.
- 1978 King Juan Carlos grants Catalonia autonomous rule.

continues

emperor dipped the fingers of the hairy warrior in his own blood and traced them down the count's shield, creating the Quatre Barres, the future flag of Catalonia. What followed was a 500-year long dynasty of Catalan count-kings with the freedom to forge a nation.

THE GOLDEN AGE & DECLINE

Catalonia entered the next millennium as a series of counties operating under the feudal system. It was gathering political strength, and artistic and artisan disciplines were beginning to flourish. Under Ramón Berenguer III (1096–1131) and his son, the region annexed the southern Tarragonese ter-

- 1981 Coup attempt by right-wing officers fails. Democracy prevails.
- 1982 Socialists gain power after 43 years of right-wing rule.
- 1986 Spain joins the European Community (now the European Union).
- 1992 Barcelona hosts the Summer Olympics.
- 1998 The Generalitat introduces controversial "linguistic normalization" laws in an effort to strengthen Catalan as the region's primary language.
- 2001 Spain moves forward as an economic powerhouse in Latin America.
- 2004 Spanish prime minister José Lluis Zapatero officially requests that Catalan, along with Basque and Galician, be recognized as working languages of the E.U.

ritories and neighboring Aragon as well. Further expansion came under Jaume I (1213–76) who conquered Sicily and the Balearic Islands and set up Catalonia as the principal maritime power of the Mediterranean. Under his long reign, the second city walls (more extensive than the old Roman ones) and the massive *drassanes* (shipyards) were built, and a code of sea trade and local parliament were established. Mercantile wealth led to the construction of such great Gothic edifices as the church of Santa María del Mar and its surrounding mansions, the Saló del Tinell at the Royal Palace, and the Saló del Cent. Catalan literature and language also greatly benefited from the city's continuing prosperity.

In 1479 this was interrupted, however, by the most far-reaching of all royal unions, that of Fernando II of Catalonia-Aragon (1452–1516) to Isabel of Castile (1451–1504). Spain was at last united, and Catalonia lost its autonomy in the shift. The pious "Catholic Kings" embarked on a bloody process of expelling all Muslims and Jews from Spain, including those remaining in Barcelona's El Call. Even though Columbus was received upon his return from the discovery of America in Barcelona, Catalans were prohibited from trading with the New World. In the early 17th century, under the rule of Felipe IV (1605–55), anti-centralist feeling was further agitated by Spain's "Thirty Year War" with France, Catalonia's neighbors, with whom Catalonia soon allied. The most emotive of all uprisings, the so-called Guerra dels Segadors (Harvesters' War), was squashed by Spanish troops and, as a final blow, in 1650 the king ceded Catalan lands north of the Pyrénées to France.

In 1700 a Bourbon prince, Philip V (1683–1746), became king, and the country fell under the influence of France. Philip V's right to the throne was challenged by a Hapsburg archduke of Austria, thus giving rise to the War of the Spanish Succession. Catalonia backed the wrong horse and Philip V, after taking the city on September 11, 1714 (still celebrated as the Diada, the Catalan national day), he outlawed the language, closed all universities, and built a citadel (on the site of the Ciutadella Park) to keep an eye of the rowdy population.

THE *RENAIXENÇA* & MODERNISM

Backed by a hard-working populace, Barcelona was the first Spanish city to embrace the industrial revolution. Textiles, with raw materials being brought in from the New World, became big business, and Barcelona gained the reputation as the "Manchester of the South." This newfound wealth led to the 19th-century *renaixença* (renaissance), a heady time of artistic and economic growth not known since the prosperous 14th century.

In cultural terms it was symbolized by the revived Jocs Florals, a poetry competition that celebrated the Catalan language; the demolition of the city walls; construction of L'Eixample (*extension,* or "new city"); and, of course, the *modernista* movement, where Gaudí and his contemporaries held sway. The international exhibition of 1888, a showcase of the glories of the new, cashed-up Catalonia, drew over two million visitors. Politically speaking, the Lliga de Catalunya, Catalonia's first pro-independence party, was founded. Anarchist and communist groups were mushrooming underground and acting above; in 1893 bombs were thrown into the audience at the Liceu Opera House by an anarchist, to the horror of the rest of Europe. As in most periods of rapid growth, the gap between rich and poor was becoming increasingly more evident, and a subculture grew, planting the seeds of the city's reputation for excess, seediness, and political action.

In 1876 Spain became a constitutional monarchy. But labor unrest, disputes with the Catholic Church, and war in Morocco combined to create political chaos in the entire country. The political polarization of Barcelona and Madrid erupted in 1909. Furious that the national government had lost the colonies in America (and therefore valuable trade) and was conscripting Catalans for an unwanted war in Morocco, rabble set fire to dozens of religious institutions in the city. Known as the Setmana Tràgica (Tragic Week), over 100 people died and many more injured. All suspected culprits, even some that had not been in Barcelona at the time, were executed.

THE 20TH CENTURY

On April 14, 1931, a revolution occurred, the second Spanish Republic was proclaimed, and King Alfonso XIII (1886–1941) and his family were forced to flee. Initially, the liberal constitutionalists ruled, but soon they were pushed aside by the socialists and anarchists. These adopted a constitution separating church and state, secularizing education, and containing several other radical provisions, including autonomous rule for Catalonia. In 1931 Francesc Macià (1859–1933) declared himself president of the Catalan republic.

But the extreme nature of these reforms fostered the growth of the conservative Falange party (*Falange española,* or "Spanish Phalanx"), modeled after Italy and Germany's fascist parties. By the 1936 elections, the country was divided equally between left and right, with Catalonia firmly to the left. In Barcelona, attacks on "bourgeois" symbols (and people) and the occupation of public buildings by collectives were common. On July 18, 1936, the army, supported by Mussolini and Hitler, tried to seize power, igniting the Spanish Civil War. General Francisco Franco, coming from Morocco to Spain, led the Nationalist (rightist) forces in fighting that ravaged the country. By October 1, Franco was clearly in charge of the leadership of nationalist Spain, abolishing popular suffrage and regional autonomy—in effect, launching a totalitarian rule for Spain. Over the next 3 years, Barcelona and the Catalan coast were bombed by German and Italian fighter planes, untold numbers of citizens were executed, and thousands fled across the Pyrénées into France. Then Franco's forces marched into Barcelona under the banner "Spain is here." The Catalan language and culture were once again forced underground, and Francesc Macià was sentenced to 30 years in prison.

Spurred on by even worse conditions in the south, where hunger and poverty were an everyday threat, millions of immigrants arrived in Barcelona in the mid-century. The 1960s saw another economic boom, this time led by tourism, which grew into an important industry on the Costa Brava and Costa Daurada. Communists formed militant trade unions, and a working class was embittered by decades of repression. Before his death, General Franco selected as his successor Juan Carlos de Borbón y Borbón (b. 1938), son of the pretender to the Spanish throne. A new constitution was approved by the electorate and the king; it guaranteed human and civil rights, as well as free enterprise, and ended the status of the Roman Catholic Church as the church of Spain. It also granted limited autonomy to several regions, including Catalonia and the Basque provinces. The election of the conservative Convergènica i Unio party, with Jordi Pujol (b. 1930) at the helm, came in 1980, spurring on decades of negotiations for even greater self-rule, a battle that still continues.

In 1981 a group of right-wing military officers seized the Cortés (parliament) in Madrid and called upon King Juan Carlos to establish a Francoist state. The king, however, refused, and the conspirators were arrested. The fledgling democracy overcame its first test, and Catalonia's morale and optimism was boosted even further when the socialists won the national elections a year later. Catalanista liberals, such as the Gauche Divine (Divine Left) party, dominated the city's counterculture for the rest of the decade, as engineers and town planners at the socialist-led city hall prepared Barcelona for the 1992 Olympic Games and its new, modern era. In 1998 Catalan became the official language of education and the judiciary, with quotas imposed on the media as well. In 1999 more than 43,000 adults enrolled for the free Catalan language courses supplied by the Generalitat.

Appendix B:
The Catalan Culture

Barcelona has always thrived on contact and commerce with countries beyond Spain's borders. From its earliest days, the city has been linked more closely to France and the rest of Europe than to Iberia. Each military and financial empire that swept through Catalonia left its cultural imprint.

1 The Language of Catalonia

Catalonia lies midway between France and Castilian Spain. The region is united by a common language, **Catalan.** Most people wrongly assume that Catalan is a dialect of Castilian Spanish. Like Spanish and all other Romance languages, it has its roots in Latin, but Spanish and Catalan developed independently of each other.

Today Catalan, alongside Spanish, is the official language of the *Països Catalans,* which include Catalonia, Andorra, the Balearic Islands, and Valencia (although the debate still rages as to whether the language of the Valencianos is a derivative of Catalan or a separate language). "Unofficial" Catalan-speaking pockets include parts of the region of Aragon, parts of the French Pyrénées, and the town of Alghero on the Italian island of Sardinia (as a result of an invasion by Catalan colonists in 1372). All in all, Catalan is spoken by nearly 11 million people, making it the seventh most widely spoken language in Europe, more than both Swedish and Greek.

The restriction and outright prohibition of the language, first at the hands of the conquering Spanish-French forces in the 1714 War of Succession and later under the iron fist of General Franco, means that language and politics have been inseparable in Catalonia. During the 13th to 15th centuries, Catalan was the *lingua franca* of the western Mediterranean; after the 18th century it enjoyed a golden period known as the *renaixença* (renaissance), when all aspects of Catalan culture, but particularly language, literature, and architecture (see below) flourished in a fervor of nationalism. Following the dictatorship, the Catalan language was reinstated as the language of education, bureaucracy, trade, and the media, with an impetus from the autonomous government to impose it as a social language as well—a plan that didn't go down well with the thousands of Spanish-speaking people residing in Catalonia.

The reality for the visitor today is that both Catalan and Spanish are freely spoken in the city with the vocabulary of the two often mixed together to form a sort of Barcelonese vernacular. The languages are extremely territorial; in El Raval, the neighborhood with the biggest immigrant population, you are more likely to hear Spanish (or Urdu, English, or Arabic), while in L'Eixample you will be greeted with a *¡Bon dia!* (as opposed to the Castilian *¡Buenos días!*) when you walk into a bar. The Catalan language is also dominant in rural areas. While all Barcelona street names are *signposted* in Catalan, most people use a mixture of the two languages when actually *referring* to them, which is the same approach I have used in this book. In museums and galleries, descriptions are in Catalan, with a translation either in Spanish, English, or both. People who understand some Spanish (or French) should not have trouble deciphering them, and those that don't will return home with a few Catalan phrases up their sleeves.

As for the media, English-language newspapers are available in most of the news kiosks along Les Ramblas. The Spanish edition of the *International Herald Tribune* contains a section with highlights from *El País,* the country's major daily newspaper, translated into English. Also be on the lookout for *Catalonia Today,* a free newspaper covering local and international news. The Catalan-language television stations (TV3 and 33) transmit in a *dual,* which means that the original language of the show can be heard at the flick of a switch. Oddly, very few hotel TVs are equipped for it.

2 Barcelona's Architecture

Like many other cities in Spain, Barcelona claims its share of Neolithic dolmens and ruins from the Roman periods. Relics of the Roman colony of Barcino can be seen (and more are being found all the time), as can monuments surviving from the Middle Ages, when the Romanesque solidity of no-nonsense barrel vaults, narrow windows, and fortified design were widely used.

In the 11th and 12th centuries, religious fervor swept through Europe, and pilgrims began to flock to Barcelona on their way west to Santiago de Compostela, bringing with them French building styles and the need for new and larger churches. The style that emerged, called Catalan Gothic, had harsher lines and more austere ornamentation than traditional Gothic. Appropriate for both civic and religious buildings, it used massive ogival (pointed) vaults, heavy columns, and gigantic sheets of sheer stone, clifflike walls, and vast rose windows set with colored glass. One of Barcelona's purest and most-loved examples of this style is the **Basilica of Santa María del Mar,** northeast of the city's harbor. Built over a period of only 54 years, it is the purest example of Catalan Gothic in the city. Other examples include the Church of Santa María del Pi, the Saló del Tinell (part of the Museu de la Ciutat), and, of course, the mesmerizing Barri Gòtic itself.

It is the *modernisme* movement however that seems to most enthrall visitors to Barcelona. Barcelona boasts the highest concentration of *modernista* architecture in the world. *Modernisme* is a confusing term, as "modernism" generally denotes 20th-century functionality. It is best known as Art Nouveau, a movement that took hold of Europe in the latter 1800s in the arts. In Barcelona, it shone in architecture with its star being **Antoni Gaudí** (see below), the eccentric and highly devout architect responsible for Barcelona's symbol: the Temple of the Sagrada Família.

The *modernistas* were obsessed with detail. They hailed the past in their architectural forms (from Arabic to Catalan Gothic) and then sublimely sprinkled them with nature-inspired features employing iron, glass, and florid ceramic motif, all of which are seen in dazzling abundance in the city. Other *modernista* architects include **Domènech i Montaner** and **Puig i Cadafalch,** whose elegant mansions and concert halls seemed perfectly suited to the enlightened, sophisticated prosperity of the 19th-century Catalonian bourgeoisie. A 19th-century economic boom coincided with the profusion of geniuses that emerged in the building business. Entrepreneurs who had made their fortunes in the fields and mines of the New World commissioned some of the beautiful and elaborate villas in Barcelona and nearby Sitges.

In 1858 the expansion of Barcelona into the northern **L'Eixample** district provided a blank canvas for *modernista* architects. The grid-like pattern of streets was intersected with broad diagonals. Although it was never endowed with the more radical details of its original design, it provided a carefully planned, elegant path in which a growing city could showcase its finest buildings.

Consistent with the general artistic stagnation in Spain during the Franco era (1939–75), the 1950s and 1960s saw a tremendous increase in the number of anonymous housing projects around the periphery of Barcelona and, in the inner city, eyesore-ridden decay. But as the last tears were being shed over the death of General Franco elsewhere in the country, Barcelona's leftfield intelligentsia were envisioning how to regenerate their city after decades of physical degradation under the dictator.

When Barcelona won its Olympic bid to host the Summer Games in 1992, work on their vision of "New Barcelona" accelerated. City planners made possible the creation of smart new urban beaches, a glitzy port and marina, city traffic-reducing ring roads, daring public sculptures and parks, and series of promenades and squares weaving through the Old City. The planners shunned a master plan and instead employed smaller, more benign projects, the sum of which made up this grand vision. The objective was to rejuvenate the *barri,* the distinct village-neighborhoods of Barcelona that often denote one's income or political stance (sometimes even the language or football team) and make up the city's peculiar territoriality. This radical and ingenious approach did not go unnoticed by the rest of the world. In 1999 the Royal Institute of British Architects presented Barcelona's City Council with their Gold Medal, the first time a city (as opposed to an architect, such as previous winners Le Corbusier and Frank Lloyd Wright) had received the accolade. Barcelona is now used as a model across Europe for town planners wishing to overhaul their own downtrodden cities.

Over a decade after the city's Olympic Year, the physical face of Barcelona is still changing in leaps and bounds. With an engaged local government still at the helm, broad swaths of industrial wasteland have been reclaimed north of the city for parkland, a new marina, and the emergence of dot-com and ritzy residential neighborhoods. A new city nucleus in the north is being created around the new AVE high-speed train terminal that will link Madrid to Barcelona and on to the French border with keynote buildings from the likes of Frank Gehry. Still a city that's not afraid to take risks with its architecture, Barcelona's skyline has been enhanced by French architect Jean Nouvel's daring and controversial **Torre Agbar** (in the outer suburb of Glòries), which has become the towering symbol of a city embracing the future with bravado.

3 Art & Artists

From the cave paintings discovered at Llerida to several true giants of the 20th century—**Picasso, Dalí,** and **Miró**—Catalonia has had a long and significant artistic tradition. Today it is the Spanish center of the plastic arts and design culture.

The first art movement to attract attention in Barcelona was **Catalan Gothic sculpture,** which held sway from the 13th to the 15th centuries and produced such renowned masters as Mestre Bartomeu and Pere Johan. Sculptors working with Italian masters brought the Renaissance to Barcelona, but few great Catalonian legacies remain from this period. The rise of baroque art in the 17th and 18th centuries saw Catalonia filled with several impressive examples but nothing worth a special pilgrimage, the great masters such as El Greco and Velázquez working in other parts of Spain (El Toledo and Madrid, respectively).

Gaudí: The Saintly Architect

June 7, 1926, started as normally as any other day in the life of the architect **Antoni Gaudí i Cornet.** Leaving his humble studio at his work in progress, the Temple of the Sagrada Família, the old man shuffled through the L'Eixample district with the help of his cane on his way to evening vespers. He did not hear the bells of the no. 30 tram as it came pelting down the Gran Vía. While waiting for an ambulance, people searched the pockets of his threadbare suit for some clue as to his identity but none was to be found. Mistaking the great architect for a vagrant, he was taken to the nearby public hospital of Santa Creu.

For the next 3 days, Gaudí lay in agony. Apart from occasionally opening his mouth to utter the words, "Jesus, my God!" his only other communication was to protest a suggestion that he be moved to a private clinic. "My place is here, with the poor," he is reported to have said.

Gaudí was born in 1852 in the rural township of Reus. The son of a metalworker, he spent long hours studying the forms of flora, fauna, and topography of the typically Mediterranean agrarian terrain. "Nature is a great book, always open, that we should make ourselves read," he once said. As well as using organic forms for his lavish decorations (over 30 species of plant are seen on the famous Nativity Facade of the Sagrada Família), he was captivated by the structure of plants and trees. As far as he was concerned, there was no shape or form that could be devised on an architect's drawing table that did not already exist in nature. "All styles are organisms related to nature," he claimed.

Apart from Mother Nature, Gaudí's two other guiding lights were religion and Catalan nationalism. When the *modernista* movement was

In the neoclassical period of the 18th century, Catalonia—and, particularly, Barcelona—arose from an artistic slumber. Art schools opened and foreign painters arrived, exerting considerable influence. The 19th century produced many Catalan artists who followed the general European trends of the time without forging any major creative breakthroughs.

The 20th century brought renewed artistic ferment in Barcelona, as reflected by the arrival of Málaga-born **Pablo Picasso.** (The Catalan capital today is the site of a major Picasso museum.) The great surrealist painters of the Spanish school, **Joan Miró** (who also has an eponymous museum in Barcelona) and **Salvador Dalí** (whose fantastical museum is along the Costa Brava, north of Barcelona), also came to the Catalan capital.

Many Catalan sculptors achieved acclaim in this century, including Casanovas, Llimon, and Blay. The Spanish Civil War brought cultural stagnation, yet against all odds many Catalan artists continued to make bold statements. **Antoni Tàpies** was one of the principal artists of this period (the Fundació Tàpies in Barcelona is devoted to his work). Among the various schools formed in Spain at the time was the **neofigurative band,** which included such artists as Vásquez Díaz and Pancho Cossio. The Museum of Modern Art in the neighborhood of El Raval (p. 153) illustrates the various 20th-century Catalan artistic movements, including

in full swing, architects such as Luis Domènech i Montaner and Josep Puig i Cadafalch were designing buildings taking florid decoration and detail to the point of delirium. Gaudí, in the latter half of his life, disapproved of their excess and their capricious, outward-reaching (that is, European) notions. He even formed a counterculture, the Artistic Circle of Saint Luke, a collective of pious creatives with a love of God and the fatherland equal to his own.

He never married and when he was close to 50, moved into a house in the Parc Güell, the planned "garden city" above Barcelona, with his ailing niece and housekeeper. After they both died, his dietary habits, always seen as somewhat eccentric by the carnivorous Catalans (Gaudí was a strict vegetarian), became so erratic that a group of Carmelite nuns who lived in the park took it upon themselves to make sure that he was properly nourished. His appearance was also starting to take on a bizarre twist. He would let his beard and hair grow for months, forget to put on underwear, and wear old slippers both indoors and out.

What became apparent by the end of his life, and long after, was that Gaudí was one of the greatest architects the world has known, whose revolutionary techniques are still the subject of theory and investigation and whose vision was an inspiration for some of today's top architects, including Spain's own Santiago Calatrava. In 2003 **Año Gaudí**, the celebration of the 150th anniversary of his birth, saw an equal number of tourists flock to Barcelona as Paris for the first time ever. Expect even greater crowds if the Temple of the Sagrada Família is finished, as predicted, for the centenary of his death in 2026.

the Dau al Set, the surrealist movement started in the 1940s by the "visual poet" Joan Brossa. His art and many other works by leading sculptors dot the streets of Barcelona, making it a vibrant outdoor museum. Watch out for Roy Lichtenstein's *Barcelona Head* opposite the main post office in the Plaça d' Antoni López, Joan Miró's phallic *Dona i Cell* in the park of the same name, and Fernando Botero's giant cat on the Rambla del Raval.

Today many Barcelona artists are making major names for themselves, and their works are sold in the most prestigious galleries of the Western world. Outstanding among these is sculptor **Susana Solano,** who ranks among the most renowned names in Spanish contemporary art, and the neo-expressionist Miguel Barceló. Design and the graphic arts have thrived in Barcelona since the heady days of *modernisme*. It seems that nothing in Barcelona, from a park bench to a mailbox, escapes the "designer touch." Leading names include the architect and interior and object designer Oscar Tusquets, and the quirky graphic artist Javier Mariscal, whose work can be seen in many of the city's designer housewares stores. The most important plastic arts schools in Spain are located in Barcelona, and the city acts as a magnet for young, European creatives who flock here to set up shop.

> **Fun Fact Picasso & *Les Demoiselles***
>
> Biographers of the 20th century's greatest artist, Spanish-born Pablo Picasso, claim that the artist was inspired to paint one of his masterpieces, *Les Demoiselles d'Avignon,* after a "glorious night" spent in a notorious bordello on Barcelona's Carrer D'Avinyó.

4 A Taste of Catalonia

Meals are an extremely important social activity in Catalonia; eating out remains a major pastime, whether in the evening with friends, at lunch in a local bar with workmates, or with the traditional Sunday family feast. Although Barcelona is a fast-paced city, mealtimes, especially lunchtime, are still respected, with the whole city shifting into first gear between the hours of 2 and 4pm. Many people either head home or crowd into a local eatery for a three-course *menú del día* (lunch of the day).

The food in Catalonia is quite different from the rest of the Spain. In Barcelona, the mainstay diet is typically Mediterranean, with an abundance of fish, legumes, and vegetables, the latter often served simply boiled with a drizzle of olive oil. Pork, in all its forms, is widely eaten whether as grilled filets, the famous Serrano ham, or delicious *embutidos* (cold cuts) from inland Catalonia. In more contemporary restaurants, portions tend to be smaller than in the U.S. Another local characteristic is the lack of tapas bars. Very good ones do exist but not in the same abundance as in the rest of Spain. Instead Catalans tend to go for *raciones* (plates of cheese, pâtés, and cured meats) if they want something to pick at.

Many restaurants in Spain close on Sunday and Monday, so check ahead of time before heading out. Hotel dining rooms are generally open 7 days a week, and there's always something open in the touristy areas. If you really want to get a true taste of Catalan cuisine, stay away from places in Les Ramblas, ask your hotel concierge for recommendations, or check chapter 5 of this book. Dining in Barcelona can range from memorable to miserable (or memorable for all the wrong reasons!), so it pays to do a bit of research. If possible, always book ahead for reputable restaurants, especially on the weekends.

MEALS

BREAKFAST   In Catalonia, as in the rest of Spain, the day starts with a light continental breakfast, usually in a bar. Most Spaniards have coffee, usually strong, served with hot milk—either a *café con leche* (half coffee, half milk) or a *cortado* (a shot of espresso "cut" with a dash of milk). If you find these too strong or bitter for your taste, you might ask for a more diluted *café americano.* Properly made tea is hard to find, but herbal infusions such as *poleo menta* (mint) or *manzanilla* (chamomile) are common. Along with these, most people just have a croissant (*cruasan*), doughnut, or *ensaimada* (a light, sugar-sprinkled pastry). If you want something more substantial, you can always ask for a *bocadillo* (roll) with cheese or grilled meat or cold cuts, or ask to see the list of *platos combinados* (combination plates). These consist of a fried egg, french fries, bacon, and a steak or a hamburger. A *bikini* is an old-fashioned, toasted ham-and-cheese sandwich.

LUNCH   The most important meal of the day everywhere in Spain, lunch is comparable to the farm-style midday "dinner" in the United States. It usually includes three or four courses, although some smarter eateries in the Old Town are now offering just one course with dessert for lighter eaters. It begins with a choice of soup, salad, or vegetables. Then follows the meat, chicken, or fish dish, simply grilled or in a rich stew or casserole. At some point, meat eaters should definitely try *botifarras,* the locally made sausages. Desserts are (thankfully) light: fruit, yogurt, or a *crema catalana* (crème brûlée). Wine and bread is always part of the meal. Lunch is served from 1:30 to 4pm, with "rush hour" at 2pm.

DINNER   Depending on what you have consumed at lunchtime, at dinner you choose either another extravaganza or a light meal.

Naturally, if you had a heavy or late lunch, you may want to simply go for a tapa or two or a few *raciones* in a wine bar. Dinner is the perfect time to try the quintessential Catalan snack *pa amb tomàquet* (rustic bread rubbed with olive oil and tomato pulp served with cheese, pâté, or cold cuts). This simple yet ingenious invention goes down extremely well with a bottle of wine.

If you choose a restaurant, expect a slightly finer version of what you had at lunch but with a larger bill, as the set-menu deal is a lunchtime-only thing.

The chic dining hour is 10 or 10:30pm. (In well-touristed regions and hardworking Catalonia, you can usually dine at 8pm, but you still may find yourself alone in the restaurant.) In most middle-class establishments, people dine around 9:30pm.

THE CUISINE
SOUPS & APPETIZERS   Soups are thick and hearty. They are divided into two categories: *sopa* (thick soup) and *potage* (a very thick, meal-in-itself soup). A *crema* is a cream soup, such as *crema de aspárrago.* A classic soup that, according to the folk singer-songwriter Lluis Llach, "reflects all the wisdom of Catalan people" is the *escudella i carn d'olla* (a meat and vegetable hot pot similar to the French *pot au feu*). Traditionally a fisherman's breakfast, a *suquet* is a hearty fish-and-potato soup. Chilled *gazpacho* is particularly refreshing during the hot months.

EGGS   These are served in countless ways. A Spanish omelet, a *tortilla española,* is made with potatoes and usually onions. Local Catalan varieties include tortillas with white beans, asparagus, and garlic shoots, often served at the bar with some *pa amb tomàquet.* A simple omelet is called a *tortilla francesa.*

FISH   As in the rest of the Peninsula, the Catalans are avid fish eaters. The consumption of fish, and particularly shellfish, holds an almost cult-like status; it is eaten at all major celebrations. Although an enormous amount is imported, there are 35 fishing ports along the Catalan coastline. Some local varieties include *dorada* (a type of bream), *mero* (grouper), and *salmonette* (red mullet). Sardines (when in season) are cheap and delicious when pan grilled with a bit of garlic and parsley. Prawns are often served in the same way (watch for prawns from Denia, which are supposedly the best), and mussels come either steamed or in a marinara sauce. Squid, octopus, and *sepia* (cuttlefish) feature heavily, from *calamari a la romana* (deep-fried squid) to *chipirones* (bite-size baby octopus, also fried) to squid cooked in its own ink. Although not native, salted cod *(bacallà)* is particularly revered by the Catalans and before you dismiss it as a poor man's fish, try the delicious *bacallà a la llauna* (baked) or *brandada de bacallà* (a creamy purée eaten with bread). Cod is a good choice in cheaper restaurants, where the fish on your *menú del día* may be frozen or of inferior quality. Premium fish and seafood in Catalonia does not come cheap, but that does not stop it being eaten in huge quantities.

PAELLA   The most internationally known Spanish dish is paella. Flavored with saffron, paella is an aromatic rice dish usually topped with shellfish and/or chicken, sausage, peppers, and local spices. Although it is widely available in Catalonia, it actually hails from Valencia. Instead you might like to try a *fideuà* (a local dish that replaces the rice with fine, angel-hair noodles) or an *arroz negre* (rice cooked in black squid ink). A true Catalan paella is made with rabbit and *botifarra,* a rich sausage. (Incidentally, what is known in the U.S. as Spanish rice isn't Spanish at all. If you ask an English-speaking waiter for Spanish rice, you'll be served paella.)

MEATS   Don't expect a steak of American proportions, but do try the spit-roasted suckling pig, so sweet and tender it can often be cut with a fork. The veal is also good, and the *lomo de cerdo* (loin of pork) is unmatched anywhere. Chicken is tender and tasty, whether a simply grilled chicken breast or spit-roasted until it turns a delectable golden brown. Catalan dishes tend to mix meat in unexpected combinations such as with seafood, fruit, or snails.

VEGETABLES & SALADS   Through more sophisticated agricultural methods and huge expanses of agrarian landscape, Spain now grows more (and, many would argue, tastier) fruit and vegetables than anywhere in Europe. On their own, they are often served simply: boiled with a drizzle of olive oil. Main dishes often don't come with vegetables, except as a simple garnish on the side. You may want to consider ordering a vegetable entree to get in your vitamin quota. A popular one is *escalivada* (strips of chargrilled sweet peppers and eggplant served cold). In traditional restaurants, salads are normally a basic combination of lettuce, tomato, onions, and olives. An *ensalada catalana* adds local cold cuts. Vegetarians and vegans should always check that no meat is included in what appears to be a vegetable dish or salad on the menu.

LEGUMES   The Catalans are big on legumes; chickpeas, lentils, white and black-eyed beans regularly pop up in all sorts of delicious ways. Chickpeas are often served with baby squid; lentils with ham, *chorizo,* and blood sausage; *habas a la catalana* mixed broad beans with Serrano ham and mint. A traditional way to eat a *botifarra* (sausage) is with *mongetes* (white beans).

DESSERTS   The Catalans do not emphasize dessert, which could explain how, in view of how much is eaten, most manage to keep their weight down. Many opt for fresh fruit, a *macedonia* (fruit salad), or even a tub of yogurt. Flan, a home-cooked egg custard, appears on all menus, as does a *crema catalana* or crème brûlée. If you really need a carb hit, you can usually find a cheesecake (baked, not the creamy kind), a *puddin,* chocolate mousse, or some other kind of traditional dessert on the menu, but in the cheaper places they tend to be of pedestrian quality. As a dining oddity—although it's not odd at all to Spaniards—many restaurants serve fresh orange juice for dessert.

OLIVE OIL & GARLIC   Olive oil is used lavishly all over Spain, the largest olive grower on the planet. It is used in all cooked dishes and even as a butter replacement on bread. Garlic is also an integral part of the Spanish diet, but you can ask them to hold it on grilled and fried dishes.

WHAT TO DRINK

WATER   Although it is safe to drink, many find the taste of Barcelona's tap water unpleasant. Mineral water, in bottles of .5 to 5 liters, is available everywhere. Bubbly water is *agua con gas;* noncarbonated is *agua sin gas.* Vichy Catalan, rather salty carbonated water that many people believe acts as a digestive aid, is very popular. Note that bottled water in some areas, bars, and cafes may cost as much as a beer.

SOFT DRINKS   Schweppes, Fanta, and, naturally, Coca-Cola are all widely available. *Bitter Kas* is a carbonated drink with a Campari-like flavor. Your cheapest bet is a liter bottle of *gaseosa,* a sort of less-sugary lemonade. In summer you should also try an *horchata.* Not to be confused with the Mexican beverage of the same name, the Spanish *horchata* is a sweet, soy milk–like beverage made of tubers called *chufas.*

COFFEE   Coffee is taken at breakfast (see above) and post-meal. After lunch or dinner, you may like to try a *carajillo,* a short coffee with a dash of brandy, cognac, rum, or Baileys.

MILK   Unfortunately, long-life milk sold in square boxes is the norm. Fresh milk can be found in larger supermarkets and *granjas,* bars that sell dairy products and drinks such as hot chocolate and (sometimes) milkshakes. *Leche merengada* is a delicious cinnamon-flavored milk that appears in the summer.

BEER   Although not native to Spain, beer *(cerveza)* is now drunk (and sold) everywhere. Local brands include San Miguel and Estrella. All beer tends to be lighter, more like the U.S. version than the British. A *clara* is a glass of beer mixed with lemon soda. A small bottle of beer is called a *mediana,* and a glass is a *caña.*

WINE   Until fairly recently, Spain was not taken particularly seriously as a winemaking region. Overshadowed by France and Italy, it was mainly associated with cheap red wine and sangria—yet thanks to the innovative practices of a handful of winemakers, and particularly those in Catalonia, Spanish wine is currently undergoing a renaissance, offering some of the best wines (both in terms of price and quality) in the world.

The undisputed king of Catalan wines is Miguel Torres, whose family has been making wines in the Penedès wine region, just 45 minutes south of Barcelona, for over 100 years. Pioneering and enigmatic, Torres turned Catalan winemaking on its head, proving that the region was capable of excellent wines and making people sit up and pay attention. Today the Penedès, known for its undulating hills, balmy Mediterranean climate, and a varied terrain, produces soft fruity reds, refreshing whites, and—the region's *pièce de résistance*—cava (sparkling wine).

Made by the same method as French champagne, most of the high-end producers will swear that *cava* is as good as, if not better than, champagne, a point that Dom Pierre Pérignon—the Benedictine monk who invented champagne in the 17th century—would no doubt have disagreed with. Regardless, in 1872 Josep Raventós Fatjó (of the bodegas Can Cordoníu) popped his first bottle of fizz and this liquid gold was soon circulating in high society, including at the royal palace.

Penedès accounts for about 75% of all the *cava* made in Spain and there are infinite different varieties, from small "garage" bodega wines (which amount to no more than somebody producing a limited number of bottles in their garden shed) to heavyweight international brands like Freixenet and Cordoníu (which account for most of the world exports). The latter are both in Sant Sadurni d'Anoia, the capital of *cava*-making, and Cordoníu is particularly interesting to visit. Housed in a spectacular *modernista* building that is part of the Spanish heritage trust, there are 15km (9 miles) of underground tunnels to explore while learning about the *cava*-making process.

For serious wine lovers, Catalan winemaking regions have far more to offer than *cava* alone, and it can make for a fascinating tour. The Romans were the first people to make wine in Penedès, and their ancient roads still crisscross the land. Recently pre-phylloxera vines have been discovered that some experts say show the way of the future. These wines are important because they use varieties of grapes that haven't been used before in modern winemaking. The Penedès winemakers feel that, rather than building an industry on known varieties, such as chardonnay and merlot, they will conquer the market with these new and, until now, undiscovered varieties that are unique to the area. For now, innovative winemakers, such as Josep Maria Noya of Albet i Noya (Spain's first organic winery) and Miguel Torres, continue to experiment with their crops, but it probably won't be long before unheard-of varieties start hitting the shelves.

Jean León—one of the region's most modern bodegas and now owned by Torres—was also responsible for shaking up a region that had hitherto made decent enough wines, though none that were particularly exciting. In the 1960s León returned to his beloved Spain from Hollywood in search of a vineyard where he could make wines suitable to serve at his restaurant, La Scala in Beverly Hills. It wasn't long before he and Miguel Torres became friends, sharing knowledge of the region, modern winemaking methods from the New World, and, most notably, new grape varieties. León introduced both chardonnay and cabernet sauvignon to the region.

The jewel in Catalonia's winemaking crown, however, is the Priorat. Wine has been produced here for at least 1,000 years, made mainly by monasteries, and for centuries it was widely acclaimed. But after phylloxera destroyed most of the crops in Europe it never really recovered—until recently, that is. In the early 1980s a troop of young winemakers began taking their craft seriously once again. The most notable of these was Carles Pastrana of Clos L'Obac, who set about establishing a set of D.O. *(denominación de origen)* standard rules and regulations. When you see the region with its impossibly rocky, vertical mountainsides and rough black soil, and couple that with the fact that many don't even water the land for fear of upsetting the delicate water-table balance, it seems impossible that anything good could ever come of it. And yet in the last 2 decades, the lush, dense reds of the Priorat have become renowned as some of the best and most exciting wines in the world.

SPIRITS   Vodkas, gins, rums, whiskeys, and brandies are available at any bar. If you don't recognize the label, it is probably local and, with the exception of brandies and cognacs, normally of an inferior quality. Measures here are about double of anywhere else, which is just as well: In some bars and nightclubs you can pay as much as 12€ ($14) for a mixed drink *(cubata)*. One of the most popular is a *cuba libre* (rum and Coca-Cola).

Appendix C:
Useful Terms & Phrases

Most Catalans are very patient with foreigners who try to speak their languages. For English speakers, Catalan pronunciation is a lot easier than Spanish pronunciation, so give it a go. If you know a little French or Italian, you will probably find it quite easy. If not, most good restaurants and hotels have English speakers on hand.

1 Useful Words & Phrases

English	Spanish/Catalan	Pronunciation
Good day	**Buenos días/Bon dia**	*bweh*-nohs *dee*-ahs/bohn *dee*-ah
How are you?	**¿Cómo está?/Com està?**	*koh*-moh es-*tah*/com ehs-*tah*
Very well	**Muy bien/Molt bé**	mwee byehn/mohl beh
Thank you	**Gracias/Gràcies**	*grah*-syahs/*grah*-syahs
You're welcome	**De nada/De res**	*deh nah*-dah/duh ress
Goodbye	**Adiós/Adéu**	ah-*dyos*/ah-*deh*-yoo
Please	**Por favor/Si us plau**	por fah-*vohr*/see yoos plow
Yes	**Sí/Sí**	see
No	**No/No**	noh
Excuse me	**Perdóneme/Perdoni'm**	pehr-*doh*-neh-meh/per-*don*-eem
Where is . . . ?	**¿Dónde está . . . ?/On és . . . ?**	*dohn*-deh es-*tah*/ohn ehs
the station	**la estación/la estació**	lah es-tah-*syohn*/la esta-*cyo*
a hotel	**un hotel/l'hotel**	oon oh-*tehl*/ehl ho-*tehl*
the market	**el mercado/el mercat**	ehl mehr-*kah*-doh/ehl mehr-*kah*
a restaurant	**un restaurante/un restaurant**	oon rehs-tow-*rahn*-teh/oon rehs-tow-*rahn*
the toilet	**el baño/el lavabo**	ehl *bah*-nyoh/ehl lah-*vah*-boh
a doctor	**un médico/un metge**	oon *meh*-dee-koh/oon meht-*jah*
the road to . . .	**el camino a/al cami per**	ehl kah-*mee*-noh ah/ahl kah-*mee* pehr
To the right	**A la derecha/A la dreta**	ah lah deh-*reh*-chah/ah lah *dreh*-tah
To the left	**A la izquierda/A l'esquerra**	ah lah ees-*kyehr*-dah/ahl ehs-kee-*ra*
I would like . . .	**Quisiera/Voldría**	kee-*syeh*-rah/vohl-*dree*-ah

English	Spanish/Catalan	Pronunciation
I want . . .	**Quiero/Vull**	*kyeh*-roh/*boo*-wee
to eat.	**Comer/Menjar**	ko-*mehr*/mehn-*jahr*
a room.	**una habitación/ un habitacion**	*oo*-nah ah-bee-tah-*syohn*/oon ah-bee-tah-*syohn*
Do you have . . . ?	**¿Tiene usted?/Té**	tyeh-neh oo-*sted*/teh
a book	**un libro/un llibre**	oon *lee*-broh/oon *yee*-breh
a dictionary	**un diccionario/ un diccionari**	oon deek-syoh-*nah*-ryoh/ oon deek-syoh-*nah*-ree
How much is it?	**¿Cuánto cuesta?/ Quant es?**	*kwahn*-toh *kwehs*-tah/ kwahnt ehs?
When?	**¿Cuándo?/Quan?**	*kwahn*-doh/kwahn
What?	**¿Qué?/Com?**	Keh/Cohm
There is (Is there . . . ?)	**(¿)Hay (. . . ?)/Hi ha? or Hi han?**	aye/ee ah/ee ahn
What is there?	**¿Qué hay?/Que hi ha?**	keh aye/keh ee ah
Yesterday	**Ayer/Ahir**	ah-*yehr*/ah-*yeer*
Today	**Hoy/Avui**	oy/ah-*wee*
Tomorrow	**Mañana/Demá**	mah-*nyah*-nah/deh-*mah*
Good	**Bueno/Bon**	*bweh*-noh/bohn
Bad	**Malo/Mal**	*mah*-loh/mahl
Better (Best)	**(Lo) Mejor/Millor**	(loh) meh-*hohr*/mee-*yohr*
More	**Más/Mes**	mahs/mehss
Less	**Menos/Menys**	*meh*-nohs/*meh*-nyus
Do you speak English?	**¿Habla inglés?/ Parla anglès?**	*ah*-blah een-*glehs*/ *pahr*-lah ahn-*glehs*
I speak a little Spanish/Catalan.	**Hablo un poco de español/Parlo una mica de Catalan**	*ah*-bloh oon *poh*-koh deh es-pah-*nyol*/*pahr*-loh *oo*-nah *mee*-kah deh kah-tah-*lahn*
I don't understand.	**No entiendo/ No comprenc**	noh ehn-*tyehn*-doh/ noh cohm-*prehnk*
What time is it?	**¿Qué hora es?/ Quina hora és?**	keh *oh*-rah ehss/ *kee*-nah *oh*-rah ehss
The check, please.	**La cuenta, por favor/El compte, si us plau**	lah *kwehn*-tah pohr fah-*vohr*/ ehl *cohmp*-tah see yoos plow

2 Numbers

Number	Spanish	Catalan
1	**uno** (*oo*-noh)	**un** (oon)
2	**dos** (dohs)	**dos** (dohs)
3	**tres** (trehs)	**tres** (trehs)
4	**cuatro** (*kwah*-troh)	**quatre** (*kwah*-trah)
5	**cinco** (*seen*-koh)	**cinc** (sink)
6	**seis** (says)	**sis** (sees)
7	**siete** (*syeh*-teh)	**set** (seht)
8	**ocho** (*oh*-choh)	**vuit** (vweet)
9	**nueve** (*nweh*-beh)	**nou** (noo)

Number	Spanish	Catalan
10	**diez** (dyehs)	**deu** (*deh*-yoo)
11	**once** (*ohn*-seh)	**onze** (*ohn*-zah)
12	**doce** (*doh*-seh)	**dotze** (*doh*-tzah)
13	**trece** (*treh*-seh)	**tretze** (*treh*-tzah)
14	**catorce** (kah-*tohr*-seh)	**catorza** (kah-*tohr*-zah)
15	**quince** (*keen*-seh)	**quinza** (*keen*-zah)
16	**dieciséis** (dyeh-see-*says*)	**setze** (*seh*-tzah)
17	**diecisiete** (dyeh-see-*syeh*-teh)	**disset** (dee-*seht*)
18	**dieciocho** (dyeh-*syoh*-choh)	**divuit** (dee-*vweet*)
19	**diecinueve** (dyeh-see-*nweh*-beh)	**dinou** (dee-*noo*)
20	**veinte** (*bayn*-teh)	**vint** (vehnt)
30	**treinta** (*trayn*-tah)	**trenta** (*trehn*-tah)
40	**cuarenta** (kwah-*rehn*-tah)	**quaranta** (kwah-*rahn*-tah)
50	**cincuenta** (seen-*kwehn*-tah)	**cinquanta** (theen-*kwahn*-tah)
60	**sesenta** (seh-*sehn*-tah)	**seixanta** (see-*shahn*-tah)
70	**setenta** (seh-*tehn*-tah)	**setanta** (seh-*tahn*-tah)
80	**ochenta** (oh-*chehn*-tah)	**vuitanta** (vwee-*tahn*-tah)
90	**noventa** (noh-*behn*-tah)	**noranta** (noh-*rahn*-tah)
100	**cien** (*syehn*)	**cent** (sent)

Index

See also Accommodations and Restaurant indexes, below.

ACCOMMODATIONS

RESTAURANTS

FROMMER'S® COMPLETE TRAVEL GUIDES

Alaska
Alaska Cruises & Ports of Call
American Southwest
Amsterdam
Argentina & Chile
Arizona
Atlanta
Australia
Austria
Bahamas
Barcelona, Madrid & Seville
Beijing
Belgium, Holland & Luxembourg
Bermuda
Boston
Brazil
British Columbia & the Canadian
   Rockies
Brussels & Bruges
Budapest & the Best of Hungary
Calgary
California
Canada
Cancún, Cozumel & the Yucatán
Cape Cod, Nantucket & Martha's
   Vineyard
Caribbean
Caribbean Ports of Call
Carolinas & Georgia
Chicago
China
Colorado
Costa Rica
Cruises & Ports of Call
Cuba
Denmark
Denver, Boulder & Colorado
   Springs
England
Europe
Europe by Rail
European Cruises & Ports of Call

Florence, Tuscany & Umbria
Florida
France
Germany
Great Britain
Greece
Greek Islands
Halifax
Hawaii
Hong Kong
Honolulu, Waikiki & Oahu
India
Ireland
Italy
Jamaica
Japan
Kauai
Las Vegas
London
Los Angeles
Maryland & Delaware
Maui
Mexico
Montana & Wyoming
Montréal & Québec City
Munich & the Bavarian Alps
Nashville & Memphis
New England
Newfoundland & Labrador
New Mexico
New Orleans
New York City
New York State
New Zealand
Northern Italy
Norway
Nova Scotia, New Brunswick &
   Prince Edward Island
Oregon
Ottawa
Paris
Peru

Philadelphia & the Amish
   Country
Portugal
Prague & the Best of the Czech
   Republic
Provence & the Riviera
Puerto Rico
Rome
San Antonio & Austin
San Diego
San Francisco
Santa Fe, Taos & Albuquerque
Scandinavia
Scotland
Seattle
Shanghai
Sicily
Singapore & Malaysia
South Africa
South America
South Florida
South Pacific
Southeast Asia
Spain
Sweden
Switzerland
Texas
Thailand
Tokyo
Toronto
Turkey
USA
Utah
Vancouver & Victoria
Vermont, New Hampshire &
   Maine
Vienna & the Danube Valley
Virgin Islands
Virginia
Walt Disney World® & Orlando
Washington, D.C.
Washington State

FROMMER'S® DOLLAR-A-DAY GUIDES

Australia from $50 a Day
California from $70 a Day
England from $75 a Day
Europe from $85 a Day
Florida from $70 a Day
Hawaii from $80 a Day

Ireland from $80 a Day
Italy from $70 a Day
London from $90 a Day
New York City from $90 a Day
Paris from $90 a Day
San Francisco from $70 a Day

Washington, D.C. from $80 a
   Day
Portable London from $90 a Day
Portable New York City from $90
   a Day
Portable Paris from $90 a Day

FROMMER'S® PORTABLE GUIDES

Acapulco, Ixtapa & Zihuatanejo
Amsterdam
Aruba
Australia's Great Barrier Reef
Bahamas
Berlin
Big Island of Hawaii
Boston
California Wine Country
Cancún
Cayman Islands
Charleston
Chicago
Disneyland®
Dominican Republic
Dublin

Florence
Frankfurt
Hong Kong
Las Vegas
Las Vegas for Non-Gamblers
London
Los Angeles
Los Cabos & Baja
Maine Coast
Maui
Miami
Nantucket & Martha's Vineyard
New Orleans
New York City
Paris

Phoenix & Scottsdale
Portland
Puerto Rico
Puerto Vallarta, Manzanillo &
   Guadalajara
Rio de Janeiro
San Diego
San Francisco
Savannah
Vancouver
Vancouver Island
Venice
Virgin Islands
Washington, D.C.
Whistler

FROMMER'S® NATIONAL PARK GUIDES

Algonquin Provincial Park
Banff & Jasper
Family Vacations in the National
  Parks

Grand Canyon
National Parks of the American
  West
Rocky Mountain

Yellowstone & Grand Teton
Yosemite & Sequoia/Kings
  Canyon
Zion & Bryce Canyon

FROMMER'S® MEMORABLE WALKS

Chicago
London

New York
Paris

San Francisco

FROMMER'S® WITH KIDS GUIDES

Chicago
Las Vegas
New York City

Ottawa
San Francisco
Toronto

Vancouver
Walt Disney World® & Orlando
Washington, D.C.

SUZY GERSHMAN'S BORN TO SHOP GUIDES

Born to Shop: France
Born to Shop: Hong Kong,
  Shanghai & Beijing

Born to Shop: Italy
Born to Shop: London

Born to Shop: New York
Born to Shop: Paris

FROMMER'S® IRREVERENT GUIDES

Amsterdam
Boston
Chicago
Las Vegas
London

Los Angeles
Manhattan
New Orleans
Paris
Rome

San Francisco
Seattle & Portland
Vancouver
Walt Disney World®
Washington, D.C.

FROMMER'S® BEST-LOVED DRIVING TOURS

Austria
Britain
California
France

Germany
Ireland
Italy
New England

Northern Italy
Scotland
Spain
Tuscany & Umbria

THE UNOFFICIAL GUIDES®

Beyond Disney
California with Kids
Central Italy
Chicago
Cruises
Disneyland®
England
Florida
Florida with Kids
Inside Disney

Hawaii
Las Vegas
London
Maui
Mexico's Best Beach Resorts
Mini Las Vegas
Mini Mickey
New Orleans
New York City
Paris

San Francisco
Skiing & Snowboarding in the
  West
South Florida including Miami &
  the Keys
Walt Disney World®
Walt Disney World® for
  Grown-ups
Walt Disney World® with Kids
Washington, D.C.

SPECIAL-INTEREST TITLES

Athens Past & Present
Cities Ranked & Rated
Frommer's Best Day Trips from London
Frommer's Best RV & Tent Campgrounds
  in the U.S.A.
Frommer's Caribbean Hideaways
Frommer's China: The 50 Most Memorable Trips
Frommer's Exploring America by RV
Frommer's Gay & Lesbian Europe
Frommer's NYC Free & Dirt Cheap

Frommer's Road Atlas Europe
Frommer's Road Atlas France
Frommer's Road Atlas Ireland
Frommer's Wonderful Weekends from
  New York City
The New York Times' Guide to Unforgettable
  Weekends
Retirement Places Rated
Rome Past & Present

Travel Tip: He who finds the best hotel deal has more to spend on facials involving knobbly vegetables.

Hello, the Roaming Gnome here. I've been nabbed from the garden and taken round the world. The people who took me are so terribly clever. They find the best offerings on Travelocity. For very little cha-ching. And that means I get to be pampered and exfoliated till I'm pink as a bunny's doodah.

travelocity®

1-888-TRAVELOCITY / travelocity.com / America Online Keyword: Travel

Travel Tip: Make sure there's customer service for any change of plans — involving friendly natives, for example.

One can plan and plan, but if you don't book with the right people you can't seize le moment and canoodle with the poodle named Pansy. I, for one, am all for fraternizing with the locals. Better yet, if I need to extend my stay and my gnome nappers are willing, it can all be arranged through the 800 number at, oh look, how convenient, the lovely company coat of arms.

travelocity®

1-888-TRAVELOCITY / travelocity.com / America Online Keyword: Travel